HISTORY OF THE GREAT WAR
BASED ON OFFICIAL DOCUMENTS

MEDICAL SERVICES

CASUALTIES AND MEDICAL STATISTICS
OF THE GREAT WAR

BY

MAJOR T. J. MITCHELL, D.S.O., M.D., Ch.M.,
ROYAL ARMY MEDICAL CORPS

AND

MISS G. M. SMITH, M.B.E., M.A.

The Naval & Military Press Ltd

Published by
The Naval & Military Press Ltd
5 Riverside, Brambleside, Bellbrook
Industrial Estate, Uckfield, East Sussex,
TN22 1QQ England
Tel: +44 (0) 1825 749494
Fax: +44 (0) 1825 765701
www.naval-military-press.com
www.military-genealogy.com
www.militarymaproom.com

In reprinting in facsimile from the original, any imperfections are inevitably reproduced and the quality may fall short of modern type and cartographic standards.

CONTENTS

CHAPTER		PAGE
	List of Diagrams	v
	List of Abbreviations	v
	Preface	vi
	Introduction	ix
I.	The Strengths of the British Expeditionary Forces from a Medical Administrative Standpoint	1
II.	A Survey of Battle and Non-battle Casualties	11
III.	The Principal Causes of Non-battle Casualties	55
IV.	Casualties among British and Dominion Troops stationed in the United Kingdom, August 1914 to December 1918	93
V.	Casualties in the British Expeditionary Force in France and Flanders, August 1914 to December 1918	106
VI.	Casualties in the British Expeditionary Force in France and Flanders, August to December 1914	120
VII.	Casualties in the British Expeditionary Force in France and Flanders, 1915	134
VIII.	Casualties in the British Expeditionary Force in France and Flanders, 1916	147
IX.	Casualties in the British Expeditionary Force in France and Flanders, 1917	156
X.	Casualties in the British Expeditionary Force in France and Flanders, 1918	166
XI.	Casualties in the British Expeditionary Force in Italy	176
XII.	Casualties in the British Salonika Force on the Macedonian Front, 1915–1918	186
XIII.	Casualties in the Mediterranean Expeditionary Force during the Dardanelles Campaign	198
XIV.	Casualties in Egypt and Palestine, 1915–1918	208
XV.	Casualties in the Mesopotamian Expeditionary Force, November 1914 to December 1918	218
XVI.	Casualties in the North Russian Expeditionary Force, 1918–1919	245
XVII.	Casualties in the Campaign in East Africa, 1914–1918	252

CONTENTS—*continued*

CHAPTER		PAGE
XVIII.	Casualties in the Campaign in South-West Africa, 1914–1915	261
XIX.	Casualties in the South African War, 1899–1902	268
XX.	Analysis of 1,043,653 British Casualties admitted to Medical Units, 1916–1920	274
XXI.	Casualties dealt with by the Ministry of Pensions	307
	Index	353

LIST OF DIAGRAMS

		PAGE
Chart of Temperatures in Mesopotamia, July 1917 .. *To face*		244
Fig. 1. Analysis of " First Awards " showing for Certain Disabilities the Percentage Proportion of each which occurred year by year in the period 1920–1926	,,	325
Fig. 2. Showing, for " Final Awards " in Certain Disabilities, the Percentage Proportion granted up to 31st May, 1923, and subsequently for each year up to 31st March, 1929	,,	328
Fig. 3. Showing, for Stabilised Awards, the Percentage Proportions in which, at 31st March, 1929, Certain Disabilities fell into the Assessment Grades	,,	331
Fig. 4. Showing, for Unstabilised Awards, the Distribution at 31st March, 1929, of the Grades of Assessment in Certain Disabilities	,,	334

LIST OF ABBREVIATIONS

A.	Admissions.
C.C.S.	Casualty Clearing Station.
D.	Deaths.
D.G.A.M.S... ..	Director-General, Army Medical Services.
D.M.S.	Director of Medical Services.
F.A.	Field Ambulance.
G.H.Q.	General Headquarters.
L. of C.	Lines of Communication.
M.A.C.	Motor Ambulance Convoy.
M.O...	Medical Officer.
N.Y.D.(N.)	Not yet diagnosed (neurological).
Off.	Officers.
O.R...	Other Ranks.
P/W..	Prisoners of War.
R.A.M.C.	Royal Army Medical Corps.
R.A.S.C.	Royal Army Service Corps.
V.D...	Venereal Diseases.

PREFACE

THIS volume records over eleven million casualties sustained by the British Expeditionary Forces at home and in the various campaigns overseas during the Great War. In that figure are included both the casualties of the battlefield and those occasioned by disease and injury. It is not the grand total, for there were many unavoidable omissions in the records. Even so, the wastage which it represents in the manhood of the British Empire alone proclaims the cost of modern warfare. Behind these figures lie tales of heroism, constant hardship and supreme sacrifice, which find no place in a bare analysis of casualties. They have nevertheless inspired this work in the hope of furthering research to alleviate suffering and prevent disease.

In the Great War few medical officers had the opportunity of studying conditions or of carrying out high administrative duties on more than one front. Experience so gained might, therefore, be limited by local surroundings, or be confined to one aspect of the war. There was, too, the risk that, with the passage of time, such knowledge might fade into oblivion. Anxiety lest this might be the fate of the medical statistics of the war was in the mind of the late Sir William Leishman, then Director-General of the Army Medical Services, when the organisation for the preparation of these statistics came unavoidably to an end in 1924. He knew that many problems associated with the prevention of disease, and the treatment and disposal of the sick and wounded, had arisen in every campaign of the War. He was aware of the time and study which had been devoted to the solution of these problems, and he realised that the results of that study were stored away among official files, not readily accessible for future guidance. He determined that the lessons to be learned from this wealth of material should be made available for all time. The statistical facts have been marshalled, and are now presented without elaboration, so that the wastage caused by war in wounds, disease and injury, may be plain to all.

All losses of personnel were, fortunately, not permanent. It has been estimated that, of the casualties admitted to medical units, 82 per cent. of the wounded and 93 per cent.

PREFACE

of the sick and injured were able to return to some form of duty in the Army. In these results were surely evident the devotion and untiring skill rendered to the nation in her time of need by the medical profession, nursing services and the men and women associated with them.

This book is primarily concerned with the wastage in manpower during the war, yet it would not have been complete without a reference to those after-effects of war service dealt with by the Ministry of Pensions. For this chapter I am indebted to Dr. Alexander Sandison, O.B.E., Principal Medical Officer of that Department, who has founded it on the documents kindly placed at his disposal by the Ministry.

The task of writing this volume would have been well-nigh impossible had I not enjoyed at the outset the understanding of the late Sir William Leishman, and, later, the confidence and encouragement of his successors in office, Lieutenant-General Sir M. H. G. Fell, K.C.B., C.M.G., F.R.C.S., K.H.P., and Lieutenant-General Sir H. B. Fawcus, K.C.B., C.M.G., D.S.O., D.C.L., K.H.P.

I am deeply indebted to Brigadier-General Sir J. E. Edmonds, C.B., C.M.G., Editor and Director of the *Official History of the War*, who read the proofs. His suggestions were valuable and his help was, as always, readily extended to me. My thanks are also due to Brigadier-General F. J. Moberly, C.B., C.S.I., D.S.O., Brigadier-General D. F. Aspinall-Oglander, C.B., C.M.G., D.S.O., and Captain Cyril Falls, for assistance in the preparation of the chapters on Mesopotamia, the Dardanelles, and Egypt and Palestine.

Major-General Sir H. T. Brooking, K.C.B., K.C.S.I., K.C.M.G., and Brigadier-General E. W. Costello, V.C., C.M.G., C.V.O., D.S.O., Director of Military Studies at Cambridge University, willingly and with enthusiasm read the manuscript. I am grateful for their advice which encouraged me to emphasise many important problems in the field which call for solution.

To Major-General H. C. R. Hime, D.S.O., and Sir Harold Stiles, K.B.E., F.R.C.S.E., LL.D., who revised the proofs and made valuable comments and criticisms, I tender my warmest thanks.

In overcoming the many technical difficulties associated with a work of this nature, I have been greatly helped by Mr. G. Biddiscombe, M.B.E., D.C.M., of the Medical Directorate in the War Office, who read all the proofs and checked all the calculations.

PREFACE

I wish also to acknowledge the assistance I have received from the Controller of H.M. Stationery Office and his Staff in the publication of the volume.

Finally, of my colleague, Miss G. M. Smith, M.B.E., M.A., I can truthfully say that without her promised help I could not have undertaken the work, and without her wholehearted loyalty, sustained enthusiasm and ability I could never have completed it.

T. J. M.

March, 1931.

INTRODUCTION

THIS, the final volume of the *Official Medical History of the War*, which deals with the statistical aspect of casualties, has had a chequered career since first it was conceived in the minds of some of our most distinguished scientists. Its production, despite an elaborate organisation, prodigious labour and a very great expenditure of money, was for a long time exceedingly doubtful. Now that it has reached publication in its present form, an introductory outline of its history may be given explaining the difficulties and alterations caused by changed conditions and the necessity to strike a balance between theoretical perfection and financial economy, so that the reasons for departing from the original scheme and the delay in production may be understood. An additional purpose will be served if, by focussing attention on the difficulties which were experienced in building up an organisation to compile the medical statistics of the Great War, a simpler method can be evolved for utilising the peace-time system in a future war, should the need arise. Prior to August 1914 no scheme had been drawn up for the collection of complete medical statistics in war, although it was realised that the peace-time system, with its complicated monthly and annual returns, would be much too elaborate for the purpose. It was apparently intended to follow the method adopted for the South African War, which was to extract the statistics from the admission and discharge books after the termination of hostilities.

The first phase of the preparation of the medical statistics of the war dates back to 1914. When the idea of establishing an organisation for the production of an official medical history of the war had been suggested by a member of the civil medical profession in September 1914, and had been adopted by the Director-General of the Army Medical Services in November 1914, the Medical Research Committee,* appointed under the National Health Insurance Acts, offered the services of their statistical staff together with money grants for additional

---

* The Medical Research Committee became the Medical Research Council on 1st April 1920, and is referred to as such in the subsequent pages of this volume.

clerical assistance with a view to the compilation of accurate medical and surgical statistics of the war. This offer was gratefully accepted by the Army Council on 17th November 1914. The value to be derived from a study of war statistics was thus early realised, and never did statistical work start with higher ideals or more influential support. The original undertaking was based on the assumption of a short war confined to the Western Front. Needless to say, the science of recording and preparing statistics in war is intricate, and there was little or no experience to guide the new organisation, because the comparatively large staff which had been engaged on the records of the South African War had been disbanded before its members were in a position to publish an official account of their labours or a comprehensive study of their results. Small wonder, then, that the unforeseen magnitude of the Great War, which tested all existing forms of record-keeping and upset all prearranged schemes, deprived the world of the complete scientific success of the undertaking.

The peace-time methods of recording army medical statistics were sufficient for the normal needs of the army, and were followed by men trained in record-keeping and routine. The Great War had not been many months in progress, however, before men trained in this work were unprocurable in France. The force, composed of Regular, Territorial and Dominion troops, was no longer homogeneous, and very often the keeping of medical records and returns fell to men neither familiar with such work nor conscious of its importance. The general work had also greatly increased, for not only had the force grown in numbers, but the exigencies of the war on the Western Front demanded that patients should be rapidly transferred from one medical unit to another, and it became rare for the treatment of any given case to be completed under one medical officer. Hence the turnover of patients in all units was very large and the amount of record-keeping proportionately increased.

With forces increasing in different parts of the world, with unwieldy, inaccurate records coming in, with growing expenditure and an ambitious general scheme to carry out, the central organisation as originally established proved insufficient. Additional financial assistance and new methods were required, and in June 1917 the War Office agreed to take over the actual cost of the routine statistical work. To overcome the numerous difficulties associated with record-keeping, the system of keeping an official medical history card for every patient admitted to a medical unit was introduced into all the forces. This card amplified all the information contained in the admission and discharge books regarding the case and reproduced it in a more easily handled form. These index cards were kept officially by general and stationary hospitals, and at the end of every six months the completed cards were sent to the statistical department of the Medical Research Council to be used later as data for the statistics regarding the medical aspects of the war. Although the revised scheme was apparently ideal, it miscarried. Mistakes were made on every side; wrong cards arrived in some theatres of war; in others, cards and instructions did not arrive together. Forces in many theatres of war were constantly moving, fighting, reorganising units and formations, or were so scattered over vast areas of country that when the right cards and full instructions were received it was well-nigh impossible to distribute them, cancel the old system and establish the new. The result was that the British Expeditionary Force in France was the only one to keep up trustworthy records; in other forces the cards were either not used or, if used, were of little value when completed, owing to inaccuracies.

The failure of this system seriously affected the preparation of the medical statistics of the war. The original laborious method of making out index cards from admission and discharge books in the statistical department of the Medical Research Council had to be resorted to before codifying or tabulating could be commenced. Further, when the war ended and all medical units were ordered to send their records to the Medical Research Council, the central statistical office was inundated with records of every conceivable sort, packed in any order, and sent from units both at home and overseas. The sorting, arranging, grading and filing of the essential records out of this overwhelming mass of documents and reports presented an almost insuperable task. To meet the needs of a rapidly expanding organisation and the growing demands for accommodation, new premises, first in the British Museum and then in Endell Street, London, had to be obtained and fitted up for the proper housing of the documents. These disturbing moves did not facilitate the work, and apart from the valuable monographs on certain subjects, issued from time to time during the war by the Medical Research Council, and the answering of thousands of medical inquiries sent in by the Ministry of Pensions, no great progress had been made by May 1919 in obtaining statistical information that would be of use for (*a*) military purposes in future wars; (b) medical purposes by the Army Medical Services; (c) medical purposes in the medical history of the war; and (d) general medical scientific purposes. On the other hand, a great advance had been made in the compilation and filing of twenty odd million individual records, which were of inestimable value to the Ministry of Pensions and to the country.

As matters then stood, the staff of this central statistical office numbered 225 and cost £18,000 annually, but it was considered insufficient for the work contemplated, and it was estimated that if an immediate increase of staff to 350 at an annual cost of £32,500 were granted, the work could be completed in three years. Three problems had now to be faced: the supplying of information to the Ministry of Pensions regarding claimants to pension; the production of a complete register of all casualties which would enable that department more readily to adjust pension schemes; and the preparation of statistical tables which would be of value to the medical services, both civil and military, and to the country in the event of a future war. It was realised that a complete register of casualties would be of the utmost value to the Ministry of Pensions, and that it would be impossible to compile detailed medical statistics until such a register had been completed. As the best solution of these problems, it was suggested early in 1920 that the Ministry of Pensions should take over the whole statistical organisation from the Medical Research Council and be responsible for the completion of the statistical information required for the volume on the medical statistics of the war.

Coincident with these problems, a reorganisation had taken place in the office of the *Official Medical History of the War*. In September 1919, Major-General Sir William Macpherson was appointed editor-in-chief and a scheme for the production of the history was drawn up and sanctioned. This scheme included a volume on the medical statistics and epidemiology of the Great War, and Dr. J. Brownlee of the Medical Research Council and Major W. R. Galwey, R.A.M.C., medical statistical officer at the War Office, were appointed to edit the volume as material became available, in accordance with a very elaborate schedule drawn up by representatives of the Medical Research Council and the War Office.

By October 1920 the central statistical organisation was transferred to the Ministry of Pensions, and sanction was given to an increase of staff, the Army Council having agreed to pay an annual sum until the register of index cards should be completed. When this agreement was reached, the members of Sir William Macpherson's Editorial Committee decided that, as the statistics then completed by the Medical Research Council covered 1914 and 1915 only, the preparation of the statistical volume of the *Official Medical History of the War* could not be undertaken by the Editorial Committee since the necessary information for the remaining years was not in their possession. They did not lose interest in the volume, for at the final meeting of the Editorial Committee in 1923, Sir Walter Fletcher was instrumental in getting a resolution passed unanimously that the preparation of a statistical volume should be undertaken at some later period, since it would constitute the final volume of the series of the *Medical History of the War*, and the statistics which it would contain would be essential for a correct interpretation of the facts in the other volumes of the series, as well as for future guidance.

No further progress in preparing the volume could be made until the register of index cards was completed. This was accomplished by December 1921, and the Ministry of Pensions was then in a position to codify and tabulate the statistical information required for it. In order to facilitate completion, it had been decided to limit statistics in detail to some fifty of the more important diseases and to group the remainder under their appropriate systems. It was also decided, in January 1922, that it would be necessary to restrict the statistical information to that relating to British troops only and not to proceed with the compilation of statistics relating to Dominion troops as was originally intended. Rising hopes were, however, doomed to disappointment. The Ministry of Pensions estimated that a further sum of £12,000 would be required to carry out the additional work essential for the final volume even on the modified scale. Eventually a compromise was effected, and it was decided to abandon the original scheme of a complete analysis of the 23 million cards. An examination of two sample sets, each of about 500,000 cards relating to British troops only, was deemed to be sufficiently satisfactory. The work was carried out on these lines, and two sets of statistical tables, compiled by the Ministry of Pensions, were given to the medical directorate in the War Office early in 1924. In May of that year, these tables, together with the statistics for 1914 and 1915, prepared by the Medical Research Council, were handed over to Major T. J. Mitchell, R.A.M.C., Assistant

Editor of the *Medical History of the War*, as the basis of the final volume of the series. As the eleven volumes of the medical history were finished and the office staff was on the eve of being disbanded, it was impossible to undertake the preparation of the final volume at that late hour, and the material was returned to the War Office. Once more the fate of the volume on statistics hung in the balance, but the late Director-General, Sir William Leishman, spurred by his belief in research, with unconquerable tenacity clung to his determination that, somehow or other, the work should be completed. He therefore persuaded Major Mitchell,* who had just joined his staff at the War Office, to continue the work on modified lines in his spare time, and when, in September 1925, he was allowed the assistance of Miss G. M. Smith, a colleague on the staff of the *Medical History of the War*, the last stage in the preparation of the statistical volume had begun with a staff of two.

As some of the statistics already prepared were of little or no value without correlation to those of the succeeding years and the strengths of the forces, and as there was neither time, nor money nor material to complete the exact scientific analysis of the medical statistics of the war, it was considered advisable and necessary to recast the original scheme. Primary attention to purely medical scientific information had to be dropped, and it was decided that the outstanding features of the volume should be associated with casualties, manpower and wastage, problems which were of the utmost importance not only to the medical services but also to the general staff during the Great War. To this end memories were racked for clues to trace some once familiar report or file. Official documents had to be reassembled from various sources. Army and War Office returns, war diaries, secret telegrams, medical reports, despatches, reports of Commissions and investigations, and various medical files, were all examined and their contents sifted, until bit by bit they yielded up sufficient information on which to build up the volume. Some of the records were of inestimable value, others less so; by using, however, all the information upon which reliance could be placed a volume on the casualties of the Great War has been produced which it is hoped will not only serve as an approximately correct record, but will also indicate the lessons to be learned from an examination of the figures.

In studying these statistics of casualties it must be borne in

---

* Major Mitchell was seconded from all duty in August, 1928, to enable him to devote his whole time to the statistical volume.

INTRODUCTION

mind that certain figures refer to admissions to medical units and not to individuals. The tables have been checked by reference to all known sources of information, and may be accepted as sufficiently accurate for use as a basis on which to calculate requirements in future wars. Readers are reminded that practically the whole of the medical profession served at one time or another in the Great War, and in many of the tables the figures are those originally produced by the profession having at its back every modern aid to diagnosis which science and the country could then give. They were compiled in good faith on the standard of knowledge of the time, and supplied the information upon which the War Office authorities and commanders in the field acted throughout the war.

Prior to the Great War, the records of Continental armies furnished most of the statistical data required in military medical calculations. An attempt is now made to record the figures of the various expeditionary forces equipped and despatched overseas by the British Empire. The opening chapters aim at giving a concise but comprehensive survey of the total casualties suffered by these forces, while the succeeding chapters deal with individual campaigns, and have been specially prepared to draw attention to the important statistical features of the campaign under review. In developing this aspect of historical research, simplicity has been aimed at, and it has been realised that chapters dealing purely with statistics will be used for reference, and that they will be studied for definite information or when assistance is required in solving some problem not necessarily peculiar to the medical services. For these reasons, the type of information which was regularly called for, or constantly used, during the war by staff, administrative and medical officers, has been tabulated in an attempt to render assistance and save the labour and time of interested workers. Hitherto such records were stored in official files and were not readily available to the general body of officers. With this end in view, all available figures have been scrutinised and collated; yearly results have been obtained by consolidating daily, weekly or monthly returns from formations, and an endeavour has been made to produce in a concise form a series of tables giving the approximate casualties in the different theatres of war.

The statistical data of the individual campaigns are presented on a uniform system throughout, due allowance being made for peculiarities of campaigns and inevitable blanks in the information available. This system is briefly summarised below, and an explanation of some of the terms used is given in order to simplify the study of the chapters.

A short précis of the principal military features of the campaign is given, more particularly as they affect the medical services. A footnote indicates where fuller details of the medical history of the campaign under review may be found.

Strength

Includes a table of the average ration strength of the whole force, divided wherever possible into British and Dominion, Indian, African and other troops, labour and followers.

Classification of Casualties

Includes tables of total casualties, including total British and Dominion casualties, analyses and percentages of British and Dominion casualties, permanent and temporary losses in the field, and the respective proportions of the different groups of casualties.

Admissions to Hospital

Includes tables of casualties admitted to medical units, analyses of admissions and disposals calculated as ratios per 1,000 of ration strength, and percentages of admissions, with the ratios per 1,000 constantly in hospital.

Hospital Accommodation on the Lines of Communication

Includes the maximum number of equipped and occupied beds, year by year or for the whole campaign, as the case may be, and the average number of equipped and occupied beds in stationary or general hospitals and convalescent depots, with the percentage of beds equipped and occupied to the ration strength of the force.

Non-battle Casualties

Includes tables of the principal causes of inefficiency, apart from wounds, and the causes of admission to hospital in detail with ratios per 1,000 of strength. The subsequent disposal is also given in the instances where it was possible of ascertainment.

After the opening précis in the chapter has recalled the main features of the campaign, it is important to have a definite idea of the numbers engaged in the respective campaigns and the numbers which had to be maintained and provided for. The term " British " has been taken to denote those who enlisted and served in the units of the British Isles, and does not include Dominion troops. When the latter are included, the reference is to " British and Dominion " troops. Indian, or other troops are referred to separately wherever possible.

In dealing with casualties a classification has been used which is as yet unfamiliar, but which seems to be the most suitable. They have been divided into " battle " and " non-

INTRODUCTION xvii

battle" casualties, and each group has been further subdivided into "permanent" and "temporary" losses "for military purposes in the field." The term "battle casualties" includes killed, missing, prisoners of war, and those who suffered injury caused by or arising from enemy action, including injuries by rifle, gunfire, bombs, bayonets and liquid fire, shock to the nervous system caused by bursting shells, although producing no visible traumata, and the effects of contact with, or inhalation of, poisonous gases. "Non-battle casualties" include all cases of sickness or injury independent of any act of the enemy. From the point of view of the military commander in the field, permanent losses include the killed, missing and prisoners of war, for although a certain number of missing and prisoners are returned to the army at the close of the campaign, until then they are lost to the force. So the expression "permanent losses for military purposes in the field" has been adopted. All battle and non-battle casualties which come under medical treatment may for a time be considered as temporary losses, but human flesh and blood being what it is, a certain proportion of these die or are discharged from the service as invalids, and must therefore be added to the permanent losses. After deducting these groups from the total casualties, the remainder can be considered as temporary losses, and their ultimate disposal is a guide to both combatant and medical officers in their preparations for battle and their schemes for the conservation of manpower. It might be argued that the casualties evacuated overseas should be considered as permanent losses. It is admitted that they have to be replaced if the force is to be kept up to strength, but the majority are not lost to the military forces, their evacuation overseas being only a temporary matter of convenience.

By the adoption of the above terms attention can be focussed more readily on all causes likely to increase the wastage of manpower in an army. By the subdivision of casualties into permanent and temporary losses, the reinforcements which may be necessary can be estimated. By deducting the numbers returned to duty from the total casualties the net casualties of a campaign are obtained. In a long and arduous campaign overseas it is important not only to reduce the number of reinforcements, which must be sent by transports, but also to facilitate, for those responsible for the future policy of the force, the estimate of the personnel that must be enlisted, trained, equipped and ready to embark on certain dates.

Following the classification and analysis of casualties, a section is devoted to the hospital and convalescent depot accommodation provided for, and used by, the different forces; and the chapters end with an analysis of non-battle casualties and the chief causes of inefficiency among the troops. The known statistical information on diseases which occurred among the troops has been tabulated after the standard method employed in the *Annual Reports on the Health of the Army*, a system both simple and easily understood. While some tables will appeal only to the military mind and others to the medical, some will interest both, promote discussion, stimulate investigation and research and aid in the adoption of sound principles for the solution of such problems as the prevention of disease, the accommodation required in hospitals and convalescent depots, and the methods of transporting casualties. The solution of these problems will encourage co-operation and efficiency, and will ultimately effect a pronounced saving in manpower.

As the United Kingdom was not only the base from which the expeditionary forces were despatched, but was itself a large military camp throughout the war, the casualties occurring among British and Dominion troops stationed there are recorded first. Thereafter the campaigns are dealt with in the order in which they are given in the *Official Names of the Battles and other Engagements fought by the Military Forces of the British Empire during the Great War 1914–1919*,* and the period covered extends from August 1914 to December 1918, except in the case of North Russia, where fighting actually continued into 1919. When possible, statistics of casualties have been given from start to finish of a campaign. In some campaigns, or parts of a campaign, the tables have been prepared from the statistical data compiled by the Medical Research Council; in others, they represent the research work of the last six years. In the former case the figures are complete for the period reviewed and give the definite numbers ultimately returned to duty or discharged from the service as invalids; in the latter there are no invaliding tables, as it was a general principle in the army not to invalid patients out of the service until after transfer to the United Kingdom, or in the case of Dominion or other troops, until after return to their own country. In a work of this nature there must necessarily be a few gaps owing to lack of information, and where these

---

* H.M. Stationery Office, 1921.

occur the fact is duly noted. It was thought advisable to devote a separate chapter to each campaign, except in the case of France and Flanders, the largest and most important campaign Great Britain has ever undertaken, and to it there has been allotted a chapter for each year and one for the totals of the period August 1914 to December 1918. In addition to the campaigns of the Great War, a chapter is included on the South African War, giving the statistics which had been prepared after the close of hostilities but which were never published. These figures have been presented as far as possible in the same form as those of the Great War, so that attention may be drawn to the diseases which, after twelve years or so, still caused a high rate of inefficiency in certain armies operating under certain conditions.

Lack of the necessary statistical data has made it impossible to prepare chapters on the operations in India, the campaign in West Africa or the minor events of the war in British garrisons abroad.

After the eleven million odd battle and non-battle casualties in the more important campaigns have been analysed and tabulated, there follows a detailed analysis of 1,043,653 British casualties which occurred during the years 1916 to 1920. This chapter summarises the statistics prepared by the Ministry of Pensions, and is intended to supplement the information given in the preceding chapters.

The medical statistics of the Great War would be incomplete without some reference to the numbers discharged from the service as invalids and the numbers who ultimately received compensation from the State for disabilities incurred owing to service. The concluding chapter of the volume is therefore devoted to a concise account of the work done by the Ministry of Pensions since its inception. The nature of war disablement, its post-war development, the post-war treatment required by the disabled and the compensating State awards are described with illustrative tables and diagrams. The after-effects of the war on one nation alone are brought home with striking force when it is realised that, exclusive of Dominion and other forces, 2,414,000 individuals, or 40 per cent. of those who served in the Great War, whether in the Navy, Army, Air Force or Nursing Services, were affected by war service in the sense of death or some form of war disablement, for which State compensation was given. If, in the event of war, these figures are remembered when preparations are being made, then questions relating to the supply of additional personnel, equipment and transport for the medical services will have a greater interest for all branches of the army, and they will be considered not only as a means of succouring sick and wounded but as important factors in preventing wastage, conserving the manpower of the nation during hostilities, and reducing expenditure after the war.

CHAPTER I

The Strengths of the British Expeditionary Forces from a Medical Administrative Standpoint

IT has been definitely laid down that " the aim of the Army is, in co-operation with the Royal Navy and the Royal Air Force, to break down the resistance of the enemy's armed forces in furtherance of the approved plan of campaign. The achievement of this result with the minimum expenditure of time, men, material and money is the object to be aimed at in the organisation of the Army." * In pursuance of this policy the conservation of manpower is an important factor with which the medical services are intimately associated in the prevention of disease, the professional treatment and care of sick and wounded, and the collection and evacuation of casualties. This leads to a wider conception of the assistance which it is within the power of the medical services to render to the State and to the army during war, and which only becomes apparent after the medical statistics of the war have been analysed and considered. The tendency in the past has been to promote an efficient medical service by the appeal to sympathy rather than by associating with it in the solution of problems of manpower and attrition, factors which are of great interest in any war, but more especially in a war of world magnitude. By preventing disease, by smoothly and quickly evacuating casualties and by reducing the number of deaths from sickness and wounds, the medical services further the ideals of medicine, create a feeling of trust among the people at home, and assist an army to maintain a high standard of morale and mobility. By shortening the period which each casualty remains in hospital, and by increasing the number of sick and wounded who are returned to duty from hospital, they play a great part in supplying trained and experienced reinforcements to maintain the strengths of formations in the field. For these same reasons an efficient medical service

---

* *Field Service Regulations* (Vol. I), 1930, Chap. I, Section 1, para. 1.

TABLE 1.—Approximate Average Ration Strength of the

Campaign	Duration of Campaign	Year	British and Dominion Troops		
			Off.	O.R.	Total
France and Flanders	4.8.14–11.11.18	1914 (a)	7,600	182,400	190,000 (b)
		1915	22,312	593,774	616,086
		1916	49,599	1,272,476	1,322,075
		1917	73,449	1,821,062	1,894,511
		1918	77,421	1,779,605	1,857,026
Italy	–.11.17–4.11.18	1917 (c)	5,064	106,932	111,996
		1918	4,405	90,229	94,634
Macedonia ...	5.10.15–11.11.18	1915 (d)	2,032	58,857	60,889
		1916	4,877	118,517	123,394
		1917	6,405	176,178	182,583
		1918	5,005	123,742	128,747
Dardanelles ...	25.4.15–8.1.16	1915	6,134	154,052	160,186 (e)
Egypt and Palestine	26.1.15–31.10.18	1915	3,405	70,728	74,133
		1916	8,387	179,539	187,926
		1917	8,767	177,782	186,549
		1918	12,286	218,804	231,090
Mesopotamia ...	6.11.14–5.11.18	1914	275	2,609	2,884
		1915	774	6,179	6,953
		1916	3,088	45,131	48,219
		1917	5,155	78,747	83,902
		1918	7,107	100,275	107,382
North Russia ...	2.8.18–12.10.19	1918	613	7,646	8,259
		1919	1,019	12,971	13,990
East Africa ...	1.9.14–11.11.18	1914 (h)	—	—	—
		1915 (h)	379	5,309	5,688
		1916	2,029	30,101	32,130
		1917	2,142	18,618	20,760
		1918	2,118	14,670	16,788
South-West Africa	20.8.14–9.7.15	— (i)	—	—	33,000
West Africa ...	8.8.14–18.2.16	1914	228	354	582
		1915 (j)	—	—	1,188
United Kingdom	4.8.14–11.11.18	1914	30,810	1,249,658	1,280,468
		1915	53,184	1,463,601	1,516,785
		1916	58,555	1,539,902	1,598,457
		1917	68,038	1,638,695	1,706,733
		1918	76,936	1,537,017	1,613,953

* Prepared in the order given in the " Official Names of the Battles and other War, 1914–1919," London, 1921.

(a) August–December; (b) British only. (c) November and December only. (f) Probably includes followers. (g) Includes Archangel and (i) Daily average over whole campaign; no detail available.

STRENGTHS

British Expeditionary Forces engaged in the Great War, 1914-1919 *

Indian, African or Other				Grand Total			
Troops			Followers or Labour	Troops		Followers or Labour	Total
Off.	O.R.	Total		Off.	O.R.		
497	24,075	24,572	6,000	8,097	206,475	6,000	220,572
767	34,801	35,568	10,688	23,079	628,575	10,688	662,342
367	11,932	12,299	2,681	49,966	1,284,408	2,681	1,337,055
355	11,108	11,463	62,905	73,804	1,832,170	62,905	1,968,879
116	14,384	14,500	117,848	77,537	1,793,989	117,848	1,989,374
—	—	—	—	5,064	106,932	—	111,996
—	—	—	4,313	4,405	90,229	4,313	98,947
—	—	—	—	2,032	58,857	—	60,889
10	2,606	2,616	—	4,887	121,123	—	126,010
13	2,095	2,108	17,574	6,418	178,273	17,574	202,265
28	3,764	3,792	27,408	5,033	127,506	27,408	159,947
60	3,220	3,280 (*f*)	—	6,194	157,272	—	163,466
327	14,911	15,238	—	3,732	85,639	—	89,371
298	30,243	30,541	7,455	8,685	209,782	7,455	225,922
271	18,619	18,890	63,329	9,038	196,401	63,329	268,768
1,298	58,068	59,366	94,871	13,584	276,872	94,871	385,327
240	8,653	8,893	2,326	515	11,262	2,326	14,103
498	16,749	17,247	7,671	1,272	22,928	7,671	31,871
1,557	65,112	66,669	50,476	4,645	110,243	50,476	165,364
2,132	99,854	101,986	121,598	7,287	178,601	121,598	307,486
2,651	137,713	140,364	163,879	9,758	237,988	163,879	411,625
—	—	—	—	613	7,646	—	8,259 (*g*)
—	—	—	—	1,019	12,971	—	13,990 (*g*)
395	20,493	20,888	18,068	774	25,802	18,068	44,644
440	25,644	26,084	40,376	2,469	55,745	40,376	98,590
319	29,623	29,942	143,959	2,461	48,241	143,959	194,661
91	24,154	24,245	87,623	2,209	38,824	87,623	128,656
—	—	—	15,000	—	—	15,000	48,000
—	2,995	2,995	5,537	228	3,349	5,537	9,114
—	—	5,927	24,184	—	—	24,184	31,299
—	—	—	—	30,810	1,249,658	—	1,280,468
—	—	—	—	53,184	1,463,601	—	1,516,785
—	—	—	—	58,555	1,539,902	—	1,598,457
—	—	—	—	68,038	1,638,695	—	1,706,733
—	—	—	—	76,936	1,537,017	—	1,613,953

Engagements fought by the Military Forces of the British Empire during the Great

(*d*) October–December. (*e*) Includes Royal Naval Division.
Murmansk Forces. (*h*) No detail available till September, 1915.
(*j*) No detail available.

TABLE 2.—Approximate Average Ration Strength of the

Campaign	British and Dominion Troops			Indian, African Troops	
	Off.	O.R.	Total	Off.	O.R.
1914 (Aug.–Dec.)					
France and Flanders	7,600	182,400	190,000 (a)	497	24,075
Mesopotamia	275	2,609	2,884	240	8,653
East Africa (b)	—	—	—	—	—
South-West Africa (c)	...	...	...	...	...
West Africa	228	354	582	—	2,995
United Kingdom	30,810	1,249,658	1,280,468	—	—
Total †	*38,913*	*1,435,021*	*1,473,934*	*737*	*35,723*
1915					
France and Flanders	22,312	593,774	616,086	767	34,801
Mesopotamia	774	6,179	6,953	498	16,749
East Africa (d)	379	5,309	5,688	395	20,493
South-West Africa	—	—	33,000	—	—
West Africa (e)	—	—	1,188	—	—
Egypt and Palestine	3,405	70,728	74,133	327	14,911
Dardanelles	6,134	154,052	160,186	60	3,220
Macedonia (f)	2,032	58,857	60,889	—	—
United Kingdom	53,184	1,463,601	1,516,785	—	—
Total	—	—	*2,474,908*	—	—
1916					
France and Flanders	49,599	1,272,476	1,322,075	367	11,932
Mesopotamia	3,088	45,131	48,219	1,557	65,112
East Africa	2,029	30,101	32,130	440	25,644
Egypt and Palestine	8,387	179,539	187,926	298	30,243
Macedonia	4,877	118,517	123,394	10	2,606
United Kingdom	58,555	1,539,902	1,598,457	—	—
Total	*126,535*	*3,185,666*	*3,312,201*	*2,672*	*135,537*
1917					
France and Flanders	73,449	1,821,062	1,894,511	355	11,108
Mesopotamia	5,155	78,747	83,902	2,132	99,854
East Africa	2,142	18,618	20,760	319	29,623
Egypt and Palestine	8,767	177,782	186,549	271	18,619
Macedonia	6,405	176,178	182,583	13	2,095
Italy (g)	5,064	106,932	111,996	—	—
United Kingdom	68,038	1,638,695	1,706,733	—	—
Total	*169,020*	*4,018,014*	*4,187,034*	*3,090*	*161,299*
1918					
France and Flanders	77,421	1,779,605	1,857,026	116	14,384
Mesopotamia	7,107	100,275	107,382	2,651	137,713
East Africa	2,118	14,670	16,788	91	24,154
Egypt and Palestine	12,286	218,804	231,090	1,298	58,068
Macedonia	5,005	123,742	128,747	28	3,764
Italy	4,405	90,229	94,634	—	—
North Russia (h)	613	7,646	8,259	—	—
United Kingdom	76,936	1,537,017	1,613,953	—	—
Total	*185,891*	*3,871,988*	*4,057,879*	*4,184*	*238,083*
1919					
North Russia	1,019	12,971	13,990	—	—

* Prepared in accordance with campaigns actually in progress.
† Excluding East and South-West Africa.
(c) Average for whole campaign under 1915.   No detail available.
(f) October–December.   (g) November–December.

STRENGTHS

British Expeditionary Forces engaged in the Great War, 1914-1919, by Years *

or Other		Grand Total			
Total	Followers or Labour	Troops Off.	Troops O.R.	Followers or Labour	Total
24,572	6,000	8,097	206,475	6,000	220,572
8,893	2,326	515	11,262	2,326	14,103
—	—	—	—	—	—
2,995	5,537	228	3,349	5,537	9,114
—	—	30,810	1,249,658	—	1,280,468
36,460	*13,863*	*39,650*	*1,470,744*	*13,863*	*1,524,257*
35,568	10,688	23,079	628,575	10,688	662,342
17,247	7,671	1,272	22,928	7,671	31,871
20,888	18,068	774	25,802	18,068	44,644
—	15,000	—	—	15,000	48,000
5,927	24,184	—	—	24,184	31,299
15,238	—	3,732	85,639	—	89,371
3,280	—	6,194	157,272	—	163,466
—	—	2,032	58,857	—	60,889
—	—	53,184	1,463,601	—	1,516,785
98,150	*75,611*	—	—	*75,611*	*2,648,667*
12,299	2,681	49,966	1,284,408	2,681	1,337,055
66,669	50,476	4,645	110,243	50,476	165,364
26,084	40,376	2,469	55,745	40,376	98,590
30,541	7,455	8,685	209,782	7,455	225,922
2,616	—	4,887	121,123	—	126,010
—	—	58,555	1,539,902	—	1,598,457
138,209	*100,988*	*129,207*	*3,321,203*	*100,988*	*3,551,398*
11,463	62,905	73,804	1,832,170	62,905	1,968,879
101,986	121,598	7,287	178,601	121,598	307,486
29,942	143,959	2,461	48,241	143,959	194,661
18,890	63,329	9,038	196,401	63,329	268,768
2,108	17,574	6,418	178,273	17,574	202,265
—	—	5,064	106,932	—	111,996
—	—	68,038	1,638,695	—	1,706,733
164,389	*409,365*	*172,110*	*4,179,313*	*409,365*	*4,760,788*
14,500	117,848	77,537	1,793,989	117,848	1,989,374
140,364	163,879	9,758	237,988	163,879	411,625
24,245	87,623	2,209	38,824	87,623	128,656
59,366	94,871	13,584	276,872	94,871	385,327
3,792	27,408	5,033	127,506	27,408	159,947
—	4,313	4,405	90,229	4,313	98,947
—	—	613	7,646	—	8,259
—	—	76,936	1,537,017	—	1,613,953
242,267	*495,942*	*190,075*	*4,110,071*	*495,942*	*4,796,088*
—	—	1,019	12,971	—	13,990

(*a*) British only.
(*b*) Not available.
(*d*) Average September to December.
(*e*) To February, 1916.
(*h*) August–December.

must mean an ultimate saving of national expenditure on transportation, post-war hospitals, treatment, appliances and war pensions.*

The magnitude of these problems is scarcely realised, rarely studied, and seldom fully appreciated; and if the history of our casualties in the Great War is to throw any light on them and provide us with guidance in the event of any future war, it is essential to commence their study by examining the strength and composition of our own forces at home and in the different campaigns of the Great War, 1914–1919, as set out in Tables 1 and 2. Although these figures, for reasons already stated, may differ in some slight degree from others previously published, they are as correct as it has been possible to make them, and not only do they form the basis of the statistical structure built up in the succeeding pages of this volume, but they also make more instructive the detailed information given in the previous volumes of the *Medical History of the War*, more particularly those devoted to the development and work of the medical services during the Great War.

These tables of strengths afford an interesting comparison when set alongside the approximate figures of some previous wars.†

TABLE 3.—Strength of Troops engaged in some previous Campaigns

Campaign	Date	Nationality	No. Mobilised	Average No. of Effectives		
				Off.	O.R.	Total
War with France	1793–1815	British	—	9,037	189,500	198,587
Walcheren Expedition	1809	British	—	—	—	21,000
Crimean War	1854–1856	French	—	—	—	309,268
,, ,,	,, ,,	British	—	—	—	97,864
Franco-German War	1870–1871	German	—	33,101	1,113,254	1,146,355
,, ,,	,, ,,	,, (garrison)	—	9,319	338,738	348,057
,, ,,	,, ,,	French	—	—	—	1,400,000 to 1,500,000
South African War	1899–1902	British	448,435	—	208,226‡	—
Russo-Japanese War	1904–1905	Russian	1,365,000	—	—	699,000
,, ,,	,, ,,	Japanese	1,200,000	—	—	650,000
Balkan Wars	1912–1913	Bulgaria	—	—	—	350,000
,,	,, ,,	Serbia	—	—	—	172,000
,,	,, ,,	Greece	—	—	—	115,000
,,	,, ,,	Montenegro	—	—	—	25,000

The expansion of the forces in the Great War was without parallel, and when one recalls the apt remark of Field-Marshal

* From its inception to the present time the total net expenditure by the Ministry of Pensions has been approximately £900,000,000.

† Taken from "Losses of Life caused by War," by S. Dumas and K. O. Vedel-Petersen, pp. 30–59. Edited by H. Westergaard.

‡ The strength on which the South African War casualties were calculated.

Sir William Robertson, that " the longer peace continues, the more difficult it is to prepare for war," * it does not require much thought to realise that one reason for this undoubtedly lies in the lack of experience in handling and making provision for large masses of men. This applies to the medical services as well as to other services, and it is just this lack of experience which sometimes narrows the outlook, dulls the mind in forming schemes of organisation, and leads to failures at the commencement of a war. The army medical officer in peace time is chiefly engaged in attending to his professional duties, and has few opportunities of studying expansive military problems. Moreover, the medical units in which he works are not organised for war, so that his study of war problems is still further limited. If one considers the approximate total strength of the British army at home and overseas year by year during the Great War, as briefly summarised in Table 4, and compares it with the total strength of the British army in 1913, and again in 1927, one sees that the medical organisation required to meet the two situations must be vastly different. It is not surprising, therefore, that when the need arises it is difficult to turn from the minor problems of peace to those born of a Great War, and to think out with imaginative foresight a broad policy that will create methodically and smoothly the medical arrangements necessary in the United Kingdom and overseas for millions of men.

TABLE 4.—Approximate Total Strength of the British Army at home and overseas, 1913–1918, and in 1927

Year	All ranks, all forces
1913	212,355†
1914 (Aug.-Dec.)	1,524,257
1915	2,666,281
1916	3,551,398
1917	4,760,788
1918	4,796,088
1927	187,084†

Take, for example, two questions of medical organisation, namely, the medical personnel and the number of hospital beds required for a war. These requirements have been carefully studied in times of peace, and on mobilisation preparations

---

* " Final Address to the Officers of the Senior Division, Staff College," 20th December, 1911. Published in the *Army Review*, vol. ii, 1912.

† " Annual Reports on the Health of the Army."

have been made to meet initial demands. As the war progresses it becomes necessary to obtain more personnel and to organise more hospitals; and if dissatisfaction at home, disorganisation of civilian life and excessive demands are to be avoided, some practical estimate of these requirements ought to be made in anticipation of the increase of the force. During the Great War, the strength of the Royal Army Medical Corps, which in August 1914 numbered 1,279 officers and 3,811 other ranks of the regular army and 1,889 officers and 12,520 other ranks of the territorial force, rose year by year until in August 1918 it numbered 10,178 officers and 100,176 other ranks of the regular forces and 2,885 officers and 30,923 other ranks of the territorial force. It is also known that 637,746 hospital beds were equipped and maintained in the United Kingdom and in the different theatres of war. Historically, these figures show the magnitude of our effort, and if they are considered in relation to the strength of the forces for which they were required, they ought to help in calculating requirements in advance, should the necessity occur again.

Herein lies the importance of these tables of strengths to administrative medical officers. In the first place, they are given some idea of the expansion of the forces, not only in the actual theatres of operation but also at home, for which advice was required in regard to problems on recruiting, training, billeting, rationing, clothing, prevention of disease, medical attendance, evacuation, hospital accommodation, invaliding, training of convalescents and the return to duty of men discharged from hospital.

Secondly, it is essential to have a basis of calculation upon which to work when estimating, both in our own and the enemy's forces, the probable numbers of sick, deaths, invalids, evacuations overseas and returned to duty. The lack of a reliable formula on which these calculations could be based was a great handicap during the late war, and it is now hoped to supply the want by including known figures in the later chapters of this volume.

Again, the attention of the student must surely be drawn to the type of operations and the variety of countries, and consequently climates, in which our troops were fighting simultaneously. This will indicate to the broadminded the advisability of studying the language, customs, local conditions and prevailing diseases of every country where operations are anticipated. Knowledge of this kind may help to prevent the recurrence of such mistakes as the despatch to the Near or Far East of immature troops unable to stand the strain of service, or of medical units, organised in personnel, medical stores, equipment and transport for a European country.

Another matter, which has received little attention in the past but calls for consideration, springs into importance on a perusal of these tables. The British army may be called on to fight in the East, and this necessitates the employment of Eastern troops and the inclusion of followers attached to the force. As far as possible, an attempt has been made in the tables of strengths to differentiate between troops and followers, because the latter constitute an important feature of a campaign, especially from a medical point of view. Prior to the Great War the Army had had experience in the treatment and care of Indian or African troops, but was inexperienced in the prejudices, habits, diets and various peculiarities of followers and carriers in large numbers. Their duties were multifarious; they were employed in laying railways, making roads, digging trenches, constructing dugouts in the vicinity of the front line and on the lines of communication, building bunds, improvising posts, and making depots, hospitals and camps for the lines of communication. They were cooks, sanitary men and personal servants, and to a very large extent they were employed in loading and unloading transport vehicles and ships, transporting food and baggage, and evacuating sick and wounded. The greater the strength of followers, the more troops there were available for combatant duties, and as a force grew in size followers became more and more indispensable. As it is essential, therefore, to employ followers in war, it is also essential that a study should be made of their different races, customs and diets, not only from the humanitarian point of view, but also from the strictly utilitarian standpoint, since even followers are not always easy to obtain, have often to be transported from distant countries, are liable to go sick and require evacuation, invaliding, repatriation and replacement.

It was not only in the East that the use of labour corps became necessary. The average ration strength of non-European labour battalions in France in 1917 and 1918 was 62,905 and 117,848 respectively, and they were composed mainly of Indians, Egyptians, South Africans, Fijians and Chinese. This diversity of nationality had its problems, not the least of which fell to the medical services to deal with. Special hospitals had to be organised for them and arrangements made for their treatment in sections of British hospitals. Climatic conditions and racial susceptibility to disease had to be considered before determining in which localities they could best be employed. Even so, large numbers had to be repatriated.

When reorganisation was urgently required in Mesopotamia in 1916, it was found that followers could be employed on certain duties more economically than British or other troops, and their numbers steadily increased until in 1918 they had an average strength of 163,879 or 39·8 per cent. of the force. A vast amount of work had to be done in making arrangements to keep them in good health. The medical services were faced with the problems of preventing the incidence of disease among them and the spread of it from them to the troops. They had to be satisfactorily housed, and there were many other difficulties which had to be overcome.

The force, however, which depended most on its followers for the success of its operations, was the East African Expeditionary Force. Its average strength in British, Indian and African troops in 1917 was 50,702, and it had attached to it a force of followers averaging 143,959, nearly three times the strength of its troops. The medical care of this native personnel threw an exceptionally heavy strain on the medical services. As elsewhere, special arrangements had to be made to deal with the sick among them, and eventually 28 mixed rest stations, 5 casualty clearing stations and 7 carrier hospitals were organised and set apart for their use, staffed by subordinate personnel drawn from the African Native Medical Corps. Experience had shown that the African native succumbed easily to disease unless well fed, and the question of suitable dieting had therefore to receive special consideration. Questions of sanitation were at all times prominent and demanded attention. It was found, too, that much of the incidence of disease might have been avoided if greater attention had been paid to the selection of the locality in which carriers were employed. Those enlisted from low-lying country should have been employed in similar parts, and those from the highlands of British East Africa should have been sent to hilly districts. Too often this was not done.

These few instances will perhaps serve to emphasise the importance of knowing even approximately the likely strength of followers required for a campaign, whether in the East or West, so that the probable sick wastage among them may be estimated and attention paid to the sociological problems connected with their employment in the force.

CHAPTER II

A SURVEY OF BATTLE AND NON-BATTLE CASUALTIES

A SURVEY of battle and non-battle casualties with special reference to the conservation of manpower in war has rarely been undertaken in connection with the British army. It is a subject that is closely associated with the work of the army medical services, yet prior to the outbreak of war in 1914 the figures used in training the personnel of the medical services in military operations were largely culled from foreign sources. If the experience gained in handling millions of casualties is not now turned to account and an attempt made to draw from and support by statistical facts the lessons to be learned from such a survey, the history of the medical services during the Great War would be incomplete. It may be well at the outset to mention three important facts which are apt to be forgotten but which have an intimate bearing on the suggestions which follow. In the first place it should be remembered that an army is but the instrument of its country's government and that it is put into the field to carry out the policy of the government. Secondly, the army is a complicated machine of which the medical services are only a small part, but both the government and the army authorities have found by experience that they are an essential part if a high level of efficiency is to be maintained in a force. Thirdly, it must be clearly understood that the medical services have no say in the prevention of battle casualties. In that the government and army commander dominate, and the casualties resulting from an action represent the price paid in personnel by the nation for the policy adopted. The medical services may, however, offer suggestions to aid the military authorities to reduce their net losses.

This survey is an introduction to the chapters dealing with the casualties in the more important campaigns conducted by Great Britain during the Great War. It aims at giving concisely the approximate total casualties suffered by the British forces in the different theatres of war; it indicates the approximate numbers and percentages treated by the medical services; it discusses some of the problems con-

TABLE 1.—Approximate Total Casualties in the British Expeditionary Forces during the Great War

Campaign	Period	Force	Killed Off.	Killed O.R.	Died of wounds Off.	Died of wounds O.R.	Died of disease or injury Off.	Died of disease or injury O.R.	Missing and prisoners of war Off.	Missing and prisoners of war O.R.	Wounded Off.	Wounded O.R.	Sick or injured Off.	Sick or injured O.R.	Grand total Off.	Grand total O.R.	Total
France and Flanders	1914	Whole force	1,038	11,971	228	3,429	12	496	783	25,728	1,877	53,812	1,910	76,139	5,848	171,575	177,423
	1915		3,032	45,572	745	14,159	110	2,797	802	23,754	7,434	217,529	15,282	561,549	27,405	865,360	892,765
	1916		6,506	100,905	1,814	35,065	229	5,612	1,628	42,047	20,345	443,352	23,187	614,893	53,709	1,241,874	1,295,583
	1917		7,659	124,102	2,627	47,205	271	8,151	2,634	51,180	20,835	494,027	40,591	993,253	74,617	1,717,898	1,792,515
	1918		5,111	75,365	3,044	43,040	635	14,785	5,066	166,222	25,733	552,669	45,076	1,124,508	84,665	1,975,589	2,060,254
Italy	1917–18	British	90	1,140	—	58	26	733	30	314	289	4,400	3,290	47,262	3,725	53,907	57,632
Macedonia	1915–18	British and Dominion	145	2,652	76	1,223	76	3,668	81	2,697	855	16,033	13,767	463,751	15,000	490,024	505,024
Dardanelles	1915–16	British	808	10,426	211	5,135	65	2,043	263	7,262	1,498	43,223	5,949	137,097	8,794	205,186	213,980
Egypt and Palestine	1915–18	British and Dominion	630	6,764	232	2,761	247	5,734	180	3,691	2,528	34,665	17,730	479,666	21,547	533,281	554,828
Mesopotamia	1914–18	Whole force	823	10,185	308	4,973	286	16,426	644	14,577	2,438	51,259	19,676	784,030	24,175	881,450	905,625
North Russia	1918–19	British and Dominion	27	160	4	20	11	110	17	160	50	455	882	8,579	991	9,484	10,475
East Africa	1914–18	All troops Followers	214	2,475 †376	56	698	125	6,433 44,911	66	1,235 635	514	7,263 1,333	*10,294	*319,938 *241,688	11,269	338,042 288,943	349,311 288,943
South-West Africa	1914–15	Dominion	21	164	3	58	7	174	44	738	62	498	809	23,756	946	25,388	26,334
Total United Kingdom	1914–18	British and Dominion	26,104	392,257	9,348	157,824	2,100	111,073	12,238	‡340,220	84,458	1,920,518	198,443 1,965,646	5,876,109 1,965,646	332,691	8,798,001	9,130,692 1,965,646
																	11,096,338

* 1916–18 only. † Includes died of wounds.
‡ These totals include 7,358 officers and 184,054 other ranks who were prisoners of war, of whom 487 officers and 15,845 other ranks died in captivity.

nected with the disposal of casualties; and it offers suggestions which may help to conserve the manpower of a force. These different points are so closely interwoven that there is bound to be a certain overlapping in the treatment of them, but this has been avoided as far as possible.

Table 1 recapitulates for the main theatres of operation the approximate total casualties in the British Expeditionary Forces during the Great War.

The various proportions of the different groups of casualties to each other, based on the figures in Table 1 exclusive of non-battle casualties in the United Kingdom, are given in Table 2.

TABLE 2.—Proportions (excluding United Kingdom)

	Officers	Other ranks	Total
1. Total battle casualties to total non-battle casualties	1 : 1·52	1 : 2·13	1 : 2·10
2. Total killed to total wounded	1 : 3·59	1 : 5·30	1 : 5·19
3. Total killed, missing, prisoners of war and died of wounds to wounded less died of wounds	1 : 1·77	1 : 2·16	1 : 2·14
4. Total died of disease or injury to total sick or injured	1 : 95·50	1 : 53·90	1 : 54·67
5. Total killed, missing, prisoners of war, died of wounds, disease or injury to total wounded, sick or injured less died of wounds, disease or injury	1 : 5·68	1 : 7·79	1 : 7·69

As already defined, casualties are either battle or non-battle, and the further subdivision of wastage in a force into permanent and temporary losses among battle and non-battle casualties determines more clearly the scope and limitations of the medical services. Permanent losses definitely include those killed in action; for military purposes during a campaign they also include the missing and those taken prisoner by the enemy. These casualties do not come under medical care, and it will be seen from Table 1 that they totalled approximately 770,819 or 26·19 per cent. of all battle casualties. Temporary losses, broadly speaking, may be taken to include all sick and wounded casualties who come under medical charge and form a large proportion of the non-effectives present in a force.* Reference to Table 3 will show that the admissions to medical units numbered 8,354,839 for the campaigns under review, representing 91·54

* In France during 1918 non-effectives, including sick and wounded, prisoners under detention, and men on light duty, formed 6 per cent. of the average ration strength of the force.

per cent. of the total casualties. Of this number, however, those who died subsequently of wounds, disease or injury,

TABLE 3.—Approximate Number of Casualties in the British Expeditionary Forces treated by the Medical Services, with Percentages of Total Casualties

Campaign	Period	Force	No. of casualties treated by the medical services			Percentages of total casualties treated		
			Battle	Non-battle	Total	Battle	Non-battle	Total
France and Flanders	1914	Whole force	59,346	78,557	137,903	33·45	44·28	77·73
	1915		239,867	579,738	819,605	26·87	64·94	91·81
	1916		500,576	643,921	1,144,497	38·64	49·70	88·34
	1917		564,694	1,042,266	1,606,960	31·50	58·15	89·65
	1918		624,486	1,184,004	1,808,490	30·31	57·47	87·78
	1914–18		1,988,969	3,528,486	5,517,455	31·98	56·74	88·73
Italy	1917–18	British	4,747	51,311	56,058	8·24	89·03	97·27
Macedonia	1915–18	British and Dominion	18,187	481,262	499,449	3·60	95·29	98·90
Dardanelles	1915–16	British	47,803	145,154	192,957	22·34	67·84	90·18
Egypt and Palestine	1915–18	British and Dominion	40,186	503,377	543,563	7·24	90·73	97·97
Mesopotamia	1914–18	Whole force	58,978	820,418	879,396	6·51	90·59	97·10
North Russia	1918–19	British and Dominion	529	9,582	10,111	5·05	91·47	96·53
East Africa *	1916–18	All troops Followers	7,728 1,324	336,540 284,891	344,268 286,215	2·23 ·46	96·91 99·29	99·14 99·76
South-West Africa	1914–15	Dominion	621	24,746	25,367	2·36	93·97	96·33
			2,169,072	6,185,767	8,354,839	23·77	67·78	91·54

* From 1916 only, the number of non-battle casualties before then being unknown.

or were invalided from the service, must in the final analysis of casualties be transferred to permanent losses.

It is with temporary losses that the medical services are intimately associated in carrying out two important duties,

SURVEY OF CASUALTIES 15

TABLE 4.—Admissions to Hospital and Disposal of Cases

Campaign	Period	Force	Admissions		Deaths		Returned to duty in the theatre of war		Evacuated overseas	
			Wounded	Sick or injured	Wounded	Sick or injured	Wounded	Sick or injured	Wounded	Sick or injured
France and Flanders	1914–18	Whole force	1,988,969	3,528,486	151,356	32,098	584,959	2,396,273	1,245,535	1,034,160
Italy	1917–18	British	4,747	51,311	58	759	1,956	35,380	2,669	13,442
Macedonia	1915–18	British and Dominion	18,187	481,262	1,299	3,744	9,919	348,230	6,849	116,190
Dardanelles ...	1915–16	British	47,803	145,154	3,082	2,108	*42,368	*141,376	Not known	
Egypt and Palestine	1915–18	British and Dominion	40,186	503,377	2,993	5,981	Not known		Not known	
Mesopotamia ...	1914–18	Whole force	58,978	820,418	5,281	16,712	25,911	634,889	26,814	154,343
North Russia ...	1918–19	British and Dominion	529	9,582	24	121	254	7,297	251	2,164
East Africa ...	1917–18	All troops	5,631	186,203	511	4,746	Not known		33,202	
South-West Africa	1914–15	Dominion	621	24,746	61	181	Not known		Not known	

* Total numbers finally returned to duty.

one to the individual concerned and the other to the army and the nation. The first of these is to the soldier who has a right to expect that, if he is willing or is compelled to run the risk of losing his life or of suffering disease or injury in war, his country will see that everything possible is done to save his life or mitigate his suffering. The second duty incumbent on the medical services is to endeavour to prevent the spread of disease in a force and to restore to health the maximum number of sick and wounded in the shortest possible space of time. In fact, the medical services of an army might rightly be regarded as a trustee for the men and the State, and the figures which emerge from a study of the casualties in the late war bear testimony to the efficient fulfilment of this trust.

Table 4 has been drawn up to show at a glance the disposal of casualties in certain theatres of operation. The table is incomplete to the extent specified owing to lack of information, but in those campaigns where the figures are known returns show that of the sick and wounded admitted to medical units 3·04 per cent. died, 58·10 per cent. were returned to duty in the theatre of war, and 37·41 per cent. were evacuated overseas.

In the final disposal of cases the numbers who die, who are discharged from the service as invalids or who are ultimately returned to duty in some capacity, must be taken into account. Taking the first of these, the percentages of the total sick and wounded casualties in the different British Expeditionary Forces during the war who died after coming into medical charge are shown in Table 5. The corresponding figures for the South African War, 1899–1902, are also shown for comparison.

TABLE 5.—Percentage of Deaths among Casualties admitted to Medical Units

Campaign	Period	Force	Percentage of deaths	
			Wounded	Sick or injured
France and Flanders	1914–18	Whole force	7·61	·91
Italy	1918	British	1·22	1·48
Macedonia	1915–18	British and Dominion	7·14	·78
Dardanelles	1915–16	British	6·45	2·84
Egypt and Palestine	1915–18	British and Dominion	7·45	1·19
Mesopotamia	1914–18	Whole force	8·95	2·04
North Russia	1918–19	British and Dominion	4·54	1·26
East Africa	1917–18	All troops	9·07	2·55
South-West Africa	1914–15	Dominion	9·82	·73
		Total	7·60	1·16
South African War	1899–1902	British and Dominion, other ranks only	8·62	3·39

SURVEY OF CASUALTIES

In all theatres of the Great War the percentage of deaths from disease or injury was lower than in the South African War. With the exception of Mesopotamia, East and South-West Africa, there is a distinct decline in the percentage of deaths from wounds, and that too despite the greater concentration, intensity and range of gun and rifle fire and the introduction of other offensive weapons of war. It is important to note that 55 per cent. of the deaths from wounds and 32 per cent. of the deaths from disease or injury occurred in casualty clearing stations or other front-line medical units. The remainder died in ambulance trains, in hospitals on the lines of communication, or at home.

Complete details of the numbers who were discharged from the service as invalids during the war are not available, but some idea of this wastage can be formed from two different groups of figures, one covering the theatres of war in 1914 and 1915 with the exception of East and South-West Africa, and the other a series of cases from 1916 onwards. Both these groups give the final disposal of the cases to which they refer. The figures in the first group have been noted in their respective chapters. The rate of invaliding for sickness or injury was high in the United Kingdom compared with that of other areas. This was probably due to a number of immature soldiers breaking down under training, as happens in peace time.*
The second group is taken from the sample cases analysed by the Ministry of Pensions. They were compiled from cards drawn from France, Italy, Africa, Egypt and Palestine, Macedonia, Mesopotamia, North Russia, Indian garrisons, and the United Kingdom, and included representatives of the following arms of the service: Cavalry, Engineers, Artillery, Infantry, Tank Corps, Machine Gun Corps, Royal Army Service Corps, Royal Army Medical Corps, Labour and other units. It must be borne in mind, however, when viewing the percentages of admissions invalided for the first seventeen months of the war alongside those of the sample figures, shown in Table 6, that the latter include cases admitted to hospital after the Armistice in November 1918, when active fighting had ceased, demobilisation was in progress and the tendency was to return men to civil life.

From the purely military aspect an analysis by campaigns

---

* During the year 1926–27, of 49,182 recruits who were medically examined 16,174 were rejected on examination and 1,083 were discharged as unfit within six months of enlistment.

TABLE 6.—Percentages of Admissions Discharged from the Service as Invalids

	Period	Wounded			Sick			Injured			Total		
		Off.	O.R.	Total	Off.	O.R.	Total	Off.	O.R.	Total	Off.	O.R.	Total
Expeditionary forces Analysis of 1,043,653 cases	1914–15	·27	5·56	5·38	·25	3·61	3·52	·29	1·76	1·73	·26	3·85	3·75
	1916–20	5·19	9·10	8·58	2·46*	4·12*	3·97*	—	—	—	3·11	5·09	4·88

* Includes injured.

of the admissions to hospital showing the numbers and percentages who returned to duty in the different theatres of operations is most important.

TABLE 7.—Numbers and Percentages Returned to Duty in Certain Theatres of War

Campaign	Period	Force	Nos. returned to duty in theatre of operations			Percentages of total admissions		
			Wounded	Sick or injured	Total	Wounded	Sick or injured	Total
France and Flanders	1914–18	Whole force	584,959	2,396,273	2,981,232	29·40	67·91	54·03
Italy	1917–18	British	1,956	35,380	37,336	41·21	68·95	66·60
Macedonia	1915–18	British and Dominion	9,919	348,230	358,149	54·54	72·36	71·71
Mesopotamia	1914–18	Whole force	25,911	634,889	660,800	43·93	77·39	75·14
North Russia	1918–19	British and Dominion	254	7,297	7,551	48·01	76·15	74·68

Prior to the Great War little had been heard of this subject. It is right, therefore, to trace briefly its development. After the initial battles in 1914, attention was mainly concentrated on the ever-increasing cost in personnel of modern warfare, on the evacuation of sick and wounded, and on the pressing need for reinforcements. It was only when battles became more extensive, submarine warfare more intensive, and hope of an early termination of hostilities had faded, that serious consideration was given to the percentages of the sick and wounded who had returned to duty. The dawn of this fresh perspective, the growing certainty that the war would drag on for months, probably years, the necessity for a more critical estimation of the enemy's losses and of our own possible future requirements, all combined to focus attention on the number of casualties rendered fit to return to duty in a theatre of operations and the assistance which it was possible for the medical services to give to the army in this connection. By increasing this number, more trained men became available in the theatre of war, fewer reinforcements were required from the United Kingdom and overseas, and less transport was required for the evacuation of invalids by sea or for the conveyance of reinforcements to the armies abroad. Over and above the high percentage returned to duty in the theatre of war a great number of those evacuated overseas or to the United Kingdom ultimately returned to duty. This detail is not available for all theatres of war, and in some campaigns it is difficult to differentiate between those who returned to duty in the war area and those who returned to duty after transfer overseas. Taking into consideration all the information available, it is calculated that during the years under review approximately 82 per cent. of wounded and 93 per cent. of sick or injured were ultimately returned to some form of duty.

A further subdivision of the numbers returned to duty is important from the administrative point of view. The percentages of wounded and sick who are fit to return to full duty in the front line have been worked out as opposed to those who are fit only for garrison duty, duty on the lines of communication, or sedentary occupations. These are points of great value in a prolonged war when many forces have to be kept up to strength, and so Table 8 has been calculated to show, in broad figures, these percentages in the final disposal of cases treated by the army medical services overseas and in the United Kingdom.*

---

* No doubt some feeling of appreciation for this practical assistance was in the minds of the Cabinet ministers, prominent politicians and army commanders, who entertained to dinner on 8th June, 1920, several regular and temporary representatives of the Army Medical Services. It was an historic occasion, and from the report of the speeches it is evident that the men who had held the destiny of the Empire in their hands during the Great War were aware of the difficulties which had beset the medical services in coping with the mass of casualties far beyond any estimate given by the best informed authorities in the army. It was interesting, too, because an outline was given of the evolution of the liaison between the medical services and the other branches of the army, commencing with the South African War, when, it was stated, the last man to hear of any intended move of the army was the senior medical officer, and terminating with the intimate relationship which existed in the final stages of the Great War. Outstanding are the expressions of admiration for the results achieved in the prevention of the spread of the enteric group of diseases, the ultimate smooth evacuation of casualties and their efficient hospitalisation and treatment, but there is no definite mention of the great service rendered to the army and the nation by the return to duty of approximately 90 per cent. of the total admissions to hospital. There is, however, the hint by the then Director-General, Army Medical Services, Lieutenant-General Sir J. Goodwin, that the very best that was done in the Great War is not the best attainable, and that as time goes on, as science advances and as knowledge progresses, the services must also advance and progress.

It cannot be denied that the figures in Table 8 are satisfactory, and, moreover, it is reasonable to assume that in future more satisfactory results will only be obtained by close attention to the following points :

(a) Better and quicker methods of evacuation.
(b) Provision of adequate hospital accommodation.
(c) Improved technique and treatment of the sick and wounded.
(d) Preventive measures against disease.

This final volume of the *Official Medical History of the War* originated in the desire for knowledge with the hope that research might influence a better result in the future. As the years pass, it will become more and more essential that a review of this kind should be available for the rising generations; for,

TABLE 8.—Final Disposal of Cases treated by the Medical Services

Disposal	Approximate percentages		
	Wounded	Sick or injured	Total
Returned to duty in front line :			
(a) From front line medical unit	7	21	18
(b) From hospital or convalescent depot	57	63	60
Returned to duty on L. of C., garrison or sedentary occupation	18	9	12
Died	7	1	3
Discharged from the service as invalids	8	4	5
Disposal otherwise, but not stated	3	2	2

although it is hoped that they may be spared the horrors of war, were such a calamity again to overtake humanity, they might be able to save thousands of lives, mitigate the sufferings of hundreds of thousands, and conserve the manhood of the Empire by avoiding the early misunderstandings and mistakes of the Great War.

It is essential, therefore, to go back to fundamental principles and ask what is actually required of the medical services in the field if the full benefits of that service are to be obtained from the very outset of a campaign. To treat the sick and wounded and prevent disease would probably be the answer to this question. This implies that the medical services are given a definite organisation, personnel and equipment with which to work, and that they are fully equipped to collect, evacuate and treat sick and wounded casualties whenever and wherever the occasion demands. In reality, however, it is by no means so simple. The difficulties and intricacies involved are not always realised. It is a known fact that a government can supply an army with the finest doctors, nurses, materials and appliances the world can produce, as witness what was accomplished in the later years of the war. This is not the place to deal with the methods of treatment or the purely professional aspects of medicine and surgery, pathology or preventive medicine. These have already been discussed in seven volumes of the *Medical History of the War*. It must suffice to mention that as the expeditionary forces were expanded and organised to meet the conditions of modern warfare, they were staffed by members of the medical profession, drawn from expert specialism, universities, hospitals, medical schools and general practice—men of ripe experience and high achievements, men devoted to their profession, who gave of their best at home and overseas in the service of the sick and wounded of their country and Empire. But of what use is such an organisation unless, in the first instance, casualties are systematically collected, rapidly evacuated and suitably accommodated ? Failure to appreciate the significance of these elementary points or impracticability to provide for them lay at the root of many mistakes and disasters.

It is advisable to examine somewhat minutely why this should be so, since the majority of combatant as well as medical officers are familiar with the general outline of the duties of the medical services in war. These duties may be summarised in a few sentences. Casualties on the field of battle receive first aid and are collected and evacuated by regimental stretcher bearers to the nearest medical post, the regimental aid post, organised by the regimental medical officer, and usually situated in a dugout or shelter in close touch with unit headquarters. Here a subdivision is made ; casualties able to walk are despatched with or without a guide to the walking wounded collecting post, if there is one, or direct to the advanced dressing station ; while the more serious cases are conveyed thither by the field ambulance bearer personnel, either by hand stretcher or by some other form of transport. At the advanced dressing station, which is formed as near the front line as military operations permit, first field dressings are readjusted, patients are treated, given hot drinks and other warm comforts before being transferred to the main dressing station where, if necessary, the slighter cases are detained, very urgent operations are performed, dressings are again adjusted, and the necessary clerical records are made. The sick and wounded requiring further treatment are then conveyed by horse-drawn or mechanical transport to the casualty clearing station which forms the first hospital link between the firing-line and the base. Cases which are likely to recover after a few days' treatment are retained in the area, if possible, to recuperate before returning to duty. Serious cases are treated by skilled surgeons or physicians before evacuation, which may be either by motor ambulance convoy, ambulance train, river steamer or barge, to the hospitals on the lines of communication and at the base. Further evacuation is effected by train, ship or other transport according to the organisation provided or the destination of the patients.

Moreover, it is probable that the combatant as well as the medical officer knows what medical units are authorised for every stage in the system of evacuation, and how they should be sited, moved and used. Wherein, then, lies the difficulty in collecting, evacuating and housing casualties, and why should there be mistakes and failures? The chief reason lies in the erroneous belief that the medical services are alone responsible. This is not the case. The second is in the inadequate provision of personnel, transport and accommodation. The medical services are only part of the complicated machinery of the army, and before they can function properly the other parts must function too. It rests with the army commander to decide whether or not an attempt is to be made to collect, protect, evacuate and treat all casualties. The medical services are not responsible for the policy; they can only render advice and carry out to the best of their ability the policy adopted. If an attempt is to be made to collect and evacuate all the casualties in an extensive and prolonged engagement, the limited regular resources of the medical services are insufficient and supplementary personnel, equipment and transport must be authorised by the staff and provided by the respective services or departments concerned. This can only follow on a close liaison between the staff and the administrative medical officer of the formation. Enemy action may, however, interfere with the collection of wounded, or it may be that the allocation of additional personnel, equipment and transport will upset the plans of the army commander and jeopardise a successful issue. In these events, it must be plainly and squarely recognised that the medical services are not responsible for the failure to attend to all the sick and wounded, and that this failure is part

SURVEY OF CASUALTIES

of the price paid for the operations. No better illustration of this principle could be given than the following, which is quoted from the official history of the campaign in Gallipoli : *

> " But no matter how many hospital ships and transports equipped as casualty carriers were available off the peninsula, it was obvious that the weakest link in the chain of evacuation must be the actual embarkation of the wounded on an open beach while fighting was still in progress in the immediate neighbourhood. The dictates of humanity, apart from the necessity of preventing the tiny beaches becoming overcrowded with non-effective men, called for the prompt embarkation of every casualty. Yet it was even more important, and in fact vital, that the disembarkation of the fighting troops, their ammunition, food and water, should not be interfered with; and all available small craft would be needed for this latter service. It was this question that offered the greatest obstacle to a satisfactory solution. It opened up a problem not only without precedent in modern war, but one which, before the inception of the Dardanelles campaign, had formed no part of the training either of the Staff or the medical services. Apart from the meagre instructions that ' sanitary and medical officers should be landed amongst the first troops of the main body,' and that in the event of a forced re-embarkation, ' wounded men, if they cannot be re-embarked during daylight, and without interfering with the re-embarkation of other troops and material, must be left on shore and the best arrangements possible made for their care,' the pre-war textbooks can be searched in vain for any reference to this important and thorny subject.
>
> " In these difficult circumstances, Sir Ian Hamilton adhered to the principle that tactical requirements must be pre-eminent. He laid down that small craft engaged on disembarking troops must on no account be diverted to take wounded to the waiting ships, and that this work must be undertaken solely by specially equipped pulling launches which the navy would make available in the afternoon of the day of the landing, as soon as steamboats to tow them could be spared. Unfortunately, only six of these launches in all were available, and each launch could carry only twelve serious cases in cots, or treble that number of light cases. It was recognised that these arrangements could not fail to inflict hardship on the wounded, but this was looked upon as unavoidable in the peculiar circumstances of the case, as indeed it probably was."

In a word, it must be clearly understood that the medical services in war have to rely on two separate organisations for the fulfilment of their functions, one the regular organisation laid down, and the other the supplementary organisation, agreed to in principle, but left to the army commander to sanction and to the force in the field to provide. Failure to realise this important fact and to act on it was partly responsible for the breakdown of the medical organisation in the

---

* *Military Operations—Gallipoli*, pp. 145–146.

Dardanelles campaign, Mesopotamia and East Africa. The reports of Parliamentary inquiries and War Office missions emphasise this, and the following passage taken from the *Report on Medical and Sanitary Matters in German East Africa*, 1917, is probably the most concise and pregnant description of the principles involved : " The medical services are dependent on other departments and if these fail them in any way, whether as regards supplies, transport facilities, disregard of advice or slowness in taking action upon a recommendation, then the responsibility does not rest with the director of medical services."

In discussing the need for the supplementary organisation the opportunity arises of showing in what ways additional help is required by the medical services and the benefits to be derived from its provision. If it is recalled that under the regular organisation combatant units have only a limited number of stretcher bearers, that a field ambulance is only equipped for 150 patients, that three field ambulances are allotted to an infantry division, and that in modern intensive warfare the casualties may amount to 60 per cent. of the effective strength of a division, the necessity for additional supplies of personnel and equipment, when occasion demands, in the collection and evacuation of casualties will be understood. One has only to picture the regimental and field ambulance stretcher bearers struggling slowly for three or four thousand yards, carrying inert and badly stricken comrades across open plains or along muddy, shell-swept trenches or roads in their heroic task of clearing wounded from the battlefield to some point where wheeled transport was available, to realise the urgent need at times for additional bearers, field stretchers, blankets, comforts, and all forms of mechanical transport. Slowly but surely this need was met, as the following three instances on the Western front show : (*a*) Regimental stretcher bearers were increased from 16 to 32 per battalion for the battles of the Somme from 1st July to 18th November 1916 ; (*b*) each division in the attack on Vimy Ridge from 9th to 14th April 1917 was allotted 100 men as extra stretcher bearers ; and (*c*) 600 fresh stretcher bearers per division were supplied every twelve hours for the third battle of Ypres, from 21st July to 10th November 1917. In addition, stores of extra stretchers and blankets were organised at convenient sites.

This increase of personnel for stretcher-bearing work was required not only for front-line work but also at casualty clearing stations, general hospitals, railway stations and ports of embarkation, to assist in loading and unloading ambulance convoys, wagons, trains and hospital ships. The need for it was not confined to France; it was required in many of the other expeditionary forces, and, as was the case in France, this personnel had to be supplied from other than medical units. Furthermore, the work of a stretcher bearer, whether on the battlefield or at the base, required fresh, fit men, for it was arduous and time was valuable. The natural desire to keep the fittest men for combatant duties at first prompted units to detail men unfit for heavy work, but this error of judgment was corrected later when it was realised that unfit men caused delay in bringing casualties to shelter and treatment, and delay meant an upsetting of convoy, railway and shipping programmes. If additional stretcher bearers, stretchers and blankets were not available, the wounded had to suffer as they did in the early days of the war, particularly in France, Mesopotamia and Gallipoli. Two illustrations will suffice to emphasise this fact. It is officially recorded that during certain battles in the Mesopotamia campaign " the bearers were insufficient in number to cope with the casualties," and that " these wounded were covered with mud . . . and after lying out for some time they were in a very exhausted condition, many dying from exposure." * In Gallipoli the numbers reported missing, presumed dead, and died before admission to medical unit,† must surely strike home the loss and suffering incurred if proper provision for collecting wounded cannot be, or is not, made.

At the beginning of the war mobile medical units were equipped with horse-drawn ambulance and transport wagons. Neither motor vehicles nor motor ambulance convoys found a place in the establishment of a force. Other units of the army were similarly handicapped. By degrees quick-moving forms of transport were taken into use, developed and extensively employed in front areas for the evacuation of casualties and the conveyance of troops, supplies, ammunition and stores. On the Western front, in addition to the convoys of general service wagons, motor omnibuses, charabancs and other petrol-driven vehicles, a network of trolleys, tramways, light and broad-gauge railways was constructed. These were primarily intended for the conveyance of troops and supplies, but economy and

---

* *General History of the Medical Services*, vol. iv, p. 209.
† p. 201.

efficiency necessitated their employment at certain periods for the evacuation of casualties, because the special transport allotted to the medical units, namely, the ambulance wagons, motor ambulances and motor ambulance convoys, proved insufficient for the numbers requiring removal. To have provided the medical services with transport reserved for their own particular use would have been extravagant and outside practical policy. This necessitated the very careful arrangement of programmes, allotments and time-tables for the transport available.

The Great War offered many illustrations of the practical importance of this system of transport in evacuating casualties, but two will suffice to emphasise the benefits to be derived from the use of utility transport for medical purposes. When the Ist and IInd Corps were advancing on Kut-al-Amara in Mesopotamia, a light railway was constructed to connect Shaikh Saad with the front-line positions, and by a simple contrivance the ordinary supply trucks were adapted for the conveyance of sick and wounded on the return journey. The numbers of sick and wounded carried by train and boat to Shaikh Saad between 13th December 1916 and 2nd April 1917, totalled 30,217, as shown in Table 9. Between 13th December 1916 and 15th February 1917, 18,874 patients were evacuated down river from Shaikh Saad by ordinary river boats and one hospital steamer, the H.S. "Sikkim."

TABLE 9.—Sick and wounded evacuated to Shaikh Saad, 13th December 1916 to 2nd April 1917

Mode of evacuation	British		Indian		Total	
	Wounded	Sick	Wounded	Sick	Wounded	Sick
Train ...	4,175	3,769	4,316	4,864	8,491	8,633
Boat ...	1,526	2,845	2,734	5,988	4,260	8,833
Total ...	5,701	6,614	7,050	10,852	12,751	17,466

The Western front supplies the second illustration. During the battle of Cambrai from 27th September 1918 to 2nd October 1918, the Canadian Corps, finding the roads congested with cars and buses, sent up a train of twelve box-cars to Quéant while the dressing-stations there were still under ground observation by the enemy. This service was kept up throughout the battle and contributed largely to the success of the evacuation. The number of wounded carried by these improvised hospital trains is shown in Table 10.

Casualty clearing stations formed the important link between field ambulances at the front and hospitals on the lines of communication, and they, too, required assistance from other branches of the army, as they had to be enlarged, suitably equipped and grouped near main railway lines with special branch lines and sidings constructed to save transport, facilitate loading and speed up evacuation. Huts, tents or buildings were erected or adapted for the accommodation of patients;

TABLE 10.—Evacuation by Broad-Gauge Trains from Quéant to Casualty Clearing Stations

Date	No. of trains	Walking wounded	Stretcher cases	Total
1918				
Sept. 27	7	1,545	659	2,204
,, 28	4	720	283	1,003
,, 29	5	965	485	1,450
,, 30	6	1,055	429	1,484
Oct. 1	5	1,275	450	1,725
,, 2	1	85	41	126
Total	28	5,645	2,347	7,992

water and lighting systems and other sanitary arrangements were provided and installed; and motor or rail transport, was detailed and provided in the event of a forward or other move being ordered. Table 11 gives an approximate idea of the numbers of casualty clearing stations and the extra medical personnel required in France for certain battles.

The functions of casualty clearing stations may be briefly defined as follows : (a) to retain all serious cases unfit to be moved or requiring operation before being evacuated ; (b) to retain all slight cases likely to be fit for duty in a short period ; (c) to evacuate all other cases which require further treatment in the theatre of operations or in the United Kingdom. For the successful performance of these functions the headquarters of the force decided the number of casualty clearing stations to be employed and their proper siting in relation to the firing-line.

The fact that 1,140,398 wounded were admitted to casualty clearing stations in France during 1917 and 1918 gives some idea of the work undertaken by these units. Of this number 30 per cent. benefited by receiving operative treatment at the

TABLE 11.—Number of Casualty Clearing Stations employed and Additional Medical Personnel required during certain Battle Periods in France and Flanders, 1915 to 1917

Battle	Period	Armies engaged	No. of divisions	No. of casualty clearing stations employed	Personnel			Additional personnel supplied by other Armies, G.H.Q. and L. of C.			No. of wounded admitted during first week
					M.Os.	Sisters	Other ranks	M.Os.	Sisters	Other ranks	
Neuve Chapelle	10th–15th March 1915	First	4	7	43	29	457	8	6	25	8,181
Ypres	22nd–28th April 1915	Second	6	7	55	39	582	7	8	5	8,081
Loos	25th Sept.–1st Oct. 1915	First	16	12	91	75	1,131	7	—	64	24,324
Somme	1st–7th July 1916	Fourth	21	15	154	130	1,895	20	7	39	42,212
Arras, including Vimy Ridge	9th–16th April 1917	First Third	17 20	11 13	100 124	99 174	1,263 1,495	15 35	23 18	62 89	}29,038
Messines	7th–14th June 1917	Second	12	13	116	141	1,342	100	118	443	18,492
Ypres	31st July–6th August 1917	Second Fifth	1 13	9 15	77 110	91 128	969 1,173	13 179	6 277	39 1,389	}25,638

hands of some of the finest surgeons in the world. Attempts were made in France to improvise or detail sections of these units as advanced operating centres, and place them in certain positions nearer and nearer the firing-line in order to shorten the interval between the time of injury and the time of operation. On the whole, the majority of consulting surgeons and administrative medical officers realised that good surgical work would not meet with the success it deserved if patients were retained in a forward shell-swept area with the noise of battle continually in their ears, or if there was constant anxiety that the enemy might break through. They recognised the importance and need of rest and quiet, the value of good nursing, and the necessity of freedom from noise and anxiety in the saving of life and the attainment of good after results.

Many may argue that what was feasible for the armies in France and Flanders, with long periods of trench warfare, might not be possible in countries where there was a more mobile form of warfare. Before considering that contention it should be remembered that 30 per cent. of the wounded admitted to casualty clearing stations required and received urgent operation, and also that 55 per cent. of the total deaths from wounds occurred at field ambulances or casualty clearing stations. It is essential, therefore, if lives are to be saved and suffering diminished, to concentrate medical and surgical skill at those units where severe cases can receive the most skilled treatment at a time when they need it most. It must be fully realised that to deprive any force of its pivotal centre for the early and modern treatment of casualties before their distribution to lines of communication hospitals is to invite the conditions which prevailed in the early days of the war in France, Gallipoli and Mesopotamia, and so increase the suffering of the wounded, the infections of the wounds, the degree of disability, and the length of stay in hospital. That it is not impossible to provide such units is shown by historical facts. As warfare became more and more mobile in France, Macedonia, Palestine, Mesopotamia, East Africa and North Russia, such pivotal units were organised, adapted to meet local conditions and successfully employed. It only meant that in the different forces operating in these countries, certain units retaining serious cases were left behind until they were cleared; that equipment was on a smaller scale owing to transport difficulties and the smaller number of cases to be treated; and that in hostile and savage countries with marauding inhabitants likely to rob and mutilate, protective measures, including suitable arrangements for guards and defences, were thought out, prepared and provided.

The medical units on the lines of communication were the second link in the chain of evacuation, and as such the importance of their medical arrangements and the supplementary assistance they required are worthy of consideration. The general hospitals were established in tents, huts or buildings, and the formation and planning of hospital bases and convalescent depots, with all the attendant accessories that made them in reality small towns with sanitary, drainage and lighting arrangements, were at all times intricate and difficult problems. The objects of this organisation may be briefly summarised : (a) the transfer of casualties with all possible speed and comfort, with the necessary facilities for professional treatment whilst *en route* from the battle area to the base hospitals ; (b) the provision of all that is necessary for the exercise of professional technique, operative skill and good nursing by the staff at these hospitals ; (c) the subsequent transfer of selected patients overseas, with provision for their continued treatment whilst on board ship ; and (d) the expeditious transfer of other patients after treatment to depots from which to rejoin their units.

Casualties were transferred by road, rail, river, canal or sea according to the resources available, the physical features of the country and the distances to be covered. On the Western front roads were only used for the evacuation of comparatively small numbers on rare occasions when railways could not be used, or were so continuously in use that it was desirable to accelerate evacuation by removing cases in motor ambulance cars or motor buses. Occasionally the nature of the wound determined the mode of transport, as for example in France, where evacuation by mechanically-propelled barges on the canals was reserved for special types of casualty, such as chest wounds. Evacuation by sea was the only possible method in the Dardanelles campaign and in the later stages of the East African campaign in the Kilwa area, when 34,730 patients were evacuated by coastal ships.

Mesopotamia stands out as the country where river evacuation, assisted later by a railway, was the method of selection. At first the force employed the archaic mahela and any river vessel available, but as personnel was scarce and equipment and transport were deficient, the wounded suffered untold misery. As the campaign developed and the conditions were made known, every type of river hospital craft was tried; some were built to a theoretical design and were elaborately equipped, but proved practically useless for certain stretches of the river. The most useful transport was the utility vessel known in the later stages of the war as ambulance transport steamers and barges. These vessels carried troops and stores up-river from Basra and conveyed sick and wounded on the return journey from Baghdad and Amara. The patients suffered little or no discomfort; there was seldom a hitch; and the force benefited by employing one vessel for several purposes, and attained efficiency by co-operation and organisation without duplication of transport or a lavish expenditure of personnel. From June 1916 to the end of December 1918, 103,229 British and 154,322 Indian casualties, and 7,162 prisoners of war, making in all a total of 264,713, were evacuated down river by ambulance transport steamers and barges.

In countries where railways were relied upon, ambulance trains were provided and reserved for the sole use of casualties, but during periods of active fighting they were insufficient and had to be supplemented by temporary and improvised ambulance trains. An example of this can be seen in the evacuation from the Aisne front in September 1914, when 3,259 cases were evacuated from Braisne by ambulance train, 1,701 by troop train, 430 by motor lorries, 58 by motor cars and 362 by French ambulance train. From August 1914 to the end of December 1918 in France the total sick and wounded evacuated from the front to the base by ambulance train or improvised ambulance train numbered 3,443,507, while from one base to another the numbers carried were 1,610,672. It is obvious that a system which has to transport such large numbers must require considerable forethought and organisation. It is common knowledge that at the outset of a campaign the British force must rely on some form of improvised transport to meet its needs, as regular ambulance trains are not required in times of peace, and it takes time to construct and equip them after the declaration of war. The improvised system in the early stages of the Great War broke down, and great was the outcry against the medical services when the wounded arrived at base hospitals, exhausted with suffering and poisoned by foully infected wounds. When in succeeding years battles became more intensive and more prolonged and the casualties grew in numbers, with increasing experience in organisation and co-operation, it was found necessary to reconsider and resuscitate the practical and economical method of employing improvised ambulance trains. The merits of both regular and improvised ambulance trains must be recognised, as in the earlier phases of a campaign the latter will be used for both sitting and lying-down cases until such time as the regular ambulance trains can be constructed, equipped and despatched to the theatre of operations.

To appreciate fully the value of ambulance trains one must see in the mind's eye a fierce battle in progress, with thousands of sick and wounded casualties waiting to be brought back, fresh troops being hurried up to the front line, and in all probability roads and railway lines in the front area congested, damaged or it may be blocked by men, animals and vehicles. The less impedimenta retained in the form of casualties in the front area the better for all. Rapid distribution of casualties is imperative, but first the patients must be fed, attended to and sorted into groups. Some cases unfit for removal must remain in casualty clearing stations; others can only be transferred lying-down; some can travel as sitting-up cases or as ordinary passengers; and others again are fit to return to duty. On occasions such as these the great object was to rid the congested area of the slight cases, and for this purpose temporary or improvised ambulance trains were often largely employed. They were composed of third-class carriages, carried one thousand cases, had a small medical staff on board, and were sent by circuitous routes taking thirty-six hours or more to reach their destination Regular halting-places were fixed beforehand for the necessary feeding, dressing and sanitary arrangements of the patients, and ambulance transport was available at each halt to convey to hospital any patient unfit for the remainder of the journey. To derive full advantage from these improvised trains, it was advisable to have them garaged in suitable places close to the forward area so that they were available in the early stages of the battle when the slight cases were the first to be brought back from the firing-line. On many occasions officers and men suffering from slight disabilities were conveyed direct from the dressing-station to the train by bus or charabanc, for distances of anything up to twenty-five miles. Such a system had several advantages; it kept patients in good cheer; it got them away quickly to hospital; it left the important casualty clearing stations free to concentrate on the patients who required more active treatment and atten-

SURVEY OF CASUALTIES

tion; and it set free the improvised trains to resume their conveyance of personnel and stores at the earliest possible hour.

Regular ambulance trains were for the most part reserved for the conveyance of the more severely wounded. Suitably equipped and staffed, they accommodated 300 to 400 patients, and ran direct to the bases. Here again, it was advisable to have a certain number of them garaged in the forward area close to casualty clearing stations in order to evacuate, as soon as possible, serious cases fit to be moved, and so prevent these units becoming overcrowded and congested.

The need for supplementary assistance at all stages in the evacuation of casualties has been clearly indicated, but in order that the greatest benefit may be derived from it there must exist, before as well as during operations, close co-operation between the medical services and those other branches of the army on which they are dependent for such assistance. Plans for modern battles, such as were fought in the late war, were not made in a day. Staffs were employed for weeks and months ahead in working out the details, or as Sir Ian Hamilton so graphically puts it : " Swiftness in war comes from slow preparations."* There had to be an estimation of requirements, consultations and co-ordination between the staffs and heads of departments before the details could be finally approved. When the plans for the allotment and employment of extra transport by the medical services were hastily, or only partially considered, or if for any other reason they proved insufficient, difficulties often arose which caused further delay before the deficiencies could be made good. Occasionally when this occurred other branches of the service were ordered to dump their valuable stores, organise their vehicles into sick convoys and carry back wounded. This resulted in the maximum of loss, discomfort and suffering. Everything was dwarfed by the compelling necessity of evacuating casualties no matter how. There was another, and minor, fault of fairly common occurrence. It happened when a staff officer suddenly came across a group of wounded awaiting transport and was stimulated into hasty action to divert to this particular group transport which was methodically evacuating casualties according to plan. By such action the waiting minutes of a few were shortened but the removal of many was delayed by hours. Such incidents, on investigation, always demonstrated more

---

* *Gallipoli Diary*, by General Sir Ian Hamilton, G.C.B., vol. i, p. 28.

and more forcibly that mistakes or delay in evacuating wounded were due to lack of liaison or co-operation between the staff and the administrative medical officer. Secrecy in the preparations of plans was all important as there was the constant danger that information might leak out to the enemy. It was, however, equally essential that certain officers should be trusted, as over-concealment tended to prevent intelligent cooperation; and if failure to supply an army with troops, ammunition, water or food was the outcome, or at a critical moment in the fighting the army found itself overloaded with casualties, the policy, plans, preparations and losses of months might have been in vain.

It is of the utmost importance that the limitations of the regular medical organisation should be clear to all, so that they may fully realise that success or failure in collecting and clearing sick and wounded in modern extensive and prolonged battles depends on the co-operation of the staff, the consideration they give to the problem, and the assistance they are prepared to authorise. The pivot on which the regular and supplementary systems turn should be the head of the medical services in the field and in certain circumstances his representatives with formations. This co-ordinating centre was sometimes lacking in the earlier years of the war in France, Gallipoli, East Africa and Mesopotamia, and the policy adopted was reminiscent of the South African War heritage. It has been recorded in the histories already published that when the British Expeditionary Force went to France in 1914 there was "no responsible administrative medical officer attached to the Commander-in-Chief's Staff, to whom important administrative questions could be referred for immediate decision, with whom questions of the strategical dispositions of medical units could be considered, and by whom a link could be formed between the medical services of the field army and the lines of communication. These were essentially functions which belonged to the D.M.S. of the Expeditionary Force. They were of extreme importance in connection with the evacuation of sick and wounded to the hospitals on the lines of communication." * The histories and official documents show that the tendency to short-circuit the senior administrative medical officer with formations died slowly. It recurred subsequent to the well-known disasters in Mesopotamia, after Commissions had inquired into the conditions there and in Gallipoli, and even after

---

* *General History of the Medical Services*, vol. ii, p. 183.

an ideal system had been established on the Western front, where experience was greater and education in war more rapid. Nor was the British army alone in its difficulties in using to the best advantage its medical services. Similar troubles beset the French army whose medical services made great efforts to impress on the army authorities the need for revised methods. The Americans, too, suffered in the same way despite the two and a half years' experience of their allies. The administrative officers of the American Medical Department had a hard struggle to obtain an organisation capable of handling the ramifications of their medical services, and to get information which they considered absolutely essential if their army and their country were to benefit by having a medical personnel in Europe, varying from 8·6 to 10 per cent. of the total strength, with provision for the hospitalisation of their cases on a 15 per cent. basis.

The organisation of the British army medical services was faulty at the beginning of the Great War. The text-book methods of evacuating casualties broke down, but the close proximity of France and Belgium to the United Kingdom, the seriousness of the casualty lists, and the strength of the enemy, all contributed to force into being a rapid and thorough reorganisation which stood the test of war. In more distant campaigns education was slower. This led to serious conditions in the field, and dissatisfaction in the United Kingdom which was only relieved by Inquiries and Commissions, with the result that ultimately satisfactory arrangements were made for the care of the sick and wounded.

An attempt has been made to emphasise the importance of the primary principles of the conservation of manpower by the medical services, namely, the early and systematic collection and evacuation of all casualties. It has been pointed out that the numbers returned to duty in the field show a striking percentage. If, therefore, it is desired that the maximum number of fully trained men should be conserved for the army in the early stages of the campaign, these figures inspire the hope that all branches of the army will continue to study the factors which brought them about. With the development of mechanised forces in the future, personnel will be more highly trained and more difficult to replace. These problems will grow more interesting and intricate, for though the effective strength of such forces may be smaller, the internal combustion engine will still be controlled by human beings and the need to conserve men will be greater. It can serve no useful purpose to forget the historical lessons of the war because the foundation of success lies in co-operation, and this means to the medical services facility to estimate requirements, ability to obtain what is required and power to use whatever is provided in the best and most economical way.

In estimating their requirements the medical services usually base their demands on a statistical foundation. Officers do not always realise this, for they have few opportunities of studying the problems owing to the lack of literature on the subject. In the first place, medical requirements in the field are calculated on the strength of the force and the approximate number of battle and non-battle casualties. Theoretically an approximate estimate of casualties should be prepared by the general staff and the administrative medical officer, but the difficulties in the way are many and are fully appreciated by officers who have served a long apprenticeship in staff employment. Many officers have not had that training, and although proficient in other subjects it is possible that this lack of experience acts like a piece of grit in a smooth-running machine. Whatever the reason, the formation commander and his staff frequently hesitate during a campaign to impart information to the administrative medical officer, and thereby fail to make full use of the medical services. The reluctance to pass on information containing an estimate of battle casualties can be understood. To win a battle is all important, and success may be marred if certain details become known either to the enemy or to the troops taking part. In the former event, the opposition is warned, the element of surprise no longer exists, enemy troops are massed and their positions strengthened for the anticipated attack. In the latter case the troops may become despondent and attack without heart, knowing that large numbers of casualties are anticipated. Moreover, the estimate may be entirely wrong and be criticised accordingly.

The commander and his staff are the only officers who can make an approximate estimate of the battle casualties. They, of all others, are in the best position to know the terrain on which they intend to fight, the estimate of the enemy's force in personnel and guns, the strong points of the position they propose to attack, and what they are prepared to lose in personnel in order to achieve their objective. These are the facts on which a calculation could be based, facts which the administrative medical officer is not given, and furthermore is not fully trained to use; yet he is expected to advise on or

SURVEY OF CASUALTIES

make preparations for the collection, evacuation, accommodation and treatment of the sick and wounded.

There is an old-fashioned formula generally used in peace for theoretical exercises, by which medical officers are encouraged to calculate the battle casualties as 10 per cent. of 3/5ths of the force, instead of being definitely informed that the casualties to be evacuated and treated have been estimated on known facts, and are likely to number approximately ten thousand or twenty thousand, or whatever the estimate is, over a certain period. Thousands of documents, working papers and war diaries belonging to headquarters of the different forces have been carefully examined to ascertain if any practical use was ever made of this formula during the Great War. In only two sets of working papers was it referred to, nor is this to be wondered at. In the Great War battles were conducted over extensive areas for prolonged periods, divisions were moved up from other formations, suffered heavily and were withdrawn from the area, and the strength of the force accordingly varied from week to week. These features are well illustrated in Tables 12 and 13. Table 12 indicates the number of divisions engaged at the opening of the battles of the Somme, Arras, Messines and Ypres 1917, with the approximate losses they sustained in the first days of each battle.

TABLE 12.—Divisions Engaged and the Casualties suffered in the first two days of Certain Battles, 1916 and 1917

Battle	Period	No. of divisions actually engaged	Total casualties for first 2 days		Average per division engaged	
			Off.	O.R.	Off.	O.R.
Somme	July 1st and 2nd 1916	17	1,718	56,440	101	3,320
Arras ...	April 9th and 10th 1917	16	894	24,329	56	1,520
Messines	June 7th and 8th 1917	12	538	13,222	45	1,102
Ypres ...	July 31st and August 1st 1917	13	844	23,377	53	1,461

Table 13 shows the approximate weekly strength of the Fifth Army during the battles of Ypres in 1917.

In actual practice a system of calculating casualties on the total strength of the force was gradually evolved, and the medical preparations for the operations on the Western front in 1917 were worked out on the information that the percentage of casualties would remain the same as in 1916, but that the number of divisions to be employed would be in the proportion of 3 to 2 as compared with 1916.

TABLE 13.—Approximate Strength of Fifth Army during the Battles of Ypres, 1917

Week ending	Average ration strength
July 7th	308,784
14th	393,497
21st	435,395
28th	492,945
Aug. 4th	537,035
11th	505,073
18th	513,994
25th	484,148
Sept. 1st	Not known
8th	Not known
15th	397,000
22nd	371,252
29th	365,965
Oct. 6th	253,696
13th	304,532
20th	266,412
27th	272,590
Nov. 3rd	282,697
10th	171,401

With regard to estimating non-battle casualties the administrative medical officer was the responsible adviser, as he was kept informed of the prevailing sick rate and could gauge the probable effect on the troops of any epidemic disease.

So far as the figures are available, the percentages of battle casualties and non-battle casualties to average strengths have been worked out, and are shown for the different campaigns in Table 14.

TABLE 14.—Percentages of Battle and Non-battle Casualties in the various Campaigns

Campaign	Percentage of average strength	
	Battle casualties	Non-battle casualties
France and Flanders	49·3	64·5
Italy	6·7	54·2
Macedonia	4·8	97·1
Dardanelles	58·8	124·0
Egypt and Palestine	7·6	74·0
Mesopotamia	14·3	86·0
North Russia	8·5	91·0
East Africa (troops only) 1916–18	7·1	224·4
South-West Africa	4·8	75·0
South African War 1899–1902 (Other ranks only)	4·8	72·8

The statistical chapters dealing with the respective campaigns are designed to give the military student some idea

SURVEY OF CASUALTIES

of the type of the individual campaign and the resulting losses in order to facilitate his calculations in future; for if ever there was common ground on which combatant and medical officers should meet sympathetically, it is in the estimation of casualties. The subject interests both; the former lose men in attaining their objective, the latter are employed in retrieving and saving men. Moreover, the administrative medical officer during actual operations is in a position to keep the formation commander and his staff regularly and methodically informed of the approximate casualties the force and its individual units are suffering. Such information may be of the greatest use to a commander during the different phases of the battle.

During the Great War there were many occasions when the value of co-operation could be seen, as, for instance, when such statistical problems as the estimation of enemy casualties, the types of wounds and their incidence by arms of the service, or the estimation of the future requirements of the force, were referred to the administrative medical staff by the General Staff.

In all campaigns an attempt was made to estimate the number of men the enemy countries could put into the field and retain up to strength. Such calculations were generally outside the province of the administrative medical officer, but occasionally he could render assistance by supplying information which the general staff required in estimating the numbers of the enemy troops likely to be admitted to hospital, to die or be discharged or invalided. On one occasion the information was asked for in the following manner:

"To D.G.A.M.S.
"I should be glad of your opinion as to the probable monthly admissions to hospital, deaths and invaliding out of the service from sickness (not from wounds) of the German Army, assuming that $3\frac{1}{2}$ million men were at the front and on the L. of C. and assuming that 1,000,000 are in depots in Germany."

Sometimes before a calculation regarding the health of the enemy troops could be completed, similar statistics for the British troops were required. The questions then put to the D.G.A.M.S. were as follows:

"(1) What is the average length of time that the sick admitted to hospital from the Depots in Germany will spend in hospital before returning to duty?

" (2) What is the average length of time that the sick evacuated from the front to hospitals in Germany will spend in hospital before returning to duty ?

" (3) How long, on an average, will wounded evacuated from the front to Germany remain in hospital before returning to duty ?

" (4) Is the German claim that 90 per cent. of their wounded return to duty unreasonable ? If so, what proportion of British wounded eventually return to duty ?

" (5) What is the normal proportion of killed to wounded ? "

Again, there are certain statistical results which interest the general staff and combatant officers and may help them in preparing for an offensive or defensive action, or in designing suitable methods of attack or defence. These are the percentage of wounds caused by different weapons, and the percentage of battle casualties occurring in the different arms of the service. It has been impossible to produce complete tables either for the different battles or for the different forces, but, by undertaking a comprehensive research, samples of this type of information have been compiled and produced to give some indication of the effect of enemy weapons on the British forces, and of the percentage of casualties in the different branches of the service. Table 15 deals with a series of 212,659 wounds admitted to casualty clearing stations, classified according to missile.

TABLE 15.—Percentages of Wounds caused by different Weapons

Wounding agent	No.	Percentage
Bullet, rifle or machine gun	82,901	38·98
Shells, trench mortars, etc.	124,425	58·51
Bombs and grenades	4,649	2·19
Bayonet	684	·32
	212,659	—

In 48,290 cases of the above series it has been possible to show the regional incidence of wounds caused by the different types of weapon. This is shown in Table 16, differentiating in each case between severe and slight wounds.

TABLE 16.—Regional Incidence of Wounds caused by different Types of Weapon in 48,290 Cases admitted to Casualty Clearing Stations

Region	Bullet, rifle or machine gun					Shells, trench mortars, etc.					Bombs and grenades				
	No. severe	No. slight	Percentage		No. severe	No. slight	Percentage		No. severe	No. slight	Percentage	
			Severe	Slight			Severe	Slight			Severe	Slight
Head, face and neck	649	1,036	5·78	9·22	1,993	3,365	6·11	10·32	162	504	3·66	11·37
Eyes	49	77	·44	·69	278	247	·85	·76	37	56	·83	1·26
Shoulder and back	414	715	3·68	6·36	1,601	1,892	4·91	5·80	111	266	2·50	6·00
Chest, front and sides	353	267	3·14	2·38	884	504	2·71	1·55	71	83	1·60	1·87
Abdomen, front and sides	329	114	2·93	1·01	750	241	2·30	·74	59	45	1·33	1·02
Buttocks	172	268	1·53	2·38	626	635	1·92	1·95	65	116	1·47	2·62
Thighs	594	681	5·29	6·06	1,727	1,560	5·29	4·78	138	266	3·11	6·00
Legs	709	995	6·31	8·85	2,556	2,412	7·84	7·39	277	510	6·25	11·51
Feet	158	353	1·41	3·14	509	807	1·56	2·47	46	156	1·04	3·52
Arms	583	814	5·19	7·24	1,524	2,008	4·67	6·16	138	396	3·11	8·94
Forearms and elbows	224	353	1·99	3·14	516	715	1·58	2·19	36	98	·81	2·21
Hands	195	579	1·74	5·15	538	1,352	1·65	4·14	75	207	1·69	4·67
Multiple	368	189	3·27	1·68	2,346	1,034	7·19	3·17	272	242	6·14	5·46
Total	4,797	6,441	42·69	57·31	15,848	16,772	48·58	51·42	1,487	2,945	33·55	66·45
Total by wounding agent	11,238					32,620					4,432			
Percentage of total cases	23·27					67·55					9·18			

Dealing with the same series, Table 17 shows the regional incidence of wounds, irrespective of the weapon causing the wound.

TABLE 17.—Regional Incidence of Wounds in 48,290 Cases admitted to Casualty Clearing Stations

Region	No. of wounds admitted			Percentage of total admitted		
	Severe	Slight	Total	Severe	Slight	Total
Head, face and neck	2,804	4,905	7,709	5·81	10·16	15·96
Eyes	364	380	744	·75	·79	1·54
Shoulder and back	2,126	2,873	4,999	4·40	5·95	10·35
Chest, front and sides	1,308	854	2,162	2·71	1·77	4·48
Abdomen, front and sides	1,138	400	1,538	2·36	·83	3·18
Buttocks	863	1,019	1,882	1·79	2·11	3·90
Thighs	2,459	2,507	4,966	5·09	5·19	10·28
Legs	3,542	3,917	7,459	7·33	8·11	15·45
Feet	713	1,316	2,029	1·48	2·73	4·20
Arms	2,245	3,218	5,463	4·65	6·66	11·31
Forearms and elbows	776	1,166	1,942	1·61	2·41	4·02
Hands	808	2,138	2,946	1·67	4·43	6·10
Multiple	2,986	1,465	4,451	6·18	3·03	9·22
Total	22,132	26,158	48,290	45·83	54·17	100·00

It is officially recorded in the *Military Effort of the British Empire during the Great War* that of the total casualties of fighting arms of the service only, " the Infantry account for 86·07 per cent., the Royal Artillery 7·58 per cent., the Royal Engineers 2·57 per cent., the Machine Gun Corps 2·46 per cent., the Cavalry 1·08 per cent., and the Tank Corps 0·24 per cent." * These figures refer to warrant officers, non-commissioned officers and men of the Regular Army and Territorial Force, and it must be remembered that they are percentages of total casualties including deaths from causes other than wounds. To give some idea of the percentages of battle casualties suffered in actual operations by the arms of the service engaged, 896,493 battle casualties resulting from certain operations on the Western front during 1916 and 1917 were analysed. The results are shown in Table 18.

Another instance in which the administrative medical staff was of service was in the calculation of an approximate estimate of future requirements in the field, which in turn was a guide to the Imperial Staff and the Government of the number of men to be called up, examined, and prepared in every way in readiness to embark for duty with an expedi-

---

* Page 247. H.M. Stationery Office, 1922.

SURVEY OF CASUALTIES

TABLE 18.—Percentage of Battle Casualties suffered by Arms of the Service engaged in certain Battles on the Western Front during 1916 and 1917

Arm of the Service	Battle of the Somme 1.7.16–27.11.16	Battle of Arras 9.4.17–20.5.17	Battle of Messines 7.6.17–13.6.17	Third Battle of Ypres 31.7.17–18.11.17	Battle of Cambrai 20.11.17–8.12.17	Percentage of total casualties in these battles
Infantry	94·79*	89·04	89·56	77·98	84·31	88·18
Royal Artillery	3·13	4·58	4·03	12·15	3·00	6·06
Machine Gun Corps	—	2·07	3·43	3·81	3·74	1·75
Royal Engineers	1·20	1·33	1·68	2·22	1·46	1·55
R.A.M.C.	·60	·63	·57	1·32	1·02	·83
Cavalry	·16	·18	·02	·11	3·18	·29
Royal Flying Corps	·08	·37	·34	·48	·49	·27
Tank Corps	—	·16	·06	·30	2·55	·25
R.A.S.C.	·04	·05	·09	·35	·04	·13
Headquarters	—	·03	·05	·06	·10	·03
Miscellaneous	—	1·56	·17	1·23	·11	·66

* Includes casualties in Machine Gun Corps and Tank Corps.

tionary force overseas. The following illustration is taken from the records of the British Expeditionary Force in France and Flanders :—

" Estimated casualties for one year (November–October), *i.e.* 6 months' battle, 6 months' ordinary at 50,000 per month, and 12 months' sick wastage would be :

	Officers	Other ranks	Total
Battle: April–Sept. (incl.)	22,464	490,788	513,252
Ordinary: Nov.–March (incl.) and October	13,400	286,600	300,000
Sick wastage: on basis of cases transferred to Base	17,280	245,025	262,305
Total	53,144	1,022,413	1,075,557

" Based on 65 divisions, or an increase from 56 divisions of approximately 16 per cent. total estimated wastage for 1 year would be :

Officers	61,647
Other ranks	1,185,999
Total	1,247,646, say, 1,250,000

" We shall require in France some 315,000 men before the end of February, and on the 1st of March 400,000 men at home trained or in training, *i.e.* 715,000 by 1st March.

" We shall require 100,000 per month from March inclusive. To allow of 4 months' training at home we must always maintain 400,000 men training in England.

" In short, we should earmark one and a half million for the forthcoming year."

The importance of an approximate estimate of casualties in relation to problems connected with the collection, evacuation and accommodation of casualties in the field, the practical use made of it by the medical services, its bearing on economy when calling for extra personnel and assistance, and the benefits derived from the resulting efficiency, do not seem to be fully appreciated. The administrative medical officer with a division or corps on being handed an estimate of battle casualties deducts the numbers likely to be killed and reported missing. He is thus able to form some idea of the numbers for which provision should be made by the respective formations. This figure is roughly subdivided according to the known percentages in the battle area into walking, sitting or lying-down cases. The percentages vary in every theatre of war and in every battle in the same theatre of war. Until experience is gained, the approximate percentages may be taken as 30 per cent. walking and 70 per cent. sitting or lying-down. By calculating the number of sitting and lying-down cases in this way, and by estimating the distance they must be carried by hand before being transferred to some form of mechanical transport, a working idea is obtained of the additional accommodation, extra bearer personnel, stretchers and blankets that will be required. At the transfer station, be it advanced dressing station, walking wounded collecting post, or main dressing station, the walking cases as a group usually disappear, as from this point onwards all casualties as a rule require conveyance of some sort. Of the total casualties sent to casualty clearing stations approximately 50 per cent. require sitting and 50 per cent. lying-down accommodation. If the transport allotted to the medical services is considered insufficient to convey the calculated number, additional transport will be required, and either extra motor ambulance convoys or general transport and utility vehicles must be provided. In both circumstances time and warning are necessary if the arrangements are to work smoothly and normal traffic is to be disturbed as little as possible.

So far as subordinate formations are concerned, their interest in the estimation of casualties is more or less confined to the preparations for and the carrying out of the collection, early or first-aid treatment and evacuation of the sick and wounded from their area. Not so with the higher formations or headquarters, who are responsible for the further treatment, housing and distribution of the casualties. The number of casualty clearing stations allotted, the sites on which they are opened, and the extra personnel and assistance given them will depend on the casualties expected from formations or areas. Like all other military movements, the concentration of medical units requires time and must be conducted with secrecy.

SURVEY OF CASUALTIES

The method of distributing patients from casualty clearing stations has been described, and only the estimation of transport is now being considered. Statistics show that, of the total sick and wounded admitted to casualty clearing stations over a long period covering both active operations and quiet times, 75 per cent. of the sick, 90 per cent. of the wounded, and 81 per cent. of the total sick and wounded, required evacuation to the base. During the periods of active operations the percentage of wounded requiring evacuation rose to 98 per cent., with a corresponding increase in the percentage of sick. Furthermore, over a long period, transport accommodation had to be provided for 58 per cent. sitting cases and 42 per cent. lying-down cases, but during active operations it was found that 51 per cent. were sitting cases and 49 per cent. lying-down cases. As the sitting cases can be more easily transported, it is possible, if simple precautions are taken, to use utility rolling-stock without detriment to the patients, and to set it free early, thereby causing little disturbance to the supply and transport services.

Finally, an estimate of total casualties is required before the hospital accommodation can be fixed. All the casualties do not reach the hospitals at the base; some die in the front areas, others are returned to duty. In addition to the number evacuated from casualty clearing stations, however, provision must be made for the non-battle casualties admitted from units and personnel stationed on the lines of communication. In France this number represented approximately 18 per cent. of the total sick admissions of the force. It has been calculated that hospital accommodation at the base must be provided on a basis of approximately 80 per cent. of the total sick admissions and 90 per cent. of the wounded.

Non-battle casualties usually outnumbered the battle casualties admitted to medical units, both in the front area and at the base, but the excess was very much greater during periods of inactivity. On the Western front, however, where the preponderance of non-battle casualties over battle casualties was not so great as in the other theatres of war, the sick admissions were sometimes less than the wounded during active periods, as is shown in Table 19. It is worth while noting, and remembering, that the farther removed a force is from conditions resembling those of service at home the greater becomes the proportion of non-battle casualties.*

---

* *See* Chapter III, Table 1, p. 56.

TABLE 19.—Comparison of Approximate Numbers of Sick and Wounded evacuated to the Base during Quiet Periods and Periods of Activity

Period	Quiet periods			Period	Periods of activity		
	Sick	Wounded	Proportion of Sick to Wounded		Sick	Wounded	Proportion of Sick to Wounded
1.11.15–26.12.15	35,276	11,665	3·1 : 1	Battle of Loos and subsidiary actions, 25.9.15–31.10.15.	21,667	35,925	1 : 1·7
27.12.15–20.1.16	16,803	5,969	2·8 : 1	Battles of the Somme : 1st–29th July, 1916.	25,503	116,207	1 : 4·6
3.12.16–20.12.16	43,405	5,214	8·3 : 1	3rd–30th Sept. 1916	34,785	71,640	1 : 2·1
31.12.16–27.1.17	42,934	6,163	7·0 : 1	Battles of Arras : 1.4.17–2.6.17.	91,026	113,311	1 : 1·2
				Cambrai operations : 4.11.17–29.12.17.	94,473	59,566	1·6 : 1
30.12.17–2.3.18	86,173	14,174	6·1 : 1	Advance to Victory : 1.9.18–2.11.18.	107,862	175,457	1 : 1·6

If the histories of the campaigns are examined, it will be found that general hospitals were among the last units of the expeditionary forces to be embarked, and were not, therefore, open and ready to receive the early cases of sickness that occurred among the troops already disembarked. Consequently, during periods of concentration before battle there were no permanent or semi-permanent medical units to which sick and wounded could be transferred, and the men drifted into an allied hospital, if concentration took place in a friendly country, as was the case in France, or into a returning transport if the attack was directed against a hostile landing, as happened in Gallipoli, Mesopotamia and East Africa. In this way the force lost men who were highly trained, who had been passed fit for duty but a few days previously and were probably only suffering from some minor disability, men who could ill be spared when the first toll of battle was taken and reinforcements were quickly and urgently needed. The provision of satisfactory hospital accommodation at the beginning of a campaign was not easily attained. Many factors combined to prevent it. Mobile medical units had been sent out with the fighting formations and general hospitals were not required in the battle area. Men whose minds were concentrated on forthcoming battles had little or no thought to spare for the slow, steady drain on manpower caused by sickness. Consequently many mobile medical units intended for the collection and evacuation of casualties were either converted into stationary units, as in the early days of the war in France and Mesopotamia, or were not sent forward with their divisions.*

---

* At the battle of Le Cateau in 1914 the medical units of one division

This policy led to disaster. It is true that with every force certain general hospitals were mobilised, which sooner or later were opened on selected sites in the theatre of operations. It is also true that the percentage of beds had been carefully calculated and was probably sufficient for the strength of the force at the time. There was, however, one outstanding fault. The hospitals were not in a position to receive and treat the early cases and so set free the mobile units for their legitimate duty.

In the Great War the hospital accommodation provided did not at first keep pace with the expansion of the different forces. This is best illustrated from the records of the British Expeditionary Force in France. The British army was limited in size in 1914 and had to be rapidly expanded; casualties were numerous and trained reinforcements for the fighting formations were difficult to supply. Attention was concentrated on keeping the front-line units up to strength, and personnel enlisted for the medical services could easily be trained and absorbed for combatant duties. Hence, for the time being it was sufficient to keep the front area medical personnel and units more or less up to war establishment, retain the hospital beds on the lines of communication at a low scale and continue the policy of rapidly evacuating all sick and wounded, whether slight or serious, to the United Kingdom whose shores were only an hour and a half from France.

The percentage of hospital beds on the lines of communication provided for the original expeditionary force in France and Flanders was 5·2 per cent. of the total strength of the force. In October 1915 it had fallen to 3·8 per cent. although as early as February of that year the Commander-in-Chief of the force had considered that 6 per cent. was required. There was no increase of beds from 1915 until 1917 when the situation became acute, as the margin of beds available was insufficient for the casualties expected from the proposed battle programme. The crisis was relieved by speeding up evacuation to the United Kingdom and by sending out to France seven general and five stationary hospitals. Both before and after 1917 temporary accommodation was provided by increasing

---

were kept back and the division went into battle without its field ambulances. It had, therefore, no medical officers except the regimental ones and the Deputy Assistant Director of Medical Services, and it had no means of removing its wounded except in requisitioned vehicles.

the number of beds in the wards of existing hospitals and by placing trestle cots and mattresses instead of hospital beds in huts for personnel, dining-rooms or other accessory buildings. Extra accommodation was provided in this way for approximately 30,000. It was designated "crisis" expansion, but it did not at first carry with it any increase in the medical personnel or nursing staff and was altogether unsuitable for the permanent treatment of patients. What happened in France was common in other forces, as the records of the different campaigns show, and as the wastage of personnel became more and more apparent in the theatres of operations, the need for increased hospital accommodation became more urgent.

The difficulties of meeting requirements in the first eighteen months of the war were not wholly confined to questions of establishment. Political and professional influence affected the situation. Two instances may be mentioned. In the first place, the retention of large well-equipped and at times lightly populated base hospitals in France did not seem to find favour with the French who felt that the British equivalent of their *hôpitaux de l'intérieur* should be in the United Kingdom. Secondly, many temporary medical officers were engaged on yearly contracts, and those who had left busy practices and were posted to base hospitals felt they were being defrauded of the glamour of front line work. It became increasingly difficult to make them realise that in war there were bound to be long periods of inactivity when purely medical work must be light and consequently boring to a man who had always enjoyed a busy professional life. This criticism drew attention to the large staff necessary for a general hospital and encouraged rumours regarding the waste of medical men and personnel, which for a time obscured the practical fact that a margin of unoccupied beds was necessary in anticipation of the periods of battle activity.

Very often the first intimation that medical units on the lines of communication received of approaching active operations was an influx of cases which had been held up by field ambulances and casualty clearing stations during the quieter periods preceding a battle, followed by a rush of crowded ambulance trains bringing in as many as 29,026 cases, as happened on 3rd and 4th July 1916 during the battle of the Somme. The majority of these cases had to be transferred overseas to provide accommodation for the fresh cases arriving daily at the respective bases. To obviate this a compensatory measure was needed, and the one most likely to prove feasible was to increase the accommodation and ensure that there was a suitable margin of unoccupied beds available. In calculating this margin, provision was made for (a) fresh cases arriving daily; (b) the retention of men too ill to be moved, such as severe cases of gunshot wounds of the thigh and fractured femurs, gunshot wounds of the chest or head; and (c) the retention of slight cases of wounds or sickness so as to prevent them being lost to the force by evacuation overseas and thereby expedite their return to duty in the field. Other factors also influenced the military authorities in fixing the margin of unoccupied beds to be maintained. Among these were the general conditions which delayed or altered the sailing of hospital ships, such as bad weather, fogs, tides, ports being closed for naval reasons, delays for coaling, the restrictions as to the number of ships using certain harbours, and the limitation of the hours when ships could enter or leave certain ports. If such factors were not taken into consideration, the turn-over when hospital ships or ambulance transport were available became rapid, and patients suffering from slight disabilities were evacuated and lost to the force for a considerable period.

There are obviously two policies with regard to the provision of hospital and convalescent depot accommodation on the lines of communication. One is to keep it down to a minimum and increase it when required by " crisis " expansion. Such accommodation can, however, only be used as a rest station in the chain of evacuation and cannot be used for the permanent treatment of cases since the majority of patients require, in addition to treatment and nursing in the acute stage of their illness, mental and physical rest during convalescence—an important preventive measure against the strain of modern warfare and essential for men returning to front-line units. The second policy is to follow the peace-time procedure and allow in war a sufficiency of beds for the grouping of injuries and diseases. Hospital administration in peace is becoming every day more important and specialised as the accommodation for officers, nursing sisters, men and women is organised into surgical, medical, infectious and venereal, and subdivided into special wards for acute and chronic, clean and septic, slight and serious, and special diseases. The actual number of vacant beds is apt to convey a wrong impression of a hospital's capacity unless this is remembered, for it would be contrary to medical principles to fill up a ward with patients suffering from a heterogeneous collection of diseases or disabilities, such as gunshot wounds, pneumonia, pulmonary tuberculosis, diphtheria, enteric fever, syphilis, gonorrhœa, mania and scabies. The allowance of vacant beds necessary for the normal fluctuation in the sick rate and the separation of cases in military hospitals in peace time is regarded as approximately 33 per cent. It will be seen from Table 20 that the percentage of equipped beds vacant in the various expeditionary forces was generally below this figure.

TABLE 20.—Percentage of Equipped Beds Vacant in Hospital Accommodation provided for British and Dominion Troops

Campaign	Year	Over 33 per cent.	Under 33 per cent.
France and Flanders	1914	—	—
	1915	37·9	—
	1916	—	27·43
	1917	—	14·30
	1918	—	16·33
Italy	1918	—	30·05
Macedonia	1915	—	26·30
	1916	—	17·86
	1917	—	26·72
	1918	—	30·09
Dardanelles	—	Not known	—
Egypt and Palestine	1916	—	—
	1917	—	17·13
	1918	—	—
Mesopotamia	1916	—	—
	1917	—	23·16
	1918	38·38	—
North Russia	1918–19	49·62	—
East Africa	October, 1917	—	24·85

In considering the question some historical facts illustrate, on the one hand, how wastage occurs if sufficient beds are not provided, and, on the other, the economic benefits of ample accommodation. In the Mediterranean Expeditionary Force at the beginning of the Dardanelles campaign, the nearest general hospital was in Alexandria, and as the accommodation there was limited, patients were distributed to other hospitals in Egypt, to Malta, and the United Kingdom. Owing to this wide distribution, the control of men suffering from minor disabilities was lost and the force was depleted of one source of reinforcements. Another instance was noted in Mesopotamia when, after attention had been drawn in 1916 to the actual conditions in the country and the hospital accommodation had been found to be gravely insufficient, the forced evacuation of thousands of cases to India became imperative.

If, on the other hand, the principle of retaining cases in the theatre of operations is adopted, there is a marked reduction in the requirements in transport and personnel for the conveyance of patients from bases to the ports of embarkation. Further, the numbers requiring evacuation overseas will be reduced and the saving in transport becomes appreciable, especially if submarine warfare is intensive and cases do not require to be transferred long distances by sea, as, for example, from Salonika to the United Kingdom, from East Africa to the United Kingdom, Egypt, India or South Africa; from Mesopotamia to India or to the United Kingdom; or from the Dardanelles to Malta, Egypt or the United Kingdom. Some idea of the numbers requiring transport to the United Kingdom only during the period of the war may be gathered from Table 21 which shows the gross totals of British, Dominion, Indian and American sick and wounded arriving in the United Kingdom from all theatres of war and miscellaneous garrisons abroad.

TABLE 21.—Sick and Wounded arriving in the United Kingdom from the British Expeditionary Forces and Miscellaneous Garrisons

From	Period	Officers	Other ranks	Total
France and Flanders	1914–18	110,433	2,150,447	2,260,880
Italy	1918	493	6,640	7,133
Mediterranean theatres of war	1915–18	8,364	156,992	165,356
Mesopotamia	1914–18	597	7,671	8,268
North Russia	1918–19	213	2,202	2,415
East Africa	1914–18	556	8,934	9,490
Miscellaneous garrisons including India	1914–18	478	5,982	6,460
Total	1914–18	121,134	2,338,868	2,460,002

Closely associated with the general hospitals in the scheme of preventing wastage are the convalescent depots, the development and extension of which were among the most interesting medical features of the Great War. Their possibilities were recognised in 1914 and one convalescent depot to accommodate 1,000 cases was actually mobilised and accompanied the expeditionary force to France. During the first four months of the war little or no thought was given to the subject, for the new environment, new experiences and the changing fortunes of war gave birth to various difficult problems and anxieties which the authorities both in the field and at home had to attend to primarily. As soon as the first furies of battle had been expended and the forces had settled down to trench warfare, the gradual drain of men from the front line stimulated commanders and units on their own initiative to experiment as to the best way of retaining the slighter cases of wounds and sickness in the front areas.* In these days the front-line trenches were lightly held in comparison with later years; there was no great concentration of reserves in back areas, nor was there any overcrowding of billets in front areas as the troops were few and billets good and plentiful. Regimental aid posts, field ambulances and casualty clearing stations retained cases likely to be fit for duty in a few days. Unit commanders improvised convalescent companies and accommodated them in billets. Army headquarters took over a jute factory at St. Omer and had it organised as a front area convalescent depot. Returns were called for at intervals to show the numbers of men who had been returned to duty in France, and these reports slowly focussed attention on the use of convalescent depots and led to additional ones being opened and expanded on the lines of communication. Then came the real clash of arms at the battle of the Somme in 1916 with the opposing forces locked in a deadly grip. The fierce struggle continued for months and the unparalleled casualties made the British army realise the full demands of modern European warfare. In totalling up the casualties both for the result and for an estimate of future requirements, the numbers shown as "returned to duty" were noted and ways and means were devised for increasing them with the result that new forms of convalescent depots were organised and came into being in 1917. Returns from France for the year 1917 show that 30 per cent. of the sick and 20 per cent. of the wounded were admitted to convalescent depots at the base. In 1918 the records for other ranks show that 33 per cent. of the sick and 27 per cent. of the wounded were admitted to convalescent depots. Information is not available for every campaign to show the development in convalescent depots, but the growth of this organisation may be seen from the figures for France and Macedonia given in Table 22.

In connection with these units the question will arise whether it is advisable to have advanced convalescent depots in the forward area. The need for these depots becomes pressing when a force has settled down in the area of operations, for they will retain many slight casualties in the front area, reduce the numbers requiring evacuation to the base and

---

* Where units had their own medical officers, lightly wounded were treated as far as possible locally; the men preferred this, and it ensured personnel being returned to their own units at an early date.

SURVEY OF CASUALTIES

the number of beds established at the base. They will prove invaluable during an epidemic of a disease such as influenza, in which the acute stage is often limited to a few days, or in a campaign where the lines of communication extend over hundreds of miles. Time after time patients have reached the base medical units, usually in hurried evacuation, in a fit and healthy condition. They did not require treatment. They were transferred at once to a convalescent depot or were returned to duty. They had taken up valuable space in the transport vehicles and had added considerably to the clerical work in the field.

TABLE 22.—Development of Convalescent Depot Accommodation for British and Dominion troops in France and Macedonia

Campaign	Year	Percentage of ration strength	
		Maximum No. of beds equipped	Maximum No. of beds occupied
France and Flanders	1916	1·6	·9
	1917	2·3	1·8
	1918	3·4	2·5
Macedonia	1916	3·2	2·6
	1917	3·4	?
	1918	11·9	6·6

As the conditions, the average strength and the battle and non-battle casualties in the different expeditionary forces are now known, the hospital and convalescent depot accommodation has been most carefully worked out in the subsequent chapters. It is hoped that these facts may be useful as a guide, and that all factors of a campaign will be taken into consideration in estimating future requirements. In using the tables, however, the possibilities connected with the development of gas and aerial warfare should not be lost to view. Nor should the human element be forgotten which demands that officers, men and women, incapacitated by wound, disease or injury, require a period of rest, comfort, recreation and hardening before being returned to active duty in a forward area. This is a fundamental precaution of the utmost importance if their vitality and energy are to be conserved and they themselves be prevented from carrying on to the breaking-point, when some functional nervous disorder or distressing illness may claim them as victims and thereby deplete the army of useful personnel, reduce individuals to wrecks, and ultimately swell the pensions burden of the State.

The outstanding lesson of the war in this respect centres round the advisability of sending 1 or 2 per cent. of the hospital accommodation and ·5 per cent. of the convalescent depot accommodation with the advance troops. By adopting such a scheme a reservoir would be formed to receive the constant trickle of men from fighting and other units, a reservoir which, once established, would supply units with the trained reinforcements that are so often urgently required after concentration and the early battles of a campaign.

CHAPTER III

THE PRINCIPAL CAUSES OF NON-BATTLE CASUALTIES

THE histories and available records of past campaigns had impressed upon the minds of combatant and medical officers the penetrating fact that non-battle casualties usually outnumbered battle casualties. The importance of this fact was always uppermost in the thoughts of medical officers prior to the Great War, and their teaching and influence had been directed towards emphasising the benefits to be obtained by attention to preventive measures against disease. The prevalence of any special disease in a campaign, productive perhaps of much suffering to individuals and inconvenience to the force at the time, had drawn attention to the lack of knowledge respecting it and the absence of any organised efforts of prevention. These diseases, therefore, became the subject of intensive study, which in time led to improvements benefiting not only the army but also the civilian population. The scourge of enteric fever which decimated the troops in the South African War has become history, and with it the investigations and researches of Wright and Leishman, whose aim was to render the individual immune from this disease and so abolish it from an army in the field. In addition they looked forward to diminishing the risk run by men, women and children who had to work or live in countries where this disease was endemic and had a high mortality rate. Their reports and their ultimate success in peace were a fresh incentive to other research workers in the prevention of disease in war, but here the study of difficult problems was sometimes handicapped by lack of a statistical survey of the diseases and disabilities which occurred during a campaign.

It was with a view to compiling a record likely to assist future administrators and investigators that seven volumes of the *Medical History of the War* were devoted to the purely professional and scientific details of wounds and diseases met with in the Great War. For various reasons already explained, it was not then possible to give a complete picture of the total wastage from wounds and sickness, and an attempt has been made in this volume to record the known casualties in their different groups. It must be borne in mind that whether personnel be killed, wounded, missing, prisoners of war, sick or injured they represent so many men absent from front line or other duties and, therefore, ineffective for the fighting machine. It is essential to subdivide these non-effectives into certain groups in order to differentiate between battle and non-battle casualties, and between permanent and temporary wastage, and by concentrating on non-battle casualties endeavour to effect a reduction in wastage in future.

It should also be remembered that when an army is mobilised and takes the field the army commander has to conduct two campaigns simultaneously, one against a visible

TABLE 1.—Proportion of Battle to Non-battle Casualties in the British Expeditionary Forces during the Great War

Campaign	Period	Force	Battle casualties	Non-battle casualties	Proportion	
					Battle casualties	Non-battle casualties
France and Flanders	1914–1918	Whole force	2,690,054	3,528,486	1 :	1·31
Italy	1917–1918	British	6,321	51,311	1 :	8·12
Macedonia	1915–1918	British and Dominion	23,762	481,262	1 :	20·25
Dardanelles	1915–1916	British	68,826	145,154	1 :	2·11
Egypt and Palestine	1915–1918	British and Dominion	51,451	503,377	1 :	9·78
Mesopotamia	1914–1918	Whole force	85,207	820,418	1 :	9·63
North Russia	1918–1919	British and Dominion	893	9,582	1 :	10·73
East Africa *	1916–1918	All troops (followers excluded)	10,717	336,540	1 :	31·40
South-West Africa	1914–1915	Dominion	1,588	24,746	1 :	15·58
		Total	2,938,819	5,900,876	1 :	2·01
South African War	1899–1902	British and Dominion, other ranks only.	26,750	404,126	1 :	15·11

* For the purposes of this table, casualties occurring in East Africa before 1916 have been omitted as the number of non-battle casualties is not known.

enemy of men and munitions of war, the other against an invisible enemy whose weapons are enervation and disease. In his preparations against the former enemy, the army commander has the assistance of a staff of officers highly trained in matters concerning intelligence and operations, discipline and reinforcements, supplies and transport. In waging war against the hidden enemy he is assisted by officers drawn from the medical services, with the additional benefit of expert professional advice from distinguished consultants attached to his staff. Both enemies cause casualties, but the losses occasioned by the shells, bullets, bombs, gas or other destructive contraptions of the human foe are equalled and often surpassed by the damage left in the track of the silent, intangible enemy ever present in battle or rest camp. The varying proportions of battle to non-battle casualties in the campaigns under review in the following chapters are shown in Table 1.

Taken all over, it will be seen that for every casualty inflicted by the visible enemy the invisible enemy claimed two. These striking figures should interest all military officers, be they commanders of an army or a company, as all are concerned in saving the strength, energy and lives of their men, while inflicting the greatest damage on the opposing troops.

It is important to realise the large numbers of non-battle casualties who are temporarily put out of action—a point worthy of constant attention, emphasis and repetition. Non-battle casualties, exclusive of those in the United Kingdom, formed 66·75 per cent. of the casualties in the above campaigns. Of the non-battle casualties, excluding those of East Africa during 1914 and 1915, 1·83 per cent. died, leaving 98·17 per cent. temporarily out of action. As the effective reduction of this temporary wastage can only be brought about by sympathetic understanding, co-operation and the action of all ranks, it is proposed to aim at simplicity, avoid scientific nomenclature as far as possible, concentrate on the chief causes of inefficiency and discuss some practical points bearing on the prevention of diseases in a body of men living under active service conditions. This is all-important if there is to be an honest grappling with problems brought into prominence by statistical research.

In civil life the prevention of disease is becoming no less important than in the army. The Ministry of Health, the Education authorities and the Press combine, year by year, to increase and widen the interest of the civilian population in the bodily well-being of the individual. While much is being done to raise the standard of this aspect of the nation's education, there are many parts where progress is slow. In the more advanced areas many believe that disease can be entirely eliminated. Whatever may happen in a future of peace, there will always be a certain sick rate in war because war is a hard profession, followed under the most arduous conditions. In peace the army is composed of men who are medically examined before enlistment, who are carefully trained, comfortably housed, well fed and clothed, and constantly looked after by medical men specially educated in all things pertaining to the preservation of health. Despite these favourable conditions, however, there is a daily sick rate, as can be seen from the records of the regular army at home and overseas in pre- and post-war years, given in Table 2.

TABLE 2.—Sick Rate among Warrant Officers, Non-commissioned Officers and Men of the Regular Army at Home and Abroad during Peace

Year	Admissions	
	Annual ratio per 1,000 of strength	Daily percentage of strength
1913	437·7	·12
::	::	::
1921	649·9	·17
1922	515·8	·14
1923	484·0	·13
1924	484·7	·13
1925	446·2	·12
1926	454·8	·12
1927	467·7	·13
1928	426·2	·12

When the Great War commenced an empirical figure of ·3 per cent. daily,* or an annual ratio per thousand of strength of 1,095, was accepted as the permissible unit of inefficiency due to sickness in an army in the field when there was neither serious fighting nor epidemic disease. The margin was a liberal one. The daily percentage of strength reporting sick and admitted to medical units for the different British Expeditionary Forces during the Great War has now been worked out on definite figures, and the result is as shown in Table 3.

It is thus possible to compare the sick rate in the various expeditionary forces with the pre- and post-war rates. Where the sick rate in an expeditionary force is lower than or closely approaches the peace rate, it is legitimate to infer that satisfactory preventive measures were instituted in that force and carried out by all ranks. In those campaigns where the sick rate exceeds the peace rate, an analysis of the admissions to hospital shows the particular disease or group of diseases which caused the higher rate. There are therefore two simple and practical methods of directing attention to the wastage caused by non-battle casualties: (a) by noting the daily percentage or ratio per thousand of strength admitted to hospital for sickness or injury; and (b) by analysing the causes of admission to hospital. Both methods have been employed in the statistical analysis of the different campaigns. Unfortunately, in all

---

* *Field Service Regulations*, Part II, 1909, p. 105. *Field Service Regulations*, 1930, vol. i, p. 195, § 3. *Official Medical History of the War, Medical Services, Hygiene of the War*, vol. i, Preface, p. ix.

campaigns the records of individual diseases are not complete, but where incomplete the gaps may be filled by the proportionate figures given in the analysis of 1,043,653 cases in Chapter XX.

The outstanding feature of this statistical review of diseases of the war, whether the ratio be high or low, is the large number

TABLE 3.—Sick Rate among the British Forces at Home and Overseas during the Great War

Campaign	Period	Admissions	
		Ratio per 1,000 of strength	Daily percentage of strength
France and Flanders	Aug.–Dec. 1914 1915 1916 1917 1918	356·15 875·28 481·60 529·37 595·16	·26 ·24 ·13 ·15 ·16
Italy	1917–18	590·03	·19
Macedonia	Oct–Dec. 1915 1916 1917 1918	166·02 1,061·18 941·80 1,306·85	·18 ·29 ·26 ·36
Dardanelles	1915–16	1,239·91	·48
Egypt and Palestine	1916 1917 1918	724·27 744·15 956·48	·20 ·20 ·26
Mesopotamia	1914–15 1916 1917 1918	902·39 1,309·10 914·32 702·69	·21 ·36 ·25 ·19
North Russia	1918–19	908·50	·19
East Africa (troops only) ...	1917 1918	2,624·35 1,432·36	·72 ·39
South-West Africa	1914–15	749·88	·23
United Kingdom	Aug.–Dec. 1914 1915 1916 1917 1918	78·94 282·19 270·37 269·39 344·14	·05 ·08 ·07 ·07 ·09

of men rendered ineffective by the simple ailments of every-day life, such as diseases of the respiratory and digestive systems, rheumatic fever and its allied conditions, local and general injuries, skin diseases, minor septic infections, and influenza. These disabilities are common in the consulting-room of the general practitioner. They form the bulk of the illnesses suffered by the seven million insured people who apply for medical treatment every year. They are equally prevalent in the army during peace as shown in the recent Reports on the Health of the Army. Wherever the available war records are complete and have been analysed, as, for example, in the United Kingdom 1914 and 1915, France and Flanders 1914 and 1915, in the Mediterranean Expeditionary Force during the Dardanelles campaign, or in the analysis of the 836,677 cases of sickness drawn from all areas from 1916 onwards, the result is the same. This has been recorded in Table 4. For comparison, the incidence of these diseases in the South African War has been recorded, showing their average annual ratio per 1,000 of strength, other ranks only.

The medical services both of the army and of the civil population have here a common enemy and a common objective. Herein lies scope for research, rich in opportunity during peace, full of possibility for the future, and well worth constant investigation if preventive medicine is to reduce the admission rate to hospital at home and abroad in peace and in war.

Another prominent group of diseases causing great inefficiency consists of venereal diseases, malaria and dysentery. These diseases were familiar to all medical officers in the British army. They had been common causes of inefficiency in the South African War, and were equally common in all Eastern armies and cantonments. They were studied by the medical profession at home and abroad, yet despite a yearly output of literature regarding the results of investigations, researches and inquiries, they hampered the attacking powers of our armies in the Great War.

There remains a third group of diseases to be mentioned, not on account of their high incidence during the war, but because they were unexpected. Just as the visible enemy sprang surprises and found his opponent unprepared for gas, flame throwers, elaborate mining and tanks, so did the invisible enemy cause havoc with his old and almost forgotten weapons, tetanus, gas gangrene, frost bite and its allied conditions, and inflict loss with such new weapons as trench fever, nephritis and poisoning from chemical warfare gas.

In theory there is no excuse for failing to recognise diseases or for being unprepared to fight them ; in practice there are many. Successful prevention depends on the state of medical knowledge at the time, the personnel and equipment provided, and the practicability of employing the defensive measures recommended. In the Great War our medical services were reinforced by members of the civil profession and graduates

TABLE 4.—Principal Causes of Admission to Hospital with the Ratios per 1,000 of Ration Strength for Disease or Injury emerging from the Analysis of Certain Complete War Records

	Troops in the United Kingdom				France and Flanders				Dardanelles campaign		Analysis of 836,677 cases, all fronts, 1916–1920		South African War, 1899–1902	
	(Aug.–Dec.) 1914		1915		(Aug.–Dec.) 1914		1915							Average annual ratio per 1,000
	No.	Ratio per 1,000	No.	Ratio per 1,000	No.	Ratio per 1,000	No.	Ratio per 1,000	No.	Ratio per 1,000	No.	Per cent. of cases analysed	No.	
Diseases of the respiratory system	8,233	6·43	31,673	21·42	4,551	23·95	31,141	52·69	3,789	32·37	55,311	6·61	10,606	19·10
Diseases of the digestive system	17,598	13·74	64,995	43·96	10,594	55·76	67,663	114·48	34,319	293·15	111,923	13·38	56,148	101·12
Rheumatic fever	1,013	·79	3,280	2·22	7,950	41·84	20,764	35·13	6,566	56·09	7,848	·94	24,460	44·05
Local and general injuries	10,411	8·13	35,314	23·89	10,612	55·85	55,080	93·19	8,464	72·30	41,810	5·00	29,063	52·34
Diseases of the skin	9,659	7·54	41,535	28·09	1,934	10·20	39,505	66·84	3,788	32·36	66,026	7·89	13,166	23·71
Diseases of the areolar tissue	1,783	1·39	18,906	12·79	3,422	18·01	35,046	59·29	4,303	36·75	68,873	8·23	7,627	13·74
Influenza	6,047	4·72	31,360	21·21	1,478	7·78	44,392	75·11	3,126	26·70	94,989	11·35	8,891	16·01
Total		42·74		153·58		213·39		496·73		549·72		53·40		270·07
Total all diseases and injuries		78·94		282·19		356·15		875·28		1,239·91		100·00		727·80

fresh from college, to the majority of whom diseases such as cholera, typhus, malaria and dysentery were unfamiliar; while new diseases born of war conditions were alike unknown to the majority of experienced practitioners and serving officers. Known, unknown or forgotten diseases, like typhus in the Serbian army, trench fever on the Western front, gas gangrene, frost bite or trench foot, may therefore attack an army before preventive measures can be initiated. There may be delay in instituting measures, not because professional knowledge is wanting but because the recognised measures require a large increase in personnel, stores and equipment, as, for example, in fighting dysentery and malaria. At the commencement of a war these may not be available, or, if available, the area of operations, the composition of the force, its distribution and activities, may all combine to prevent or negative the efficient application of the known preventive measures.

Scientific facts concerning disease and detailed measures for its prevention are essential for the medical services, but unaccompanied by actual figures they make little or no appeal to the army as a whole. The best method, therefore, of enlisting the interest and co-operation of all ranks towards further progress is to show plainly the wastage caused by individual diseases or groups of diseases. This can be done by consolidating them into simple tables.* Such tables, deprived of all scientific clothing, will by their sheer nakedness interest military staffs who should view them as records of casualties and inefficients for whom provision must be made and reinforcements obtained. Recommendations regarding measures calculated to diminish the numbers will then be surveyed in a new light, and the practical lessons from the Great War will be more easily appreciated and remembered.

As the majority of preventable diseases come under the heading of diseases due to infection, it is convenient to subdivide them into groups.

Ordinary Infectious Diseases

Every one has at one time or another in his career heard of or experienced some of the ordinary infectious diseases common

---

* It is regretted that it has not been possible to compile complete tables for all diseases in the various expeditionary forces owing to lack of records. Only the known figures have been recorded, the years and campaigns being omitted where records were lacking or incomplete.

TABLE 5.—Incidence of Cerebro-spinal Fever, Chicken-pox, Diphtheria, Measles, Mumps, Rubella, Scarlet Fever and Small-pox during the Great War, with Deaths and Ratios per 1,000 of Ration Strength

Campaign	Period	Force	Cerebro-spinal fever			Chicken-pox			Diphtheria			Measles			Mumps			Rubella			Scarlet fever			Small-pox		
			A.	D.	Per 1,000	A.	D.	Per 1,000	A.	D.	Per 1,000	A.	D.	Per 1,000	A.	D.	Per 1,000	A.	D.	Per 1,000	A.	D.	Per 1,000	A.	D.	Per 1,000
France and Flanders	Aug.–Dec. 1914	British and Dominion	2	1	·01	4		·02	37	6	·19	103	1	·54	22		·12	1		·01	79					
	1915		357	169	·60	43		·07	439	7	·74	1,929	123	3·26	399		·67	1,613		2·73	808	14	1·37	1		·00
	1916		393	138	·30	83		·06	1,175	8	·89	1,912	51	1·45	4,333		3·28	5,490		4·15	749	7	·57	4		·00
	1917		692	192	·37	139		·07	2,273	20	1·20	1,221	14	1·14	18,203		4·33	9,418		4·97	563	2	·30	6	3	·00
	1918		176	69	·09	124		·07	1,657	24	·89	4	1	·66	2,165	14	1·30	1,698	5	·91	496	4	·27	2		·00
Italy	Oct.–Dec. 1915	British	7		·07	1		·01	154		1·63				125	1	1·32	37		·39	73		·77			·02
	1916	British and Dominion	8	4	·06	1		·02	40		·32	66		·53	7		·11	2		·03	4		·07			
Macedonia	1916																										
	1916		8	4	·06				40		·32	66		·53	22		·18	142		1·15	14	1	·11	3		·02
	1917		14	6	·08	11		·06	92	3	·50	309	1	1·69	97		·53	633	1	3·47	62		·34	11	1	·06
	1918		17	8	·13	4		·03	14	1	·11	17		·13	48	1	·37	121	1	·94	19		·15			
Dardanelles	Apr. 1915–Jan. 1916	British	9	4	·08	4		·03	275	18	2·35	120		1·03	41	1	·35	116	1	·99	283	3	2·42	17	4	·15
Mesopotamia	1914–15	Whole force	399	238	1·30																						
	1916		349	210	·85			·01							14		1·87							17		·10
	1917		295	177	·82				2		·27	6		·80	2	1	·50	6		1·50	1		·13	633	98	2·06
	1918		1,240	75	3·49				7		1·74													1,225	163	2·98
North Russia	1918–19	Archangel		70	1·71																						
		Murmansk	75	18	8·61																						
East Africa	1917	Troops	1,240	75	3·49																			301	121	7·34
		Followers		83	2·31																			443	106	5·06
	1918	Troops	263	202	3·00																					2·95
		Followers	22	12	2·01																			1		1·21
United Kingdom	Aug.–Dec. 1914	British and Dominion				17		·01	407	3	·32	516	41	·40	160		·12	33		·03	681	12	·53			·00
	1915		1,088	434	·74	98		·07	1,206	12	·82	17,216	62	4·88	1,046	2	·71	3,600		2·44	2,014	47	1·36	13		·01
	1916		967		·60						·17															
	1917		1,337		·78																		·03			
	1918		689		·43																					
South African War	1899–1902	British and Dominion, other ranks only.							32	2	·06	1,218		2·19							338	1	·61	10		·02

NOTE. A = Admissions; D = Deaths. Blank spaces denote no information available. The ratios for the South African War are the average annual ratios per 1,000.

to every family in the kingdom during peace or war. This group includes cerebro-spinal fever, chicken-pox, diphtheria, measles, mumps, rubella, scarlet fever and small-pox. The precautionary measures adopted to prevent the spread of infection become familiar whenever a case occurs. On active service the risks are increased as the troops may have come from infected areas or may be specially liable to contract certain infectious diseases, and have to live together in close contact. The precautionary measures taken to prevent infection spreading to others include notification, isolation and treatment of the case, disinfection of billets and transport, segregation and treatment of contacts; and these measures may be difficult to put into practice while interfering as little as possible with the normal routine of the units in the field.

Where records were available the returns for these infectious diseases from the different armies at home and in the field have been consolidated and the totals and ratios per 1,000 of strength are shown year by year by campaigns in Table 5.

For comparison the highest ratios per 1,000 of strength admitted to hospital for corresponding diseases among warrant officers, non-commissioned officers and men of the regular army at home and abroad during the years 1924 to 1928 are given in Table 6.

TABLE 6.—Highest Ratios per 1,000 of the Ordinary Infectious Diseases among Warrant Officers, Non-commissioned Officers and Men of the Regular Army, 1924 to 1928

Disease	Year	Ratio per 1,000	
		Admissions	Deaths
Cerebro-spinal fever	1926	·1	·03
Diphtheria	1927	1·9	·01
Measles	1924	1·4	—
Mumps	1925	2·1	—
Scarlet fever	1924	1·1	·01
Small-pox	1924	·2	·02

It will be seen that the incidence in many theatres of war was remarkably low and compares favourably with that of peace time. The figures are interesting because they extend over a period of years and demonstrate the good results obtained by the very thorough preventive measures enforced in the various armies during the period of the war. Where the incidence is outstandingly high, as in the case of cerebro-spinal fever in the United Kingdom and East Africa or small-pox in Mesopotamia, full details appear in the volumes already published.

Infectious Diseases Associated with the East

The second group of diseases due to infection includes enteric fever, cholera, typhus, relapsing fever and plague, diseases which are more commonly associated with Eastern countries and previous wars. There was a grim mortality about these diseases which struck a hard blow against maintaining a high morale in an army. Fortunately, little was heard of them during the Great War and they are fast disappearing from the health reports of the British army. Nevertheless, as a potential danger they still exist, and care must be exercised lest over-confidence may result in preventive measures being neglected until the insidious germs have gained a favourable foothold and the army is startled into action by the sudden appearance of one or other of these diseases.

It is with justifiable pride that the British army point to their work in the prevention of the enteric group of fevers during the Great War and compare their results with the incidence and mortality of typhoid fever in the South African War (Table 7). It is with pleasure, too, that the statistical record is now given, as the figures show the marvellous results of the preventive measures brought about by the work of Sir Almwroth Wright and the late Lieutenant-General Sir William B. Leishman, a Director-General of the Army Medical Services and the determined enthusiast who made it possible for this survey to be completed. All the cases recorded here were not scrutinised by Leishman, nor did they pass his critical laboratory tests, but they indicate the general standard of medical diagnosis at the time. They do not err on the side of leniency, but represent rather the maximum number of cases reported.

The British Expeditionary Forces remained singularly free of Mediterranean fever, cholera, typhus, relapsing fever and plague. In the European theatres of war particular attention was directed against the possible introduction of these diseases from the East where conditions favoured the spread of infection. The majority of cases of cholera, typhus, relapsing fever and plague occurring in British forces were reported from Mesopotamia (Table 8). The reasons are not far to seek. The area occupied had almost unlimited boundaries; native cities were densely populated, over-crowded and insanitary; pilgrims traversed the land to and from the

TABLE 7.—Incidence of the Enteric Group of Fevers during the Great War, with Deaths and Ratios per 1,000 of Ration Strength

Campaign	Period	Force	Admissions	Deaths	Discharged as invalids	Ratio per 1,000 of strength			Average No. of days in hospital per patient	
						Admissions	Deaths	Discharged as invalids	Officers	Other ranks
France and Flanders	Aug.–Dec. 1914	British and Dominion	466	57		2·45	·30		32·8	85·6
	1915		3,462	153		5·86	·26			
	1916		2,738	30		2·07	·02			
	1917		1,275	24	4	·67	·01	·02		
	1918		376	22	18	·20	·01	·03		
Italy	1918	British	142	14		1·50	·15			
Macedonia	Oct.–Dec. 1915	British and Dominion	170	5		2·79	·08		57·5	103·0
	1916		1,105	40		8·96	·32			
	1917		529	19		2·90	·10			
	1918		135	6		1·05	·05			
Dardanelles	1915–16	British	9,423	330	49	80·49	2·82	·42		
Egypt and Palestine	1916	British and Dominion	3,108	70		16·54	·37			
	1917		573	27		3·07	·14			
	1918		437	51		1·89	·22			
Mesopotamia	1914–15	Whole force	197			6·18				
	1916		3,060	157		18·50	·51			
	1917		1,535	148		4·99	·36			
	1918		1,071	24		2·60				
North Russia	1918–19	Archangel	1			3·21				
		Murmansk				·25				
East Africa	June–Dec. 1916	Troops	142	33		2·91	·68			
	"	Followers	9	1		·11	·01			
	1917	Troops	124	24		2·45	·47			
	"	Followers	40	5		·28	·03			
	1918	Troops	69	13		1·68	·32			
	"	Followers	42	7		·48	·08			
South-West Africa	1914–15	Dominion	230	26		6·97	·79		46·55	
United Kingdom	Aug.–Dec. 1914	British and Dominion	208	26	5	·16	·02	·00	38·3	61·1
	1915		320	29	9	·22	·02	·01		
South African War	1899–1902	British and Dominion, other ranks only	57,684	8,022	19,454	103·88	14·45			

NOTE.—Blank spaces in the table denote no information available. The ratios for the South African War are average annual ratios per 1,000.

NON-BATTLE CASUALTIES

TABLE 8.—Incidence of Mediterranean Fever, Plague, Cholera, Typhus Fever, Relapsing Fever and Sand-fly Fever during the Great War, with Deaths and Ratios per 1,000 of Ration Strength

Campaign	Period	Force	Mediterranean Fever			Plague			Cholera			Typhus Fever			Relapsing Fever			Sand-fly Fever		
			A.	D.	Per 1,000 A. D.	A.	D.	Per 1,000 A. D.	A.	D.	Per 1,000 A. D.	A.	D.	Per 1,000 A. D.	A.	D.	Per 1,000 A. D.	A.	D.	Per 1,000 A. D.
France and Flanders	Aug.–Dec. 1914	British and Dominion	3	—	·02 —										1	—	·01 —			
	1915											4	—	·00 —	10	—	·01 ·00	6	—	·01 —
	1916	British and Dominion													9	—	·00 ·79			
	1917	Indian										—	—	— ·02	16	—	·25 ·00			
	1918	Native Labour													6	—	·00 ·00			
		British and Dominion													10	—	·00 ·03			
		Indian										—	1	— ·01	3	1	·03 ·01			
Italy	1918	Native Labour	1	—	·01 —															
Macedonia	1915	British	2	—	·02 —										17	—	·14 ·02	236	—	1·91 —
	1916	British and Dominion	3	1	·02 ·01										73	4	·40 ·01	1,374	—	7·58 —
	1917											1	—	·01 ·00	12	—	·09 —	495	—	3·84 —
	1918											1	—	·00 —				77	—	·66 —
Dardanelles	Apr. 1915–Jan. 1916	British																		
Mesopotamia	1914–15	Whole force				102	—	·62 —	1,918	345	11·60 2·09									
	1916					98	49	·32 ·16	345	209	·68 ·23	21	11	·07 ·04						
	1917					164	106	·40 ·26	450	194	1·09 ·47	515	121	1·25 ·27	1,712	—	4·16 ·28			
	1918														114	—	·25 —			
North Russia	1918–19	Murmansk	14	—	·42 —										1	—	— —			
South-West Africa	1914–15	Dominion	5	—	·00 —				1	—	·00 —									
United Kingdom	Aug.–Dec. 1914	British and Dominion																		
	1915																			
South African War	1899–1902	British and Dominion, other ranks only	35	—	·06 —	23	—	4·04 ·00												

NOTE. A=Admissions; D=Deaths. Blank spaces denote no information available. The ratios for the South African War are the average annual ratios per 1,000.

religious centres; starved and half-clad refugees crowded to the protection of the British authorities; local labourers and natives of other Eastern countries in organised labour corps came often in contact with the troops; the sterilisation of water supplies was always difficult; and perhaps, most of all, the enemy force itself was a constant focus of infection.

The first outbreak of cholera among front-line troops in Mesopotamia passed unexpectedly from the Turkish army to the British troops in the spring of 1916. The cause was an infected water supply. The British force being unprepared could not take the necessary precautions to ensure that sterilised drinking water was distributed to the troops—a reflection on the administration of a force which, of all others, should have been forewarned, since it was composed largely of experienced officers with a life-long knowledge of the East and the disturbing consequences of epidemic diseases. No other named disease causes such despondency among troops as does cholera, and when it breaks out with any severity its depressing effect on morale is difficult to overcome. This outbreak came at a very trying time, but fortunately the authorities made up for their unpreparedness by their knowledge of and energy in establishing preventive measures. Despite many trials and difficulties they managed to keep the disease under control.

Typhus and relapsing fever were constant sources of danger to the troops in Mesopotamia and Egypt, as from time to time Turkish prisoners of war and local labourers were found to be suffering from these diseases. The infection is spread by lice. Preventive measures consist of early diagnosis of suspected cases, their isolation and treatment, segregation of contacts, disinfestation and insistence on general cleanliness. The early application of these measures was not easy as the clinical manifestations of typhus and relapsing fever were not always recognised by all medical officers, and the forces at first were not properly equipped either for the isolation of cases or for the disinfestation of clothing. Both difficulties were overcome, the first by clinical teaching and the dissemination of literature on the subject, the second by the substitution of suitable plant for the early improvised methods.

The few cases of plague that were reported from the different forces demonstrate the value of the elaborate methods directed against sources of infection at ports and in the occupied areas. In Mesopotamia 364 cases were reported, and there is no doubt that this disease caused the military authorities

TABLE 9.—Incidence of Tuberculosis in the British Expeditionary Forces during the Great War, with Deaths and Ratios per 1,000 of Ration Strength

Campaign	Period	Force	Pulmonary tuberculosis				Other tuberculosis				Total			
			Adms.	Deaths	Ratio per 1,000 Adms.	Deaths	Adms.	Deaths	Ratio per 1,000 Adms.	Deaths	Adms.	Deaths	Ratio per 1,000 Adms.	Deaths
France and Flanders	Aug.–Dec. 1914	British and Dominion	325	10	1·71	·05	26	2	·14	·01	351	12	1·85	·06
	1915		1,541	60	2·61	·10	359	25	·61	·04	1,900	85	3·22	·14
	1916		1,203		·91		140		·11		1,343	37	1·02	·03
	1917		1,512		·80		148		·08		1,660	91	·88	·05
	1918										1,221	74	·66	·04
Italy	1918	British	81		1·03									
Macedonia	Oct.–Dec. 1915	British and Dominion	29	2	·48	·03								
	1916		220		1·78									
	1917		390	1	2·14	·01								
	1918		231	10	1·79	·07								
Dardanelles	Apr. 1915–Jan. 1916	British	434	32	3·71	·27	69	4	·59	·03	503	36	4·30	·30
North Russia	1918–19	Archangel Murmansk	6		·80									
			11		2·74									
United Kingdom	Aug.–Dec. 1914	British and Dominion	957	30	·75	·02	151	7	·12	·01	1,108	37	·87	·03
	1915		3,893	166	2·63	·11	820	55	·55	·04	4,713	221	3·18	·15
South African War	1899–1902	British and Dominion, other ranks only	1,509	122	2·72	·22	194	24	·35	·04	1,703	146	3·07	·26

NOTE.—Blank spaces in the table denote no information available. The ratios for the South African War are average annual ratios per 1,000.

more anxiety than many of the other infectious diseases. The reason is obvious. The disease is spread by rats, and rats abounded in the densely populated riverside towns and villages. If they got aboard the supply ships on the rivers Tigris and Euphrates they could carry infection to the British camps and native settlements. Fortunately for the force, there were serving in it officers of the Indian Medical Service who had had extensive experience in combating plague in infested areas and towns by rat-destruction and by preventive inoculation. These officers fought hard to prevent the spread of the disease to the troops. As a result of their efforts the force suffered little damage, while thousands of the local inhabitants in the crowded cities benefited by the knowledge, zeal and courage of the officers who lived in the disease-stricken areas and opened special dispensaries and inoculation centres.

Although the figures are incomplete, there is sufficient information in Tables 5, 7 and 8 to justify the contention that non-battle casualties resulting from infectious or epidemic diseases, known at home and abroad during peace, formed only a small portion of the total cases admitted to hospital for sickness during the Great War.

Before turning to the diseases due to infection which produce a high incidence rate, it is interesting to record the available figures of two well-known diseases, tuberculosis and pneumonia.

Tuberculosis

The known incidence of tuberculosis, pulmonary or otherwise, in the British armies during the Great War is shown in Table 9.

Comparison with Table 10 will show that there was in certain areas an increase in the peace-time ratios, but this increase is negligible from a wastage point of view in a world war.

The smallness of the increase during active service is a

TABLE 10.—Tuberculosis among Warrant Officers, Non-commissioned Officers and Men of the Regular Army at Home and Abroad, Ratios per 1,000 of Strength, 1921–1928

Year	Pulmonary tuberculosis		Other tuberculosis	
	Admissions	Deaths	Admissions	Deaths
1921	1·6	·18	·4	·05
1922	1·3	·18	·3	·01
1923	1·4	·15	·4	·04
1924	1·2	·14	·3	·05
1925	1·3	·11	·3	·04
1926	1·1	·12	·4	·05
1927	1·3	·14	·4	·03
1928	1·1	·14	·3	·02

tribute to the physical stamina of the troops who were called on to face heat and cold, wind and rain, trench mud and desert sand, wounds and sickness. It is also a tribute to the medical services and the careful consideration given by the army authorities to the provision of proper clothing, rations and all that pertains to the comfort and well-being of the troops. The latent development of tuberculosis among troops, worn out by war, disease and service conditions, who have returned to civil life and, perhaps, overcrowded surroundings, is shown in Chapter XXI. While it can be truthfully said that the wastage from this disease is negligible during war, the pensions burden to the State on its account after war is high.

Pneumonia

What has been said of tuberculosis is applicable generally when the figures for pneumonia during the Great War are reviewed.

TABLE 11.—Incidence of Pneumonia in the British Expeditionary Forces during the Great War, with Deaths and Ratios per 1,000 of Ration Strength

Campaign	Period	Force	Admissions	Deaths	Ratio per 1,000	
					Admissions	Deaths
France and Flanders	Aug.–Dec. 1914	British and Dominion	378	53	1·99	·28
	1915		1,925	241	3·26	·41
	1916		1,497	135	1·13	·10
	1917		2,157	193	1·14	·10
	1918		1,921	352	1·03	·19
Italy	1918	British	173		2·20	
Macedonia	Oct.–Dec. 1915	British and Dominion	49	5	·80	·08
	1916		73	10	·59	·08
	1917		279	43	1·53	·24
	1918		48		·37	
Dardanelles	April 1915–Jan. 1916	British	677	98	5·78	·84
Egypt and Palestine	1916	British and Dominion	1,080	115	5·75	·61
	1917		228	55	1·22	·29
	1918		1,510	1,027	6·53	4·44
North Russia	1918–19	Archangel	26		3·43	
		Murmansk	23		5·73	
East Africa	June–Dec. 1916	All troops	463	119	9·48	2·44
		Followers	1,957	372	24·80	4·72
	1917	All troops	1,653	444	32·60	8·76
		Followers	10,009	3,013	69·53	20·93
	1918	All troops	2,023	516	49·30	12·58
		Followers	3,116	873	35·56	9·96
South-West Africa	1914–15	Dominion	124	12	3·76	·36
United Kingdom	Aug.–Dec. 1914	British and Dominion	1,352	177	1·06	·14
	1915		4,852	653	3·28	·44
	1916		4,104		2·57	
	1917		4,924		2·89	
	1918		9,484		5·88	
South African War	1899–1902	British and Dominion, other ranks only	2,591	466	4·57	·85

NOTE.—Blank spaces in the table denote no information available.
The ratios for the South African War are average annual ratios per 1,000.

As will be seen from Tables 11 and 12, in certain areas the increase on the peace-time ratio was slight, and in others it was much greater.

TABLE 12.—Pneumonia among Warrant Officers, Non-commissioned Officers and Men of the Regular Army at Home and Abroad, Ratios per 1,000 of Strength, 1921–1928

Year	Admissions	Deaths
1921	4·5	·52
1922	4·2	·44
1923	3·5	·30
1924	3·9	·33
1925	2·7	·33
1926	2·6	·31
1927	3·6	·39
1928	3·3	·32

The slight increase is noticeable in the Mediterranean Expeditionary Force during the Dardanelles campaign, in Egypt and Palestine in 1916 and 1918, in North Russia, and in the United Kingdom during 1918. On the other hand, the increase was very marked in East Africa. In the Dardanelles and North Russia depression and extreme cold were no doubt predisposing causes; in Egypt and Palestine the potent factors for evil were the malarial and influenza infections, while in the United Kingdom in 1918 the chief cause was influenza. In East Africa the African troops and followers were heavily infected with malaria and dysentery, and pneumonia was usually associated with these diseases, especially the former.

There now remain only the diseases due to infection which caused marked inefficiency and which are troublesome to control both in peace and in war—venereal diseases, malaria, dysentery and influenza.

Venereal Diseases

In all other infectious diseases the medical services endeavour to prevent infection reaching the personnel of an army. Indirectly this is also true of venereal diseases, but the medical services cannot be held responsible for a high incidence of these diseases among the troops because the causes are well known and officers and men, knowing how infection is contracted, individually take the risk. Preventive measures, therefore, must be viewed from an entirely different angle, and a comprehensive anti-venereal policy for adoption in war should be carefully worked out in times of peace. If such a policy was lacking during the whole period of the

TABLE 13.—Incidence of Venereal Diseases in the British Expeditionary Forces during the Great War with Ratios per 1,000 of Ration Strength

Campaign	Period	Force	Gonorrhœa Admissions	Gonorrhœa Ratio per 1,000	Syphilis Admissions	Syphilis Ratio per 1,000	Other Venereal Diseases Admissions	Other Venereal Diseases Ratio per 1,000	Total Admissions	Total Ratio per 1,000
France and Flanders	Aug.–Dec. 1914	British and Dominion	2,272	11·96	599	3·15	420	2·21	3,291	17·32
	1915		12,378	20·94	3,849	6·51	1,298	2·20	17,525	29·65
	1916		16,209	12·26	3,583	2·71	4,316	3·26	24,108	18·23
	1917		30,683	16·20	8,983	4·74	8,842	4·67	48,508	25·60
	1918								60,099	32·36
Italy	Oct.–Dec. 1915	British							415	41·80
Macedonia		British and Dominion							3,956	6·82
	1916								2,566	20·80
	1917								2,020	11·06
	1918								1,895	14·72
Dardanelles	Apr. 1915–Jan. 1916	British	1,774	15·15	415	3·54	556	4·75	2,745	23·45
Egypt and Palestine	1916	British and Dominion							14,153	75·31
	1917								5,242	28·10
	1918								11,656	50·44
Mesopotamia	1914–15	Whole force							619	19·42
	1916								3,491	21·11
	1917								6,144	19·98
	1918								6,636	16·12
North Russia	1918–19	Archangel	167	22·36	75	10·04	—	—	242	32·40
		Murmansk	75	18·69	35	8·72	1	·25	111	27·66
South-West Africa	1914–15	Dominion	1,130	34·24	227	6·88	—	—	1,357	41·12
United Kingdom	Aug.–Dec. 1914	British and Dominion	6,745	5·27	1,670	1·30	692	·54	9,107	7·11
	1915		24,877	16·83	8,117	5·49	1,764	1·19	34,758	23·51
	1916		34,337	21·48	10,434	6·53	2,748	1·72	47,519	29·73
	1917		34,495	20·21	17,986	10·54	2,015	1·18	54,496	31·93
	1918		35,480	21·98	16,733	10·37	1,626	1·01	53,839	33·36
South African War	1899–1902	British and Dominion other ranks only	8,538	15·38	8,620	15·52	1,969	3·54	19,127	34·45

NOTE.—Blank spaces denote no information available. The ratios for the South African War are average annual ratios per 1,000.

Great War, it can truly be said that persevering efforts were made in all areas to check or prevent increasing numbers falling victims to these diseases, for not only were they a great source of wastage in personnel in the national struggle but they also incurred the likelihood of permanent damage to the individual, infection to others, and a heritage which might stain an innocent life. Some idea of the wastage can be obtained by surveying the recorded figures for venereal diseases in the British forces at home and overseas during the Great War, shown in Table 13. The total of 416,891 admissions to hospital includes in the majority of countries mentioned cases occurring among British and Dominion troops only.

Administrators and scientists require more detailed information than is shown in the above table if they are to combine in furthering measures for the prevention of venereal diseases. The administrator responsible for the personnel of a force must have some idea of (a) the area in which infection is most likely to occur; (b) the approximate highest number of men off duty in hospital on this account; and (c) the average time spent in hospital per patient. The scientist on his part, in order to make headway on the professional side, will be interested in (a) the proportional incidence of the different types of the disease, as a knowledge of this kind may guide him in recommending preventive applications and appliances; and (b) the percentage of relapses among cases admitted to hospital, giving him some idea of the result of treatment when patients come under

TABLE 14.—Analysis of 91,231 Fresh Admissions to Hospital in France for Venereal Diseases from January 1915 to May 1918, showing Country in which disease was contracted

Disease contracted in	Fresh admissions				Percentage of fresh admissions			
	Gonorrhœa	Syphilis	Other V.D.	Total	Gonorrhœa	Syphilis	Other V.D.	Total
France	27,180	5,847	7,793	40,820	46·79	36·05	46·05	44·74
United Kingdom	24,665	7,821	6,076	38,562	42·46	48·22	35·90	42·27
Other countries	1,834	804	580	3,218	3·16	4·96	3·43	3·53
Source unknown	4,410	1,746	2,475	8,631	7·59	10·77	14·62	9·46
Total	58,089	16,218	16,924	91,231	—	—	—	—

medical charge; and (c) the potential infectivity of those who have been treated and discharged as apparently cured.

Table 14 is an analysis of 91,231 fresh admissions to hospital for venereal diseases in France from January 1915 to May 1918 showing the country in which the different types of disease were contracted.

This information is given separately in Tables 15 and 16 for the total fresh cases occurring in France in 1916 and 1917.

In a series of 7,010 British and Indian cases admitted to hospital in Mesopotamia from July 1917 to June 1918

TABLE 15.—Fresh Admissions to Hospital for Venereal Diseases in France in 1916 showing Country in which the disease was contracted

Disease con- tracted in	Fresh admissions				Percentage of fresh admissions			
	Gonorrhœa	Syphilis	Other V.D.	Total	Gonorrhœa	Syphilis	Other V.D.	Total
France	6,600	1,189	1,952	9,741	51·95	41·04	50·47	50·03
United Kingdom	4,191	1,002	1,180	6,373	32·99	34·59	30·51	32·73
Other countries	604	239	178	1,021	4·75	8·25	4·60	5·24
Source unknown	1,309	467	558	2,334	10·30	16·12	14·43	11·99
Total	12,704	2,897	3,868	19,469	—	—	—	—

the records show that the disease was contracted in Mesopotamia in 19·17 per cent. of the cases, in India in 64·47 per cent., in other countries in 6·32 per cent., and in 10·04 per cent. the source of infection was unknown.

From the point of view of the hospitalisation of cases, the maximum number of British and Dominion venereal patients in hospital on one day in France during 1917 was 8,392, or 5·50 per 1,000 of the ration strength. The maximum number for 1918 cannot be definitely stated, as some returns are not

TABLE 16.—Fresh Admissions to Hospital for Venereal Diseases in France in 1917 showing Country in which Disease was contracted

Disease con- tracted in	Fresh admissions				Percentage of fresh admissions			
	Gonorrhœa	Syphilis	Other V.D.	Total	Gonorrhœa	Syphilis	Other V.D.	Total
France	11,460	2,738	3,348	17,546	44·92	34·64	42·54	42·50
United Kingdom	11,851	4,151	3,072	19,074	46·45	52·52	39·03	46·20
Other countries	740	346	237	1,323	2·90	4·38	3·01	3·20
Source unknown	1,462	669	1,214	3,345	5·73	8·46	15·42	8·10
Total	25,513	7,904	7,871	41,288	—	—	—	—

available, but it is estimated that the number was approximately 11,000.

The completed records of cases for all years and forces are not known, but those of patients admitted to hospital at home and in certain theatres of war during 1915 show that the average time spent in hospital per patient for gonorrhœa was 28·6 days, for syphilis 37·6 days, and for other venereal diseases 31·3 days.

TABLE 17.—Percentages of Admissions for Venereal Diseases due to Gonorrhœa, Syphilis and Other Forms of the Disease.

	Period	Force	Cases analysed	Percentage of admissions for venereal diseases			Proportion
				Gonorrhœa	Syphilis	Other V.D.	Syphilis : Gonorrhœa
South African War	1899–1902	British and Dominion (other ranks)	19,127	44·64	45·07	10·29	1 : ·99
At home and abroad Great War (a)	1913 Aug. 1914–May 1918	British army British and Dominion troops in France and Flanders	12,509 117,203	56·49 65·20	26·56 18·72	16·96 16·08	1 : 2·13 1 : 3·48
(b)	Aug. 1914–Dec. 1918	British and Dominion troops in the United Kingdom *Total (a) and (b)*	199,719 *316,922*	68·06 *67·00*	27·51 *24·26*	4·43 *8·74*	1 : 2·47 *1 : 2·76*
(c) (d)	1918 April 1917–Dec. 1919	British troops in Italy American troops in United States and Europe *	3,602 338,746	62·69 71·11	14·08 18·70	23·23 10·19	1 : 4·45 1 : 3·80
At home and abroad " " At home	1921–24 1925–28 1921–24	British army British army British army, other ranks	52,507 32,796 13,820	66·55 72·08 72·04	17·08 9·91 20·09	16·37 18·01 7·87	1 : 3·90 1 : 7·27 1 : 3·59
" "	1925–28	British army, other ranks	8,259	81·74	10·99	7·26	1 : 7·44

* *The Medical Department of the United States Army in the World War*, Vol. XV, *Statistics*, Part Two, *Medical and Casualty Statistics*, p. 576.

Table 17 has been compiled from known figures to give some idea of the percentages of admissions for venereal diseases due to gonorrhœa, syphilis and other forms of the disease. The figures for the South African War and for the British army at home and abroad in pre- and post-war years have also been included for purposes of comparison.

All admissions to hospital for venereal diseases are not necessarily fresh cases, and until this research was undertaken statistics were not available, except perhaps those kept by individual surgeons, to show the percentage of admissions that were due to relapses. Fortunately the medical records of the British Expeditionary Forces in France and Italy can throw some light on this important subject. From August 1914 to December 1918 there were recorded in France, among British and Dominion troops, 153,531 admissions to hospital for venereal diseases. There is no data to show the percentage of total admissions in 1914 and 1915 due to relapses, but in 1916 they formed 19·24 per cent. of admissions, in 1917 the percentage was 14·88, and in 1918 it was 15·79. In order to show the percentage of relapses occurring in the different types of venereal disease an analysis was made of

TABLE 18.—Percentage of Relapses in the Different Types of Venereal Disease

Year	Gonorrhœa			Syphilis			Other venereal diseases			Total		
	Cases	Relapses	Per cent.	Cases	Relapses	Per cent.	Cases	Relapses	Per cent.	Cases	Relapses	Per cent.
France 1915	9,193	1,541	16·76	1,462	361	24·69	2,054	123	5·99	12,709	2,025	15·93
1916	16,209	3,505	21·62	3,583	686	19·15	4,316	448	10·38	24,108	4,639	19·24
1917	30,683	5,170	16·85	8,983	1,079	12·01	8,842	971	10·98	48,508	7,220	14·88
Jan.-May 1918	14,877	2,657	17·86	4,925	609	12·37	3,969	715	18·01	23,771	3,981	16·75
Total	*70,962*	*12,873*	*18·14*	*18,953*	*2,735*	*14·43*	*19,181*	*2,257*	*11·77*	*109,096*	*17,865*	*16·38*
Italy, 1918	2,258	272	12·05	507	58	11·44	837	66	7·89	3,602	396	10·99

109,096 cases occurring in France from January 1915 to May 1918, forming 71·06 per cent. of the total admissions, and of 3,602 cases in Italy during 1918. The results are shown in Table 18.

The known preventive measures are moral persuasion, the issue of preventive outfits, the establishment of early treatment centres and the provision of special hospitals. Before these can be employed to the best advantage, the psychology of the serving soldier must be studied and understood. There can be no doubt that during war the sexual instinct is stimulated in both sexes, and gratification of the impulse is more easily obtained. Personnel have more money to spend and there is a tendency towards slackening of moral principles. A soldier population may be divided into three types—the man who by nature or training is endowed to resist incontinence; the man who falls to temptation; and the man who deliberately sets out to gratify his sexual appetite. The first requires no help; he is fortunate in his strength and may be used as an influence for good among his companions. The second type requires sympathetic help, for in the solution of his problem lies hope for the future. It is unlikely that he will calmly seek protection by carrying and using a preventive outfit. Such an idea might not be feasible or it might be repulsive to his finer instincts. Picture him, however, stranded in a strange town, having been granted leave or even a few hours' respite from trench life, active fighting or military duties. He naturally seeks gaiety, brightness and laughter, therein to find for the time being the antidote to all he wishes to forget. Provided these recreative hours are spent in wholesome company and pursuits, they will have a stimulating effect on war-worn nerves. The danger is that, in the grip of loneliness or boredom, or because he is temporarily unstrung by the horrors of war, he may associate with the wrong company and run the risk of infection.

This typical picture seems to suggest one method of prevention. The weaker a man's nature, the greater is his tendency to rely on outside influences. Left to his own resources at any time he is miserable, but combined with the sudden transition from trench life to comparative freedom he finds himself helpless to direct his own energies along right channels and becomes an easy prey to the ills that attend this frame of mind. The efforts to attract officers and men to pleasing and health-giving recreation huts, fields of sport and places of healthy amusement during their hours off duty or during leave in a modern town should be redoubled. For these duties there are many men and women, unable to take an active share in the preparations for war, whose stimulating personality can be most usefully turned to account for their country's good in organising counter-attractions to keep men and women from temptation. Should these efforts fail and the risk of infection be run, the sufferer should be encouraged to report to an early-treatment centre, and if necessary to a hospital where modern skill and science may cut short the disease and so reduce the period of inefficiency and prevent damage to others.

For men of the third category the only sure method of minimising the risks they so willingly run is the use of a preventive outfit and attendance at an early-treatment centre.

In civil life there are several schools of thought regarding the best methods of diminishing venereal diseases. In the army during war men are so valuable that every possible means of successful prevention, early diagnosis and treatment should be investigated and employed if men are to be protected, the inefficiency caused by the disease reduced and army personnel returned to their own kith and kin in good health mentally, morally, and physically.

Malaria

Malaria is well known as an old enemy of the fighting machine and is expensive to control. As far as can be traced, the total admissions to hospital for this disease in the British Expeditionary Forces during the Great War numbered 497,659, distributed as shown in Table 19. They formed 8·04 per cent. of the non-battle casualties suffered in the same forces.

The greatest incidence occurred in Macedonia, East Africa, Mesopotamia, Egypt and Palestine. The severity of the disease in Macedonia can be realised by comparing the total battle casualties, numbering 23,762 killed, died of wounds, missing, prisoners of war, and wounded, with the total of 162,517 admissions to hospital for malaria alone, or from the records of one division in which it is stated that there were 5,000 admissions to hospital for malaria in one month.

The medical features of malaria and the preventive measures adopted have been fully described in two previous volumes.* The statistical survey is concerned with the wastage resulting and its bearing on the preliminary administrative measures required to lessen the incidence in an endemic area. The following practical questions stand out prominently for answer when a force is being mobilised for a particular theatre of war:

---

* *General History of the Medical Services, Diseases of the War*, vol. i, chaps. ix and x ; and *Hygiene of the War*, vol. ii, chap. viii.

1. Must troops be employed in a malarious district?
2. Has the force sufficient personnel and equipment for anti-malarial measures?
3. If the force is not organised or equipped to meet a high incidence of malaria, are steps being taken to make it so?

TABLE 19.—Incidence of Malaria in the British Expeditionary Forces during the Great War, with Deaths and Ratios per 1,000 of Ration Strength

Campaign	Period	Force	Admissions	Deaths	Ratio per 1,000 Admissions	Ratio per 1,000 Deaths
France and Flanders	Aug.–Dec. 1914	British and Dominion	1,147	4	6·04	·02
	1915		4,297	4	7·27	·01
	1916		58		·04	
	1917		781	2	·41	·00
	1918		2,739	4	1·47	·00
Italy	1918	British	279		2·95	
Macedonia	Oct.–Dec. 1915	British and Dominion	—	—	—	—
	1916		32,018	287	259·48	2·33
	1917		71,412	228	391·12	1·25
	1918		59,087	272	458·94	2·11
Dardanelles	Apr. 1915–Jan. 1916	British	1,473	5	12·58	·04
Egypt and Palestine	1916	British and Dominion	1,423	8	7·57	·04
	1917		8,480	73	45·46	·39
	1918		30,241	773	130·86	3·35
Mesopotamia	1914–15	Whole force	4,856		152·36	
	1916		16,957		102·54	
	1917		16,063	118	52·24	·38
	1918		21,447	166	52·10	·40
North Russia	1918–19	Archangel	—	—	—	—
		Murmansk	35		8·72	
East Africa	June–Dec. 1916	Troops	50,768	263	1,039·11	5·38
		Followers	7,127	187	90·33	2·37
	1917	Troops	72,141	499	1,422·84	9·84
		Followers	40,527	2,291	281·52	15·91
	1918	Troops	22,941	69	559·09	1·68
		Followers	21,260	361	242·63	4·12
South-West Africa	1914–15	Dominion	518	2	15·70	·06
United Kingdom	Aug.–Dec. 1914	British and Dominion	678	4	·53	·00
	1915		1,837	4	1·24	·00
	1916		1,072		·67	
	1917		3,088		1·81	
	1918		2,820		1·75	
South African War	1899–1902	British and Dominion, other ranks only	25,156	85	45·30	·15

NOTE.—Blank spaces denote no information available.
The ratios for the South African War are the average annual ratios per 1,000.

If these questions are not carefully considered and if measures of prevention are not organised with the same clear-cut anticipation as is given to the prevention of gas casualties, then the disease will attack fresh troops the moment they enter an endemic area. This happened in all the countries where statistics

NON-BATTLE CASUALTIES 81

show the incidence to have been high during the war. Valuable men will be lost to the force, time will be wasted, and the growing casualty list will necessitate demands for greater effort and more expense in endeavours to control the disease and cure its ravages.

Dysentery

Dysentery, with its allies diarrhœa, colitis and enteritis, is another old enemy of war and a constant source of trouble to armies in the field. Table 20 gives some idea of its incidence in the British armies during the war. The known figures show a total of 203,421 admissions to hospital.

TABLE 20.—Incidence of Dysentery in the British Expeditionary Forces during the Great War, with Deaths and Ratios per 1,000 of Ration Strength

Campaign	Period	Force	Admissions	Deaths	Ratio per 1,000	
					Admissions	Deaths
France and Flanders	Aug.–Dec. 1914	British and Dominion	861	4	4·53	·02
	1915		1,559	24	2·64	·04
	1916		5,776	40	4·37	·03
	1917		6,025	46	3·18	·02
	1918		12,211	46	6·58	·02
Italy	1918	British	901	17	9·52	·18
Macedonia	Oct.–Dec. 1915	British and Dominion	811	14	13·32	·23
	1916		8,204	169	66·49	1·37
	1917		5,792	124	31·72	·68
	1918		9,438	173	73·31	1·34
Dardanelles	Apr. 1915–Jan. 1916	British	29,728	811	253·94	6·93
Egypt and Palestine	1916	British and Dominion	5,597	81	29·78	·43
	1917		4,341	139	23·27	·75
	1918		4,906	264	21·23	1·14
Mesopotamia	1914–15	Whole force	3,476	33	109·06	1·04
	1916		15,270		92·34	
	1917		11,959	286	38·89	·93
	1918		12,290	303	29·86	·74
North Russia	1918–19	Archangel	8		1·07	
		Murmansk	6		1·50	
East Africa	June–Dec. 1916	Troops	8,902	306	182·21	6·26
		Followers	3,795	1,008	48·10	12·78
	1917	Troops	14,045	429	277·01	8·46
		Followers	26,607	7,277	184·82	50·55
	1918	Troops	3,294	86	80·28	2·10
		Followers	3,740	681	42·68	7·77
South-West Africa	1914–15	Dominion	715	13	21·67	·39
United Kingdom	Aug.–Dec. 1914	British and Dominion	220	3	·17	·00
	1915		570	2	·39	·00
	1916		421		·26	
	1917		485		·28	
	1918		353		·22	
South African War	1899–1902	British and Dominion, other ranks only.	38,108	1,343	68·60	2·42

NOTE.—Blank spaces denote no information available.
The ratios for the South African War are average annual ratios per 1,000.

The statistics of the disease during the operations in Gallipoli, Macedonia, Mesopotamia, East Africa, Egypt and Palestine, form a background to the descriptions written from time to time by army commanders or popular authors on the devitalising effects of dysentery. Any one who has served in an Eastern theatre of war, or studied the history of such campaigns, or has treated dysentery cases, will be in hearty agreement with the following words of General Sir Ian Hamilton :

> " Oh, energy, to what distant clime have you flown ? I used to be energetic ; . . . Yet, see me to-day, when a poor cousin to the cholera—this cursed enteritis—lays me by the heels ; fills me with desperate longing to lie down and do nothing but rest. More than half my Staff and troops are in the same state of indescribable slackness, and this, I think, must be the reason the Greeks were ten long years taking Troy." *

Or, again, with A. P. Herbert when he writes of dysentery in Gallipoli in like strain :

> " It became universal ; everybody had it, and everybody could not be sent away . . . The men could not be spared. . . . In the worst stage there was . . . only a dull misery of recurrent pain and lassitude and disgust . . . finally there came a terrible debility, a kind of paralysing lassitude when it needed a genuine flogging of the will for him to lift himself and walk across the camp." †

The cause of dysentery is well known, and the preventive measures are directed against flies and filth. Officers and men were trained from their earliest days in the army to wage an incessant war against these objective signs of insanitary conditions. Why, then, should the figures for the Eastern campaigns given in Table 20 compare unfavourably with those of the South African War ? Must medical science and army organisation accept defeat and plead that these diseases are a necessary concomitant of war ? The figures for the individual years help to dissipate that notion, for they show a gradual improvement in the incidence of the disease. The reason is simple. The sanitary services of an army improved year by year. It is easy to make excuses for the high incidence in the early days of the war and say that the army personnel was insufficient for the demands made upon it. If it is left at that, there will be little or no improvement in the future. Urgent reinforcements will be sent to infected areas and in time will

---

* *Gallipoli Diary*, by General Sir Ian Hamilton, G.C.B., vol. ii, pp. 7-8.

† *The Secret Battle*, by A. P. Herbert.

fall victims to the disease, and so the vicious circle will be continued. If for a moment we turn back to elementary principles it will be found that dysentery is indicative of bad sanitation. This was specially noted at two crucial periods, first when troops fought their earlier battles, particularly in trench warfare, and secondly when troops had fought hard, marched hard and fought again. Success and occupation of an enemy's position under these conditions were more often productive of dysentery owing to contamination from the enemy position, than failure and retreat to a prepared position on fresh ground.

Taking the first of these periods, there were several reasons for bad sanitation in the earlier stages of a campaign. There was the preliminary excitement of meeting the enemy in battle. All else was apt to be forgotten, and man, a civilised member of society by training, rapidly reverted to a primitive being when actual war occurred and he took the field of battle. It was not until the first excitement had passed that training re-asserted itself and sanitary principles were re-instated. The damage done, however, by a preliminary contamination of an area is not easily made good. All admit and recognise that sanitation in the line is difficult. The difficulties are not, however, insuperable, and if a force wishes to maintain its fighting ranks fit and free from dysentery, sanitary perfection must be its goal. This would be an easier task if troops were only kept in the front line for a brief period at each tour.

The second crucial period was more apparent and more important in the Eastern theatres of war where enemy positions were insanitary and consequently heavily infected. When such a position was taken, defences against a counter-attack were hurriedly prepared. Approaching darkness usually added to the commander's difficulties and entirely upset all sanitary arrangements, although even under the most favourable conditions there was a certain amount of confusion and the troops were usually tired, weary, hungry and thirsty. In these circumstances there was no known stimulus to convert the men into enthusiastic sanitarians. If the medical history of these attacks and operations is studied, it will be found that the numbers admitted to hospital suffering from dysentery were higher during the periods of operations than at other times. In Table 21 the monthly incidence of dysentery in Mesopotamia is shown during periods of successful operations. It was practically double the monthly incidence at other periods, for which the average number of admissions per period of four weeks during 1917 and 1918 were 717 with 14 deaths.

To discover a practical solution to this constantly recurring problem on active service is difficult, though worthy of a great effort. Good sanitation will not only diminish the risks of dysentery but also of many other diseases which reduce the

TABLE 21.—Incidence of Dysentery in Mesopotamia in Four-Weekly periods during successful Operations

Period	Operations	Admissions	Deaths
21.10.16–18.11.16		1,149	22
19.11.16–16.12.16	Operations for the capture of Kut	1,483	23
17.12.16–13. 1.17	,, ,, ,,	1,061	24
26. 8.17–29. 9.17	Capture of Ramadi	1,563	31
30. 9.17–27.10.17	Tigris operations	1,441	34
28.10.17–24.11.17	,, ,,	1,850	15
25.11.17–29.12.17	,, ,,	1,661	25
28. 4.18– 1. 6.18	Kirkuk operations	1,309	49
29. 9.18– 2.11.18	Advance to and occupation of Mosul	1,352	33
3.11.18–30.11.18	,, ,, ,,	1,489	33
1.12.18–28.12.18	,, ,, ,,	1,268	31

fighting value of front-line troops. Before discussing two historical developments in the sanitary organisation of the forces during the war that point the way to further evolution of the defensive measures against dysentery at these weak points, it is well to quote the words of General Sir Stanley Maude: " It is not development in preventive medical work, but rather greater efficiency in the manner in which the existing system is carried out that is required." Further let us recall to mind the definite principles of sanitary organisation of field units and divisions, viz : (1) Every unit, through its commander, is responsible for its own sanitation and for the condition of the area which it occupies ; (2) divisional sanitary sections are included in each division and cavalry division to supervise and carry out measures of a technical nature.

When sanitary sections were first employed in France with mobile troops, that is to say with divisions, they formed part of the divisions and moved with them. It was found, however, that under the conditions existing in France there was no continuity of effort, and in the interval of divisions changing over scrupulous attention to sanitary details was in partial or temporary abeyance. Reorganisation then took place, sanitary sections were appointed to areas and no longer moved with divisions. This ensured continuity of policy and minimised the lapses from sanitary grace.

NON-BATTLE CASUALTIES

In Mesopotamia some units and sanitary sections were treated very sympathetically by divisional commanders, and every effort was made to allow them additional sanitary personnel and transport to carry extra equipment so that the greatest sanitary effort might be made when it was most required.

The outstanding lessons in defensive measures against dysentery during a war may be summarised briefly as follows:

1. Preventive measures, including the provision of proper food, clothing, comforts, satisfactory water supply and good conservancy, must be very carefully and strictly attended to from the very outset of the campaign.
2. The greater the difficulties in the way, the more strenuous must be the efforts to overcome them.
3. Additional sanitary personnel with equipment should be organised and kept prepared to play the part of shock troops and attack the focus of infection before tired or insufficient sanitary personnel can prevent it getting a hold on the fighting troops.

Influenza

Apart from reproducing in Table 22 the recorded figures for influenza in the British armies at home and abroad during the Great War little need be said about this disease. The medical profession in allied and enemy armies waged a common war against it. They may have mitigated the suffering of many; they were powerless to prevent the spread of the epidemics. The same may be said in peace time even in the most advanced civilised states in the world. When influenza is rife it is no uncommon procedure for the general practitioner to struggle day and night to cover his rounds in his endeavour to prevent the disease spreading. Very often whole families are stricken, and he has to carry with him the front-door keys to let himself into his patients' houses.

Elaborate measures of prevention have been suggested, but at the present time they are impracticable for an army in the field to adopt. There is, however, one practical measure for conserving men which might be considered. It sometimes happens that units are scattered over a large area or that fighting is not imminent. Under such circumstances it will only crowd transport and hospitals to evacuate the slighter cases which in all probability will recover in a day or two.

It was possible in France to limit evacuation and in Mesopotamia to detail extra medical personnel and supply medical comforts to combatant and other units, and for these units to convert themselves temporarily into improvised hospitals

TABLE 22.—Incidence of Influenza in the British Expeditionary Forces during the Great War, with Deaths and Ratios per 1,000 of Ration Strength

Campaign	Period	Force	Admissions	Deaths	Ratio per 1,000	
					Admissions	Deaths
France and Flanders	Aug.–Dec. 1914 1915 (24 weeks) 1918	British and Dominion	1,478 44,392 313,938	2 23	7·78 75·11 157·81	·01 ·04
Italy (Forward Area)	1918	British	11,514	481	146·72	6·12
Macedonia	Oct.–Dec. 1915 1916 1917 1918	British and Dominion	795 252 984 19,862	262	13·06 2·04 5·39 154·27	2·03
Dardanelles	Apr. 1915– Jan. 1916	British	3,126	3	26·70	·03
Egypt and Palestine	1918	British and Dominion	9,709	34	42·01	·15
Mesopotamia	Aug.–Dec. 1918	Whole force	24,987 (incomplete)	169		
North Russia	1918–19	Archangel Murmansk	506 442		67·76 110·14	
South-West Africa	1914–15	Dominion	1,052		31·88	
United Kingdom	Aug.–Dec. 1914 1915 1916 1917 1918	British and Dominion	6,047 31,360 36,072 28,980 139,682	5 67	4·72 21·21 22·57 16·98 86·55	·00 ·05
South African War	1899–1902	British and Dominion, other ranks only	8,891	3	16·01	·00

NOTE.—Blank spaces denote no information available.
The ratios for the South African War are average annual ratios per 1,000.

to look after their own influenza cases. All the more serious cases were evacuated to regular medical units. By adopting these measures the epidemic was weathered with the minimum of discomfort and disturbance.

With the exception of trench fever, all the important diseases due to infection recorded from the various expeditionary forces have been noted either in this survey or in the chapters dealing with the individual campaigns. It is to be regretted that the total number of cases of trench fever and their distribution among the different campaigns have had to be omitted owing to lack of reliable figures. The few detailed statistical tables available, apart from those shown in the detailed analysis

NON-BATTLE CASUALTIES 87

of 836,677 cases in Chapter XX, are small and unimportant, and do not add any information to the chapter on trench fever published in a previous volume.*

With regard to the general diseases and disabilities not due to infection, the high incidence caused by the common everyday ailments which affect rich and poor alike, in peace or in war, has already been indicated.

It is outside the scope of this volume to discuss all the other diseases which occurred and were responsible for little wastage and a low admission ratio per 1,000 of strength. The outstanding disabilities of each campaign have been recorded in their respective chapters. Some were common to many campaigns, others had a purely local interest. Of the former three are important, frost bite and trench foot, war nephritis and epidemic jaundice. They were either unfamiliar or new to medical officers serving during the Great War, and consequently require prominence in this brief summary on account of the anxiety they produced and the constant care and attention devoted to their prevention.

Frost Bite and Trench Foot

The total admissions and geographical distribution of these disabilities are shown in Table 23.

Table 24 shows the weekly admissions to medical units in France and the numbers requiring evacuation to the base from March 1916 to June 1918. No returns were called for during the summer months. The weekly returns for 1917 show 429 cases more than the recorded totals of admissions to hospital for that year. As these were field returns the difference may be due to a faulty diagnosis. Of the total admissions 87·36 per cent. required evacuation to the base.

The greatest incidence occurred on the Western front and in Gallipoli. Few medical officers had had any experience of these conditions. Consequently the preventive measures so fully described in a previous volume † had to be hastily organised, methodically developed and stringently supervised by unit commanders. The beneficial results are reflected by the marked reduction in the yearly ratio per 1,000 of troops affected by these disabilities. During the war the figures day

---

* *General History of the Medical Services, Diseases of the War*, vol. i, chap. xvi.

† *General History of the Medical Services, Hygiene of the War*, vol. ii, chap. x.

TABLE 23.—Incidence of Frost Bite and Trench Foot in the British Expeditionary Forces during the Great War, with Deaths and Ratios per 1,000 of Strength

Campaign	Period	Force	Frost Bite				Trench Foot				Total			
			Admissions	Deaths	Ratio per 1,000		Admissions	Deaths	Ratio per 1,000		Admissions	Deaths	Ratio per 1,000	
					Admissions	Deaths			Admissions	Deaths			Admissions	Deaths
France and Flanders	Aug.–Dec. 1914	British and Dominion	6,447	12	33·93	·06	8	—	·04	—	6,455	12	33·97	·06
	1915		16,256	19	27·50	·03	6,462	6	10·93	·01	22,718	25	38·43	·04
	1916										16,955	1	12·82	·00
	1917										21,487	3	11·34	·00
	1918										7,096	—	3·82	—
Italy	1918	British (Forward area)	12	—	·15	—	14	—	·18	—	26	—	·33	—
Macedonia	Oct.–Dec. 1915	British and Dominion	1,014	—	16·65	—	111	—	1·82	—	1,125	—	18·48	—
	1916										66	—	·53	—
	1917										123	—	·67	—
	1918										254	—	1·97	—
Dardanelles ..	Apr. 1915–Jan. 1916	British	6,602	68	56·39	·58	1,380	10	11·79	·09	7,982	78	68·18	·67
North Russia ..	1918–19	Murmansk	48	—	11·96	—	—	—	—	—	48	—	11·96	—
United Kingdom ..	Aug.–Dec. 1914	British and Dominion	24	1	·02	·00	1	—	·00	—	25	1	·02	·00
	1915		288	—	·19	—	22	—	·01	—	310	—	·20	—

NOTE.—An analysis of the figures for 1914 and 1915 differentiated between frost bite and trench foot. This was not possible for the succeeding years.

NON-BATTLE CASUALTIES 89

TABLE 24.—Weekly Incidence of Frost Bite or Trench Foot in the British Expeditionary Force in France and Flanders

Week ending	Admissions to medical units	Evacuated to Base	Week ending	Admissions to medical units	Evacuated to Base	Week ending	Admissions to medical units	Evacuated to base
1916 March 25	78	100	1917 Feb. 3	551	424	1918 Jan. 5	698	718
April 1	148	120	10	491	309	12	921	632
8	9	74	17	573	546	19	2,321	1,691
15	39	14	24	1,708	635	26	1,211	1,145
22	83	27	March 3	2,159	2,312	Feb. 2	198	253
29	208	178	10	651	675	9	135	157
May 6	18	17	17	592	302	16	98	75
13	3	2	24	291	290	23	89	71
20	4	4	31	105	100	March 2	48	47
27	—	2	April 7	338	336	9	106	61
(No returns)			14	397	429	16	25	36
Oct. 7	38	14	21	667	574	23	19	17
14	11	4	28	225	362	30	27	41
21	98	11	May 5	54	67	April 6	123	44
28	707	662	12	16	21	13	613	396
Nov. 4	1,099	638	(No returns)			20	153	125
11	1,417	1,151	Oct. 13	1,022	1,032	27	155	167
18	536	618	20	1,088	711	May 4	43	49
25	960	799	27	725	1,097	11	96	89
Dec. 2	1,754	1,561	Nov. 3	1,223	392	18	14	12
9	666	837	10	1,298	1,003	25	2	3
16	3,104	2,521	17	1,117	469	June 1	1	1
23	2,486	2,692	24	391	337	(No returns)		
30	1,360	1,195	Dec. 1	479	457			
1917 Jan. 6	1,080	1,128	8	460	841	Total 18.3.16 to 1.6.18	43,838	38,298
13	930	419	15	909	565			
20	1,235	1,052	22	588	497			
27	860	823	29	546				

by day and week by week were diligently scrutinised by combatant and administrative officers. When the daily and weekly percentage of cases were seen to rise in a unit or formation a report was called for. These reports are instructive by drawing attention to the following important factors which tend to increase the daily admission rate and are sometimes overlooked even when the best preventive measures known and understood are applied :

1. The increased liability to trench foot caused by a prolonged period of trench warfare.
2. A long, rapid march to the trenches where the men arrived with hot, swollen feet and had to stand in cold, wet mud.
3. Inadequate provision of well-fitting boots.
4. Alternating frost, thaw and rain.

The first three predisposing causes are brought about by the inability of commanders to relieve strained and tired troops, provide transport or supply proper boots. The last depends on a power over which man has no control.

War Nephritis

The etiology of war nephritis was never quite satisfactorily explained, and the different theories have been fully dealt with elsewhere.* Certain conclusions stand out from the reports examined. (1) In the majority of cases the attack was not due to an exacerbation of a chronic or latent lesion of the kidneys nor to the previous occurrence of nephritis. (2) The incidence was greater during the winter months. (3) 95 per cent. of the cases occurred in front-line troops. (4) 75 per cent. of the cases occurred among the men and 25 per cent. among officers. Table 25 shows the recorded incidence of nephritis in some of the theatres of war.

It seems feasible to suggest that the predisposing causes are cold and humidity, hard work and overloading the soldier with heavy equipment. Any administrative measures that can mitigate these conditions in war time will not only increase the well-being of front-line troops, but will also tend to diminish war nephritis, trench foot, bronchitis and rheumatism—ailments which all cause a high sick rate.

---

* *General History of the Medical Services, Diseases of the War*, vol. i, chap. xxii.

TABLE 25.—Incidence of Nephritis in the British Expeditionary Forces during the Great War, with Deaths and Ratios per 1,000 of Ration Strength

Campaign	Period	Force	Admissions	Deaths	Ratio per 1,000	
					Admissions	Deaths
France and Flanders	Aug.–Dec. 1914	British and Dominion	104	4	·55	·02
	1915		4,010	97	6·78	·16
	1916		9,813	92	7·42	·07
	1917		15,214	201	8·03	·11
	1918		6,422		3·46	
Italy (Forward Area)	1918	British	512		6·53	
Dardanelles ..	Apr. 1915–Jan. 1916	British	626	20	5·35	·17
United Kingdom ..	Aug.–Dec. 1914	British and Dominion	270	21	·21	·02
	1915		1,373	84	·93	·06
South African War	1899–1902	British and Dominion, other ranks only	492	32	·88	·06

NOTE.—Blank spaces denote no information available.
The ratios for the South African War are average annual ratios per 1,000.

Jaundice

Campaign jaundice broke out in many of the Eastern theatres of war, but unfortunately the recorded figures are far from complete. Those given in Table 26 come under the broad heading of jaundice, as it was impossible to subdivide them and classify them more scientifically. They must, there-

TABLE 26.—Incidence of Jaundice in the British Expeditionary Forces during the Great War, with Deaths and Ratios per 1,000 of Ration Strength

Campaign	Period	Force	Admissions	Deaths	Ratio per 1,000	
					Admissions	Deaths
France and Flanders	Aug.–Dec. 1914	British and Dominion	94	—	·49	—
	1915		1,492	14	2·52	·02
	1916		181	2	·14	·00
	1917		940	9	·50	·00
	1918		1,268	6	·68	·00
Italy (Forward Area)	1918	British	599		7·63	
Macedonia ..	Oct.–Dec. 1915	British and Dominion	380	—	6·24	—
	1916		582	1	4·72	·01
	1917		320	1	1·75	·01
	1918		134	2	1·04	·02
Dardanelles ..	Apr. 1915–Jan. 1916	British	8,030	31	68·59	·26
United Kingdom ..	Aug.–Dec. 1914	British and Dominion	204	—	·16	—
	1915		492	7	·33	·00
South African War	1899–1902	British and Dominion, other ranks only	6,194	3	11·16	·00

NOTE.—Blank spaces denote no information available.
The ratios for the South African War are average annual ratios per 1,000.

fore, serve merely as a reminder of the wastage caused by diseases whose etiology is still indefinite.

It is not unreasonable in summing up to say, after surveying all the figures and reports, that when a force was fully equipped and prepared to fight diseases such as cholera, the enteric fevers, typhus, plague and relapsing fever, or the ordinary troubles of everyday life, they caused comparatively little wastage and could be kept under control. When, on the other hand, diseases such as venereal diseases, trench fever, dysentery and malaria, were allowed early to pierce faulty defences, they gained a firm footing, greatly increased the disability rate and swelled the number of admissions to hospital.

For the conquest of unfamiliar or new diseases brought about by war the medical services must be prepared to continue research and disseminate knowledge. The figures in this volume indicate the work to be done. Enthusiasm must be the stimulus if the science of medicine is to continue her victories in the prevention and cure of disease.

CHAPTER IV

CASUALTIES AMONG BRITISH AND DOMINION TROOPS STATIONED IN THE UNITED KINGDOM, AUGUST 1914 TO DECEMBER 1918

THE primary intention of this volume was to draw a statistical picture of the casualties suffered by the British forces in the different theatres of war. Casualties are, however, not confined to the wounds inflicted by the enemy; sickness and accidental injuries swell the numbers of personnel thrown temporarily out of action in the training camps and garrisons at home as well as in the armies overseas. Before these numbers can be fully appreciated or their further study stimulated in the interests of mankind, it is essential to scrutinise the records of diseases and disabilities occurring in the great national reservoir of troops in the United Kingdom, formed by the conversion of a nation at peace to one at war, and to compare the figures with those in the campaigns overseas.

During the years of the Great War almost every recruitable man in the country was medically examined either by a recruiting medical officer or medical board. This was a new experience for the British people, and the rather startling results tended to alter existing opinions of the physical efficiency of the nation. There arose in the minds of scientists doubts as to whether it would be possible to form and keep up to strength the large armies required for a modern world war, and whether the recruits accepted for service would deteriorate and break down on transfer from the comparative comfort of civil life to the new conditions of billeting, rationing, clothing, training and hard work. As every one knows, the armies required for service overseas were formed and kept up to strength with troops that were second to none. Statistically, the total admissions for sickness or injury for troops stationed in the United Kingdom for the period August 1914 to December 1918 show the low average annual ratio of 289·82 per 1,000 of strength in a force averaging a little over one and a half million troops per year. This ratio and the annual ratios year by year compare more than favourably with the pre- or post-war peace time ratios for sickness among troops in the United Kingdom. Indeed, as the following figures show, they have never been bettered:

Ratio per 1,000 of Strength

1914–1918		1908–13 and 1921–27	
(Aug.–Dec.) 1914 ...	78·94	1908–12	368·9
1915 ...	282·19	1912	346·4
1916 ...	270·37	1913	357·4
1917 ...	269·39	1921	434·5
1918 ...	344·14	1922	376·4
		1923	346·0
		1924	362·8
		1925	335·1
		1926	333·1
		1927	333·1
		1928	304·8

It seems, therefore, reasonable to assume that the physical standard of the recruits was high, or sufficiently so for the strenuous work they had to undertake, and, moreover, that they suffered no deleterious effects from service at home.

It is regretted that a complete analysis of all admissions to hospital is not available. Only the periods August to December 1914 and the whole of 1915 were completed, but these in themselves help to bridge the gap in army records created by the war. The analyses for these years, along with the records of diseases which are now available for 1916, 1917 and 1918, form a useful guide, and taken in conjunction with the detailed figures for France 1914 and 1915, for the Mediterranean Expeditionary Force during the Dardanelles campaign, and for the South African War, they give a reliable indication of the diseases and disabilities, apart altogether from diseases due to war, climate or country, that are common to troops both at home and in the field. This chapter necessarily refers only to non-battle casualties, and there are many unavoidable gaps in the information available; it is nevertheless safe to say that the outstanding causes of inefficiency were diseases of the digestive and respiratory systems and of the organs of locomotion, venereal diseases, rheumatic fever, skin affections and local and general injuries.

Strength

Table 1 shows the average ration strength of the troops stationed in the United Kingdom from August 1914 to December 1918.

TABLE 1.—Average Ration Strength

Year		Officers	Other Ranks	Total
(Aug.–Dec.) 1914	British and Dominion troops	30,810	1,249,658	1,280,468
1915	British troops only	51,566	1,426,825	1,478,391
,,	British and Dominion troops	53,184	1,463,601	1,516,785
1916	,, ,, ,,	58,555	1,539,902	1,598,457
1917	,, ,, ,,	63,038	1,638,695	1,706,733
1918	,, ,, ,,	76,936	1,537,017	1,613,953

Classification of Non-battle Casualties

The total non-battle casualties suffered by the troops in the United Kingdom are shown year by year in Table 2, with the actual ratios per 1,000 of strength and the average annual ratio per 1,000.

TABLE 2.—Total Non-battle Casualties

Year		Off.	O.R.	Total	Ratio per 1,000		
					Off.	O.R.	Total
(Aug.–Dec.) 1914	British and Dominion troops	1,152	99,926	101,078	37·39	79·96	78·94
1915	British troops only ...	10,285	406,902	417,187	199·45	285·18	282·19
1916	British and Dominion troops	—	—	432,168	—	—	270·37
1917	,, ,, ,,	—	—	459,781	—	—	269·39
1918	,, ,, ,,	—	—	555,432	—	—	344·14
Total (excluding Dominion troops, 1915)		..		1,965,646	Average annual ratio per 1,000		289·82

An analysis of non-battle casualties occurring among British and Dominion troops in the United Kingdom from August to December 1914 is given in Table 3 with the corresponding percentages.

TABLE 3.—Classification and Percentages of Total Non-battle Casualties, August–December, 1914

	Off.	O.R.	Total	Percentage of non-battle casualties		
				Off.	O.R.	Total
Non-battle casualties:						
Died of disease	6	706	712	·52	·71	·70
Died of injury	4	73	77	·35	·07	·08
Sick less died of disease	980	88,975	89,955	85·07	89·04	89·00
Injured less died of injury	162	10,172	10,334	14·06	10·18	10·22
Total	1,152	99,926	101,078	—	—	—

Table 4 shows a similar analysis for 1915 for British troops only.

TABLE 4.—Classification and Percentages of Total Non-battle Casualties among British Troops in 1915

	Off.	O.R.	Total	Percentage of non-battle casualties		
				Off.	O.R.	Total
Non-battle casualties:						
Died of disease	95	2,940	3,035	·92	·72	·73
Died of injury	32	269	301	·31	·07	·07
Sick less died of disease	8,894	369,944	378,838	86·48	90·92	90·81
Injured less died of injury	1,264	33,749	35,013	12·29	8·29	8·39
Total	10,285	406,902	417,187	—	—	—

Admissions to Hospital

The available information for the years 1916, 1917 and 1918 is confined to the total admissions to hospital for sickness or injury. It has not been possible to ascertain how many died, were returned to duty, or were invalided out of the service. The final disposal of admissions to hospital is, however, complete in respect of British and Dominion troops for August 1914 to December 1914, and for British troops only for 1915. The analysis of the former is given in Tables 5 (*a*), 5 (*b*) and 5 (*c*) with the corresponding ratios per 1,000 of strength and percentages of total admissions.

TABLE 5 (a).—Admissions to Hospital and Final Disposal of Cases, British and Dominion Troops, August to December, 1914

	Sick			Injured			Total		
	Off.	O.R.	Total	Off.	O.R.	Total	Off.	O.R.	Total
Admissions	986	89,681	90,667	166	10,245	10,411	1,152	99,926	101,078
Deaths	6	706	712	4	73	77	10	779	789
Returned to duty	972	82,060	83,032	161	9,858	10,019	1,133	91,918	93,051
Discharged as invalids	8	6,915	6,923	1	314	315	9	7,229	7,238

TABLE 5 (b).—Ratios per 1,000 of Ration Strength

	Sick			Injured			Total		
	Off.	O.R.	Total	Off.	O.R.	Total	Off.	O.R.	Total
Admissions	32·00	71·76	70·81	5·39	8·20	8·13	37·39	79·96	78·94
Deaths	·19	·56	·56	·13	·06	·06	·32	·62	·62
Returned to duty	31·55	65·67	64·85	5·23	7·89	7·82	36·77	73·55	72·67
Discharged as invalids	·26	5·53	5·41	·03	·25	·25	·29	5·78	5·65

TABLE 5 (c).—Percentages of Total Admissions

	Sick			Injured			Total		
	Off.	O.R.	Total	Off.	O.R.	Total	Off.	O.R.	Total
Deaths	·61	·79	·79	2·41	·71	·74	·87	·78	·78
Returned to duty	98·58	91·50	91·58	96·99	96·22	96·23	98·35	91·99	92·06
Discharged as invalids	·81	7·71	7·64	·60	3·06	3·03	·78	7·23	7·16

Table 6(a) shows the final disposal of cases admitted to hospital in 1915 among British troops stationed in the United Kingdom, with the corresponding ratios per 1,000 of strength in Table 6 (b) and the percentages of admissions in Table 6 (c).

TABLE 6 (a).—Admissions to Hospital and Final Disposal of Cases, British Troops only, 1915

	Sick			Injured			Total		
	Off.	O.R.	Total	Off.	O.R.	Total	Off.	O.R.	Total
Admissions	8,989	372,884	381,873	1,296	34,018	35,314	10,285	406,902	417,187
Deaths	95	2,940	3,035	32	269	301	127	3,209	3,336
Returned to duty	8,848	347,116	355,964	1,253	32,760	34,013	10,101	379,876	389,977
Discharged as invalids	46	22,828	22,874	11	989	1,000	57	23,817	23,874

TABLE 6 (b).—Ratios per 1,000 of Ration Strength

	Sick			Injured			Total		
	Off.	O.R.	Total	Off.	O.R.	Total	Off.	O.R.	Total
Admissions	174·32	261·34	258·30	25·13	23·84	23·89	199·45	285·18	282·19
Deaths	1·84	2·06	2·05	·62	·19	·20	2·46	2·25	2·26
Returned to duty	171·59	243·28	240·78	24·30	22·96	23·01	195·88	266·24	263·78
Discharged as invalids	·89	16·00	15·47	·21	·69	·68	1·11	16·69	16·15

UNITED KINGDOM, 1914–1918

TABLE 6 (c).—Percentages of Total Admissions

	Sick			Injured			Total		
	Off.	O.R.	Total	Off.	O.R.	Total	Off.	O.R.	Total
Deaths	1·06	·79	·79	2·47	·79	·85	1·23	·79	·80
Returned to duty	98·43	93·09	93·22	96·68	96·30	96·32	98·21	93·36	93·48
Discharged as invalids	·51	6·12	5·99	·85	2·91	2·83	·55	5·85	5·72

The average numbers constantly in hospital for sickness or injury during 1914 and 1915 are shown in Table 7 with the ratios per 1,000 of strength.

TABLE 7.—Average Numbers constantly in Hospital, 1914 and 1915

	1914 (Aug.–Dec.)				1915			
	Average Numbers		Ratio per 1,000		Average Numbers		Ratio per 1,000	
	Off.	O.R.	Off.	O.R.	Off.	O.R.	Off.	O.R.
Sick	83·7	10,093·6	2·72	8·08	374·7	22,529·2	7·27	15·79
Injured	17·5	1,235·0	·57	·99	64·8	2,426·1	1·26	1·70
Total	101·2	11,328·6	3·28	9·07	439·5	24,955·3	8·52	17·49

Table 8 shows the percentage of admissions among British troops in 1915 whose records were complete in respect of the time spent in hospital, with the average number of days in hospital per patient.

TABLE 8.—Average Period in Hospital per Patient in 1915

	Percentage of Admissions with completed records		Average No. of days in hospital per patient	
	Off.	O.R.	Off.	O.R.
Sick	96·53	95·83	15·8	23·0
Injured	96·14	97·08	19·0	26·8
Total	96·48	95·93	16·2	23·3

Hospital Accommodation

The hospitals and convalescent depots in the United Kingdom were open to receive not only cases from the troops stationed in the United Kingdom but also the sick and wounded casualties evacuated from the expeditionary forces overseas. It is therefore impossible to state what accommodation was reserved for the troops at home, or what percentage of beds to strength they occupied.*

---

* Hospital accommodation in the United Kingdom has been fully dealt with in the *General History of the Medical Services*, Vol. I, Chap. v

Non-battle Casualties

The principal causes of inefficiency among British and Dominion troops in the United Kingdom from August to December 1914, and among British troops in 1915, are shown in Table 9.

TABLE 9.—Principal Causes of Inefficiency, 1914 and 1915

1914 (Aug.-Dec.)			1915		
Cause	No.	Actual ratio per 1,000	Cause	No.	Actual ratio per 1,000
Diseases of the—			Diseases of the—		
Digestive system	17,598	13·74	Digestive system	64,995	43·96
Local and general injuries	10,411	8·13	Skin	41,535	28·09
Diseases of the skin	9,659	7·54	Organs of locomotion	37,244	25·19
Venereal diseases	9,107	7·11	Local and general injuries	35,314	23·89
Diseases of the—			Venereal diseases	34,758	23·51
Organs of locomotion	8,441	6·59	Diseases of the—		
Respiratory system (excluding pneumonia)	8,233	6·43	Respiratory system (excluding pneumonia)	31,673	21·42
			Influenza	31,360	21·21

For the succeeding years, 1916 to 1918, it has only been possible to obtain records of admissions for the more important diseases, infectious and otherwise, affecting the troops. The principal recorded causes of inefficiency among the troops stationed in the United Kingdom from August 1914 to December 1918 are given in Table 10 with the average annual ratios per 1,000 of strength.

TABLE 10.—Principal Recorded Causes of Inefficiency among Troops in the United Kingdom, August 1914 to December 1918

	Admissions	Average annual ratio per 1,000
Diseases of the digestive system	247,727	36·52
Influenza	242,141	35·70
Venereal diseases	199,719	29·44
Local and general injuries	136,362	20·11

Table 11 is a detailed analysis of the admissions to hospital for sickness or injury among British and Dominion troops from August to December 1914, showing the ultimate disposal of the cases and the ratios per 1,000 of strength.

Table 12 is a similar analysis in respect of British troops only for 1915, showing in addition the average number of days spent in hospital per patient for the different diseases or injuries.

TABLE 11.—Analysis of Admissions to Hospital of British and Dominion Troops stationed in the United Kingdom, August to December 1914, showing Disposal of Cases and Ratios per 1,000 of Strength

	Admissions	Deaths	Returned to duty	Discharged as invalids	Ratio per 1,000 Admissions	Ratio per 1,000 Deaths	Ratio per 1,000 Returned to duty	Ratio per 1,000 Discharged as invalids
Specific diseases due to infection								
Anthrax ...	7	2	5	—	·01	·00	·00	—
Blackwater fever ...	1	—	1	—	·00	—	·00	—
Cerebro-spinal fever	22	12	10	—	·02	·01	·01	—
Chicken-pox ...	17	—	17	—	·01	—	·01	—
Diphtheria ...	407	3	401	3	·32	·00	·31	·00
Dysentery ...	220	3	209	8	·17	·00	·16	·01
Enteric group of fevers	208	26	177	5	·16	·02	·14	·00
Erysipelas ...	127	3	123	1	·10	·00	·10	·00
Influenza ...	6,047	5	5,999	43	4·72	·00	4·69	·03
Malaria ...	678	4	651	23	·53	·00	·51	·02
Measles ...	616	41	475	—	·40	·03	·37	—
Mediterranean fever	5	—	4	1	·00	—	·00	·00
Mumps ...	160	—	159	—	·12	—	·12	—
Pneumonia (including broncho-pneumonia)	1,352	177	1,138	37	1·06	·14	·89	·03
Pyrexia of uncertain origin	310	—	307	3	·24	—	·24	·00
Rheumatic fever ...	1,013	8	864	141	·79	·01	·67	·11
Rubella ...	33	—	33	—	·03	—	·03	—
Scarlet fever ...	681	12	667	2	·53	·01	·52	·00
Septic diseases, major	118	7	102	9	·09	·01	·08	·01
Small-pox ...	1	—	1	—	·00	—	·00	—
Sprue ...	3	1	—	1	·00	·00	—	·00
Tetanus ...	3	—	3	—	·00	—	·00	—
Tuberculosis {Pulmonary	957	30	346	581	·75	·02	·27	·45
{Other	151	7	77	67	·12	·01	·06	·05
Venereal diseases {Gonorrhœa	6,745	—	6,601	144	5·27	—	5·16	·11
{Syphilis	1,670	5	1,535	130	1·30	·00	1·20	·10
{Soft chancre	573	—	564	5	·45	—	·44	·01
{Other	119	—	114	5	·09	—	·09	·00
Whooping-cough ...	8	—	8	—	·01	—	·01	—

TABLE 11.—continued.

	Admissions	Deaths	Returned to duty	Discharged as invalids	Ratio per 1,000 Admissions	Ratio per 1,000 Deaths	Ratio per 1,000 Returned to duty	Ratio per 1,000 Discharged as invalids
Diseases classified under systems								
Diseases of the nervous system	2,583	66	1,876	641	2·02	·05	1·47	·50
Mental diseases	609	12	200	397	·48	·01	·16	·31
Diseases of the—								
Eye	1,852	—	1,558	294	1·45	—	1·22	·23
Ear	1,453	9	1,149	295	1·13	·01	·90	·23
Nose	388	—	368	20	·30	—	·29	·02
Circulatory system {Valvular disease of the heart	863	22	389	452	·67	·02	·30	·35
Disordered action of the heart	548	2	387	159	·43	·00	·30	·12
Other	1,832	24	1,480	328	1·43	·02	1·16	·26
Respiratory system	8,233	61	7,653	519	6·43	·05	5·98	·41
Blood	117	2	94	21	·09	·00	·07	·02
Spleen	6	—	5	1	·00	—	·00	·00
Lymphatic system	566	—	548	18	·44	—	·43	·01
Endocrine glands	59	—	41	18	·05	—	·03	·01
Breast	6	—	5	1	·00	—	·00	·00
Teeth and gums	808	—	722	86	·63	—	·56	·07
Digestive system {Tonsillitis	6,967	1	6,926	40	5·44	·00	5·41	·03
Indigestion	820	—	753	67	·64	—	·59	·05
Inflammation and ulceration of the stomach	1,520	14	1,359	147	1·19	·01	1·06	·11
Other diseases of the stomach	131	—	122	8	·10	—	·10	·01
Appendicitis	1,053	24	992	37	·82	·02	·77	·03
Inflammation of the intestines	433	6	418	9	·34	·00	·33	·01
Other diseases of the intestines	1,468	10	1,367	91	1·15	·01	1·07	·07
Diarrhœa	816	—	816	—	·64	—	·64	—
Jaundice	204	—	202	2	·16	—	·16	·00
Other diseases of the digestive system	4,186	19	3,787	380	3·27	·01	2·96	·30
Generative system	2,373	1	2,235	137	1·85	·00	1·75	·11

UNITED KINGDOM, 1914–1918

	Admissions	Deaths						
Skin { Eczema	899	—	882	17	·70	—	·69	·01
Skin { Impetigo contagiosa	584	—	580	4	·46	—	·45	·00
Skin { Scabies	3,341	9	3,329	12	2·61	—	2·60	·01
Skin { Other	4,835	4	4,752	74	3·78	·01	3·71	·06
Areolar tissue	1,783	—	1,744	35	1·39	·00	1·36	·03
Organs of locomotion { Myalgia	1,074	3	1,014	60	·84	—	·79	·05
Organs of locomotion { Other	7,367	—	6,618	746	5·75	·02	5·17	·58
Urinary system { Nephritis	270	21	158	91	·21	·02	·12	·07
Urinary system { Other	705	6	601	98	·55	·00	·47	·08

Miscellaneous diseases

Debility	797	—	699	98	·62	·00	·55	·08
Diseases due to disorders of nutrition or of metabolism { Beri-beri	42	—	41	1	·03	—	·03	·00
Diseases due to disorders of nutrition or of metabolism { Other	103	5	77	21	·08	·01	·06	·02
Tumours and cysts	384	10	334	40	·30	·01	·26	·03
Poisons	312	8	283	21	·24	·01	·22	·02
Parasites	845	—	836	9	·66	—	·65	·01
Diseases unclassified	5,280	26	5,040	214	4·12	·02	3·94	·17

Injuries

Frost bite	24	1	22	1	·02	·00	·02	·00
Trench foot	1	—	1	—	·00	—	·00	—
Local and general injuries { Effects of heat or cold	313	1	304	8	·24	·00	·24	·01
Local and general injuries { Other	10,073	75	9,692	306	7·87	·06	7·57	·24
Grand total of diseases and injuries	101,078	789	93,051	7,238	78·94	·62	72·67	5·65

TABLE 12.—Analysis of Admissions to Hospital of British Troops stationed in the United Kingdom during 1915, showing Disposal of Cases, Ratios per 1,000 of Strength, and Average Number of Days in Hospital

	Admissions	Deaths	Returned to duty	Discharged as invalids	Ratio per 1,000 Admissions	Ratio per 1,000 Deaths	Ratio per 1,000 Returned to duty	Ratio per 1,000 Discharged as invalids	Average No. of days in hospital per patient Off.	Average No. of days in hospital per patient O.R.
Specific diseases due to infection										
Cerebro-spinal fever	1,088	434	617	37	·74	·29	·42	·03	14·8	43·2
Chicken-pox	98	—	98	—	·07	—	·07	—	15·5	21·3
Cholera	1	—	1	—	·00	—	·00	—	—	31·0
Diphtheria	1,206	12	1,190	4	·82	·01	·80	·00	27·3	34·1
Dysentery	570	2	527	41	·39	·00	·36	·03	22·8	38·1
Enteric group of fevers	320	29	282	9	·22	·02	·19	·01	38·3	61·1
Influenza	31,360	67	31,172	121	21·21	·05	21·09	·08	9·5	16·2
Malaria	1,837	4	1,781	52	1·24	·00	1·20	·04	12·3	30·8
Measles	7,216	62	7,143	11	4·88	·04	4·83	·01	13·4	22·6
Mumps	1,046	2	1,043	1	·71	·00	·71	·00	22·2	19·9
Pneumonia (including broncho-pneumonia)	4,852	653	4,073	126	3·28	·44	2·76	·09	20·4	38·1
Pyrexia of uncertain origin	812	2	807	3	·55	·00	·55	·00	12·0	11·4
Rheumatic fever	3,280	14	2,878	388	2·22	·01	1·95	·26	26·9	38·9
Rubella	3,600	7	3,589	4	2·44	·00	2·43	·00	12·0	18·5
Scarlet fever	2,014	47	1,959	8	1·36	·03	1·33	·01	38·5	47·6
Septic diseases, major	712	52	630	30	·48	·04	·43	·02	53·9	30·7
Small-pox	13	—	13	—	·01	—	·01	—	11·0	18·1
Tetanus	125	11	114	—	·08	·01	·08	—	—	12·1
Trench fever	4	—	4	—	·00	—	·00	—	—	36·3
Tuberculosis {Pulmonary	3,893	166	1,190	2,537	2·63	·11	·80	1·72	20·9	36·9
{Other	820	55	503	262	·55	·04	·34	·18	36·2	54·0
Venereal diseases {Gonorrhoea	24,877	2	24,759	116	16·83	·00	16·75	·08	33·4	26·4
{Syphilis	8,117	11	7,949	157	5·49	·01	5·38	·11	27·3	38·9
{Other	1,764	—	1,759	5	1·19	—	1·19	·00	27·0	30·3
Other diseases due to infection	3,736	8	3,714	14	2·53	·01	2·51	·01	8·8	13·7

UNITED KINGDOM, 1914-1918

Diseases classified under systems								
Diseases of the nervous system	13,184	180	10,130	2,874	8·92	·12	6·85	1·94	21·6	28·2
Mental diseases	1,871	30	663	1,178	1·27	·02	·45	·80	25·3	31·6
Diseases of the—										
Eye	6,599	4	5,578	1,017	4·46	·00	3·77	·69	16·1	20·1
Ear	6,597	29	5,409	1,159	4·46	·02	3·66	·78	20·7	26·4
Nose	2,845	10	2,784	51	1·92	·01	1·88	·03	10·8	23·6
Circulatory system { Valvular disease of the heart	3,934	80	1,878	1,976	2·66	·05	1·27	1·34	27·2	30·7
Disordered action of the heart	3,103	30	2,583	490	2·10	·02	1·75	·33	13·0	23·0
Other	8,400	63	7,380	957	5·68	·04	4·99	·65	22·5	32·3
Respiratory system	31,673	264	29,509	1,900	21·42	·18	19·96	1·29	11·8	22·0
Blood	631	18	542	71	·43	·01	·37	·05	20·6	31·8
Spleen	18	2	14	2	·01	·00	·01	·00	—	42·0
Lymphatic system	1,879	2	1,851	26	1·27	·00	1·25	·02	24·0	28·9
Endocrine glands	309	3	204	102	·21	·00	·14	·07	20·0	29·9
Breast	43	—	43	—	·03	—	·03	—	—	24·8
Teeth and gums	3,028	5	2,900	123	2·05	·00	1·96	·08	14·2	14·5
Digestive system { Tonsillitis	21,389	21	21,295	73	14·47	·01	14·40	·05	10·3	13·0
Indigestion	3,450	4	3,278	168	2·33	·00	2·22	·11	13·4	20·1
Inflammation and ulceration of the stomach	7,939	62	7,336	541	5·37	·04	4·96	·37	13·4	25·1
Other diseases of the stomach	704	14	634	56	·48	·01	·43	·04	15·0	27·8
Inflammation of the intestines	5,849	94	5,626	129	3·95	·06	3·81	·09	25·9	34·3
Other diseases of the intestines	20,104	84	19,295	725	13·60	·06	13·05	·49	25·2	29·5
Diarrhoea	2,198	—	2,185	13	1·49	—	1·48	·01	7·4	11·3
Jaundice	492	7	480	5	·33	·00	·32	·00	14·9	26·1
Other diseases of the digestive system	2,870	72	2,690	108	1·94	·05	1·82	·07	24·2	23·8
Generative system	11,923	17	11,608	298	8·06	·01	7·85	·20	22·2	26·6
Skin { Scabies	28,494	—	28,461	33	19·27	—	19·25	·02	13·8	11·8
Other	13,041	9	12,854	178	8·82	·01	8·69	·12	16·6	16·0
Areolar tissue	18,906	39	18,660	207	12·79	·03	12·62	·14	17·5	19·7
Organs of locomotion { Myalgia	5,087	4	4,837	246	3·44	·00	3·27	·17	16·9	23·1
Other	32,157	27	29,362	2,768	21·75	·02	19·86	1·87	21·4	28·3
Urinary system { Nephritis	1,373	84	951	338	·93	·06	·64	·23	29·6	41·6
Other	3,500	18	3,120	362	2·37	·01	2·11	·24	24·2	28·1

TABLE 12.—continued.

	Admissions	Deaths	Returned to duty	Discharged as invalids	Ratio per 1,000 Admissions	Ratio per 1,000 Deaths	Ratio per 1,000 Returned to duty	Ratio per 1,000 Discharged as invalids	Average No. of days in hospital per patient Off.	Average No. of days in hospital per patient O.R.
Miscellaneous diseases										
Debility	3,867	2	3,576	289	2·62	·00	2·42	·20	16·6	20·0
Diseases due to disorders of nutrition or of metabolism {Scurvy	4	—	4	—	·00	—	·00	—	—	13·7
{Beri-beri	9	—	8	1	·01	—	·01	·00	—	72·8
{Other	668	38	513	117	·45	·03	·35	·08	12·1	22·1
Tumours and cysts	1,066	17	939	110	·72	·01	·64	·07	22·2	25·2
Poisons	1,280	17	1,199	64	·87	·01	·81	·04	11·8	12·9
Parasites {Bilharzia haematobia	34	—	26	8	·02	—	·02	·01	—	22·5
{Other	1,666	—	1,662	4	1·13	—	1·12	·00	14·3	11·6
Other diseases unclassified	6,328	45	6,102	181	4·28	·03	4·13	·12	6·5	10·1
Injuries										
Frost bite	288	—	262	26	·19	—	·18	·02	23·0	41·3
Trench foot	22	—	22	—	·01	—	·01	—	—	32·4
Local and general injuries {Effects of heat	262	4	250	8	·18	·00	·17	·01	13·3	14·4
{Other	1,736	56	1,645	35	1·17	·04	1·11	·02	10·8	20·5
Other injuries accidental or undefined	33,006	241	31,834	931	22·33	·16	21·53	·63	19·3	27·1
Grand total of diseases and injuries	417,187	3,336	389,977	23,874	282·19	2·26	263·78	16·15	16·2	23·3

UNITED KINGDOM, 1914–1918

Table 13 gives the principal recorded admissions for sickness or injury among British and Dominion troops in the United Kingdom for the years 1916, 1917 and 1918, with the corresponding ratios per 1,000 of strength.

TABLE 13.—Principal Recorded Admissions to Hospital, 1916–18

	1916	1917	1918	Ratio per 1,000		
				1916	1917	1918
Specific diseases due to infection						
Cerebro-spinal fever	967	1,337	689	·60	·78	·43
Dysentery	421	485	353	·26	·28	·22
Influenza	36,072	28,980	139,682	22·57	16·98	86·55
Malaria	1,072	3,088	2,820	·67	1·81	1·75
Pneumonia	4,104	4,924	9,484	2·57	2·89	5·88
Rheumatic fever	5,944	3,828	2,363	3·72	2·24	1·46
Venereal diseases { Gonorrhœa	34,337	34,495	35,480	21·48	20·21	21·98
Syphilis	10,434	17,986	16,733	6·53	10·54	10·37
Other	2,748	2,015	1,626	1·72	1·18	1·01
Other diseases or injuries						
Diseases of the digestive system { Tonsillitis	17,743	19,361	18,865	11·10	11·34	11·69
Other	32,863	37,761	38,181	20·56	22·12	23·66
Local and general injuries	29,726	33,102	27,809	18·60	19·39	17·23
Other diseases and injuries unclassified	255,737	272,419	261,347	159·99	159·61	161·93
Total diseases and injuries	432,168	459,781	555,432	270·37	269·39	344·14

Table 14 shows the total recorded admissions to hospital for the above diseases for the period August 1914 to December 1918 with the average annual ratio per 1,000.

TABLE 14.—Total Recorded Admissions to Hospital, 1914–18

	Admissions 1914–1918	Average annual ratio per 1,000
Specific diseases due to infection		
Cerebro-spinal fever	4,103	·60
Dysentery	2,049	·30
Influenza	242,141	35·70
Malaria	9,495	1·40
Pneumonia	24,716	3·64
Rheumatic fever	16,428	2·42
Venereal diseases { Gonorrhœa	135,934	20·04
Syphilis	54,940	8·10
Other	8,845	1·30
Other diseases or injuries		
Diseases of the digestive system { Tonsillitis	84,325	12·43
Other	163,402	24·09
Local and general injuries	136,362	20·11
Total admissions for diseases and injuries	1,965,646*	289·82

* Excluding Dominion troops in 1915.

CHAPTER V

CASUALTIES IN THE BRITISH EXPEDITIONARY FORCE IN FRANCE AND FLANDERS, AUGUST 1914 TO DECEMBER 1918

THE Western Front was essentially the main theatre of operations during the Great War, and so continuous was the fighting, so intense the struggle, and so numerous the casualties, that no single chapter could do justice to the medical statistical aspect of over four years of warfare in that area. Each year presented its own medical picture of problems to be solved, difficulties to be overcome, successes and failures to be recorded, a précis of which, together with the chief battle events of the year, forms the introduction to the tabulated statistical results year by year. Some are given in greater detail than others. The statistics for 1914 and 1915 are as complete as modern scientific methods could produce, and the decision not to continue the detailed analysis of medical cards for the succeeding years is indeed to be regretted. With such degree of accuracy, however, as has been possible, the composite picture would be incomplete and difficult to compare with that of other campaigns if it did not include a summary of the six million odd battle and non-battle casualties incurred by the British Expeditionary Force in France and Flanders over the whole period of the war. A separate chapter has been devoted, therefore, to the production of this summary from such data as could be utilised, and the results are so striking that it has been decided to adopt the unusual method of presenting the summary first and the details in succeeding chapters.

It is not possible to refer, even briefly, to all that these millions represent in manpower, organisation, transport, feeding, housing and so on, but there are two outstanding features of the survey. With regard to the transportation of patients, the records show that some 4,000,000 cases required evacuation from the casualty clearing stations to the base by ambulance transport, and that 1,160,672 required evacuation from bases to ports of evacuation overseas. From the point of view of the conservation of manpower the second important point is the fact that 2,981,232 cases of wounds or disease, or 54·03 per cent. of the total admissions, were returned to duty in the theatre of war. To this total must be added the numbers who returned to duty after evacuation to the United Kingdom if the true value of the medical services to the state is to be appreciated.

A further point of interest lies in the chief causes of admission to hospital. The known statistics for 1914 and 1915 and the medical reports of the various armies for the later years indicate that the greatest temporary wastage was caused by the digestive, respiratory and other everyday diseases commonly met with in civil and military life, together with those peculiar to trench warfare, and not by the diseases which were anticipated or which attracted particular attention by their severity or sudden onset. Even so, the relative inefficiency caused by disease in France, where constant fighting resulted in heavy battle casualties, may be judged by comparing the 2,690,054 battle casualties with the 3,528,486 non-battle casualties. The average annual sick admission ratio of 646·55 per 1,000 of ration strength is remarkably low, testifying to the value of the precautionary measures adopted by the force to ensure a healthy army.

It is a matter for regret that the records of gas poisoning, nervous disorders and skin diseases, three important causes of inefficiency, are incomplete, but valuable samples have been prepared from available records to give some idea of the incidence of these diseases in relation to other admissions. Two sample tables are also included in this survey to indicate the extent of the dental work necessary in the force.

While it must be remembered that the figures represent admissions and not individuals, the results of modern warfare in a civilised country, as summarised for 1914–1918 in France, are without parallel. However viewed, they arrest attention and rouse the imagination. They demonstrate very forcibly the importance of medical problems in a titanic struggle, and drive home, as mere words will never do, the desirability of paying particular attention from the very outset of a campaign to the organisation which plays such an important part in the conservation of manpower.

Classification of Casualties

The total casualties sustained by the British Expeditionary Force in France and Flanders from August 1914 to December 1918 are shown in Table 1, with the average annual ratios per 1,000 of ration strength.

TABLE 1.—Total Casualties

	Off.	O.R;	Total	Average annual ratio per 1,000		
				Off.	O.R.	Total
Battle casualties ...	118,941	2,571,113	2,690,054	579·18	489·54	492·92
Non-battle casualties	127,303	3,401,183	3,528,486	619·89	647·59	646·55
Total	246,244	5,972,296	6,218,540	1,199·07	1,137·13	1,139·46

The proportion of battle casualties to non-battle casualties in the whole force was 1 to 1·07 officers ; 1 to 1·32 other ranks ; and 1 to 1·31 all ranks.

An analysis of the total casualties occurring in the British

Expeditionary Force in France for the period August 1914 to December 1918 is given in Table 2.

TABLE 2.—Classification and Percentages of Total Casualties

	Off.	O.R.	Total	Percentage of total casualties		
				Off.	O.R.	Total
A. *Battle Casualties:*						
(a) Killed	23,346	357,915	381,261	9·48	5·99	6·13
(b) Died of wounds	8,458	142,898	151,356	3·43	2·39	2·43
(c) Missing	4,265	140,633	144,898	1·73	2·35	2·33
(d) Prisoners of war	6,648	168,278	174,926	2·70	2·82	2·81
(e) Wounded less (b)	76,224	1,761,389	1,837,613	30·95	29·49	29·55
B. *Non-battle Casualties:*						
(f) Died of disease or injury	1,257	30,841	32,098	·51	·52	·52
(g) Sick or injured less (f)	126,046	3,370,342	3,496,388	51·19	56·43	56·23
Total A. and B.	246,244	5,972,296	6,218,540	—	—	—

Table 3 (*a*) shows this detail as percentages of battle casualties, and Table 3 (*b*) shows similarly the percentages of non-battle casualties.

TABLE 3 (*a*).—Percentages of Total Battle Casualties

	Off.	O.R.	Total
(a) Killed	19·63	13·92	14·17
(b) Died of wounds	7·11	5·56	5·63
(c) Missing	3·59	5·47	5·39
(d) Prisoners of war	5·59	6·54	6·50
(e) Wounded less (b)	64·08	68·51	68·31

TABLE 3 (*b*).—Percentages of Total Non-battle Casualties

	Off.	O.R.	Total
(f) Died of disease or injury	·99	·91	·91
(g) Sick or injured less (f)	99·01	99·09	99·09

The casualties sustained by the British Expeditionary Force in France from August 1914 to December 1918 may be further classified into permanent and temporary losses for military purposes in the field.

FRANCE AND FLANDERS, 1914–1918

TABLE 4 (a).—Permanent Losses for Military Purposes in the Field

	Off.	O.R.	Total	Percentage of total casualties		
				Off.	O.R.	Total
A. *Battle Casualties* :						
Killed	23,346	357,915	381,261	9·48	5·99	6·13
Died of wounds	8,458	142,898	151,356	3·43	2·39	2·43
Missing	4,265	140,633	144,898	1·73	2·35	2·33
Prisoners of war	6,648	168,278	174,926	2·70	2·82	2·81
Total	*42,717*	*809,724*	*852,441*	*17·35*	*13·56*	*13·71*
B. *Non-battle Casualties* :						
Died of disease or injury	1,257	30,841	32,098	·51	·52	·52
Total permanent losses	43,974	840,565	884,539	17·86	14·07	14·22

TABLE 4 (b).—Temporary Losses for Military Purposes in the Field

	Off.	O.R.	Total	Percentage of total casualties		
				Off.	O.R.	Total
A. *Battle Casualties* :						
Wounded less died of wounds	76,224	1,761,389	1,837,613	30·95	29·49	29·55
B. *Non-battle Casualties* :						
Sick or injured less died of disease or injury	126,046	3,370,342	3,496,388	51·19	56·43	56·23
Total temporary losses	202,270	5,131,731	5,334,001	82·14	85·93	85·78

The relative proportions of the various classes of casualties to each other for the whole force in France from August 1914 to December 1918 are shown in Table 5.

TABLE 5.—Proportions

	Officers	Other Ranks	Total
1. Total battle casualties to total non-battle casualties	1 : 1·07	1 : 1·32	1 : 1·31
2. Total killed to total wounded including died of wounds	1 : 3·63	1 : 5·32	1 : 5·22
3. Permanent losses among battle casualties to total wounded less died of wounds	1 : 1·78	1 : 2·18	1 : 2·16
4. Permanent losses among non-battle casualties to total sick and injured less died of disease or injury	1 : 100·27	1 : 109·28	1 : 108·93
5. Total permanent losses to total temporary losses	1 : 4·60	1 : 6·11	1 : 6·03

Admissions to Hospital

Of the total casualties suffered by the British Expeditionary Force in France and Flanders from August 1914 to December 1918, the numbers admitted to hospital and treated by the medical services are shown in Table 6.

TABLE 6.—Numbers admitted to Hospital

	Off.	O.R.	Total	Percentage of total casualties		
				Off.	O.R.	Total
Wounded	84,682	1,904,287	1,988,969	34·39	31·89	31·98
Sick or injured	127,303	3,401,183	3,528,486	51·70	56·95	56·74
Total	211,985	5,305,470	5,517,455	86·09	88·83	88·73

The proportion of wounded to sick and injured treated by the medical services was 1 to 1·5 officers; 1 to 1·8 other ranks; and 1 to 1·8 all ranks.

The casualties which were not treated by the medical services are shown in Table 7.

TABLE 7.—Casualties in the British Expeditionary Force not treated by the Medical Services

	Off.	O.R.	Total	Percentage of total casualties		
				Off.	O.R.	Total
Killed	23,346	357,915	381,261	9·48	5·99	6·13
Missing	4,265	140,633	144,898	1·73	2·35	2·33
Prisoners of war	6,648	168,278	174,926	2·70	2·82	2·81
Total	34,259	666,826	701,085	13·91	11·17	11·27

The numbers of sick and wounded admitted to hospital, and the disposal of cases, are shown in Table 8 (a), while the average annual ratios per 1,000 of ration strength and the

TABLE 8 (a).—Admissions to Hospital and Disposal of Cases, British Expeditionary Force, France, 1914–18

	Wounded			Sick or injured			Total		
	Off.	O.R.	Total	Off.	O.R.	Total	Off.	O.R.	Total
Admissions	84,682	1,904,287	1,988,969	127,303	3,401,183	3,528,486	211,985	5,305,470	5,517,455
Deaths	8,458	142,898	151,356	1,257	30,841	32,098	9,715	173,739	183,454
Returned to duty in theatre of war	15,920	569,039	584,959	74,243	2,322,030	2,396,273	90,163	2,891,069	2,981,232
Evacuated overseas	60,215	1,185,320	1,245,535	50,391	983,769	1,034,160	110,606	2,169,089	2,279,695

percentages of total admissions are given in Tables 8 (b) and 8 (c) respectively. In order to complete these tables, the figures for 1914 and 1915, which show the ultimate disposal of cases in their respective chapters, have been brought into line with those of the succeeding years.

TABLE 8 (b).—Average Annual Ratio per 1,000 of Ration Strength

	Wounded			Sick or injured			Total		
	Off.	O.R.	Total	Off.	O.R.	Total	Off.	O.R.	Total
Admissions	412·35	362·58	364·45	619·89	647·59	646·55	1,032·26	1,010·17	1,011·00
Deaths	41·19	27·21	27·73	6·11	5·87	5·88	47·31	33·08	33·62
Returned to duty in theatre of war	77·53	108·35	107·19	361·53	442·12	439·08	439·04	550·46	546·27
Evacuated overseas	293·22	225·69	228·23	245·37	187·32	189·50	538·59	413·00	417·72

TABLE 8 (c).—Percentages of Total Admissions

	Wounded			Sick or injured			Total		
	Off.	O.R.	Total	Off.	O.R.	Total	Off.	O.R.	Total
Deaths	9·99	7·50	7·61	·99	·91	·91	4·58	3·27	3·32
Returned to duty in theatre of war	18·80	29·88	29·40	58·32	68·27	67·91	42·53	54·49	54·03
Evacuated overseas	71·11	62·24	62·62	39·58	28·92	29·31	52·18	40·88	41·32
Remaining in medical charge on 31.12.18	·11	·37	·36	1·11	1·90	1·87	·71	1·35	1·32

Gas Casualties

In estimating the total number of gas casualties in France from 1915 to the end of the war, it must be remembered that very many were probably included under the heading killed in action, especially in the first surprise attacks of 1915. Table 9, therefore, shows the approximate numbers admitted to hospital suffering from the effects of gas warfare and the number of deaths, with the corresponding annual ratios per 1,000 of ration strength and percentage of total wounded year by year.

TABLE 9.—Approximate Total Gas Casualties admitted to Medical Units in France, with Deaths and Ratios per 1,000 of Ration Strength, 1915–1918

Year	Admissions	Deaths	Annual ratio per 1,000		Percentage of total wounded
			Admissions	Deaths	
1915	12,792*	307*	21·64	·52	5·79
1916	6,698	1,123	5·01	·84	1·34
1917	52,452	1,796	26·64	·91	9·29
1918	113,764	2,673	57·19	1·34	18·22
1915–18	185,706	5,899	31·55	1·00	9·72

* British troops only; the ratios and percentage are calculated accordingly. The admissions and deaths among Dominion troops are not known.

Two samples have been taken from the records of armies in the field to give some idea of the disposal of cases of gas poisoning admitted to casualty clearing stations. Table 10 shows the admissions to casualty clearing stations of the First

TABLE 10.—Disposal of Cases of Gas Poisoning admitted to Casualty Clearing Stations of the First Army, 22.4.17–7.12.18

	Off.	O.R.	Total	Percentage of total " gas " admissions		
				Off.	O.R.	Total
Deaths in C.C.S. ...	8	393	401	·63	1·10	1·08
Returned to duty	45	1,843	1,888	3·55	5·14	5·09
Evacuated to base	1,215	33,607	34,822	95·82	93·76	93·83
Total " gas " admissions	1,268	35,843	37,111	—	—	—

Army over a period of 85 consecutive weeks from 22nd April, 1917 to 7th December, 1918. Table 11 treats of admissions to Fourth Army casualty clearing stations from 26th November, 1916 to 29th December, 1917.

TABLE 11.—Disposal of Cases of Gas Poisoning admitted to Casualty Clearing Stations of the Fourth Army, 26.11.16–29.12.17

	Off.	O.R.	Total	Percentage of total " gas " admissions		
				Off.	O.R.	Total
Deaths in C.C.S. ...	1	137	138	·31	1·58	1·54
Returned to duty	4	76	80	1·26	·88	·89
Evacuated to base	299	8,120	8,419	94·03	93·71	93·72
Disposal not stated	14	332	346	4·40	3·83	3·85
Total " gas " admissions	318	8,665	8,983	—	—	—

The proportion of gas casualties to the approximate total number of wounded received during these periods in the casualty clearing stations of the armies concerned is shown in Table 12.

TABLE 12.—Proportion of Gas Casualties to Wounded admitted to Casualty Clearing Stations during Periods covered by Tables 10 and 11

Army	Gas casualties			Wounded			Proportion of gas casualties to wounded		
	Off.	O.R.	Total	Off.	O.R.	Total	Off.	O.R.	Total
First	1,268	35,843	37,111	6,671	145,754	152,425	1 : 5·26	1 : 4·07	1 : 4·11
Fourth	318	8,665	8,983	2,301	52,002	54,503	1 : 7·24	1 : 6·00	1 : 6·07

Military students of chemical gas warfare will regret the decision not to continue the detailed analysis of medical cards after 1915, which has thereby deprived science of ascertaining the ultimate results of cases of gas poisoning during the war. The final disposal of cases admitted to hospital in 1915 for this cause is shown in Table 13, while Table 14 shows the

TABLE 13.—Admissions to Hospital of British Troops suffering from Gas Poisoning in France, 1915, with Final Disposal of Cases

	Off.	O.R.	Total	Percentage of total " gas " admissions		
				Off.	O.R.	Total
Deaths	16	291	307	5·80	2·33	2·40
Returned to duty	260	12,122	12,382	94·20	96·85	96·79
Discharged as invalids	—	103	103	—	·82	·81
Total " gas " admissions	276	12,516	12,792	—	—	—

results obtained from an analysis of two sets of sample cards amounting to 23,626 cases for the years 1916 onwards. It will be noted that although slightly over 93 per cent. of those admitted to casualty clearing stations required evacuation to the base, the percentage ultimately returned to duty is very high, being 96·79 in 1915 and 92·90 for the later years according to the samples.

TABLE 14.—Final Disposal of 23,626 Cases of Gas Poisoning admitted to Hospital from 1916 onwards

	Off.	O.R.	Total	Percentage of total " gas " admissions		
				Off.	O.R.	Total
Deaths	48	687	735	1·96	3·24	3·11
Returned to duty	2,241	19,708	21,949	91·47	93·07	92·90
Discharged as invalids	43	297	340	1·76	1·40	1·44
Discharged from hospital indefinite	5	3	8	·20	·01	·03
Records incomplete	104	404	508	4·24	1·91	2·15
Disease changed	9	77	86	·37	·36	·36
Total admissions	2,450	21,176	23,626	—	—	—

The average number of days in hospital either in France or in the United Kingdom of the cases that occurred among British troops in 1915 was 12·2 in the case of officers and 27·6 in the case of other ranks, while the average number constantly in hospital on account of gas poisoning was 8·27 officers and 883·04 other ranks.

Non-battle Casualties

It has not been possible to obtain a complete record of admissions to hospital for disease or injury, nor is it possible from the records available to state numerically the chief causes of admission for the period August 1914 to December 1918. As already explained, the records for 1914 and 1915 in respect of an analysis of the causes of admission are as complete as they can be, and if they may be taken as a guide, along with the medical reports rendered from time to time by the directors of medical services of armies in the field, it is safe to assume

TABLE 15.—Principal Recorded Causes of Admission to Hospital of British and Dominion Troops in France, 1914–18, with Deaths and Average Annual Ratios per 1,000 of Ration Strength

	Admissions	Deaths	Average annual ratio per 1,000	
			Admissions	Deaths
Specific diseases due to infection				
Cerebro-spinal meningitis	1,620	569	·31	·11
Chicken-pox	393	—	·08	—
Diphtheria	5,581	65	1·08	·01
Dysentery	26,432	160	5·11	·03
Enteric fever — Typhoid	2,431	208	·47	·04
Enteric fever — Paratyphoid A	1,051	12	·20	·00
Enteric fever — Paratyphoid B	3,000	40	·58	·01
Enteric fever — Group	941	6	·18	·00
Malaria	9,022	14	1·74	·00
Measles	7,330	36	1·42	·01
Mumps	15,367	—	2·97	—
Pneumonia	7,878	974	1·52	·19
Rubella	18,220	16	3·52	·00
Scarlet fever	2,695	27	·52	·01
Small-pox	12	3	·00	·00
Tuberculosis	6,475	299	1·25	·06
Venereal diseases	153,531	14	29·69	·00
Other diseases or disabilities				
Jaundice	3,975	31	·77	·01
Nephritis	35,563	394	6·88	·08
Trench foot or frost bite	74,711	41	14·45	·01

that diseases of the digestive system and of the respiratory system, together with local and general injuries, were the prevailing causes of inefficiency among the troops. The known statistics of admission to hospital over the whole period are mainly confined to infectious diseases, of which Table 15 shows the approximate total number of admissions and deaths, and the average annual ratios per 1,000 of ration strength. It should be remembered that the detailed statistics for 1915 refer to British troops only.

Nervous Disorders

There is unfortunately little information regarding the wastage due to nervous disorders in France other than that for the period August to December 1914 and for 1915. Table 16 shows the admissions to hospital of British troops suffering from nervous or mental diseases up to the end of 1915.

TABLE 16.—Admissions to Hospital of British Troops suffering from Nervous Disorders, August 1914 to December 1915

Period	Admissions	Percentage of total British admissions for disease or injury	Proportion of nervous disorders to total British admissions	
			Wounded	Sick or injured
1914 (Aug.–Dec.)	1,906	2·55	1 : 29·54	1 : 39·15
1915	20,327	3·84	1 : 10·88	1 : 26·06

With regard to the years 1916 to 1918, the records are very incomplete, and it has only been possible to compile sample tables indicative of the incidence of nervous disorders in the force and the disposal of cases. Table 17 represents the admissions to medical units in army areas for the whole force for 28 weeks in 1918, 26 of which are consecutive.

TABLE 17.—Admissions and Disposal of Cases of Nervous Disorders in Army Areas for the weeks ending 30.3.18 and 13.4.18, and from 8.6.18 to 7.12.18

Diagnosis	Disposal	Off.	O.R.	Total	Percentage of admissions		
					Off.	O.R.	Total
Neurasthenia or other nervous complaint ...	To duty	27	2,064	2,091	5·53	26·91	25·63
,, ,,	,, base	324	2,761	3,085	66·39	36·00	37·82
Shell-shock (wound)	,, duty	5	191	196	1·02	2·49	2·40
,, ,,	,, base	33	452	485	6·76	5·89	5·95
No appreciable disease ...	,, duty	10	522	532	2·05	6·81	6·52
Not yet diagnosed (nervous)	,, base	66	1,305	1,371	13·52	17·02	16·81
	Not stated	23	374	397	4·71	4·88	4·87
Total admissions ...	—	488	7,669	8,157	—	—	—

Table 18 shows the diagnosis and final disposal of cases sent from armies in the field to the base labelled " N.Y.D.(N.) "* for a period of seven months from June to December 1917.

* Not yet diagnosed (neurological).

TABLE 18.—Diagnosis and Final Disposal of "N.Y.D.(N.)" Cases sent from Armies to the Base, June to December, 1917

Diagnosis	Disposal	Off.	O.R.	Total	Percentage of admissions		
					Off.	O.R.	Total
Neurasthenia	To duty	25	384	409	16·13	15·72	15·74
,, ...	,, U.K.	53	139	192	34·19	5·69	7·39
Shell-shock (wound) ...	,, duty	21	1,184	1,205	13·55	48·47	46·38
,, ,, ...	,, U.K.	39	449	488	25·16	18·38	18·78
No appreciable disease ...	,, duty	—	1	1	—	·04	·04
Other casualty	,, duty	7	191	198	4·52	7·82	7·62
,, ,, ...	,, U.K.	8	89	97	5·16	3·64	3·73
	Died	—	2	2	—	·08	·08
	Not stated	2	4	6	1·29	·16	·23
Total admissions ...		155	2,443	2,598	—	—	—

Table 19 shows the proportions of the cases in Tables 17 and 18 to the total number of sick and wounded admitted from the same armies for the same periods.

TABLE 19.—Proportion of Nervous Disorders to Sick and Wounded Admitted

Nervous disorders			Sick and wounded			Proportion of nervous disorders to sick and wounded admitted		
Off.	O.R.	Total	Off.	O.R.	Total	Off.	O.R.	Total
488	7,669	8,157	40,336	1,116,858	1,157,194	1 : 82·64	1 : 145·63	1 : 141·87
155	2,443	2,598	35,708	1,051,009	1,086,717	1 : 230·37	1 : 430·21	1 : 418·28

Diseases of the Skin and Areolar Tissue

Although it is a well-known fact that diseases of the skin and areolar tissue were a common cause of inefficiency among the troops during the war, the only complete record of admissions for British troops covers the period from August 1914 to the end of December 1915. These are shown in Table 20 as a proportion of the total sick or injured admitted and as a ratio per 1,000 of ration strength.

TABLE 20.—Admissions to Hospital of British Troops suffering from Diseases of the Skin or Areolar Tissue, with Ratios per 1,000 of Ration Strength, August 1914 to December 1915

Period	Cause of Admission	No.	Proportion of skin and areolar tissue diseases to total sick and injured admitted	Ratio per 1,000
(Aug.–Dec. 1914)	Diseases of the skin ...	1,934	1 : 38·60	10·18
	,, ,, areolar tissue	3,422	1 : 21·81	18·01
	Total ...	*5,356*	*1 : 13·93*	*28·19*
1915	Diseases of the skin ...	39,505	1 : 13·41	66·84
	,, ,, areolar tissue	35,046	1 : 15·11	59·29
	Total ...	*74,551*	*1 : 7·11*	*126·13*

FRANCE AND FLANDERS, 1914–1918

The returns from the First Army for 1918 shed some light on the amount of wastage due to skin troubles in the field. This is shown in Table 21.

TABLE 21.—Admissions to Field Ambulances of the First Army for Scabies and Other Skin Diseases, January to December, 1918

Period	Cause	Admissions	Proportion of skin diseases to approximate total sick and injured admitted to F.As. First Army	Ratio per 1,000
1918	Scabies Other skin diseases	9,345 6,739	1 : 30·32 1 : 42·04	27·45 19·80
	Total	16,084	1 : 17·61	47·25

Ambulance Transport

The development of the ambulance transport services required for the evacuation of sick and wounded by rail, road or canal, throughout the war has been described in previous volumes of the *Medical History of the War*. It remains only to emphasise the extent of the work undertaken by giving in Table 22 an analysis of the methods of evacuation, as far as possible, and the total numbers carried from front to base, and from base to base, in France, from August 1914 to December 1918.

TABLE 22.—Ambulance Transport of Sick and Wounded of the British Expeditionary Force, France, 1914–18

Year	Front to Base				Base to Base
	Ambulance Train *	Ambulance Barge	Motor Ambulance Convoy	Total	Ambulance Train *
1914 (Aug.–Dec.)	85,327	—	Not available	85,327**	7,544
1915	383,810	4,156	,,	387,966**	87,642 †
1916	744,616	18,042	,,	762,658**	253,907
1917	1,038,993	10,112	30,196	1,079,301	493,280 ‡
1918	1,190,761	21,451	22,645	1,234,857 §	768,299 ‖
1914–18	3,443,507	53,761	52,841 ¶	3,550,109 **	1,610,672

* Includes improvised and temporary ambulance trains.
† Includes 5,732 by barge from Versailles to Rouen and Havre.
‡ Includes 6,466 from Mediterranean Expeditionary Force and 959 repatriated British prisoners of war from Switzerland.
§ Includes 79,429 other nationalities.
‖ Includes 20,387 from other expeditionary forces and 2,572 repatriated British prisoners of war.
¶ 1917 and 1918 only.
** Excluding M.A.C. 1914–1916.

Table 23 shows the proportion of wounded to sick evacuated from front to base for 1916, 1917 and 1918.

TABLE 23.—Proportion of Wounded to Sick Evacuated from Front to Base

Method of evacuation	Year	Wounded	Sick	Proportion of Wounded to Sick
Ambulance trains	1916	391,651	352,965	1·11 : 1
,, ,,	1917	499,491	539,502	1 : 1·08
,, ,,	1918	550,718	561,261	1 : 1·02
Ambulance barge	1917	6,612	3,500	1·89 : 1
,, ,,	1918	8,953	12,035	1 : 1·34
Motor ambulance convoy	1918	9,939	12,522	1 : 1·26

There are no complete records to show the proportion of lying down cases to sitting cases evacuated to the base by ambulance transport except for the year 1916. This figure is given in Table 24 along with the results obtained from an examination of the records for a period of nine months from June 1917 to February 1918.

TABLE 24.—Proportion of Lying-down Cases to Sitting Cases Evacuated from Front to Base

Period	Lying-down Cases	Sitting Cases	Proportion of lying-down to sitting cases
1916	306,690	437,926	1 : 1·43
June 1917 to February 1918	368,711	356,657	1·03 : 1

Unfortunately the records do not show the proportion of sick and wounded among either lying-down or sitting cases.

Work of the Army Dental Service

With regard to the dental work carried out among the troops in France, two sample tables have been prepared from the information now available. Table 25 shows the work done month by month at the base for the year 1917.

TABLE 25.—Return of Dental Work at the Base, British Expeditionary Force, France, 1917

Month	Fillings	Repairs	New Dentures	Total cases treated during month
January	6,319	2,873	6,226	43,682
February	6,067	2,696	4,936	37,552
March	7,996	2,866	6,271	51,367
April	6,919	2,704	6,486	46,670
May	7,452	3,672	6,346	53,971
June	7,665	3,751	7,236	58,370
July	8,896	3,864	7,279	61,932
August	9,583	4,455	7,060	61,442
September	10,274	4,660	7,097	59,430
October	9,126	2,687	5,242	48,434
November	7,841	2,820	4,333	44,040
December	8,091	2,103	3,391	39,085
Total	96,229	39,151	71,903	605,975

The other sample table gives some indication of the extent of the work done in army areas for six months during 1918.

TABLE 26.—Dental Work in Army Areas for Six Months in 1918

Nature of Work	Number
Fillings	40,692
Extractions	79,434
Dentures sent down for repairs	6,421
Sundries	47,139
New dentures made	10,966
Dentures repaired	8,293
Cases evacuated to Army Dental Centres	3,004
,, ,, ,, Base	214

These tables give some idea of the development of the work of the Army Dental Service when it is recalled that there were no dental officers attached to the original expeditionary force on mobilisation and an organised service had not been anticipated. Although they are but a meagre representation of the total work done, they provide ample illustration of the dental treatment required to assist the army authorities in maintaining the health of the troops.

CHAPTER VI

CASUALTIES IN THE BRITISH EXPEDITIONARY FORCE IN FRANCE
AND FLANDERS, AUGUST TO DECEMBER, 1914

GREAT BRITAIN entered the Great War on the side of France against Germany on 4th August, 1914, and twelve days later the original British Expeditionary Force had concluded its disembarkation in France. A few days' concentration of troops was followed by a march north into Belgium on 21st August, and the battle of Mons two days later. Overwhelmed by the superior numbers of the enemy, the troops retreated, marching day and night with short halts and one day's rest, from 24th August until 5th September. During this period the battle of Le Cateau was fought and a series of rearguard actions which caused a considerable number of casualties; large numbers of the troops fell out from exhaustion, especially during the heat of the last few days of August, but the numbers reported missing formed the bulk of the casualties at this time. On 6th September the offensive was resumed in the advance towards the Aisne, in the course of which the battles of the Marne and the Aisne were fought, operations continuing until 1st October. Plans were then made to extend the British line farther north towards the sea; assistance was given to the Belgians in the defence of Antwerp, and there began on 10th October a series of operations in Flanders lasting until 22nd November. These included the battles of La Bassée, Messines, Armentières, and the first battles of Ypres, 1914. The remainder of the year was practically spent in trench warfare.

It will thus be seen that many severe tests for the medical services were crowded into the first few months of the war. Mobilisation at home was followed by frequent and rapid changes; embarkation of the troops in England and disembarkation in France; the concentration, advance and opening battle against highly trained, fully armed and well-organised European troops over cultivated agricultural land; the trying retreat, halt, attack and advance; the change of front and lines of communication; and finally the war of movement terminating in trench warfare which was to last not for months but for years. Handicapped by lack of experience, co-operation, information and motor transport, the medical services were poorly equipped to meet these sudden changes and trying conditions at the outset of the war, and consequently the arrangements made for the evacuation and subsequent care of the sick and wounded were rudimentary and unsatisfactory. With growing experience, fuller consideration was given to the medical situation and its pressing problems, not only by the general staff but by the whole medical profession, as there came to all a sudden, startling awakening from the confidence begotten of the limited experience

FRANCE AND FLANDERS, 1914

in the South African War, and the dreams and teaching of aseptic surgery. Tetanus and gas gangrene, grim ghosts of a forgotten age, re-appeared, claimed many victims, and reminded all that the neglect of a medical service and medical science might cause more individual damage than the shells and bullets of the enemy.

The outstanding features of this period of the war from the medical point of view were the reorganisation at general headquarters and the development of a better liaison between the staff and administrative medical officers; the ready adaptation of units organised during peace but untried in war to meet one contingency after another; the success of the measures adopted to prevent the spread of enteric fever from the civil population of Belgium to the troops; the low sick rate of 356·15 per 1,000 of strength of the force; and the institution of research and other methods to cope with the known and unfamiliar diseases which might assail the British Army.*

Strength

The average ration strength of the British Expeditionary Force in France and Flanders from August to December, 1914, is shown in Table 1.

TABLE 1.—Average Ration Strength

Period	Force	Officers	Other ranks	Total
4.8.14 to 31.12.14	British Expeditionary Force	8,097	212,475	220,572
	British troops only	7,600	182,400	190,000

Classification of Casualties

The total casualties sustained by the British Expeditionary Force during this period are given in Table 2, with the ratios per 1,000 of the ration strength.

TABLE 2.—Total Casualties

	Off.	O.R.	Total	Ratio per 1,000		
				Off.	O.R.	Total
Battle casualties	3,926	94,940	98,866	484·87	446·83	448·23
Non-battle casualties	1,922	76,635	78,557	237·37	360·68	356·15
Total	5,848	171,575	177,423	722·24	807·51	804·38

---

* The history of the Medical Services in France and Flanders during 1914 is fully dealt with in the *General History of the Medical Services*, vol. ii, chaps. i–xv.

Table 3 shows the total casualties among British troops only for the same period, with the ratios per 1,000 of average British ration strength.

TABLE 3.—Casualties among British Troops only

	Off.	O.R.	Total	Ratio per 1,000		
				Off.	O.R.	Total
Battle casualties	3,710	90,189	93,899	488·16	494·46	494·21
Non-battle casualties	1,748	72,867	74,615	230·00	399·49	392·71
Total	5,458	163,056	168,514	718·16	893·95	886·92

The proportion of battle casualties to non-battle casualties in the whole force was 2·0 to 1 officers; 1·2 to 1 other ranks; and 1·3 to 1 all ranks. For British troops only, the proportion of battle to non-battle casualties was 2·1 to 1 officers; 1·2 to 1 other ranks; and 1·3 to 1 all ranks.

An analysis of the total casualties occurring in the British Expeditionary Force from August to December, 1914, is given in Table 4. Figures for disease and injury have been shown separately in order to give some indication of the relative incidence.

TABLE 4.—Classification and Percentages of Total Casualties

	Off.	O.R.	Total	Percentage of total casualties		
				Off.	O.R.	Total
A. *Battle Casualties:*						
(a) Killed	1,038	11,971	13,009	17·75	6·98	7·33
(b) Died of wounds	228	3,429	3,657	3·90	2·00	2·06
(c) Missing	253	6,343	6,596	4·32	3·70	3·72
(d) Prisoners of war	530	19,385	19,915	9·06	11·30	11·22
(e) Wounded less (b)	1,877	53,812	55,689	32·10	31·36	31·39
B. *Non-battle Casualties:*						
(f) Died of disease	4	368	372	·07	·21	·21
(g) Died of injury	8	128	136	·14	·07	·08
(h) Sick less (f)	1,568	58,670	60,238	26·81	34·20	33·95
(i) Injured less (g)	342	17,469	17,811	5·85	10·18	10·04
Total A. and B.	5,848	171,575	177,423	—	—	—

Table 5 shows a similar analysis for British troops only. It is not possible, however, to differentiate between missing and prisoners of war for this period, and these figures have been treated as one total.

TABLE 5.—Classification and Percentages of Total British Casualties

	Off.	O.R.	Total	Percentage of total British casualties		
				Off.	O.R.	Total
A. *Battle Casualties*:						
(a) Killed	995	10,942	11,937	18·23	6·71	7·08
(b) Died of wounds	219	3,343	3,562	4·01	2·05	2·11
(c) Missing (d) Prisoners of war	} 748	24,913	25,661	13·70	15·28	15·23
(e) Wounded less (b)	1,748	50,991	52,739	32·03	31·27	31·30
B. *Non-Battle Casualties*:						
(f) Died of disease	4	320	324	·07	·20	·19
(g) Died of injury	8	121	129	·15	·07	·08
(h) Sick less (f)	1,429	55,806	57,235	26·18	34·23	33·96
(i) Injured less (g)	307	16,620	16,927	5·63	10·19	10·05
Total A. and B.	5,458	163,056	168,514	—	—	—

Table 6 (a) shows this detail as percentages of battle casualties for the whole force and for British troops only, while Table 6 (b) shows similarly the percentages of non-battle casualties.

TABLE 6 (a).—Percentages of Battle Casualties

	Whole Force			British troops only		
	Off.	O.R.	Total	Off.	O.R.	Total
(a) Killed	26·44	12·61	13·16	26·82	12·13	12·71
(b) Died of wounds	5·81	3·61	3·70	5·90	3·71	3·79
(c) Missing	6·44	6·68	6·67 }	20·16	27·62	27·33
(d) Prisoners of war	13·50	20·42	20·14 }			
(e) Wounded less (b)	47·81	56·68	56·33	47·12	56·54	56·17

TABLE 6 (b).—Percentages of Non-battle Casualties

	Whole Force			British troops only		
	Off.	O.R.	Total	Off.	O.R.	Total
(f) Died of disease	·21	·48	·48	·23	·44	·43
(g) Died of injury	·42	·17	·17	·46	·16	·17
(h) Sick less (f)	81·58	76·56	76·68	81·75	76·59	76·71
(i) Injured less (g)	17·79	22·79	22·67	17·56	22·81	22·69

The casualties sustained by the British Expeditionary Force, and by the British troops only, during the period August to December, 1914, may be further classified into permanent and temporary losses for military purposes in the field.

TABLE 7 (a).—Permanent Losses for Military Purposes in the Field—Whole Force

	Off.	O.R.	Total	Percentage of total casualties		
				Off.	O.R.	Total
A. *Battle Casualties*:						
Killed...	1,038	11,971	13,009	17·75	6·98	7·33
Died of wounds	228	3,429	3,657	3·90	2·00	2·06
Missing	253	6,343	6,596	4·32	3·70	3·72
Prisoners of war	530	19,385	19,915	9·06	11·30	11·22
Total	*2,049*	*41,128*	*43,177*	*35·04*	*23·97*	*24·34*
B. *Non-battle Casualties*:						
Died of disease	4	368	372	·07	·21	·21
Died of injury	8	128	136	·14	·07	·08
Total	*12*	*496*	*508*	*·21*	*·29*	*·29*
Total Permanent Losses	2,061	41,624	43,685	35·24	24·26	24·62

TABLE 7 (b).—Temporary Losses for Military Purposes in the Field—Whole Force

	Off.	O.R.	Total	Percentage of total casualties		
				Off.	O.R.	Total
A. *Battle Casualties*:						
Wounded less died of wounds	1,877	53,812	55,689	32·10	31·36	31·39
B. *Non-battle Casualties*:						
Sick less died of disease	1,568	58,670	60,238	26·81	34·20	33·95
Injured less died of injury	342	17,469	17,811	5·85	10·18	10·04
Total	*1,910*	*76,139*	*78,049*	*32·66*	*44·38*	*43·99*
Total temporary losses	3,787	129,951	133,738	64·76	75·74	75·38

Tables 8 (a) and 8 (b) show the same sub-division in respect of British troops only.

TABLE 8 (a).—Permanent Losses for Military Purposes in the Field—British troops only

	Off.	O.R.	Total	Percentage of total British casualties		
				Off.	O.R.	Total
A. *Battle Casualties*:						
Killed	995	10,942	11,937	18·23	6·71	7·08
Died of wounds	219	3,343	3,562	4·01	2·05	2·11
Missing and prisoners of war	748	24,913	25,661	13·70	15·28	15·23
Total	*1,962*	*39,198*	*41,160*	*35·95*	*24·04*	*24·43*
B. *Non-battle Casualties*:						
Died of disease	4	320	324	·07	·20	·19
Died of injury	8	121	129	·15	·07	·08
Total	*12*	*441*	*453*	*·22*	*·27*	*·27*
Total permanent British losses	1,974	39,639	41,613	36·17	24·31	24·69

FRANCE AND FLANDERS, 1914

TABLE 8 (b).—Temporary Losses for Military Purposes in the Field—British troops only

	Off.	O.R.	Total	Percentage of total British casualties		
				Off.	O.R.	Total
A. *Battle Casualties*: Wounded less died of wounds	1,748	50,991	52,739	32·03	31·27	31·30
B. *Non-battle Casualties*:						
Sick less died of disease	1,429	55,806	57,235	26·18	34·23	33·96
Injured less died of injury	307	16,620	16,927	5·63	10·19	10·05
Total	*1,736*	*72,426*	*74,162*	*31·81*	*44·42*	*44·01*
Total temporary British losses	3,484	123,417	126,901	63·83	75·69	75·31

The relative proportions of the various classes of casualties to each other for the whole force and for British troops only are shown in Tables 9 and 10.

TABLE 9.—Proportions—Whole Force

	Officers	Other ranks	Total
1. Total battle casualties to total non-battle casualties	2·0 : 1	1·2 : 1	1·3 : 1
2. Total killed to total wounded including died of wounds	1 : 2·0	1 : 4·8	1 : 4·6
3. Permanent losses among battle casualties to total wounded less died of wounds	1·1 : 1	1 : 1·3	1 : 1·3
4. Permanent losses among non-battle casualties to total sick and injured less died of disease or injury	1 : 159·2	1 : 153·5	1 : 153·6
5. Total permanent losses to total temporary losses	1 : 1·8	1 : 3·1	1 : 3·1

TABLE 10.—Proportions—British Troops only

	Officers	Other ranks	Total
1. Total battle casualties to total non-battle casualties	2·1 : 1	1·2 : 1	1·3 : 1
2. Total killed to total wounded, including died of wounds	1 : 2·0	1 : 5·0	1 : 4·7
3. Permanent losses among battle casualties to total wounded less died of wounds	1·1 : 1	1 : 1·3	1 : 1·3
4. Permanent losses among non-battle casualties to total sick and injured less died of disease or injury	1 : 144·7	1 : 164·2	1 : 163·7
5. Total permanent losses to total temporary losses	1 : 1·8	1 : 3·2	1 : 3·0

Admissions to Hospital

Of the total casualties suffered by the British Expeditionary Force in France and Flanders during the period August to

December, 1914, the numbers admitted to hospital and treated by the medical services are shown in Table 11.

TABLE 11.—Numbers admitted to Hospital—Whole Force

	Off.	O.R.	Total	Percentage of total casualties		
				Off.	O.R.	Total
Wounded	2,105	57,241	59,346	36·00	33·36	33·45
Sick	1,572	59,038	60,610	26·88	34·41	34·16
Injured	350	17,597	17,947	5·98	10·26	10·12
Total	4,027	133,876	137,903	68·86	78·03	77·73

Table 12 shows the admissions to hospital for British troops only.

TABLE 12.—Numbers admitted to Hospital—British Troops only

	Off.	O.R.	Total	Percentage of total British casualties		
				Off.	O.R.	Total
Wounded	1,967	54,334	56,301	36·04	33·32	33·41
Sick	1,433	56,126	57,559	26·26	34·42	34·16
Injured	315	16,741	17,056	5·77	10·27	10·12
Total	3,715	127,201	130,916	68·07	78·01	77·69

The proportion of wounded to sick and injured treated by the medical services was 1·1 to 1 officers; 1 to 1·3 other ranks; and 1 to 1·3 all ranks, both for the whole force and for British troops only.

The casualties which were not treated by the medical services are shown in Tables 13 and 14 for the whole force and British troops respectively.

TABLE 13.—Casualties in the British Expeditionary Force not treated by the Medical Services

	Off.	O.R.	Total	Percentage of total casualties		
				Off.	O.R.	Total
Killed	1,038	11,971	13,009	17·75	6·98	7·33
Missing	253	6,343	6,596	4·32	3·70	3·72
Prisoners of war	530	19,385	19,915	9·06	11·30	11·22
Total	1,821	37,699	39,520	31·14	21·97	22·27

TABLE 14.—Casualties among British Troops not treated by the Medical Services

	Off.	O.R.	Total	Percentage of total British casualties		
				Off.	O.R.	Total
Killed	995	10,942	11,937	18·23	6·71	7·08
Missing and prisoners of war	748	24,913	25,661	13·70	15·28	15·23
Total	1,743	35,855	37,598	31·93	21·99	22·31

An analysis of the admissions to hospital of troops in the British Expeditionary Force in France during this period is given in Table 15 (*a*), showing the ultimate disposal of the cases and the numbers discharged from the service as invalids. Tables 15 (*b*) and 15 (*c*) give the corresponding ratios per 1,000 of ration strength and percentages of total admissions re-

TABLE 15 (*a*).—Admissions to Hospital and Disposal of Cases—Whole Force

	Wounded			Sick			Injured			Grand total		
	Off.	O.R.	Total	Off.	O.R.	Total	Off.	O.R.	Total	Off.	O.R.	Total
Admissions	2,105	57,241	59,346	1,572	59,038	60,610	350	17,597	17,947	4,027	133,876	137,903
Deaths	228	3,429	3,657	4	368	372	8	128	136	240	3,925	4,165
Returned to duty	1,869	50,614	52,483	1,559	57,299	58,858	342	17,187	17,529	3,770	125,100	128,870
Discharged as invalids	8	3,198	3,206	9	1,371	1,380	—	282	282	17	4,851	4,868

TABLE 15 (*b*).—Ratios per 1,000 of Ration Strength—Whole Force

	Wounded			Sick			Injured			Grand total		
	Off.	O.R.	Total	Off.	O.R.	Total	Off.	O.R.	Total	Off.	O.R.	Total
Admissions	259·97	269·40	269·06	194·15	277·86	274·79	43·23	82·82	81·37	497·34	630·08	625·21
Deaths	28·16	16·14	16·58	·49	1·73	1·69	·99	·60	·62	29·64	18·47	18·88
Returned to duty	230·83	238·21	237·94	192·54	269·67	266·84	42·24	80·89	79·47	465·60	588·78	584·25
Discharged as invalids	·99	15·05	14·53	1·11	6·45	6·26	—	1·33	1·28	2·10	22·83	22·07

TABLE 15 (*c*).—Percentages of Total Admissions—Whole Force

	Wounded			Sick			Injured			Grand total		
	Off.	O.R.	Total	Off.	O.R.	Total	Off.	O.R.	Total	Off.	O.R.	Total
Deaths	10·83	5·99	6·16	·26	·62	·61	2·29	·73	·76	5·96	2·93	3·02
Returned to duty	88·79	88·42	88·44	99·17	97·06	97·11	97·71	97·67	97·67	93·62	93·45	93·45
Discharged as invalids	·38	5·59	5·40	·57	2·32	2·28	—	1·60	1·57	·42	3·62	3·53

spectively. Similar information is given for British troops only in Tables 16 (a), 16 (b) and 16 (c).

TABLE 16 (a).—Admissions to Hospital and Disposal of Cases—British troops only

	Wounded			Sick			Injured			Grand total		
	Off.	O.R.	Total	Off.	O.R.	Total	Off.	O.R.	Total	Off.	O.R.	Total
Admissions	1,967	54,334	56,301	1,433	56,126	57,559	315	16,741	17,056	3,715	127,201	130,916
Deaths	219	3,343	3,562	4	320	324	8	121	129	231	3,784	4,015
Returned to duty	1,744	47,977	49,721	1,427	54,616	56,043	307	16,383	16,690	3,478	118,976	122,454
Discharged as invalids	4	3,014	3,018	2	1,190	1,192	—	237	237	6	4,441	4,447

TABLE 16 (b).—Ratio per 1,000 of British Ration Strength

	Wounded			Sick			Injured			Grand total		
	Off.	O.R.	Total	Off.	O.R.	Total	Off.	O.R.	Total	Off.	O.R.	Total
Admissions	258·82	297·88	296·32	188·55	307·71	302·94	41·45	91·78	89·77	488·82	697·37	689·03
Deaths	28·82	18·33	18·75	·53	1·75	1·71	1·05	·66	·68	30·39	20·75	21·13
Returned to duty	229·47	263·03	261·69	187·76	299·43	294·96	40·39	89·82	87·84	457·63	652·28	644·49
Discharged as invalids	·53	16·52	15·88	·26	6·52	6·27	—	1·30	1·25	·79	24·35	23·41

TABLE 16 (c).—Percentages of Total British Admissions

	Wounded			Sick			Injured			Grand total		
	Off.	O.R.	Total	Off.	O.R.	Total	Off.	O.R.	Total	Off.	O.R.	Total
Deaths	11·14	6·15	6·33	·28	·57	·56	2·54	·72	·76	6·22	2·98	3·07
Returned to duty	88·66	88·30	88·31	99·58	97·31	97·37	97·46	97·86	97·85	93·62	93·53	93·54
Discharged as invalids	·20	5·55	5·36	·14	2·12	2·07	—	1·42	1·39	·16	3·49	3·40

The records of admissions in the case of 1,169 wounded, 1,909 sick, and 542 injured are incomplete as regards the number constantly in hospital, but for the remainder of admissions the ratio per 1,000 of strength constantly in hospital, either in France or in the United Kingdom, for the whole force and for British troops only, is shown in Table 17.

TABLE 17.—Ratio per 1,000 of Strength constantly in Hospital

	British Expeditionary Force			British troops only		
	Off.	O.R.	Total	Off.	O.R.	Total
Wounded	43·29	72·28	71·22	41·63	79·16	77·66
Sick	15·86	36·91	36·14	14·32	40·52	39·47
Injured	4·86	13·48	13·17	4·78	14·71	14·31
Total	64·01	122·68	120·52	60·74	134·38	131·44

From 25th September to 31st December, 1914, the average number of British sick and wounded constantly in hospital in France was 7,150 or 37·63 per 1,000 of the British ration strength.

Hospital Accommodation

Table 18 shows the maximum number of equipped hospital beds in France for British troops, and the maximum number occupied on any one date during the period August to December, 1914, with the percentage of average British ration strength.

TABLE 18.—Accommodation provided in Hospitals on the Lines of Communication

Period	Average ration strength	Maximum No. equipped beds	Maximum No. occupied beds	Average No. occupied beds	Percentage of ration strength		
					Equipped beds	Max. No. occupied	Average No. occupied
August–December, 1914	190,000	9,000	9,000	7,150	4·7	4·7	3·7

In addition there was one convalescent depot of 1,000 beds, but there are no records to show the percentage occupied.

Non-battle Casualties

The statistics of admissions to hospital for disease or injury among British and Dominion troops of the British Expeditionary Force in France from August to December, 1914, are as complete and as accurate as it was possible for the Medical Research Council to make them by codifying and tabulating the medical records. Considerable detail is given, including the ultimate disposal of the cases. The chief causes of admission for non-battle casualties during this period are shown in Table 19, with the ratios per 1,000 of strength.

TABLE 19.—Principal Causes of Inefficiency

	Admissions	Ratio per 1,000
Local and general injuries	10,612	55·85
Diseases of the digestive system	10,594	55·76
Rheumatic fever	7,950	41·84
Frost bite	6,447	33·93
Diseases of the organs of locomotion	5,328	28·04
Diseases of the respiratory system	4,551	23·95
Diseases of the areolar tissue	3,422	18·01
Venereal diseases	3,291	17·32
Diseases of the teeth and gums	2,495	13·13

TABLE 20.—Analysis of Admissions to Hospital, British * Troops of the British Expeditionary Force, France, August to December, 1914, showing Disposal of Cases and Ratios per 1,000 of Strength

	Admissions*	Deaths	Returned to duty*	Discharged as Invalids	Ratio per 1,000 Admissions*	Ratio per 1,000 Deaths	Ratio per 1,000 Returned to duty*	Ratio per 1,000 Discharged as Invalids
Specific diseases due to infection								
Cerebro-spinal fever	2	1	—	—	·01	·01	—	—
Chicken-pox	4	—	1	—	·02	—	·02	—
Diphtheria	37	—	4	—	·19	—	·16	—
Dysentery	861	6	31	11	4·53	·03	4·45	·06
Enteric fever { Typhoid	438	4	846	4	2·31	·02	1·99	·02
Paratyphoid A	11	55	379	—	·06	·29	·05	—
Paratyphoid B	2	1	10	—	·01	·01	·01	—
Group	10	—	2	—	·05	—	·05	—
Erysipelas	5	1	9	—	·03	—	·03	—
Glanders	21	—	5	—	·11	·01	·11	—
Influenza	1	—	20	—	·01	—	·01	—
Malaria	1,478	2	1	2	7·78	·01	7·76	·01
Measles	1,147	4	1,474	1	6·04	·02	6·01	·01
Mediterranean fever	103	1	1,142	—	·54	·01	·54	—
Mumps	3	—	1,102	—	·02	—	·02	—
Pneumonia	22	—	3	3	·12	—	·12	·02
Pyrexia of uncertain origin	378	53	22	—	1·99	·28	1·69	—
Relapsing fever	192	—	322	—	1·01	—	1·01	—
Rheumatic fever	1	—	192	—	·01	—	·01	—
Rubella	7,950	—	1	123	41·84	—	41·19	·65
Scarlet fever	1	—	7,827	—	·01	—	—	—
Septic diseases, major	79	—	1	3	·42	—	·42	·02
Tetanus †	38	5	79	—	·20	·03	·16	—
Tuberculosis { Pulmonary	11	9	30	140	·06	·05	·01	·74
Other	325	10	2	4	1·71	·05	·92	·02
	26	2	175		·14	·01	·11	
			20					

Disease								
Venereal diseases — Gonorrhoea	2,272	—	2,272	—	11·96	—	11·96	—
Syphilis	599	1	584	14	3·15	·01	3·07	·07
Other	420	—	420	—	2·21	—	2·21	—
Whooping-cough	3	—	3	—	·02	—	·02	—
Diseases classified under systems								
Diseases of the nervous system	1,810	15	1,681	114	9·53	·08	8·85	·60
Mental diseases	96	2	52	42	·51	·01	·27	·22
Diseases of the—								
Eye	920	—	890	30	4·84	—	4·68	·16
Ear	1,083	—	1,001	82	5·70	—	5·27	·43
Nose	81	—	80	1	·43	—	·42	·01
Circulatory system — Valvular disease of the heart	444	6	330	108	2·34	·03	1·74	·57
Disordered action of the heart	508	—	485	23	2·67	—	2·55	·12
Other	1,016	7	942	67	5·35	·04	4·96	·35
Respiratory system	4,551	13	4,454	84	23·95	·07	23·44	·44
Blood	30	—	30	—	·16	—	·16	—
Spleen	4	—	4	—	·02	—	·02	—
Lymphatic system	205	—	202	3	1·08	—	1·06	·02
Endocrine glands	18	1	14	3	·09	·01	·07	·02
Breast	2	—	2	—	·01	—	·01	—
Teeth and gums	2,495	—	2,464	31	13·13	—	12·97	·16
Digestive system — Tonsillitis	1,582	—	1,581	1	8·33	—	8·32	·01
Indigestion	643	—	639	4	3·38	—	3·36	·02
Inflammation and ulceration of the stomach	756	1	730	25	3·98	·01	3·84	·13
Other diseases of the stomach	72	—	68	4	·38	—	·36	·02
Appendicitis	358	11	340	7	1·88	·06	1·79	·04
Inflammation of the intestines	723	3	717	3	3·81	·02	3·77	·02
Other diseases of the intestines	1,022	9	1,007	6	5·38	·05	5·30	·03
Diarrhoea	2,307	1	2,304	—	12·14	·01	12·13	·01
Jaundice	94	—	94	—	·49	—	·49	—
Other diseases of the digestive system	3,037	18	2,933	86	15·98	·09	15·44	·45
Generative system	981	1	968	12	5·16	·01	5·09	·06
Skin — Eczema	405	—	405	—	2·13	—	2·13	—
Impetigo contagiosa	210	—	210	—	1·11	—	1·11	—
Scabies	860	—	860	—	4·53	—	4·53	—
Other	459	—	456	3	2·42	—	2·40	·02

TABLE 20.—continued

	Admissions*	Deaths	Returned to duty*	Discharged as invalids	Ratio per 1,000 Admissions*	Deaths	Returned to duty*	Discharged as invalids
Diseases of the—								
Areolar tissue	3,422	3	3,413	6	18·01	·02	17·96	·03
Organs of locomotion } Myalgia	2,369	—	2,359	10	12·47	—	12·42	·05
Other	2,959	3	2,876	80	15·57	·02	15·14	·42
Urinary system } Nephritis	104	4	85	15	·55	·02	·45	·08
Other	274	3	263	8	1·44	·02	1·38	·04
Miscellaneous diseases								
Debility	1,080	—	1,076	4	5·68	—	5·66	·02
Diseases due to disorders of nutrition or of metabolism { Scurvy	1	—	1	—	·01	—	·01	—
Beri-beri	32	—	32	—	·17	—	·17	—
Other	60	—	49	9	·32	—	·26	·05
Tumours and cysts	103	2	97	5	·54	·01	·51	·03
Poisons	65	1	62	1	·34	·01	·33	·01
Parasites	222	2	220	2	1·17	·01	1·16	·01
Diseases unclassified	3,744	62	3,676	6	19·71	·33	19·35	·03
Injuries								
Frost bite	6,447	12	6,350	85	33·93	·06	33·42	·45
Trench foot	8	—	8	—	·04	—	·04	—
Local and general injuries { Effects of heat or cold	1,003	6	992	5	5·28	·03	5·22	·03
Other	9,609	111	9,351	147	50·57	·58	49·22	·77
Grand Total of Diseases and Injuries	74,714*	453	72,832*	1,429	393·23*	2·38	383·33*	7·52

* Includes 99 Canadians who were admitted and discharged to duty (*see* p. 133).
† Direct admissions. See Table 21 for complications arising from wounds in action.

Table 20 gives an analysis of the direct causes of admission to hospital with the ultimate disposal of the cases. These figures include 99 Canadian cases admitted and 99 returned to duty, but as this figure is so small and no strength for Canadian troops is available for this period, the ratios per 1,000 have been calculated on the strength of the British troops. No Indian cases are included in the table.

In a number of cases where the primary cause of admission to hospital was gunshot wounds, a secondary disease or disability supervened. A further analysis of the medical records for this period was undertaken by the Medical Research Council with a view to finding the diseases or disabilities most frequently associated with gunshot wounds, and the results are given in Table 21.

TABLE 21.—Diseases or Disabilities most frequently associated with Gunshot Wounds, British Troops in France, August–December, 1914

Disease or Disability	No. of Cases
Dysentery	29
Enteric, including paratyphoid	41
Gangrene	184
Malaria	70
Septicæmia	49
Syphilis	20
Tetanus	273 (183 fatal)
Tuberculosis, pulmonary	26
Neurasthenia	115
Epilepsy or fits	66
Meningitis	42
Hemiplegia	64
Paraplegia	58
Paralysis, local	452
Otitis media	63
Deafness	116
Valvular disease of the heart	65
Disordered action of the heart	34
Aneurysm	73
Varicose veins	46
Pneumonia, including broncho-pneumonia	114
Bronchitis	108
Empyema	108
Hæmothorax	76
Tonsillitis or sore throat	51
Hernia	51
Rheumatism	420
Myalgia	114
Ankylosis or stiff joint	481
Frost bite or trench foot	170

CHAPTER VII

CASUALTIES IN THE BRITISH EXPEDITIONARY FORCE IN FRANCE AND FLANDERS, 1915

THE opening of the year 1915 found the British army in France and Flanders settling down to the period of trench warfare which had begun in November 1914, and was to last until the more open warfare at the commencement of the battles of the Somme in July 1916. This period was, however, punctuated by battles of increasing size and importance, although in view of the more extensive and intensive battles of the later years of the war they may now be looked upon as experimental efforts. The battle of Neuve Chapelle and the affair at St. Eloi from 10th to 15th March 1915 opened the summer operations; then followed a series of actions extending from 22nd April to 25th May, known as the battles of Ypres 1915; while the battles of Aubers Ridge on 9th May and Festubert from 15th to 25th May were being fought on another section of the British front. Thereafter, except for minor actions, trench warfare ensued until the battle of Loos from 25th September to 8th October, followed by an enemy counter-attack from 13th to 19th October, which brought to a conclusion the severe fighting of 1915.

The outstanding features of military medical interest during the year were (a) the preparations and developments for the collection, evacuation and treatment of casualties in premeditated or deliberate attacks with massed artillery support when opposing trench lines and defences were in close proximity to each other; (b) the use of gas by the enemy as a weapon of warfare; (c) the experience of the British troops in using gas for the first time as an offensive weapon in the battle of Loos; (d) the appointment of a consulting surgeon to army headquarters and the development of surgical treatment and operations at casualty clearing stations. The first German gas attack on 22nd April 1915 took the British completely by surprise, and spasmodically throughout the year the troops were subjected to this new form of warfare. Casualties from gas are included in the total battle casualties, but the hospital returns for British troops show 12,792 admissions for gas poisoning during 1915, of whom 307 were fatal. The prevention and treatment of this new type of casualty were problems which demanded, and received, immediate attention, not only in 1915 but throughout the subsequent development of gas warfare.*

The difficulties experienced in 1914 had not been without effect, and a review of the work of the medical services during 1915 shows the efforts made to put into practice the lessons learned from each successive battle. The period was one of co-ordination and of further experiment. It was, however, not without its difficulties, of which the most important were associated with the gradual increase in the number of battle

---

* See *Diseases of the War*, vol. ii, chaps. vii–xvii, for fuller details of the medical aspects of gas warfare.

casualties and in the strength of the force in France. The numbers of wounded admitted to medical units for the main battles in 1915 rose from 9,256 in the battle of Neuve Chapelle and the affair at St. Eloi and 7,433 at Aubers Ridge to 12,419 at the battle of Festubert, 15th to 25th May; 32,334 at Ypres, 22nd April to 31st May; and 33,500 at the battle of Loos from 25th September to 1st October. The expansion of the strength of the force from approximately 300,000 in January 1915 to three times that number by the end of the year caused the medical services considerable anxiety on the matters of adequate hospital accommodation and the supply of medical personnel.

The first winter of the war was cold, wet and foggy, and life in the early type of exposed trench in such inclement weather was largely responsible for the higher sick rate of 875·28 per 1,000 of ration strength. Frost bite and trench foot, influenza, rheumatic fever and diseases of the respiratory system all show a high admission rate. It must, however, be remembered that a large proportion of the troops were drawn from reservists, and that it was not until later in the year that men of the Territorial Force and New Armies formed a considerable proportion of the force in France. Furthermore, thanks to the work of the Medical Research Council in codifying the medical records, the figures for 1915 in respect of British troops only are the most complete record of hospital admissions in any force during the Great War, and the picture they represent of the health of a force in the field is worthy of study. Trench fever and trench nephritis began to make their appearance in the force, and there was an increased number of nervous cases; there was little epidemic disease, and it is interesting to note from the tables on page 143 that the principal causes of inefficiency among British troops in 1915 were, in varying order and in increased ratios, the same as those reported for the British army at home and abroad in 1927.*

Strength

The average ration strength of the British Expeditionary Force in France and Flanders during 1915 is shown in Table 1.

TABLE 1.—Average Ration Strength

Period	Force	Officers	Other Ranks	Total
1915	British Expeditionary Force	23,079	639,263	662,342
	British troops only ...	21,405	569,643	591,048

Classification of Casualties

The total casualties sustained by the British Expeditionary Force in France during 1915 are given in Table 2, with the ratios per 1,000 of ration strength.

---

* The history of the Medical Services with the British Expeditionary Force in France and Flanders during 1915 is dealt with in the *General History of the Medical Services*, vol. ii, chap. xvi. *et seq.*

TABLE 2.—Total Casualties

	Off.	O.R.	Total	Ratio per 1,000		
				Off.	O.R.	Total
Battle casualties	12,013	301,014	313,027	520·52	470·88	472·61
Non-battle casualties	15,392	564,346	579,738	666·93	882·81	875·28
Total	27,405	865,360	892,765	1,187·44	1,353·68	1,347·89

Table 3 shows the total casualties among British troops only for the same period, with the ratios per 1,000 of average British ration strength.

TABLE 3.—Casualties among British Troops only

	Off.	O.R.	Total	Ratio per 1,000		
				Off.	O.R.	Total
Battle casualties	11,106	275,362	286,468	518·85	483·39	484·68
Non-battle casualties	14,154	515,554	529,708	661·25	905·05	896·22
Total	25,260	790,916	816,176	1,180·10	1,388·44	1,380·90

The proportion of battle casualties to non-battle casualties in the whole force was 1 to 1·3 officers; 1 to 1·9 other ranks; and 1 to 1·9 all ranks. For British troops only the proportion of battle to non-battle casualties was 1 to 1·3 officers; 1 to 1·9 other ranks; 1 to 1·8 all ranks.

An analysis of the total casualties occurring in the British Expeditionary Force in France during 1915 is given in Table 4.

TABLE 4.—Classification and Percentages of Total Casualties

	Off.	O.R.	Total	Percentage of total casualties		
				Off.	O.R.	Total
A. *Battle Casualties:*						
(a) Killed	3,032	45,572	48,604	11·06	5·27	5·44
(b) Died of wounds	745	14,159	14,904	2·72	1·64	1·67
(c) Missing	412	15,523	15,935	1·51	1·79	1·78
(d) Prisoners of war	390	8,231	8,621	1·42	·95	·97
(e) Wounded less (b)	7,434	217,529	224,963	27·13	25·14	25·20
B. *Non-battle Casualties:*						
(f) Died of disease or injury	110	2,797	2,907	·40	·32	·33
(g) Sick or injured less (f)	15,282	561,549	576,831	55·76	64·89	64·61
Total A. and B.	27,405	865,360	892,765	—	—	—

Table 5 shows a similar analysis for British troops only, but in this case the figures for disease and injury are given separately. It has not been possible, however, to differentiate between missing and prisoners of war for this period, and these figures have been treated as one total.

TABLE 5.—Classification and Percentages of Total British Casualties

	Off.	O.R.	Total	Percentage of total British casualties		
				Off.	O.R.	Total
A. Battle Casualties:						
(a) Killed	2,828	41,791	44,619	11·20	5·28	5·47
(b) Died of wounds	703	13,445	14,148	2·78	1·70	1·73
(c) Missing (d) Prisoners of war	727	20,048	20,775	2·88	2·53	2·55
(e) Wounded less (b)	6,848	200,078	206,926	27·11	25·30	25·35
B. Non-battle Casualties:						
(f) Died of disease	60	1,637	1,697	·24	·21	·21
(g) Died of injury	41	543	584	·16	·07	·07
(h) Sick less (f)	12,421	437,792	450,213	49·17	55·35	55·16
(i) Injured less (g)	1,632	75,582	77,214	6·46	9·56	9·46
Total A. and B.	25,260	790,916	816,176	—	—	—

Table 6 (a) shows this detail as percentages of battle casualties for the whole force and for British troops only, while Table 6 (b) shows similarly the percentages of non-battle casualties.

TABLE 6 (a).—Percentages of Battle Casualties

	Whole Force			British troops only		
	Off.	O.R.	Total	Off.	O.R.	Total
(a) Killed	25·24	15·14	15·53	25·46	15·18	15·58
(b) Died of wounds	6·20	4·70	4·76	6·33	4·88	4·94
(c) Missing	3·43	5·16	5·09	6·55	7·28	7·25
(d) Prisoners of war	3·25	2·73	2·75			
(e) Wounded less (b)	61·88	72·27	71·87	61·66	72·66	72·23

TABLE 6 (b).—Percentages of Non-battle Casualties

	Whole Force			British troops only		
	Off.	O.R.	Total	Off.	O.R.	Total
(f) Died of disease	·71	·50	·50	·42	·32	·32
(g) Died of injury				·29	·10	·11
(h) Sick less (f)	99·29	99·50	99·50	87·76	84·92	84·99
(i) Injured less (g)				11·53	14·66	14·58

The casualties sustained by the British Expeditionary Force and by British troops only, in France and Flanders during

1915, may be further classified into permanent and temporary losses for military purposes in the field.

TABLE 7 (a).—Permanent Losses for Military Purposes in the Field—Whole Force

	Off.	O.R.	Total	Percentage of total casualties		
				Off.	O.R.	Total
A. Battle Casualties:						
Killed	3,032	45,572	48,604	11·06	5·27	5·44
Died of wounds	745	14,159	14,904	2·72	1·64	1·67
Missing	412	15,523	15,935	1·51	1·79	1·78
Prisoners of war	390	8,231	8,621	1·42	·95	·97
Total	4,579	83,485	88,064	16·71	9·65	9·86
B. Non-battle Casualties:						
Died of disease or injury	110	2,797	2,907	·40	·32	·33
Total permanent losses	4,689	86,282	90,971	17·11	9·97	10·19

TABLE 7 (b).—Temporary Losses for Military Purposes in the Field—Whole Force

	Off.	O.R.	Total	Percentage of total casualties		
				Off.	O.R.	Total
A. Battle Casualties:						
Wounded less died of wounds	7,434	217,529	224,963	27·13	25·14	25·20
B. Non-battle Casualties:						
Sick or injured less died of disease or injury	15,282	561,549	576,831	55·76	64·89	64·61
Total temporary losses	22,716	779,078	801,794	82·89	90·03	89·81

Table 8 (a) and 8 (b) show the same subdivision for British troops only.

TABLE 8 (a).—Permanent Losses for Military Purposes in the Field—British Troops only

	Off.	O.R.	Total	Percentage of total British casualties		
				Off.	O.R.	Total
A. Battle Casualties:						
Killed	2,828	41,791	44,619	11·20	5·28	5·47
Died of wounds	703	13,445	14,148	2·78	1·70	1·73
Missing } Prisoners of war }	727	20,048	20,775	2·88	2·53	2·55
Total	4,258	75,284	79,542	16·86	9·52	9·75
B. Non-battle Casualties:						
Died of disease	60	1,637	1,697	·24	·21	·21
Died of injury	41	543	584	·16	·07	·07
Total	101	2,180	2,281	·40	·28	·28
Total permanent British losses	4,359	77,464	81,823	17·26	9·79	10·03

TABLE 8 (b).—Temporary Losses for Military Purposes in the Field—British Troops only

	Off.	O.R.	Total	Percentage of total British casualties		
				Off.	O.R.	Total
A. *Battle Casualties:* Wounded less died of wounds	6,848	200,078	206,926	27·11	25·30	25·35
B. *Non-battle Casualties:* Sick less died of disease	12,421	437,792	450,213	49·17	55·35	55·16
Injured less died of injury	1,632	75,582	77,214	6·46	9·56	9·46
Total	*14,053*	*513,374*	*527,427*	*55·63*	*64·91*	*64·62*
Total temporary British losses	20,901	713,452	734,353	82·74	90·21	89·97

The relative proportions of the various classes of casualties to each other in respect of the whole force and of British troops only during 1915 are shown in Tables 9 and 10.

TABLE 9.—Proportions—Whole Force

	Officers	Other ranks	Total
1. Total battle casualties to total non-battle casualties	1 : 1·3	1 : 1·9	1 : 1·9
2. Total killed to total wounded including died of wounds	1 : 2·7	1 : 5·1	1 : 4·9
3. Permanent losses among battle casualties to total wounded less died of wounds	1 : 1·6	1 : 2·6	1 : 2·6
4. Permanent losses among non-battle casualties to total sick and injured less died of disease or injury	1 : 138·9	1 : 200·8	1 : 198·4
5. Total permanent losses to total temporary losses	1 : 4·8	1 : 9·0	1 : 8·8

TABLE 10.—Proportions—British Troops only

	Officers	Other ranks	Total
1. Total battle casualties to total non-battle casualties	1 : 1·3	1 : 1·9	1 : 1·8
2. Total killed to total wounded including died of wounds	1 : 2·7	1 : 5·1	1 : 5·0
3. Permanent losses among battle casualties to total wounded less died of wounds	1 : 1·6	1 : 2·7	1 : 2·6
4. Permanent losses among non-battle casualties to total sick and injured less died of disease or injury	1 : 139·1	1 : 235·5	1 : 231·2
5. Total permanent losses to total temporary losses	1 : 4·8	1 : 9·2	1 : 9·0

Admissions to Hospital

Of the total casualties suffered by the British Expeditionary Force in France and Flanders during 1915, the numbers admitted to hospital and treated by the medical services are shown in Table 11.

TABLE 11.—Numbers admitted to Hospital—Whole Force

	Off.	O.R.	Total	Percentage of total casualties		
				Off.	O.R.	Total
Wounded	8,179	231,688	239,867	29·84	26·77	26·87
Sick or injured	15,392	564,346	579,738	56·16	65·22	64·94
Total	23,571	796,034	819,605	86·01	91·99	91·81

Table 12 shows the admissions to hospital for British troops only.

TABLE 12.—Numbers admitted to Hospital—British troops only

	Off.	O.R.	Total	Percentage of total British casualties		
				Off.	O.R.	Total
Wounded	7,551	213,523	221,074	29·89	27·00	27·09
Sick	12,481	439,429	451,910	49·41	55·56	55·37
Injured	1,673	76,125	77,798	6·62	9·62	9·53
Total	21,705	729,077	750,782	85·93	92·18	91·99

The proportion of wounded to sick and injured treated by the medical services was 1 to 1·9 officers; 1 to 2·4 other ranks; and 1 to 2·4 all ranks, both for the whole force and for British troops only.

The casualties which were not treated by the medical services are shown in Tables 13 and 14 for the whole force and for British troops only, respectively.

TABLE 13.—Casualties in the British Expeditionary Force not treated by the Medical Services

	Off.	O.R.	Total	Percentage of total casualties		
				Off.	O.R.	Total
Killed	3,032	45,572	48,604	11·06	5·27	5·44
Missing	412	15,523	15,935	1·51	1·79	1·78
Prisoners of war	390	8,231	8,621	1·42	·95	·97
Total	3,834	69,326	73,160	13·99	8·01	8·19

FRANCE AND FLANDERS, 1915

TABLE 14.—Casualties among British Troops only not treated by the Medical Services

	Off.	O.R.	Total	Percentage of total British casualties		
				Off.	O.R.	Total
Killed	2,828	41,791	44,619	11·20	5·28	5·47
Missing and prisoners of war	727	20,048	20,775	2·88	2·53	2·55
Total	3,555	61,839	65,394	14·07	7·82	8·01

Owing to the lack of information regarding the ultimate disposal of Dominion and Indian troops admitted to hospital, the following analysis refers to British troops only. Tables 15 (b) and 15 (c) show the corresponding ratios per 1,000 of British ration strength and percentages of total British admissions respectively.

TABLE 15 (a).—Admissions to Hospital and Disposal of Cases—British Troops only

	Wounded			Sick			Injured			Total		
	Off.	O.R.	Total	Off.	O.R.	Total	Off.	O.R.	Total	Off.	O.R.	Total
Admissions	7,551	213,523	221,074	12,481	439,429	451,910	1,673	76,125	77,798	21,705	729,077	750,782
Deaths	703	13,445	14,148	60	1,637	1,697	41	543	584	804	15,625	16,429
Returned to duty	6,827	187,962	194,789	12,415	429,994	442,409	1,632	74,694	76,326	20,874	692,650	713,524
Discharged as invalids	21	12,116	12,137	6	7,798	7,804	—	888	888	27	20,802	20,829

TABLE 15 (b).—Ratios per 1,000 of British Ration Strength

	Wounded			Sick			Injured			Total		
	Off.	O.R.	Total	Off.	O.R.	Total	Off.	O.R.	Total	Off.	O.R.	Total
Admissions	352·77	374·84	374·04	583·09	771·41	764·59	78·16	133·64	131·63	1,014·02	1,279·88	1,270·26
Deaths	32·84	23·60	23·94	2·80	2·87	2·87	1·92	·95	·99	37·56	27·43	27·80
Returned to duty	318·94	329·96	329·57	580·00	754·85	748·52	76·24	131·12	129·14	975·19	1,215·94	1,207·22
Discharged as invalids	·98	21·27	20·53	·28	13·69	13·20	—	1·56	1·50	1·26	36·52	35·24

TABLE 15 (c).—Percentages of Total British Admissions

	Wounded			Sick			Injured			Total		
	Off.	O.R.	Total	Off.	O.R.	Total	Off.	O.R.	Total	Off.	O.R.	Total
Deaths	9·31	6·30	6·40	·48	·37	·37	2·45	·71	·75	3·70	2·14	2·19
Returned to duty	90·41	88·03	88·11	99·47	97·85	97·90	97·55	98·12	98·11	96·17	95·01	95·04
Discharged as invalids	·28	5·67	5·49	·05	1·78	1·73	—	1·17	1·14	·13	2·85	2·77

Table 16 shows the percentage of the above admissions whose records were complete in respect of the total number of days spent in hospital in France and in the United Kingdom, and of that percentage the ratio per 1,000 of strength constantly in hospital and the average number of days in hospital per patient.

TABLE 16.—Ratio per 1,000 of Strength constantly in Hospital, with the average stay in Hospital per patient, British Troops only

	Percentage of admissions with completed records		Ratio per 1,000 constantly in hospital			Average No. of days in hospital per patient	
	Off.	O.R.	Off.	O.R.	Total	Off.	O.R.
Wounded	82·8	90·0	26·09	55·81	54·74	32·6	60·4
Sick	87·2	94·3	22·01	42·06	41·34	15·8	21·1
Injured	85·8	92·7	3·24	7·19	7·05	17·6	21·2
Total	85·6	92·8	51·35	105·07	103·12	21·6	32·2

The ratio per 1,000 of total strength constantly in hospital in France over the period May to December, 1915, for which records are available, for all ranks sick and wounded, was 12·03 per 1,000 in the forward area and 23·85 per 1,000 in lines of communication hospitals, making a total of **35·88** per 1,000.

Hospital Accommodation

Table 17 shows the hospital accommodation provided for the British and Dominion troops of the British Expeditionary Force in France in 1915, with the percentage of average ration strength of British and Dominion troops.

TABLE 17.—Accommodation provided in Hospitals on the Lines of Communication for British and Dominion Troops

Period	Average ration strength	Max. No. equipped beds	Max. No. occupied beds	Average No. equipped beds	Average No. occupied beds	Percentage of Ration Strength			
						Maximum No.		Average No.	
						Equipped	Occup.	Equipped	Occup.
1915	616,086	36,057	22,391	31,705	13,576	5·9	3·6	5·1	2·2

On the date of the maximum number of equipped beds, the percentage of equipped beds to actual strength was 4·0.

Three convalescent depots were open for British and Dominion troops early in 1915, and this number had increased to seven by August of that year. There are no details of the number of beds occupied or equipped until August, when there was accommodation for 8,525 British and Dominion troops. The percentage of equipped beds to strength of the British and Dominion troops at that time was 1·2.

Non-battle Casualties

The statistics of admissions to hospital for sickness or injury among British troops only of the British Expeditionary Force in France during 1915 are again a very complete record, as indicated in Table 20. The chief causes of admission for non-battle casualties during this period, given in Table 18 with the corresponding ratios per 1,000 of ration strength, are very similar to those of 1914, while Table 19 sets out the chief causes of inefficiency in the British army at home and abroad in 1927 alongside those of 1915 for purposes of comparison.

TABLE 18.—Principal Causes of Inefficiency

	Admissions	Ratio per 1,000
Diseases of the digestive system	67,663	114·48
Local and general injuries	55,080	93·19
Influenza	44,392	75·11
Diseases of the organs of locomotion	40,648	68·77
Diseases of the skin	39,505	66·84
Diseases of the areolar tissue	35,046	59·29
Diseases of the respiratory system	31,141	52·69
Diseases of the teeth and gums	24,703	41·80
Frost bite (16,256) and trench foot (6,462)	22,718	38·44
Rheumatic fever	20,764	35·13
Diseases of the nervous system	20,327	34·39
Venereal diseases	17,525	29·65

TABLE 19.—Comparison between Principal Causes of Inefficiency among British Troops in 1915 and 1927

British Troops in France, 1915		British Army at home and abroad, 1927	
Principal causes of admission to hospital	Ratio per 1,000	Principal causes of admission to hospital	Ratio per 1,000
Diseases of the—		Diseases of the—	
Digestive system	114·48	Digestive system	91·8
Local and general injuries	93·19	Local and general injuries	52·2
Influenza	75·11	Malaria	48·1
Diseases of the—		Venereal diseases	46·7
Organs of locomotion	68·77	Diseases of the—	
Skin	66·84	Areolar tissue	33·1
Areolar tissue	59·29	Teeth and gums	32·2
Respiratory system	52·69	Influenza	23·8
Teeth and gums	41·80	Diseases of the—	
Frost bite and trench foot	38·44	Skin	22·3
Rheumatic fever	35·13	Organs of locomotion	20·4
		Respiratory system	19·9

TABLE 20.—Analysis of Admissions to Hospital, British troops only, of the British Strength, and the Average number

#	Disease	Admissions	Deaths	Returned to duty
	Specific diseases due to infection			
1	Cerebro-spinal fever	357	169	183
2	Chicken-pox	43	—	43
3	Diphtheria	439	7	432
4	Dysentery	1,559	24	1,517
5	Enteric group of fevers	3,462	153	3,291
6	Influenza	44,392	23	44,339
7	Malaria	4,297	4	4,281
8	Measles	1,929	12	1,916
9	Mumps	399	—	399
10	Pneumonia *	1,925	241	1,653
11	Pyrexia of uncertain origin	9,929	8	9,919
12	Rheumatic fever	20,764	19	20,173
13	Rubella	1,613	1	1,611
14	Sand-fly fever	6	—	6
15	Scarlet fever	808	14	793
16	Septic diseases, major	358	33	310
17	Small-pox	1	—	1
18	Tetanus †	14	5	9
19	Trench fever	256	1	254
20	Tuberculosis { Pulmonary	1,541	60	879
21	{ Other	359	25	273
22	Venereal diseases { Gonorrhœa	12,378	4	12,360
23	{ Syphilis	3,849	6	3,827
24	{ Other	1,298	3	1,295
25	Other diseases due to infection	459	24	433
	Diseases classified under systems			
26	Diseases of the nervous system	19,540	106	17,963
27	Mental diseases	787	19	363
	Diseases of the—			
28	Eye { Trachoma	26	—	24
29	{ Other	12,425	2	12,185
30	Ear	8,897	24	8,422
31	Nose	922	1	911
32	Circulatory { Valvular disease of the heart	3,476	44	2,683
33	system { Disordered action of the heart	4,485	12	4,280
34	{ Other	5,188	27	4,943
35	Respiratory system	31,141	94	30,415
36	Blood	575	4	556
37	Spleen	13	—	13
38	Lymphatic system	1,304	4	1,295
39	Endocrine glands	210	1	195
40	Breast	72	—	72
41	Teeth and gums	24,703	6	24,655
42	{ Tonsillitis	11,682	13	11,660
43	{ Indigestion	3,731	—	3,703
44	{ Inflammation and ulceration of stomach	7,858	22	7,693
45	Digestive { Other diseases of the stomach	417	—	408
46	system { Inflammation of the intestines	8,898	77	8,770
47	{ Diarrhœa	12,852	3	12,840
48	{ Other diseases of the intestines	18,954	39	18,721
49	{ Jaundice	1,492	14	1,475
50	{ Other	1,779	30	1,734
51	Generative system	6,786	11	6,718
52	Skin { Scabies	25,242	2	25,233
53	{ Other	14,263	7	14,224
54	Areolar tissue { Septic diseases, minor	17,099	14	17,061
55	{ Other	17,947	11	17,916
56	{ Myalgia	21,915	5	21,756
57	Organs of locomotion { Lumbago	2,439	2	2,422
58	{ Other	16,294	12	15,881
59	Urinary system { Nephritis	4,010	97	3,473
60	{ Other	2,403	8	2,323
	Miscellaneous diseases			
61	Debility	14,810	12	14,665
62	Diseases due to disorders of nutrition or { Scurvy	9	—	9
63	of metabolism { Beri-beri	3	—	2
64	{ Other	397	13	357
65	Tumours and cysts	1,240	26	1,171
66	Poisons	618	13	599
67	Parasites { Bilharziasis	22	—	20
68	{ Other	2,585	1	2,583
69	Diseases unclassified	9,966	85	9,818
	Injuries			
70	Frostbite	16,256	19	16,010
71	Trench foot	6,462	6	6,416
72	Local and general { Effects of heat	256	—	255
73	injuries { Other	7,403	53	7,336
74	Other injuries accidental or undefined	47,421	506	46,309
	Grand Total of Diseases and Injuries	529,708	2,281	518,735

* Includes broncho-pneumonia.

Expeditionary Force in France, 1915, showing Disposal of Cases, Ratio per 1,000 of of Days in Hospital per Patient

Discharged as invalids	Ratio per 1,000				Average No. of days in hospital per patient		
	Admissions	Deaths	Returned to duty	Discharged as invalids	Off.	O.R.	
5	·60	·29	·31	·01	48·8	53·0	1
—	·07	—	·07	—	32·2	32·2	2
—	·74	·01	·73	—	22·6	52·8	3
18	2·64	·04	2·57	·03	17·0	37·7	4
18	5·86	·26	5·57	·03	32·8	85·6	5
30	75·11	·04	75·02	·05	6·0	15·3	6
12	7·27	·01	7·24	·02	12·4	18·9	7
1	3·26	·02	3·24	·00	17·1	24·5	8
—	·67	—	·67	—	21·8	26·6	9
31	3·26	·41	2·80	·05	20·1	46·8	10
2	16·80	·01	16·78	·00	8·6	8·3	11
572	35·13	·03	34·13	·97	21·2	27·8	12
1	2·73	·00	2·73	·00	12·0	17·2	13
—	·01	—	·01	—	—	15·0	14
1	1·37	·02	1·34	·00	41·0	52·1	15
13	·61	·06	·52	·02	16·5	43·8	16
—	·00	—	·00	—	—	6·0	17
—	·02	·01	·02	—	—	34·8	18
1	·43	·00	·43	·00	10·9	3·0	19
602	2·61	·10	1·49	1·02	20·7	56·5	20
61	·61	·04	·46	·10	65·8	72·8	21
14	20·94	·01	20·91	·02	—	32·4	22
16	6·51	·01	6·47	·03	46·6	33·2	23
—	2·20	·01	2·19	—	25·4	31·6	24
2	·78	·04	·73	·00	14·7	18·9	25
1,471	33·06	·18	30·39	2·49	14·2	38·5	26
405	1·33	·03	·61	·69	51·3	7·3	27
2	·04	—	·04	·00	2·0	60·5	28
238	21·02	·00	20·62	·40	12·0	15·2	29
451	15·05	·04	14·25	·76	14·4	25·6	30
10	1·56	·00	1·54	·01	13·6	26·4	31
749	5·88	·07	4·54	1·27	22·2	48·4	32
193	7·59	·02	7·24	·33	25·7	27·4	33
218	8·78	·05	8·36	·37	20·4	29·9	34
632	52·69	·16	51·46	1·07	10·0	22·5	35
15	·97	·01	·94	·03	6·4	32·4	36
—	·02	—	·02	—	—	35·6	37
5	2·21	·01	2·19	·01	15·7	24·6	38
14	·36	·00	·33	·02	9·0	48·8	39
—	·12	—	·12	—	16·0	19·5	40
42	41·80	·01	41·71	·07	4·9	7·5	41
9	19·76	·02	19·73	·02	9·1	11·9	42
28	6·31	—	6·27	·05	10·4	14·7	43
143	13·30	·04	13·02	·24	14·9	23·1	44
9	·71	—	·69	·02	11·6	19·4	45
51	15·05	·13	14·84	·09	10·4	29·0	46
9	21·74	·01	21·72	·02	9·8	7·9	47
194	32·07	·07	31·67	·33	19·9	27·9	48
3	2·52	·02	2·50	·01	15·7	31·3	49
15	3·01	·05	2·93	·03	12·5	17·5	50
57	11·48	·02	11·37	·10	24·1	23·3	51
7	42·71	·00	42·69	·01	10·7	10·9	52
32	24·13	01	24·07	·05	13·5	20·2	53
24	28·93	·02	28·87	·04	13·1	18·6	54
20	30·36	·02	30·31	·03	11·8	14·2	55
154	37·08	·01	36·81	·26	17·7	18·8	56
15	4·13	·00	4·10	·03	13·0	16·3	57
401	27·57	·02	26·87	·68	22·4	28·1	58
440	6·78	·16	5·88	·74	31·7	81·0	59
72	4·07	·01	3·93	·12	24·6	30·7	60
133	25·06	·02	24·81	·23	76·1	20·0	61
—	·02	—	·02	—	—	21·3	62
1	·01	—	·00	·00	—	90·0	63
27	·67	·02	·60	·05	12·1	29·2	64
43	2·10	·04	1·98	·07	16·6	28·5	65
6	1·05	·02	1·01	·01	14·3	14·2	66
2	·04	—	·03	·00	29·0	33·1	67
1	4·37	·00	4·37	·00	8·4	5·1	68
63	16·86	·14	16·61	·11	5·9	7·1	69
227	27·50	·03	27·09	·38	26·0	40·0	70
40	10·93	·01	10·86	·07	19·7	30·3	71
1	·43	—	·43	·00	10·4	13·8	72
14	12·53	·09	12·41	·02	15·7	16·8	73
606	80·23	·86	78·35	1·03	17·0	14·5	74
8,692	896·22	3·86	877·65	14·71	16·0	21·1	

† Direct admissions; *see* note in text.

Table 20 gives a detailed analysis of the causes of admission to hospital of British troops in France during 1915, with their ultimate disposal and the average length of stay in hospital per patient. Two points require some explanation. In the original compilation of the table, admissions for pneumonia and broncho-pneumonia were grouped together, and have had to be reproduced here as one total. With regard to admissions for tetanus, the figure quoted in the table refers to direct admissions to hospital. Other records, however, show that there were in addition 93 cases of tetanus among the British troops in France, and that 138 cases of the disease occurred in the United Kingdom during 1915 as a result of wounds in France.

CHAPTER VIII

CASUALTIES IN THE BRITISH EXPEDITIONARY FORCE IN FRANCE AND FLANDERS, 1916

THE state of trench warfare, which existed on the Western front for the first six months of 1916, was broken by minor actions at the Bluff and St. Eloi Craters in March and April, at Vimy Ridge in May, and at Mount Sorrel in June, and gave place to mobile warfare when operations on the Somme commenced on 1st July. From that date until 10th November, the British force was engaged in the most extensive and prolonged battles it had as yet undertaken, in which the casualties sustained were without parallel in any previous fighting, and accounted for 63·1 per cent. of the total battle casualties for the year. Some idea of the work which was thrown upon the medical services can be gained from the fact that 73·8 per cent. of the battle casualties in the Somme operations were admitted to medical units.

From the military medical point of view the year is chiefly remarkable for the arrangements made for the collection of the casualties from a large force fighting a series of battles and advancing by slow degrees, and for their evacuation in summer and winter, by day or night, through a heavy barrage, across barren and exposed country, deficient in roads, ploughed by shells, and occasionally churned into a morass by heavy rain and the passage of men, guns and transport. To cope with the increasing casualties, several improvements in their collection and evacuation were introduced. The number of regimental stretcher bearers per battalion was doubled ; more accommodation and better shelter were provided in regimental aid posts and advanced dressing stations ; a system of relay posts every 1,000 yards was established for stretcher bearers ; and extensive use was made of buses, charabancs, light railways, and general service transport. Casualty clearing stations were formed into groups of two or three, and an attempt was made to set apart special units for special types of cases, such as nervous disorders, skin troubles or specific varieties of wounds. The system of admitting 150 to 300 cases to casualty clearing stations in rotation facilitated evacuation and benefited the surgical treatment of wounds, the advance in which was one of the outstanding features of the work of the medical services. For the extensive operative surgery which was now undertaken at casualty clearing stations, additional surgical teams and equipment were supplied during battles. The lack of sufficient hospital accommodation at the base to meet the increased demands resulted in the use of improvised accommodation, known as " crisis " beds, which are explained later in the chapter, and also in the evacuation to the United Kingdom of a large number of patients suffering from slight disabilities.

The health of the troops was good; the admission rate for sickness or injury during the year was 481·60 per 1,000 of strength, which testified to the success of the preventive measures adopted in the force. Increasing numbers of casualties, which included 6,698 gas cases, called for investigation into the best methods of treatment; and the continuance of the diseases associated with modern warfare and trench life necessitated careful clinical study and laboratory research by skilled specialists.*

Strength

The average ration strength of the British Expeditionary Force in France and Flanders during 1916 is shown in Table 1.

TABLE 1.—Average Ration Strength

Period	Force	Officers	Other Ranks	Total
1916	British Expeditionary Force British and Dominion troops	49,966 49,599	1,287,089 1,272,476	1,337,055 1,322,075

Classification of Casualties

The total casualties sustained by the British Expeditionary Force operating in France and Flanders during 1916 are given in Table 2, with the ratios per 1,000 of average ration strength.

TABLE 2.—Total Casualties

	Off.	O.R.	Total	Ratio per 1,000		
				Off.	O.R.	Total
Battle casualties ...	30,293	621,369	651,662	606·27	482·77	487·39
Non-battle casualties	23,416	620,505	643,921	468·64	482·10	481·60
Total ...	53,709	1,241,874	1,295,583	1,074·91	964·87	968·98

The proportion of battle casualties to non-battle casualties in the whole force was 1·3 to 1 officers; 1·00 to 1 other ranks; and 1·01 to 1 all ranks.

---

* The history of the medical services in France during 1916 is dealt with in the *General History of the Medical Services*, vol. iii, pp. 1–53.

FRANCE AND FLANDERS, 1916

An analysis of the total casualties occurring in the British Expeditionary Force during 1916 is given in Table 3.

TABLE 3.—Classification and Percentages of Total Casualties

	Off.	O.R.	Total	Percentage of total casualties		
				Off.	O.R.	Total
A. *Battle casualties:*						
(a) Killed	6,506	100,905	107,411	12·11	8·13	8·29
(b) Died of wounds	1,814	35,065	36,879	3·38	2·82	2·85
(c) Missing	878	27,281	28,159	1·63	2·20	2·17
(d) Prisoners of war	750	14,766	15,516	1·40	1·19	1·20
(e) Wounded less (b)	20,345	443,352	463,697	37·88	35·70	35·79
B. *Non-battle casualties:*						
(f) Died of disease or injury	229	5,612	5,841	·43	·45	·45
(g) Sick or injured less (f)	23,187	614,893	638,080	43·17	49·51	49·25
Total A. and B.	53,709	1,241,874	1,295,583	—	—	—

Table 4 (a) shows this detail as percentages of battle casualties, and Table 4 (b) shows similarly the percentages of non-battle casualties.

TABLE 4 (a).—Percentages of Battle Casualties

	Off.	O.R.	Total
(a) Killed	21·48	16·24	16·48
(b) Died of wounds	5·99	5·64	5·66
(c) Missing	2·90	4·39	4·32
(d) Prisoners of war	2·48	2·38	2·38
(e) Wounded less (b)	67·16	71·35	71·16

TABLE 4 (b).—Percentages of Non-battle Casualties

	Off.	O.R.	Total
(f) Died of disease or injury	·98	·90	·91
(g) Sick or injured less (f)	99·02	99·10	99·09

The casualties in the British Expeditionary Force in France and Flanders during 1916 may be further subdivided into permanent and temporary losses for military purposes in the field.

TABLE 5 (a).—Permanent Losses for Military Purposes in the Field

	Off.	O.R.	Total	Percentage of total casualties		
				Off.	O.R.	Total
A. Battle casualties:						
Killed	6,506	100,905	107,411	12·11	8·13	8·29
Died of wounds	1,814	35,065	36,879	3·38	2·82	2·85
Missing	878	27,281	28,159	1·63	2·20	2·17
Prisoners of war	750	14,766	15,516	1·40	1·19	1·20
Total	*9,948*	*178,017*	*187,965*	*18·52*	*14·33*	*14·51*
B. Non-battle casualties:						
Died of disease or injury	229	5,612	5,841	·43	·45	·45
Total permanent losses	10,177	183,629	193,806	18·95	14·79	14·96

TABLE 5 (b).—Temporary Losses for Military Purposes in the Field

	Off.	O.R.	Total	Percentage of total casualties		
				Off.	O.R.	Total
A. Battle casualties:						
Wounded less died of wounds	20,345	443,352	463,697	37·88	35·70	35·79
B. Non-battle casualties:						
Sick or injured less died of disease or injury	23,187	614,893	638,080	43·17	49·51	49·25
Total temporary losses	43,532	1,058,245	1,101,777	81·05	85·21	85·04

The relative proportions of the various classes of casualties to each other for the whole force in France during 1916 are indicated in Table 6.

TABLE 6.—Proportions

	Officers	Other ranks	Total
1. Total battle casualties to total non-battle casualties	1·3 : 1	1·0 : 1	1·01 : 1
2. Total killed to total wounded including died of wounds	1 : 3·4	1 : 4·7	1 : 4·7
3. Permanent losses among battle casualties to total wounded less died of wounds	1 : 2·0	1 : 2·5	1 : 2·5
4. Permanent losses among non-battle casualties to total sick and injured less deaths from disease or injury	1 : 101·3	1 : 109·6	1 : 109·2
5. Total permanent losses to total temporary losses	1 : 4·3	1 : 5·8	1 : 5·7

Admissions to Hospital

Of the total casualties suffered by the British Expeditionary Force in France and Flanders during 1916, the numbers admitted to hospital and treated by the medical services are shown in Table 7.

TABLE 7.—Numbers admitted to Hospital

	Off.	O.R.	Total	Percentage of total casualties		
				Off.	O.R.	Total
Wounded	22,159	478,417	500,576	41·26	38·52	38·64
Sick or injured	23,416	620,505	643,921	43·60	49·97	49·70
Total	45,575	1,098,922	1,144,497	84·86	88·49	88·34

The proportion of wounded to sick and injured treated by the medical services was 1 to 1·1 officers; 1 to 1·3 other ranks; and 1 to 1·3 all ranks.

The casualties which were not treated by the medical services are shown in Table 8.

TABLE 8.—Casualties not treated by the Medical Services

	Off.	O.R.	Total	Percentage of total casualties		
				Off.	O.R.	Total
Killed	6,506	100,905	107,411	12·11	8·13	8·29
Missing	878	27,281	28,159	1·63	2·20	2·17
Prisoners of war	750	14,766	15,516	1·40	1·19	1·20
Total	8,134	142,952	151,086	15·14	11·51	11·66

The numbers of sick and wounded admitted to hospital, and the disposal of cases, are shown in Table 9 (*a*); while the corresponding ratios per 1,000 of strength and percentages of total admissions are given in Tables 9 (*b*) and 9 (*c*). With regard to Table 9 (*c*) it should be remembered that the calculations are the percentages of total admissions for the year plus the numbers remaining in hospital on the last day of the previous year.

TABLE 9 (a).—Admissions to Hospital and Disposal of Cases, British Expeditionary Force, France, 1916

	Wounded			Sick or injured			Total		
	Off.	O.R.	Total	Off.	O.R.	Total	Off.	O.R.	Total
Admissions	22,159	478,417	500,576	23,416	620,505	643,921	45,575	1,098,922	1,144,497
Deaths	1,814	35,065	36,879	229	5,612	5,841	2,043	40,677	42,720
Returned to duty in theatre of war	6,636	161,719	168,355	9,724	352,418	362,142	16,360	514,137	530,497
Evacuated overseas	13,634	278,314	291,948	12,759	220,677	233,436	26,393	498,991	525,384

TABLE 9 (b).—Ratios per 1,000 of Ration Strength

	Wounded			Sick or injured			Total		
	Off.	O.R.	Total	Off.	O.R.	Total	Off.	O.R.	Total
Admissions	443·48	371·70	374·39	468·64	482·10	481·60	912·12	853·80	855·98
Deaths	36·30	27·24	27·58	4·58	4·36	4·37	40·89	31·60	31·95
Returned to duty in theatre of war	132·81	125·65	125·91	194·61	273·81	270·85	327·42	399·46	396·77
Evacuated overseas	272·87	216·24	218·35	255·35	171·45	174·59	528·22	387·69	392·94

TABLE 9 (c).—Percentages of Total Admissions*

	Wounded			Sick or injured			Total		
	Off.	O.R.	Total	Off.	O.R.	Total	Off.	O.R.	Total
Deaths	8·14	7·26	7·30	·96	·88	·88	4·43	3·63	3·66
Returned to duty in theatre of war	29·77	33·49	33·32	40·74	55·28	54·76	35·44	45·89	45·48
Evacuated overseas	61·17	57·63	57·79	53·45	34·62	35·30	57·18	44·54	45·04
Remaining in medical charge on 31.12.16	·92	1·62	1·59	4·85	9·22	9·06	2·95	5·94	5·82

Of the British Expeditionary Force in France and Flanders during 1916, the ratios per 1,000 of ration strength constantly in medical units in France for wounds, disease or injury, are shown in Table 10.

TABLE 10.—Ratio per 1,000 of Strength constantly in Medical Units

Year	Army Areas				Lines of Communication			Total
	Field Amb.	Rest Stn.	C.C.S.	Total	Hospital	Conval. Depot	Total	
1916	3·50	4·76	5·72	13·98	19·16	6·03	25·19	39·17

Hospital Accommodation

Table 11 shows the maximum number of equipped hospital beds for British and Dominion troops of the expeditionary force in France, the maximum number of occupied beds on

* Including numbers remaining in medical charge on 31st December, 1915.

any one date, and the average number of equipped beds throughout the year, with the corresponding percentages of the average strength of British and Dominion troops. To meet the increased demands for hospital accommodation, occasioned by the heavy casualties in the Somme fighting, approximately 30,000 additional beds were provided by increasing the number of beds in the wards of existing hospitals, and by appropriating the huts for personnel, dining-rooms and other accessory buildings, and placing trestle cots and mattresses in them instead of hospital beds. This "crisis" expansion, as it was called, made extra provision for 2·27 per cent. of the strength, but as extra medical and nursing personnel were not provided for this improvised accommodation, it was unsuitable for the permanent treatment of patients.

TABLE 11.—Accommodation provided in Hospitals on the Lines of Communications for British and Dominion Troops

Year	Average British and Dom. Str.	Max. No. equipped beds	Max. No. occupied beds	Average No. equipped beds	Average No. occupied beds	Percentage of ration strength			
						Maximum No.		Average No.	
						Equip.	Occup.	Equip.	Occup.
1916	1,322,075	49,000	35,561	47,977	25,109	3·7	2·6	3·6	1·8

Table 12 shows the hospital accommodation provided for Indian troops in France during 1916.

TABLE 12.—Accommodation provided in Hospitals on the Lines of Communications for Indian Troops

Year	Average ration strength	Max. No. equipped beds	Max. No. occupied beds	Average No. equipped beds	Average No. occupied beds	Percentage of ration strength			
						Maximum No.		Average No.	
						Equip.	Occup.	Equip.	Occup.
1916	14,980	2,100	1,402	1,297	576	14·02	9·36	8·66	3·84

The convalescent depot accommodation provided on the lines of communication for British and Dominion troops of the force in France during 1916 is shown in Table 13, and that

TABLE 13.—Accommodation provided in Convalescent Depots for British and Dominion Troops

Year	Average British and Dom. Str.	Max. No. equipped beds	Max. No. occupied beds	Average No. equipped beds	Average No. occupied beds	Percentage of ration strength			
						Maximum No.		Average No.	
						Equip.	Occup.	Equip.	Occup.
1916	1,322,075	20,872	12,546	15,904	8,069	1·6	·9	1·2	·6

for Indians for the period May to December, for which records are available, is given in Table 14.

TABLE 14.—Accommodation provided in Convalescent Depots for Indians, May to December, 1916

Year	Average ration strength	Max. No. equipped beds	Max. No. occupied beds	Average No. equipped beds	Average No. occupied beds	Percentage of ration strength			
						Maximum No.		Average No.	
						Equip.	Occup.	Equip.	Occup.
1916 (May–Dec.)	14,980	500	65	303	46	3·34	·43	2·02	·31

Non-battle Casualties

The following tables of admissions to hospital for sickness or injury in France during 1916 refer to British and Dominion troops only, as there is little reliable information regarding the detail of admissions for Indian or other troops. Unfortunately the figures for 1916, 1917 and 1918 are not so complete as those for the first seventeen months of the war. Records were kept only of infectious diseases or other diseases which were likely to spread or cause the greatest wastage among the troops. The admission rate for the year, however, compares very favourably with the peace-time figures for the British army in pre- and post-war years,* and it may be assumed therefore that the number of admissions unspecified represents the ordinary sick admissions to be expected in an army of European troops stationed at home and abroad. Among the specified causes, the following diseases or disabilities caused the greatest wastage during 1916.

TABLE 15.—Principal Recorded Causes of Inefficiency among British and Dominion Troops

	Admissions	Ratio per 1,000
Venereal diseases	24,108	18·23
Frostbite and trench foot	16,955	12·82
Nephritis	9,813	7·42
Dysentery	5,776	4·37
Rubella	5,490	4·15
Mumps	4,333	3·28

* 1913..437·7 per 1,000.
 1921..649·9 ,, ,,

Table 16 shows the admissions and deaths occurring among British and Dominion troops of the British Expeditionary Force in France during 1916 for certain infectious and other diseases and disabilities, with the ratios per 1,000 of ration strength.

TABLE 16.—Principal Recorded Causes of Admission to Hospital of British and Dominion Troops in France, 1916, with Deaths and Ratios per 1,000 of ration strength

	Admissions	Deaths	Ratio per 1,000 Admissions	Ratio per 1,000 Deaths
Specific diseases due to infection				
Anthrax	9	—	·01	—
Cerebro-spinal meningitis	393	138	·30	·10
Chicken-pox	83	—	·06	—
Diphtheria	1,175	8	·89	·01
Dysentery	5,776	40	4·37	·03
Enteric fever ⎰ Typhoid	778	17	·59	·01
⎨ Paratyphoid	1,588	13	1·20	·01
⎱ Group	372	—	·28	—
Erysipelas	239	9	·18	·01
Malaria	58	—	·04	—
Measles	1,912	5	1·45	·00
Mumps	4,333	—	3·28	—
Pneumonia	1,497	135	1·13	·10
Poliomyelitis	1	—	·00	—
Relapsing fever	10	—	·01	—
Rubella	5,490	1	4·15	·00
Scarlet fever	749	7	·57	·01
Small-pox	4	—	·00	—
Tetanus	254	146	·19	·11
Tuberculosis ⎰ Pulmonary	1,203	⎰ 37 ⎱	·91	⎰ ·03 ⎱
⎱ Other	140		·11	
Typhus	4	—	·00	—
Venereal diseases ⎰ Gonorrhœa	16,209	—	12·26	—
⎨ Syphilis	3,583	—	2·71	—
⎱ Other	4,316	—	3·26	—
Whooping-cough	15	—	·01	—
Other diseases or disabilities				
Jaundice	181	2	·14	·00
Nephritis	9,813	92	7·42	·07
Frostbite and trench foot	16,955	1	12·82	·00

CHAPTER IX

CASUALTIES IN THE BRITISH EXPEDITIONARY FORCE IN FRANCE AND FLANDERS, 1917

THE allied offensive which had begun with the battles of the Somme in 1916 was continued throughout 1917 in a number of important battles. Operations on the Ancre from 11th January to 13th March, with the subsequent German retreat from 14th March to 5th April, constituted the advance to the Hindenburg Line. Then followed the Arras offensive with the battle of Arras from 9th April to 4th May, and concurrently the battle of Vimy Ridge from 9th to 14th April, while flanking operations were continued on this sector of the front line during the summer months. Further north, preparations on a large scale had been undertaken in readiness for the Flanders offensive which opened with the battle of Messines, 7th to 14th June. This attack was remarkable for the deep mining offensive measures adopted, whereby without previous bombardment 19 large mines were exploded beneath the enemy defences, after which the troops advanced on their objectives under a creeping artillery barrage. In the Dunkirk-Nieuport area of Flanders, preparations had also been made for combined operations with the Navy should the opportunity arise, but no active offensive was undertaken. On 31st July, in conjunction with French troops, operations began against enemy positions in the Ypres Salient, which, in a series of severe battles known as the battles of Ypres 1917, brought the Flanders offensive to a close on 10th November. The final offensive operations for the year were undertaken at the battle of Cambrai, from 20th November to 7th December, at which a further surprise method of attack was launched upon the enemy by the use of tanks to lead the assault and prepare the way for the attacking infantry.

The winter of 1916–17 was very severe; weeks of hard frost, during which transport was easy but the making of dugouts and shelters was difficult, were followed by a rapid thaw which rendered roads impassable, flooded low-lying ground and waterlogged the trenches. Rain, hail, sleet and snow interfered with the Spring operations, and in August and September incessant rain interrupted the offensive in Flanders.

The ratio of total battle casualties per 1,000 of strength was not so high as in 1916, but the total number of wounded admitted to medical units, namely 564,694, was the highest yet reached on the Western front and represented no light task for the medical services to undertake. To meet the growing casualty list, the medical arrangements which had taken shape during the offensive in 1916 were developed and improved during 1917. The chief features of military medical interest centred round the evacuation and treatment of casualties in the forward area, and the problems of hospital accommodation at the base. To speed up evacuation, routes were more distinctly marked;

additional stretcher bearers up to 600 per division were supplied during the battles ; ample reserves of stretchers and blankets were provided ; bearers worked in relays ; and tramways, trollies, general service motor and other vehicles and temporary ambulance trains were used to advantage. The system of grouping casualty clearing stations and admitting cases in rotation proved successful and was continued. The increasing importance of casualty clearing stations as pivotal units for the distribution of casualties and as operating centres for urgent cases led to the extension of branch railway lines and the construction of railway sidings for their special use ; to the garaging of regular and temporary ambulance trains in convenient areas ; and to a further development in the organisation and institution of attaching surgical teams to the casualty clearing stations in action. Hospital accommodation at the base was a source of considerable anxiety to the medical services at the beginning of 1917. The policy of retaining sick and wounded in France, other than those who would obviously not be fit for duty within a reasonable time, had been adopted at the close of the operations on the Somme in 1916, so that with the existing accommodation the margin of vacant beds was very small when the Spring offensive was pending. To meet this critical situation it was decided to increase the convalescent depot accommodation and to double the evacuation of sick and wounded to the United Kingdom until further general hospitals could be sent out to France. For a considerable period, therefore, this policy resulted in a reduction in the number of wounded officers and other ranks returned to duty in the theatre of war.

Generally speaking, the improvement in the health of the troops was maintained in 1917, although the admission rate of 529·37 per 1,000 of strength was slightly higher than in 1916. Reports throughout the year point to the fact that venereal diseases, trench fever, pyrexia of uncertain origin, trench foot, nephritis, digestive disorders and minor skin troubles were included in the principal causes of inefficiency among the troops, although in some cases there are no complete records. There were 52,452 shell gas casualties admitted to casualty clearing stations during the year, of whom 1,168 died in these units; 40,566 gas casualties, of whom 628 subsequently died, were admitted to hospitals on the lines of communication suffering from the effects of " mustard " gas.*

Strength

The average ration strength of the British Expeditionary Force in France and Flanders during 1917 is shown in Table 1.

TABLE 1.—Average Ration Strength

Period	Force	Officers	Other Ranks	Total
1917	British Expeditionary Force British and Dominion troops	73,804 73,449	1,895,075 1,821,062	1,968,879 1,894,511

* The history of the Medical Services with the British Expeditionary Force in France during 1917 is dealt with in the *General History of the Medical Services*, vol. iii, pp. 54–200.

Classification of Casualties

The total casualties sustained by the British Expeditionary Force in France during 1917 are shown in Table 2, with the ratios per 1,000 of ration strength.

TABLE 2.—Total Casualties

	Off.	O.R.	Total	Ratio per 1,000		
				Off.	O.R.	Total
Battle casualties	33,755	716,494	750,249	457·36	378·08	381·05
Non-battle casualties	40,862	1,001,404	1,042,266	553·66	528·42	529·37
Total	74,617	1,717,898	1,792,515	1,011·02	906·51	910·42

The proportion of battle casualties to non-battle casualties in the whole force was 1 to 1·2 officers; 1 to 1·4 other ranks; and 1 to 1·4 all ranks.

An analysis of the total casualties occurring in the British Expeditionary Force in France during 1917 is given in Table 3.

TABLE 3.—Classification and Percentages of Total Casualties

	Off.	O.R.	Total	Percentage of total casualties		
				Off.	O.R.	Total
A. *Battle casualties:*						
(a) Killed	7,659	124,102	131,761	10·26	7·22	7·35
(b) Died of wounds	2,627	47,205	49,832	3·52	2·75	2·78
(c) Missing	1,405	29,162	30,567	1·88	1·70	1·71
(d) Prisoners of war	1,229	21,998	23,227	1·65	1·28	1·30
(e) Wounded less (b)	20,835	494,027	514,862	27·92	28·76	28·72
B. *Non-battle casualties:*						
(f) Died of disease or injury	271	8,151	8,422	·36	·47	·47
(g) Sick or injured less (f)	40,591	993,253	1,033,844	54·40	57·82	57·68
Total A. and B.	74,617	1,717,898	1,792,515	—	—	—

Table 4 (a) shows this detail as percentages of battle casualties and Table 4 (b) shows similarly the percentages of non-battle casualties.

TABLE 4 (a).—Percentages of Battle Casualties

	Off.	O.R.	Total
(a) Killed	22·69	17·32	17·56
(b) Died of wounds	7·78	6·59	6·64
(c) Missing	4·16	4·07	4·07
(d) Prisoners of war	3·64	3·07	3·10
(e) Wounded less (b)	61·72	68·95	68·63

TABLE 4 (b).—Percentages of Non-battle Casualties

	Off.	O.R.	Total
(f) Died of disease or injury	·66	·81	·81
(g) Sick or injured less (f)	99·34	99·19	99·19

The casualties sustained by the British Expeditionary Force in France during 1917 may be further classified into permanent and temporary losses for military purposes in the field.

TABLE 5 (a).—Permanent Losses for Military Purposes in the Field

	Off.	O.R.	Total	Percentage of total casualties		
				Off.	O.R.	Total
A. *Battle casualties*.						
Killed	7,659	124,102	131,761	10·26	7·22	7·35
Died of wounds	2,627	47,205	49,832	3·52	2·75	2·78
Missing	1,405	29,162	30,567	1·88	1·70	1·71
Prisoners of war	1,229	21,998	23,227	1·65	1·28	1·30
Total	*12,920*	*222,467*	*235,387*	*17·32*	*12·95*	*13·13*
B. *Non-battle casualties:*						
Died of disease or injury	271	8,151	8,422	·36	·47	·47
Total permanent losses	13,191	230,618	243,809	17·68	13·42	13·60

TABLE 5 (b).—Temporary Losses for Military Purposes in the Field

	Off.	O.R.	Total	Percentage of total casualties		
				Off.	O.R.	Total
A. *Battle casualties*:						
Wounded less died of wounds	20,835	494,027	514,862	27·92	28·76	28·72
B. *Non-battle casualties:*						
Sick or injured less died of disease or injury	40,591	993,253	1,033,844	54·40	57·82	57·68
Total temporary losses	61,426	1,487,280	1,548,706	82·32	86·58	86·40

The relative proportions of the various classes of casualties to each other for the whole force in France during 1917 are shown in Table 6.

160   MEDICAL HISTORY OF THE WAR

TABLE 6.—Proportions

	Officers	Other ranks	Total
1. Total battle casualties to total non-battle casualties	1 : 1·2	1 : 1·4	1 : 1·4
2. Total killed to total wounded including died of wounds	1 : 3·1	1 : 4·4	1 : 4·3
3. Permanent losses among battle casualties to total wounded less died of wounds	1 : 1·6	1 : 2·2	1 : 2·2
4. Permanent losses among non-battle casualties to total sick and injured less died of disease or injury	1 : 149·8	1 : 121·8	1 : 122·8
5. Total permanent losses to total temporary losses	1 : 4·7	1 : 6·4	1 : 6·4

Admissions to Hospital

Of the total casualties suffered by the British Expeditionary Force in France and Flanders during 1917, the numbers admitted to hospital and treated by the medical services are shown in Table 7.

TABLE 7.—Numbers admitted to Hospital

	Off.	O.R.	Total	Percentage of total casualties		
				Off.	O.R.	Total
Wounded	23,462	541,232	564,694	31·44	31·51	31·50
Sick or injured	40,862	1,001,404	1,042,266	54·76	58·29	58·15
Total	64,324	1,542,636	1,606,960	86·21	89·80	89·65

The proportion of wounded to sick and injured treated by the medical services was 1 to 1·7 officers; 1 to 1·9 other ranks; and 1 to 1·8 all ranks.

The casualties which were not treated by the medical services are shown in Table 8.

TABLE 8.—Casualties in the British Expeditionary Force not treated by the Medical Services

	Off.	O.R.	Total	Percentage of total casualties		
				Off.	O.R.	Total
Killed	7,659	124,102	131,761	10·26	7·22	7·35
Missing	1,405	29,162	30,567	1·88	1·70	1·71
Prisoners of war	1,229	21,998	23,227	1·65	1·28	1·30
Total	10,293	175,262	185,555	13·80	10·20	10·35

The numbers of sick and wounded admitted to hospital, and the disposal of cases, are shown in Table 9 (a), while the corresponding ratios per 1,000 of strength and percentages of total admissions are given in Tables 9 (b) and 9 (c) respectively. With regard to the numbers returned to duty in the theatre of operations, it should be remembered that, owing to the pressing need for hospital beds in France for the offensive operations in the Spring, a large number of slight cases of wounds or disease were evacuated to the United Kingdom instead of being kept in France until convalescent and able to return to duty. In Table 9 (c) the percentages are calculated on the total admissions for the year plus the numbers remaining in medical charge on 31st December, 1916.

TABLE 9 (a).—Admissions to Hospital and Disposal of Cases, British Expeditionary Force, France, 1917

	Wounded			Sick or injured			Total		
	Off.	O.R.	Total	Off.	O.R.	Total	Off.	O.R.	Total
Admissions	23,462	541,232	564,694	40,862	1,001,404	1,042,266	64,324	1,542,636	1,606,960
Deaths	2,627	47,205	49,832	271	8,151	8,422	2,898	55,356	58,254
Returned to duty in theatre of war	3,144	135,625	138,769	24,935	647,889	672,824	28,079	783,514	811,593
Evacuated overseas	17,339	347,064	364,403	15,326	322,976	338,302	32,665	670,040	702,705

TABLE 9 (b).—Ratios per 1,000 of Ration Strength

	Wounded			Sick or injured			Total		
	Off.	O.R.	Total	Off.	O.R.	Total	Off.	O.R.	Total
Admissions	317·90	285·60	286·81	553·66	528·42	529·37	871·55	814·02	816·18
Deaths	35·59	24·91	25·31	3·67	4·30	4·28	39·27	29·21	29·59
Returned to duty in theatre of war	42·60	71·57	70·48	337·85	341·88	341·73	380·45	413·45	412·21
Evacuated overseas	234·93	183·14	185·08	207·66	170·43	171·82	442·59	353·57	356·91

TABLE 9 (c).—Percentages of Total Admissions *

	Wounded			Sick or injured			Total		
	Off.	O.R.	Total	Off.	O.R.	Total	Off.	O.R.	Total
Deaths	11·10	8·60	8·70	·64	·77	·76	4·41	3·44	3·48
Returned to duty in theatre of war	13·28	24·70	24·23	59·34	61·11	61·05	42·75	48·69	48·46
Evacuated overseas	73·27	63·21	63·63	36·47	30·47	30·69	49·73	41·64	41·95
Remaining in medical charge 29.12.17	2·35	3·49	3·44	3·54	7·65	7·50	3·11	6·23	6·11

* Including numbers remaining in medical charge on 31st December, 1916.

The ratios per 1,000 of strength of the British Expeditionary Force in France constantly in medical units in the theatre of war for wounds, disease or injury, are shown in Table 10.

TABLE 10.—Ratio per 1,000 of Strength constantly in Medical Units in France

Year	Army Areas				Lines of Communication				Total
	Field Amb.	Rest Stn.	C.C.S.	Total	Hospital	Conval.	Depot	Total	
1917	3·28	4·65	6·86	14·78	22·77	10·70		33·47	48·25

Hospital Accommodation

Table 11 shows the maximum number of equipped hospital beds for British and Dominion troops of the expeditionary force in France during 1917, the maximum number of occupied beds on any one date, and the average number occupied throughout the year, with the corresponding percentages of the average strength of British and Dominion troops. There was in addition an average of 12,026 " crisis " beds throughout the year, making extra provision for ·64 per cent. of the strength, and an average of 3,695 beds was also available in hospitals in the front area, which provided for ·2 per cent. of the strength. Of these the average number occupied represented ·13 per cent. of British and Dominion strength.

TABLE 11.—Accommodation provided in Hospitals on the Lines of Communication for British and Dominion Troops

Year	Average British and Dom. Str.	Max. No. equipped beds	Max. No. occupied beds	Average No. equipped beds	Average No. occupied beds	Percentage of ration strength			
						Maximum No.		Average No.	
						Equip.	Occup.	Equip.	Occup.
1917	1,894,511	75,723	64,897	63,484	43,871	4·00	3·43	3·35	2·32

Table 12 shows the hospital accommodation provided for Indian troops and followers in France during 1917.

TABLE 12.—Accommodation provided in Hospitals on the Lines of Communication for Indian Troops and Followers

Year	Average ration strength	Max. No. equipped beds	Max. No. occupied beds	Average No. equipped beds	Average No. occupied beds	Percentage of ration strength			
						Maximum No.		Average No.	
						Equip.	Occup.	Equip.	Occup.
1917	19,317	2,303	2,236	1,073	957	11·92	11·58	5·55	4·95

The convalescent depot accommodation provided on the lines of communication for British and Dominion troops in

France during 1917 is shown in Table 13. Arrangements were made in November for a further 5,000 beds, but these were not required.

TABLE 13.—Accommodation provided in Convalescent Depots for British and Dominion Troops

Year	Average British and Dom. Str.	Max. No. equipped beds	Max. No. occupied beds	Average No. equipped beds	Average No. occupied beds	Percentage of ration strength			
						Maximum No.		Average No.	
						Equip.	Occup.	Equip.	Occup.
1917	1,894,511	43,735	34,817	30,690	20,936	2·31	1·84	1·62	1·11

Table 14 shows the convalescent depot accommodation provided for Indian troops and followers.

TABLE 14.—Accommodation provided in Convalescent Depots for Indian Troops and Followers

Year	Average ration strength	Max. No. equipped beds	Max. No. occupied beds	Average No. equipped beds	Average No. occupied beds	Percentage of ration strength			
						Maximum No.		Average No.	
						Equip.	Occup.	Equip.	Occup.
1917	19,317	686	580	243	140	3·55	3·00	1·26	·72

Non-battle Casualties

As was the case in 1916, records were kept of infectious diseases only, or of those likely to cause the greatest wastage among the troops, and of the recorded admissions to hospital for British and Dominion troops the principal causes are shown in Table 15. The similarity between the figures for 1916 and 1917 is striking.

TABLE 15.—Principal Recorded Causes of Inefficiency among British and Dominion Troops

	Admissions	Ratio per 1,000
Venereal diseases	48,508	25·60
Frostbite and trench foot	21,487	11·34
Nephritis	15,214	8·03
Rubella	9,418	4·97
Mumps	8,203	4·33
Dysentery	6,025	3·18

The principal causes of admission to hospital for infectious disease among Indian troops and native labour corps are shown in Table 16 with the ratios per 1,000 of ration strength.

TABLE 16.—Principal Causes of Inefficiency among Indian Troops and Native Labour Corps

Indian Troops only			Native Labour Corps		
	Admissions	Ratio per 1,000		Admissions	Ratio per 1,000
Mumps	983	85·75	Trachoma	6,094	96·88
Tuberculosis	235	20·50	Venereal diseases	955	15·18
Venereal diseases	198	17·27	Mumps	950	15·10
			Tuberculosis	245	3·89

Table 17 shows the admissions and deaths occurring among British and Dominion troops in France during 1917 for certain infectious and other diseases or disabilities, with the corresponding ratios per 1,000 of ration strength.

TABLE 17.—Principal Recorded Causes of Admission to Hospital of British and Dominion Troops in France, 1917, with Deaths and Ratios per 1,000 of ration strength

	Admissions	Deaths	Ratio per 1,000	
			Admissions	Deaths
Specific diseases due to infection				
Anthrax	8	1	·00	·00
Cerebro-spinal meningitis	692	192	·37	·10
Chicken-pox	139	—	·07	—
Diphtheria	2,273	20	1·20	·01
Dysentery	6,025	46	3·18	·02
Enteric fever — Typhoid	259	15	·14	·01
Enteric fever — Paratyphoid A	190	2	·10	·00
Enteric fever — Paratyphoid B	517	4	·27	·00
Enteric fever — Group	309	3	·16	·00
Erysipelas	271	7	·14	·00
Malaria	781	2	·41	·00
Measles	2,165	14	1·14	·01
Mumps	8,203	—	4·33	—
Pneumonia, lobar	2,157	193	1·14	·10
Relapsing fever	1	—	·00	—
Rubella	9,418	9	4·97	·00
Scarlet fever	563	2	·30	·00
Small-pox	1	—	·00	—
Tetanus *	271	134	·14	·07
Tuberculosis — Pulmonary	1,512	} 91	·80	} ·05
Tuberculosis — Other	148		·08	
Venereal diseases — Gonorrhœa	30,683	—	16·20	—
Venereal diseases — Syphilis	8,983	—	4·74	—
Venereal diseases — Other	8,842	—	4·67	—
Whooping-cough	19	—	·01	—
Other diseases or disabilities				
Trachoma	138	—	·07	—
Jaundice	940	9	·50	·00
Nephritis	15,214	201	8·03	·11
Frostbite and trench foot	21,487	3	11·34	·00
Scurvy	1	—	·00	—
Beri-beri	1	—	·00	—

* In addition 358 cases occurred in the United Kingdom during 1917 from wounds received in France.

Table 18 gives a similar analysis of admissions to hospital for Indian troops and native labour corps separately with the ratios per 1,000 of ration strength.

TABLE 18.—Principal Causes of Admission to Hospital of Indian Troops and Native Labour Corps in France, 1917, with Deaths and Ratios per 1,000 of strength

	Indian Troops only				Native Labour Corps			
	Admissions	Deaths	Ratio per 1,000		Admissions	Deaths	Ratio per 1,000	
			Admissions	Deaths			Admissions	Deaths
Specific diseases due to infection								
Cerebro-spinal meningitis	6	2	·52	·17	19	7	·30	·11
Chicken-pox	1	—	·09	—	34	—	·54	—
Diphtheria	—	—	—	—	1	—	·02	—
Dysentery	25	—	2·18	—	56	2	·89	·03
Enteric fever — Typhoid	1	1	·09	·09	3	2	·05	·03
Enteric fever — Paratyphoid	—	—	—	—	1	—	·02	—
Enteric fever — Group	1	—	·09	—	2	1	·03	·02
Erysipelas	1	—	·09	—	5	—	·08	—
Leprosy	—	—	—	—	1	—	·02	—
Malaria	12	—	1·05	—	49	2	·78	·03
Measles	38	1	3·32	·09	118	16	1·88	·25
Mumps	983	—	85·75	—	950	—	15·10	—
Pneumonia (lobar)	14	5	1·22	·44	59	19	·94	·30
Relapsing fever	9	—	·79	—	16	—	·25	—
Rubella	1	—	·09	—	3	—	·05	—
Small-pox	1	—	·09	—	—	—	—	—
Tetanus	—	—	—	—	3	1	·05	·02
Tuberculosis	235	44	20·50	3·84	245	108	3·89	1·72
Typhus	—	—	—	—	1	—	·02	—
Venereal diseases — Gonorrhœa	90	—	7·85	—	} 955	—	15·18	—
Venereal diseases — Syphilis	11	—	·96	—				
Venereal diseases — Other	97	—	8·46	—				
Other diseases or disabilities								
Trachoma	22	—	1·92	—	6,094	—	96·88	—
Jaundice	4	—	·35	—	3	—	·05	—
Nephritis	7	—	·61	—	17	—	·27	—
Scurvy	14	—	1·22	—	124	—	1·97	—
Beri-beri	—	—	—	—	169	1	2·69	·02
Ankylostomiasis	—	—	—	—	17	—	·27	—
Bilharziasis	—	—	—	—	29	—	·46	—
Frostbite and trench foot	—	—	—	—	26	—	·41	—

CHAPTER X

CASUALTIES IN THE BRITISH EXPEDITIONARY FORCE IN FRANCE AND FLANDERS, 1918

THE operations in France and Flanders during the closing year of the Great War were in many respects reminiscent of the fighting in 1914, with its memorable British retreat in face of overwhelming odds and its ultimate advance, but whereas then the one British army numbered roughly 150,000 men, the force in 1918 comprised five armies with a total average strength of nearly 2,000,000, with the experience of three and a half years of modern warfare behind them. Even so, the British and French troops were again outnumbered by the enemy massed in preparation for the great German offensives of 1918. The initial attack was launched on 21st March against the British Fifth and Third Armies on the front between the Sensée, south of Arras, and the Oise, and died down on 5th April. The series of battles fought by the British troops between these dates in their thirty-odd mile retreat are known as the First Battles of the Somme, 1918. The second German attack was directed against the British First and Second Armies in Flanders, in the Battles of the Lys from 9th to 29th April, when the British line was withdrawn some seven miles. The third and last German offensive, from 27th May to 8th June, in Champagne, was directed against the French Sixth Army, of which the British IXth Corps formed part, at the battle of the Aisne. The French counter-attack at the battles of the Marne, 20th July to 2nd August, 1918, with the British XXIInd Corps assisting, marked the turning-point in the operations. The British Army, heartened and re-equipped, commenced on 8th August the historic advance which proved to be the Advance to Victory. The first phase of this offensive included the battle of Amiens, the Second Battles of the Somme, 1918, and the Second Battles of Arras, 1918—a series of battles from one entrenched position to another over the devastated areas of the recent fighting, until finally the Hindenburg Line was broken in the beginning of October. The second phase was the final advance over open country until Mons was retaken and hostilities ceased on 11th November.

Despite the varying changes from trench warfare to retreat and from retreat to advance, the medical services were well prepared, and had schemes carefully considered and outlined to meet all contingencies, and although some units were lost in the retreat, and there occurred minor failures and slight confusions, inevitable either in retirement or rapid advance of a large force, the wounded were quickly and expeditiously evacuated by motor and other mechanical vehicles. During the twelve weeks of German offensive operations, upwards of 335,000 sick and wounded were evacuated from the front line to the base. The statistics for the year reflect both the nature of the operations and the preparedness of the medical services. The large numbers reported missing and prisoners of war indicate the enemy advance; the ratios per 1,000 constantly in medical units show the extent to which casualty clearing stations functioned as centres for recording, treating and distributing casualties; and that the accommodation provided in hospitals and convalescent depots on the lines of communication was ample is borne out by the high percentage of sick and wounded who were returned to duty in the theatre of operations.

The general sick rate of the troops was low, being 595·16 per 1,000 of ration strength. There was little or no infectious disease until influenza broke out with startling suddenness, first in June and July and again in October, in a world-wide epidemic which no medical service could control, and which laid low both friend and foe alike. The complete figures for the year are not available, but from 18th May to 10th August there were 226,615 admissions, including pyrexia of uncertain origin, and from 5th October to 28th December there were 87,323 admissions, including 6,627 cases of broncho-pneumonia, with 5,377 deaths. These totals alone over a period of 24 weeks show a ratio of 157·81 per 1,000 of ration strength, and give some idea of the extent of the epidemic.

In reviewing the figures for 1918, it should be remembered that there was no fighting after 11th November, and that there was considerable evacuation of sick and wounded repatriated prisoners of war.*

Strength

The average ration strength of the British Expeditionary Force in France and Flanders during 1918 is shown in Table 1.

TABLE 1.—Average Ration Strength

Period	Force	Officers	Other Ranks	Total
1918	British Expeditionary Force	77,537	1,911,837	1,989,374
	British and Dominion troops	77,421	1,779,605	1,857,026

Classification of Casualties

The total casualties sustained by the British Expeditionary Force in France during 1918 are shown in Table 2, with the ratios per 1,000 of ration strength.

TABLE 2.—Total Casualties

	Off.	O.R.	Total	Ratio per 1,000		
				Off.	O.R.	Total
Battle casualties ...	38,954	837,296	876,250	502·39	437·95	440·47
Non-battle casualties	45,711	1,138,293	1,184,004	589·54	595·39	595·16
Total ...	84,665	1,975,589	2,060,254¶	1,091·93	1,033·35	1,035·63

* The history of the Medical Services with the British Expeditionary Force in France during 1918 is dealt with in the *General History of the Medical Services*, vol. iii, pp. 201–326.

The proportion of battle casualties to non-battle casualties in the whole force was 1 to 1·2 officers; 1 to 1·4 other ranks; and 1 to 1·4 all ranks.

An analysis of the total casualties occurring in the British Expeditionary Force in France during 1918 is given in Table 3.

TABLE 3.—Classification and Percentages of Total Casualties

	Off.	O.R.	Total	Percentage of total casualties		
				Off.	O.R.	Total
A. *Battle casualties*:						
(a) Killed	5,111	75,365	80,476	6·04	3·81	3·91
(b) Died of wounds	3,044	43,040	46,084	3·60	2·18	2·24
(c) Missing	1,317	62,324	63,641	1·56	3·15	3·09
(d) Prisoners of war	3,749	103,898	107,647	4·43	5·26	5·22
(e) Wounded less (b)	25,733	552,669	578,402	30·39	27·97	28·07
B. *Non-battle casualties*:						
(f) Died of disease or injury	635	13,785	14,420	·75	·70	·70
(g) Sick or injured less (f)	45,076	1,124,508	1,169,584	53·24	56·92	56·77
Total A. and B.	84,665	1,975,589	2,060,254	—	—	—

Table 4 (*a*) shows this detail as percentages of battle casualties, and Table 4 (*b*) shows similarly the percentages of non-battle casualties.

TABLE 4 (*a*).—Percentages of Battle Casualties

	Off.	O.R.	Total
(a) Killed	13·12	9·00	9·18
(b) Died of wounds	7·81	5·14	5·26
(c) Missing	3·38	7·44	7·26
(d) Prisoners of war	9·62	12·41	12·28
(e) Wounded less (b)	66·06	66·01	66·01

TABLE 4 (*b*).—Percentages of Non-battle Casualties

	Off.	O.R.	Total
(f) Died of disease or injury	1·39	1·21	1·22
(g) Sick or injured less (f)	98·61	98·79	98·78

The casualties sustained by the British Expeditionary Force in France during 1918 may be further classified into permanent and temporary losses for military purposes in the field.

FRANCE AND FLANDERS, 1918

TABLE 5 (a).—Permanent Losses for Military Purposes in the Field

	Off.	O.R.	Total	Percentage of total casualties		
				Off.	O.R.	Total
A. *Battle casualties:*						
Killed	5,111	75,365	80,476	6·04	3·81	3·91
Died of wounds	3,044	43,040	46,084	3·60	2·18	2·24
Missing	1,317	62,324	63,641	1·56	3·15	3·09
Prisoners of war	3,749	103,898	107,647	4·43	5·26	5·22
Total	*13,221*	*284,627*	*297,848*	*15·62*	*14·41*	*14·46*
B. *Non-battle casualties:*						
Died of disease or injury	635	13,785	14,420	·75	·70	·70
Total permanent losses	13,856	298,412	312,268	16·37	15·10	15·16

TABLE 5 (b).—Temporary Losses for Military Purposes in the Field

	Off.	O.R.	Total	Percentage of total casualties		
				Off.	O.R.	Total
A. *Battle casualties:*						
Wounded less died of wounds	25,733	552,669	578,402	30·39	27·97	28·07
B. *Non-battle casualties:*						
Sick or injured less died of disease or injury	45,076	1,124,508	1,169,584	53·24	56·92	56·77
Total temporary losses	70,809	1,677,177	1,747,986	83·63	84·90	84·84

The relative proportions of the various classes of casualties to each other for the whole force in France during 1918 are shown in Table 6.

TABLE 6.—Proportions

	Officers	Other ranks	Total
1. Total battle casualties to total non-battle casualties	1 : 1·2	1 : 1·4	1 : 1·4
2. Total killed to total wounded including died of wounds	1 : 5·6	1 : 7·9	1 : 7·8
3. Permanent losses among battle casualties to total wounded less died of wounds	1 : 1·9	1 : 1·9	1 : 1·9
4. Permanent losses among non-battle casualties to total sick and injured less died of disease or injury	1 : 71·0	1 : 81·6	1 : 81·1
5. Total permanent losses to total temporary losses	1 : 5·1	1 : 5·6	1 : 5·6

Admissions to Hospital

Of the total casualties suffered by the British Expeditionary Force in France and Flanders during 1918, the numbers admitted to hospital and treated by the medical services are shown in Table 7.

TABLE 7.—Numbers admitted to Hospital

	Off.	O.R.	Total	Percentage of total casualties		
				Off.	O.R.	Total
Wounded	28,777	595,709	624,486	33·99	30·15	30·31
Sick or injured	45,711	1,138,293	1,184,004	53·99	57·62	57·47
Total	74,488	1,734,002	1,808,490	87·98	87·77	87·78

The proportion of wounded to sick and injured treated by the medical services was 1 to 1·6 officers; 1 to 1·9 other ranks; and 1 to 1·9 all ranks.

The casualties which were not treated by the medical services are shown in Table 8.

TABLE 8.—Casualties in the British Expeditionary Force not treated by the Medical Services

	Off.	O.R.	Total	Percentage of total casualties		
				Off.	O.R.	Total
Killed	5,111	75,365	80,476	6·04	3·81	3·91
Missing	1,317	62,324	63,641	1·56	3·15	3·09
Prisoners of war	3,749	103,898	107,647	4·43	5·26	5·22
Total	10,177	241,587	251,764	12·02	12·23	12·22

The numbers of sick and wounded admitted to hospital, and the disposal of cases, are shown in Table 9 (*a*), while the corresponding ratios per 1,000 of strength and percentages of total admissions are given in Tables 9 (*b*) and 9 (*c*) respectively. It must be remembered that the percentages in Table 9 (*c*) are calculated on the total admissions for the year plus the numbers remaining in medical charge on 29th December, 1917.

FRANCE AND FLANDERS, 1918

TABLE 9 (a).—Admissions to Hospital and Disposal of Cases, British Expeditionary Force, France 1918

	Wounded			Sick or injured			Total		
	Off.	O.R.	Total	Off.	O.R.	Total	Off.	O.R.	Total
Admissions	28,777	595,709	624,486	45,711	1,138,293	1,184,004	74,488	1,734,002	1,808,490
Deaths	3,044	43,040	46,084	635	13,785	14,420	3,679	56,825	60,504
Returned to duty in theatre of war	4,500	184,045	188,545	30,064	870,287	900,351	34,564	1,054,332	1,088,896
Evacuated overseas	21,700	380,764	402,464	15,088	270,812	285,900	36,788	651,576	688,364

TABLE 9 (b).—Ratios per 1,000 of Ration Strength

	Wounded			Sick or injured			Total		
	Off.	O.R.	Total	Off.	O.R.	Total	Off.	O.R.	Total
Admissions	371·14	311·59	313·91	589·54	595·39	595·16	960·68	906·98	909·07
Deaths	39·26	22·51	23·17	8·19	7·21	7·25	47·45	29·72	30·41
Returned to duty in theatre of war	58·04	96·27	94·78	387·74	455·21	452·58	445·77	551·48	547·36
Evacuated overseas	279·87	199·16	202·31	194·59	141·65	143·71	474·46	340·81	346·02

TABLE 9 (c).—Percentages of Total Admissions *

	Wounded			Sick or injured			Total		
	Off.	O.R.	Total	Off.	O.R.	Total	Off.	O.R.	Total
Deaths	10·38	7·00	7·15	1·35	1·13	1·14	4·81	3·10	3·17
Returned to duty in theatre of war	15·34	29·93	29·27	63·70	71·37	71·08	45·16	57·48	56·99
Evacuated overseas	73·98	61·93	62·47	31·97	22·21	22·57	48·07	35·52	36·02
Remaining in medical charge 31.12.18	·30	1·14	1·11	2·99	5·29	5·21	1·96	3·90	3·82

* Including numbers remaining in medical charge on 29th December, 1917.

The ratios per 1,000 of strength of the British Expeditionary Force in France constantly in medical units in the theatre of war for wounds, disease or injury, are shown in Table 10.

TABLE 10.—Ratio per 1,000 of Strength constantly in Medical Units in France

Year	Army Areas				Lines of Communication			Total
	Field Amb.	Rest Stn.	C.C.S.	Total	Hospital	Conval. Depot	Total	
1918	·18	·26	7·40	7·84	27·81	17·82	45·63	53·47

Hospital Accommodation

Table 11 shows the maximum number of equipped hospital beds for British and Dominion troops of the expeditionary force in France during 1918, the maximum number occupied on any one date and the average number occupied throughout the year, with the corresponding percentages of the average strength of British and Dominion troops. There was in addition an average of 10,390 " crisis " beds, making extra provision for ·56 per cent. of the strength. The hospital accommodation in the front area for British and Dominion troops averaged 5,660 beds, or ·3 per cent. of the strength, and the average number occupied represented ·17 per cent. of the strength.

The available records for 1918 make it possible to give some indication of the variety of nationalities housed and tended in the hospitals reserved for British and Dominion troops at one time or another during the year. Over a period of 38 weeks which the record covers, the average numbers in medical charge in hospitals included 91·2 per cent. British and Dominion, 2·3 per cent. American, 2·5 per cent. prisoners of war, and ·5 per cent. other nationalities, made up of Portuguese, Italians, Belgians, French, Russians, Serbs, Roumanians and Siamese. The hospitals set apart for the accommodation of Indian troops and native labour corps provided for Indians, Chinese, Cape Boys, Kaffirs, Egyptians and Fijians.

TABLE 11.—Accommodation provided in Hospitals on the Lines of Communication for British and Dominion Troops

Year	Average British and Dom. Str.	Max. No. equipped beds	Max. No. occupied beds	Average No. equipped beds	Average No. occupied beds	Percentage of ration strength			
						Maximum No.		Average No.	
						Equip.	Occup.	Equip.	Occup.
1918	1,857,026	87,933	73,572	76,050	54,766	4·74	3·96	4·10	2·95

Table 12 shows the hospital accommodation provided for Indian troops and native labour corps in France during 1918.

TABLE 12.—Accommodation provided in Hospitals on the Lines of Communication for Indian Troops and Native Labour Corps

Year	Average ration strength	Max. No. equipped beds	Max. No. occupied beds	Average No. equipped beds	Average No. occupied beds	Percentage of ration strength			
						Maximum No.		Average No.	
						Equip.	Occup.	Equip.	Occup.
1918	132,348	7,027	6,652	6,441	4,215	5·31	5·03	4·87	3·18

The convalescent depot accommodation provided on the lines of communication for British and Dominion troops in France during 1918 is shown in Table 13, while that for Indian troops and native labour corps is shown in Table 14.

TABLE 13.—Accommodation provided in Convalescent Depots for British and Dominion troops

Year	Average British and Dom. Str.	Max. No. equipped beds	Max. No. occupied beds	Average No. equipped beds	Average No. occupied beds	Percentage of ration strength			
						Maximum No.		Average No.	
						Equip.	Occup.	Equip.	Occup.
1918	1,857,026	62,142	46,427	55,421	35,586	3·35	2·50	2·98	1·92

TABLE 14.—Accommodation provided in Convalescent Depots for Indian troops and Native Labour Corps

Year	Average ration strength	Max. No. equipped beds	Max. No. occupied beds	Average No. equipped beds	Average No. occupied beds	Percentage of ration strength			
						Maximum No.		Average No.	
						Equip.	Occup.	Equip.	Occup.
1918	132,348	1,200	1,044	975	505	·91	·79	·74	·38

Non-battle Casualties

As was the case in both 1916 and 1917, records were kept only of infectious diseases or of those likely to cause the greatest wastage among the troops, and of the recorded admissions to hospital for British and Dominion troops in France during 1918 the principal causes are shown in Table 15. Influenza probably accounted for the greatest wastage during the year, but, as already explained, there are no complete records.

TABLE 15.—Principal Recorded Causes of Inefficiency among British and Dominion Troops

	Admissions	Ratio per 1,000
Venereal diseases...	60,099	32·36
Dysentery...	12,211	6·58
Frost bite and trench foot	7,096	3·82
Nephritis	6,422	3·46

The principal causes of admission to hospital for infectious diseases among Indian troops and native labour corps are shown in Table 16, with the ratios per 1,000 of ration strength.

TABLE 16.—Principal Causes of Inefficiency among Indian troops and Native Labour Corps

	Indian Troops			Native Labour Corps	
	Admissions	Ratio per 1,000		Admissions	Ratio per 1,000
Mumps	1,610	111·03	Mumps	1,715	14·55
Tuberculosis	136	9·38	Trachoma	1,449	12·30
			Dysentery	1,187	10·07
			Tuberculosis	661	5·61

Table 17 shows the admissions and deaths occurring among British and Dominion troops in France during 1918 for certain infectious and other diseases or disabilities, with the corresponding ratios per 1,000 of ration strength.

TABLE 17.—Principal Recorded Causes of Admission to Hospital of British and Dominion Troops in France, 1918, with Deaths and Ratios per 1,000 of ration strength

	Admissions	Deaths	Ratio per 1,000	
			Admissions	Deaths
Specific diseases due to infection				
Anthrax	1	—	·00	—
Cerebro-spinal meningitis	176	69	·09	·04
Chicken-pox	124	—	·07	—
Diphtheria	1,657	24	·89	·01
Dysentery	12,211	46	6·58	·02
Enteric fever Typhoid	98	17	·05	·01
Paratyphoid A	45	1	·02	·00
Paratyphoid B	182	1	·10	·00
Group	51	3	·03	·00
Erysipelas	280	7	·15	·00
Malaria	2,739	4	1·47	·00
Measles	1,221	4	·66	·00
Mumps	2,410	—	1·30	—
Pneumonia, lobar	1,921	352	1·03	·19
Relapsing fever	6	—	·00	—
Rubella	1,698	5	·91	·00
Scarlet fever	496	4	·27	·00
Small-pox	6	3	·00	·00
Tetanus	112	59	·06	·03
Tuberculosis	1,221	74	·66	·04
Venereal diseases	60,099	?	32·36	?
Whooping-cough	10	—	·01	—
Other diseases or disabilities				
Trachoma	105	—	·06	—
Jaundice	1,268	6	·68	·00
Nephritis	6,422	—	3·46	—
Frost bite and trench foot	7,096	—	3·82	—

Table 18 gives a similar analysis of admissions to hospital for Indian troops and native labour corps separately, with the ratios per 1,000 of ration strength.

TABLE 18.—Principal Causes of Admission to Hospital of Indian Troops and Native Labour Corps in France, 1918, with Deaths and Ratios per 1,000 of strength

	Indian Troops				Native Labour Corps			
	Admissions	Deaths	Ratio per 1,000		Admissions	Deaths	Ratio per 1,000	
			Admissions	Deaths			Admissions	Deaths
Specific diseases due to infection								
Cerebro-spinal fever	4	4	·28	·28	5	2	·04	·02
Chicken-pox	2	—	·14	—	21	—	·18	—
Diphtheria	1	—	·07	—	1	—	·01	—
Dysentery	38	—	2·62	—	1,187	5	10·07	·04
Enteric fever {Typhoid	—	—	—	—	5	1	·04	·01
Paratyphoid	—	—	—	—	15	2	·13	·02
Group	—	—	—	—	1	—	·01	
Erysipelas	—	—	—	—	15	—	·13	—
Leprosy	—	—	—	—	22	—	·19	—
Malaria	7	—	·48	—	78	—	·66	—
Measles	10	1	·69	·07	83	7	·70	·06
Mumps	1,610	—	111·03	—	1,715	—	14·55	—
Pneumonia, lobar	34	7	2·34	·48	72	14	·61	·12
Relapsing fever	10	—	·69	—	3	1	·03	·01
Rubella	1	—	·07	—	13	1	·11	·01
Scarlet fever	—	—	—	—	6	1	·05	·01
Tetanus	4	3	·28	·21	2	2	·02	·02
Tuberculosis	136	26	9·38	1·79	661	393	5·61	3·33
Venereal diseases	40	—	2·76	—	455	—	3·86	—
Other diseases								
Trachoma	5	—	·34	—	1,449	—	12·30	—
Jaundice	1	—	·07	—	—	—	—	—
Nephritis	1	—	·07	—	19	3	·16	·03
Scurvy	2	—	·14	—	199	1	1·69	·01
Beri-beri	—	—	—	—	65	4	·55	·03
Kala-azar	—	—	—	—	2	—	·02	—

CHAPTER XI

CASUALTIES IN THE BRITISH EXPEDITIONARY FORCE IN ITALY

IN November 1917, following the Austrian Caporetto offensive against Italy, a British and a French expeditionary force were sent from France to reinforce the Italian armies. The British force then absorbed the two British brigades of heavy artillery which had been attached to the Italian force since April of that year, and the casualties incurred during the period April to November 1917 have been included in the total for the campaign which lasted until 4th November 1918. The outstanding operations were the Austrian offensive in June 1918, which found the British troops engaged on the Asiago plateau, and the Italian offensive in October and November 1918, when the passage of the River Piave and the fighting in the Val d'Assa were the important incidents in which the British troops were concerned. Both kinds of terrain presented difficulties in the evacuation of casualties; the mountain roads of Alpine steepness with hairpin bends were too narrow and in places dangerous for the heavy type of motor ambulance car in use, and arrangements had to be made for the supply of a more suitable type; in the plains, the crossing of the Piave River entailed the evacuation of sick and wounded partly by boat and partly by hand carriage. Fortunately, casualties were few in number. Influenza was the chief cause of sick wastage among the troops, and although the prevalence of typhoid, dysentery and allied complaints among the civil population of the district was at all times a source of anxiety to the medical services, the incidence of these diseases among British troops remained comparatively low. In other respects the campaign in Italy presented no outstanding military medical features.*

Strength

The average ration strength of the total British force in Italy, and of British troops only, for the period November 1917 to December 1918 is shown in Table 1.

TABLE 1.—Average Ration Strength

Period	Force	Officers	Other Ranks	Labour	Total
November, 1917 to December, 1918	Total British Force	4,405	90,229	4,313	98,947
	British troops only	4,405	90,229	—	94,634

* The history of the medical services with the British troops in Italy is dealt with in the *General History of the Medical Services*, vol. iii, chap. xviii.

ITALY, 1918

Classification of Casualties

The total casualties sustained by the British Expeditionary Force in Italy for the period November 1917 to December 1918 are tabulated below, with the ratios per 1,000 of ration strength, and include, as already stated, battle casualties occurring prior to November 1917 among the British artillery.

TABLE 2.—Total Casualties

	British	Labour	Total	Ratio per 1,000		
				British	Labour	Total
Battle casualties	6,321	—	6,321	66·79	—	63·88
Non-battle casualties	51,311	7,071	58,382	542·20	1,639·46	590·03
Total	57,632	7,071	64,703	609·00	1,639·46	653·92

Casualties among the British troops only have been analysed in the following tables, but a separate analysis is made of labour casualties at the end of the chapter from the information available. Table 3 shows the number of British casualties and the ratios per 1,000 of strength for the duration of the campaign.

TABLE 3.—Casualties among British Troops

	Off.	O.R.	Total	Ratio per 1,000		
				Off.	O.R.	Total
Battle casualties	409	5,912	6,321	92·85	65·52	66·79
Non-battle casualties	3,316	47,995	51,311	752·78	531·92	542·20
Total	3,725	53,907	57,632	845·63	597·45	609·00

TABLE 4.—Classification and Percentages of Total British Casualties

	Off.	O.R.	Total	Percentage of total British casualties		
				Off.	O.R.	Total
A. *Battle casualties:*						
(a) Killed	90	1,140	1,230	2·41	2·11	2·13
(b) Died of wounds	—	58	58	—	·11	·10
(c) Missing	4	62	66	·11	·12	·11
(d) Prisoners of war *	26	252	278	·70	·47	·48
(e) Wounded less (b)	289	4,400	4,689	7·76	8·16	8·14
B. *Non-battle casualties:*						
(f) Died of disease or injury	26	733	759	·70	1·36	1·32
(g) Sick or injured less (f)	3,290	47,262	50,552	88·32	87·67	87·72
Total A. and B.	3,725	53,907	57,632	—	—	—

* Includes 1 officer and 3 other ranks who died as prisoners of war.

The proportion of battle casualties to non-battle casualties among British troops in Italy was 1 to 8·1 for officers, for other ranks and for all ranks.

An analysis of the total British casualties, excluding labour, is given in Table 4.

Table 5 (a) shows this detail as percentages of battle casualties, and Table 5 (b) shows similarly the percentages of non-battle casualties.

TABLE 5 (a).—Percentages of Battle Casualties

	Off.	O.R.	Total
(a) Killed	22·00	19·28	19·46
(b) Died of wounds	—	·98	·92
(c) Missing	·98	1·05	1.04
(d) Prisoners of war	6·36	4·26	4·40
(e) Wounded less (b)	70·66	74·43	74·18

TABLE 5 (b).—Percentages of Non-battle Casualties

	Off.	O.R.	Total
(f) Died of disease or injury	·78	1·53	1·48
(g) Sick or injured less (f)	99·22	98·47	98·52

The casualties sustained by the British troops during the campaign in Italy may be further classified into permanent and temporary losses for military purposes in the field.

TABLE 6 (a).—Permanent Losses for Military Purposes in the Field

	Off.	O.R.	Total	Percentage of total British casualties		
				Off.	O.R.	Total
A. Battle casualties:						
Killed	90	1,140	1,230	2·41	2·11	2·13
Died of wounds	—	58	58	—	·11	·10
Missing	4	62	66	·11	·12	·11
Prisoners of war	26	252	278	·70	·47	·48
Total	120	1,512	1,632	3·21	2·80	2·83
B. Non-battle casualties:						
Died of disease or injury	26	733	759	·70	1·36	1·32
Total permanent losses	146	2,245	2,391	3·92	4·16	4·15

ITALY, 1918

TABLE 6 (b).—Temporary Losses for Military Purposes in the Field

	Off.	O.R.	Total	Percentage of total British casualties		
				Off.	O.R.	Total
A. *Battle casualties:* Wounded less died of wounds	289	4,400	4,689	7·76	8·16	8·14
B. *Non-battle casualties:* Sick or injured less died of disease or injury	3,290	47,262	50,552	88·32	87·67	87·72
Total temporary losses	3,579	51,662	55,241	96·08	95·84	95·85

The relative proportions of the various classes of casualties to each other for British troops only are shown in Table 7.

TABLE 7.—Proportions

	Officers	Other Ranks	Total
1. Total battle casualties to total non-battle casualties	1 : 8·1	1 : 8·1	1 : 8·1
2. Total killed to total wounded including died of wounds	1 : 3·2	1 : 3·9	1 : 3·9
3. Permanent losses among battle casualties to total wounded less died of wounds	1 : 2·4	1 : 2·9	1 : 2·9
4. Permanent losses among non-battle casualties to total sick and injured less deaths from disease or injury	1 : 126·5	1 : 64·5	1 : 66·6
5. Total permanent losses to total temporary losses	1 : 24·5	1 : 23·0	1 : 23·1

Admissions to Hospital

Of the total casualties suffered by the British troops in Italy, the numbers admitted to hospital and treated by the medical services are shown in Table 8.

TABLE 8.—Numbers admitted to Hospital

	Off.	O.R.	Total	Percentage of total British casualties		
				Off.	O.R.	Total
Wounded	289	4,458	4,747	7·76	8·27	8·24
Sick or injured	3,316	47,995	51,311	89·02	89·03	89·03
Total	3,605	52,453	56,058	96·79	97·30	97·27

The proportion of wounded to sick and injured treated by the medical services was 1 to 11·5 officers; 1 to 10·8 other ranks; and 1 to 10·8 all ranks.

The casualties which were not treated by the medical services are shown in Table 9.

TABLE 9.—Casualties not treated by the Medical Services

	Off.	O.R.	Total	Percentage of total British casualties		
				Off.	O.R.	Total
Killed	90	1,140	1,230	2·41	2·11	2·13
Missing	4	62	66	·11	·12	·11
Prisoners of war	26	252	278	·70	·47	·48
Total	120	1,454	1,574	3·21	2·70	2·73

The numbers of sick and wounded admitted to hospital and their disposal are shown in Table 10 (*a*), while the corresponding ratios per 1,000 of ration strength, and the percentages of total admissions are given in Tables 10 (*b*) and 10 (*c*) respectively.

TABLE 10 (*a*).—Admissions to Hospital and Disposal of Cases—British Troops only

	Wounded			Sick or injured			Total		
	Off.	O.R.	Total	Off.	O.R.	Total	Off.	O.R.	Total
Admissions	289	4,458	4,747	3,316	47,995	51,311	3,605	52,453	56,058
Deaths	—	58	58	26	733	759	26	791	817
Returned to duty in the theatre of war	99	1,857	1,956	2,504	32,876	35,380	2,603	34,733	37,336
Evacuated:									
(*a*) To France	45	1,093	1,138	330	7,510	7,840	375	8,603	8,978
(*b*) To U.K. via France	143	1,388	1,531	350	5,252	5,602	493	6,640	7,133
Total evacuated	*188*	*2,481*	*2,669*	*680*	*12,762*	*13,442*	*868*	*15,243*	*16,111*

TABLE 10 (*b*).—Ratios per 1,000 of Ration Strength

	Wounded			Sick or injured			Total		
	Off.	O.R.	Total	Off.	O.R.	Total	Off.	O.R.	Total
Admissions	65·61	49·41	50·16	752·73	531·92	542·20	818·39	581·33	592·39
Deaths	—	·64	·61	5·90	8·12	8·02	5·90	8·77	8·63
Returned to duty in the theatre of war	22·47	20·58	20·67	568·44	364·36	373·86	590·92	384·94	394·53
Evacuated:									
(*a*) To France	10·22	12·11	12·03	74·91	83·23	82·85	85·13	95·35	94·87
(*b*) To U.K. via France	32·46	15·38	16·18	79·46	58·21	59·20	111·92	73·59	75·37
Total evacuated	*42·68*	*27·50*	*28·21*	*154·37*	*141·44*	*142·04*	*197·05*	*168·94*	*170·25*

ITALY, 1918

TABLE 10 (c).—Percentages of Total Admissions

	Wounded			Sick or injured			Total		
	Off.	O.R.	Total	Off.	O.R.	Total	Off.	O.R.	Total
Deaths	—	1·30	1·22	·78	1·53	1·48	·72	1·51	1·46
Returned to duty in the theatre of war	34·26	41·66	41·21	75·51	68·50	68·95	72·20	66·22	66·60
Evacuated :									
(a) To France	15·57	24·52	23·97	9·95	15·65	15·28	10·40	16·40	16·02
(b) To U.K. via France	49·48	31·13	32·25	10·55	10·94	10·92	13·68	12·66	12·72
Total evacuated	*65·05*	*55·65*	*56·22*	*20·51*	*26·59*	*26·20*	*24·08*	*29·06*	*28·74*
Remaining in medical charge on 31.12.18	·69	1·39	1·35	3·20	3·38	3·37	3·00	3·21	3·20

Table 11 shows the admissions to hospital and disposal of cases, with the ratios per 1,000 of the strength, for labour battalions attached to the British force in Italy.

TABLE 11.—Admissions to Hospital and Disposal of Cases—Labour Battalions only

	Number	Ratio per 1,000
Admissions	7,071	1,639·46
Deaths	143	33·16
Returned to duty in theatre of war	6,135	1,422·44
Evacuated to France	261	60·51
In medical charge on 31.12.18	353	81·85
Unaccounted for	159	36·87

For the whole British force in Italy, inclusive of labour, the ratios per 1,000 of ration strength constantly in medical units are shown in Table 12.

TABLE 12.—Ratios per 1,000 of Strength constantly in Medical Units

	Total Force		British only, in Italy
	In Italy	Marseilles	
In hospitals	30·76	15·68	30·21
„ convalescent depots	10·24	?	10·71

Hospital Accommodation

Table 13 shows the maximum number of equipped hospital beds provided for the British Expeditionary Force in Italy, inclusive of labour, the maximum number of occupied beds and the average number of occupied beds on any one date, with percentages of the average ration strength of the whole force.

TABLE 13.—Accommodation Provided in Hospitals on the Lines of Communication

Period		Average ration strength 98,947	Maximum No. equipped beds	Maximum No. occupied beds	Average No. occupied beds	Percentage of ration strength		
						Maximum No.		Average No. occupied
						Equip.	Occup.	
Nov. 1917 to Dec. 1918	Italy		6,823	4,221	3,223	6·90	4·27	3·26
	Marseilles		3,000	2,650	1,552	3·03	2·68	1·57
	Total ...		9,823	6,871	4,775	9·93	6·94	4·83

The convalescent depot accommodation provided for the force, exclusive of Marseilles, is shown in Table 14.

TABLE 14.—Accommodation Provided in Convalescent Depots

Period	Average ration strength	Maximum No. equipped beds	Maximum No. occupied beds	Average No. occupied beds	Percentage of ration strength		
					Maximum No.		Average No. occupied
					Equip.	Occup.	
Nov. 1917 to Dec. 1918	98,947	2,603	1,369	1,014	2·63	1·38	1·02

Non-battle Casualties

Information regarding the admissions to hospital for the base and lines of communication area, excluding Taranto, is confined to infectious diseases only. Table 15, therefore, shows the principal infectious diseases causing inefficiency in the British force in Italy, with the corresponding ratios per 1,000 of ration strength. The figures for influenza, on the other hand, include Taranto and as the strength of troops there is not known, it is not possible to give a correct ratio for this disease.

TABLE 15.—Principal Causes of Inefficiency from Infectious Diseases

	Admissions	Ratio per 1,000
Influenza	17,088*	?
Venereal diseases	3,956	41·80
Dysentery	901	9·52
Malaria	279	2·95
Pneumonia	229	2·42

* Taranto included

It has been possible for this campaign to give an analysis of the causes of admissions to hospital for British troops occupying the forward area, and the chief of these are shown in Table 16, together with the deaths occurring and the ratios per 1,000 of the average strength of front-line troops.

TABLE 16.—Principal Causes of Inefficiency among Troops in the Forward Area

Cause	Admissions	Deaths	Ratio per 1,000	
			Adms.	Deaths
Influenza	11,514	481	146·72	6·12
Inflammation of connective tissue	3,722	—	47·43	—
Diarrhœa	3,129	4	39·87	·05
Pyrexia of uncertain origin	2,754	—	35·09	—
Venereal diseases	1,888	—	24·06	—
Dental caries	1,029	—	13·11	—
Dysentery	859	17	10·95	·22

As in most theatres of war the returns from forward areas and lines of communication are combined, the information contained in Table 17 is both interesting and valuable as showing the diseases from which the front-line troops in Italy suffered during the campaign.

TABLE 17.—Principal Causes of Admissions to Hospital of British Troops in the Forward Area, November 1917 to December 1918, with the ratios per 1,000 of average front-line strength

Average Ration Strength, Forward Area 78,477	Admissions	Ratio per 1,000
Specific diseases due to infection		
Anthrax	2	·03
Cerebro-spinal fever	6	·08
Chicken-pox	1	·01
Diphtheria	141	1·80
Dysentery	859	10·95
Enteric fever — Typhoid	32	·41
Enteric fever — Paratyphoid A	22	·28
Enteric fever — Paratyphoid B	58	·74
Enteric fever — Group	22	·28
Erysipelas	21	·27
Influenza	11,514	146·72
Malaria	88	1·12
Measles	27	·34
Mediterranean fever	1	·01
Mumps	111	1·41
Pneumonia	173	2·20
Pyrexia of uncertain origin	2,754	35·09
Rheumatic fever	21	·27
Rubella	25	·32
Scarlet fever	58	·74
Small-pox	1	·01
Tetanus	3	·04
Tuberculosis, pulmonary	81	1·03
Venereal diseases	1,888	24·06
Diseases classified under systems		
Diseases of the		
Eye — Conjunctivitis	19	·24
Eye — Trachoma	1	·01
Eye — Other	145	1·85
Ear — Middle ear disease	42	·54
Ear — Otitis media	38	·48
Ear — Otorrhœa	5	·06
Circulatory system — Valvular disease of the heart	37	·47
Circulatory system — Disordered action of the heart	261	3·33
Circulatory system — Varix	5	·06
Respiratory system — Bronchitis and broncho-pneumonia	607	7·73
Respiratory system — Pleurisy	157	2·00
Lymphatic system	31	·40
Teeth and gums	1,029	13·11
Digestive system — Tonsillitis	455	5·80
Digestive system — Gastritis	90	1·15
Digestive system — Gastralgia	22	·28
Digestive system — Enteritis	11	·14
Digestive system — Diarrhœa	3,129	39·87
Digestive system — Appendicitis	74	·94
Digestive system — Jaundice	599	7·63
Digestive system — Hernia	112	1·43
Digestive system — Hæmorrhoids	189	2·41
Skin — Scabies	580	7·39
Skin — Impetigo	188	2·40
Skin — Psoriasis	10	·13
Areolar tissue — Inflammation of connective tissue	3,722	47·43
Areolar tissue — Boils	279	3·56
Areolar tissue — Abscesses	60	·76
Organs of locomotion — Myalgia	739	9·42
Organs of locomotion — Synovitis	142	1·81
Organs of locomotion — Lumbago	5	·06
Urinary system — Albuminuria	320	4·08
Urinary system — Nephritis	192	2·45
Urinary system — Urethritis	23	·29
Miscellaneous diseases		
Debility	425	5·42
Injuries		
Trench foot or frost bite	26	·33
Sprains	97	1·24
Contusions	19	·24
Total diseases and disabilities reported	31,794	405·14

Work of the Army Dental Service

Records of the dental work carried out by a monthly average number of six dental surgeons and eight dental mechanics attached to the British force in Italy have been analysed, and are summarised in Table 18 for the year January to December 1918.

TABLE 18.—Records of Dental Treatment in the British Force in Italy from January to December 1918

	Total number	Monthly average
Extractions	13,429	1,119
Fillings	6,801	567
Impressions taken	4,176	348
Scalings	1,245	104
Dressings	6,512	543
As_2O_3 dressings	920	77
Root treatment	1,279	107
$AgNO_3$ treatment	663	55
Number of repairs finished	1,464	122
Number of dentures finished	3,008	251
Daily average number of cases treated	117·41	

CHAPTER XII

CASUALTIES IN THE BRITISH SALONIKA FORCE ON THE MACEDONIAN FRONT, 1915–1918

THE British Salonika Force, consisting of British and Dominion troops, some Indian troops and a large following of labour enrolled locally, carried on operations in Macedonia from October 1915 until the end of October 1918, in conjunction with the allied forces of French, Serbs, Greeks, Russians and Italians against the Central Powers. The principal fighting occurred from August to October 1916 in the Struma Valley; in April and May 1917 on the Doiran front; and the final offensive along the Doiran to the Monastir line in September 1918. During the remainder of the campaign fighting was spasmodic. Hills, valleys, rivers, lakes and marshes comprised the greater part of the country occupied by the troops. Road and rail communications were bad and to a large extent dominated military operations. The climate was extreme; intense cold in winter accompanied by a wet season, and great heat in summer, broken by heavy thunder and rain storms. The average temperature varied in winter from 38° F. to 52° F. and in summer from 70° F. to 90° F., though greater extremes were experienced in various parts. The greatest enemy of the force was malaria, which, always endemic in the country, was intensified by conditions of warfare.*

Strength

The average ration strength of the total British Salonika Force year by year is shown in Table 1.

TABLE 1.—Average Ration Strength

Year	British and Dominion Troops			Indian Troops			Labour raised locally	Grand Total		
	Off.	O.R.	Total	Off.	O.R.	Total		Off.	O.R.	Total
1915†	2,032	58,857	60,889	—	—	—	—	2,032	58,857	60,889
1916	4,877	118,517	123,394	10	2,606	2,616	—	4,887	121,123	126,010
1917	6,405	176,178	182,583	13	2,095	2,108	17,574	6,418	195,847	202,265
1918	5,005	123,742	128,747	28	3,764	3,792	27,408	5,033	154,914	159,947

† October to December.

---

* The history of the Medical Services on the Macedonian Front is dealt with in the *General History of the Medical Services*, vol. iv, pp. 62–148.

Classification of Casualties

Reliable information regarding the battle casualties among Indian troops and native labour battalions is lacking, but the numbers are believed to have been small and are probably included in the non-battle casualties. From all the available data it is estimated that the approximate total casualties for all ranks in the British Salonika Force from October 1915 to December 1918, with the corresponding average annual ratios per 1,000 of strength, were as shown in Table 2.

TABLE 2.—Total Casualties

	British and Dominion troops	Indian troops	Labour	Total	Average annual ratio per 1,000			
					British and Dominion	Indian	Labour	Total
Battle casualties	23,762	20	5	23,787	59·01	2·47	·13	53·31
Non-battle casualties	481,262	4,044	17,237	502,543	1,195·14	474·82	383·18	1,126·39
Total ...	505,024	4,064	17,242	526,330	1,254·14	477·28	383·31	1,179·71

As the information regarding the casualties among British and Dominion troops throughout the campaign is at once more accurate and more extensive, the following tables of casualties deal solely with them, and calculations have been based on the average strength of these troops only. In greater detail, therefore, the total casualties among the British and Dominion troops for the period October 1915 to December 1918 are given in Table 3.

TABLE 3.—Casualties among British and Dominion Troops

	Officers	Other Ranks	Total	Average annual ratio per 1,000		
				Off.	O.R.	Total
Battle casualties ...	1,157	22,605	23,762	77·73	58·29	59·01
Non-battle casualties	13,843	467,419	481,262	929·91	1,205·31	1,195·14
Total	15,000	490,024	505,024	1,007·64	1,263·60	1,254·14

The proportion of battle casualties to non-battle casualties among British and Dominion troops was 1 to 11·9 officers; 1 to 20·7 other ranks; and 1 to 20·3 all ranks.

An analysis of the total casualties among British and Dominion troops during the campaign is given in Table 4.

TABLE 4.—Classification and Percentages of Total British and Dominion Casualties

	Off.	O.R.	Total	Percentage of total British and Dominion casualties		
				Off.	O.R.	Total
A. Battle Casualties:						
(a) Killed	145	2,652	2,797	·97	·54	·55
(b) Died of wounds	76	1,223	1,299	·51	·25	·26
(c) Missing	74	1,510	1,584	·49	·31	·31
(d) Prisoners of war	7	1,187	1,194	·04	·24	·24
(e) Wounded less (b)	855	16,033	16,888	5·70	3·27	3·35
B. Non-battle Casualties:						
(f) Died of disease or injury	76	3,668	3,744	·51	·75	·74
(g) Sick or injured less (f)	13,767	463,751	477,518	91·78	94·64	94·55
Total A. and B.	15,000	490,024	505,024	—	—	—

Table 5 (*a*) shows this detail as percentages of battle casualties, and Table 5 (*b*) shows similarly the percentages of non-battle casualties.

TABLE 5 (*a*).—Percentages of Battle Casualties

	Off.	O.R.	Total
(a) Killed	12·53	11·73	11·77
(b) Died of wounds	6·57	5·41	5·47
(c) Missing	6·40	6·68	6·67
(d) Prisoners of war	·60	5·25	5·02
(e) Wounded less (b)	73·90	70·93	71·07

TABLE 5 (*b*).—Percentages of Non-battle Casualties

	Off.	O.R.	Total
(f) Died of disease or injury	·55	·78	·78
(g) Sick or injured less (f)	99·45	99·22	99·22

The casualties sustained by the British and Dominion troops during the campaign in Macedonia may be further classified into permanent and temporary losses for military purposes in the field.

MACEDONIA, 1915–1918

TABLE 6 (a).—Permanent Losses for Military Purposes in the Field

	Off.	O.R.	Total	Percentage of total British & Dominion casualties		
				Off.	O.R.	Total
A. Battle Casualties:						
Killed	145	2,652	2,797	·97	·54	·55
Died of wounds	76	1,223	1,299	·51	·25	·26
Missing	74	1,510	1,584	·49	·31	·31
Prisoners of war	7	1,187	1,194	·04	·24	·24
Total	*302*	*6,572*	*6,874*	*2·01*	*1·34*	*1·36*
B. Non-battle Casualties:						
Died of disease or injury	76	3,668	3,744	·51	·75	·74
Total permanent losses	378	10,240	10,618	2·52	2·09	2·10

TABLE 6 (b).—Temporary Losses for Military Purposes in the Field

	Off.	O.R.	Total	Percentage of total British & Dominion casualties		
				Off.	O.R.	Total
A. Battle Casualties:						
Wounded less died of wounds	855	16,033	16,888	5·70	3·27	3·35
B. Non-battle Casualties:						
Sick or injured less died of disease or injury	13,767	463,751	477,518	91·78	94·64	94·55
Total temporary losses	14,622	479,784	494,406	97·48	97·91	97·90

The relative proportions of the various classes of casualties to each other for British and Dominion troops of the British Salonika Force are indicated in Table 7.

TABLE 7.—Proportions

	Officers	Other ranks	Total
1. Total battle casualties to total non-battle casualties	1 : 11·9	1 : 20·7	1 : 20·3
2. Total killed to total wounded including died of wounds	1 : 6·4	1 : 6·5	1 : 6·5
3. Permanent losses among battle casualties to total wounded less died of wounds	1 : 2·6	1 : 2·3	1 : 2·3
4. Permanent losses among non-battle casualties to total sick and injured less deaths from disease or injury	1 : 181·1	1 : 126·4	1 : 127·5
5. Total permanent losses to total temporary losses	1 : 38·7	1 : 46·9	1 : 46·6

Admissions to Hospital

Of the total casualties among the British and Dominion troops, the numbers admitted to hospital and treated by the medical services are shown in Table 8.

TABLE 8.—Numbers admitted to Hospital

	Off.	O.R.	Total	Percentage of total British and Dominion casualties		
				Off.	O.R.	Total
Wounded	931	17,256	18,187	6·21	3·52	3·60
Sick or injured	13,843	467,419	481,262	92·29	95·39	95·29
Total	14,774	484,675	499,449	98·49	98·91	98·90

The proportion of wounded to sick or injured treated by the medical services was 1 to 14·9 officers; 1 to 27·1 other ranks; and 1 to 26·5 all ranks.

The casualties which were not treated by the medical services are shown in Table 9.

TABLE 9.—Casualties not treated by the Medical Services

	Off.	O.R.	Total	Percentage of total British and Dominion casualties		
				Off.	O.R.	Total
Killed	145	2,652	2,797	·97	·54	·55
Missing	74	1,510	1,584	·49	·31	·31
Prisoners of war	7	1,187	1,194	·04	·24	·24
Total	226	5,349	5,575	1·51	1·09	1·10

Table 10 gives an analysis of the numbers treated by the medical services in the theatre of operations, arranged by years under the different headings of disposal for purposes of comparison. Particular attention should be paid to the numbers evacuated overseas in 1916 compared with subsequent years, with the resulting increase in the numbers returned to duty in the theatre of war in the later years.

The numbers of sick and wounded admitted to hospital and the disposal of cases in the same year are shown in Table 11 (*a*), while the corresponding ratios per 1,000 of ration strength and the percentages of total admissions are shown in Tables 11 (*b*) and 11 (*c*) respectively.

191

TABLE 10.—Numbers Admitted to Hospital and their Disposal by Years—British and Dominion Troops

	Year	Wounded			Sick or injured			Total		
		Off.	O.R.	Total	Off.	O.R.	Total	Off.	O.R.	Total
Admissions	1915*	34	481	515	363	9,746	10,109	397	10,227	10,624
	1916	323	4,675	4,998	4,400	126,543	130,943	4,723	131,218	135,941
	1917	336	7,421	7,757	4,607	167,350	171,957	4,943	174,771	179,714
	1918	238	4,679	4,917	4,473	163,780	168,253	4,711	168,459	173,170
	Total	931	17,256	18,187	13,843	467,419	481,262	14,774	484,675	499,449
Deaths	1915*	—	11	11	—	39	39	—	50	50
	1916	26	314	340	22	704	726	48	1,018	1,066
	1917	29	576	605	14	723	737	43	1,299	1,342
	1918	21	322	343	40	2,202	2,242	61	2,524	2,585
	Total	76	1,223	1,299	76	3,668	3,744	152	4,891	5,043
Returned to duty in the theatre of operations	1915*	10	163	173	188	2,888	3,076	198	3,051	3,249
	1916	52	947	999	2,435	70,898	73,333	2,487	71,845	74,332
	1917	206	5,169	5,375	3,870	141,676	145,546	4,076	146,845	150,921
	1918	120	3,252	3,372	3,595	122,680	126,275	3,715	125,932	129,647
	Total	388	9,531	9,919	10,088	338,142	348,230	10,476	347,673	358,149
Evacuated overseas	1915*	23	246	269	102	3,695	3,797	125	3,941	4,066
	1916	227	3,078	3,305	1,888	50,758	52,646	2,115	53,836	55,951
	1917	109	1,728	1,837	618	12,850	13,468	727	14,578	15,305
	1918	105	1,333	1,438	481	11,036	11,517	586	12,369	12,955
	Total	464	6,385	6,849	3,089	78,339	81,428	3,553	84,724	88,277
To U.K. under "Y" scheme †	1917	—	—	—	7	300	307	7	300	307
	1918	—	—	—	335	34,120	34,455	335	34,120	34,455
	Total	—	—	—	342	34,420	34,762	342	34,420	34,762

* October to December. † This was a scheme for sending malarial convalescents to England.

TABLE 11(a).—Admissions to Hospital and Disposal of Cases in each Year—British and Dominion Troops

Year		Wounded			Sick or injured			Total		
		Off.	O.R.	Total	Off.	O.R.	Total	Off.	O.R.	Total
1915*	Admissions	34	481	515	363	9,746	10,109	397	10,227	10,624
	Deaths	—	11	11	—	39	39	—	50	50
	Returned to duty in theatre of war	10	163	173	188	2,888	3,076	198	3,051	3,249
	Evacuated overseas	23	246	269	102	3,695	3,797	125	3,941	4,066
1916	Admissions	323	4,675	4,998	4,400	126,543	130,943	4,723	131,218	135,941
	Deaths	26	314	340	22	704	726	48	1,018	1,066
	Returned to duty in theatre of war	52	947	999	2,435	70,898	73,333	2,487	71,845	74,332
	Evacuated overseas	227	3,078	3,305	1,888	50,758	52,646	2,115	53,836	55,951
1917	Admissions	336	7,421	7,757	4,607	167,350	171,957	4,943	174,771	179,714
	Deaths	29	576	605	14	723	737	43	1,299	1,342
	Returned to duty in theatre of war	206	5,169	5,375	3,870	141,676	145,546	4,076	146,845	150,921
	Evacuated overseas	109	1,728	1,837	618	12,850	13,468	727	14,578	15,305
	To U.K. " Y " scheme	—	—	—	7	300	307	7	300	307
1918	Admissions	238	4,679	4,917	4,473	163,780	168,253	4,711	168,459	173,170
	Deaths	21	322	343	40	2,202	2,242	61	2,524	2,585
	Returned to duty in theatre of war	120	3,252	3,372	3,595	122,680	126,275	3,715	125,932	129,647
	Evacuated overseas	105	1,333	1,438	481	11,036	11,517	586	12,369	12,955
	To U.K. " Y " scheme	—	—	—	335	34,120	34,455	335	34,120	34,455
Total	Admissions	931	17,256	18,187	13,843	467,419	481,262	14,774	484,675	499,449
	Deaths	76	1,223	1,299	76	3,668	3,744	152	4,891	5,043
	Returned to duty in theatre of war	388	9,531	9,919	10,088	338,142	348,230	10,476	347,673	358,149
	Evacuated overseas	464	6,385	6,849	3,089	78,339	81,428	3,553	84,724	88,277
	To U.K. " Y " scheme	—	—	—	342	34,420	34,762	342	34,420	34,762

* October–December.

TABLE 11 (b).—Ratios per 1,000 of Ration Strength

Year		Wounded			Sick or injured			Total		
		Off.	O.R.	Total	Off.	O.R.	Total	Off.	O.R.	Total
1915*	Admissions	16·73	8·17	8·46	178·64	165·59	166·02	195·37	173·76	174·48
	Deaths	—	·19	·18	—	·66	·64	—	·85	·82
	Returned to duty in theatre of war	4·92	2·77	2·84	92·52	49·07	50·52	97·44	51·84	53·36
	Evacuated overseas	11·32	4·18	4·42	50·20	62·78	62·36	61·52	66·96	66·78
1916	Admissions	66·23	39·45	40·50	902·19	1,067·72	1,061·18	968·42	1,107·17	1,101·68
	Deaths	5·33	2·65	2·76	4·51	5·94	5·88	9·84	8·59	8·64
	Returned to duty in theatre of war	10·66	7·99	8·10	499·28	598·21	594·30	509·94	606·20	602·40
	Evacuated overseas	46·55	25·97	26·78	387·12	428·28	426·65	433·67	454·25	453·43
1917	Admissions	52·46	42·12	42·48	719·28	949·89	941·80	771·74	992·01	984·29
	Deaths	4·53	3·27	3·31	2·19	4·10	4·04	6·71	7·37	7·35
	Returned to duty in theatre of war	32·16	29·34	29·44	604·22	804·16	797·15	636·38	833·50	826·59
	Evacuated overseas	17·02	9·81	10·06	96·49	72·94	73·76	113·51	82·75	83·82
	To U.K. "Y" scheme	—	—	—	1·09	1·70	1·68	1·09	1·70	1·68
1918	Admissions	47·55	37·81	38·19	893·71	1,323·56	1,306·85	941·26	1,361·37	1,345·04
	Deaths	4·20	2·60	2·66	7·99	17·80	17·41	12·19	20·40	20·08
	Returned to duty in theatre of war	23·98	26·28	26·19	718·28	991·42	980·80	742·26	1,017·70	1,006·99
	Evacuated overseas	20·98	10·77	11·17	96·10	89·19	89·45	117·08	99·96	100·93
	To U.K. "Y" scheme	—	—	—	66·93	275·73	267·62	66·93	275·73	267·62
Average annual ratio per 1,000	Admissions	62·45	44·50	43·10	929·91	1,205·31	1,195·14	992·58	1,249·81	1,230·30
	Deaths	5·02	3·15	3·23	5·02	9·46	9·30	10·26	12·61	12·53
	Returned to duty in theatre of war	26·20	24·58	24·63	677·73	871·95	864·77	703·71	896·52	889·41
	Evacuated overseas	31·22	16·47	17·01	207·42	202·01	202·21	238·65	218·47	219·22
	To U.K. "Y" scheme	—	—	—	22·93	88·76	86·33	22·93	88·76	86·33

* October–December.

TABLE 11 (c).—Percentages of Total Admissions

Year		Wounded			Sick or injured			Total		
		Off.	O.R.	Total	Off.	O.R.	Total	Off.	O.R.	Total
1915*	Deaths	—	2·29	2·14	—	·40	·39	—	·49	·47
	Returned to duty in theatre of war	29·41	33·89	33·59	51·79	29·63	30·43	49·87	29·83	30·58
	Evacuated overseas	67·65	51·14	52·23	28·10	37·91	37·56	31·49	38·54	38·27
	In medical charge 31.12.15	2·94	12·68	12·04	20·11	32·06	31·62	18·64	31·14	30·68
1916	Deaths	8·02	6·63	6·72	·49	·54	·54	1·00	·76	·77
	Returned to duty in theatre of war	16·05	20·00	19·74	54·44	54·68	54·67	51·84	53·45	53·40
	Evacuated overseas	70·06	64·99	65·32	42·21	39·14	39·25	44·09	40·06	40·19
	In medical charge 30.12.16	5·87	8·38	8·22	2·86	5·64	5·54	3·07	5·73	5·64
1917	Deaths	8·17	7·37	7·40	·30	·41	·41	·84	·71	·72
	Returned to duty in theatre of war	58·03	66·12	65·76	81·73	81·12	81·11	80·08	80·47	80·46
	Evacuated overseas	30·70	22·10	22·48	13·05	7·36	7·51	14·28	7·99	8·16
	To U.K. " Y " scheme	—	—	—	·15	·17	·17	·14	·16	·16
	In medical charge 29.12.17	3·10	4·41	4·36	4·77	10·94	10·80	4·66	10·67	10·50
1918	Deaths	8·43	6·41	6·50	·85	1·20	1·20	1·23	1·34	1·34
	Returned to duty in theatre of war	48·19	64·73	63·95	76·51	67·08	67·31	75·08	67·02	67·22
	Evacuated overseas	42·17	26·53	27·27	10·24	6·03	6·14	11·84	6·58	6·72
	To U.K. " Y " scheme	—	—	—	7·12	18·66	18·37	6·77	18·16	17·87
	In medical charge 31.12.18	1·21	2·33	2·28	5·28	7·03	6·98	5·08	6·90	6·85
Total	Deaths	8·16	7·09	7·14	·55	·78	·78	1·03	1·01	1·01
	Returned to duty in theatre of war	41·68	55·23	54·54	72·87	72·34	72·36	70·91	71·73	71·71
	Evacuated overseas	49·84	37·00	37·66	22·31	16·76	16·92	24·05	17·48	17·67
	To U.K. " Y " scheme	—	—	—	2·47	7·36	7·22	2·31	7·10	6·96
	In medical charge 31.12.18	·32	·68	·66	1·80	2·76	2·72	1·70	2·68	2·65

* October–December.

Of the whole British Salonika Force, including Indian troops and labour, the ratios per 1,000 of strength constantly in medical units are shown in Table 12.

TABLE 12.—Ratio per 1,000 of Strength constantly in Medical Units

	British Salonika Force	British & Dominion Troops only
In divisional medical units	3·69	4·09
,, hospitals	60·36	65·23
,, convalescent depots	27·96	30·98
Total	92·01	100·30

Hospital Accommodation

Table 13 shows the maximum number of equipped hospital beds provided year by year for the whole British Salonika Force, the maximum number of occupied beds on any one date, and the average number of occupied beds throughout the year with the corresponding percentages of the total strength of the force.

TABLE 13.—Accommodation provided in Hospitals on the Lines of Communication

Year	Average ration strength	Maximum No. equipped beds	Maximum No. occupied beds	Average No. occupied beds	Percentage of ration strength		
					Equipped beds	Maximum No. occupied	Average No. occupied
1915 (Oct.–Dec.)	60,889	4,859	3,581	3,359	8·0	5·9	5·5
1916	126,010	14,000	11,500	6,237	11·1	9·1	4·9
1917	202,265	29,000	21,250	13,020	14·3	10·5	6·4
1918	159,947	28,250	19,750	12,559	17·7	12·3	7·9

The convalescent depot accommodation provided for the British Salonika Force is shown in Table 14.

TABLE 14.—Accommodation provided in Convalescent Depots

Year	Average ration strength	Maximum No. equipped beds	Maximum No. occupied beds	Average No. occupied beds	Percentage of ration strength		
					Equipped beds	Maximum No. occupied	Average No. occupied
1915 (Oct.–Dec.)	60,889	—	—	—	—	—	—
1916	126,010	4,000	3,250	1,027	3·2	2·6	·8
1917	202,265	17,000	16,000	6,409	3·4	7·9	3·2
1918	159,947	19,000	10,500	7,921	11·9	6·6	5·0

Non-battle Casualties

It has already been pointed out that non-battle casualties exceeded battle casualties in the proportion of twenty to one for all ranks. Table 15 shows the chief causes of admission to hospital for the duration of the campaign with the corresponding average annual ratios per 1,000 of ration strength. The average annual ratio per 1,000 for malaria alone was higher than the ratio per 1,000 for all diseases admitted to hospital from troops stationed in the United Kingdom for the years 1914–1918.

TABLE 15.—Principal Causes of Inefficiency

Cause	Admissions	Average annual ratio per 1,000
Malaria	162,517	403·58
Dysentery	24,245	60·21
Diarrhœa	22,598	56·12
Influenza	21,893	54·37
Venereal diseases	6,896	17·21
Scabies	5,819	14·45
Pyrexia of uncertain origin	5,502	13·66
Pneumonia	3,239	8·05

The more important diseases or disabilities causing admission to hospital in each year from October 1915 to December 1918 are given in Tables 16 and 17, with the number of deaths and the corresponding ratios per 1,000 of strength. In a very large number of cases the specific cause of admission was not stated. Evidently these cases caused no undue anxiety, and it has been assumed that they represent the ordinary sick admissions to be expected in any British army. They have been entered in the table as one comprehensive total.

TABLE 16.—Principal Causes of Admission to Hospital of British and Dominion Troops in Macedonia, October to December 1915 and 1916, with Deaths and Ratios per 1,000 of Strength

	1915 (Oct.–Dec.)				1916			
	Adms.	Deaths	Ratio per 1,000		Adms.	Deaths	Ratio per 1,000	
			Adms.	Deaths			Adms.	Deaths
Specific diseases due to infection								
Anthrax	—	—	—	—	2	—	·02	—
Blackwater fever	—	—	—	—	—	—	—	—
Cerebro-spinal fever	—	—	—	—	8	4	·06	·03
Chicken-pox	1	—	·02	—	—	—	—	—
Diphtheria	4	—	·07	—	40	—	·32	—
Dysentery	811	14	13·32	·23	8,204	169	66·49	1·37
Enteric fever	170	5	2·79	·08	1,105	40	8·96	·32
Erysipelas	—	—	—	—	10	—	·08	—
Influenza	795	—	13·06	—	252	—	2·04	—
Malaria	—	—	—	—	32,018	287	259·48	2·33
Measles	4	1	·07	·02	66	—	·53	—
Mediterranean fever	—	—	—	—	2	—	·02	—
Mumps	7	—	·11	—	22	—	·18	—
Pneumonia	49	5	·80	·08	73	10	·59	·08
Pyrexia of uncertain origin	76	—	1·25	—	2,635	14	21·35	·11
Relapsing fever	—	—	—	—	17	—	·14	—
Rubella	2	—	·03	—	142	—	1·15	—
Sand-fly fever	—	—	—	—	236	—	1·91	—
Scarlet fever	4	—	·07	—	14	—	·11	—
Small-pox	—	—	—	—	3	—	·02	—
Trench fever	—	—	—	—	—	—	—	—
Tuberculosis, pulmonary	29	2	·48	·03	220	—	1·78	—
Typhus fever	—	—	—	—	—	—	—	—
Venereal diseases	415	—	6·82	—	2,566	—	20·80	—
Other diseases classified under systems								
Eye—Trachoma	1	—	·02	—	2	—	·02	—
Digestive ⎰ Jaundice	380	—	6·24	—	582	1	4·72	·01
system ⎱ Diarrhœa	543	1	8·92	·02	7,699	12	62·39	·10
Skin—Scabies	317	—	5·21	—	1,010	—	8·19	—
Miscellaneous diseases or disabilities								
Trench foot or frost bite	1,125	—	18·48	—	66	—	·53	—
Effects of heat	6	—	·10	—	452	3	3·66	·02
Other diseases or injuries not specified	5,370	11	88·19	·18	73,497	186	595·63	1·51
Grand Total of Diseases and Injuries	10,109	39	166·02	·64	130,943	726	1,061·18	5·88

TABLE 17.—Principal Causes of Admission to Hospital of British and Dominion Troops in Macedonia, 1917 and 1918, with Deaths and Ratios per 1,000 of Strength

	1917				1918			
			Ratio per 1,000				Ratio per 1,000	
	Adms.	Deaths	Adms.	Deaths	Adms.	Deaths	Adms.	Deaths
Specific diseases due to infection								
Anthrax	8	—	·04	—	2	—	·02	—
Blackwater fever	43	12	·24	·07	133	28	1·03	·22
Cerebro-spinal fever	14	6	·08	·03	17	8	·13	·06
Chicken-pox	11	—	·06	—	4	—	·03	—
Diphtheria	92	3	·50	·02	14	1	·11	·01
Dysentery	5,792	124	31·72	·68	9,438	173	73·31	1·34
Enteric fever	529	19	2·90	·10	135	6	1·05	·05
Erysipelas	26	1	·14	·06	16	—	·12	—
Influenza	984	—	5·39	—	19,862	262	154·27	2·03
Malaria	71,412	228	391·12	1·25	59,087	272	458·94	2·11
Measles	309	—	1·69	—	17	—	·13	—
Mediterranean fever	3	1	·02	·01	—	—	—	—
Mumps	97	—	·53	—	48	—	·37	—
Pneumonia	279	43	1·53	·24	2,838	1,024	22·04	7·95
Pyrexia of uncertain origin	1,782	—	9·76	—	1,009	2	7·84	·02
Relapsing fever	73	4	·40	·02	12	—	·09	—
Rubella	633	—	3·47	—	121	1	·94	·01
Sand-fly fever	1,374	—	7·58	—	495	—	3·84	—
Scarlet fever	62	—	·34	—	19	—	·15	—
Small-pox	11	1	·06	·01	—	—	—	—
Trench fever	1,372	—	7·51	—	11	—	·09	—
Tuberculosis, pulmonary	390	1	2·14	·01	231	10	1·79	·07
Typhus fever	—	—	—	—	1	—	·01	—
Venereal diseases	2,020	2	11·06	·01	1,895	—	14·72	—
Other diseases classified under systems								
Eye—Trachoma	—	—	—	—	3	—	·02	—
Digestive { Jaundice	320	1	1·75	·01	134	2	1·04	·02
system { Diarrhœa	6,993	4	38·30	·02	7,363	—	57·19	—
Skin—Scabies	2,624	—	14·37	—	1,868	—	14·51	—
Miscellaneous diseases or disabilities								
Trench foot or frost bite	123	—	·67	—	254	—	1·97	—
Effects of heat	44	—	·24	—	4	—	·03	—
Other diseases or injuries not specified	74,537	287	408·24	1·57	63,222	453	491·06	3·52
Grand Total of Diseases and Injuries	171,957	737	941·80	4·04	168,253	2,242	1,306·85	17·41

TABLE 18.—Summary of the Principal Causes of Admission to Hospital of British and Dominion Troops in Macedonia, October 1915 to December 1918, with Deaths and Average Annual Ratios per 1,000 of Strength

	Total Oct. 1915–Dec. 1918			
	Adms.	Deaths	Average annual ratio per 1,000	
			Adms.	Deaths
Specific diseases due to infection				
Anthrax	12	—	·03	—
Blackwater fever	176	40	·44	·10
Cerebro-spinal fever	39	18	·10	·05
Chicken-pox	16	—	·04	—
Diphtheria	150	4	·37	·01
Dysentery	24,245	480	60·21	1·19
Enteric fever	1,939	70	4·82	·18
Erysipelas	52	1	·13	·00
Influenza	21,893	262	54·37	·65
Malaria	162,517	787	403·58	1·95
Measles	396	1	·98	·00
Mediterranean fever	5	1	·02	·00
Mumps	174	—	·44	—
Pneumonia	3,239	1,082	8·05	2·69
Pyrexia of uncertain origin	5,502	16	13·66	·04
Relapsing fever	102	4	·25	·01
Rubella	898	1	2·23	·00
Sand-fly fever	2,105	—	5·23	—
Scarlet fever	99	—	·24	—
Small-pox	14	1	·03	·00
Trench fever	1,383	—	3·44	—
Tuberculosis, pulmonary	870	13	2·16	·03
Typhus fever	1	—	·00	—
Venereal diseases	6,896	2	17·21	·01
Other diseases classified under systems				
Eye—Trachoma	6	—	·02	—
Digestive system { Jaundice	1,416	4	2·52	·01
Digestive system { Diarrhœa	22,598	17	56·12	·04
Skin—Scabies	5,819	—	14·45	—
Miscellaneous diseases or disabilities				
Trench foot or frost bite	1,568	—	3·89	—
Effects of heat	506	3	1·26	·01
Other diseases or injuries not specified	216,626	937	537·95	2·32
Grand Total of Diseases and Injuries	481,262	3,744	1,195·14	9·31

CHAPTER XIII

CASUALTIES IN THE MEDITERRANEAN EXPEDITIONARY FORCE DURING THE DARDANELLES CAMPAIGN

AFTER an unsuccessful attempt had been made by the British and French navies, early in 1915, to force a passage through the Dardanelles into the Sea of Marmora, it was decided to send out a combined British and French military force to co-operate with the navies, in the hope that by clearing the Gallipoli Peninsula of Turkish troops the Straits might be forced. This force was termed the Mediterranean Expeditionary Force. In the meantime, however, the enemy had been given time to prepare his defences so effectively that when the combined naval and military operations commenced on 25th April, 1915, they met with determined resistance, and the several landings on the Peninsula were only carried out at a cost of thousands of casualties. The Mediterranean Expeditionary Force gained a footing on the Gallipoli Peninsula, but further progress was slow, as the Peninsula was intersected with well-planned and well-constructed trenches, and the opposing forces were in close contact. There was no room to manœuvre; trench warfare had to be undertaken and every few yards of ground fought for. Throughout the summer fighting was practically continuous as attacks and counter-attacks were planned and carried out; further advances were made, but the real objective was never attained. A final effort on a large scale took place in August, when attacks were made on the Helles and Anzac fronts, simultaneously with a surprise landing at Suvla Bay. Although in part successful, these combined operations failed to dislodge the Turks from their commanding positions. A state of trench warfare ensued until the final evacuation of troops from the Peninsula, which was accomplished almost without casualty by 8th January, 1916.

The outstanding features of the Dardanelles campaign were the comparative shortness of its duration, the intensity of the struggle in a confined area, and the exceptionally large numbers of battle and non-battle casualties. From the medical services' point of view its chief characteristics were difficulties in the evacuation of sick and wounded, and in preserving a state of health among the troops. At the outset of the campaign the estimates of probable casualties fell far short of the actual numbers, and the medical arrangements were inadequate. This was due to the lack of training in handling casualties from combined naval and military operations, to the want of sufficient ambulance launches, and also to the great difficulties of removing the wounded, under heavy fire, from beaches within a few yards of the front line when every available boat was required for bringing ashore fresh troops. As time wore on, the arrangements improved, but at no time did the Gallipoli Peninsula afford the regular routes of evacuation from front line to the base such as other theatres of war enjoyed. Rough tracks and gullies were substitutes for roads, down which casualties were conveyed to the beaches, for the most part by hand-carriage but occasionally by ambulance wagon. Small sea craft played the part of ambulance convoys to the ships waiting to transport the sick and wounded to hospitals in Mudros or Egypt, there to be retained or, if need be, despatched still farther by sea to Malta or to the United Kingdom.

The health of the troops and the problems of sanitation were constant sources of anxiety to the medical services. Local water supplies were insufficient for the needs of the force and had to be supplemented from Egypt. The fact that the area of operations was separated from its base in Egypt by a two to three days' voyage of approximately 700 miles added to the difficulties of obtaining supplies and comforts for the sick and wounded. Climatic conditions tried the troops to the uttermost; the discomfort of the heat in summer with its attendant dust and flies was equalled in intensity by that of the blizzard in November, which alone caused some thousands of casualties from exposure. Dysentery and diseases of the digestive system accounted for approximately 50 per cent. of the admissions to hospital for sickness among British troops, which showed a ratio of 1,239·91 per 1,000 of strength for non-battle casualties. One of the most trying features of the campaign for the troops was their inability to get beyond the range of enemy fire while out of the trenches. The establishment of rest camps at Imbros and elsewhere in the later stages of the campaign was no doubt the means of restoring to health many war-worn men.*

Strength

The average ration strength of the British Mediterranean Expeditionary Force in Gallipoli and at the base for the duration of the Dardanelles campaign is shown in Table 1. It includes British, Dominion, Royal Naval Division and Indian troops, but excludes native followers enlisted locally or overseas.

TABLE 1.—Average Ration Strength

Period	Force	Officers	Other ranks	Total
25.4.15 to 8.1.16	Mediterranean Expeditionary Force	6,194	157,272	163,466
	British troops only	4,461	112,607	117,068

Classification of Casualties

The total battle casualties sustained by the Mediterranean Expeditionary Force operating in the Dardanelles campaign

* The history of the Medical Services during the Dardanelles Campaign is given in the *General History of the Medical Services*, vol. iv, chap. i, pp. 1–61.

from 25th April, 1915, to 8th January, 1916, are given in Table 2, with the corresponding ratios per 1,000 of ration strength.

TABLE 2.—Total Battle Casualties

	Off.	O.R.	Total	Ratio per 1,000		
				Off.	O.R.	Total
Battle casualties	4,531	110,212	114,743	731·51	700·77	701·94

A further analysis of these casualties from such information as is available shows the following detail:

TABLE 3.—Classification of Total Battle Casualties showing British, Dominion and Indian Troops separately

Troops	Killed	Died of wounds	Wounded	Missing and Prisoners of war	Total
British	11,234	5,346	44,721	7,525*	68,826
Royal Naval Division	1,653	600	5,037	2	7,292
Australian	5,790	2,000	17,900	70	25,760
New Zealand	1,902	543	4,752	—	7,197
Newfoundland	18	13	93	—	124
Indian	1,285	397	3,761	101	5,544
Total	21,882	8,899	76,264	7,698	114,743

Owing to the lack of reliable figures at the present time of admissions to hospital for disease or injury among Dominion or Indian troops, it has not been possible to compile a table of the total non-battle casualties which occurred during the campaign. The subsequent tables therefore refer only to the British troops, exclusive of the Royal Naval Division, of the Mediterranean Expeditionary Force.

TABLE 4.—Casualties among British troops only

	Off.	O.R.	Total	Ratio per 1,000		
				Off.	O.R.	Total
Battle casualties	2,780	66,046	68,826	623·18	586·52	587·91
Non-battle casualties	6,014	139,140	145,154	1,348·13	1,235·62	1,239·91
Total	8,794	205,186	213,980	1,971·31	1,822·14	1,827·83

The proportion of battle casualties to non-battle casualties was 1 to 2·2 officers; 1 to 2·1 other ranks; and 1 to 2·1 all ranks.

* Includes 7,221 missing.

DARDANELLES CAMPAIGN

An analysis of the total British casualties is given in Table 5.

TABLE 5.—Classification and Percentages of Total British Casualties

	Off.	O.R.	Total	Percentage of total British casualties		
				Off.	O.R.	Total
A. *Battle Casualties:*						
(a) Killed	808	10,426	11,234	9·19	5·08	5·25
(b) Died of wounds, injury or exposure before admission to hospital	60	2,204	2,264	·68	1·07	1·06
(c) Died of wounds in hospital	151	2,931	3,082	1·72	1·43	1·44
(d) Missing	244	6,977	7,221	2·77	3·40	3·37
(e) Prisoners of war *	19	285	304	·22	·14	·14
(f) Wounded less (c)	1,498	43,223	44,721	17·03	21·06	20·90
B. *Non-battle Casualties:*						
(g) Died of disease in hospital	60	1,821	1,881	·68	·89	·88
(h) Died of injury in hospital	5	222	227	·06	·11	·11
(i) Sick less (g)	5,564	121,263	126,827	63·27	59·10	59·27
(j) Injured less (h)	385	15,834	16,219	4·38	7·72	7·58
Total *A*. and *B*.	8,794	205,186	213,980	—	—	—

Table 6 (a) shows this detail as percentages of battle casualties, while Table 6 (b) shows the percentages of non-battle casualties.

TABLE 6 (a).—Percentages of Battle Casualties

	Off.	O.R.	Total
(a) Killed	29·06	15·79	16·32
(b) Died of wounds, etc., before admission to hospital	2·16	3·34	3·29
(c) Died of wounds in hospital	5·43	4·44	4·48
(d) Missing	8·78	10·56	10·49
(e) Prisoners of war	·68	·43	·44
(f) Wounded less (c)	53·89	65·44	64·98

TABLE 6 (b).—Percentages of Non-battle Casualties

	Off.	O.R.	Total
(g) Died of disease	1·00	1·31	1·30
(h) Died of injury	·08	·16	·16
(i) Sick less (g)	92·52	87·15	87·37
(j) Injured less (h)	6·40	11·38	11·17

The casualties sustained by the British troops during the Dardanelles campaign may be further classified into permanent and temporary losses for military purposes in the field.

* Includes 1 officer and 95 other ranks who died as prisoners of war.

TABLE 7 (a).—Permanent Losses for Military Purposes in the Field

	Off.	O.R.	Total	Percentage of total British casualties		
				Off.	O.R.	Total
A. Battle Casualties:						
Killed	808	10,426	11,234	9·19	5·08	5·25
Died before admission to hospital	60	2,204	2,264	·68	1·07	1·06
Died of wounds in hospital	151	2,931	3,082	1·72	1·43	1·44
Missing	244	6,977	7,221	2·77	3·40	3·37
Prisoners of war	19	285	304	·22	·14	·14
Total	1,282	22,823	24,105	14·58	11·12	11·26
B. Non-battle Casualties:						
Died of disease	60	1,821	1,881	·68	·89	·88
Died of injury	5	222	227	·06	·11	·11
Total	65	2,043	2,108	·74	1·00	·99
Total permanent losses	1,347	24,866	26,213	15·32	12·12	12·25

TABLE 7 (b).—Temporary Losses for Military Purposes in the Field

	Off.	O.R.	Total	Percentage of total British casualties		
				Off.	O.R.	Total
A. Battle Casualties:						
Wounded less died of wounds	1,498	43,223	44,721	17·03	21·06	20·90
B. Non-battle Casualties:						
Sick less died of disease	5,564	121,263	126,827	63·27	59·10	59·27
Injured less died of injury	385	15,834	16,219	4·38	7·72	7·58
Total	5,949	137,097	143,046	67·65	66·82	66·85
Total temporary losses	7,447	180,320	187,767	84·68	87·88	87·75

The relative proportions of the various classes of casualties to each other for British troops of the Mediterranean Expeditionary Force are given in Table 8.

TABLE 8.—Proportions

	Officers	Other ranks	Total
1. Total battle casualties to total non-battle casualties	1 : 2·2	1 : 2·1	1 : 2·1
2. Total killed and died before admission to hospital to total wounded including died of wounds in hospital	1 : 1·9	1 : 3·7	1 : 3·5
3. Permanent losses among battle casualties to total wounded less died of wounds in hospital	1 : 1·2	1 : 1·9	1 : 1·9
4. Permanent losses among non-battle casualties to total sick and injured less deaths from disease or injury	1 : 91·5	1 : 67·1	1 : 67·9
5. Total permanent losses to total temporary losses	1 : 5·5	1 : 7·2	1 : 7·2

Admissions to Hospital

Of the total casualties suffered by the British troops of the Mediterranean Expeditionary Force during the Dardanelles campaign, the numbers admitted to hospital and treated by the medical services are shown in Table 9.

TABLE 9.—Numbers admitted to Hospital—British Troops only

	Off.	O.R.	Total	Percentage of total British casualties		
				Off.	O.R.	Total
Wounded	1,649	46,154	47,803	18·75	22·49	22·34
Sick	5,624	123,084	128,708	63·95	59·99	60·15
Injured	390	16,056	16,446	4·44	7·83	7·69
Total	7,663	185,294	192,957	87·14	90·31	90·18

The proportion of wounded to sick and injured treated by the medical services was 1 to 3·6 officers; 1 to 3·0 other ranks; and 1 to 3·0 all ranks.

The casualties which were not treated by the medical services are shown in Table 10.

TABLE 10.—Casualties among British Troops not treated by the Medical Services

	Off.	O.R.	Total	Percentage of total British casualties		
				Off.	O.R.	Total
Killed and died before admission to hospital	868	12,630	13,498	9·87	6·15	6·31
Missing	244	6,977	7,221	2·77	3·40	3·37
Prisoners of war	19	285	304	·22	·14	·14
Total	1,131	19,892	21,023	12·86	9·69	9·82

An analysis of the admissions to hospital is given in Table 11 (a), with the corresponding ratios per 1,000 of strength and percentages of total admissions in Table 11 (b) and Table 11 (c) respectively. These figures show the ultimate disposal of cases, and, for this campaign, it has been possible to give the numbers of sick and wounded who were discharged from the service as invalids. On the other hand, complete information regarding the numbers who were evacuated from the Gallipoli Peninsula is not available, so that it has not been possible to include that figure nor the number of men who returned to duty in the theatre of operations.

TABLE 11 (a).—Admissions to Hospital and Final Disposal of Cases—British troops only

	Wounded			Sick			Injured			Total		
	Off.	O.R.	Total	Off.	O.R.	Total	Off.	O.R.	Total	Off.	O.R.	Total
Admissions	1,649	46,154	47,803	5,624	123,084	128,708	390	16,056	16,446	7,663	185,294	192,957
Deaths	151	2,931	3,082	60	1,821	1,881	5	222	227	216	4,974	5,190
Returned to duty	1,495	40,873	42,368	5,559	119,923	125,482	385	15,509	15,894	7,439	176,305	183,744
Discharged as invalids	3	2,350	2,353	5	1,340	1,345	—	325	325	8	4,015	4,023

TABLE 11 (b).—Ratios per 1,000 of British Ration Strength

	Wounded			Sick			Injured			Total		
	Off.	O.R.	Total	Off.	O.R.	Total	Off.	O.R.	Total	Off.	O.R.	Total
Admissions	369·65	409·87	408·34	1,260·70	1,093·04	1,099·43	87·42	142·58	140·48	1,717·78	1,645·49	1,648·25
Deaths	33·85	26·03	26·33	13·45	16·17	16·07	1·12	1·97	1·94	48·42	44·17	44·33
Returned to duty	335·13	362·97	361·91	1,246·13	1,064·97	1,071·87	86·30	137·73	135·77	1,667·56	1,565·67	1,569·55
Discharged as invalids	·67	20·87	20·10	1·12	11·90	11·49	—	2·89	2·78	1·79	35·65	34·36

TABLE 11 (c).—Percentages of Total British Admissions

	Wounded			Sick			Injured			Total		
	Off.	O.R.	Total	Off.	O.R.	Total	Off.	O.R.	Total	Off.	O.R.	Total
Deaths	9·16	6·35	6·45	1·07	1·48	1·46	1·28	1·38	1·38	2·82	2·68	2·69
Returned to duty	90·66	88·56	88·63	98·84	97·43	97·49	98·72	96·60	96·64	97·08	95·17	95·23
Discharged as invalids	·18	5·09	4·92	·09	1·09	1·05	—	2·02	1·98	·10	2·15	2·08

Table 12 shows the percentages of the above admissions whose records were complete as regards the total number of days spent in hospital with the Mediterranean Expeditionary Force and in the United Kingdom, and of that percentage the ratios per 1,000 of strength constantly in hospital, and the average number of days in hospital per patient.

TABLE 12.—Ratio per 1,000 of Strength constantly in Hospital, with the Average Stay in Hospital per patient, British Troops only

	Percentage of admissions with completed records		Ratio per 1,000 constantly in hospital			Average No. of days in hospital per patient	
	Off.	O.R.	Off.	O.R.	Total	Off.	O.R.
Wounded	74·89	86·24	44·78	74·93	73·78	44·0	67·1
Sick	73·90	89·11	105·22	131·89	130·87	30·1	44·2
Injured	71·79	89·27	6·39	19·23	18·74	26·1	49·3
Total	74·00	88·41	156·39	226·05	223·39	32·9	50·2

Hospital Accommodation

There is no definite information available to show what hospital accommodation was provided for the sick and wounded of the Mediterranean Expeditionary Force during the Dardanelles campaign. It is known to have been inadequate at the commencement of operations, and that cases were sent to Egypt, Malta and the United Kingdom. As the campaign progressed, hospitals were organised in Mudros, and extra accommodation was provided in Egypt. The necessity to use hospitals wherever they were available, no matter how far distant from the peninsula, and the fact that the base, Egypt, was itself a theatre of war with casualties of its own to contend with, explain the lack of reliable data as to the beds actually set apart for the casualties of the Mediterranean Expeditionary Force.

Non-battle Casualties

The statistics of admissions to hospital for sickness or injury among British troops of the Mediterranean Expeditionary Force during the Dardanelles campaign in 1915 are as complete a record as it was possible to obtain. Table 13 shows the principal causes of admission to hospital with the corresponding ratios per 1,000 of ration strength.

TABLE 13.—Principal Causes of Inefficiency

	Admissions	Ratio per 1,000
Dysentery	29,728	253·94
Diarrhœa	10,383	88·69
Enteric group of fevers	9,423	80·49
Local and general injuries	8,464	72·30
Jaundice	8,030	68·59
Frost bite (6,602) and trench foot (1,380)	7,982	68·18
Inflammation of the intestines	7,551	64·50
Rheumatic fever	6,566	56·09
Diseases of the organs of locomotion	4,334	37·02
Debility	3,844	32·84
Diseases of the respiratory system	3,789	32·37
Skin diseases	3,788	32·36
Other diseases of the intestines	3,560	30·41
Influenza	3,126	26·70

Table 14 gives a detailed analysis of the causes of admission to hospital of British troops during the Dardanelles campaign in 1915, with their ultimate disposal, the corresponding ratios per 1,000 of average British ration strength, and the average length of stay in hospital per patient. In the original compilation of these figures pneumonia and broncho-pneumonia were grouped together, and have therefore had to be reproduced here as one total.

TABLE 14.—Analysis of Admissions to Hospital, British Troops only, of the Mediterranean
Average No. of Days

		Admissions	Deaths	Returned to duty
	Specific diseases due to infection			
1	Cerebro-spinal fever	9	4	5
2	Chicken-pox	4	—	4
3	Cholera	7	—	7
4	Diphtheria	275	18	256
5	Dysentery	29,728	811	28,793
6	Enteric group of fevers	9,423	330	9,044
7	Influenza	3,126	3	3,120
8	Malaria	1,473	5	1,464
9	Measles	120	—	120
10	Mumps	41	1	40
11	Pneumonia	677	98	572
12	Pyrexia of uncertain origin	2,390	14	2,374
13	Rheumatic fever	6,566	17	6,465
14	Rubella	116	1	115
15	Sand-fly fever	77	—	77
16	Scarlet fever	283	3	280
17	Septic diseases, major	98	16	81
18	Small-pox	17	4	13
19	Tetanus	9	6	3
20	Trench fever	6	—	6
21	Tuberculosis { Pulmonary	434	32	224
22	{ Other	69	4	50
23	{ Gonorrhœa	1,774	—	1,773
24	Venereal diseases { Syphilis	415	1	414
25	{ Other	556	—	556
26	Other infectious diseases	191	5	183
	Other diseases classified under systems			
27	Diseases of the nervous system	2,936	24	2,733
28	Mental diseases	118	5	73
	Diseases of the—			
29	Eye	1,759	2	1,717
30	Ear	1,340	3	1,282
31	Nose	98	—	97
32	Circulatory { Valvular disease of the heart	1,020	26	839
33	system { Disordered action of the heart	533	13	496
34	{ Other diseases	1,023	20	990
35	Respiratory system	3,789	35	3,667
36	Blood	98	2	94
37	Spleen	8	1	7
38	Lymphatic system	283	2	280
39	Endocrine glands	62	—	51
40	Breast	3	—	3
41	Teeth and gums	1,180	1	1,173
42	{ Tonsillitis	2,003	5	1,995
43	{ Inflammation and ulceration of the stomach	1,680	8	1,661
44	Digestive { Inflammation of the intestines	7,551	62	7,478
45	system { Diarrhœa	10,383	29	10,348
46	{ Other diseases of the intestines	3,560	16	3,516
47	{ Jaundice	8,030	31	7,986
48	{ Other diseases	1,112	23	1,079
49	Generative system	1,099	4	1,093
50	Skin { Scabies	2,544	—	2,542
51	{ Other	1,244	2	1,237
52	Areolar tissue { Minor septic diseases	2,227	3	2,220
53	{ Other	2,076	5	2,068
54	Organs of locomotion	4,407	5	4,351
55	Urinary system	1,168	25	1,086
	Miscellaneous diseases			
56	Debility	3,844	12	3,819
57	Diseases due to disorders of nutrition or { Scurvy	7	—	7
58	of metabolism { Other	44	—	41
59	Tumours and cysts	65	2	61
60	Poisons	110	1	108
61	Parasites	216	1	214
62	Diseases unclassified	3,204	140	3,031
	Injuries			
63	Frost bite	6,602	68	6,368
64	Trench foot	1,380	10	1,303
65	Effects of heat	686	—	673
66	Other local and general injuries	7,778	149	7,550
	Grand total of diseases and injuries	145,154	2,108	141,376

Expeditionary Force, showing Disposal of Cases, Ratios per 1,000 of Strength, and the in Hospital per Patient

Discharged as Invalids	Ratio per 1,000				Average No. of days in hospital per patient		
	Admissions	Deaths	Returned to duty	Discharged as invalids	Off.	O.R.	
—	·08	·03	·04	—	11·0	52·7	1
—	·03	—	·03	—	—	63·0	2
—	·06	—	·06	—	—	24·2	3
1	2·35	·15	2·19	·01	59·3	58·6	4
124	253·94	6·93	245·95	1·06	38·7	61·5	5
49	80·49	2·82	77·25	·42	57·5	103·0	6
3	26·70	·03	26·65	·03	21·5	24·2	7
4	12·58	·04	12·51	·03	35·2	40·6	8
—	1·03	—	1·03	—	30·7	22·7	9
—	·35	·01	·34	—	25·5	35·3	10
7	5·78	·84	4·89	·06	26·3	54·9	11
2	20·42	·12	20·28	·02	24·2	20·1	12
84	56·09	·15	55·22	·72	38·0	49·3	13
—	·99	·01	·98	—	16·6	11·4	14
—	·66	—	·66	—	6·3	25·2	15
—	2·42	·03	2·39	—	51·8	58·9	16
1	·84	·14	·69	·01	37·6	30·8	17
—	·15	·03	·11	—	—	24·5	18
—	·08	·05	·03	—	—	6·5	19
—	·05	—	·05	—	—	76·6	20
178	3·71	·27	1·91	1·52	25·3	66·8	21
15	·59	·03	·43	·13	14·0	85·8	22
1	15·15	—	15·15	·01	26·6	34·6	23
—	3·54	·01	3·54	—	53·8	48·0	24
—	4·75	—	4·75	—	—	32·0	25
3	1·63	·04	1·56	·03	25·2	34·1	26
179	25·08	·21	23·35	1·53	30·8	54·4	27
40	1·01	·04	·62	·34	—	95·0	28
40	15·03	·02	14·67	·34	21·6	43·3	29
55	11·45	·03	10·95	·47	30·2	39·7	30
1	·84	—	·83	·01	26·0	13·6	31
155	8·71	·22	7·17	1·32	30·7	66·5	32
24	4·55	·11	4·24	·21	29·1	65·0	33
13	8·74	·17	8·46	·11	30·0	44·8	34
87	32·37	·30	31·32	·74	22·9	40·8	35
2	·84	·02	·80	·02	16·5	47·5	36
—	·07	·01	·06	—	—	59·8	37
1	2·42	·02	2·39	·01	19·9	29·8	38
11	·53	—	·44	·09	—	66·0	39
—	·03	—	·03	—	—	17·6	40
6	10·08	·01	10·02	·05	14·7	24·5	41
3	17·11	·04	17·04	·03	12·8	19·9	42
11	14·35	·07	14·19	·09	27·0	37·5	43
11	64·50	·53	63·88	·09	20·5	33·3	44
6	88·69	·25	88·39	·05	8·4	17·2	45
28	30·41	·14	30·03	·24	38·5	35·4	46
13	68·59	·26	68·22	·11	31·8	34·3	47
10	9·50	·20	9·22	·09	16·2	27·5	48
2	9·39	·03	9·34	·02	21·7	43·9	49
2	21·73	—	21·71	·02	13·0	18·8	50
5	10·63	·02	10·57	·04	25·3	27·8	51
4	19·02	·03	18·97	·03	34·7	27·7	52
3	17·73	·04	17·66	·03	16·4	24·3	53
51	37·64	·04	37·16	·44	27·4	25·1	54
57	9·98	·21	9·28	·49	52·1	75·2	55
13	32·84	·10	32·62	·11	19·5	33·8	56
—	·06	—	·06	—	6·0	6·5	57
3	·38	—	·35	·03	31·0	34·1	58
2	·56	·02	·52	·02	4·5	32·7	59
1	·94	·01	·92	·01	40·3	22·8	60
1	1·85	·01	1·83	·01	60·0	13·0	61
33	27·37	1·20	25·89	·28	4·9	8·2	62
166	56·39	·58	54·40	1·42	17·3	62·3	63
67	11·79	·09	11·13	·57	38·6	75·6	64
13	5·86	—	5·75	·11	19·5	36·3	65
79	66·44	1·27	64·49	·67	12·9	14·1	66
1,670	1,239·91	18·01	1,207·64	14·27	29·9	44·7	

CHAPTER XIV

CASUALTIES IN EGYPT AND PALESTINE, 1915–1918

THROUGHOUT the war Egypt played a three-fold part in military operations. It was organised for the defence of its own boundaries; it acted as a base for the operations in the Dardanelles, Macedonia and Palestine; and it formed an intermediate base for troops passing to and from the Eastern theatres of war. In so far as the campaign in Egypt itself is concerned, the defence of the Suez Canal was the primary concern, but except for patrol work and raids, which in February 1915 assumed major proportions as 20–25,000 Turks crossed the Sinai desert, the first active hostilities on its Eastern frontier took place at the battle of Romani in August, 1916. On the Western frontier operations were conducted against the Senussi from November 1915 to February 1917, while in the South a force from the Sudan operated against the Sultan of Darfur from March to December, 1916. Offensive operations were afterwards confined to the Eastern frontier. After the evacuation of Gallipoli in January, 1916, reorganisation of troops in Egypt took place and the Egyptian Expeditionary Force came into being. Following the defeat of the Turks at Romani, the force advanced steadily along the North coast of the Sinai Peninsula and invaded Palestine. Two attempts to take Gaza in March and April 1917, failed, and the attack was resumed in October 1917, this time with success. Jerusalem was captured on 9th December. During 1918 the offensive operations against the Turks were continued with little effect in and beyond the Jordan Valley, but as the result of a successful attack, mainly along the coastal plain, commencing on 19th September, operations were brought to a close in the final pursuit of the enemy through Syria, the capture of Damascus and the occupation of Aleppo on 26th October, 1918.

From the military medical point of view British troops have so long been stationed in Egypt that conditions there are well known, and there is little of outstanding note to contribute from the years of war. The average annual sick ratio per 1,000 for other ranks in Egypt and Palestine during the war was 750·40, which compares very favourably with the post-war rates of 741·8 and 682·3 in 1921 and 1922 respectively. The work of the medical services and the modes of transport used with success in evacuating casualties across the desert have been described elsewhere.* During the operations in Palestine in 1918, 91·79 per cent. of the total sick and wounded admissions were evacuated. There are no complete records of sick admissions or of specific diseases for the whole force, and in order to give some idea of the health of the force recourse has been made to samples for certain periods. Statistics of

---

* *General History of the Medical Services*, vol. iii, pp. 362–483, and vol. iv, chap. xxiii.

EGYPT AND PALESTINE, 1915-1918

evacuation overseas are of little value owing to the fact that Egypt housed the sick and wounded of other campaigns. For British and Dominion troops the average annual sick admission rate was 740·59 per 1,000 of strength, the chief recorded causes of inefficiency being malaria, diarrhœa and dysentery, and venereal diseases.

As there is no reliable information regarding Indian casualties, the tables refer to British and Dominion troops unless otherwise stated.

Strength

The average ration strength of the force in Egypt and Palestine from 1915 to 1918 is shown in Table 1. The figures for 1915 are exclusive of the troops of the Mediterranean Expeditionary Force base in Egypt.

TABLE 1.—Average Ration Strength

Year	British and Dominion troops			Indian or Other troops			Labour	Total			
	Off.	O.R.	Total	Off.	O.R.	Total		Off.	O.R.	Labour	Total
1915	3,405	70,728	74,133	327	14,911	15,238	—	3,732	85,639	—	89,371
1916	8,387	179,539	187,926	298	30,243	30,541	7,455	8,685	209,782	7,455	225,922
1917	8,767	177,782	186,549	271	18,619	18,890	63,329	9,038	196,401	63,329	268,768
1918	12,286	218,804	231,090	1,298	58,068	59,366	94,871	13,584	276,872	94,871	385,327

Classification of Casualties

The total casualties sustained by British and Dominion troops in Egypt and Palestine from 1915 to 1918 are given in Table 2 with the average annual ratios per 1,000 of ration strength.

TABLE 2.—Total British and Dominion Casualties

	Off.	O.R.	Total	Average annual ratio per 1,000		
				Off.	O.R.	Total
Battle casualties ...	3,570	47,881	51,451	108·76	74·02	75·70
Non-battle casualties	17,977	485,400	503,377	547·31	750·40	740·59
Total ...	21,547	533,281	554,828	656·07	824·42	816·29

The proportion of battle casualties to non-battle casualties was 1 to 5·04 officers; 1 to 10·14 other ranks; and 1 to 9·78 all ranks.

An analysis of the total British and Dominion casualties occurring in Egypt and Palestine from 1915 to 1918 is given in Table 3.

TABLE 3.—Classification and Percentages of Total British and Dominion Casualties

	Off.	O.R.	Total	Percentage of total British and Dominion casualties		
				Off.	O.R.	Total
A. *Battle casualties*:						
(a) Killed	630	6,764	7,394	2·92	1·27	1·33
(b) Died of wounds	232	2,761	2,993	1·08	·52	·54
(c) Missing	100	2,386	2,486	·46	·45	·45
(d) Prisoners of war	80*	1,305*	1,385	·37	·24	·25
(e) Wounded less (b)	2,528	34,665	37,193	11·73	6·50	6·70
B. *Non-battle casualties*:						
(f) Died of disease or injury	247	5,734	5,981	1·15	1·08	1·08
(g) Sick or injured less (f)	17,730	479,666	497,396	82·29	89·95	89·65
Total A. and B.	21,547	533,281	554,828	—	—	—

* Of these 5 officers and 291 other ranks died as prisoners of war.

Table 4 (a) shows this detail as percentages of battle casualties, while Table 4 (b) shows similarly the percentages of non-battle casualties.

TABLE 4 (a).—Percentages of Battle Casualties

	Off.	O.R.	Total
(a) Killed	17·65	14·13	14·37
(b) Died of wounds	6·50	5·77	5·82
(c) Missing	2·80	4·98	4·83
(d) Prisoners of war	2·24	2·73	2·69
(e) Wounded less (b)	70·81	72·40	72·29

TABLE 4 (b).—Percentages of Non-battle Casualties

	Off.	O.R.	Total
(f) Died of disease or injury	1·37	1·18	1·19
(g) Sick or injured less (f)	98·63	98·82	98·81

The casualties among British and Dominion troops in Egypt and Palestine from 1915 to 1918 may be further subdivided into permanent and temporary losses for military purposes in the field.

EGYPT AND PALESTINE, 1915-1918

TABLE 5 (a).—Permanent Losses for Military Purposes in the Field

	Off.	O.R.	Total	Percentage of total British and Dominion casualties		
				Off.	O.R.	Total
A. *Battle casualties*:						
Killed	630	6,764	7,394	2·92	1·27	1·33
Died of wounds ...	232	2,761	2,993	1·08	·52	·54
Missing	100	2,386	2,486	·46	·45	·45
Prisoners of war ...	80	1,305	1,385	·37	·24	·25
Total	*1,042*	*13,216*	*14,258*	*4·84*	*2·48*	*2·57*
B. *Non-battle casualties*:						
Died of disease or injury	247	5,734	5,981	1·15	1·08	1·08
Total permanent losses	1,289	18,950	20,239	5·98	3·55	3·65

TABLE 5 (b).—Temporary Losses for Military Purposes in the Field

	Off.	O.R.	Total	Percentage of total British and Dominion casualties		
				Off.	O.R.	Total
A. *Battle casualties*:						
Wounded less died of wounds ...	2,528	34,665	37,193	11·73	6·50	6·70
B. *Non-battle casualties*:						
Sick or injured less died of disease or injury	17,730	479,666	497,396	82·29	89·95	89·65
Total temporary losses	20,258	514,331	534,589	94·02	96·45	96·35

The relative proportions of the different classes of casualties to each other for British and Dominion troops in Egypt and Palestine from 1915 to 1918 are shown in Table 6.

TABLE 6.—Proportions

	Officers	Other Ranks	Total
1. Total battle casualties to total non-battle casualties	1 : 5·04	1 : 10·14	1 : 9·78
2. Total killed to total wounded, including died of wounds	1 : 4·38	1 : 5·53	1 : 5·43
3. Permanent losses among battle casualties to total wounded less died of wounds ...	1 : 2·43	1 : 2·62	1 : 2·61
4. Permanent losses among non-battle casualties to total sick and injured less died of disease or injury	1 : 71·78	1 : 83·65	1 : 83·16
5. Total permanent losses to total temporary losses	1 : 15·72	1 : 27·14	1 : 26·41

Admissions to Hospital

Of the total casualties suffered by British and Dominion troops in Egypt and Palestine from 1915 to 1918, the numbers admitted to hospital and treated by the medical services are shown in Table 7.

TABLE 7.—Numbers admitted to Hospital

	Off.	O.R.	Total	Percentage of total British and Dominion casualties		
				Off.	O.R.	Total
Wounded	2,760	37,426	40,186	12·81	7·02	7·24
Sick or injured	17,977	485,400	503,377	83·43	91·02	90·73
Total	20,737	522,826	543,563	96·24	98·04	97·97

The proportion of wounded to sick and injured treated by the medical services was 1 to 6·51 officers; 1 to 12·97 other ranks; and 1 to 12·53 all ranks.

The casualties which were not treated by the medical services are shown in Table 8.

TABLE 8.—Casualties not treated by the Medical Services

	Off.	O.R.	Total	Percentage of total British and Dominion casualties		
				Off.	O.R.	Total
Killed	630	6,764	7,394	2·92	1·27	1·33
Missing	100	2,386	2,486	·46	·45	·45
Prisoners of war	80	1,305	1,385	·37	·24	·25
Total	810	10,455	11,265	3·76	1·96	2·03

Table 9 (*a*) shows the yearly admissions to hospital for sick and wounded, and the deaths. The ratios per 1,000 of strength and the mortality percentage of admissions are given in Tables 9 (*b*) and 9 (*c*) respectively. As already pointed out, the fact that Egypt was a base for other campaigns and an intermediate base for troops passing to or from the East renders such figures as there are for evacuations overseas of little value when dealing with the disposal of sick and wounded of the force in Egypt and Palestine. There are likewise no records to show the numbers who returned to duty in the theatre of operations.

EGYPT AND PALESTINE, 1915–1918

TABLE 9 (a).—Admissions to Hospital and Deaths, British and Dominion Troops, 1916–1918

	Year	Wounded			Sick or injured			Total		
		Off.	O.R.	Total	Off.	O.R.	Total	Off.	O.R.	Total
Admissions	1916	186	1,422	1,608	3,762	132,348	136,110	3,948	133,770	137,718
	1917	1,854	27,488	29,342	5,440	133,381	138,821	7,294	160,869	168,163
	1918	704	8,464	9,168	8,500	212,534	221,034	9,204	220,998	230,202
Deaths	1916	20	120	140	51	1,043	1,094	71	1,163	1,234
	1917	162	2,069	2,231	77	1,623	1,700	239	3,692	3,931
	1918	48	567	615	111	2,998	3,109	159	3,565	3,724

TABLE 9 (b).—Ratios per 1,000 of Ration Strength

	Year	Wounded			Sick or injured			Total		
		Off.	O.R.	Total	Off.	O.R.	Total	Off.	O.R.	Total
Admissions	1916	22·18	7·92	8·56	448·55	737·15	724·27	470·73	745·07	732·83
	1917	211·47	154·62	157·29	620·51	750·25	744·15	831·98	904·87	901·44
	1918	57·30	38·68	39·67	691·84	971·34	956·48	749·15	1,010·03	996·16
Deaths	1916	2·38	·67	·74	6·08	5·81	5·82	8·47	6·48	6·57
	1917	18·48	11·64	11·96	8·78	9·13	9·11	27·26	20·77	21·07
	1918	3·91	2·59	2·66	9·03	13·70	13·45	12·94	16·29	16·11

TABLE 9 (c).—Percentages of Admissions

	Year	Wounded			Sick or injured			Total		
		Off.	O.R.	Total	Off.	O.R.	Total	Off.	O.R.	Total
Deaths	1916	10·75	8·44	8·71	1·36	·79	·80	1·80	·87	·90
	1917	8·74	7·53	7·60	1·42	1·22	1·22	3·28	2·30	2·34
	1918	6·82	6·70	6·71	1·31	1·41	1·41	1·73	1·61	1·62

Table 10 shows the ratios per 1,000 of strength constantly in medical units for the years 1916, 1917 and 1918. As the figures for 1915 are chiefly casualties from the Dardanelles, it would be misleading to represent them as ratios per 1,000 of the force in Egypt.

TABLE 10.—Ratio per 1,000 of Strength constantly in Medical Units

	British and Dominion	Indian	Total
1916	72·13	35·43	67·00
1917	65·10	44·47	63·21
1918	79·51	64·97	76·54

Hospital Accommodation

Table 11 shows the maximum number of equipped hospital beds for British and Dominion troops in Egypt and Palestine, the maximum number of beds occupied on any one date, and the average number of beds equipped and occupied throughout the year, with the corresponding percentages of the average strength of British and Dominion troops.

The percentages for 1915 have not been worked out as the numbers in hospital include the sick and wounded evacuated from the Gallipoli Peninsula. The maximum number in hospital in 1918 probably includes a large number of influenza cases.

TABLE 11.—Accommodation provided in Hospitals for British and Dominion Troops in Egypt and Palestine

Year	Average ration strength	Maximum No. equipped beds	Maximum No. occupied beds	Average No. equipped beds	Average No. occupied beds	Percentage of strength			
						Maximum No.		Average No.	
						Equip.	Occup.	Equip.	Occup.
1915	74,133	19,142	23,273	13,810	15,766	—	—	—	—
1916	187,926	21,460	22,656	?	13,555	11·42	12·06	?	7·21
1917	186,549	29,851	24,738	19,377	12,145	16·00	13·26	10·39	6·51
1918	231,090	28,659	30,658	25,523	18,375	12·40	13·27	11·04	7·95

Table 12 shows the hospital accommodation provided for Indian troops in Egypt and Palestine. No information is available for 1916.

TABLE 12.—Accommodation provided in Hospitals for Indian Troops in Egypt and Palestine

Year	Average ration strength	Maximum No. equipped beds	Maximum No. occupied beds	Average No. equipped beds	Average No. occupied beds	Percentage of strength			
						Maximum No.		Average No.	
						Equip.	Occup.	Equip.	Occup.
1915	15,238	1,556	2,709	1,464	1,748	—	—	—	—
1916	30,541	—	—	—	—	—	—	—	—
1917	18,890	2,044	1,816	1,263	840	10·82	9·61	6·69	4·45
1918	59,366	10,634	14,759	6,412	3,857	17·91	24·86	10·80	6·50

The convalescent depot accommodation provided for British and Dominion troops in Egypt and Palestine is given in Table 13. No information is available regarding the convalescent depot accommodation for Indian troops.

TABLE 13.—Convalescent Depot Accommodation provided for British and Dominion Troops in Egypt and Palestine

Year	Average ration strength	Maximum No. equipped beds	Maximum No. occupied beds	Average No. equipped beds	Average No. occupied beds	Percentage of strength			
						Maximum No.		Average No.	
						Equip.	Occup.	Equip.	Occup.
1915	74,133	9,305	—	4,949	—	—	—	—	—
1916	187,926	4,646	3,264	?	2,884	2·47	1·74	?	1·53
1917	186,549	6,605	4,904	6,040	3,381	3·54	2·63	3·24	1·81
1918	231,090	7,359	6,471	6,968	4,366	3·18	2·80	3·02	1·89

Non-battle Casualties

There are no complete records of the causes of admission to hospital for sickness or injury among British and Dominion troops in Egypt and Palestine during the war. Records are only available of the more important special diseases causing inefficiency, and these, together with the number of deaths and the corresponding ratios per 1,000 of ration strength, are shown in Tables 14 and 15. The records for influenza are incomplete.

The increase of malaria cases in 1918 is due to the severe infection suffered by the troops operating in malarious areas during the advance and final operations against the Turks.

TABLE 14.—Principal Recorded Causes of Admission to Hospital, British and Dominion Troops, 1916 and 1917

Cause	1916				1917			
	Admissions	Deaths	Ratio per 1,000		Admissions	Deaths	Ratio per 1,000	
			Adms.	Deaths			Adms.	Deaths
Diarrhœa	5,889	—	31·34	—	14,117	5	75·67	·03
Dysentery.. ..	5,597	81	29·78	·43	4,341	139	23·27	·75
Enteric ⎧ Typhoid	100	6	·53	·03	14	3	·08	·02
fever ⎨ Para. A	202	7	1·07	·04	75	—	·40	—
⎩ Para. B	145	3	·77	·02	80	—	·43	—
⎩ Group ..	2,661	54	14·16	·29	404	24	2·17	·13
Total ..	3,108	70	16·54	·37	573	27	3·07	·14
Malaria	1,423	8	7·57	·04	8,480	73	45·46	·39
Pneumonia ..	1,080	115	5·75	·61	228	55	1·22	·25
Venereal diseases..	14,153	—	75·31	—	5,242	—	28·10	—

TABLE 15.—Principal Recorded Causes of Admission to Hospital, British and Dominion Troops, in 1918 and Totals 1916–1918

Cause	1918				Total 1916–1918			
	Admissions	Deaths	Ratio per 1,000		Admissions	Deaths	Average Annual Ratio per 1,000	
			Adms.	Deaths			Adms.	Deaths
Diarrhœa	14,487	11	62·69	·05	34,493	16	56·96	·02
Dysentery.. ..	4,906	264	21·23	1·14	14,844	484	24·51	·80
Enteric ⎧ Typhoid	31	13	·13	·06	145	22	·24	·03
fever ⎨ Para. A	75	4	·32	·02	352	11	·58	·02
⎩ Para. B	46	4	·20	·02	271	7	·45	·01
⎩ Group ..	285	30	1·23	·13	3,350	108	5·53	·18
Total ..	437	51	1·89	·22	4,118	148	6·80	·24
Influenza	9,709	34	42·01	·15	—	—	—	—
Malaria	30,241	773	130·86	3·35	40,144	854	66·29	1·41
Pneumonia ..	1,510	1,027	6·53	4·44	2,818	1,197	4·65	1·98
Venereal diseases ..	11,656	—	50·44	—	31,051	—	51 27	—

In order to give some idea of the incidence of infectious diseases in the whole force, three sample periods, each of three months' duration, have been selected. Table 16 shows the numbers of infectious diseases notified during each period, and the ratios per 1,000 of strength for the period in question.

TABLE 16.—Incidence of Diseases due to Infection in the Egyptian Expeditionary Force at Certain Periods

	April to June, 1916		April to June, 1917		July to Sept., 1917	
	Adms.	Ratio per 1,000	Adms.	Ratio per 1,000	Adms.	Ratio per 1,000
Anthrax	—	—	2	·01	1	·00
Bilharziasis	1	·01	62	·36	50	·22
Cerebro-spinal fever	18	·08	11	·05	7	·03
Chicken-pox	35	·17	7	·04	4	·02
Diphtheria	96	·43	743	4·20	958	4·20
Dysentery	2,057	9·05	1,213	7·00	2,698	12·00
Enterica	893	3·93	159	·91	189	·84
Epidemic jaundice	12	·05	1	·01	1	·00
Malaria	160	·70	608	3·50	3,035	13·50
Measles	278	1·23	31	·18	40	·17
Mumps	407	1·80	63	·37	136	·60
Plague	—	—	19	·11	—	—
Relapsing fever	130	·57	99	·49	32	·14
Rubella	12	·05	140	·84	42	·19
Scarlet fever	58	·27	169	·97	97	·43
Small-pox	73	·32	6	·03	10	·04
Typhus	7	·04	6	·03	3	·01

Table 17 is a sample showing the diseases affecting the force during 1918, the records being those of the XXth Corps and XXIst Corps for the year.

TABLE 17.—Diseases affecting the XXth Corps and XXIst Corps, Egyptian Expeditionary Force, 1918

	XXth Corps		XXIst Corps	
	Admissions	Ratio per 1,000	Admissions	Ratio per 1,000
Anthrax	—	—	6	·11
Bilharziasis	—	—	2	·04
Cerebro-spinal fever	9	·16	2	·04
Chicken-pox	—	—	9	·16
Cholera	—	—	1	·02
Diarrhœa	2,500	44·69	—	—
Diphtheria	333	5·95	324	5·76
Dysentery	1,500	26·81	1,449	25·75
Enterica	90	1·61	61	1·08
Erysipelas	—	—	15	·27
Jaundice	—	—	24	·43
Malaria	7,556	135·07	8,603	152·88
Measles	93	1·66	57	1·01
Mumps	—	—	140	2·49
Pyrexia of uncertain origin	11,930	213·25	—	—
Relapsing fever	—	—	371	6·59
Rubella	—	—	15	·27
Scarlet fever	109	1·95	59	1·05
Septic sores	1,027	18·36	—	—
Tonsillitis	1,288	23·02	—	—
Trench foot	165	2·95	—	—
Tuberculosis, pulmonary	—	—	11	·20
Typhus	—	—	35	·62
Venereal diseases	780	13·94	—	—

Table 18 has been compiled from available records to show the sick admission rate in different forces or units of the force over shorter or longer periods during the war.

TABLE 18.—Sick Admission Rates in Certain Operations

Force	Average ration strength	Period	Sick admissions	Ratio per 1,000
Western Frontier Force	15,300	25.3.16–10.3.17	15,161	990·92
Eastern Force	89,930	4.11.16–4.8.17	50,461	561·11
XXIst Army Corps	56,274	30.12.17–28.12.18	62,705	1,114·28
Desert Column	34,007	13.1.17–4.8.17	14,686	431·85
Force in Palestine	195,220	1918	180,818	926·23

Table 19 shows the total admissions for sick and wounded of the force in Palestine during 1918, and the numbers requiring evacuation. The ratios per 1,000 are calculated on the average ration strength of the force in Palestine only. The totals include British, Dominion and Indian troops.

TABLE 19.—Total Sick and Wounded admitted to Medical Units of the Force in Palestine, 1918

	Admissions		Evacuations		Percentage of Admissions
	Nos.	Ratio per 1,000	Nos.	Ratio per 1,000	
Wounded	13,782	70·60	12,635	64·72	91·68
Sick or injured	180,818	926·23	165,984	850·24	91·80
Total	194,600	996·82	178,619	914·96	91·79

CHAPTER XV

CASUALTIES IN THE MESOPOTAMIAN EXPEDITIONARY FORCE, NOVEMBER 1914 TO DECEMBER 1918

THE campaign against the Turks in Mesopotamia commenced early in November 1914 and extended over a period of four years. It was undertaken in the first instance by an expeditionary force despatched and controlled by the Government of India in order to protect British interests in the Persian Gulf. Reinforcements were sent out later from the United Kingdom, and in July 1916 the British Government assumed administrative control of the Mesopotamian Expeditionary Force. Briefly outlined, the campaign falls into four phases. The first phase, the campaign in Lower Mesopotamia, included the Basra operations and the advance of the force up the rivers Tigris and Euphrates. The second phase, the campaign for Baghdad, opened with the battle of Ctesiphon in November 1915 and the subsequent defence of Kut-al-Amara, and covered the period of repeated but unsuccessful efforts to relieve the beleaguered force. After the fall of Kut in April 1916, the absence of military activity during the summer months enabled the force to be reorganised and reconditioned prior to entering upon the third phase of the campaign, the capture and consolidation of Baghdad. These operations lasted from December 1916 to the end of April 1917. The final phase, the campaign in Upper Mesopotamia, included the Euphrates operations from July 1917 to April 1918, the Tigris operations from October to December 1917, and the Kirkuk operations in April and May 1918, and terminated with the advance on Mosul in October and its subsequent occupation in November 1918.

The preparation of the medical statistics of the campaign in Mesopotamia has presented many unusual difficulties owing to the composition of the force and the nature of the operations. The force was a mixed one, comprising a minority of British troops, a majority of Indian troops of various castes drawn from different parts of India, and an ever-increasing army of followers, mainly Indian, but including Arabs, Egyptians, Kurds, Chinese and many of other nationalities. To obtain the best results, therefore, statistics had to be compiled separately for the British troops, the Indian troops and followers, and for the whole force. In addition, the early operations did not permit of records being carefully kept, and there were many omissions and overlappings in the reports. These had to be noted and a subsequent search had to be made through masses of documents for some odd clue to other sources of information which would elucidate or confirm approximate figures hastily jotted down in periods of advance and victory, retreat and defeat, confusion, disorder and imperfect organisation.

The nature of the operations and the type of country and climate in which they were conducted give an added interest to the campaign, and explain in part the difficulties encountered by the medical services. There were periods of mobile warfare and manœuvre, by day and night, intensive trench warfare, cavalry actions and raids by mechanised forces. In 1915–16 success, failure, administrative breakdown and reorganisation followed in quick succession. Extreme heat in summer and great cold in winter attended the operations by land and river, through marsh and mud or over sandy desert, in the plains and in the mountains. Casualties had to be evacuated great distances. At first there was no broad-gauge railway to link up the various posts on the lines of communication and facilitate the evacuation of sick and wounded. Such roads as existed were bad, and the rivers and waterways forming the main lines of communication with the base, although navigable, were difficult to navigate. Many of the native towns were situated on the river banks and, one and all being over-populated and insanitary, constituted a fertile focus for the spread of disease. Basra, the base, was unhealthy, malarious, intersected by creeks and embedded in date groves. By river it was 132 miles from Amara, 243 from Shaikh Saad, 285 from Kut-al-Amara, 467 from Ctesiphon, and 498 from Baghdad. By sea it was several days' journey to India and many weeks to the United Kingdom.

The expeditionary force operating in such a country and under such conditions was bound to have problems peculiar to itself. Knowledge, resource and ingenuity were all required to preserve the health of the troops, collect and evacuate casualties, accommodate and treat them. The medical history of the campaign and the statistics of the different years forcibly demonstrate the losses which accrue from neglect and lack of foresight, and the benefits derived from adequate provision and proper organisation. The original force was well organised and trained for the initial operations. It fought with success for a year, but that very success was the undoing of its medical services. As long as the operations conformed to the type practised during peace the medical services did yeoman work. They were, however, being gradually undermined by improvisation and a strategical policy which broke down the principles of medical work in the field. Casualties were evacuated forwards with the force instead of backwards to the lines of communication and the base; mobile medical units were depleted by having medical personnel and equipment detached; and the lines of communication were not properly organised for the evacuation, reception and treatment of casualties. Just when the most ambitious part of the operations was put to the test at Ctesiphon in November 1915, the medical services, instead of being at their strongest, were at their weakest. The plan failed, a large force was besieged in Kut,* and when the Indian divisions arrived from France they were hurried to the front without their full complement of medical units. The strained and inadequate medical units at the front and on the lines of communication could not cope with the influx of sick and wounded. The transportation and treatment of casualties broke down, and the resulting conditions are well described by the late Sir Victor Horsley as " grossly insanitary and inhuman."

---

* The medical statistics of the garrison in Kut are included in this chapter. For separate details see the *General History of the Medical Services*, vol. iv, chap. ix.

In the following tables there are some points worthy of special comment.

(1) The percentage of deaths among sick and wounded admitted to hospital from 1916 onwards is high.

Year	British Wounded	Sick	Indian Wounded	Sick	British and Indian Wounded	Sick
1914–15	5·88	1·76	3·41	1·56	4·01	1·62
1916	9·94	2·77	10·82	1·85	10·46	2·16
1917	11·36	1·12	6·47	2·02	8·57	1·66
1918	9·30	1·10	11·28	2·68	10·66	2·14

The first reason for the high percentage of deaths from wounds was the great difficulty experienced in collecting and transporting the wounded from the firing-line over bad country to a fully equipped operating centre where they could receive attention and nursing. The second responsible factor was the time that elapsed before it was possible to operate on certain cases.

(2) The total numbers returned to duty in the theatre of operations show a high percentage of the total admissions. The lowest was in 1916.

Year	Nos. returned to duty	Percentage of admissions
1914–15	26,478	60·03
1916	135,889	55·65
1917	239,101	75·54
1918	259,332	83·66
	660,800	75·14

(3) The high sick rate in 1916 was followed by a great reduction in the succeeding years.

Year	Sick admissions	Ratio per 1,000
1914–15	33,553	902·39
1916	216,478	1,309·10
1917	281,141	914·32
1918	289,246	702·69

The high sick rate in 1916 is easily explained. After a trying period of intensive warfare lasting from January to April, the Tigris force failed to relieve the garrison at Kut. The total battle casualties in these operations were approximately 24,000. One division was reduced to a total effective fighting strength of 4,000; another had lost 273 officers out of 558 and 4,189 other ranks out of 9,439. The sanitary conditions were bad, and despite all peace-time training the troops were without the necessary appliances, materials and chemicals for providing an adequate supply of good water, or for preventing an outbreak of waterborne diseases. Officers and men were worn out by work and operations under trying conditions with often a daily shortage of rations and fuel. For the greater part of the ensuing summer most of the troops were concentrated in the front area with inadequate protection from a relentless sun. Little wonder, then, that they went sick, and as if to add to the general depression in a force inactive and subdued, the sick had to be retained in field units as they could not be evacuated regularly from the front at this period. The following figures show the actual sick admissions for the whole force for six months from March to August with the monthly percentage of strength affected.

1916	Sick admissions	Percentage of strength
March	8,500	7·73
April	14,025	11·22
May	19,935	15·33
June	25,606	18·30
July	34,778	24·84
August	19,249	13·75

The sick admissions from the Tigris Corps alone from 1st July to 2nd September 1916 numbered 21,256. With the onset of cooler weather and as a result of the many benefits of successful reorganisation, the old feeling of élan and will to win returned, and sickness began to diminish. For the forthcoming operations medical schemes were carefully considered and worked smoothly and efficiently when put to the test. Transport, hospitals and convalescent depots were constructed on most modern and up-to-date lines. Sanitation improved by leaps and bounds, and everything that was possible was done for the comfort and well-being of all ranks. The sick rate was reduced, evacuation overseas became less, and more patients were retained in the country and were ultimately returned to their units fit and well.

One of the most beneficial measures was the formation of the River Sick Convoy Unit and the establishment of a more or less regular system of evacuating sick and wounded by river. From its inception in June 1916 to the end of December 1918, 264,713 patients were evacuated by this means, as is shown in somewhat greater detail in the following table:

Period	Front to Amara				Amara to Basra				Total numbers carried			
	Brit.	Ind.	P/W.*	Total	Brit.	Ind.	P/W.*	Total	Brit.	Ind.	P/W.*	Total
June–Dec. 1916	15,671	27,582	—	43,253	15,749	25,902	—	41,651	31,420	53,484	—	84,904
1917	33,888	39,501	1,850	75,239	17,217	27,370	1,690	46,277	51,105	66,871	3,540	121,516
Jan.–June 1918	4,681	8,904	456	14,041	3,078	5,775	1,408	10,261	7,759	14,679	1,864	24,302
July–Dec. 1918	—	—	—	—	—	—	—	—	12,945	19,288	1,758	33,991
	—	—	—	—	—	—	—	—	103,229	154,322	7,162	264,713

* Prisoners of War

Despite the numerous improvements it would have been unnatural to expect that a mixed force could be kept entirely free from the virulent endemic diseases, such as cholera, small-pox, typhus, relapsing fever and plague, or from the less virulent troubles such as oriental sore and the effects of the trying heat. They were a constant source of anxiety in the force and were held in check only by systematised and careful measures of prevention. The statistical records will point a warning finger to their potential danger and should stimulate all concerned to make provision for them in a force operating in an eastern country.*

* The history of the Medical Services with the Mesopotamian Expeditionary Force is dealt with in the *General History of the Medical Services*, vol. iv, chaps. vi–xvi, pp. 163–415.

Strength

The average ration strength of the Mesopotamian Expeditionary Force year by year throughout the campaign is shown in Table 1.

TABLE 1.—Average Ration Strength

Year	British			Indian				Total			
	Off.	O.R.	Total	Off.	O.R.	Follrs.	Total	Off.	O.R.	Follrs.	Total
1914 1915 *	774	6,179	6,953	498	16,749	7,671	24,918	1,272	22,928	7,671	31,871
1916	3,088	45,131	48,219	1,557	65,112	50,476	117,145	4,645	110,243	50,476	165,364
1917	5,155	78,747	83,902	2,132	99,854	121,598	223,584	7,287	178,601	121,598	307,486
1918	7,107	100,275	107,382	2,651	137,713	163,879	304,243	9,758	237,988	163,879	411,625

* Refers throughout the chapter to the period 6th November, 1914, to the end of December 1915.

Classification of Casualties

The total casualties sustained by the Mesopotamian Expeditionary Force during the campaign are shown in Table 2. In calculating the ratios per 1,000 of strength for battle and non-battle casualties the very large proportion of non-combatant followers had to be taken into account. As there was no way of differentiating between Indian troops and followers in the reports, the figures for battle casualties probably include a few followers, but these numbers must have been very small and would not alter the ratio to any great extent. The method adopted has been to calculate the Indian battle casualties on the strength of the Indian troops, and the Indian non-battle casualties on the total Indian strength. In this way it is hoped that a more accurate ratio for battle and non-battle casualties has been obtained. The tables have accordingly been slightly modified to meet this departure from the usual formula.

TABLE 2.—Total Casualties

	British			Indian			Total		
	Off.	O.R.	Total	Off.	O.R.	Total	Off.	O.R.	Total
Battle casualties	2,944	28,405	31,349	1,269	52,589	53,858	4,213	80,994	85,207
Non-battle casualties	15,710	283,064	298,774	4,252	517,392*	521,644*	19,962	800,456*	820,418*
Total ..	18,654	311,469	330,123	5,521	569,981*	575,502*	24,175	881,450*	905,625*

* Includes followers.

The proportion of total battle casualties to non-battle casualties among British troops was 1 to 5·34 officers; 1 to 9·97 other ranks; and 1 to 9·53 all ranks. For Indian troops and followers it was 1 to 3·35 officers; 1 to 9·84 other ranks;

MESOPOTAMIA, 1914–1918

and 1 to 9·69 all ranks. For the whole force the proportion was 1 to 4·74 officers ; 1 to 9·88 other ranks ; and 1 to 9·63 all ranks.

Table 3 gives the battle casualties in the Mesopotamian Expeditionary Force year by year, with the average annual ratios per 1,000 of ration strength.

TABLE 3.—Battle Casualties by Years

Force	Year	Off.	O.R.	Total	Average annual ratio per 1,000		
					Off.	O.R.	Total
British ...	1914–15	456	2,723	3,179	505·17	377·73	391·92
	1916	1,406	13,243	14,649	455·31	293·43	303·80
	1917	959	11,506	12,465	186·03	146·11	148·57
	1918	123	933	1,056	17·31	9·30	9·83
	Total	*2,944*	*28,405*	*31,349*	*175·39*	*118·39*	*122·12*
Indian ...	1914–15	253	9,628	9,881	435·74	492·75	491·04
	1916	633	24,267	24,900	406·55	372·70	373·49
	1917	357	16,611	16,968	167·45	166·35	166·38
	1918	26	2,083	2,109	9·81	15·13	15·03
	Total	*1,269*	*52,589*	*53,858*	*178·36*	*158·05*	*158·47*
Total force	1914–15	709	12,351	13,060	477·99	461·71	462·56
	1916	2,039	37,510	39,549	438·97	340·25	344·24
	1917	1,316	28,117	29,433	180·60	157·43	158·34
	1918	149	3,016	3,165	15·27	12·67	12·78
	Total	*4,213*	*80,994*	*85,207*	*176·10*	*141·44*	*142·83*

Similarly, Table 4 shows the non-battle casualties in the force by years with the average annual ratios per 1,000 of strength.

TABLE 4.—Non-battle Casualties by Years

Force	Year	Off.	O.R.	Total	Average annual ratio per 1,000		
					Off.	O.R.	Total
British ...	1914–15	308	10,210	10,518	341·09	1,416·25	1,296·56
	1916	5,365	69,746	75,111	1,737·37	1,545·41	1,557·71
	1917	4,974	109,438	114,412	964·89	1,389·74	1,363·64
	1918	5,063	93,670	98,733	712·40	934·13	919·46
	Total	*15,710*	*283,064*	*298,774*	*935·25*	*1,179·78*	*1,163·79*
Indian ...	1914–15	148	22,887	23,035	255·02	803·32	792·36
	1916	1,624	139,743	141,367	1,043·03	1,208·97	1,206·77
	1917	1,475	165,254	166,729	691·84	746·23	745·71
	1918	1,005	189,508	190,513	379·10	628·36	626·19
	Total	*4,252*	*517,392*	*521,644*	*596·49*	*749·11*	*747·55*
Total force	1914–15	456	33,097	33,553	307·39	927·12	902·39
	1916	6,989	209,489	216,478	1,504·63	1,303·45	1,309·10
	1917	6,449	274,692	281,141	885·00	915·03	914·32
	1918	6,068	283,178	289,246	621·85	704·66	702·69
	Total	*19,962*	*800,456*	*820,418*	*834·52*	*860·14*	*859·50*

An analysis of the total casualties occurring in the Mesopotamian campaign is given in Table 5 (*a*) for British troops, in Table 5 (b) for Indian troops and followers, and for the whole force in Table 5 (c).

TABLE 5 (a).—Classification and Percentages of Total British Casualties

	Off.	O.R.	Total	Percentage of total British casualties		
				Off.	O.R.	Total
A. Battle Casualties:						
(a) Killed	629	4,403	5,032	3·37	1·41	1·52
(b) Died of wounds	221	2,156	2,377	1·18	·69	·72
(c) Missing	87	446	533	·47	·14	·16
(d) Prisoners of war *	313	2,735	3,048	1·68	·88	·92
(e) Wounded less (b)	1,694	18,665	20,359	9·08	5·99	6·17
B. Non-battle Casualties:						
(f) Died of disease or injury	241	4,534	4,775	1·29	1·46	1·45
(g) Sick or injured less (f)	15,469	278,530	293,999	82·93	89·42	89·06
Total A. and B.	18,654	311,469	330,123	—	—	—

TABLE 5 (b).—Classification and Percentages of Total Indian Casualties

	Off.	O.R.	Total	Percentage of total Indian casualties		
				Off.	O.R.	Total
A. Battle Casualties:						
(a) Killed	194	5,782	5,976	3·51	1·01	1·04
(b) Died of wounds	87	2,817	2,904	1·58	·49	·50
(c) Missing	15	1,794	1,809	·27	·31	·31
(d) Prisoners of war †	229	9,602	9,831	4·15	1·68	1·71
(e) Wounded less (b)	744	32,594	33,338	13·48	5·72	5·79
B. Non-battle casualties: ‡						
(f) Died of disease or injury	45	11,892	11,937	·82	2·09	2·07
(g) Sick or injured less (f)	4,207	505,500	509,707	76·20	88·69	88·57
Total A. and B.	5,521	569,981	575,502	—	—	—

TABLE 5 (c).—Classification and Percentages of Total Casualties

	Off.	O.R.	Total	Percentage of total casualties		
				Off.	O.R.	Total
A. Battle Casualties:						
(a) Killed	823	10,185	11,008	3·40	1·16	1·22
(b) Died of wounds	308	4,973	5,281	1·27	·56	·58
(c) Missing	102	2,240	2,342	·42	·25	·26
(d) Prisoners of war	542	12,337	12,879	2·24	1·40	1·42
(e) Wounded less (b)	2,438	51,259	53,697	10·08	5·82	5·93
B. Non-battle Casualties: ‡						
(f) Died of disease or injury	286	16,426	16,712	1·18	1·86	1·85
(g) Sick or injured less (f)	19,676	784,030	803,706	81·39	88·95	88·75
Total A. and B.	24,175	881,450	905,625	—	—	—

* Includes 22 officers and 1,654 other ranks who died as prisoners of war.
† Includes 10 officers and 1,698 other ranks who died as prisoners of war.
‡ Includes followers.

Table 6 (a) shows this detail as percentages of total battle casualties for British troops and Indian troops, while Table 6 (b) shows similarly the percentages of non-battle casualties.

TABLE 6 (a).—Percentages of Battle Casualties

	British			Indian			Total		
	Off.	O.R.	Total	Off.	O.R.	Total	Off.	O.R.	Total
(a) Killed	21·37	15·50	16·05	15·29	10·99	11·10	19·53	12·58	12·92
(b) Died of wounds	7·51	7·59	7·58	6·86	5·36	5·39	7·31	6·14	6·20
(c) Missing	2·96	1·57	1·70	1·18	3·41	3·36	2·42	2·77	2·75
(d) Prisoners of war	10·63	9·63	9·72	18·05	18·26	18·25	12·86	15·23	15·11
(e) Wounded less (b)	57·54	65·71	64·94	58·63	61·98	61·90	57·87	63·29	63·02

TABLE 6 (b).—Percentages of Non-battle Casualties

	British			Indian *			Total		
	Off.	O.R.	Total	Off.	O.R.	Total	Off.	O.R.	Total
(f) Died of disease or injury	1·53	1·60	1·60	1·06	2·30	2·29	1·43	2·05	2·04
(g) Sick or injured less (f)	98·47	98·40	98·40	98·94	97·70	97·71	98·57	97·95	97·96

* Includes followers.

The casualties sustained by the Mesopotamian Expeditionary Force may be further classified into permanent and temporary losses for military purposes in the field.

TABLE 7 (a).—Permanent Losses for Military Purposes in the Field expressed as Percentages of Total Casualties

	British			Indian			Total		
	Off.	O.R.	Total	Off.	O.R.	Total	Off.	O.R.	Total
A. *Battle Casualties*:									
Killed	3·37	1·41	1·52	3·51	1·01	1·04	3·40	1·16	1·22
Died of wounds	1·18	·69	·72	1·58	·49	·50	1·27	·56	·58
Missing	·47	·14	·16	·27	·31	·31	·42	·25	·26
Prisoners of war	1·68	·88	·92	4·15	1·68	1·71	2·24	1·40	1·42
Total	*6·70*	*3·13*	*3·33*	*9·51*	*3·51*	*3·57*	*7·34*	*3·37*	*3·48*
B. *Non-battle Casualties*: *									
Died of disease or injury	1·29	1·46	1·45	·82	2·09	2·07	1·18	1·86	1·85
Total permanent losses	7·99	4·58	4·78	10·32	5·59	5·64	8·53	5·24	5·32

TABLE 7 (b).—Temporary Losses for Military Purposes in the Field expressed as Percentages of Total Casualties

	British			Indian			Total		
	Off.	O.R.	Total	Off.	O.R.	Total	Off.	O.R.	Total
A. *Battle Casualties*:									
Wounded less died of wounds	9·08	5·99	6·17	13·48	5·72	5·79	10·08	5·82	5·93
B. *Non-battle Casualties*: *									
Sick or injured less died of disease or injury	82·93	89·42	89·06	76·20	88·69	88·57	81·39	88·95	88·75
Total temporary losses	92·01	95·42	95·22	89·68	94·41	94·36	91·47	94·76	94·68

* Includes followers.

The relative proportions of the various classes of casualties to each other in respect of British troops, Indian troops and followers and of the whole force during the campaign in Mesopotamia are shown in Tables 8 (a), 8 (b) and 8 (c) respectively.

TABLE 8 (a).—Proportions—British Troops only

	Officers	Other ranks	Total
1. Total battle casualties to total non-battle casualties	1 : 5·34	1 : 9·97	1 : 9·53
2. Total killed to total wounded including died of wounds	1 : 3·04	1 : 4·73	1 : 4·52
3. Permanent losses among battle casualties to total wounded less died of wounds	1 : 1·36	1 : 1·92	1 : 1·85
4. Permanent losses among non-battle casualties to total sick and injured less died of disease or injury	1 : 64·19	1 : 61·43	1 : 61·57
5. Total permanent losses to total temporary losses	1 : 11·51	1 : 20·82	1 : 19·94

TABLE 8 (b).—Proportions—Indian Troops and Followers

	Officers	Other ranks	Total
1. Total battle casualties to total non-battle casualties	1 : 3·35	1 : 9·84	1 : 9·69
2. Total killed to total wounded including died of wounds	1 : 4·28	1 : 6·12	1 : 6·06
3. Permanent losses among battle casualties to total wounded less died of wounds	1 : 1·42	1 : 1·63	1 : 1·62
4. Permanent losses among non-battle casualties to total sick and injured less died of disease or injury	1 : 93·49	1 : 42·51	1 : 42·70
5. Total permanent losses to total temporary losses	1 : 8·69	1 : 17·19	1 : 16·73

TABLE 8 (c).—Proportions—Whole Force

	Officers	Other ranks	Total
1. Total battle casualties to total non-battle casualties	1 : 4·74	1 : 9·88	1 : 9·63
2. Total killed to total wounded including died of wounds	1 : 3·34	1 : 5·52	1 : 5·36
3. Permanent losses among battle casualties to total wounded less died of wounds	1 : 1·37	1 : 1·72	1 : 1·70
4. Permanent losses among non-battle casualties to total sick and injured less died of disease or injury	1 : 68·80	1 : 47·73	1 : 48·09
5. Total permanent losses to total temporary losses	1 : 10·73	1 : 18·10	1 : 17·78

Admissions to Hospital

Of the total casualties suffered by the Mesopotamian Expeditionary Force from November 1914 to the end of December 1918, the numbers admitted to hospital and treated by the medical services are shown in Table 9 (a) for British troops, Table 9 (b) for Indian troops and followers, and Table 9 (c) for the whole force.

TABLE 9 (a).—Numbers admitted to Hospital—British Troops

	Off.	O.R.	Total	Percentage of total British casualties		
				Off.	O.R.	Total
Wounded	1,915	20,821	22,736	10·27	6·68	6·89
Sick or injured	15,710	283,064	298,774	84·22	90·88	90·50
Total	17,625	303,885	321,510	94·48	97·57	97·39

TABLE 9 (b).—Numbers admitted to Hospital—Indian Troops and Followers

	Off.	O.R.	Total	Percentage of total Indian casualties		
				Off.	O.R.	Total
Wounded	831	35,411	36,242	15·05	6·21	6·30
Sick or injured	4,252	517,392	521,644	77·02	90·77	90·64
Total	5,083	552,803	557,886	92·07	96·99	96·94

TABLE 9 (c).—Numbers admitted to Hospital—Whole Force

	Off.	O.R.	Total	Percentage of total casualties		
				Off.	O.R.	Total
Wounded	2,746	56,232	58,978	11·36	6·38	6·51
Sick or injured	19,962	800,456	820,418	82·57	90·81	90·59
Total	22,708	856,688	879,396	93·93	97·19	97·10

The proportion of wounded to sick and injured treated by the medical services in the case of British troops was 1 to 8·20 officers; 1 to 13·60 other ranks; and 1 to 13·14 all ranks. For Indian troops and followers the proportion was 1 to 5·12 officers; 1 to 14·61 other ranks; and 1 to 14·39 all ranks. The proportion for the whole force was 1 to 7·27 officers; 1 to 14·23 other ranks; and 1 to 13·91 all ranks.

The casualties which were not treated by the medical services are shown in Table 10 (a) for British troops, Table 10 (b) for Indian troops, and Table 10 (c) for the whole force.

TABLE 10 (a).—Casualties among British Troops not treated by the Medical Services

	Off.	O.R.	Total	Percentage of total British casualties		
				Off.	O.R.	Total
Killed	629	4,403	5,032	3·37	1·41	1·52
Missing	87	446	533	·47	·14	·16
Prisoners of war	313	2,735	3,048	1·68	·88	·92
Total	1,029	7,584	8,613	5·52	2·43	2·61

TABLE 10 (b).—Casualties among Indian Troops not treated by the Medical Services

	Off.	O.R.	Total	Percentage of total Indian casualties		
				Off.	O.R.	Total
Killed	194	5,782	5,976	3·51	1·01	1·04
Missing	15	1,794	1,809	·27	·31	·31
Prisoners of war	229	9,602	9,831	4·15	1·68	1·71
Total	438	17,178	17,616	7·93	3·01	3·06

TABLE 10 (c).—Casualties in the Mesopotamian Expeditionary Force not treated by the Medical Services

	Off.	O.R.	Total	Percentage of total casualties		
				Off.	O.R.	Total
Killed	823	10,185	11,008	3·40	1·16	1·22
Missing	102	2,240	2,342	·42	·25	·26
Prisoners of war	542	12,337	12,879	2·24	1·40	1·42
Total	1,467	24,762	26,229	6·07	2·81	2·90

The numbers of sick and wounded admitted to hospital and the disposal of cases in each year, with the corresponding ratios per 1,000 of strength and the percentages of total admissions, are given for British troops of the Mesopotamian Expeditionary Force in Tables 11 (a), 11 (b) and 11 (c). In the table of percentages it must be remembered that, with the exception of the period November 1914 to December 1915, the percentages are calculated on the total admissions for each year plus the numbers remaining in hospital at the end of the previous year.

TABLE 11 (a).—Admissions to Hospital and Disposal of Cases in each Year—British Troops only

Year		Wounded			Sick or injured			Total		
		Off.	O.R.	Total	Off.	O.R.	Total	Off.	O.R.	Total
1914–1915	Admissions	341	2,211	2,552	308	10,210	10,518	649	12,421	13,070
	Deaths	26	124	150	6	179	185	32	303	335
	Returned to duty in theatre of war	160	1,167	1,327	127	8,071	8,198	287	9,238	9,525
	Evacuated overseas	109	658	767	145	1,455	1,600	254	2,113	2,367
1916	Admissions	819	9,050	9,869	5,365	69,746	75,111	6,184	78,796	84,980
	Deaths	97	915	1,012	71	2,024	2,095	168	2,939	3,107
	Returned to duty in theatre of war	205	3,261	3,466	3,224	42,451	45,675	3,429	45,712	49,141
	Evacuated overseas	530	4,707	5,237	1,904	22,069	23,973	2,434	26,776	29,210
1917	Admissions	677	8,813	9,490	4,974	109,438	114,412	5,651	118,251	123,902
	Deaths	89	1,042	1,131	68	1,256	1,324	157	2,298	2,455
	Returned to duty in theatre of war	219	4,264	4,483	3,979	90,670	94,649	4,198	94,934	99,132
	Evacuated overseas	391	3,869	4,260	875	14,227	15,102	1,266	18,096	19,362
1918	Admissions	78	747	825	5,063	93,670	98,733	5,141	94,417	99,558
	Deaths	9	75	84	96	1,075	1,171	105	1,150	1,255
	Returned to duty in theatre of war	30	258	288	4,429	86,951	91,380	4,459	87,209	91,668
	Evacuated overseas	35	370	405	547	7,245	7,792	582	7,615	8,197
1914–1918	Admissions	1,915	20,821	22,736	15,710	283,064	298,774	17,625	303,885	321,510
	Deaths	221	2,156	2,377	241	4,534	4,775	462	6,690	7,152
	Returned to duty in theatre of war	614	8,950	9,564	11,759	228,143	239,902	12,373	237,093	249,466
	Evacuated overseas	1,065	9,604	10,669	3,471	44,996	48,467	4,536	54,600	59,136

TABLE 11 (b).—Annual Ratios per 1,000 of British Ration Strength

Year		Wounded			Sick or injured			Total		
		Off.	O.R.	Total	Off.	O.R.	Total	Off.	O.R.	Total
1914–1915	Admissions	377·26	306·68	314·54	341·09	1,416·25	1,296·56	718·35	1,723·09	1,611·25
	Deaths	28·42	17·15	18·55	6·46	24·76	22·87	34·88	42·08	41·28
	Returned to duty in theatre of war	177·00	161·84	163·53	140·83	1,119·60	1,010·64	317·83	1,281·44	1,174·17
	Evacuated overseas	120·16	91·28	94·49	160·21	201·81	197·18	281·65	293·09	291·82
1916	Admissions	265·22	200·53	204·67	1,737·37	1,545·41	1,557·71	2,002·59	1,745·94	1,762·38
	Deaths	31·41	20·27	20·99	22·99	44·85	43·45	54·40	65·12	64·44
	Returned to duty in theatre of war	66·39	72·26	71·88	1,044·04	942·02	947·24	1,110·43	1,012·87	1,019·12
	Evacuated overseas	171·63	104·30	108·61	616·58	489·00	497·17	788·21	593·30	605·78
1917	Admissions	131·33	111·92	113·11	964·89	1,389·74	1,363·64	1,096·22	1,501·66	1,476·75
	Deaths	17·26	13·23	13·48	13·19	15·95	15·78	30·46	29·18	29·26
	Returned to duty in theatre of war	42·48	54·15	53·43	771·87	1,151·41	1,128·09	814·35	1,205·56	1,181·52
	Evacuated overseas	75·85	49·13	50·77	169·74	180·67	180·00	245·59	229·80	230·77
1918	Admissions	10·98	7·45	7·68	712·40	934·13	919·46	723·37	941·58	927·14
	Deaths	1·27	·75	·78	13·51	10·72	10·90	14·77	11·47	11·69
	Returned to duty in theatre of war	4·22	2·57	2·68	623·19	867·13	850·98	627·41	869·70	853·66
	Evacuated overseas	4·92	3·69	3·77	76·97	72·25	72·56	81·89	75·94	76·33
Average annual ratio per 1,000	Admissions	114·12	86·78	88·57	935·25	1,179·78	1,163·79	1,049·37	1,266·55	1,252·35
	Deaths	13·15	8·98	9·25	14·39	18·89	18·60	27·54	27·89	27·85
	Returned to duty in theatre of war	36·47	37·30	37·25	700·07	950·87	934·46	736·79	988·17	971·73
	Evacuated overseas	63·51	40·03	41·57	206·65	187·54	188·79	270·16	227·57	230·35

TABLE 11 (c).—Percentages of Total British Admissions

Year		Wounded			Sick or injured			Total		
		Off.	O.R.	Total	Off.	O.R.	Total	Off.	O.R.	Total
1914–1915	Deaths	7·62	5·61	5·88	1·95	1·75	1·76	4·93	2·44	2·56
	Returned to duty in theatre of war	46·92	52·78	52·00	41·23	79·05	77·94	44·22	74·37	72·88
	Evacuated overseas	31·96	29·76	30·05	47·08	14·25	15·21	39·14	17·01	18·11
	Remaining in medical charge	13·49	11·85	12·07	9·74	4·95	5·09	11·71	6·18	6·45
1916	Deaths	11·21	9·83	9·94	1·32	2·88	2·77	2·68	3·69	3·62
	Returned to duty in theatre of war	23·70	35·02	34·06	59·76	60·43	60·38	54·78	57·45	57·26
	Evacuated overseas	61·27	50·55	51·46	35·29	31·41	31·69	38·88	33·65	34·04
	Remaining in medical charge	3·82	4·61	4·54	3·63	5·28	5·16	3·66	5·20	5·09
1917	Deaths	12·54	11·27	11·36	1·32	1·11	1·12	2·67	1·88	1·91
	Returned to duty in theatre of war	30·85	46·14	45·05	76·96	80·14	80·00	71·39	77·57	77·29
	Evacuated overseas	55·07	41·86	42·81	16·92	12·57	12·76	21·53	14·79	15·10
	Remaining in medical charge	1·55	·72	·78	4·80	6·18	6·12	4·40	5·77	5·71
1918	Deaths	10·11	9·21	9·30	1·81	1·07	1·10	1·94	1·13	1·17
	Returned to duty in theatre of war	33·71	31·70	31·89	83·39	86·38	86·23	82·57	85·94	85·77
	Evacuated overseas	39·33	45·45	44·85	10·30	7·20	7·35	10·78	7·50	7·67
	Remaining in medical charge	16·85	13·64	13·95	4·50	5·36	5·31	4·70	5·42	5·39
1914–1918	Deaths	11·54	10·35	10·45	1·53	1·60	1·60	2·62	2·20	2·22
	Returned to duty in theatre of war	32·06	42·99	42·07	74·85	80·60	80·30	70·20	78·02	77·59
	Evacuated overseas	55·61	46·13	46·93	22·09	15·90	16·22	25·74	17·97	18·39
	Remaining in medical charge	·78	·53	·55	1·52	1·90	1·88	1·44	1·81	1·79

MESOPOTAMIA, 1914-1918

TABLE 12 (a).—Admissions to Hospital and Disposal of Cases in each Year—Indian Troops and Followers

Year		Wounded (troops only)			Sick and injured (includes followers)			Total		
		Off.	O.R.	Total	Off.	O.R.	Total	Off.	O.R.	Total
1914–1915	Admissions	187	7,814	8,001	148	22,887	23,035	335	30,701	31,036
	Deaths	10	263	273	5	354	359	15	617	632
	Returned to duty in theatre of war	80	3,464	3,544	72	13,337	13,409	152	16,801	16,953
	Evacuated overseas	78	3,210	3,288	54	6,528	6,582	132	9,738	9,870
1916	Admissions	348	13,084	13,432	1,624	139,743	141,367	1,972	152,827	154,799
	Deaths	45	1,505	1,550	14	2,644	2,658	59	4,149	4,208
	Returned to duty in theatre of war	199	6,765	6,964	813	78,971	79,784	1,012	85,736	86,748
	Evacuated overseas	113	5,420	5,533	727	52,646	53,373	840	58,066	58,906
1917	Admissions	272	12,727	12,999	1,475	165,254	166,729	1,747	177,981	179,728
	Deaths	28	831	859	13	3,519	3,532	41	4,350	4,391
	Returned to duty in theatre of war	70	5,135	5,205	1,116	133,648	134,764	1,186	138,783	139,969
	Evacuated overseas	179	6,879	7,058	358	25,703	26,061	537	32,582	33,119
1918	Admissions	24	1,786	1,810	1,005	189,508	190,513	1,029	191,294	192,323
	Deaths	4	218	222	13	5,375	5,388	17	5,593	5,610
	Returned to duty in theatre of war	10	624	634	594	166,436	167,030	604	167,060	167,664
	Evacuated overseas	13	253	266	443	19,417	19,860	456	19,670	20,126
1914–1918	Admissions	831	35,411	36,242	4,252	517,392	521,644	5,083	552,803	557,886
	Deaths	87	2,817	2,904	45	11,892	11,937	132	14,709	14,841
	Returned to duty in theatre of war	359	15,988	16,347	2,595	392,392	394,987	2,954	408,380	411,334
	Evacuated overseas	383	15,762	16,145	1,582	104,294	105,876	1,965	120,056	122,021

TABLE 12 (b).—Annual Ratios per 1,000 of Indian Ration Strength

Year		Wounded (troops only)			Sick and injured (includes followers)		
		Off.	O.R.	Total	Off.	O.R.	Total
1914–1915	Admissions	321·29	399·90	397·63	255·02	803·32	792·36
	Deaths	18·07	13·43	13·57	8·03	12·41	12·36
	Returned to duty in theatre of war	138·55	177·26	176·15	124·50	468·14	461·23
	Evacuated overseas	134·54	164·25	163·39	92·37	229·12	226·42
1916	Admissions	223·51	200·95	201·47	1,043·03	1,208·97	1,206·77
	Deaths	28·90	23·11	23·25	8·99	22·87	22·69
	Returned to duty in theatre of war	127·81	103·90	104·46	522·16	683·21	681·07
	Evacuated overseas	72·58	83·24	82·99	466·92	455·46	455·61
1917	Admissions	127·58	127·46	127·46	691·84	746·23	745·71
	Deaths	13·13	8·32	8·42	6·10	15·89	15·80
	Returned to duty in theatre of war	32·83	51·43	51·04	523·45	603·51	602·74
	Evacuated overseas	83·96	68·89	69·21	167·92	116·07	116·56
1918	Admissions	9·05	12·97	12·90	379·10	628·36	626·19
	Deaths	1·51	1·58	1·58	4·90	17·82	17·71
	Returned to duty in theatre of war	3·77	4·53	4·52	224·07	551·86	549·00
	Evacuated overseas	4·90	1·84	1·90	167·11	64·38	65·28
Average annual ratio per 1,000	Admissions	116·37	106·43	106·64	596·49	749·11	747·55
	Deaths	12·28	8·47	8·55	6·43	17·22	17·11
	Returned to duty in theatre of war	50·29	48·05	48·10	364·33	568·12	566·04
	Evacuated overseas	53·80	47·37	47·51	222·22	151·00	151·73

Tables 12 (a), 12 (b) and 12 (c) give similar information in respect of Indian troops and followers year by year during the campaign. Here again it must be noted that in the case of Indian wounded the ratios per 1,000 are calculated on the strength of the Indian troops only. The ratios for sick and injured are calculated on the total Indian strength. It is therefore impossible to show a combined ratio of Indian sick and wounded.

TABLE 12 (c).—Percentages of Total Indian Admissions

Year		Wounded (troops only)			Sick or injured (includes followers)			Total		
		Off.	O.R.	Total	Off.	O.R.	Total	Off.	O.R.	Total
1914–1915	Deaths	5·35	3·37	3·41	3·38	1·55	1·56	4·48	2·01	2·04
	Returned to duty in theatre of war	42·78	44·33	44·29	48·65	58·27	58·21	45·37	54·72	54·62
	Evacuated overseas	41·71	41·08	41·09	36·49	28·52	28·57	39·40	31·72	31·80
	Remaining in medical charge	10·16	11·22	11·20	11·49	11·66	11·66	10·75	11·55	11·54
1916	Deaths	12·26	10·78	10·82	·85	1·86	1·85	2·94	2·65	2·66
	Returned to duty in theatre of war	54·22	48·46	48·60	49·54	55·45	55·39	50·40	54·83	54·77
	Evacuated overseas	30·79	38·82	38·62	44·30	36·97	37·05	41·83	37·13	37·19
	Remaining in medical charge	2·72	1·94	1·96	5·30	5·72	5·72	4·83	5·39	5·38
1917	Deaths	9·93	6·39	6·47	·83	2·03	2·02	2·22	2·33	2·33
	Returned to duty in theatre of war	24·82	39·51	39·19	71·45	77·07	77·02	64·32	74·45	74·35
	Evacuated overseas	63·48	52·92	53·15	22·92	14·82	14·89	29·12	17·48	17·59
	Remaining in medical charge	1·77	1·18	1·19	4·80	6·07	6·06	4·34	5·73	5·72
1918	Deaths	13·79	11·24	11·28	1·20	2·69	2·68	1·53	2·77	2·76
	Returned to duty in theatre of war	34·48	32·18	32·22	55·00	83·20	83·05	54·46	82·71	82·56
	Evacuated overseas	44·83	13·05	13·52	41·02	9·71	9·87	41·12	9·74	9·91
	Remaining in medical charge	6·90	43·53	42·99	2·78	4·41	4·40	2·89	4·78	4·77
1914–1918	Deaths	10·47	7·96	8·01	1·06	2·30	2·29	2·60	2·66	2·66
	Returned to duty in theatre of war	43·20	45·15	45·11	61·03	75·84	75·72	58·12	73·87	73·73
	Evacuated overseas	46·09	44·51	44·55	37·21	20·16	20·30	38·66	21·72	21·87
	Remaining in medical charge	·24	2·38	2·33	·71	1·70	1·70	·63	1·75	1·74

Tables 13 (a), 13 (b) and 13 (c) show the total admissions to hospital and disposal of cases year by year for the whole force in Mesopotamia. The ratios per 1,000 of total wounded are again calculated on the strength of British and Indian troops, while the ratios for sick and injured are calculated on the strength of the whole force.

It is unfortunately not possible to show the average numbers constantly in medical charge for the whole campaign, but records have been kept for longer or shorter periods in each year which give some idea of the approximate figures. These are given in Table 14, the ratio per 1,000 being calculated on the average strength of the force for the period in question.

MESOPOTAMIA, 1914–1918

TABLE 13 (a).—Admissions to Hospital and Disposal of Cases in each Year—Whole Force

Year		Wounded (troops only)			Sick or injured (includes followers)			Total		
		Off.	O.R.	Total	Off.	O.R.	Total	Off.	O.R.	Total
1914–1915	Admissions	528	10,025	10,553	456	33,097	33,553	984	43,122	44,106
	Deaths	36	387	423	11	533	544	47	920	967
	Returned to duty in theatre of war	240	4,631	4,871	199	21,408	21,607	439	26,039	26,478
	Evacuated overseas	187	3,868	4,055	199	7,983	8,182	386	11,851	12,237
1916	Admissions	1,167	22,134	23,301	6,989	209,489	216,478	8,156	231,623	239,779
	Deaths	142	2,420	2,562	85	4,668	4,753	227	7,088	7,315
	Returned to duty in theatre of war	404	10,026	10,430	4,037	121,422	125,459	4,441	131,448	135,889
	Evacuated overseas	643	10,127	10,770	2,631	74,715	77,346	3,274	84,842	88,116
1917	Admissions	949	21,540	22,489	6,449	274,692	281,141	7,398	296,232	303,630
	Deaths	117	1,873	1,990	81	4,775	4,856	198	6,648	6,846
	Returned to duty in theatre of war	289	9,399	9,688	5,095	224,318	229,413	5,384	233,717	239,101
	Evacuated overseas	570	10,748	11,318	1,233	39,930	41,163	1,803	50,678	52,481
1918	Admissions	102	2,533	2,635	6,068	283,178	289,246	6,170	285,711	291,881
	Deaths	13	293	306	109	6,450	6,559	122	6,743	6,865
	Returned to duty in theatre of war	40	882	922	5,023	253,387	258,410	5,063	254,269	259,332
	Evacuated overseas	48	623	671	990	26,662	27,652	1,038	27,285	28,323
1914–1918	Admissions	2,746	56,232	58,978	19,962	800,456	820,418	22,708	856,688	879,396
	Deaths	308	4,973	5,281	286	16,426	16,712	594	21,399	21,993
	Returned to duty in theatre of war	973	24,938	25,911	14,354	620,535	634,889	15,327	645,473	660,800
	Evacuated overseas	1,448	25,366	26,814	5,053	149,290	154,343	6,501	174,656	181,157

TABLE 13 (b).—Annual Ratios per 1,000 of Total Ration Strength

Year		Wounded (troops only)			Sick or injured (whole force)		
		Off.	O.R.	Total	Off.	O.R.	Total
1914–1915	Admissions	356·13	374·78	373·76	307·39	927·12	902·39
	Deaths	24·37	14·48	15·00	7·08	14·94	14·62
	Returned to duty in theatre of war	161·95	173·11	172·52	134·43	599·69	581·09
	Evacuated overseas	125·79	144·58	143·64	134·43	223·63	220·04
1916	Admissions	251·24	200·77	202·81	1,504·63	1,303·45	1,309·10
	Deaths	30·57	21·95	22·30	18·30	29·04	28·74
	Returned to duty in theatre of war	86·98	90·94	90·78	869·11	755·49	758·68
	Evacuated overseas	138·43	91·86	93·74	566·42	464·88	467·73
1917	Admissions	130·23	120·60	120·98	885·00	915·03	914·32
	Deaths	16·06	10·49	10·71	11·12	15·91	15·79
	Returned to duty in theatre of war	39·66	52·63	52·12	699·19	747·23	746·09
	Evacuated overseas	78·22	60·18	60·89	169·21	133·01	133·87
1918	Admissions	10·45	10·64	10·64	621·85	704·66	702·69
	Deaths	1·33	1·23	1·24	11·17	16·05	15·93
	Returned to duty in theatre of war	4·10	3·71	3·72	514·76	630·52	627·78
	Evacuated overseas	4·92	2·62	2·71	101·46	66·35	67·18
Average annual ratio per 1,000	Admissions	114·79	98·20	98·86	834·52	860·14	859·50
	Deaths	12·89	8·69	8·85	12·02	17·65	17·51
	Returned to duty in theatre of war	40·76	43·55	43·43	600·07	666·80	665·13
	Evacuated overseas	60·62	44·30	44·94	211·29	160·42	161·69

TABLE 13 (c).—Percentages of Total Admissions

Year		Wounded (troops only)			Sick or injured (includes followers)			Total		
		Off.	O.R.	Total	Off.	O.R.	Total	Off.	O.R.	Total
1914–1915	Deaths	6·82	3·86	4·01	2·41	1·61	1·62	4·78	2·13	2·19
	Returned to duty in theatre of war	45·45	46·19	46·16	43·64	64·68	64·40	44·61	60·38	60·03
	Evacuated overseas	35·42	38·58	38·43	43·64	24·12	24·39	39·23	27·48	27·74
	Remaining in medical charge	12·31	11·36	11·41	10·31	9·59	9·60	11·38	10·00	10·03
1916	Deaths	11·53	10·40	10·46	1·21	2·20	2·16	2·75	3·00	3·00
	Returned to duty in theatre of war	32·79	43·08	42·56	57·38	57·10	57·11	53·71	55·71	55·65
	Evacuated overseas	52·19	43·51	43·95	37·39	35·13	35·21	39·60	35·96	36·08
	Remaining in medical charge	3·49	3·01	3·03	4·02	5·58	5·53	3·94	5·32	5·28
1917	Deaths	11·79	8·42	8·57	1·20	1·67	1·66	2·56	2·15	2·16
	Returned to duty in theatre of war	29·13	42·26	41·70	75·68	78·28	78·22	69·70	75·69	75·54
	Evacuated overseas	57·46	48·33	48·72	18·32	13·93	14·04	23·34	16·41	16·58
	Remaining in medical charge	1·61	·99	1·02	4·80	6·12	6·09	4·39	5·75	5·71
1918	Deaths	11·02	10·64	10·66	1·71	2·14	2·14	1·87	2·22	2·21
	Returned to duty in theatre of war	33·90	32·04	32·11	78·59	84·26	84·15	77·78	83·79	83·66
	Evacuated overseas	40·68	22·63	23·37	15·49	8·87	9·00	15·95	8·99	9·14
	Remaining in medical charge	14·41	34·69	33·86	4·21	4·72	4·71	4·39	5·00	4·98
1914–1918	Deaths	11·22	8·84	8·95	1·43	2·05	2·04	2·62	2·50	2·50
	Returned to duty in theatre of war	35·43	44·35	43·93	71·91	77·52	77·39	67·50	75·35	75·14
	Evacuated overseas	52·73	45·11	45·46	25·31	18·65	18·81	28·63	20·39	20·60
	Remaining in medical charge	·62	1·70	1·65	1·35	1·77	1·76	1·26	1·77	1·76

TABLE 14.—Average Numbers Constantly in Medical Charge over Certain Periods during the Mesopotamia Campaign

Period	British		Indian				Total	
			Troops		Followers			
	Nos.	Ratio per 1,000	Nos.	Ratio per 1,000	Nos.	Ratio per 1,000	Nos.	Ratio per 1,000
July–October, 1915	638	102·56	1,588	79·00	922	114·25	3,148	91·53
29th April, 1916	3,062	77·81	6,932	115·50	812	31·29	10,806	86·23
July–December, 1916	5,106	96·06	9,523*	71·89*			14,629	78·81
May–December, 1917	7,185	75·88	4,541	37·86	4,998	36·28	16,724	47·46
January–December, 1918	6,507	60·60	4,267	30·40	6,385	38·96	17,159	41·69

* Includes followers.

Hospital Accommodation

From the information available regarding the hospital accommodation provided for the British and Indian troops and followers in Mesopotamia it has only been possible to show in Table 15 the average numbers of hospital beds equipped and occupied each year, with the corresponding percentages of ration strength. What is probably of considerable value is the greater detail given in Table 16 to show the very limited hospital accommodation which was available to meet the needs of the force augmented at the end of 1915 and early in 1916 by the arrival of the Indian divisions from France, and the gradual increase in the number of equipped beds until the deficiency had been made good by the beginning of the following cold weather.

TABLE 15.—Average Hospital Accommodation provided for the Mesopotamian Expeditionary Force on the Lines of Communication

Year	Force	Average ration strength	Average No. equipped beds	Average No. occupied beds	Percentage of ration strength	
					Equipped beds	Occupied beds
1915	British	6,953	500		7·19	
	Indian	24,918	1,050		4·21	
	Total	*31,871*	*1,550*	*1,930*	*4·86*	*6·06*
1916	British	48,219	3,330	4,085	6·91	8·47
	Indian	117,145	5,404	7,619	4·61	6·50
	Total	*165,364*	*8,734*	*11,704*	*5·28*	*7·08*
1917	British	83,902	6,968	5,354	8·30	6·38
	Indian	223,584	11,908	7,223	5·33	3·23
	Total	*307,486*	*18,876*	*12,577*	*6·14*	*4·09*
1918	British	107,382	7,303	4,500	6·80	4·19
	Indian	304,243	12,000	7,670	3·94	2·52
	Total	*411,625*	*19,303*	*12,170*	*4·69*	*2·96*

TABLE 16.—Development of Hospital Accommodation in the Mesopotamian Expeditionary Force during 1916

Date 1916	Force	Ration strength	Equipped beds	Occupied beds	Percentage of strength	
					Equipped beds	Occupied beds
January	British		1,050			
	Indian		2,550			
	Total	*71,112*	*3,600*	*4,686*	*5·06*	*6·59*
May	British	39,352	2,790		7·09	
	Indian	85,964	3,110		3·62	
	Total	*125,316*	*5,900*		*4·71*	
1st July	British	42,624	6,310	6,320	14·80	14·83
	Indian	108,033	7,110	9,208	6·58	8·52
	Total	*150,657*	*13,420*	*15,528*	*8·91*	*10·31*
6th Oct.	British	50,119	5,820	3,275	11·61	6·53
	Indian	126,816	9,030	7,249	7·12	5·72
	Total	*176,935*	*14,850*	*10,514*	*8·39*	*5·94*
23rd Dec.	British	70,837	6,260	3,492	8·84	4·93
	Indian	178,263	9,880	6,815	5·54	3·82
	Total	*249,700*	*16,140*	*10,307*	*6·48*	*4·14*

Table 17 shows the average convalescent depot accommodation provided for the force in Mesopotamia from 1916 onwards. No note has been taken of the temporary convalescent depots organised by corps and divisions during the summer months in the areas they occupied.

TABLE 17.—Convalescent Depot Accommodation provided for the Mesopotamian Expeditionary Force, 1916–1918

Year	Force	Average ration strength	Equipped beds	Occupied beds	Percentage of ration strength	
					Equipped beds	Occupied beds
1916	British	48,219	1,625		3·37	
	Indian	117,145	2,025		1·73	
	Total	*165,364*	*3,650*		*2·21*	
1917	British	83,902	2,498		2·98	
	Indian	223,584	3,080		1·38	
	Total	*307,486*	*5,578*		*1·81*	
1918	British	107,382	3,965	1,837	3·69	1·71
	Indian	304,243	3,500	2,663	1·15	·88
	Total	*411,625*	*7,465*	*4,500*	*1·81*	*1·09*

Non-battle Casualties

It has not been possible to obtain a complete record of all the causes of admission to hospital for disease or injury during the campaign in Mesopotamia owing to loss of records, inconsistence in preparing reports in the field, and the difficulty of keeping complete records at certain periods of the campaign. The principal diseases recorded year by year among British troops and Indian troops and followers are shown in Tables 18, 19, 20, 21 and 22, with the number of deaths, where these are known, and the corresponding actual ratios per 1,000 of strength.

At first sight these tables of special diseases occurring in the Mesopotamian Expeditionary Force may appear small and insignificant, but they indicate the incidence of the virulent infectious diseases, such as plague, cholera, small-pox and typhus, which are always a potential source of trouble in a force operating in the East. Apart from drawing attention to their comparatively low admission rate, it is important to note that the greatest number of cases of cholera occurred in 1916 when the force was unprepared to combat the disease.

According to the medical reports, the high sick rate was chiefly caused by the commoner diseases of everyday life,

TABLE 18.—Principal Diseases in the Mesopotamian Expeditionary Force from November 1914 to December 1915

	British		Indian		Total		Ratio per 1,000					
							British		Indian		Total	
	Admissions	Deaths	Admissions	Deaths	Admissions	Deaths	Admissions	Deaths	Admissions	Deaths	Admissions	Deaths
Cerebro-spinal fever	—	—	—	—	—	—	—	—	—	—	—	—
Cholera	604	12	2,872	21	3,476	33	86·87	1·73	115·26	·84	109·06	1·04
Dysentery	127	13	70	—	197	—	18·27	1·87	2·81	—	6·18	—
Enteric group of fevers	2,457	12	2,399	—	4,856	—	353·37	1·73	96·28	—	152·36	—
Malaria	—	—	—	—	—	—	—	—	—	—	—	—
Plague	—	—	—	—	—	—	—	—	—	—	—	—
Small-pox	—	—	—	—	—	—	—	—	—	—	—	—
Typhus	—	—	—	—	—	—	—	—	—	—	—	—
Venereal diseases	125	—	494	—	619	—	17·98	—	19·83	—	19·42	—
Scurvy	1	—	450	—	451	—	·14	—	18·06	—	14·15	—
Beri-beri	319	5	—	—	319	5	45·88	·72	—	—	10·01	·16
Effects of heat	538	1	52	—	590	1	77·39	·14	2·09	—	18·51	·03

TABLE 19.—Principal Diseases in the Mesopotamian Expeditionary Force in 1916

| | British | | Indian | | Total | | Ratio per 1,000 | | | | | |
| | | | | | | | British | | Indian | | Total | |
	Admissions	Deaths	Admissions	Deaths	Admissions	Deaths	Admissions	Deaths	Admissions	Deaths	Admissions	Deaths
Cerebro-spinal fever	5	2	48	8	53	10	(Figures incomplete)		—	—	—	—
Cholera	182	72	1,736	273	1,918	345	3·77	1·49	14·82	2·33	11·60	2·09
Dysentery	5,493	—	9,777	—	15,270	—	113·92	—	83·46	—	92·34	—
Enteric group of fevers	2,649	—	411	—	3,060	—	54·94	—	3·51	—	18·50	—
Malaria	5,318	—	11,639	—	16,957	—	110·29	—	99·36	—	102·54	—
Plague	—	—	102	—	102	—	—	—	·87	—	·62	—
Small-pox	2	—	15	—	17	—	·04	—	·13	—	·10	—
Typhus	—	—	—	—	—	—	—	—	—	—	—	—
Venereal diseases	709	—	2,782	—	3,491	—	14·70	—	23·75	—	21·11	—
Scurvy	15	—	16,637	1	16,662	1	·31	—	142·02	·01	100·76	—
Beri-beri	131	2	10	—	141	3	2·72	·04	·09	—	·85	·02
Effects of heat	2,459	—	56	—	2,515	—	51·00	—	·48	—	15·21	—

TABLE 20.—Principal Diseases in the Mesopotamian Expeditionary Force in 1917

| | British | | Indian | | Total | | Ratio per 1,000 | | | | | |
| | | | | | | | British | | Indian | | Total | |
	Admissions	Deaths	Admissions	Deaths	Admissions	Deaths	Admissions	Deaths	Admissions	Deaths	Admissions	Deaths
Cerebro-spinal fever	21	8	378	230	399	238	·25	·10	1·69	1·03	1·30	·77
Cholera	46	18	163	53	209	71	·55	·21	·73	·24	·68	·23
Dysentery	5,408	126	6,551	160	11,959	286	64·46	1·50	29·30	·72	38·89	·93
Enteric ⎧ Typhoid	49	17	57	16	106	33	·58	·20	·25	·07	·34	·11
fever ⎨ Paratyphoid A	152	8	39	5	191	13	1·81	·10	·17	·02	·62	·04
⎩ Paratyphoid B	13	—	7	2	20	2	·15	—	·03	·01	·07	·01
Group	862	66	356	43	1,218	109	10·27	·79	1·59	·19	3·96	·35
Malaria	7,171	46	8,892	72	16,063	118	85·47	·55	39·77	·32	52·24	·38
Plague	6	3	92	46	98	49	·07	·04	·41	·21	·32	·16
Small-pox	360	71	273	27	633	98	4·29	·85	1·22	·12	2·06	·32
Typhus	12	7	9	4	21	11	·14	·08	·04	·02	·07	·04
Venereal diseases	1,609	—	4,535	—	6,144	—	19·18	—	20·28	—	19·98	—
Scurvy	8	—	2,558	5	2,566	5	·10	—	11·44	·02	8·35	·02
Beri-beri	91	—	83	10	174	10	1·08	—	·37	·04	·57	·03
Effects of heat	6,242	524	896	89	7,138	613	74·40	6·25	4·01	·40	23·21	1·99

TABLE 21.—Principal Diseases in the Mesopotamian Expeditionary Force in 1918

| | British | | Indian | | Total | | Ratio per 1,000 | | | | | |
| | | | | | | | British | | Indian | | Total | |
	Admissions	Deaths	Admissions	Deaths	Admissions	Deaths	Admissions	Deaths	Admissions	Deaths	Admissions	Deaths
Cerebro-spinal fever	15	10	334	200	349	210	·14	·09	1·10	·66	·85	·51
Cholera	80	35	370	159	450	194	·75	·33	1·22	·52	1·09	·47
Dysentery	6,545	109	5,745	194	12,290	303	60·95	1·02	18·88	·64	29·86	·74
Enteric { Typhoid	87	9	117	30	204	39	·81	·08	·38	·10	·50	·09
fever { Paratyphoid A	142	5	71	6	213	11	1·32	·05	·23	·02	·52	·03
{ Paratyphoid B	51	3	52	8	103	11	·47	·03	·17	·03	·25	·03
{ Group	360	53	191	34	551	87	3·35	·49	·63	·11	1·34	·21
Malaria	10,887	68	10,560	98	21,447	166	101·39	·63	34·71	·32	52·10	·40
Plague	13	4	151	102	164	106	·12	·04	·50	·34	·40	·26
Relapsing fever	137	8	1,575	106	1,712	114	1·28	·07	5·18	·35	4·16	·28
Small-pox	597	111	628	52	1,225	163	5·56	1·03	2·06	·17	2·98	·40
Typhus	138	27	377	85	515	112	1·29	·25	1·24	·28	1·25	·27
Venereal diseases	1,759	—	4,877	—	6,636	—	16·38	—	16·03	—	16·12	—
Scurvy	8	—	933	—	941	—	·07	—	3·07	—	2·29	—
Beri-beri	129	7	157	20	286	27	1·20	·07	·52	·07	·69	·07
Effects of heat	574	31	172	14	746	45	5·35	·29	·57	·05	1·81	·11

TABLE 22.—Summary of the Principal Diseases in the Mesopotamian Expeditionary Force from November 1914 to December 1918

	British		Indian		Total		Average annual ratio per 1,000					
							British		Indian		Total	
	Admissions	Deaths	Admissions	Deaths	Admissions	Deaths	Admissions	Deaths	Admissions	Deaths	Admissions	Deaths
Cholera	308	125	2,269	485	2,577	610	1·20	·49	3·25	·69	2·70	·64
Dysentery	18,050	—	24,945	—	42,995	—	70·31	—	35·75	—	45·04	—
Enteric group of fevers	4,492	—	1,371	—	5,863	—	17·50	—	1·96	—	6·14	—
Malaria	25,833	—	33,490	—	59,323	—	100·63	—	48·00	—	62·15	—
Plague	19	11	345	105	364	116	·08	·05	·50	·15	·38	·12
Small-pox	959	182	916	79	1,875	261	3·73	·71	1·31	·11	1·96	·28
Typhus	150	34	386	89	536	123	·58	·13	·56	·13	·56	·13
Venereal diseases	4,202	—	12,688	—	17,013	—	16·36	—	18·18	—	17·82	—
Scurvy	32	—	20,578	31	20,610	31	·13	—	29·49	—	21·59	—
Beri-beri	670	14	250	31	920	45	2·61	·05	·36	·04	·96	·05
Effects of heat	9,813	—	1,176	—	10,989	—	38·22	—	1·68	—	11·51	—

which can be placed at approximately 55 per cent. of admissions, and at certain periods by other diseases, such as sand-fly fever, of which the records are incomplete. That sand-fly fever was very prevalent is shown by the fact that 29,089 cases were admitted at the base from July 1917 to the end of December 1918. Of these, 13,987 were British and 15,102 Indian or followers. The figures for relapsing fever are incomplete until 1918, but it is known that there were about 250 cases among Indians at the base during 1917. Influenza was not noted among the special diseases until the epidemic in 1918, when the returns from August to the end of the year show 11,670 British cases with 29 deaths and 13,317 Indian cases with 140 deaths. Here again the figures are misleading and give no idea of the total numbers stricken. To meet the needs of the moment many regiments and units were given extra medical personnel and comforts, and turned themselves into temporary hospitals for a brief period. They attended to their own men stricken by a mild infection until they were fit to resume their ordinary duties. The more serious cases were evacuated to medical units. Jaundice, colitis and other intestinal diseases were constant causes of inefficiency, but apart from dysentery there are no complete records. Oriental sore was probably responsible for about 12,000 admissions to hospital, or an average annual ratio of 12·57 per 1,000. It is recorded that there were only 7 cases of tetanus in the whole campaign.

Of the remaining important diseases dysentery and malaria have been referred to in a previous chapter and require no further comment here. The high incidence of scurvy among Indians in 1916 shows what happens when Indian troops, having lived for many years on a bare subsistence diet in their own country, are called upon to participate in a trying campaign, ill-supplied with suitable rations. It is not possible to give the monthly incidence of the disease, but the records of three divisions over a period of three weeks in July 1916 are worthy of note.

Week ending 1916	Percentages of admissions to total Indian ration strength			Percentage of admissions to total Indian sick		
	III Div.	VII Div.	XIV Div.	III Div.	VII Div.	XIV Div.
2nd July	·69	·70	1·18	—	—	—
9th ,, ...	·60	·64	1·73	11·2	18·3	34·0
16th ,, ...	·67	1·03	1·91	20·2	24·7	39·7

Table 23 shows the percentages of cases of scurvy to the total fresh sick admissions among Indians each week for each of these divisions and for the whole Indian force from 1st July to 9th September, 1916.

TABLE 23.—Percentages of Cases of Scurvy to Total Indian Sick Admissions

Week ending 1916	III Divison	VII Division	XIV Division	Total Indian Force
	Per cent.	Per cent.	Per cent.	Per cent.
8th July	—	18	33	7
15th ,,	20	25	23	18
22nd ,,	33	43	46	17
29th ,,	44	34	46	19
5th Aug.	48	29	65	13
12th ,,	66	32	65	35
19th ,,	58	40	65	20
26th ,,	46	39	67	18
2nd Sept.	54	37	70	20
9th ,,	60	37	75	22

As the force became reorganised and rations improved in quantity and quality there was a gradual decrease in the number of cases admitted to hospital.

The effects of heat were another important source of inefficiency in the force. This was to be expected in a country like Mesopotamia, and measures had to be adopted to afford as much protection to the troops as possible. In July 1917 the heat was perhaps the most trying experienced by any troops. Table 24 shows the distribution of admissions and deaths from the effects of heat from 7th to 28th July. In this period 48·26 per cent. of the total cases for the year were admitted to hospital. The table should be read in conjunction with the chart of temperatures in July 1917, and the following quotation from the diary of the director of medical services of the force :

" The maximum and minimum temperatures for July are shown in the attached chart. It will be seen that the highest shade temperatures were reached at Baghdad on 10th (122°) and on 20th (122·8°) and at Basra on 11th (121·5°) and on 21st (122°). The highest minimum temperatures were reached at Baghdad (84°) on 10th and (82·5°) on 20th, and at Basra (86·4°) on 10th and (87·8°) on 21st. On 25th there was 70 per cent. humidity at Basra. The maximum temperatures were higher than those recorded since the beginning of the war. Indeed, so far as our information goes, 122·8° is a record high shade temperature for Baghdad. From 8th to 24th inclusive the maximum at Baghdad never fell below 116°. Fortunately there were no important military operations in progress during the period of intense heat, and the whole of the troops were either in billets or in double fly tents. The majority of the men (British and Indian) slept in the open. The men who suffered most were British other ranks employed on works, mechanical transport, signalling, military police and in kitchens. It is a general impression that the older men (*i.e.* those over 35) were less able to stand the strain than the younger soldiers, and one was struck by the high proportion of these older men in the wards where heatstroke cases were treated."

TABLE 24.—Admissions and Deaths from Effects of Heat from 7th July to 28th July, 1917

Area	British		Indian		Total	
	Admissions	Deaths	Admissions	Deaths	Admissions	Deaths
III Division	391	18	128	2	519	20
VII ,,	168	16	11	1	179	17
XIII ,,	352	50	1	—	353	50
XIV ,,	152	12	113	—	265	12
XV ,,	66	9	2	—	68	9
Cavalry Division	32	—	—	—	32	—
Base	835	131	176	32	1,011	163
Amara	215	27	7	2	222	29
Advanced Base	474	145	31	14	505	159
Euphrates Front	22	3	3	1	25	4
Ahwaz	—	—	—	—	—	—
Qurna	41	3	74	3	115	6
Kut-al-Amara	137	9	14	4	151	13
Total	2,885	423	560	59	3,445	482

To face p. 244.

Chart of Temperatures in Mesopotamia, July 1917.

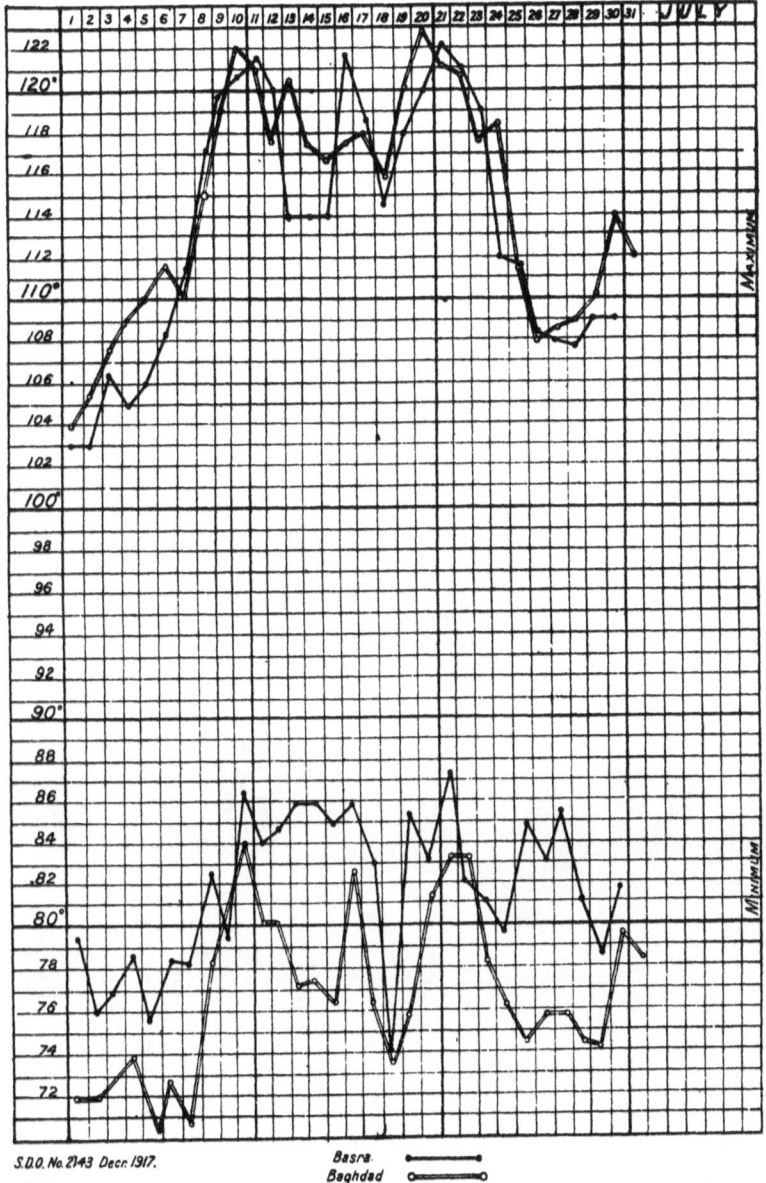

CHAPTER XVI

CASUALTIES IN THE NORTH RUSSIAN EXPEDITIONARY FORCE, 1918–1919

THE last expeditionary force to be organised during the Great War was destined for North Russia consequent upon the Allies' decision that such a campaign was essential if Germany, having concluded a separate peace with Russia, was to be prevented from transferring large numbers of troops from her Eastern to her Western theatre of war. The campaign was launched by landing a small force at Murmansk on the north coast of Russia in April 1918. It assumed greater proportions as it became involved in Russian affairs, and by July 1918, when actual operations may be said to have commenced, the North Russian Expeditionary Force comprised two forces of allied British, French, Italian, American, Serbian and "loyal" Russian troops, one force based on Archangel and the other on Murmansk. The original occupation of these towns, the consolidation of positions around them, initial advances and capture of several other towns, defensive measures against Bolshevik attacks, and the final operations to cover the withdrawal of the troops from the country, which was accomplished by 12th October, 1919, mark the salient military features of the campaign.

It was not, however, in the actual operations but in the isolation of the troops, and in the nature of the country and the climate that the greatest danger lay. Although relieved later by fresher and fitter volunteers, the British force at the outset of the campaign was composed for the most part of war-worn troops from other fronts. Many had experienced extremes of heat and cold in other countries, with heat predominating, but in North Russia they were operating in an Arctic climate where the winter was long, dreary, dark and very cold—conditions which were likely to have a very depressing effect upon troops who had already experienced war and its hardships. The country consisted either of vast open spaces with bogs, rivers, marshes and lakes, frozen hard in winter, or of endless snowclad forests. Distances were long, journeys were wearisome and transport was difficult and slow, necessitating special arrangements for the evacuation of cases over trackless wastes.

The chief difficulties of the campaign from the medical point of view included the use of special transport for ice and snow; the treatment of wounds under exposed and trying circumstances; the grave risk of contracting infectious disease from the cosmopolitan inhabitants of the towns or from their insanitary surroundings; and the anxiety lest debilitating diseases, nervous or otherwise, brought about by war weariness, distance from home, trying conditions and the depression of an Arctic winter, should beset the troops. The force was, however, well equipped to combat all the consequences of active service in such a country, and it speaks well for the stamina of the men and for the measures adopted that only a few cases of neurasthenia were reported as admissions to hospital. All things considered, the comparatively low ratio of 908·50 per 1,000 of ration strength of the British troops admitted to hospital for the period of the campaign on account of disease or injury must be taken as indicative of the success of the preventive methods employed by the force.*

Strength

The average ration strength of the North Russian Expeditionary Force for the period July 1918 to October 1919 is shown in Table 1.

TABLE 1.—Average Ration Strength

Period	Force	Officers	Other Ranks	Total
July 1918 to October 1919	British and Dominion troops in North Russia	713	9,834	10,547

Classification of Casualties

The total casualties sustained by the British and Dominion troops in North Russia during the period of the campaign are shown in Table 2 with the ratios per 1,000 of average ration strength.

TABLE 2.—Total Casualties

	Off.	O.R.	Total	Ratio per 1,000		
				Off.	O.R.	Total
Battle casualties	98	795	893	137·45	80·84	84·67
Non-battle casualties ...	893	8,689	9,582	1,252·45	883·57	908·50
Total	991	9,484	10,475	1,389·90	964·41	993·17

The proportion of battle casualties to non-battle casualties among British and Dominion troops in North Russia was 1 to 9·1 officers; 1 to 10·9 other ranks; and 1 to 10·7 all ranks.

An analysis of the total casualties occurring among British

---

* The history of the Medical Services with the North Russian Expeditionary Force is dealt with in the *General History of the Medical Services*, vol. iv, pp. 512–559.

and Dominion troops in North Russia from July 1918 to October 1919 is given in Table 3.

TABLE 3.—Classification and Percentages of Total Casualties

	Off.	O.R.	Total	Percentage of total casualties		
				Off.	O.R.	Total
A. *Battle casualties*:						
(a) Killed	27	160	187	2·72	1·69	1·79
(b) Died of wounds	4	20	24	·40	·21	·23
(c) Missing	3	41	44	·30	·43	·42
(d) Prisoners of war	14	119	133	1·41	1·25	1·27
(e) Wounded less (b)	50	455	505	5·05	4·80	4·82
B. *Non-battle casualties*:						
(f) Died of disease or injury	11	110	121	1·11	1·16	1·16
(g) Sick or injured less (f)	882	8,579	9,461	89·00	90·46	90·32
Total A. and B.	991	9,484	10,475	—	—	—

Table 4 (a) shows this detail as percentages of battle casualties, and Table 4 (b) shows similarly the percentages of non-battle casualties.

TABLE 4 (a).—Percentages of Battle Casualties

	Off.	O.R.	Total
(a) Killed	27·55	20·13	20·94
(b) Died of wounds	4·08	2·52	2·69
(c) Missing	3·06	5·16	4·93
(d) Prisoners of war	14·29	14·97	14·89
(e) Wounded less (b)	51·02	57·23	56·55

TABLE 4 (b).—Percentages of Non-battle Casualties

	Off.	O.R.	Total
(f) Died of disease or injury	1·23	1·27	1·26
(g) Sick or injured less (f)	98·77	98·73	98·74

The casualties sustained by the British and Dominion troops in North Russia may be further classified into permanent and temporary losses for military purposes in the field.

TABLE 5 (a).—Permanent Losses for Military Purposes in the Field

	Off.	O.R.	Total	Percentage of total casualties		
				Off.	O.R.	Total
A. Battle casualties:						
Killed	27	160	187	2·72	1·69	1·79
Died of wounds	4	20	24	·40	·21	·23
Missing	3	41	44	·30	·43	·42
Prisoners of war	14	119	133	1·41	1·25	1·27
Total	48	340	388	4·84	3·58	3·70
B. Non-battle casualties:						
Died of disease or injury	11	110	121	1·11	1·16	1·16
Total permanent losses	59	450	509	5·95	4·74	4·86

TABLE 5 (b).—Temporary Losses for Military Purposes in the Field

	Off.	O.R.	Total	Percentage of total casualties		
				Off.	O.R.	Total
A. Battle casualties:						
Wounded less died of wounds	50	455	505	5·05	4·80	4·82
B. Non-battle casualties:						
Sick or injured less died of disease or injury	882	8,579	9,461	89·00	90·46	90·32
Total temporary losses	932	9,034	9,966	94·05	95·26	95·14

The relative proportions of the various classes of casualties to each other for the British and Dominion troops in North Russia for the period of the campaign are shown in Table 6.

TABLE 6.—Proportions

	Officers	Other Ranks	Total
1. Total battle casualties to total non-battle casualties	1 : 9·11	1 : 10·93	1 : 10·73
2. Total killed to total wounded including died of wounds	1 : 2·00	1 : 2·97	1 : 2·83
3. Permanent losses among battle casualties to total wounded less died of wounds	1 : 1·04	1 : 1·34	1 : 1·30
4. Permanent losses among non-battle casualties to total sick and injured less deaths from disease and injury	1 : 80·18	1 : 77·99	1 : 78·19
5. Total permanent losses to total temporary losses	1 : 15·80	1 : 20·08	1 : 19·58

Admissions to Hospital

Of the total casualties suffered by the British and Dominion troops in North Russia, the numbers admitted to hospital and treated by the medical services are shown in Table 7.

NORTH RUSSIA, 1918–1919

TABLE 7.—Numbers admitted to Hospital

	Off.	O.R.	Total	Percentage of total casualties		
				Off.	O.R.	Total
Wounded	54	475	529	5·45	5·01	5·05
Sick or injured	893	8,689	9,582	90·11	91·62	91·47
Total	947	9,164	10,111	95·56	96·63	96·53

The proportion of wounded to sick and injured treated by the medical services was 1 to 16·54 officers; 1 to 18·29 other ranks; and 1 to 18·11 all ranks.

The casualties which were not treated by the medical services are shown in Table 8.

TABLE 8.—Casualties among British and Dominion Troops in North Russia not treated by the Medical Services

	Off.	O.R.	Total	Percentage of total casualties		
				Off.	O.R.	Total
Killed	27	160	187	2·72	1·69	1·79
Missing	3	41	44	·30	·43	·42
Prisoners of war	14	119	133	1·41	1·25	1·27
Total	44	320	364	4·44	3·37	3·47

The numbers of sick and wounded admitted to hospital, and the disposal of cases, are shown in Table 9 (a), while the corresponding ratios per 1,000 of strength and percentages of total admissions are given in Tables 9 (b) and 9 (c) respectively.

TABLE 9 (a).—Admissions to Hospital and Disposal of Cases, British and Dominion Troops in North Russia

	Wounded			Sick and injured			Total		
	Off.	O.R.	Total	Off.	O.R.	Total	Off.	O.R.	Total
Admissions	54	475	529	893	8,689	9,582	947	9,164	10,111
Deaths	4	20	24	11	110	121	15	130	145
Returned to duty in theatre of war	9	245	254	710	6,587	7,297	719	6,832	7,551
Evacuated overseas	41	210	251	172	1,992	2,164	213	2,202	2,415

TABLE 9 (b).—Ratio per 1,000 of Ration Strength

	Wounded			Sick and injured			Total		
	Off.	O.R.	Total	Off.	O.R.	Total	Off.	O.R.	Total
Admissions	75·74	48·30	50·16	1,252·45	883·57	908·50	1,328·19	931·87	958·66
Deaths	5·61	2·03	2·28	15·43	11·19	11·47	21·04	13·22	13·75
Returned to duty in theatre of war	12·62	24·91	24·08	995·79	669·82	691·86	1,008·42	694·73	715·94
Evacuated overseas	57·50	21·35	23·80	241·23	202·56	205·18	298·74	223·92	228·98

TABLE 9 (c).—Percentages of Total Admissions

	Wounded			Sick and injured			Total		
	Off.	O.R.	Total	Off.	O.R.	Total	Off.	O.R.	Total
Deaths	7·14	4·21	4·54	1·23	1·27	1·26	1·58	1·42	1·43
Returned to duty in theatre of war	16·67	51·58	48·02	79·51	75·81	76·15	75·92	74·55	74·68
Evacuated overseas	75·92	44·21	47·45	19·26	22·92	22·58	22·49	24·03	23·88

The ratios per 1,000 of strength of the British and Dominion troops constantly in hospital in North Russia during the period of the campaign are shown in Table 10.

TABLE 10.—Ratio per 1,000 of Ration Strength constantly in Hospital in North Russia

Wounded		Sick and injured		Total	
Off.	O.R.	Off.	O.R.	Off.	O.R.
4·21	3·25	35·06	43·93	39·27	47·18

Hospital Accommodation

Table 11 shows the maximum number of equipped beds, the maximum number occupied on any one date, and the average number occupied throughout the period of the campaign for the British and Dominion troops of the North Russian Expeditionary Force. It must be remembered, however, that in a campaign of this nature hospital accommodation reserved for British and Dominion troops had of necessity to be extended to allied troops, of whom there was a daily average of 4 officers and 108 other ranks occupying British beds at Archangel and 4 officers and 129 other ranks at Murmansk.

TABLE 11.—Accommodation provided in Hospitals for British and Dominion Troops of the North Russian Expeditionary Force

Period	Average ration strength	Max. No. equipped beds	Max. No. occupied beds	Average No. equipped beds	Average No. occupied beds	Percentage of ration strength			
						Maximum No.		Average No.	
						Equip.	Occup.	Equip.	Occup.
July 1918 to Oct. 1919	10,547	3,569	1,798	1,996	859	33·84	17·05	18·92	8·14

Non-battle Casualties

It is not possible to state numerically the chief causes of admission to hospital as the records are incomplete, but from such information as is available it would appear that influenza and venereal diseases caused the greatest inefficiency, and that intestinal diseases and diseases of the respiratory system were also prevalent. The incidence of other infectious diseases was comparatively low, and there were no outbreaks of disease of a serious nature among the British and Dominion troops. Table 12 shows the principal recorded causes of admission to hospital for disease in the Archangel Force for the period June 1918 to May 1919, and in the Murmansk Force from September 1918 to September 1919.

TABLE 12.—Principal Causes of Admission to Hospital of British and Dominion Troops at Archangel and Murmansk, with Ratios per 1,000 of Average Ration Strength of each Force.

	"Elope" Force, Archangel (June 1918–May 1919)		"Syren" Force, Murmansk (Sept. 1918–Sept. 1919)	
	Admissions	Ratio per 1,000	Admissions	Ratio per 1,000
Specific diseases due to infection				
Cerebro-spinal fever	1	·13	1	·25
Diphtheria	2	·27	7	1·74
Dysentery	8	1·07	6	1·50
Enteric fever ⎰ Typhoid	10	1·34	—	—
⎱ Paratyphoid	8	1·07	1	·25
⎱ Group	6	·80		
Influenza	506	67·76	442	110·14
Malaria	—	—	35	8·72
Measles	6	·80	3	·75
Mumps	14	1·87	2	·50
Pneumonia	26	3·48	23	5·73
Relapsing fever	—	—	1	·25
Rubella	—	—	6	1·50
Scarlet fever	1	·13	—	—
Tuberculosis, pulmonary	6	·80	11	2·74
Venereal diseases ⎰ Gonorrhœa	167	22·36	75	18·69
⎱ Syphilis	75	10·04	35	8·72
⎱ Other	—	—	1	·25
Other diseases				
Diarrhœa	Not stated		118	29·40
Enteritis	”		5	1·25
Scurvy	”		3	·75
Scabies	”		173	43·11
Frost bite	”		48	11·96

CHAPTER XVII

CASUALTIES IN THE CAMPAIGN IN EAST AFRICA, 1914—1918

THE campaign in East Africa was conducted almost entirely in the territory known as German East Africa, which extended over an area of roughly 384,000 square miles, with a coast line 620 miles in length. When war broke out in 1914 the total British force in British East Africa numbered only a few hundreds. In November 1914 an Indian Expeditionary Force, approximately 7,000 rifles strong, attacked the port of Tanga in German East Africa, but was driven off. During the remainder of 1914 and the whole of 1915 there were minor raids and engagements, chiefly on the Uganda side. Reorganisation of the British force in East Africa took place in 1916. In the Spring of that year active offensive operations were commenced in the Kilimanjaro area and these continued intermittently until September when the Uluguru Mountains were cleared of the enemy. While these operations were in progress other detachments of the force operated in the Northern and Eastern areas and in the Southern and Western areas of the theatre of war. By the beginning of 1917 the greater part of the country had been cleared, and thereafter the main operations took place in the Kilwa and Lindi areas. These were followed by an advance to the Portuguese frontier. At the end of November 1917 the German commander, accompanied by a small force, escaped into Portuguese territory, and ten months later he recrossed the River Rovuma into German East Africa. This force was pursued until the German commander surrendered a few days after the close of hostilities on 12th November, 1918.

The East Africa campaign presented many difficulties, both military and medical. It was a campaign of manœuvre and hard marching over mountains, through bush, and across rivers, lakes and swamps. Periods of drought and dust were followed by seasons of torrential rains and mud. At all times the fierce heat and luxuriant vegetation were productive of parasitic life which caused many diseases. Transport and supplies presented the gravest difficulties, and in many of the operations reliance had to be placed on a large force of carriers who were only human and an easy prey to disease. The lines of communication were long, and the evacuation of sick and wounded casualties was fraught with difficulties. The struggle was one where, in the early stages, an efficient medical service would have been invaluable, as General Smuts is reported to have described it as a " campaign against nature, in which climate, geography and disease fought more effectively against us than the well-trained forces of the enemy." *

The force was a mixed one, comprising British and Dominion troops, Indian, African, and British West Indian troops, and a large force of

---

* *A History of the Great War,* by John Buchan, Vol. IV, p. 108.

followers, Indian and African, drawn from diverse races and districts and speaking different languages. Casualties from wounds were not numerous, but the excessive sick rate and the constant care exercised to prevent the spread of disease, threw a heavy strain on the medical services. *

Strength

The average ration strength of the East African Expeditionary Force from September 1915 to the end of the campaign is shown in Table 1. There are no definite figures available to show the average strength of the force prior to that date.

TABLE 1.—Average Ration Strength

	British and Dominion troops			Indian, African or other troops			Followers or labour	Total force			
	Off.	O.R.	Total	Off.	O.R.	Total		Off.	O.R.	Follrs.	Total
Sept.–Dec. 1915	379	5,309	5,688	395	20,493	20,888	18,068	774	25,802	18,068	44,644
1916	2,029	30,101	32,130	440	25,644	26,084	40,376	2,469	55,745	40,376	98,590
1917	2,142	18,618	20,760	319	29,623	29,942	143,959	2,461	48,241	143,959	194,661
1918	2,118	14,670	16,788	91	24,154	24,245	87,623	2,209	38,824	87,623	128,656

Classification of Casualties

In preparing the statistical tables for the campaign in East Africa it has been found necessary to divide the casualties into two periods, one dealing with 1914–15 for which only the battle casualties are definitely known, and the other with 1916–1918 when battle, non-battle casualties and strengths are available. Table 2 shows, therefore, the analysis of battle casualties in the East African Expeditionary Force during 1914–1915 with percentages.

TABLE 2.—Casualties in the East African Expeditionary Force, 1914–15

	Troops			Followers	Percentage of battle casualties			
	Off.	O.R.	Total		Off.	O.R.	Total	Follrs.
A. Battle casualties:								
(a) Killed	50	550	600	} 41 {	35.46	33.07	33.26	}12.77
(b) Died of wounds	3	46	49		2.13	2.77	2.72	
(c) Missing	13	289	302	} 271 {	9.22	17.38	16.74	}84.42
(d) Prisoners of war	5	94	99		3.55	5.65	5.49	
(e) Wounded less (b)	70	684	754	9	49.65	41.13	41.80	2.80
Total	141	1,663	1,804	321	—	—	—	—
B. Non-battle casualties:								
(f) Died of disease or injury	3	247	250	1,708	—	—	—	—
(g) Sick or injured	Not known		—	—	—	—	—	—

* The history of the Medical Services in East Africa is dealt with in the *General History of the Medical Services*, vol. iv, chaps. xvii–xx, pp. 416–504.

The casualties sustained by the East African Expeditionary Force from 1916 to the end of 1918 are shown in Table 3 with the average annual ratios per 1,000 of ration strength.

TABLE 3.—Casualties in the East African Expeditionary Force, 1916–18

	Troops			Fol-lowers	Average annual ratio per 1,000			
	Off.	O.R.	Total		Off.	O.R.	Total	Follrs.
Battle casualties	709	10,008	10,717	2,023	99·16	70·08	71·46	7·44
Non-battle casualties	10,416	326,124	336,540	284,891	1,458·82	2,283·64	2,244·36	1,047·57
Total	11,125	336,132	347,257	286,914	1,557·98	2,353·72	2,315·83	1,055·00

The proportion of battle casualties to non-battle casualties among the troops was 1 to 14·69 officers; 1 to 32·59 other ranks; and 1 to 31·40 all ranks. Among followers it was 1 to 140·83.

An analysis of the casualties occurring in the East African Expeditionary Force from 1916 to 1918 is given in Table 4.

TABLE 4.—Classification and Percentages of Casualties 1916–1918

	Troops			Fol-lowers	Percentage of total casualties, 1916–18			
					Troops			Fol-lowers
	Off.	O.R.	Total		Off.	O.R.	Total	
A. *Battle casualties:*								
(a) Killed	164	1,925	2,089	{ 335 }	1·47	·57	·60	{ ·12
(b) Died of wounds	53	652	705		·48	·19	·20	
(c) Missing	31	655	686	{ 364 }	·28	·19	·20	{ ·13
(d) Prisoners of war	17	197	214		·15	·06	·06	
(e) Wounded less (b)	444	6,579	7,023	1,324	3·99	1·96	2·02	·46
B. *Non-battle casualties:*								
(f) Died of disease or injury	122	6,186	6,308	43,203	1·10	1·84	1·82	15·06
(g) Sick or injured less (f)	10,294	319,938	330,232	241,688	92·53	95·18	95·10	84·24
Total A. and B.	11,125	336,132	347,257	286,914	—	—	—	—

Table 5 (a) shows this detail as percentages of battle casualties and Table 5 (b) shows similarly the percentages of non-battle casualties.

TABLE 5 (a).—Percentages of Battle Casualties

	Troops			Followers
	Off.	O.R.	Total	
(a) Killed	23·13	19·23	19·49	{ 16·56
(b) Died of wounds	7·48	6·51	6·58	
(c) Missing	4·37	6·54	6·40	{ 17·99
(d) Prisoners of war	2·40	1·97	2·00	
(e) Wounded less (b)	62·62	65·74	65·53	65·45

EAST AFRICA, 1914–1918

TABLE 5 (b).—Percentages of Non-battle Casualties

	Troops			Followers
	Off.	O.R.	Total	
(f) Died of disease or injury	1·17	1·90	1·87	15·16
(g) Sick or injured less (f)	98·83	98·10	98·13	84·84

The casualties sustained by the East African Expeditionary Force from 1916 to 1918 may be further classified into permanent and temporary losses for military purposes in the field.

TABLE 6 (a).—Permanent Losses for Military Purposes in the Field

	Troops			Fol-lowers	Percentage of total casualties, 1916–18			
	Off.	O.R.	Total		Off.	O.R.	Total	Follrs.
A. *Battle casualties:*								
Killed	164	1,925	2,089	} 335 }	1·47	·57	·60	} ·12
Died of wounds	53	652	705		·48	·19	·20	
Missing	31	655	686	} 364 }	·28	·19	·20	} ·13
Prisoners of war	17	197	214		·15	·06	·06	
Total	*265*	*3,429*	*3,694*	699	2·38	1·02	1·06	·24
B. *Non-battle casualties:*								
Died of disease or injury	122	6,186	6,308	43,203	1·10	1·84	1·82	15·06
Total permanent losses	387	9,615	10,002	43,902	3·48	2·86	2·88	15·30

TABLE 6 (b).—Temporary Losses for Military Purposes in the Field

	Troops			Fol-lowers	Percentage of total casualties, 1916–18			
	Off.	O.R.	Total		Off.	O.R.	Total	Follrs.
A. *Battle casualties:*								
Wounded less died of wounds	444	6,579	7,023	1,324	3·99	1·96	2·02	·46
B. *Non-battle casualties:*								
Sick or injured less died of disease or injury	10,294	319,938	330,232	241,688	92·53	95·18	95·10	84·24
Total temporary losses	10,738	326,517	337,255	243,012	96·52	97·14	97·12	84·70

The relative proportions of the various classes of casualties to each other for the East African Expeditionary Force from 1916 to 1918 are shown in Table 7.

TABLE 7.—Proportions

	Officers	Other ranks	Total	Followers
1. Total battle casualties to total non-battle casualties	1 : 14·69	1 : 32·59	1 : 31·40	1 : 140·83
2. Total killed to total wounded including died of wounds	1 : 3·03	1 : 3·76	1 : 3·70	?
3. Permanent losses among battle casualties to total wounded less died of wounds	1 : 1·68	1 : 1·92	1 : 1·90	1 : 1·89
4. Permanent losses among non-battle casualties to total sick and injured less died of disease or injury	1 : 84·38	1 : 51·72	1 : 52·35	1 : 5·59
5. Total permanent losses to total temporary losses	1 : 27·75	1 : 33·96	1 : 33·72	1 : 5·54

Admissions to Hospital

Of the total casualties suffered by the East African Expeditionary Force from 1916 to 1918, the numbers admitted to hospital and treated by the medical services are shown in Table 8.

TABLE 8.—Numbers admitted to Hospital

	Troops			Fol-lowers	Percentage of total casualties, 1916–18			
	Off.	O.R.	Total		Off.	O.R.	Total	Follrs.
Wounded	497	7,231	7,728	1,324*	4·47	2·15	2·23	·46
Sick or injured	10,416	326,124	336,540	284,891	93·63	97·02	96·91	99·29
Total	10,913	333,355	344,268	286,215	98·09	99·17	99·14	99·76

* Excludes died of wounds, the number of which is not known apart from killed.

The proportion of wounded to sick and injured treated by the medical services was 1 to 20·96 officers; 1 to 45·10 other ranks; and 1 to 43·55 all ranks. For followers it was 1 to 215·17.

The casualties which were not treated by the medical services are shown in Table 9.

TABLE 9.—Casualties not treated by the Medical Services

	Troops			Fol-lowers	Percentage of total casualties, 1916–18			
	Off.	O.R.	Total		Off.	O.R.	Total	Follrs.
Killed	164	1,925	2,089	335*	1·47	·57	·60	·12
Missing	31	655	686	} 364 {	·28	·19	·20	} ·13
Prisoners of war	17	197	214		·15	·06	·06	
Total	212	2,777	2,989	699	1·91	·83	·86	·24

* Includes died of wounds.

Owing to the lack of sufficient detail for 1916, the disposal of cases admitted to hospital, as far as it is known, is given only for 1917 and 1918 in Table 10, with the corresponding ratios per 1,000 of strength and the percentages of admissions. It is not possible to state the numbers returned to duty in the field, but from various records it is estimated that 65 per cent. of the troops and 76 per cent. of the followers admitted to hospital returned to duty in East Africa. These percentages include 25 per cent. of those evacuated to coastal bases and 10 per cent. of those evacuated overseas. In addition to the numbers shown as admitted to hospital there were large numbers repatriated as unfit, and of the followers many deserted and were lost to the force. It is impossible, however, to give even approximate figures for these two classes.

TABLE 10.—Admissions to Hospital for Sick and Wounded of the East African Expeditionary Force, 1917 and 1918, and Disposal of Cases

		Troops			Followers		
		Nos.	Ratio per 1,000	Per cent. of Adms.*	Nos.	Ratio per 1,000	Per cent. of Adms.*
1917	Admissions	133,060	2,624·35	—	181,511	1,260·85	—
	Deaths	3,009	59·35	2·15	23,777	165·17	12·90
	Evacuated overseas	28,118	554·57	20·09	6,575	45·67	3·57
	Evacuated to coastal bases	28,379	559·72	20·28	6,351	44·12	3·45
	Remaining in medical charge	10,750	212·02	7·68	7,910	54·95	4·29
1918	Admissions	58,774	1,432·36	—	69,560	793·86	—
	Deaths	2,248	54·79	3·23	14,946†	170·57	19·29
	Evacuated overseas	5,084	123·90	7·31	1,040	11·87	1·34
	Evacuated to coastal bases	13,472	328·32	19·38	10,826	123·55	13·97

* Calculated on total admissions for the year plus the numbers remaining in hospital at the end of the previous year.
† Excludes died of wounds, the numbers of which are not known.

The average numbers constantly in hospital during 1916, 1917 and 1918 are shown in Table 11 with the ratios per 1,000 of ration strength.

TABLE 11.—Average Numbers constantly in Hospital

Year	Troops			Fol-lowers	Ratio per 1,000 of strength			Fol-lowers
	British and Dominion	Indian, African, or other	Total		British and Dominion	Indian, African, or other	Total	
1916	3,554	1,979	5,533	2,235	110·61	75·87	95·05	55·35
1917	3,168	4,287	7,455	7,264	152·60	143·18	147·04	50·46
1918	—	—	5,143	6,165	—	—	125·34	70·36
Average	..	..	6,044	5,221	Average annual ratio		120·92	57·59

Hospital Accommodation

The only definite figures of the hospital accommodation provided for the East African Expeditionary Force are those for October 1917, shown in Table 12. As the maximum number of occupied beds, both for troops and for followers, was reached during this period, the former representing 19·03 per cent. of strength and the latter 7·21 per cent., it will be noted that the accommodation provided was by that date sufficient to meet the requirements of the force.

TABLE 12.—Hospital Accommodation provided for the East African Expeditionary Force, October 1917

Date	Force	Average ration strength	No. of equipped beds	No. of occupied beds	Percentage of ration strength	
					Equipped beds	Occupied beds
October 1917	British and Dominion	16,293	4,080	3,066	25·04	18·82
	Indian, African, etc.	40,369	8,572	5,868	21·23	14·54
	Total	56,662	12,652	8,934	22·33	15·77
	Followers	157,900	12,850	9,886	8·14	6·26

Non-battle Casualties

Records of the special diseases affecting the East African Expeditionary Force are only available from June 1916 onwards, and of these diseases only a few have been recorded throughout. Their importance, however, lies in the high ratio of admissions for malaria, which dwarfs interest in the other diseases and makes this terrible cause of wastage stand out prominently. Dysentery was the next most frequent cause of inefficiency. The African troops suffered in greater proportion than the British or Indian. Pneumonia likewise affected the African troops chiefly, the Indians slightly and the British only occasionally, and when it did it was probably associated with malaria. Cerebro-spinal fever and small-pox were prevalent among the civilian population, and it was not surprising, therefore, that African recruits and carriers coming from infected areas should suffer from these diseases. Unfortunately the records are incomplete. The comparatively small known ratios were due to the precautionary methods and segregation measures adopted. In 1918 it is reported that the pandemic spread of influenza to East Africa affected both troops and followers throughout the country. It taxed the resources of the medical services, but the approximate number of cases has not been recorded. Occasional cases of enteric fever occurred every month, mostly among British troops, but now and again among Africans and Indians.

The very high death-rate among followers, due mainly to dysentery, pneumonia and malaria, can be readily explained. A large force of African carriers was required. It was hastily organised and at first the organisation was imperfect. Moreover, the personnel were of poor physique and predisposed to disease. Inattention to sanitary details, incorrect dieting, hard work and the climatic rigours of the campaign increased this predisposition and made the personnel more liable to contract dysenteric infections. The transfer of men from the cool and comparatively healthy highlands of German East Africa to the hot, unhealthy, malarious areas on the coast was responsible for many contracting a severe malaria infection; the transfer of others, already highly infected with malaria, from the warm, low-lying districts to the highlands was responsible for the majority of deaths from pneumonia.

TABLE 13.—Principal recorded Causes of Admission to Hospital in the East African Expeditionary Force, June to December 1916, with Deaths and Ratios per 1,000 of ration strength

| | Troops | | Followers | | Ratio per 1,000 | | | |
| | | | | | Troops | | Followers | |
	Admissions	Deaths	Admissions	Deaths	Adms.	Deaths	Adms.	Deaths
Dysentery	8,902	306	3,795	1,008	182·21	6·26	48·10	12·78
Enteric fever	142	33	9	1	2·91	·68	·11	·01
Malaria	50,768	263	7,127	187	1,039·11	5·38	90·33	2·37
Pneumonia	463	119	1,957	372	9·48	2·44	24·80	4·72

TABLE 14.—Principal recorded Causes of Admission to Hospital in the East African Expeditionary Force, 1917, with Deaths and Ratios per 1,000 of ration strength

| | Troops | | Followers | | Ratio per 1,000 | | | |
| | | | | | Troops | | Followers | |
	Admissions	Deaths	Admissions	Deaths	Adms.	Deaths	Adms.	Deaths
Cerebro-spinal fever	295	177	1,240	—	5·82	3·49	8·61	—
Dysentery	14,045	429	26,607	7,277	277·01	8·46	184·82	50·55
Enteric fever	124	24	40	5	2·45	·47	·28	·03
Malaria	72,141	499	40,527	2,291	1,422·84	9·84	281·52	15·91
Pneumonia	1,653	444	10,009	3,013	32·60	8·76	69·53	20·93

TABLE 15.—Principal recorded Causes of Admission to Hospital in the East African Expeditionary Force, 1918, with Deaths and Ratios per 1,000 of ration strength

	Troops		Followers		Ratio per 1,000			
					Troops		Followers	
	Admissions	Deaths	Admissions	Deaths	Adms.	Deaths	Adms.	Deaths
Cerebro-spinal fever	75	70	263	202	1·83	1·71	3·00	2·31
Dysentery	3,294	86	3,740	681	80·28	2·10	42·68	7·77
Enteric fever	69	13	42	7	1·68	·32	·48	·08
Malaria	22,941	69	21,260	361	559·09	1·68	242·63	4·12
Pneumonia	2,023	516	3,116	873	49·30	12·58	35·56	9·96
Small-pox	301	121	443	106	7·34	2·95	5·06	1·21

CHAPTER XVIII

CASUALTIES IN THE CAMPAIGN IN SOUTH-WEST AFRICA, 1914–1915

THE operations in German South-West Africa, undertaken by the Dominion troops of South Africa, formed one of the early campaigns of the Great War. Fighting commenced on 20th August, 1914, and continued intermittently until the final surrender of the German forces on 9th July, 1915. The initial operations on the Orange River lasted until 10th November and included the affair at Raman's Drift on 25th September, when a small force of Dominion troops was cut off by the enemy and suffered heavy losses in prisoners and missing. The main incidents of the Southern Operations from 15th September, 1914 to 30th April, 1915, were the landing at Lüderitz Bay on 19th September, the occupation of Aus on 30th March, and the action of Gibeon on 25th and 26th April. The Northern Operations, which commenced on 21st December, 1914, and brought hostilities to a close on 9th July, 1915, fell into two phases: the advance on Windhuk from 22nd February with its ultimate occupation on 13th May, and the advance on Otavifontein from 19th June with its capture on 1st July.

The organisation of the Force was at first hurriedly built up to meet the immediate needs of the different columns of which it was constituted. The outstanding requirements in the early days of the campaign were mobility and the power to endure heat, thirst and sand-storms in traversing difficult country until the desert strip, sand dunes and rocky gradients had been negotiated and the troops were in possession of the railways. It was a campaign of movement and manœuvre under trying conditions, climatic and geographical, with a constant battle against the want of a proper water supply.

From the medical aspect the chief difficulties were the supply of pure drinking water, the prevention of disease, and the evacuation of sick and wounded casualties over inferior roads with such transport as was available. As the campaign developed and control of the sea and the railway was gained, the medical organisation was perfected to meet all demands, ensure comfort for the patients, and effect their transfer to stationary or base hospitals by ambulance train and hospital ship. Considering the nature of the country and the rigours of the campaign, the sick rate of 749·88 per 1,000 of the average strength of Dominion troops over the period of hostilities is remarkably low.

Native labour was to a large extent employed throughout the campaign on work connected with railways, transport and remount duties. Although there are no exact figures, it is reported that the average daily number so employed was 15,000 and that the amount of sickness was small. Special arrangements had to be made by the medical services for their hospital accommodation and medical care, and it is noteworthy that there were no serious outbreaks of disease among them.*

Strength

The average ration strength of the Dominion troops engaged in operations in South-West Africa during the period of the campaign is shown in Table 1. It has not been possible to obtain a separate strength for officers and other ranks.

Table 1.—Average Ration Strength

Period	Force	All ranks
Aug. 1914—July 1915	Dominion troops	33,000

Classification of Casualties

The total casualties sustained by the Dominion troops operating in South-West Africa are shown in Table 2 with the ratios per 1,000 of average ration strength.

TABLE 2.—Total Casualties

	Off.	O.R.	Total	Ratio per 1,000		
				Off.	O.R.	Total
Battle casualties	130	1,458	1,588			48·12
Non-battle casualties	816	23,930	24,746			749·88
Total	946	25,388	26,334			798·00

The proportion of battle casualties to non-battle casualties among Dominion troops in South-West Africa was 1 to 6·28 officers; 1 to 16·41 other ranks; and 1 to 15·58 all ranks.

An analysis of the total casualties occurring among Dominion troops in South-West Africa during the period of the campaign is given in Table 3.

---

* The history of the Medical Services during operations in South-West Africa is dealt with in the *General History of the Medical Services*, vol. i, pp. 323–356.

TABLE 3.—Classification and Percentages of Total Casualties

	Off.	O.R.	Total	Percentage of total casualties		
				Off.	O.R.	Total
A. *Battle casualties*:						
(a) Killed	21	164	185	2·22	·65	·70
(b) Died of wounds	3	58	61	·32	·23	·23
(c) Missing }	44	738	782	4·65	2·91	2·97
(d) Prisoners of war }						
(e) Wounded less (b)	62	498	560	6·55	1·96	2·13
B. *Non-battle casualties*:						
(f) Died of disease or injury	7	174	181	·74	·69	·69
(g) Sick or injured less (f)	809	23,756	24,565	85·52	93·57	93·28
Total A. and B.	946	25,388	26,334	—	—	—

Table 4 (a) shows this detail as percentages of battle casualties, and Table 4 (b) shows similarly the percentages of of non-battle casualties.

TABLE 4 (a).—Percentages of Battle Casualties

	Off.	O.R.	Total
(a) Killed	16·15	11·25	11·65
(b) Died of wounds	2·31	3·98	3·84
(c) Missing }	33·85	50·62	49·24
(d) Prisoners of war }			
(e) Wounded less (b)	47·69	34·16	35·26

TABLE 4 (b).—Percentages of Non-battle Casualties

	Off.	O.R.	Total
(f) Died of disease or injury	·86	·73	·73
(g) Sick or injured less (f)	99·14	99·27	99·27

The casualties sustained by the Dominion troops in the South-West African campaign may be further classified into permanent and temporary losses for military purposes in the field.

TABLE 5 (a).—Permanent Losses for Military Purposes in the Field

	Off.	O.R.	Total	Percentage of total casualties		
				Off.	O.R.	Total
A. *Battle casualties*:						
Killed	21	164	185	2·22	·65	·70
Died of wounds	3	58	61	·32	·23	·23
Missing	} 44	738	782	4·65	2·91	2·97
Prisoners of war						
Total	*68*	*960*	*1,028*	*7·19*	*3·78*	*3·90*
B. *Non-battle casualties*:						
Died of disease or injury	7	174	181	·74	·69	·69
Total permanent losses	75	1,134	1,209	7·93	4·47	4·59

TABLE 5 (b).—Temporary Losses for Military Purposes in the Field

	Off.	O.R.	Total	Percentage of total casualties		
				Off.	O.R.	Total
A. *Battle casualties*:						
Wounded less died of wounds	62	498	560	6·55	1·96	2·13
B. *Non-battle casualties*:						
Sick or injured less died of disease or injury	809	23,756	24,565	85·52	93·57	93·28
Total temporary losses	871	24,254	25,125	92·07	95·53	95·41

The relative proportions of the various classes of casualties to each other for Dominion troops in South-West Africa for the period of the campaign are shown in Table 6.

Table 6.—Proportions

	Officers	Other Ranks	Total
1. Total battle casualties to total non-battle casualties	1 : 6·28	1 : 16·41	1 : 15·58
2. Total killed to total wounded including died of wounds	1 : 3·10	1 : 3·39	1 : 3·36
3. Permanent losses among battle casualties to total wounded less died of wounds	1·10 : 1	1·93 : 1	1·84 : 1
4. Permanent losses among non-battle casualties to total sick and injured less died of disease or injury	1 : 115·57	1 : 136·53	1 : 135·72
5. Total permanent losses to total temporary losses	1 : 11·61	1 : 21·39	1 : 20·78

Admissions to Hospital

Of the total casualties suffered by the Dominion troops in South-West Africa, the numbers admitted to hospital and treated by the medical services are shown in Table 7.

TABLE 7.—Numbers admitted to Hospital

	Off.	O.R.	Total	Percentage of total casualties		
				Off.	O.R.	Total
Wounded	65	556	621	6·87	2·19	2·36
Sick or injured	816	23,930	24,746	86·26	94·26	93·97
Total	881	24,486	25,367	93·13	96·45	96·33

The proportion of wounded to sick and injured treated by the medical services was 1 to 12·55 officers; 1 to 43·04 other ranks; and 1 to 39·85 all ranks.

The casualties which were not treated by the medical services are shown in Table 8.

TABLE 8.—Casualties among Dominion Troops in South-West Africa not treated by the Medical Services

	Off.	O.R.	Total	Percentage of total casualties		
				Off.	O.R.	Total
Killed	21	164	185	2·22	·65	·70
Missing Prisoners of war	44	738	782	4·65	2·91	2·97
Total	65	902	967	6·87	3·55	3·67

There is unfortunately no information available to show the disposal of cases admitted to hospital for wounds or disease. Table 9 shows the number of admissions and deaths, the ratios per 1,000 of strength for all ranks admitted, and the mortality percentage.

TABLE 9.—Admissions to Hospital, Deaths and Mortality Percentage

		Wounded			Sick and injured			Total		
		Off.	O.R.	Total	Off.	O.R.	Total	Off.	O.R.	Total
Numbers	Admissions	65	556	621	816	23,930	24,746	881	24,486	25,367
	Deaths	3	58	61	7	174	181	10	232	242
Ratio per 1,000	Admissions			18·82			749·88			768·70
	Deaths			1·85			5·48			7·33
Percentage Total Adms.	Deaths	4·62	10·43	9·82	·86	·73	·73	1·14	·95	·95

From 26th December 1914 to 14th August 1915 the average number constantly in hospital was 1,304 or 31·66 per 1,000 of the average strength of the Dominion troops for that period. The average length of stay in hospital per patient for wounds and disease was 12·8 days, and the average duration of each case of sickness was 16·65 days.

Hospital Accommodation

There is unfortunately no information available to show the hospital accommodation provided for the Dominion troops in South-West Africa. The maximum number in hospital on any one date was 1,745 or 5·29 per cent. of the average strength, while the average number in hospital for the whole period was 1,090 or 3·30 per cent. of the average strength.

Non-battle Casualties

Of the recorded and classified causes of admission, Table 10 shows the principal causes of inefficiency among the Dominion troops during the South-West African campaign.

TABLE 10.—Principal Causes of Inefficiency

	Admissions	Ratio per 1,000
Diseases of the digestive system	6,304	191·03
Diseases of the nervous system and organs of special sense	1,698	51·45
Diseases of the circulatory system	1,672	50·67
Diseases of the respiratory system, excluding pneumonia	1,394	42·24
Diseases of the skin and cellular tissue	1,279	38·76
Influenza	1,052	31·88

Table 11 shows a more detailed analysis of admissions to hospital on account of sickness or injury among the Dominion troops in South-West Africa, with the number of deaths, the ratios per 1,000 of average strength over the period, and the average duration of treatment in hospital for some of the more important diseases.

TABLE 11.—Analysis of Admissions to Hospital, Deaths, and Average Duration in Hospital for the more important Diseases among Dominion Troops in South-West Africa

	Admissions	Deaths	Ratio per 1,000 Admissions	Ratio per 1,000 Deaths	Average No. of days in hospital
Specific diseases due to infection					
Dysentery	715	13	21·67	·39	15·52
Enteric fever (typhoid)	230	26	6·97	·79	46·55
Influenza	1,052	—	31·88	—	8·12
Malaria	518	2	15·70	·06	12·91
Mediterranean fever	14	—	·42	—	44·64
Pneumonia, lobar and broncho-	124	12	3·76	·36	26·30
Venereal diseases { Gonorrhœa	1,130	—	34·24	—	21·67
Syphilis	227	—	6·88	—	37·12
Diseases classified under systems					
Diseases of the—					
Nervous system and organs of special sense	1,698	3	51·45	·09	19·24
Circulatory system	1,672	7	50·67	·21	19·73
Respiratory system, excluding pneumonia	1,394	3	42·24	·09	?
Digestive system { Diarrhœa and enteritis	2,927	2	88·70	·06	9·71
Appendicitis	374	6	11·33	·18	27·81
Other	3,003	12	91·00	·36	?
Skin and cellular tissue	1,279	—	38·76	—	15·97
Bones and organs of locomotion	929	—	28·15	—	24·46
Other diseases or injuries					
Scurvy	10	—	·30	—	10·80
Bilharziasis	153	—	4·64	—	15·19
Effects of heat	406	1	12·30	·03	10·65
Unclassified	6,891	94	208·82	2·85	?
Total diseases and injuries	24,746	181	749·88	5·48	16·65

CHAPTER XIX

CASUALTIES IN THE SOUTH AFRICAN WAR, 1899-1902

FOR purposes of comparison the approximate casualties in the South African War, 1899–1902, have been tabulated on lines similar to those of the campaigns in the Great War. The figures for battle casualties are those published by the War Office ; the figures for non-battle casualties are the work of a staff instituted to compile the medical statistics of the campaign, but hitherto unpublished. The tables are not entirely comparable with those of the Great War owing to lack of certain information, such as the average strength of officers engaged, the admissions to hospital of officers suffering from disease or injury, and the number of prisoners of war captured by the enemy during the campaign. With the exception, therefore, of the table of analysed casualties, which are the final results given by the War Office, the tables in this chapter refer to other ranks only.

Strength

The average ration strength of warrant officers, non-commissioned officers and men of the force in South Africa, including colonial troops, is shown in Table 1.

TABLE 1.—Average Ration Strength

Period	Other Ranks
October 1899 to May 1902	208,226

Classification of Casualties

The total casualties among other ranks of the force in South Africa from October 1899 to May 1902 are given in Table 2, with the average annual ratios per 1,000 of strength.

SOUTH AFRICAN WAR, 1899-1902

TABLE 2.—Total Casualties, other ranks only

	Other ranks	Average annual ratio per 1,000 Other ranks
Battle casualties	26,750	48·17
Non-battle casualties	404,126	727·80
Total	430,876	775·97

The proportion of battle casualties to non-battle casualties among other ranks was 1 to 15·1.

An analysis of the total casualties is given in Table 3.

TABLE 3.—Classification and Percentages of Total Casualties

	Off.	O.R.	Total	Percentage of total casualties		
				Off.	O.R.	Total
A. *Battle casualties:*						
(a) Killed	518	5,256	5,774		1·22	
(b) Died of wounds	183	1,835	2,018		·42	
(c) Missing, presumed dead	—	105	105		·02	
(d) Died as prisoners of war	5	97	102		·02	
(e) Wounded less (b)		19,457			4·52	
B. *Non-battle casualties:*						
(f) Died of disease or injury	366	13,682	14,048		3·18	
(g) Sick or injured less (f)		390,444			90·62	
Total A. and B.		430,876			—	

Table 4 (a) shows this detail as percentages of battle casualties, and Table 4 (b) as percentages of non-battle casualties.

TABLE 4 (a).—Percentages of Battle Casualties

	Other ranks
(a) Killed	19·65
(b) Died of wounds	6·86
(c) Missing, presumed dead	·39
(d) Died as prisoners of war	·36
(e) Wounded less (b)	72·74

TABLE 4 (b).—Percentages of Non-battle Casualties

	Other ranks
(f) Died of disease or injury	3·38
(g) Sick or injured less (f)	96·62

The casualties sustained by the troops during the South African War may be further classified into permanent losses (exclusive of prisoners of war who did not die in captivity) and temporary losses for military purposes in the field.

TABLE 5 (a).—Permanent Losses for Military Purposes in the Field

	Other ranks	Percentage of total casualties — Other ranks
A. *Battle casualties:*		
Killed	5,256	1·22
Died of wounds	1,835	·42
Missing, presumed dead	105	·02
Died as prisoners of war	97	·02
Total	7,293	1·68
B. *Non-battle casualties:*		
Died of disease or injury	13,682	3·18
Total permanent losses	20,975	4·86

TABLE 5 (b).—Temporary Losses for Military Purposes in the Field

	Other ranks	Percentage of total casualties — Other ranks
A. *Battle casualties:*		
Wounded less died of wounds	19,457	4·52
B. *Non-battle casualties:*		
Sick or injured less died of disease or injury	390,444	90·62
Total temporary losses	409,901	95·14

The relative proportions of the various classes of casualties to each other for other ranks in the South African War are indicated in Table 6.

TABLE 6.—Proportions

	Other ranks
1. Total battle casualties to total non-battle casualties	1 : 15·1
2. Total killed to total wounded including died of wounds	1 : 4·5
3. Permanent losses among battle casualties to total wounded less died of wounds	1 : 2·6
4. Permanent losses among non-battle casualties to total sick and injured less deaths from disease or injury	1 : 28·5
5. Total permanent losses to total temporary losses	1 : 19·5

Admissions to Hospital

Of the total casualties among other ranks of the force in South Africa, the numbers admitted to hospital and treated by the medical service are given in Table 7.

TABLE 7.—Numbers admitted to Hospital

	Other ranks	Percentage of total casualties — Other ranks
Wounded	21,292	4·94
Sick or injured	404,126	93·80
Total	425,418	98·74

The proportion of wounded to sick and injured treated by the medical services was 1 to 18·9.

The casualties which were not treated by the medical services are shown in Table 8.

TABLE 8.—Casualties not treated by the Medical Services

	Other ranks	Percentage of total casualties — Other ranks
Killed	5,256	1·22
Missing, presumed dead	105	·02
Died as prisoners of war	97	·02
Total	5,458*	1·26

The numbers of sick and wounded admitted to hospital and their disposal are shown in Table 9 (a), while the average annual ratios per 1,000 of ration strength, and the percentages of total admissions are given in Tables 9 (b) and 9 (c) respectively.

TABLE 9 (a).—Admissions to Hospital and Disposal of Cases—Other Ranks only

	Wounded	Sick or injured	Total
Admissions	21,292	404,126	425,418
Deaths	1,835	13,682	15,517
Returned to duty	12,523	324,828	337,351
Invalided overseas	6,934	65,617	72,551 †

TABLE 9 (b).—Average Annual Ratio per 1,000 of Ration Strength—Other Ranks only

	Wounded	Sick or injured	Total
Admissions	38·35	727·80	766·15
Deaths	3·30	24·64	27·95
Returned to duty	22·65	585·00	607·55
Invalided overseas	12·49	118·17	130·66

* Prisoners of war during the campaign not included.

† Of these 5,879 were discharged from the service as unfit, giving a ratio of 28·23 per 1,000 of the strength.

TABLE 9 (c).—Percentages of total Admissions—Other Ranks only

	Wounded	Sick or injured	Total
Deaths	8·62	3·39	3·65
Returned to duty	58·81	80·38	79·30
Invalided overseas	32·57	16·23	17·05

The ratios per 1,000 other ranks constantly in hospital are shown in Table 10.

TABLE 10.—Ratio per 1,000 constantly in Medical Units

	Wounded	Sick or injured	Total
In hospitals	4·53	56·69	61·22

Hospital Accommodation

Definite information concerning the number of hospital beds provided for the British troops in South Africa during the campaign has not been obtained.

Non-battle Casualties

The following figures for disease or injury among other ranks in the South African War were compiled from the admission and discharge books by a specially detailed staff in the War Office after the close of the campaign. The chief causes of admission to hospital with the average annual ratios per 1,000 of strength are shown in Table 11.

TABLE 11.—Principal Causes of Inefficiency

	Admissions	Average annual ratio per 1,000
Enteric fever	57,684	103·88
Diseases of the digestive system	56,148	101·12
Dysentery	38,108	68·60
Pyrexia of uncertain origin (simple continued fever)	33,033	59·49
Injuries, local and general	29,063	52·34
Malaria	25,156	45·30
Rheumatic fever	24,460	44·05
Debility	20,767	37·40
Venereal diseases	19,127	34·45
Diseases of the skin	13,166	23·71

Table 12 gives a detailed analysis of the causes of admission to hospital of British troops, other ranks only, during the South African War.

TABLE 12.—Admissions to Hospital during the South African War, 1899-1902, and Deaths in South Africa, and the Numbers Invalided Overseas for Diseases or Injuries, Other Ranks only, with the Average Annual Ratios per 1,000 of the strength

	Admissions	Deaths	Invalided overseas	Average annual ratio per 1,000		
				Admissions	Deaths	Invalided
Specific diseases due to infection						
Dengue	335	—	6	·61	—	·01
Diphtheria	32	2	3	·06	·00	·00
Dysentery	38,108	1,343	5,776	68·60	2·42	10·40
Enteric fever	57,684	8,022	19,454	103·88	14·45	35·03
Erysipelas	496	12	27	·89	·02	·05
Influenza	8,891	3	357	16·01	·00	·64
Malaria	25,156	85	2,428	45·30	·15	4·37
Measles	1,218	4	11	2·19	·00	·02
Mediterranean fever	35	—	15	·06	—	·03
Plague	23	4	10	·04	—	·02
Pneumonia	2,591	466	397	4·67	·85	·72
Pyæmia	19	9	2	·03	·01	·00
Pyrexia of uncertain origin (simple continued fever)	33,033	23	2,131	59·49	·04	3·84
Rheumatic fever	24,460	25	4,305	44·05	·04	7·75
Scarlet fever	338	1	5	·61	·00	·01
Septicæmia	476	6	29	·85	·01	·05
Small-pox	10	—	2	·02	—	·00
Tetanus	6	3	—	·01	·00	—
Tuberculosis { Pulmonary	1,509	122	843	2·72	·22	1·52
Tuberculosis { Other	194	24	105	·35	·04	·19
Venereal diseases { Gonorrhœa	8,538	—	262	15·38	—	·47
Venereal diseases { Syphilis	8,620	6	1,690	15·52	·01	3·04
Venereal diseases { Soft chancre	1,969	—	59	3·54	—	·11
Other diseases due to infection	1,501	23	288	2·70	·04	·52
Diseases classified under systems						
Diseases of the nervous system	4,327	79	1,366	7·79	·14	2·46
Mental diseases	781	12	620	1·41	·02	1·11
Diseases of the						
Eye { Conjunctivitis	2,363	—	231	3·65	—	·42
Eye { Other diseases	2,716	—	928	4·89	—	1·67
Ear { Middle ear disease	1,716	3	663	3·09	·00	1·20
Ear { Other diseases	2,050	—	422	3·69	—	·76
Nose	199	—	24	·36	—	·04
Circulatory system { Valvular disease of the heart	2,613	75	1,895	4·71	·13	3·41
Circulatory system { Disordered action of the heart	3,631	3	1,470	6·54	·00	2·65
Circulatory system { Other diseases	2,496	89	690	4·50	·16	1·24
Respiratory system { Bronchitis	8,087	22	692	14·57	·04	1·24
Respiratory system { Other diseases	2,519	52	463	4·54	·09	·84
Spleen and lymphatic system	2,245	—	189	4·04	—	·34
Endocrine glands	40	—	25	·07	—	·04
Teeth and gums	6,942	—	2,274	12·50	—	4·10
Digestive system { Tonsillitis	10,987	2	201	19·79	·00	·36
Digestive system { Inflammation and ulceration of the stomach	2,201	10	265	3·96	·02	·48
Digestive system { Enteritis, typhlitis and colitis	1,738	46	256	3·13	·08	·46
Digestive system { Diarrhœa	18,716	20	750	33·70	·03	1·35
Digestive system { Jaundice	6,194	3	316	11·16	·00	·57
Digestive system { Other diseases	16,312	208	1,873	24·57	·37	3·37
Generative system	5,649	3	704	10·17	·00	1·27
Skin	13,166	—	505	23·71	—	·91
Areolar tissue	7,627	2	339	13·74	·00	·61
Organs of locomotion	6,741	7	1,151	12·14	·01	2·07
Urinary System { Nephritis	492	32	248	·88	·06	·45
Urinary System { Other diseases	1,337	28	403	2·41	·05	·73
Miscellaneous diseases						
Debility	20,767	12	5,365	37·40	·02	9·66
Scurvy	152	11	21	·27	·02	·04
Poisons (includes alcoholism)	698	59	24	1·26	·10	·04
Parasites { Bilharzia hæmatobia	187	—	100	·34	—	·18
Parasites { Other	3,075	1	12	5·54	·00	·02
No appreciable disease	1,057	—	—	1·90	—	—
Injuries						
Effects of heat	1,528	13	309	2·75	·02	·56
Other general injuries	452	163	82	·81	·29	·15
Local injuries	27,083	209	2,536	48·77	·33	4·57
Total Diseases and Injuries	404,126	11,347*	65,617	727·80	20·43	118·17

* Deaths in hospital during the campaign; the War Office figure 13,682 denotes ultimate results.

CHAPTER XX

ANALYSIS OF 1,043,653 BRITISH CASUALTIES ADMITTED TO MEDICAL UNITS 1916–1920

IN the preceding chapters the casualties occurring in the Great War have been treated from the standpoint of the administrative medical officer, as adminstrative action must always initiate broad preventive measures against disease in an expeditionary force. An attempt has been made to use the results of research and focus attention on the important lessons of the war in each campaign, indicate the way towards further progress, and provide a working basis for future calculations. No volume of medical statistics would, however, be complete without a scientific analysis of the cases admitted to hospital for wounds, disease or injury, and the originators of the *Medical History of the War* had this in view when they outlined their elaborate scheme of tabulating results under a thousand and fifty headings. The chapters dealing with the United Kingdom, France and Flanders, 1914 and 1915, the Mediterranean Expeditionary Force during the Dardanelles campaign, and the South African War include the detailed statistics of disease in a final form. This information is, however, not available for the remaining years of the war as it was found impracticable to complete the analysis of some twenty-three million cards. In order to bridge the gap a modified scheme was drawn up which, in the opinion of the Army Council, reduced to a minimum the statistics required. Under this new scheme the analysis was confined to the medical cards of British troops only, from which information on the following lines was to be extracted :—

1. A general table showing the numbers of admissions to hospital, deaths, invalids from the service, and average constantly sick for the diseases, wounds and injuries, or groups of diseases, wounds and injuries, specified, with the ratios per 1,000 of the strength under each heading.
2. A table showing the numbers of admissions to hospital, deaths, invalids, and average constantly sick on account of wounds, classified according to site of wound, with ratios per 1,000 of the strength under each heading.
3. A table showing the number of admissions for wounds classified according to the nature of the wounds and their site.
4. The foregoing information to be extracted separately for each force and for the United Kingdom.
5. The average number of days in hospital for the various diseases to be calculated by sampling a series of cards in which this information is shown completely.
6. To enable the Medical Research Council to complete the study of the minor epidemiology of the war, records of the following diseases to be codified by months in addition to the information required for the completion of the tables referred to in paragraph 1 :—

(a) Pyrexia of uncertain origin
(b) Rheumatic fever and allied disorders
(c) Sand-fly fever
(d) Trench fever
(e) Tonsillitis
(f) Scurvy
(g) Scabies
(h) Nephritis (acute and chronic)
(i) Trench nephritis

It was estimated that an analysis of the medical cards for the remaining years on these lines would occupy thirty clerks for three years and cost many thousands of pounds in addition to the expenditure incurred in editing and publishing. Unfortunately, the urgent need for economy at the time compelled the authorities to seek an alternative and still less expensive proposition. It was suggested that adequate results would be obtained from an examination of sample cards in place of an analysis of the complete register, that the results would show a sufficiently high degree of accuracy in matters of importance; and that while unreliable results might be expected in minor directions, it did not necessarily follow that this would be remedied by a 100 per cent. examination of the cards. Moreover, it was not considered that the results were likely to influence appreciably the practical arrangements necessary for the prevention of disease or for the replacement of casualties and wastage. This further modification of the scheme was ultimately adopted. Two sets of sample cards, representing 1,043,653 cases, or about 18·5 per cent. of the total cards for the years 1916 onwards, were taken as closely as possible in proportion to the approximate strength of the various arms comprising the British army, and as the record cards were filed under regiments and in regimental numerical order, the samples were taken one-third from the beginning, one-third from the middle, and one-third from the end of the files.

The tables in this chapter are the result of the scientific analysis of these two sets of samples. They cover the period from 1916 to 1920, and therefore include the transition stage from war to peace, a time when men were not required for active fighting, and it was desirable to have them demobilised and reinstated in civil employment. Read in conjunction with the previous chapters they should prove of value both to the administrative officer and to the scientific investigator of disease, as they fill some gaps and bridge others in a more comprehensive manner than is possible with isolated samples. It is not possible to reduce any of the figures to ratios per 1,000 of strength, but certain percentages have been introduced as a guide. The tables do not follow the usual formula. They are self-explanatory and require no prefatory remarks.

TABLE 1.—Summary of Wounds, Diseases and Injuries under Examination

	Officers	Other ranks	Total
Wounds	24,669	182,307	206,976
Diseases or injuries	78,760	757,917	836,677
Total	103,429	940,224	1,043,653

TABLE 2.—Number of Cases of Wounds, Disease or Injury, Analysed by Arms of the Service

Arms of the Service	Wounds			Disease or injury			Total		
	Off.	O.R.	Total	Off.	O.R.	Total	Off.	O.R.	Total
Infantry	16,519	122,850	139,369	38,289	328,918	367,207	54,808	451,768	506,576
Cavalry	875	3,212	4,087	2,784	24,542	27,326	3,659	27,754	31,413
Artillery	3,242	20,842	24,084	11,070	101,023	112,093	14,312	121,865	136,177
R.A.S.C.	725	7,508	8,233	7,879	82,448	90,327	8,604	89,956	98,560
R.A.M.C.	321	2,872	3,193	3,802	33,869	37,671	4,123	36,741	40,864
Engineers	1,459	9,814	11,273	7,199	66,891	74,090	8,658	76,705	85,363
Labour	236	5,965	6,201	2,723	66,407	69,130	2,959	72,372	75,331
Tanks	327	2,435	2,762	755	9,235	9,990	1,082	11,670	12,752
Machine Gun Corps	498	4,092	4,590	1,630	14,295	15,925	2,128	18,387	20,515
Others	467	2,717	3,184	2,629	30,289	32,918	3,096	33,006	36,102
Total	24,669	182,307	206,976	78,760	757,917	836,677	103,429	940,224	1,043,653

TABLE 3.—Percentages of Total Cases Analysed by Arms of the Service

Arms of the Service	Wounds	Disease or injury	Total	Percentage of total cases analysed		
				Wounds	Disease	Total
Infantry	139,369	367,207	506,576	67·34	43·89	48·54
Cavalry	4,087	27,326	31,413	1·97	3·27	3·01
Artillery	24,084	112,093	136,177	11·64	13·40	13·05
R.A.S.C.	8,233	90,327	98,560	3·98	10·80	9·44
R.A.M.C.	3,193	37,671	40,864	1·54	4·50	3·92
Engineers	11,273	74,090	85,363	5·45	8·86	8·18
Labour	6,201	69,130	75,331	3·00	8·26	7·22
Tanks	2,762	9,990	12,752	1·33	1·19	1·22
Machine Gun Corps	4,590	15,925	20,515	2·22	1·90	1·97
Others	3,184	32,918	36,102	1·54	3·93	3·46
Total	206,976	836,677	1,043,653	—	—	—

TABLE 4.—Number of Cases of Wounds and Disease or Injury Analysed by Geographical Areas

Country	Wounds			Disease or injury			Total		
	Off.	O.R.	Total	Off.	O.R.	Total	Off.	O.R.	Total
France	21,175	159,423	180,598	43,954	419,634	463,588	65,129	579,057	644,186
Italy	142	1,056	1,198	1,026	10,831	11,857	1,168	11,887	13,055
Africa	10	21	31	277	3,004	3,281	287	3,025	3,312
Palestine and Egypt	571	4,348	4,919	4,018	46,004	50,022	4,589	50,352	54,941
Macedonia	439	1,739	2,178	4,284	33,418	37,702	4,723	35,157	39,880
Mesopotamia	392	1,486	1,878	3,799	19,080	22,879	4,191	20,566	24,757
North Russia	14	49	63	77	1,259	1,336	91	1,308	1,399
United Kingdom	1,742	12,881	14,623	18,684	202,029	220,713	20,426	214,910	235,336
India	98	748	846	1,599	14,871	16,470	1,697	15,619	17,316
Miscellaneous and uncertain	86	556	642	1,042	7,787	8,829	1,128	8,343	9,471
Total	24,669	182,307	206,976	78,760	757,917	836,677	103,429	940,224	1,043,653

ANALYSIS OF 1,043,653 CASUALTIES

TABLE 5.—Number of Cases of Wounds, Disease or Injury Analysed by Age Groups

Age	Wounds			Disease or injury			Total		
	Off.	O.R.	Total	Off.	O.R.	Total	Off.	O.R.	Total
Under 20 years	1,231	16,500	17,731	2,980	78,740	81,720	4,211	95,240	99,451
20–29	14,990	104,001	118,991	41,295	382,191	423,486	56,285	486,192	542,477
30–39	5,271	41,984	47,255	21,010	183,581	204,591	26,281	225,565	251,846
40–49	1,068	10,464	11,532	7,169	71,039	78,208	8,237	81,503	89,740
50–59	147	640	787	1,608	9,513	11,121	1,755	10,153	11,908
60 and over	13	32	45	176	631	807	189	663	852
Not recorded	1,949	8,686	10,635	4,522	32,222	36,744	6,471	40,908	47,379
Total	24,669	182,307	206,976	78,760	757,917	836,677	103,429	940,224	1,043,653

TABLE 6.—Number of Cases of Wounds, Disease or Injury, according to Year of Admission to Hospital

Year	Wounds			Disease or injury			Total		
	Off.	O.R.	Total	Off.	O.R.	Total	Off.	O.R.	Total
1916	6,048	54,882	60,930	17,580	210,623	228,203	23,628	265,505	289,133
1917	8,530	61,730	70,260	22,139	203,347	225,486	30,669	265,077	295,746
1918	8,973	59,370	68,343	28,183	253,964	282,147	37,156	313,334	350,490
1919	868	4,807	5,675	8,898	72,253	81,151	9,766	77,060	86,826
1920	250	1,518	1,768	1,960	17,730	19,690	2,210	19,248	21,458
Total	24,669	182,307	206,976	78,760	757,917	836,677	103,429	940,224	1,043,653

TABLE 7.—Number of Cases of Wounds, Disease or Injury, according to Period in Hospital

Period	Wounds			Disease or injury			Total		
	Off.	O.R.	Total	Off.	O.R.	Total	Off.	O.R.	Total
1 week and under	3,994	28,643	32,637	15,228	164,814	180,042	19,222	193,457	212,679
1–2 weeks	2,311	15,808	18,119	17,667	146,447	164,114	19,978	162,255	182,233
2–4 weeks	1,936	11,503	13,439	9,854	83,485	93,339	11,790	94,988	106,778
1 month	2,353	16,596	18,949	8,367	81,207	89,574	10,720	97,803	108,523
2 months	4,052	37,155	41,207	10,967	128,389	139,356	15,019	165,544	180,563
3 months	2,347	21,525	23,872	4,675	60,178	64,853	7,022	81,703	88,725
3–6 months	3,026	24,873	27,899	4,200	49,193	53,393	7,226	74,066	81,292
6–9 months	1,159	8,186	9,345	888	8,282	9,170	2,047	16,468	18,515
9–12 months	500	3,934	4,434	239	2,599	2,838	739	6,533	7,272
12 months	52	306	358	20	176	196	72	482	554
Over 12 months	543	3,358	3,901	120	1,007	1,127	663	4,365	5,028
Incomplete	2,396	10,420	12,816	6,535	32,140	38,675	8,931	42,560	51,491
Total	24,669	182,307	206,976	78,760	757,917	836,677	103,429	940,224	1,043,653

TABLE 8.—Percentages of Total Cases Analysed according to Period in Hospital

Period	Wounds	Disease or injury	Total	Percentage of total cases analysed		
				Wounds	Disease	Total
1 week and under	32,637	180,042	212,679	15·77	21·52	20·38
1–2 weeks	18,119	164,114	182,233	8·75	19·61	17·46
2–4 weeks	13,439	93,339	106,778	6·49	11·16	10·23
1 month	18,949	89,574	108,523	9·16	10·71	10·40
2 months	41,207	139,356	180,563	19·91	16·66	17·30
3 months	23,872	64,853	88,725	11·53	7·75	8·50
3–6 months	27,899	53,393	81,292	13·48	6·38	7·79
6–9 months	9,345	9,170	18,515	4·52	1·10	1·77
9–12 months	4,434	2,838	7,272	2·14	·34	·70
12 months	358	196	554	·17	·02	·05
Over 12 months	3,901	1,127	5,028	1·88	·13	·48
Incomplete	12,816	38,675	51,491	6·19	4·62	4·93
Total	206,976	836,677	1,043,653	—	—	—

TABLE 9.—Number of Cases of Wounds, Disease or Injury, according to Final Disposal

Disposal	Wounds			Disease or injury			Total		
	Off.	O.R.	Total	Off.	O.R.	Total	Off.	O.R.	Total
Deaths	2,088	10,850	12,938	801	7,536	8,337	2,889	18,386	21,275
Returned to duty	19,691	148,330	168,021	71,609	696,269	767,878	91,300	844,599	935,899
Discharged as invalids	1,281	16,486	17,767	1,936	31,255	33,191	3,217	47,741	50,958
Discharged from hospital (indefinite)	185	427	612	470	2,291	2,761	655	2,718	3,373
Incomplete records	1,364	5,665	7,029	3,698	17,599	21,297	5,062	23,264	28,326
Disease changed	60	549	609	246	2,967	3,213	306	3,516	3,822
Total	24,669	182,307	206,976	78,760	757,917	836,677	103,429	940,224	1,043,653

TABLE 10.—Percentages of Total Cases Analysed according to Final Disposal

Disposal	Wounds	Disease or injury	Total	Percentage of total cases analysed		
				Wounds	Disease	Total
Deaths	12,938	8,337	21,275	6·25	1·00	2·04
Returned to duty	168,021	767,878	935,899	81·18	91·78	89·68
Discharged as invalids	17,767	33,191	50,958	8·58	3·97	4·88
Discharged from hospital (indefinite)	612	2,761	3,373	·30	·33	·32
Incomplete records	7,029	21,297	28,326	3·40	2·55	2·71
Disease changed	609	3,213	3,822	·29	·38	·37
Total	206,976	836,677	1,043,653	—	—	—

ANALYSIS OF 1,043,653 CASUALTIES

TABLE 11.—Cause of Wounds, with Percentages

Cause of wounds	Officers	Other ranks	Total	Percentage of total wounds analysed		
				Off.	O.R.	Total
Rifle bullet, shrapnel, bomb, bayonet or other instrument of war ...	18,653	136,908	155,561	75·61	75·10	75·16
Accidental or undefined	5,441	41,677	47,118	22·06	22·86	22·76
Self-inflicted	8	265	273	·03	·15	·13
Old wound or injury ...	567	3,457	4,024	2·30	1·90	1·94
Total	24,669	182,307	206,976	—	—	—

TABLE 12.—Nature of Wounds, with Percentages

Nature of wounds	Officers	Other Ranks	Total	Percentage of total wounds analysed		
				Off.	O.R.	Total
Flesh wound or contusion	19,145	145,030	164,175	77·61	79·55	79·32
Wound with fracture, major	2,577	16,253	18,830	10·45	8·92	9·10
Wound with fracture, minor	1,345	8,326	9,671	5·45	4·57	4·67
Dislocation or sprain ...	1,444	11,354	12,798	5·85	6·23	6·18
Undefined	158	1,344	1,502	·64	·74	·73
Total	24,669	182,307	206,976	—	—	—

TABLE 13.—Regional Incidence of Wounds, with Percentages

Site of wounds	Officers	Other ranks	Total	Percentage of total wounds analysed		
				Off.	O.R.	Total
Head, face or neck ...	4,509	29,804	34,313	18·28	16·35	16·58
Chest	1,315	6,503	7,818	5·33	3·57	3·78
Abdomen	856	3,852	4,708	3·47	2·11	2·27
Back	1,383	11,586	12,969	5·61	6·36	6·27
Upper extremity, not involving amputation ...	6,486	54,343	60,829	26·29	29·81	29·39
Lower extremity not involving amputation ...	9,310	69,889	79,199	37·74	38·34	38·26
Upper extremity with amputation	113	1,039	1,152	·46	·57	·56
Lower extremity with amputation	326	2,758	3,084	1·32	1·51	1·49
Undefined	371	2,533	2,904	1·50	1·39	1·40
Total	24,669	182,307	206,976	—	—	—

TABLE 14.—Analysis of Wounds, showing Cause, Nature and Site of Wounds, by Arms of the Service

	Infantry	Cavalry	Artillery	R.A.S.C.	R.A.M.C.	Engineers	Labour	Tanks	Machine Gun Corps	Others	Total
A. Cause of Wounds:											
Rifle bullet, shrapnel, bomb, bayonet or other instrument of war	118,594	2,166	15,851	1,679	1,922	6,218	2,485	2,156	3,658	832	155,561
Accidental or undefined	18,411	1,829	7,865	6,244	1,214	4,739	3,148	575	879	2,214	47,118
Self-inflicted	197	2	15	18	—	13	13	1	7	7	273
Old wound or injury	2,167	90	353	292	55	303	555	30	46	133	4,024
Total	139,369	4,087	24,084	8,233	3,193	11,273	6,201	2,762	4,590	3,184	206,976
B. Nature of Wounds:											
Flesh wound or contusion	115,292	2,929	18,394	4,758	2,267	8,152	4,397	2,314	3,754	1,918	164,175
Wound with fracture, major	13,850	250	1,944	550	187	856	424	179	377	213	18,830
Wound with fracture, minor	3,169	411	1,804	1,545	271	986	653	123	172	537	9,671
Dislocation or sprain	6,423	444	1,666	1,192	414	1,134	656	127	271	471	12,798
Undefined	635	53	276	188	54	145	71	19	16	45	1,502
Total	139,369	4,087	24,084	8,233	3,193	11,273	6,201	2,762	4,590	3,184	206,976
C. Site of Wounds:											
Head, face or neck	22,114	664	4,304	1,523	532	2,002	1,129	591	815	639	34,313
Chest	5,392	166	875	279	120	430	210	90	144	112	7,818
Abdomen	3,173	91	607	180	56	258	108	48	104	83	4,708
Back	8,521	215	1,727	500	217	765	392	154	283	195	12,969
Upper extremity, not involving amputation	43,193	1,075	6,201	2,186	757	2,884	1,671	825	1,298	739	60,829
Lower extremity, not involving amputation	52,046	1,767	9,461	3,397	1,393	4,564	2,515	965	1,774	1,317	79,199
Upper extremity, with amputation	874	14	103	25	8	52	30	12	25	9	1,152
Lower extremity, with amputation	2,290	35	349	59	31	113	63	43	77	24	3,084
Undefined	1,766	60	457	84	79	205	83	34	70	66	2,904
Total	139,369	4,087	24,084	8,233	3,193	11,273	6,201	2,762	4,590	3,184	206,976

ANALYSIS OF 1,043,653 CASUALTIES 281

TABLE 15.—Analysis of Wounds, showing Cause, Nature and Site of Wounds, by Geographical Areas

	France	Italy	Africa	Palestine or Egypt	Macedonia	Mesopotamia	North Russia	United Kingdom	India	Miscellaneous and uncertain	Total
A. *Cause of Wounds*:											
Rifle bullet, shrapnel, bomb, bayonet or other instrument of war	147,610	626	8	3,110	1,086	1,334	21	1,266	239	261	155,561
Accidental or undefined	30,071	554	22	1,584	1,015	482	38	12,404	585	363	47,118
Self-inflicted	210	1	—	5	—	1	—	52	2	2	273
Old wound or injury	2,707	17	1	220	76	61	4	901	20	17	4,024
Total	*180,598*	*1,198*	*31*	*4,919*	*2,178*	*1,878*	*63*	*14,623*	*846*	*642*	*206,976*
B. *Nature of Wounds*:											
Flesh wound or contusion	148,156	845	20	3,808	1,478	1,456	40	7,494	481	397	164,175
Wound with fracture, major	17,327	82	4	350	192	148	4	647	43	33	18,830
Wound with fracture, minor	5,857	101	2	311	179	124	4	2,917	88	88	9,671
Dislocation or sprain	8,181	155	4	418	295	135	14	3,261	219	116	12,798
Undefined	1,077	15	1	32	34	15	1	304	15	8	1,502
Total	*180,598*	*1,198*	*31*	*4,919*	*2,178*	*1,878*	*63*	*14,623*	*846*	*642*	*206,976*
C. *Site of Wounds*:											
Head, face or neck	30,387	177	7	704	340	277	8	2,209	106	98	34,313
Chest	6,959	31	1	230	115	99	4	327	27	25	7,818
Abdomen	4,163	41	—	134	59	51	3	233	13	11	4,708
Back	11,558	85	2	279	122	99	4	757	35	28	12,969
Upper extremity, not involving amputation	54,066	318	6	1,319	523	520	18	3,713	174	172	60,829
Lower extremity, not involving amputation	66,966	521	13	2,156	956	786	24	7,075	422	280	79,199
Upper extremity, with amputation	1,076	—	—	18	17	5	1	30	3	2	1,152
Lower extremity, with amputation	2,922	15	1	48	22	20	1	47	4	4	3,084
Undefined	2,501	10	1	31	24	21	—	232	62	22	2,904
Total	*180,598*	*1,198*	*31*	*4,919*	*2,178*	*1,878*	*63*	*14,623*	*846*	*642*	*206,976*

TABLE 16.—Analysis of Wounds, showing Cause, Nature and Site of Wounds, by Age Groups

	Under 20 years	20–29	30–39	40–49	50–59	60 years and over	Not recorded	Total
A. Cause of Wounds:								
Rifle bullet, shrapnel, bomb, bayonet or other instrument of war	13,827	93,159	33,682	6,122	134	7	8,630	155,561
Accidental or undefined	3,656	23,285	12,595	5,025	606	35	1,916	47,118
Self-inflicted	41	155	40	29	1	—	7	273
Old wound or injury	207	2,392	938	356	46	3	82	4,024
Total	17,731	118,991	47,255	11,532	787	45	10,635	206,976
B. Nature of Wounds:								
Flesh wound or contusion	14,337	96,355	36,238	8,042	405	17	8,781	164,175
Wound with fracture, major	1,548	10,989	4,396	943	41	3	910	18,830
Wound with fracture, minor	626	4,399	2,951	1,293	203	15	184	9,671
Dislocation or sprain	1,131	6,603	3,358	1,142	123	10	431	12,798
Undefined	89	645	312	112	15	—	329	1,502
Total	17,731	118,991	47,255	11,532	787	45	10,635	206,976
C. Site of Wounds:								
Head, face or neck	2,755	18,781	7,926	2,013	111	7	2,720	34,313
Chest	580	4,208	1,789	445	34	1	761	7,818
Abdomen	309	2,218	848	187	7	—	1,139	4,708
Back	872	7,182	3,089	910	88	7	821	12,969
Upper extremity, not involving amputation	5,668	36,543	13,611	3,097	171	9	1,730	60,829
Lower extremity, not involving amputation	7,023	46,102	18,434	4,528	355	20	2,737	79,199
Upper extremity, with amputation	80	682	310	57	1	—	22	1,152
Lower extremity, with amputation	266	1,859	726	156	6	—	71	3,084
Undefined	178	1,416	522	139	14	1	634	2,904
Total	17,731	118,991	47,255	11,532	787	45	10,635	206,976

TABLE 17.—Analysis of Wounds, showing Cause, Nature and Site of Wounds, according to Year of Admission to Hospital

	1916	1917	1918	1919	1920	Total
A. Cause of Wounds:						
Rifle bullet, shrapnel, bomb, bayonet or other instrument of war	46,477	54,807	52,815	1,037	425	155,561
Accidental or undefined	13,487	14,254	14,133	4,059	1,185	47,118
Self-inflicted	100	68	90	11	4	273
Old wound or injury	866	1,131	1,305	568	154	4,024
Total	60,930	70,260	68,343	5,675	1,768	206,976
B. Nature of Wounds:						
Flesh wound or contusion	49,342	56,175	54,393	3,272	993	164,175
Wound with fracture, major	4,514	6,862	6,962	380	112	18,830
Wound with fracture, minor	2,461	2,856	2,962	1,056	336	9,671
Dislocation or sprain	4,135	3,852	3,621	879	311	12,798
Undefined	478	515	405	88	16	1,502
Total	60,930	70,260	68,343	5,675	1,768	206,976
C. Site of Wounds:						
Head, face or neck	10,251	11,819	10,815	1,102	326	34,313
Chest	2,290	2,727	2,597	164	40	7,818
Abdomen	1,377	1,708	1,505	91	27	4,708
Back	4,117	4,636	3,877	214	125	12,969
Upper extremity, not involving amputation	17,739	20,717	20,195	1,657	521	60,829
Lower extremity, not involving amputation	23,150	26,053	26,970	2,320	706	79,199
Upper extremity, with amputation	306	454	371	19	2	1,152
Lower extremity, with amputation	783	1,069	1,166	58	8	3,084
Undefined	917	1,077	847	50	13	2,904
Total	60,930	70,260	68,343	5,675	1,768	206,976

ANALYSIS OF 1,043,653 CASUALTIES 283

TABLE 18.—Analysis of Wounds, showing Cause, Nature and Site of Wounds, according to Period in Hospital

	1 Week and under	1–2 weeks	2–4 weeks	1 month	2 months	3 months	3–6 months	6–9 months	9–12 months	12 months	Over 12 months	Incomplete	Total
A. Cause of Wounds:													
Rifle bullet, shrapnel, bomb, bayonet or other instrument of war	22,537	9,566	7,904	13,009	31,523	19,502	24,012	8,542	4,153	335	3,724	10,754	155,561
Accidental or undefined	9,294	8,011	5,161	5,494	8,857	3,957	3,497	701	248	22	144	1,732	47,118
Self-inflicted	39	18	16	23	54	36	56	7	4	—	4	16	273
Old wound or injury	767	524	358	423	773	377	334	95	29	1	29	314	4,024
Total	32,637	18,119	13,439	18,949	41,207	23,872	27,899	9,345	4,434	358	3,907	12,816	206,976
B. Nature of Wounds:													
Flesh wound or contusion	26,838	14,318	10,785	15,819	34,469	19,556	21,242	6,087	2,567	205	1,764	10,525	164,175
Wound with fracture, major	1,877	343	292	452	1,859	1,805	4,302	2,748	1,654	144	2,014	1,340	18,830
Wound with fracture, minor	562	473	521	960	2,497	1,640	1,760	422	179	5	109	543	9,671
Dislocation or sprain	2,680	2,747	1,697	1,612	2,237	808	534	81	25	4	12	361	12,798
Undefined	680	238	144	106	145	63	61	7	9	—	2	47	1,502
Total	32,637	18,119	13,439	18,949	41,207	23,872	27,899	9,345	4,434	358	3,907	12,816	206,976
C. Site of Wounds:													
Head, face or neck	8,127	4,188	2,809	3,536	5,830	2,900	3,453	961	383	30	252	1,844	34,313
Chest	1,575	516	389	544	1,457	992	1,239	359	137	10	78	522	7,818
Abdomen	2,181	269	163	227	486	352	531	154	67	4	41	233	4,708
Back	2,528	1,382	937	1,200	2,554	1,570	1,500	380	145	8	74	691	12,969
Upper extremity, not involving amputation	6,860	4,511	3,834	6,319	14,307	7,666	8,369	2,665	1,226	92	998	3,982	60,829
Lower extremity, not involving amputation	9,922	6,886	5,065	6,866	16,121	10,014	11,924	3,931	1,774	147	1,547	5,002	79,199
Upper extremity, with amputation	40	10	18	32	58	84	252	235	158	9	142	114	1,152
Lower extremity, with amputation	172	55	47	52	95	93	376	575	508	56	752	303	3,084
Undefined	1,232	302	177	173	299	201	255	85	36	2	17	125	2,904
Total	32,637	18,119	13,439	18,949	41,207	23,872	27,899	9,345	4,434	358	3,907	12,816	206,976

TABLE 19.—Analysis of Wounds, showing Cause, Nature and Site of Wounds, according to Final Disposal, with Percentages of Admissions

	Deaths	Returned to duty	Discharged as invalids	Discharged from hospital (indefinite)	Records incomplete	Disease changed	Total	Percentage of Admissions					
								Deaths	Returned to duty	Discharged as invalids	Discharged from hospital (indefinite)	Records incomplete	Disease changed
A. Cause of Wounds:													
Rifle bullet, shrapnel, bomb, bayonet or other instrument of war	12,263	120,968	15,654	404	5,834	438	155,561	7·88	77·76	10·06	·26	3·75	·28
Accidental or undefined	637	43,580	1,523	186	1,039	153	47,118	1·35	92·49	3·23	·39	2·21	·32
Self-inflicted	25	212	21	1	12	2	273	9·16	77·66	7·69	·37	4·40	·73
Old wound or injury	13	3,261	569	21	144	16	4,024	·32	81·04	14·14	·52	3·58	·40
Total	*12,938*	*168,021*	*17,767*	*612*	*7,029*	*609*	*206,976*	*6·25*	*81·18*	*8·58*	*·30*	*3·40*	*·29*
B. Nature of Wounds:													
Flesh wound or contusion	10,063	137,430	10,047	424	5,722	489	164,175	6·13	83·71	6·12	·26	3·49	·30
Wound with fracture, major	2,292	9,075	6,632	75	721	35	18,830	12·17	48·19	35·22	·40	3·83	·19
Wound with fracture, minor	187	8,208	860	47	336	33	9,671	1·93	84·87	8·89	·49	3·47	·34
Dislocation or sprain	10	12,304	167	50	216	51	12,798	·08	96·14	1·30	·39	1·69	·40
Undefined	386	1,004	61	16	34	1	1,502	25·70	66·84	4·06	1·07	2·26	·07
Total	*12,938*	*168,021*	*17,767*	*612*	*7,029*	*609*	*206,976*	*6·25*	*81·18*	*8·58*	*·30*	*3·40*	*·29*
C. Site of Wounds:													
Head, face or neck	2,954	28,153	2,034	96	984	92	34,313	8·61	82·05	5·93	·28	2·87	·27
Chest	1,271	5,672	530	22	304	19	7,818	16·26	72·55	6·78	·28	3·89	·24
Abdomen	2,042	2,192	311	10	141	12	4,708	43·37	46·56	6·61	·21	2·99	·25
Back	1,171	10,797	561	44	360	36	12,969	9·03	83·25	4·33	·34	2·78	·28
Upper extremity, not involving amputation	922	52,410	5,019	145	2,145	188	60,829	1·52	86·16	8·25	·24	3·53	·31
Lower extremity, not involving amputation	3,258	66,685	5,923	249	2,830	254	79,199	4·11	84·20	7·48	·31	3·57	·32
Upper extremity, with amputation	75	138	873	13	52	1	1,152	6·51	11·98	75·78	1·13	4·51	·09
Lower extremity, with amputation	344	202	2,388	18	128	4	3,084	11·15	6·55	77·43	·58	4·15	·13
Undefined	901	1,772	128	15	85	3	2,904	31·03	61·02	4·41	·52	2·93	·10
Total	*12,938*	*168,021*	*17,767*	*612*	*7,029*	*609*	*206,976*	*6·25*	*81·18*	*8·58*	*·30*	*3·40*	*·29*

ANALYSIS OF 1,043,653 CASUALTIES

TABLE 20.—Number of Cases of Disease or Injury Analysed, arranged by Diseases or Groups of Diseases

	Officers	Other ranks	Total	
1. Cerebro-spinal fever	40	549	589	1
2. Chicken-pox	50	116	166	2
3. Cholera	7	105	112	3
4. Diphtheria	217	1,580	1,797	4
5. Dysentery	1,290	10,538	11,828	5
6. Enteric group of fevers	403	1,948	2,351	6
7. Influenza	9,603	85,386	94,989	7
8. Malaria	3,284	30,619	33,903	8
9. Measles	548	2,870	3,418	9
10. Mumps	254	1,274	1,528	10
11. Pyrexia of uncertain origin	3,956	42,149	46,105	11
12. Rheumatic fever or acute rheumatism	165	2,519	2,684	12
13. Rheumatism	316	4,848	5,164	13
14. Fibrositis	9	51	60	14
15. Myositis	6	51	57	15
16. Myalgia	1,149	22,650	23,799	16
17. Pleurodynia	18	363	381	17
18. Lumbago	194	1,760	1,954	18
19. Sciatica	292	1,370	1,662	19
20. Sand-fly fever	1,216	4,823	6,039	20
21. Scarlet fever	117	922	1,039	21
22. Small-pox	14	98	112	22
23. Tubercle of lung	314	3,539	3,853	23
24. Tubercular diseases, other	53	882	935	24
25. Tetanus, following gunshot wound	3	32	35	25
26. Tetanus, idiopathic, or following other injury	3	23	26	26
27. Trench fever	1,227	11,785	13,012	27
28. Venereal diseases ⎰ Gonorrhœa	2,779	22,647	25,426	28
29. Venereal diseases ⎨ Syphilis	1,377	11,076	12,453	29
30. Venereal diseases ⎱ Other	156	3,503	3,659	30
31. Other diseases caused by infection	1,639	9,599	11,238	31
32. Debility	2,945	17,308	20,253	32
33. Functional diseases of the nervous system (including neurasthenia and shell-shock)	4,692	16,857	21,549	33
34. Epilepsy	90	2,562	2,652	34
35. Organic diseases of the nervous system	125	895	1,020	35
36. Mental diseases	145	3,063	3,208	36
37. Trachoma	1	96	97	37
38. Other diseases of the eye	722	12,838	13,560	38
39. Diseases of the ear	727	9,368	10,095	39
40. Diseases of the nose	588	2,016	2,604	40
41. Functional diseases of the heart	983	12,425	13,408	41
42. Organic diseases of the heart	287	5,688	5,975	42
43. Diseases of the arteries, veins and capillaries	405	4,148	4,553	43
44. Anæmia and other diseases of the blood	109	1,357	1,466	44
45. Diseases of the spleen	2	21	23	45
46. Diseases of the lymphatic system	203	2,015	2,218	46
47. Diseases of the thymus, thyroid, adrenals and pituitary body	41	805	846	47
48. Diseases of the breast	4	140	144	48
49. Pneumonia and broncho-pneumonia	859	8,484	9,343	49
50. Other diseases of the respiratory system	3,889	42,079	45,968	50
51. Caries of dentine	825	10,124	10,949	51
52. Inflammation of periosteum and alveoli	506	2,342	2,848	52
53. Other diseases of the teeth and gums	262	1,725	1,987	53
54. Tonsillitis and sore throat	3,236	23,180	26,416	54
55. Inflammation and ulceration of the stomach	1,491	9,989	11,480	55
56. Other diseases of the stomach	646	4,497	5,143	56
57. Inflammation of the intestines	2,589	10,627	13,216	57
58. Diarrhœa	1,871	22,399	24,270	58
59. Other diseases of the intestines	1,965	22,448	24,413	59
60. Jaundice	800	2,491	3,291	60
61. Other diseases of the liver	137	381	518	61
62. Diseases of the gall bladder and ducts	74	183	257	62

TABLE 20.—continued

	Officers	Other ranks	Total	
63. Peritonitis and other diseases of the peritoneum	21	187	208	63
64. Other diseases of the digestive system	409	2,302	2,711	64
65. Scurvy	—	5	5	65
66. Beri-beri	3	40	43	66
67. Other diseases due to disorders of nutrition or of metabolism	103	699	802	67
68. Diseases of the generative system	800	7,577	8,377	68
69. Diseases of the bones and periosteum	105	859	964	69
70. Diseases of the joints	1,728	12,610	14,338	70
71. Diseases of the spine	21	304	325	71
72. Diseases of the muscles and fascia	104	621	725	72
73. Flat foot	40	783	823	73
74. Other deformities of the feet	198	2,911	3,109	74
75. Other diseases of the organs of locomotion	73	1,116	1,189	75
76. Diseases of the areolar tissue	3,665	65,208	68,873	76
77. Diseases of the skin	1,616	23,188	24,804	77
78. Scabies	1,842	39,380	41,222	78
79. Bilharzia hæmatobia	8	60	68	79
80. Other parasitic diseases	140	3,421	3,561	80
81. Nephritis (acute and chronic)	247	5,585	5,832	81
82. Trench nephritis	6	278	284	82
83. Other diseases of the kidney	227	1,391	1,618	83
84. Other diseases of the ureter	16	276	292	84
85. Diseases of the bladder	201	1,929	2,130	85
86. Other diseases of the urinary organs	278	2,877	3,155	86
87. Malignant new growths (including cancer, carcinoma, epithelioma, sarcoma and rodent ulcer)	52	352	404	87
88. Non-malignant new growths	67	740	807	88
89. Tumour or growth, undefined (including malformations)	106	1,021	1,127	89
90. Alcoholism	67	174	241	90
91. Other poisons and intoxications	104	690	794	91
92. Heat-stroke and sunstroke	206	1,557	1,763	92
93. Burns and scalds	234	3,743	3,977	93
94. Gas poisoning	2,450	21,176	23,626	94
95. Other general injuries	163	1,615	1,778	95
96. Frost bite	21	485	506	96
97. Trench foot	124	5,391	5,515	97
98. Other local injuries	464	4,181	4,645	98
99. Other miscellaneous indefinite diseases	933	10,959	11,892	99
Grand Total of Diseases and Injuries	78,760	757,917	836,677	

TABLE 21.—Principal Causes of Admission to Hospital among Cases of Disease or Injury analysed, with percentages

	Admissions	Percentage of total diseases analysed
Diseases of the digestive system	111,923	13·38
Influenza	94,989	11·35
Diseases of the areolar tissue	68,873	8·23
Diseases of the skin, including scabies	66,026	7·89
Diseases of the respiratory system, including pneumonia	55,311	6·61
Diseases of the organs of locomotion	54,550	6·52
Pyrexia of uncertain origin	46,105	5·51
Local and general injuries	41,810	5·00
Venereal diseases	41,538	4·96
Malaria	33,903	4·05
Nervous disorders	28,429	3·40

ANALYSIS OF 1,043,653 CASUALTIES   287

TABLE 22.—Analysis of Admissions to Hospital for Disease or Injury by Arms of the Service

	Infantry	Cavalry	Artillery	R.A.S.C.	R.A.M.C.	Engineers	Labour	Tanks	Machine Gun Corps	Others	Total	
1. Cerebro-spinal fever	261	28	88	55	18	58	32	3	8	38	589	1
2. Chicken-pox	74	9	21	22	8	8	5	6	1	12	166	2
3. Cholera	67	1	18	9	4	9	—	—	1	3	112	3
4. Diphtheria	811	70	103	293	73	96	37	257	20	37	1,797	4
5. Dysentery	5,510	552	1,503	1,356	683	1,152	465	67	186	354	11,828	5
6. Enteric group of fevers	1,327	118	234	214	155	186	32	4	17	64	2,351	6
7. Influenza	33,872	3,309	13,240	12,087	6,197	8,934	10,181	1,375	1,799	3,995	94,989	7
8. Malaria	14,093	926	4,948	5,881	1,669	3,776	1,060	27	317	1,206	33,903	8
9. Measles	1,564	214	544	373	130	207	55	25	142	164	3,418	9
10. Mumps	660	85	198	177	75	101	79	30	33	90	1,528	10
11. Pyrexia of uncertain origin	20,920	877	6,811	3,631	3,004	4,035	3,989	472	1,251	1,115	46,105	11
12. Rheumatic fever or acute rheumatism	1,258	63	167	271	111	132	93	453	42	94	2,684	12
13. Rheumatism	1,407	1,060	435	731	262	380	496	200	47	146	5,164	13
14. Fibrositis	20	1	9	10	5	9	3	1	1	1	60	14
15. Myositis	25	1	5	11	3	4	5	—	—	3	57	15
16. Myalgia	10,453	527	3,223	2,238	829	2,250	2,818	138	312	1,011	23,799	16
17. Pleurodynia	139	9	57	52	27	30	40	1	7	19	381	17
18. Lumbago	668	74	259	270	104	225	208	8	13	125	1,954	18
19. Sciatica	555	55	232	249	75	181	167	14	12	122	1,662	19
20. Sand-fly fever	2,173	144	582	1,252	528	916	51	20	137	236	6,039	20
21. Scarlet fever	542	75	94	111	53	72	31	8	12	41	1,039	21
22. Small-pox	49	5	6	32	6	8	1	—	1	4	112	22
23. Tubercle of lung	1,524	126	440	454	212	355	485	19	45	193	3,853	23
24. Tubercular diseases, other	365	22	58	83	35	52	63	214	15	28	935	24
25. Tetanus, following gunshot wound	23	1	4	2	—	3	1	—	—	1	35	25
26. Tetanus, idiopathic, or following other injury	14	—	4	—	1	2	1	1	1	2	26	26
27. Trench fever	6,981	132	2,208	424	559	907	1,209	100	323	169	13,012	27
28. Venereal diseases {Gonorrhœa	10,137	788	3,216	3,998	675	2,444	2,127	400	429	1,212	25,426	28
29. Syphilis	4,904	381	1,482	1,928	307	1,156	1,253	150	253	639	12,453	29
30. Other	1,476	104	442	665	82	397	269	37	38	149	3,659	30
31. Other diseases caused by infection	5,233	703	1,226	1,319	539	865	412	52	180	709	11,238	31
32. Debility	8,484	530	2,533	2,252	1,001	2,041	2,176	127	305	804	20,253	32

TABLE 22.—continued

	Infantry	Cavalry	Artillery	R.A.S.C.	R.A.M.C.	Engineers	Labour	Tanks	Machine Gun Corps	Others	Total	
33. Functional diseases of the nervous system (including neurasthenia and shell-shock)	11,386	461	2,762	1,717	751	1,600	1,734	171	306	661	21,549	33
	1,131	66	304	305	84	185	411	26	32	108	2,652	34
34. Epilepsy	364	27	135	129	39	96	147	5	10	68	1,020	35
35. Organic diseases of the nervous system	1,287	65	312	366	126	271	617	20	24	120	3,208	36
36. Mental diseases	32	1	5	13	3	14	24	—	—	5	97	37
37. Trachoma	5,071	372	1,457	1,796	576	1,458	1,855	104	171	700	13,560	38
38. Other diseases of the eye	1,081	358	1,444	961	355	874	1,128	62	136	397	10,095	39
39. Diseases of the ear	1,081	118	306	319	151	234	177	26	32	160	2,604	40
40. Diseases of the nose	5,341	354	1,683	1,340	573	1,279	1,972	96	213	557	13,408	41
41. Functional diseases of the heart	2,361	154	646	658	284	471	945	43	49	364	5,975	42
42. Organic diseases of the heart												
43. Diseases of the arteries, veins and capillaries	2,123	114	269	407	167	291	261	721	52	148	4,553	43
44. Anæmia and other diseases of the blood	641	33	100	151	69	96	68	230	36	42	1,466	44
45. Diseases of the spleen	12	1	2	1	1	1	2	—	1	2	23	45
46. Diseases of the lymphatic system	1,027	79	298	222	80	174	173	27	56	82	2,218	46
47. Diseases of the thymus, thyroid, adrenals and pituitary body	366	27	121	92	33	67	85	1	12	42	846	47
48. Diseases of the breast	76	5	18	10	4	10	8	3	7	3	144	48
49. Pneumonia and broncho-pneumonia	3,569	271	1,278	1,250	354	887	1,113	105	130	386	9,343	49
50. Other diseases of the respiratory system	18,404	1,522	5,761	5,337	2,287	4,266	5,130	325	591	2,345	45,968	50
	4,429	299	1,842	1,088	480	1,409	809	96	164	333	10,949	51
51. Caries of dentine	1,269	88	388	290	113	258	248	28	63	103	2,848	52
52. Inflammation of periosteum and alveoli												
53. Other diseases of the teeth and gums	1,040	48	179	172	93	148	86	140	35	46	1,987	53
54. Tonsillitis and sore throat	12,033	1,239	3,089	2,961	1,608	2,078	1,281	307	522	1,298	26,416	54
55. Inflammation and ulceration of the stomach	4,394	412	1,465	1,415	617	1,197	1,138	85	137	620	11,480	55
56. Other diseases of the stomach	1,922	160	687	664	319	471	465	42	78	335	5,143	56

ANALYSIS OF 1,043,653 CASUALTIES

#	Disease											Total	#
57.	Inflammation of the intestines	5,800	523	1,760	1,468	851	1,178	774	121	208	533	13,216	57
58.	Diarrhoea	10,816	863	3,467	2,415	1,114	2,312	1,811	145	591	736	24,270	58
59.	Other diseases of the intestines	10,061	823	3,064	3,055	996	2,285	2,391	209	346	1,183	24,413	59
60.	Jaundice	1,503	160	404	438	143	322	106	18	52	145	3,291	60
61.	Other diseases of the liver	249	18	62	45	28	45	36	1	4	30	518	61
62.	Diseases of the gall bladder and ducts	77	—	30	40	21	28	22	2	—	27	257	62
63.	Peritonitis and other diseases of the peritoneum	96	10	21	23	12	20	12	—	2	12	208	63
64.	Other diseases of the digestive system	1,132	109	322	358	162	255	175	26	43	129	2,711	64
65.	Scurvy	2	1	1	1	—	—	—	—	—	—	5	65
66.	Beri-beri	21	2	13	1	2	3	1	—	—	—	43	66
67.	Other diseases due to disorders of nutrition or metabolism	282	22	94	129	30	76	63	3	6	97	802	67
68.	Diseases of the generative system	3,526	339	1,174	1,063	276	725	608	100	130	436	8,377	68
69.	Diseases of the bones and periosteum	389	30	137	124	48	78	101	3	10	44	964	69
70.	Diseases of the joints	5,999	572	2,045	1,588	559	1,379	1,104	176	268	648	14,338	70
71.	Diseases of the spine	124	9	30	33	14	15	71	2	5	22	325	71
72.	Diseases of the muscles and fascia	284	27	115	89	36	83	48	5	11	27	725	72
73.	Flat foot	429	26	70	81	29	57	75	2	19	35	823	73
74.	Other deformities of the feet	1,458	139	395	290	119	257	246	20	37	148	3,109	74
75.	Other diseases of the organs of locomotion	559	37	152	118	56	101	87	9	32	38	1,189	75
76.	Diseases of the areolar tissue	35,835	2,096	8,836	5,378	2,189	5,242	4,837	656	1,837	1,967	68,873	76
77.	Diseases of the skin	12,100	908	3,220	2,332	729	1,912	1,769	261	528	1,045	24,804	77
78.	Scabies	21,057	1,629	4,920	3,687	810	2,778	2,861	537	1,170	1,873	41,222	78
79.	Bilharzia haematobia	29	10	4	9	2	4	2	7	—	1	68	79
80.	Other parasitic diseases	1,732	205	493	284	90	236	326	28	66	101	3,561	80
81.	Nephritis (acute and chronic)	2,484	129	1,020	426	284	484	651	49	106	199	5,832	81
82.	Trench nephritis	126	6	48	30	7	25	28	2	6	6	284	82
83.	Other diseases of the kidney	604	56	227	209	110	147	151	10	28	76	1,618	83
84.	Other diseases of the ureter	73	9	57	42	13	50	27	5	1	15	292	84
85.	Diseases of the bladder	898	71	243	229	88	185	245	14	38	119	2,130	85
86.	Other diseases of the urinary organs (including cancer, carcinoma, epithelioma, sarcoma and rodent ulcer)	1,227	90	375	440	107	307	345	35	43	186	3,155	86
87.	Malignant new growths	147	16	47	41	18	33	45	7	1	49	404	87
88.	Non-malignant new growths	311	32	118	120	28	78	60	2	19	39	807	88

TABLE 22.—continued

	Infantry	Cavalry	Artillery	R.A.S.C.	R.A.M.C.	Engineers	Labour	Tanks	Machine Gun Corps	Others	Total	
89. Tumour or growth, undefined (including malformations)	439	46	177	124	41	99	93	13	27	68	1,127	89
90. Alcoholism	99	5	25	40	14	23	18	2	2	13	241	90
91. Other poisons and intoxications	297	34	106	91	53	73	74	6	14	46	794	91
92. Heat-stroke and sunstroke	894	94	180	222	106	145	30	5	30	57	1,763	92
93. Burns and scalds	1,398	84	766	542	144	348	288	183	77	147	3,977	93
94. Gas poisoning	12,335	131	6,137	209	828	2,137	516	296	955	82	23,626	94
95. Other general injuries	774	58	271	248	61	135	111	23	32	65	1,778	95
96. Frost bite	386	12	35	25	4	17	15	—	5	7	506	96
97. Trench foot	4,972	53	202	30	21	49	61	5	112	10	5,515	97
98. Other local injuries	1,787	171	680	723	131	491	291	39	67	265	4,645	98
99. Other miscellaneous indefinite diseases	5,068	399	1,609	1,473	700	1,047	834	91	192	481	11,892	99
TOTAL	367,207	27,326	112,093	90,327	37,671	74,090	69,130	9,990	15,925	32,918	836,677	

ANALYSIS OF 1,043,653 CASUALTIES

TABLE 23.—Analysis of Admissions to Hospital for Disease or Injury by Geographical Areas

	France	Italy	Africa	Palestine or Egypt	Macedonia	Mesopotamia	North Russia	United Kingdom	India	Miscellaneous and uncertain	Total	
1. Cerebro-spinal fever	189	—	1	7	6	7	—	373	2	4	589	1
2. Chicken-pox	55	1	1	9	2	2	—	91	1	4	166	2
3. Cholera	4	—	—	3	1	85	—	1	18	—	112	3
4. Diphtheria	836	61	74	300	55	92	32	281	29	37	1,797	4
5. Dysentery	3,692	143	184	2,761	2,326	1,659	9	357	450	247	11,828	5
6. Enteric group of fevers	654	24	16	345	227	737	—	124	158	66	2,351	6
7. Influenza	51,951	1,804	81	2,809	1,803	1,003	84	34,149	450	855	94,989	7
8. Malaria	2,627	119	1,690	6,634	14,386	2,721	72	1,707	3,182	765	33,903	8
9. Measles	1,040	9	8	75	26	29	3	2,185	33	10	3,418	9
10. Mumps	663	23	1	41	27	21	1	723	16	12	1,528	10
11. Pyrexia of uncertain origin	38,692	1,194	36	2,842	1,182	505	17	1,275	138	224	46,105	11
12. Rheumatic fever or acute rheumatism	1,191	72	151	142	106	142	100	568	60	152	2,684	12
13. Rheumatism	1,350	1,076	10	223	263	144	38	1,124	895	41	5,164	13
14. Fibrositis	39	—	—	5	2	—	—	14	—	—	60	14
15. Myositis	28	1	—	5	—	2	—	19	1	1	57	15
16. Myalgia	17,121	229	9	557	624	231	24	4,604	294	106	23,799	16
17. Pleurodynia	192	1	—	18	3	1	—	155	5	6	381	17
18. Lumbago	1,078	18	1	91	68	22	—	635	20	21	1,954	18
19. Sciatica	828	11	1	80	36	28	1	651	16	10	1,662	19
20. Sand-fly fever	113	2	4	1,465	484	2,699	—	88	882	302	6,039	20
21. Scarlet fever	318	7	1	85	12	13	—	554	43	6	1,039	21
22. Small-pox	6	—	—	20	8	34	—	22	18	4	112	22
23. Tubercle of lung	1,447	24	8	209	103	53	3	1,900	77	29	3,853	23
24. Tubercular diseases, other	396	18	47	78	40	40	40	237	13	26	935	24
25. Tetanus, following gunshot wound	29	—	—	1	—	—	—	5	—	—	35	25
26. Tetanus, idiopathic, or following other injury	19	—	—	—	2	—	—	5	—	—	26	26
27. Trench fever	12,702	102	16	20	69	6	—	104	4	5	13,012	27
28. Venereal diseases {Gonorrhoea	11,550	351	10	933	325	288	13	10,915	525	510	25,426	28
29. {Syphilis	5,364	229	9	364	108	144	6	5,880	184	164	12,453	29
30. {Other	1,633	55	—	521	140	113	2	841	179	166	3,659	30

TABLE 23.—continued

		France	Italy	Africa	Palestine or Egypt	Macedonia	Mesopotamia	North Russia	United Kingdom	India	Miscellaneous and uncertain	Total	
31.	Other diseases caused by infection	4,275	40	18	589	187	191	9	5,508	329	92	11,238	31
32.	Debility	12,420	181	30	1,752	924	1,030	25	3,178	498	215	20,253	32
33.	Functional diseases of the nervous system (including neurasthenia and shell-shock)	14,771	80	21	766	435	274	21	4,747	280	154	21,549	33
34.	Epilepsy	1,038	12	1	111	31	38	2	1,367	30	22	2,652	34
35.	Organic diseases of the nervous system	479	10	—	43	29	17	1	419	16	6	1,020	35
36.	Mental diseases	1,511	17	3	186	112	65	6	1,219	46	43	3,208	36
37.	Trachoma	52	—	—	8	2	1	—	29	3	2	97	37
38.	Other diseases of the eye	8,342	144	16	946	313	266	8	3,221	201	103	13,560	38
39.	Diseases of the ear	5,788	106	12	629	283	200	11	2,687	293	86	10,095	39
40.	Diseases of the nose	1,028	13	2	99	54	38	2	1,322	16	30	2,604	40
41.	Functional diseases of the heart	8,335	116	29	746	341	338	17	3,122	260	104	13,408	41
42.	Organic diseases of the heart	2,654	47	17	304	149	152	8	2,477	114	53	5,975	42
43.	Diseases of the arteries, veins and capillaries	1,988	82	246	369	159	263	269	897	83	197	4,553	43
44.	Anaemia and other diseases of the blood	684	26	85	122	86	96	73	241	21	32	1,466	44
45.	Diseases of the spleen	7	—	1	2	2	—	—	11	—	—	23	45
46.	Diseases of the lymphatic system	1,164	22	4	150	67	45	1	681	62	22	2,218	46
47.	Diseases of the thymus, thyroid, ad-renals and pituitary body	383	7	6	41	23	22	—	328	20	16	846	47
48.	Diseases of the breast	83	3	—	5	7	2	—	39	3	2	144	48
49.	Pneumonia and broncho-pneumonia	4,369	113	7	542	258	147	5	3,720	99	83	9,343	49
50.	Other diseases of the respiratory system	24,229	382	23	1,641	848	573	75	17,373	524	300	45,958	50
51.	Caries of dentine	9,590	265	—	255	321	124	13	269	70	42	10,949	51
52.	Inflammation of periosteum and alveoli	1,973	43	—	107	75	33	3	568	32	14	2,848	52
53.	Other diseases of the teeth and gums	1,145	35	123	171	93	104	54	179	25	58	1,987	53

ANALYSIS OF 1,043,653 CASUALTIES

54		10,962	255	18	1,980	487	470	21	11,290	666	267	26,416
54.	Tonsillitis and sore throat											
55.	Inflammation and ulceration of the stomach	5,487	103	15	660	351	341	9	4,288	194	132	11,480
56.	Other diseases of the stomach	2,101	53	6	298	151	140	9	2,132	183	70	5,143
57.	Inflammation of the intestines	6,273	99	19	1,069	800	983	13	3,386	417	157	13,216
58.	Diarrhœa	14,357	915	50	3,230	1,686	1,176	32	1,871	600	353	24,270
59.	Other diseases of the intestines	12,757	204	32	1,258	653	577	27	8,140	518	247	24,413
60.	Jaundice	905	171	1	479	329	666	1	510	166	63	3,291
61.	Other diseases of the liver	100	1	1	43	22	60	1	149	124	17	518
62.	Diseases of the gall bladder and ducts	100	1	—	25	9	8	1	101	6	6	257
63.	Peritonitis and other diseases of the peritoneum	101	2	—	12	1	4	—	81	6	1	208
64.	Other diseases of the digestive system	1,261	15	3	128	74	71	3	1,069	54	33	2,711
65.	Scurvy	—	—	—	—	—	1	1	1	2	—	5
66.	Beri-beri	3	—	1	—	2	21	—	2	13	1	43
67.	Other diseases due to disorders of nutrition or of metabolism	296	2	—	17	7	7	—	449	17	7	802
68.	Diseases of the generative system	3,977	90	10	543	164	125	4	3,146	185	133	8,377
69.	Diseases of the bones and periosteum	469	9	—	48	20	16	—	372	19	11	964
70.	Diseases of the joints	8,202	149	12	673	349	215	15	4,409	208	106	14,338
71.	Diseases of the spine	146	5	—	13	7	4	—	141	7	2	325
72.	Diseases of the muscles and fascia	354	1	2	30	13	9	1	301	7	7	725
73.	Flat foot	468	4	1	49	26	27	—	230	11	7	823
74.	Other deformities of the feet	1,405	17	3	190	67	43	1	1,325	30	28	3,109
75.	Other diseases of the organs of locomotion	649	14	1	72	22	23	2	366	26	14	1,189
76.	Diseases of the areolar tissue	45,715	1,209	39	3,501	1,498	1,304	33	14,183	915	476	68,873
77.	Diseases of the skin	13,553	264	13	939	377	283	19	8,782	345	229	24,804
78.	Scabies	19,737	540	8	1,299	925	189	38	17,942	108	436	41,222
79.	Bilharzia hæmatobia	21	1	2	31	4	4	2	6	—	—	68
80.	Other parasitic diseases	1,652	37	2	592	51	39	7	1,004	122	55	3,561
81.	Nephritis (acute and chronic)	4,460	43	2	150	161	50	4	909	29	24	5,832
82.	Trench nephritis	258	3	—	—	7	—	—	16	—	—	284
83.	Other diseases of the kidney	909	28	1	89	37	41	2	478	18	15	1,618
84.	Other diseases of the ureter	142	4	—	15	5	2	1	119	2	2	292
85.	Diseases of the bladder	991	18	—	102	60	28	1	898	18	14	2,130
86.	Other diseases of the urinary organs	1,446	18	3	195	55	50	1	1,310	49	28	3,155

TABLE 23.—continued

	France	Italy	Africa	Palestine or Egypt	Macedonia	Mesopotamia	North Russia	United Kingdom	India	Miscellaneous and uncertain	Total	
87. Malignant new growths (including cancer, carcinoma, epithelioma, sarcoma and rodent ulcer)	130	2	—	30	6	10	—	212	11	3	404	87
88. Non-malignant new growths	410	9	—	46	18	9	1	295	12	7	807	88
89. Tumour or growth, undefined (including malformations)	500	8	1	53	27	14	1	500	8	15	1,127	89
90. Alcoholism	78	5	—	13	10	7	1	110	8	9	241	90
91. Other poisons and intoxications	373	6	—	58	15	19	—	269	47	7	794	91
92. Heat-stroke or sunstroke	182	—	5	338	213	519	5	86	348	67	1,763	92
93. Burns and scalds	2,831	52	4	155	87	59	3	732	24	30	3,977	93
94. Gas poisoning	23,432	22	3	6	2	2	1	127	2	10	23,626	94
95. Other general injuries	1,075	8	1	88	21	26	2	480	33	15	1,778	95
96. Frost bite	294	4	—	50	50	36	13	31	2	24	506	96
97. Trench foot	5,350	8	—	38	52	13	2	48	2	15	5,515	97
98. Other local injuries	2,532	39	4	202	136	59	3	1,550	70	50	4,645	98
99. Other miscellaneous indefinite diseases	5,029	101	15	988	1,378	289	7	3,778	120	187	11,892	99
TOTAL	463,588	11,857	3,281	50,022	37,702	22,879	1,336	220,713	16,470	8,829	836,677	

ANALYSIS OF 1,043,653 CASUALTIES 295

TABLE 24.—Analysis of Admissions to Hospital for Disease or Injury by Age Groups

	Under 20 years	20–29	30–39	40–49	50–59	60 years and over	Not recorded	Total	
1. Cerebro-spinal fever	134	284	113	31	3	—	24	589	1
2. Chicken-pox	36	84	32	8	2	—	4	166	2
3. Cholera	6	62	23	5	—	—	16	112	3
4. Diphtheria	324	1,126	246	43	4	7	54	1,797	4
5. Dysentery	725	6,560	3,107	973	78	—	378	11,828	5
6. Enteric group of fevers	242	1,423	488	128	14	—	56	2,351	6
7. Influenza	11,383	47,663	22,568	7,548	746	38	5,043	94,989	7
8. Malaria	952	19,258	8,647	2,982	307	5	1,752	33,903	8
9. Measles	923	1,875	488	76	4	—	52	3,418	9
10. Mumps	332	830	249	70	—	1	45	1,528	10
11. Pyrexia of uncertain origin	3,655	25,440	10,779	2,915	171	3	3,142	46,105	11
12. Rheumatic fever or acute rheumatism	226	1,005	742	517	154	9	31	2,684	12
13. Rheumatism	251	1,706	1,459	1,269	300	30	149	5,164	13
14. Fibrositis	1	18	20	15	3	1	2	60	14
15. Myositis	1	20	15	12	3	—	6	57	15
16. Myalgia	997	7,804	7,330	5,689	1,256	84	639	23,799	16
17. Pleurodynia	40	185	100	38	5	—	13	381	17
18. Lumbago	50	494	673	550	122	2	63	1,954	18
19. Sciatica	30	406	652	467	83	4	20	1,662	19
20. Sand-fly fever	477	3,495	1,391	387	35	1	253	6,039	20
21. Scarlet fever	288	567	128	24	—	—	32	1,039	21
22. Small-pox	4	56	34	11	2	—	5	112	22
23. Tubercle of lung	262	1,817	1,176	504	60	5	29	3,853	23
24. Tubercular diseases, other	99	510	230	80	6	1	9	935	24
25. Tetanus, following gunshot wound	3	18	6	4	—	—	4	35	25
26. Tetanus, idiopathic, or following other injury	1	14	5	2	—	—	4	26	26
27. Trench fever	1,045	6,899	3,829	1,010	48	1	181	13,012	27
28. Venereal diseases — Gonorrhoea	1,752	15,893	5,122	1,106	69	—	1,483	25,426	28
29. Venereal diseases — Syphilis	609	7,156	3,176	943	72	4	493	12,453	29
30. Venereal diseases — Other	242	2,141	738	208	20	—	310	3,659	30
31. Other diseases caused by infection	2,031	5,620	2,303	883	112	11	278	11,238	31
32. Debility	1,366	8,743	5,259	3,122	891	89	783	20,253	32

TABLE 24.—continued

	Under 20 years	20-29	30-39	40-49	50-59	60 years and over	Not recorded	Total	
33. Functional diseases of the nervous system (including neurasthenia and shell-shock)	1,582	11,488	5,621	2,066	270	14	508	21,549	33
34. Epilepsy	359	1,414	608	202	24	3	42	2,652	34
35. Organic diseases of the nervous system	75	350	304	196	59	5	31	1,020	35
36. Mental diseases	223	1,291	1,038	547	72	3	34	3,208	36
37. Trachoma	12	49	26	6	2	1	1	97	37
38. Other diseases of the eye	1,088	6,442	3,377	1,589	297	14	753	13,560	38
39. Diseases of the ear	1,187	5,741	2,213	609	71		274	10,095	39
40. Diseases of the nose	410	1,396	569	152	25	1	51	2,604	40
41. Functional diseases of the heart	1,327	6,862	3,457	1,326	188	14	234	13,408	41
42. Organic diseases of the heart	549	2,848	1,526	797	165	13	77	5,975	42
43. Diseases of the arteries, veins and capillaries	171	1,605	1,477	893	310	29	68	4,553	43
44. Anaemia and other diseases of the blood	179	734	332	152	34	1	34	1,466	44
45. Diseases of the spleen	5	7	9		2			23	45
46. Diseases of the lymphatic system	260	1,289	466	137	17		49	2,218	46
47. Diseases of the thymus, thyroid, adrenals and pituitary body	126	477	171	51	2	1	18	846	47
48. Diseases of the breast	13	76	33	13	3		6	144	48
49. Pneumonia and broncho-pneumonia	930	4,399	2,549	871	121	12	461	9,343	49
50. Other diseases of the respiratory system	4,109	19,559	13,046	6,667	1,311	144	1,132	45,968	50
51. Caries of dentine	383	5,098	2,786	992	94	3	1,593	10,949	51
52. Inflammation of periosteum and alveoli	241	1,511	628	208	21	2	237	2,848	52
53. Other diseases of the teeth and gums	85	878	482	172	20		350	1,987	53
54. Tonsillitis and sore throat	4,969	15,354	4,131	866	72	4	1,020	26,416	54
55. Inflammation and ulceration of the stomach	736	4,992	3,510	1,636	275	12	319	11,480	55
56. Other diseases of the stomach	414	2,160	1,490	814	115	8	142	5,143	56
57. Inflammation of the intestines	1,333	7,096	3,140	1,068	143	5	431	13,216	57
58. Diarrhoea	1,934	12,439	5,952	2,023	185	11	1,726	24,270	58
59. Other diseases of the intestines	1,700	10,509	7,828	3,404	422	36	514	24,413	59
60. Jaundice	239	2,044	704	180	17	1	106	3,291	60
61. Other diseases of the liver	13	165	172	118	31	3	16	518	61
62. Diseases of the gall bladder and ducts	6	73	83	72	16	4	3	257	62
63. Peritonitis and other diseases of the peritoneum	26	102	46	21	7		6	208	63
64. Other diseases of the digestive system	406	1,393	563	202	20	2	125	2,711	64

ANALYSIS OF 1,043,653 CASUALTIES

No.										No.
65.	Scurvy	—	—	—	—	—	—	—	5	802	65
66.	Beri-beri	—	1	—	—	—	1	1	43	8,377	66
67.	Other diseases due to disorders of nutrition or of metabolism	24	138	254	282	82	11	11	—	802	67
68.	Diseases of the generative system	971	4,534	1,782	619	117	11	343	8,377	8,377	68
69.	Diseases of the bones and periosteum	99	452	285	94	13	11	20	964	964	69
70.	Diseases of the joints	1,082	7,247	3,872	1,516	286	25	310	14,338	14,338	70
71.	Diseases of the spine	34	173	81	29	2	2	4	325	325	71
72.	Diseases of the muscles and fascia	48	325	195	108	26	1	22	725	725	72
73.	Flat foot	102	410	195	74	13	1	28	823	823	73
74.	Other deformities of the feet	475	1,649	683	200	24	3	75	3,109	3,109	74
75.	Other diseases of the organs of locomotion	94	553	356	137	23	2	24	1,189	1,189	75
76.	Diseases of the areolar tissue	7,071	36,671	16,438	5,419	452	27	2,795	68,873	68,873	76
77.	Diseases of the skin	3,843	12,600	5,220	1,772	178	12	1,199	24,804	24,804	77
78.	Scabies	7,375	21,482	7,129	2,259	210	7	2,760	41,222	41,222	78
79.	Bilharzia haematobia	10	37	17	3	—	—	1	68	68	79
80.	Other parasitic diseases	481	1,626	713	249	19	—	473	3,561	3,561	80
81.	Nephritis (acute and chronic)	281	2,237	2,248	893	90	9	74	5,832	5,832	81
82.	Trench nephritis	9	—	17	41	3	—	1	284	284	82
83.	Other diseases of the kidney	81	704	526	243	29	4	31	1,618	1,618	83
84.	Other diseases of the ureter	11	91	91	84	4	1	10	292	292	84
85.	Diseases of the bladder	262	864	582	303	68	1	50	2,130	2,130	85
86.	Other diseases of the urinary organs	224	1,276	923	523	102	5	102	3,155	3,155	86
87.	Malignant new growths (including cancer, carcinoma, epithelioma, sarcoma, and rodent ulcer)	9	81	110	134	57	10	3	404	404	87
88.	Non-malignant new growths	74	370	208	89	15	1	50	807	807	88
89.	Tumour or growth, undefined (including malformations)	93	526	314	116	25	2	51	1,127	1,127	89
90.	Alcoholism	9	51	103	51	11	—	16	241	241	90
91.	Other poisons and intoxications	86	369	194	72	9	1	63	794	794	91
92.	Heat-stroke and sunstroke	125	963	432	142	26	—	74	1,763	1,763	92
93.	Burns and scalds	318	2,179	983	298	22	4	173	3,977	3,977	93
94.	Gas poisoning	2,094	13,921	5,806	1,086	24	1	694	23,626	23,626	94
95.	Other general injuries	133	945	403	135	19	—	142	1,778	1,778	95
96.	Frost bite	73	283	92	29	2	1	27	506	506	96
97.	Trench foot	877	3,338	1,010	190	8	—	92	5,515	5,515	97
98.	Other local injuries	475	2,317	1,064	434	72	7	276	4,645	4,645	98
99.	Other miscellaneous indefinite diseases	1,199	5,926	2,680	911	108	13	1,055	11,892	11,892	99
	TOTAL	81,720	423,486	204,591	78,208	11,121	807	36,744	836,677		

TABLE 25.—Analysis of Admissions to Hospital for Disease or Injury according to Year of Admission

	1916	1917	1918	1919	1920	Total	
1. Cerebro-spinal fever	199	245	115	21	9	589	1
2. Chicken-pox	38	43	60	20	5	166	2
3. Cholera	93	7	2	10	—	112	3
4. Diphtheria	497	616	479	160	45	1,797	4
5. Dysentery	4,126	2,502	4,216	805	179	11,828	5
6. Enteric group of fevers	1,550	355	319	97	30	2,351	6
7. Influenza	18,894	9,287	54,563	11,251	994	94,989	7
8. Malaria	8,617	7,633	12,574	4,227	852	33,903	8
9. Measles	1,202	1,352	685	150	29	3,418	9
10. Mumps	331	506	503	138	50	1,528	10
11. Pyrexia of uncertain origin	9,737	14,747	19,760	1,583	278	46,105	11
12. Rheumatic fever or acute rheumatism	1,205	702	545	182	50	2,684	12
13. Rheumatism	2,566	1,259	876	380	83	5,164	13
14. Fibrositis	23	16	15	4	2	60	14
15. Myositis	17	18	16	3	3	57	15
16. Myalgia	7,390	8,202	6,317	1,478	412	23,799	16
17. Pleurodynia	92	102	120	58	9	381	17
18. Lumbago	703	513	495	192	51	1,954	18
19. Sciatica	483	485	480	169	45	1,662	19
20. Sand-fly fever	1,150	1,260	1,960	776	893	6,039	20
21. Scarlet fever	485	199	230	95	30	1,039	21
22. Small-pox	38	13	34	24	3	112	22
23. Tubercle of lung	1,061	1,094	1,195	412	91	3,853	23
24. Tubercular diseases, other	270	286	252	104	23	935	24
25. Tetanus, following gunshot wound	13	12	7	3	—	35	25
26. Tetanus, idiopathic, or following other injury	11	5	8	1	1	26	26
27. Trench fever	2,155	6,366	4,372	114	5	13,012	27
28. Venereal diseases {Gonorrhoea	6,273	5,442	6,757	5,347	1,607	25,426	28
29. Syphilis	2,807	2,886	3,519	2,502	739	12,453	29
30. Other	881	567	781	1,048	382	3,659	30
31. Other diseases caused by infection	4,651	3,735	2,069	580	203	11,238	31
32. Debility	5,200	5,304	6,941	2,564	244	20,253	32
33. Functional diseases of the nervous system (including neurasthenia and shell-shock)	8,710	5,958	5,120	1,404	357	21,549	33
34. Epilepsy	761	803	723	281	84	2,652	34
35. Organic diseases of the nervous system	255	302	303	120	40	1,020	35

ANALYSIS OF 1,043,653 CASUALTIES

No.	Disease								Total	No.
36.	Mental diseases	...	697	975	1,049	393	94	3,208	36
37.	Trachoma	...	20	41	25	10	1	97	37
38.	Other diseases of the eye	...	4,257	3,768	3,611	1,482	442	13,560	38
39.	Diseases of the ear	...	3,190	2,742	2,630	1,183	350	10,095	39
40.	Diseases of the nose	...	762	636	711	346	149	2,604	40
41.	Functional diseases of the heart	...	3,107	3,959	4,461	1,587	294	13,408	41
42.	Organic diseases of the heart	...	1,759	1,822	1,650	617	127	5,975	42
43.	Diseases of the arteries, veins and capillaries	...	1,753	1,214	1,058	422	106	4,553	43
44.	Anaemia and other diseases of the blood	...	375	419	439	159	74	1,466	44
45.	Diseases of the spleen	...	10	3	7	1	2	23	45
46.	Diseases of the lymphatic system	...	651	615	646	229	77	2,218	46
47.	Diseases of the thymus, thyroid, adrenals and pituitary body	...	235	263	236	98	14	846	47
48.	Diseases of the breast	...	46	49	36	11	2	144	48
49.	Pneumonia and broncho-pneumonia	...	1,478	1,621	4,476	1,582	186	9,343	49
50.	Other diseases of the respiratory system	...	13,207	13,619	13,432	4,722	986	45,968	50
51.	Caries of dentine	...	4,421	3,017	2,357	985	169	10,949	51
52.	Inflammation of periosteum and alveoli	...	752	771	871	385	69	2,848	52
53.	Other diseases of the teeth and gums	...	505	567	595	288	32	1,987	53
54.	Tonsillitis and sore throat	...	7,997	6,994	6,994	3,334	1,184	26,416	54
55.	Inflammation and ulceration of the stomach	...	3,412	3,275	3,358	1,118	317	11,480	55
56.	Other diseases of the stomach	...	1,706	1,396	1,366	521	154	5,143	56
57.	Inflammation of the intestines	...	4,721	3,574	3,624	1,022	275	13,216	57
58.	Diarrhœa	...	5,348	7,764	9,451	1,260	447	24,270	58
59.	Other diseases of the intestines	...	7,505	6,974	6,859	2,479	598	24,413	59
60.	Jaundice	...	1,400	513	896	351	131	3,291	60
61.	Other diseases of the liver	...	180	116	141	63	18	518	61
62.	Diseases of the gall bladder and ducts	...	80	54	82	35	6	257	62
63.	Peritonitis and other diseases of the peritoneum	...	65	55	59	26	3	208	63
64.	Other diseases of the digestive system	...	794	706	728	338	145	2,711	64
65.	Scurvy	...	1	1	—	—	—	5	65
66.	Beri-beri	...	31	5	4	2	—	43	66
67.	Other diseases due to disorders of nutrition or of metabolism	...	296	278	167	3	17	802	67
68.	Diseases of the generative system	...	2,628	2,046	2,234	1,154	315	8,377	68
69.	Diseases of the bones and periosteum	...	284	297	263	84	36	964	69
70.	Diseases of the joints	...	4,171	4,350	4,241	1,287	289	14,338	70
71.	Diseases of the spine	...	99	99	89	27	11	325	71
72.	Diseases of the muscles and fascia	...	252	216	185	55	17	725	72
73.	Flat foot	...	337	199	176	77	34	823	73
74.	Other deformities of the feet	...	1,130	816	780	271	112	3,109	74
75.	Other diseases of the organs of locomotion	...	359	361	350	90	29	1,189	75
76.	Diseases of the areolar tissue	...	16,674	23,814	22,140	4,885	1,360	68,873	76

TABLE 25.—continued

		1916	1917	1918	1919	1920	Total	
77.	Diseases of the skin	7,493	7,233	7,060	2,310	708	24,804	77
78.	Scabies	14,824	11,027	9,095	5,063	1,213	41,222	78
79.	Bilharzia haematobia	14	28	16	8	2	68	79
80.	Other parasitic diseases	1,111	1,179	827	364	80	3,561	80
81.	Nephritis (acute and chronic)	1,669	2,403	1,439	272	49	5,832	81
82.	Trench nephritis	79	145	55	5	—	284	82
83.	Other diseases of the kidney	403	557	468	150	40	1,618	83
84.	Other diseases of the ureter	65	65	91	60	11	292	84
85.	Diseases of the bladder	620	625	634	184	67	2,130	85
86.	Other diseases of the urinary organs	841	856	918	429	111	3,155	86
87.	Malignant new growths (including cancer, carcinoma, epithelioma, sarcoma and rodent ulcer)	96	124	127	48	9	404	87
88.	Non-malignant new growths	238	185	245	110	29	807	88
89.	Tumour or growth, undefined (including malformations)	311	324	298	156	38	1,127	89
90.	Alcoholism	89	66	50	24	12	241	90
91.	Other poisons and intoxications	275	263	190	57	9	794	91
92.	Heat-stroke and sunstroke	899	446	179	191	48	1,763	92
93.	Burns and scalds	860	1,350	1,327	347	93	3,977	93
94.	Gas poisoning	1,609	7,712	14,186	107	12	23,626	94
95.	Other general injuries	527	542	530	134	45	1,778	95
96.	Frost bite	222	173	81	25	5	506	96
97.	Trench foot	2,102	2,651	737	20	5	5,515	97
98.	Other local injuries	1,506	1,310	1,144	465	220	4,645	98
99.	Other miscellaneous indefinite diseases	3,171	3,483	3,561	1,295	382	11,892	99
	TOTAL	228,203	225,486	282,147	81,151	19,690	836,677	

ANALYSIS OF 1,043,653 CASUALTIES 301

TABLE 26.—Analysis of Admissions to Hospital for Disease or Injury according to Period in Hospital

	1 Week and under	1-2 weeks	2-4 weeks	1 month	2 months	3 months	3-6 months	6-9 months	9-12 months	12 months	Over 12 months	Incomplete	Total	
1. Cerebro-spinal fever	140	64	32	34	90	69	100	22	14	—	2	22	589	1
2. Chicken-pox	2	23	42	62	24	6	2	—	1	—	—	4	166	2
3. Cholera	34	4	7	6	21	9	10	2	—	—	—	18	112	3
4. Diphtheria	45	91	141	308	589	235	198	32	3	1	3	151	1,797	4
5. Enteric group of fevers	461	830	913	1,215	2,098	1,473	2,171	611	167	7	96	1,786	11,828	5
6. Dysentery	95	81	78	120	413	353	463	96	24	1	8	620	2,351	6
7. Influenza	24,904	28,439	12,753	9,730	11,425	3,620	1,756	159	23	6	9	2,165	94,989	7
8. Malaria	4,977	6,843	4,197	3,895	4,924	2,088	2,333	598	282	18	111	3,637	33,903	8
9. Measles	107	848	1,325	664	297	60	26	2	—	2	—	87	3,418	9
10. Mumps	62	158	516	502	197	39	19	3	1	—	—	31	1,528	10
11. Pyrexia of uncertain origin	14,981	11,295	4,829	3,988	5,760	2,393	1,353	108	22	6	5	1,365	46,105	11
12. Rheumatic fever or acute rheumatism	194	267	215	241	602	391	508	73	34	1	3	155	2,684	12
13. Rheumatism	787	838	569	615	952	528	474	65	20	—	6	309	5,164	13
14. Fibrositis	9	13	3	6	6	7	11	—	—	—	—	5	60	14
15. Myositis	10	13	2	9	8	3	7	—	—	—	—	5	57	15
16. Myalgia	4,869	4,698	2,632	2,662	4,132	1,974	1,596	224	70	5	8	929	23,799	16
17. Pleurodynia	97	112	40	43	47	17	6	1	3	1	—	18	381	17
18. Lumbago	476	475	249	240	253	88	82	13	3	—	1	73	1,954	18
19. Sciatica	135	202	143	218	328	219	240	52	11	1	7	107	1,662	19
20. Sand-fly fever	2,005	2,121	631	399	313	51	62	2	—	—	—	482	6,039	20
21. Scarlet fever	23	45	46	75	570	156	8	7	3	—	1	51	1,039	21
22. Small-pox	12	13	6	13	25	14	8	2	—	—	—	19	112	22
23. Tubercle of lung	144	207	298	526	1,075	565	577	118	36	—	18	289	3,853	23
24. Tubercular diseases, other	66	61	59	87	210	137	166	41	28	2	18	60	935	24
25. Tetanus, following gunshot wound	11	6	3	2	6	3	4	1	—	—	—	2	35	25
26. Tetanus, idiopathic or following other injury	8	5	1	—	3	5	4	—	—	—	—	—	26	26
27. Trench fever	421	805	810	1,353	3,895	2,742	2,162	292	80	8	12	432	13,012	27
28. Venereal diseases {Gonorrhoea	864	1,152	1,553	3,246	8,404	4,321	3,284	448	130	3	38	1,983	25,426	28
29. Syphilis	362	454	661	1,174	4,748	2,775	1,349	101	27	2	18	782	12,453	29
30. Other	237	460	402	581	948	403	186	17	4	—	—	419	3,659	30
31. Other diseases caused by infection	1,371	4,507	1,951	1,145	1,034	419	343	67	21	3	10	367	11,238	31
32. Debility	4,699	3,996	2,397	2,299	3,232	1,221	877	95	37	2	5	1,393	20,253	32
33. Functional diseases of the nervous system (including neurasthenia and shell-shock)	3,827	2,962	1,758	2,102	3,471	1,926	2,516	797	293	20	161	1,716	21,549	33
34. Epilepsy	374	330	272	321	612	287	256	30	8	3	6	153	2,652	34
35. Organic diseases of the nervous system	188	84	73	82	184	105	148	44	10	2	17	83	1,020	35

(130)—L

TABLE 26.—continued

		1 Week and under	1–2 weeks	2–4 weeks	1 month	2 months	3 months	3–6 months	6–9 months	9–12 months	12 months	Over 12 months	Incomplete	Total	
36.	Mental diseases	134	125	125	162	387	311	704	395	251	17	159	438	3,208	36
37.	Trachoma	13	12	5	14	27	10	4	2				10	97	37
38.	Other diseases of the eye	4,492	2,351	1,434	1,343	1,858	730	606	123	30	3	13	597	13,560	38
39.	Diseases of the ear	2,157	1,676	1,151	1,203	1,730	788	697	117	27		8	539	10,095	39
40.	Diseases of the nose	524	488	336	345	454	183	118	22	8	3	5	124	2,604	40
41.	Functional diseases of the heart	1,680	1,623	1,232	1,570	2,863	1,629	1,565	278	73	3	17	875	13,408	41
42.	Organic diseases of the heart	718	1,522	502	699	1,339	852	768	126	40	2	12	395	5,975	42
43.	Diseases of the arteries, veins and capillaries	944	461	361	583	1,102	485	335	51	14		3	214	4,553	43
44.	Anæmia and other diseases of the blood	173	226	153	187	327	146	125	17	8			104	1,466	44
45.	Diseases of the spleen		3	4	2	7	3	1	1					23	45
46.	Diseases of the lymphatic system	331	374	252	266	434	215	183	33	8	1	3	118	2,218	46
47.	Diseases of the thymus, thyroid, adrenals and pituitary body	139	99	77	99	169	81	107	16	7		2	50	846	47
48.	Diseases of the breast	28	26	14	18	33	5	5	1	2			7	144	48
49.	Pneumonia and broncho-pneumonia	1,573	966	544	809	2,294	1,322	1,161	147	36		11	480	9,343	49
50.	Other diseases of the respiratory system	7,852	9,211	5,405	5,353	8,504	3,976	3,283	465	125	9	40	1,745	45,968	50
51.	Caries of dentine	5,661	2,602	960	629	539	177	60	8				313	10,949	51
52.	Inflammation of periosteum and alveoli	1,079	704	310	241	282	86	61	11	3		1	70	2,848	52
53.	Other diseases of the teeth and gums	881	455	185	162	152	44	39	4			1	64	1,987	53
54.	Tonsillitis and sore throat	7,271	8,688	3,696	2,563	2,430	706	399	44	8		1	610	26,416	54
55.	Inflammation and ulceration of the stomach	2,208	2,197	1,283	1,218	1,924	997	880	185	41	3	10	534	11,480	55
56.	Other diseases of the stomach	1,424	1,153	611	543	693	267	213	20	9	2	2	206	5,143	56
57.	Inflammation of the intestines	2,095	1,700	1,645	1,386	2,659	1,466	1,179	215	51	3	14	803	13,216	57
58.	Diarrhœa	9,474	5,936	2,651	2,012	2,146	671	408	47	8	2	2	914	24,270	58
59.	Other diseases of the intestines	5,006	3,101	1,944	2,661	5,722	2,808	1,869	222	55	1	17	1,007	24,413	59
60.	Jaundice	211	488	505	506	700	259	196	24	4		3	395	3,291	60
61.	Other diseases of the liver	72	89	57	67	77	36	54	11	4	1	6	45	518	61
62.	Diseases of the gall bladder and ducts	28	27	33	33	41	40	35	4	2			13	257	62
63.	Peritonitis and other diseases of the peritoneum	42	33	12	14	43	15	28	10			1	10	208	63
64.	Other diseases of the digestive system	790	772	357	262	299	97	59	8	5			61	2,711	64
65.	Scurvy		1		1	1							1	5	65
66.	Beri-beri	4	4	5	1	11	4	5	1	1			7	43	66
67.	Other diseases due to disorders of nutrition or of metabolism	111	127	106	104	176	72	57	9	3	1		36	802	67

ANALYSIS OF 1,043,653 CASUALTIES

No.	Disease															
68	Diseases of the generative system	1,600	1,402	1,095	1,189	1,732	576	343	61	11	—	—	3	365	8,377
69	Diseases of the bones and periosteum	129	126	87	103	174	105	133	35	7	—	—	5	60	964
70	Diseases of the joints	1,887	2,196	1,572	1,748	2,867	1,501	1,508	269	77	8	—	36	669	14,338
71	Diseases of the spine	76	30	19	14	58	43	42	13	8	1	—	5	16	325
72	Diseases of the muscles and fascia	162	138	74	89	114	54	60	8	3	—	—	1	22	725
73	Flat foot	312	106	84	79	95	47	47	9	3	—	—	1	40	823
74	Other deformities of the feet	733	391	340	479	622	227	170	25	11	—	—	4	107	3,109
75	Other diseases of the organs of locomotion	200	177	143	175	233	104	73	16	2	—	—	3	63	1,189
76	Diseases of the areolar tissue	13,365	14,301	8,916	8,865	12,412	5,056	3,233	394	127	10	—	42	2,152	68,873
77	Diseases of the skin	4,504	5,252	3,600	3,292	4,326	1,653	1,288	169	51	8	—	17	644	24,804
78	Scabies	16,745	11,760	4,876	3,382	2,791	697	383	33	7	5	—	3	540	41,222
79	Bilharzia haematobia	10	5	9	11	9	6	11	2	—	—	—	1	4	68
80	Other parasitic diseases	2,122	621	253	215	197	52	51	7	1	4	—	17	42	3,561
81	Nephritis (acute and chronic)	231	181	174	294	812	980	2,128	505	119	—	—	2	387	5,832
82	Trench nephritis	4	5	7	11	33	52	119	34	6	—	—	2	11	284
83	Other diseases of the kidney	179	198	123	156	284	217	275	64	12	1	—	7	103	1,618
84	Other diseases of the ureter	54	47	33	35	73	18	23	2	—	—	—	—	7	292
85	Other diseases of the bladder	384	384	260	250	390	170	156	23	9	—	—	7	96	2,130
86	Other diseases of the urinary organs	644	599	339	382	581	214	197	34	7	1	—	3	154	3,155
87	Malignant new growths (including cancer, carcinoma, epithelioma, sarcoma and rodent ulcer)	28	30	31	49	74	65	63	26	8	1	—	3	26	404
88	Non-malignant new growths	116	131	113	121	174	69	48	9	2	1	—	—	23	807
89	Tumour or growth undefined (including malformations)	208	218	158	168	191	81	52	10	3	—	—	3	35	1,127
90	Alcoholism	116	46	28	14	16	4	7	1	—	—	—	—	9	241
91	Other poisons and intoxications	208	131	59	55	45	23	10	—	1	1	—	2	43	794
92	Heat-stroke and sunstroke	424	398	153	125	145	64	54	6	4	—	—	1	249	1,763
93	Burns and scalds	563	544	472	564	937	418	263	54	17	2	—	5	161	3,977
94	Gas poisoning	540	2,202	1,878	2,874	6,706	3,629	2,838	396	102	4	—	30	726	23,626
95	Other general injuries	2,241	367	211	161	223	71	43	3	1	—	—	1	56	1,778
96	Frost bite	641	48	47	53	105	50	47	15	4	—	—	2	71	506
97	Trench foot	64	357	313	458	1,474	1,080	959	164	49	3	—	26	321	5,515
98	Other local injuries	311	1,089	552	463	544	178	125	25	7	1	—	5	138	4,645
99	Other miscellaneous indefinite diseases	1,519 / 5,820	1,892	1,757	681	604	161	110	16	2	1	—	—	848	11,892
	TOTAL	180,042	164,114	93,339	89,574	139,356	64,853	53,393	9,170	2,838	196	—	1,127	38,675	836,677

304 MEDICAL HISTORY OF THE WAR

TABLE 27.—Analysis of Admissions to Hospital for Disease or Injury according to Final Disposal

	Deaths	Returned to duty	Discharged as invalids	Discharged from hospital (indefinite)	Records incomplete	Disease changed	Total	
1. Cerebro-spinal fever	245	272	45	8	16	3	589	1
2. Chicken-pox	—	161	1	—	2	2	166	2
3. Cholera	45	46	—	—	17	4	112	3
4. Diphtheria	23	1,631	23	7	99	14	1,797	4
5. Dysentery	172	10,352	334	33	877	60	11,828	5
6. Enteric group of fevers	90	1,754	44	23	423	17	2,351	6
7. Influenza	1,073	91,625	520	241	1,213	317	94,989	7
8. Malaria	167	31,312	691	61	1,548	124	33,903	8
9. Measles	12	3,268	8	31	64	35	3,418	9
10. Mumps	—	1,488	2	9	18	11	1,528	10
11. Pyrexia of uncertain origin	47	44,903	130	29	924	72	46,105	11
12. Rheumatic fever or acute rheumatism	10	2,209	356	15	77	17	2,684	12
13. Rheumatism	6	4,591	342	51	155	19	5,164	13
14. Fibrositis	—	50	8	—	3	—	60	14
15. Myositis	1	50	2	1	3	—	57	15
16. Myalgia	16	22,028	1,109	63	501	82	23,799	16
17. Pleurodynia	1	359	5	1	13	2	381	17
18. Lumbago	—	1,843	56	10	41	4	1,954	18
19. Sciatica	2	1,397	185	17	56	5	1,662	19
20. Sand-fly fever	3	5,647	10	6	338	35	6,039	20
21. Scarlet fever	11	970	6	8	30	14	1,039	21
22. Small-pox	9	84	—	1	17	—	112	22
23. Tubercle of lung	262	796	2,618	25	144	8	3,853	23
24. Tubercular diseases, other	84	408	399	12	29	3	935	24
25. Tetanus, following gunshot wound	16	14	3	—	2	—	35	25
26. Tetanus, idiopathic, or following other injury	11	14	1	—	—	—	26	26
27. Trench fever	4	12,506	191	21	249	41	13,012	27
28. Venereal diseases {Gonorrhœa	5	23,809	67	33	1,360	152	25,426	28
29. Syphilis	18	11,793	73	16	479	74	12,453	29
30. Other	—	3,328	7	3	302	19	3,659	30
31. Other diseases caused by infection	114	10,533	188	105	217	81	11,238	31

ANALYSIS OF 1,043,653 CASUALTIES

		17	18,605	796	92	684	59	20,253	
32.	Debility								32
33.	Functional diseases of the nervous system (including neurasthenia and shell-shock)	35	17,384	3,323	98	652	57	21,549	33
34.	Epilepsy	26	1,542	981	15	79	9	2,652	34
35.	Organic diseases of the nervous system	175	503	283	8	46	5	1,020	35
36.	Mental diseases	76	603	2,249	23	245	12	3,208	36
37.	Trachoma	1	56	32	—	7	1	97	37
38.	Other diseases of the eye	6	12,118	1,021	35	343	37	13,560	38
39.	Diseases of the ear	32	8,754	975	47	268	19	10,095	39
40.	Diseases of the nose	6	2,436	87	16	49	10	2,604	40
41.	Functional diseases of the heart	63	11,403	1,428	45	421	48	13,408	41
42.	Organic diseases of the heart	213	3,321	2,171	42	200	28	5,975	42
43.	Diseases of the arteries, veins and capillaries	22	3,841	536	34	100	20	4,553	43
44.	Anaemia and other diseases of the blood	29	1,275	101	12	43	6	1,466	44
45.	Diseases of the spleen	1	19	3	—	—	—	23	45
46.	Diseases of the lymphatic system	16	2,036	79	4	76	7	2,218	46
47.	Diseases of the thymus, thyroid, adrenals and pituitary body	10	665	145	3	22	1	846	47
48.	Diseases of the breast	1	136	2	—	5	—	144	48
49.	Pneumonia and broncho-pneumonia	2,522	6,043	402	36	280	60	9,343	49
50.	Other diseases of the respiratory system	357	41,319	2,995	229	882	186	45,968	50
51.	Caries of dentine	—	10,621	45	8	235	40	10,949	51
52.	Inflammation of periosteum and alveoli	3	2,769	18	8	39	11	2,848	52
53.	Other diseases of the teeth and gums	—	1,929	12	4	35	7	1,987	53
54.	Tonsillitis and sore throat	21	25,758	116	104	316	101	26,416	54
55.	Inflammation and ulceration of the stomach	73	10,199	845	47	272	44	11,480	55
56.	Other diseases of the stomach	22	4,752	230	30	93	16	5,143	56
57.	Inflammation of the intestines	225	12,048	383	50	464	46	13,216	57
58.	Diarrhoea	17	23,478	83	34	572	86	24,270	58
59.	Other diseases of the intestines	87	22,962	645	121	497	101	24,413	59
60.	Jaundice	21	2,952	43	10	249	16	3,291	60
61.	Other diseases of the liver	45	393	43	8	26	3	518	61
62.	Diseases of the gall bladder and ducts	8	214	20	4	8	3	257	62
63.	Peritonitis and other diseases of the peritoneum	40	135	28	—	5	—	208	63
64.	Other diseases of the digestive system	18	2,600	36	11	35	11	2,711	64
65.	Scurvy	1	3	—	—	—	1	5	65
66.	Beri-beri	3	33	3	1	3	—	43	66
67.	Other diseases due to disorders of nutrition or metabolism								67
68.	Diseases of the generative system	32	7,961	147	9	14	29	8,377	68
69.	Diseases of the bones and periosteum	13	801	127	27	220	3	964	69

TABLE 27.—continued

	Deaths	Returned to duty	Discharged as invalids	Discharged from hospital (indefinite)	Records incomplete	Disease changed	Total	
70. Diseases of the joints	14	12,945	914	64	355	46	14,338	70
71. Diseases of the spine	10	170	130	4	9	2	325	71
72. Diseases of the muscles and fascia	2	643	64	4	9	3	725	72
73. Flat foot	—	706	97	5	14	1	823	73
74. Other deformities of the feet	2	2,843	191	15	52	6	3,109	74
75. Other diseases of the organs of locomotion	3	1,096	54	6	27	3	1,189	75
76. Diseases of the areolar tissue	78	66,714	496	150	1,198	237	68,873	76
77. Diseases of the skin	8	23,844	365	100	374	113	24,804	77
78. Scabies	3	40,489	38	116	318	258	41,222	78
79. Bilharzia haematobia	—	57	9	—	2	—	68	79
80. Other parasitic diseases	—	3,502	16	7	25	11	3,561	80
81. Nephritis (acute and chronic)	235	4,048	1,293	43	195	18	5,832	81
82. Trench nephritis	6	196	72	1	8	1	284	82
83. Other diseases of the kidney	26	1,321	190	10	62	9	1,618	83
84. Other diseases of the ureter	2	275	8	2	5	—	292	84
85. Diseases of the bladder	10	1,884	171	10	51	4	2,130	85
86. Other diseases of the urinary organs	19	2,858	163	6	97	12	3,155	86
87. Malignant new growths (including cancer, carcinoma, epithelioma, sarcoma and rodent ulcer)	138	138	115	1	12	—	404	87
88. Non-malignant new growths	6	769	17	3	8	4	807	88
89. Tumour, or growth, undefined (incl. malformations)	10	1,029	56	5	22	5	1,127	89
90. Alcoholism	11	214	8	2	5	1	241	90
91. Other poisons and intoxications	32	728	10	6	15	3	794	91
92. Heat-stroke and sunstroke	49	1,555	15	1	133	10	1,763	92
93. Burns and scalds	70	3,715	67	6	103	16	3,977	93
94. Gas poisoning	735	21,949	340	8	508	86	23,626	94
95. Other general injuries	50	1,644	23	17	39	5	1,778	95
96. Frost bite	1	447	16	6	32	4	506	96
97. Trench foot	5	5,173	123	26	167	21	5,515	97
98. Other local injuries	23	4,441	64	24	79	14	4,645	98
99. Other miscellaneous indefinite diseases	92	10,977	87	67	647	22	11,892	99
TOTAL	8,337	767,878	33,191	2,761	21,297	3,213	836,677	

CHAPTER XXI

CASUALTIES DEALT WITH BY THE MINISTRY OF PENSIONS

THE *Medical History of the War* is essentially a record of the wounds, injuries and diseases, due to or associated with the conflict, and of the way in which these casualties were dealt with medically. To confine this history to the period of active hostilities would be to give an incomplete picture of the full effects of war on the health and capacity, physical and mental, of those who served. The survey must extend into the decade following the Armistice in order to obtain a true perspective. For this purpose the records of the Ministry of Pensions provide the needed material, and they have been studied and analysed with the object of extracting the basic facts and figures of medical interest. The aim of this chapter is to give a broad presentation of the Ministry's medical tasks and accomplishments with a general analysis of the outstanding medical characteristics of post-war disablement and the manner and extent to which such disablement has been compensated by the State. It may be regarded as a bird's-eye view of a wide landscape, revealing only the prominent features. As far as possible verbal and administrative technicalities have been avoided, but except where otherwise stated, it has not been possible, in the statistical reports, to distinguish between Army, Navy and Air Force cases. The numerical size of the Army was, however, so much greater than that of the Navy and Air Force together, that in considering the large totals here analysed a combination of the figures for all Services does not appreciably alter or affect the results, which may therefore be taken as produced essentially by the Army alone. Unless otherwise stated, the figures comprise other ranks only, officers and nurses being excluded.

The Main Task of the Ministry of Pensions

The primary duty placed upon the Ministry of Pensions by Statute and Royal Warrant is to award compensation for physical or mental disablement arising from a wound, injury or disease caused by war service. This duty, in its medical aspect, necessitated consideration of whether the particular disability from which the discharged man was found to be suffering was either due to, or if not due to, had been increased by, his war service. If the disability was either due to or had been increased by war service, the extent to which the man was disabled by war service had then to be determined.

The powers and duties of making " provision for the care of disabled officers and men after they have left the service, including provision for their health, training, etc.," rested until 1917 upon the Statutory Committee constituted by the Naval and Military War Pensions, etc., Act, 1915. By the Transfer of Powers Act, 1917, these powers and duties of the Statutory Committee were transferred to the Ministry of Pensions, and thus the Ministry, in connection with its task of awarding compensation proportionate to the degree of war service disablement, were empowered to provide medical and surgical treatment, with the object of reducing as far as possible the disabling effects of war service wounds and diseases.

Medical Organisation of the Ministry of Pensions.—A medical branch was first formed in December, 1917, with Sir John Collie as director. Medical boards were at that time functioning under the Ministry of National Service for the medical examination of men of the various categories called up for enlistment, and, owing to the need for economy in medical personnel, use was made of these boards by the Ministry of Pensions for the medical examination of pensioners and claimants to pension. At the same time medical men in private practice throughout the country were appointed by the Ministry to examine and certify, on the basis of a fee per certificate, as to the condition of disabled men referred to them for the purpose by Local War Pensions Committees, mainly in connection with the need for medical treatment. As regards the actual provision of treatment, little more could be done by the medical branch during the war than to secure, on the basis of a capitation payment by the Ministry, such accommodation in civil hospitals as was available, and to establish a number of homes for the medical care and treatment of men suffering from some form of paralysis. In the main the Ministry had still to rely upon naval and military hospitals for the treatment of pensioners. This preparatory work continued until the commencement of general demobilisation soon after the Armistice. Sir John Collie then resigned, and in January, 1919, Colonel A. Lisle Webb * of the Army Medical Service, was

---

* Now Sir A. Lisle Webb, K.B.E.

MINISTRY OF PENSIONS MEDICAL REVIEW

appointed Director-General of Medical Services of the Ministry of Pensions.

The unprecedented number of claims to pension that poured in upon the Ministry consequent upon general demobilisation, and the need for the Department to take under its direct charge the sick and wounded in the service hospitals, called for an immediate expansion of the Medical Services Division. The medical work was accordingly regrouped and branches were created to deal with the following duties:

(a) Medical boards, and the selection and appointment of medical personnel.
(b) The provision of medical and surgical treatment, including the management of Ministry hospitals and clinics.
(c) The provision of treatment concurrently with training, and the establishment of special institutions for the purpose.
(d) The provision of medical supplies and equipment, including hospital accommodation, and artificial limbs and surgical appliances.
(e) Nursing services.

In June, 1919, to meet the overwhelming pressure of work, the Ministry introduced a scheme of decentralisation, by which large sections of the work were transferred from headquarters to eleven regional offices. This transfer included much of the work of the Medical Services Division, which in each region was placed under the control of a Commissioner of Medical Services. The Commissioner was made responsible under the Director-General at Headquarters for the conduct of medical boards, the supervision of the arrangements for the provision of treatment, and in general for the whole medical administration of the region. Each region was divided into a number of medical areas, in which the medical work was under the charge of a Deputy Commissioner of Medical Services responsible directly to the Commissioner at the regional office. The maintenance of the regional offices was a temporary expedient intended to meet the heaviest years of the Ministry's work. When the crest of the wave was past, the regional offices were disbanded, the post of Commissioner of Medical Services was discontinued, and the medical areas were finally adopted as the unit for the Ministry's medical work. Additional responsibilities and duties, comparable to those formerly exercised by the regional Commissioner of Medical Services, were thus assigned to the area Deputy Commissioners of Medical Services, and additional medical personnel was rendered available to assist them. This personnel continues to consist partly of full-time medical officers, partly of medical officers working on the basis of a fee for a sessional service on medical boards or at Ministry clinics, and partly of medical men in private practice, specialists and others, whose services are available on the basis of a fee per report or certificate. The area Deputy Commissioner of Medical Services is guided and directed in his activities by the Director-General of Medical Services, Ministry of Pensions, at Ministry Headquarters, working through the Medical Director of the particular Headquarters Medical Branch concerned.

Medical Boards.—On the 1st April, 1919, the medical boards of the Ministry of National Service were taken over by the Ministry of Pensions and reconstituted in order to adapt them to the different functions they were required to serve. Three main types of Board were formed, viz :—

(a) " Primary Awards " Boards which examined claimants to pension and advised the Ministry as to whether the disability was either attributable to or aggravated by war service, and as to the degree of the claimant's disablement therefrom.

(b) " Re-Survey " Boards which examined men shortly before the expiration of the period of their current pension, and also men who during the period of current pension claimed that their condition had become worse.

(c) " Appeal " Boards which examined men who were dissatisfied with the award made as a result of their examination by either a " Primary Awards " Board or a " Re-Survey " Board.

Each medical board was originally composed of three medical men, one of whom acted as chairman. The services of specialists were available to boards, either in the capacity of member of the board, or for the purpose of making a special examination and report. In appeal boards a specialist in the disability from which the man was suffering was invariably one of the members. A shortage of available specialists in neurasthenic conditions and heart conditions was met by the training of specially selected medical men. The doctors, before whom the claimant appeared at medical boards, were usually ex-service men themselves, and their medical judgment was unfettered. To function with equity and uniformity, however, the boards required guidance, and this was afforded by the whole-time medical officers who co-ordinated and advised the boards in order to ensure an adherence to the technical regulations inseparable from the administration of a large organisation deriving its authority from specific Warrants and Acts.

Arising directly from a decision that a particular disability was consequent upon war service came the problem of assessing the degree of disablement caused thereby. A problem of this kind was new to the majority of the profession. It was found to be by no means easy, and afforded opportunity for divergence of opinion. The experience of former wars gave only limited assistance, since the basis on which the State decided to accept responsibility for disabilities traceable to the Great War was, owing to the fact that there had been compulsory enlistment of the general civil population, different in principle and wider in scope than in any previous war pension scheme. Formerly, compensation had been in the main limited to the wounds and direct injuries due to warfare and endemic diseases, other diseases and general physical effects being relatively excluded. Compensation, moreover, had been assessed on the basis of the effect on earning capacity. Following the Great War the State was prepared not only to consider all conditions arising from wound, injury or disease caused by war service, but also conditions of disablement of pre-war origin which had been made worse by war service. At the same time a more generous standard for the assessment of compensation was adopted. The Ministry, therefore, took as its standard the normal healthy man of the same age as the pensioner and assessed the degree of disablement arising from the wound or disease according to the extent to which war service had reduced him below that standard. Whilst, therefore, the Royal Warrant had laid down certain fixed assessments for a few well-defined disabilities, such as amputations of different degree, it was necessary to ensure that other assessments were made by the boards in conformity with the new principles. To secure this uniformity and equity a special branch of whole-time medical officers, known as assessors, was formed to scrutinise the assessments and discuss with individual boards any instances where their assessments and opinions on entitlement were out of harmony with what experience had shown to be the more general medical opinion.

The final development of the boarding and assessing medical services thus resulted in a harmonious combination of the medical experience of the independent general practitioner, the specialist and the administrator. On the one hand, the pensioner was assured of the primary consideration of his case by independent medical men, and, on the other, of general uniformity and equity of judgment.

In 1919 the Minister of Pensions appointed a Ministry of Pensions Disability Committee, having as its members the Presidents of the Royal Colleges of Physicians and Surgeons, the Secretary of the Medical Research Council, and other eminent medical men, with the Director-General of Medical Services, Ministry of Pensions, as Chairman. The function of this committee was to consider in detail, in conjunction with senior officials of the Ministry, the medical aspect of the existing principles and regulations relating to the connection of the various forms of disability with war service and the assessment of the degree of disablement therefrom. The committee, with its specialist sub-committees, held frequent meetings throughout 1920, 1921 and 1922. As the outcome of its labours the practice of the Ministry in entitlement and assessment became based upon the highest medical authority.

A summary of the total boarding work done by the Ministry up to 1929 is given in Table 1, from which the magnitude of the numbers boarded in the early years is at once apparent. The totals include 29,380 officers in 1919–20, 50,796 in 1920–21, and 34,195 in 1921–22.

TABLE 1.—Ministry of Pensions Medical Boards held from 1919 to 1929

Financial year	Numbers boarded
1919–20	1,051,102
1920–21	1,259,899
1921–22	888,026
1922–23	613,171
1923–24	457,555
1924–25	288,012
1925–26	137,132
1926–27	89,837
1927–28	46,127
1928–29	47,424
Total ..	4,878,285

Medical Treatment.—Side by side with the development of medical boarding, arrangements had to be made to meet the current and future needs of the Ministry for providing medical and surgical treatment. The limbless wanted limbs, face wounds required plastic surgery, "shell-shocks" demanded a remedy for their multitudinous complexes and complications. The insane needed mental institutions, and the tuberculous sanatoria. Men from the East brought with them malaria, dysentery, bilharziasis, and other tropical diseases. The blind sought training, the paralysed a home. The situation was without precedent, analogies were few, and doctors, whether clinicians or administrators, found themselves launched on a little-charted sea. Guiding principles, however, soon emerged, and the appropriate treatment was provided, whether it was in-patient, out-patient or at home.

It was at once clear that the resources of civil hospitals were altogether inadequate for the Ministry's requirements, and arrangements were therefore made to take over for the treatment of pensioners a number of the best equipped and most suitably situated hospitals that had been used by the service departments. In addition, the Ministry established a number of out-patient clinics for the treatment of special forms of disability, such as orthopædic, neurological, tropical diseases, aural, cardiac and ophthalmic, for which other facilities either did not exist or were insufficient for Ministry requirements.

The provision of vocational training for men whose war service disablement prevented them from resuming their pre-war occupation was one of the duties of the Ministry of Pensions in its early days, but this duty was transferred in 1919 to the Ministry of Labour. The Ministry of Pensions, however, remained responsible for the training of men whose need for medical treatment would interfere with their regular attendance at a continuous course of training on ordinary industrial lines, and also for those men who on account of their disability were likely to break down, or had broken down, in training or employment under ordinary industrial conditions. For the purpose of this combination of training with medical treatment a number of convalescent centres, with accommodation for 3,800 patients, were established by the Ministry in convenient parts of the country. The training, which was not carried out at the expense of treatment but was regulated in accordance with the man's physical ability as determined by the medical officer in charge, was in the hands of expert instructors, and was both theoretical and practical in character. Sick quarters were provided for temporary cases of illness. Nursing and massage services were available, and each centre included a dispensary and a large massage room fitted with modern apparatus, electrical and otherwise.

The Ministry also established a number of limb-fitting centres throughout the country where officers and men who had suffered amputation of a limb through war service attended for the supply, repair and renewal of their artificial limbs. The limb-makers' workshops were stationed either at the limb-fitting centre itself or close by. Each centre was under the supervision of a surgeon-in-charge, who was assisted by a number of other surgeons specially selected and trained for the work.

Table 2 shows the total number of pensioners receiving institutional treatment at the close of each financial year, 1918–1929.

TABLE 2.—Number of Pensioners receiving Institutional Treatment at the end of each Financial Year, 1918–1929

Date	Numbers receiving institutional treatment		
	In-patients	Out-patients	Total
At 3.4.18		10,743	10,743
,, 31.3.19		35,948	35,948
,, 31.3.20	24,007	94,206	118,213
,, 31.3.21	26,342	106,005	132,347
,, 31.3.22	23,894	119,494	143,388
,, 31.3.23	18,402	43,574	61,976
,, 31.3.24	15,046	29,047	44,093
,, 31.3.25	10,727	22,179	32,906
,, 31.3.26	8,921	10,279	19,200
,, 31.3.27	7,550	5,919	13,469
,, 31.3.28	6,121	3,736	9,857
,, 31.3.29	5,106	2,388	7,494

Table 3 shows the extent of hospital in-patient accommodation provided by the Ministry of Pensions for the period 1919–1929.

TABLE 3.—Extent of Hospital In-patient Accommodation provided by the Ministry of Pensions, 1919–1929

Year ending 31st March	Hospitals directly controlled by the Ministry of Pensions		Hospitals reserving beds for the Ministry of Pensions		Total No. of beds available
	No.	Beds	No.	Beds	
1919	9	374	32	1,786	2,160
1920	46	9,845	26	2,461	12,306
1921	67	13,225	46	5,378	18,603
1922	55	13,396	40	2,630	16,026
1923	37	10,047	36	2,672	12,719
1924	33	7,843	46	3,024	10,867
1925	29	6,919	40	2,566	9,485
1926	22	5,038	33	2,715	7,753
1927	19	4,138	27	2,497	6,635
1928	19	3,686	25	2,363	6,049
1929	17	3,093	22	2,005	5,098

MINISTRY OF PENSIONS MEDICAL REVIEW

Summary of War Disablement

Before proceeding to a detailed consideration of the disbilities for which State compensation was given, it is desirable to give some general idea of the total disablement effect of the war up to the year 1930. For this purpose the total British officers, nursing sisters and other ranks, excluding Dominion and Indian troops, who served between 4th August, 1914, and 11th November, 1918, may be taken as approximately 6,000,000. At the time of the Armistice, of this total some 750,000, or 12·5 per cent., had become death casualties, and 600,000, or 10 per cent., had been discharged from the service as disabled with some form of pension or gratuity.

By the end of March, 1920, demobilisation and discharge had been mainly completed, and contemporaneously a very large number of men had been medically examined for disabilities claimed as due to or aggravated by war service. Between 11th November, 1918, and 31st March, 1920, 335,000 were discharged from army hospitals as disabled by war service and were awarded pension or gratuity at the time of discharge; and 485,000 were granted pension or gratuity as the result of an accepted claim in respect of war disablement made at the time of or after demobilisation. Thus, by 31st March, 1920, 1,420,000, or 23·6 per cent. of the total who served, had been awarded pensions or gratuities.

By 31st March, 1925, this total had increased to 1,654,000, and by 31st March, 1930, to 1,664,000, or 27·7 per cent. of those who served. If to this total is added the 750,000 death casualties, the total numbers affected by war service, in the sense of death or some form of war disablement for which State compensation was given, may be estimated at approximately 2,414,000 or 40·2 per cent. of those who served.

The Nature of Post-War Disablements and the Compensation Therefor

Disabilities traceable to the war, whether by wound or disease, may be broadly classified as follows :—
- (A) Immediately obvious, and with clearly circumscribed sequelæ, such as a clean bullet wound.
- (B) Immediately obvious, but with liability to prolonged and widespread sequelæ, for example, head wounds, dysentery.
- (C) Not immediately obvious, but emerging after a latent period of varied length, as, for example, tuberculosis.

These classes are not, of course, precise nor mutually exclusive; an apparently clean and healed wound may flare up, after many years, in acute osteitis; tuberculosis may be sudden and miliary almost from infection. They afford, however, a useful general division for the consideration of war disablements as a whole. For the most part wounds and injuries fall into Classes (A) and (B) and diseases into Classes (B) and (C). With the termination of hostilities additions to Classes (A) and (B) tend to cease, but Class (C) continues to increase, and this class has formed a major problem of the Ministry. Further, it is clear that for the most part, the conditions in Class (A) will tend towards cure or stabilisation at an early date, whilst those in Class (B) will be likely to persist and remain unstable for a more or less prolonged period. Thus, from the point of view of compensation by the State, it could be anticipated that for Class (A) some form of compensation by gratuity or permanent pension could be given within a reasonably short time after the end of the war, whilst for Class (B), finality in award of pension would be deferred for some years. For Class (C) an early final award would be appropriate for a small number only, since, for the most part, it would comprise unstable and progressive conditions.

In order to survey to the full the extent to which some form of gratuity or pension has been granted to ex-service men as compensation for war disablement, however slight, the following statement of the position as at 31st March, 1929, reduces the types of award to the simplest possible categories. No attempt is here made to give an account of the various technical details in "awards," and they are defined in broad outline only.

The total number of disabled ex-service men who have received some form of gratuity or pension as the result of war service may be taken up to 31st March, 1929, in round numbers, as 1,600,000.

This total can be sub-divided as shown in Table 4.

Class I of this table comprises the cases which became medically stabilised within a short time after discharge from service. The medical records concerning them are, in the main, not susceptible to any useful analysis, as the conditions were mostly slight, often merely temporary, and such cases can thus be ignored in estimating the real effect of the war from a medical standpoint. About 70,000, however, consisted of wounds, amputations and injuries of serious degree.

This medical stabilisation enabled the extent of war service

TABLE 4.—Main Types of Disablement and Corresponding Form of Compensation, at 31st March, 1929

Nature of disablement	Form of compensation awarded	No. at 31.3.29
I. Immediately obvious in kind and rapidly stabilised in degree of disablement.	Early stabilised grants of pension or gratuity.	790,000*
II. Tending towards cure or stabilisation within a limited time.	"Final award" under Act of 1921.	572,000
III. Remaining uncured and unstabilised.	Unstabilised pension at amount adjusted periodically to correspond with the current degree of disablement.	113,000
		1,475,000
Died whilst in receipt of pension		120,000
	Total ..	1,595,000

* This figure is approximate only, as it contains a certain proportion of duplication.

disablement to be appraised finally, and consequently the early stabilised grants came in due course within the scope of the War Pensions Act of 1921.

The figures in Class II represent the cases, not included in Class I, to which, as medical stabilisation occurred, final awards were given in accordance with the War Pensions Act, 1921. Together with Class I, they comprise the total of all final awards in the technical sense of that Act.

Class III comprises those cases in which a stabilised condition had not been reached by 31st March, 1929, and in which, therefore, the award of compensation remained unstabilised at that date.

The Ministry mortality statistics refer only to those pensioners who died whilst in receipt of some continuing monetary compensation. They do not, therefore, include deaths amongst those whose award had taken the form of a gratuity or of a temporary allowance which had expired at the time of death, the number of these and the cause being generally unknown. Broadly speaking, therefore, these 120,000 deaths occurred amongst Classes II and III, but they were not all either due to or hastened by the disability for which pension was being paid. The extent to which this was so necessarily varied with the nature of the war service disability, but it has been estimated that in some 60 to 70 per cent. of the total 120,000 the pensionable disability was a major factor in the cause of death.

Table 4 thus gives in a generalised form the nature and

extent of State compensation up to 31st March, 1929. It demonstrates the three main phases of the Ministry's work in the determination of appropriate compensation, namely :—
  (1) The early disposal of the obviously stable and permanent and the minor conditions (Class I).
  (2) The gradually increasing disposal of conditions in which stabilisation was effected (Class II).
  (3) The continuing adjustment of the remaining unstabilised conditions (Class III).

The Conspicuous Disablements and their Variations.—The classification of wounds and diseases used in the following tables was introduced in 1920; before that date certain conditions, now separated, were combined for statistical purposes. When this change affects the main conclusions to be reached from the totals an appropriate note is made. Certain of the classes are still wide and lack precise definition as, for example, neurasthenia, which comprises all functional diseases of the nervous system.

Although these tables provide precise figures for these various conditions and awards, yet, owing to their inevitable complexity, they fail to emphasise at sight the salient features they contain. They are, therefore, dissected later into percentages to show the chief facts they present. Such an analysis reveals certain conditions as constantly present to a considerable degree, and as the variations and extent of these are of particular interest, they are here briefly summarised. The conditions thus commonly recurring in appreciable amount may be broadly classified as follows :—
  (a) Wounds, injuries and amputations.
  (b) Tuberculosis, including surgical tuberculosis.
  (c) Respiratory diseases, excluding tuberculosis and gas injury.
  (d) Organic diseases of the heart.
  (e) Functional diseases of the heart.
  (f) Neurasthenia.
  (g) Malaria.
  (h) Rheumatism, including fibrositis, myositis, myalgia, pleurodynia, lumbago and sciatica.
  (i) Diseases of the ear.
  (j) Psychoses.
  (k) Dysentery.
  (l) Nephritis.

These conditions constitute over 80 per cent. of the total disabilities.

Table 5 gives a summary of the proportions in which these disabilities occur in the different classes given above.

TABLE 5.—Percentage Proportions of the Chief Disabilities in Classes II and III of Table 4, at 31st March, 1929

Disability	Percentage in Class II	Percentage in Class III
Wounds	40·4	16·3
Amputations	1·2	·6
Tuberculosis	2·3	20·7
Respiratory diseases	5·3	13·5
Organic diseases of the heart	2·2	8·8
Functional diseases of the heart	6·8	4·0
Neurasthenia	8·6	6·9
Malaria	7·6	·5
Rheumatism	4·9	2·3
Diseases of the ear	3·4	2·6
Psychoses	·7	7·3
Dysentery	1·1	·8
Nephritis	1·4	4·7
Other disabilities	14·1	11·0
Total percentage	100·0	100·0
Approximate total analysed	572,000	113,000

From this table it is clear that wounds, neurasthenia, malaria and functional diseases of the heart constitute the bulk of the stabilised Class II, whilst tuberculosis, wounds, respiratory diseases and organic diseases of the heart form a major proportion of the unstabilised Class III.

Comparative Analysis of War Disablement

Under this heading an attempt is made to present in a more precise form the main characteristics in the nature and development of post-war disablement. The present distribution of the various disabilities among stabilised and unstabilised awards is first dealt with in detail, and having shown the general position as at 31st March, 1929, the stages by which it has been reached are next considered. First, the conditions which did not appear in evidence as war disablement until after demobilisation are analysed—in other words, the post-war emergence of war disablement. By this means a broad indication is given of the extent to which there was a continuous unknown factor in the summation of the State's responsibilities, due to delayed but acceptable claims for compensation for war disablement.

Next is considered the rate at which it was possible, owing to stabilisation or cure of the disability produced or accentuated by war service, to stabilise or terminate the State's liability.

Finally, the existing groups of stabilised and unstabilised conditions are then separately considered in further detail as to severity of disablement.

The distribution of disabilities amongst stabilised and unstabilised awards.—This has already been broadly considered in reference to Tables 4 and 5. The detailed figures on which that consideration was based are now given in Tables 6 and 7.

TABLE 6.—Analysis of the Stabilised Awards made up to 31st March, 1929, in so far as Detailed Classification by Disabilities is practicable

Disability	Totals
Wounds :	
Complete blindness	794
Head	18,109
Face	14,130
Neck	2,890
Chest	11,491
Abdomen	4,487
Perineum	1,563
Back	9,063
Upper extremities (not amputation)	94,716
Lower extremities (not amputation)	79,468
Fracture of femur	6,090
Multiple	5,450
Amputations :	
Amputation of one upper extremity	9,074
Amputation of both upper extremities	46
Other amputations of upper extremities	6,501
Amputation of one lower extremity	22,887
Amputation of both lower extremities	940
Other amputations of lower extremities	1,525
Amputation of one upper and one lower extremity	160
Other multiple amputations	75
Total	289,459
Diseases :	
Dysentery	6,019
Enteric	222
Malaria	43,197
Trench fever	2,054
Rheumatism	26,416
Pulmonary tuberculosis	9,439
Tuberculosis not pulmonary	1,930
Affections of the respiratory system	28,832
Organic diseases of the heart	11,705
Functional diseases of the heart	38,367
Nephritis	7,464
Gastric ulcer	2,270
Appendicitis	1,044
Other diseases of the alimentary system	6,881
Hernia	4,205
Neurasthenia	47,669
Epilepsy	2,590
Tabes dorsalis	545
Other organic nervous diseases	2,750
Psychoses	4,163
Diseases of the eye resulting in complete blindness	124
Other diseases of the eye	7,206
Diseases of the ear	19,346
Debility	12,456
Diabetes	157
Flat foot	1,907
Frost bite	2,691
Gas poisoning	6,717
Miscellaneous	9,491
Diseases of the veins	6,566
Diseases of the joints	5,858
Arteriosclerosis	409
Bilharziasis	11
Loss of eye	9,146
Not recorded	2,666
Total	332,513
Grand Total	621,972

When considering Table 4 it was stated that the medical records relating to the " early stabilised grants of pension or gratuity " were, in the main, not susceptible to any useful analysis. On the other hand, the final awards of Class II of Table 4 can be fully analysed from a medical standpoint. In order to give the maximum amount of accurate medical information relative to stabilised awards as a whole (*i.e.* Classes I

TABLE 7.—Analysis of Unstabilised Pensions in Payment at 31st March, 1929
(*Vide* Class III of Table 4)

Disability	Totals
Wounds :	
Complete blindness	2
Head	4,188
Face	961
Neck	249
Chest	2,800
Abdomen	795
Perineum	177
Back	983
Upper extremities (not amputation)	2,509
Lower extremities (not amputation)	4,791
Fracture of femur	886
Multiple	83
Amputations :	
Amputation of one upper extremity	96
Amputation of both upper extremities	1
Other amputations of upper extremities	134
Amputation of one lower extremity	423
Amputation of both lower extremities	7
Other amputations of lower extremities	69
Amputation of one upper and one lower extremity	9
Other multiple amputations	—
Total	19,163
Diseases :	
Dysentery	1,021
Enteric	18
Malaria	572
Trench fever	111
Rheumatism	2,567
Pulmonary tuberculosis	22,300
Tuberculosis not pulmonary	1,215
Affections of the respiratory system	15,311
Organic diseases of the heart	10,001
Functional diseases of the heart	4,581
Nephritis	5,265
Gastric ulcer	744
Appendicitis	126
Other diseases of the alimentary system	1,256
Hernia	349
Neurasthenia	7,800
Epilepsy	1,284
Tabes dorsalis	246
Other organic nervous diseases	876
Psychoses	8,208
Diseases of the eye resulting in complete blindness	3
Other diseases of the eye	1,332
Diseases of the ear	2,987
Debility	533
Diabetes	123
Flat foot	66
Frost bite	115
Gas poisoning	699
Miscellaneous	1,654
Diseases of the veins	923
Diseases of the joints	1,732
Arteriosclerosis	125
Bilharziasis	2
Loss of eye	207
Not recorded	—
Total	94,352
Grand Total	113,515

and II of Table 4) those cases in Class I for which accurate medical records are available have been added to Class II and are included in the figures in Table 6. This table, therefore, can be taken as a general analysis, by disabilities, of those conditions which by 31st March, 1929, had become stabilised. It is a fair presentation of the stabilisation of definite war disablement. A more detailed analysis is given later on. It is here sufficient to point out that wounds and amputations make up 45 per cent. of the total, the next highest proportion being neurasthenia (7·2 per cent.), followed by malaria (6·9 per cent.) and functional diseases of the heart (6·2 per cent.).

Table 7 gives a complete analysis by disabilities of the cases remaining unstabilised at 31st March, 1929, and thus still in receipt of a pension periodically adjusted to the current degree of disablement. It represents Class III of Table 4.

A more detailed analysis is given later, but it may be noted here that wounds and amputations comprise only 16·9 per cent. of the total, tuberculosis 20·7 per cent., respiratory diseases 13·5 per cent., and malaria ·5 per cent.

The additions to war disablement after demobilisation.—In addition to the war disablement which became manifest during and immediately after the hostilities, there was a succession of post-war claims for disablement which were accepted for pension purposes. These were especially numerous in the first years after the Armistice, and to a considerable extent were in respect of conditions in which there is a preliminary latent period before their nature is made clear. The incidence of these conditions thus merits analysis, for they indicate the delayed effects of war service, and afford information not previously known on any similar scale.

Whilst it is not possible accurately to study from this point of view all the conditions arising after demobilisation for which awards were made, there is a group known technically as " First Awards," totalling 140,223 up to 31st March, 1926,* which affords a reliable indication of the main characteristics of post-demobilisation awards. The group consists of awards made after March, 1920, but only of those made to men who had received no previous award of any kind. For instance, an award for tuberculosis following a previous award for debility is not included ; each first award represents the first appearance of the man as a recipient of any form of compensation for

---

* The numbers between 1926 and 1929 are relatively few and the general characteristics of the group are adequately shown in the period up to 1926.

war-disablement. These first awards afford, by study of their yearly incidence, a good indication of the latent period of certain conditions associated with war service.

TABLE 8.—" First Awards " of Pension in each Financial Year, 1st April to 31st March, 1920–1926

Disability	Financial Year							Totals
	1920–21		1921–22	1922–23	1923–24	1924–25	1925–26	
	New Code	Chelsea Code						
Wounds:								
Complete blindness	—	—	2	2	—	—	—	4
Head	601	}1,266	{ 266	102	76	112	91	}3,884
Face	563		{ 249	110	65	90	83	
Neck	104		33	14	22	21	16	
Chest	494	}2,321	183	107	61	80	64	}4,413
Abdomen	134		75	20	15	9	18	
Perineum	50		23	8	8	11	6	
Back	395		136	60	34	53	48	
Upper extremities (not amputation)	2,104	1,895	1,077	411	173	222	191	6,073
Lower extremities (not amputation)	2,654	5,012	1,389	481	224	304	289	}10,516
Fracture of femur	95	—	43	14	1	5	5	
Multiple	258	—	102	32	20	13	5	430
Amputations:								
Amputation of one upper extremity	84	}128	{ 41	10	—	1	—	}273
Amputation of both upper extremities	5		{ 3	1	—	—	—	
Other amputations of upper extremities	79	1,185	46	29	12	17	6	1,374
Amputation of one lower extremity	313	}901	{ 103	40	3	6	2	}1,456
Amputation of both lower extremities	14		{ 7	1	—	—	1	
Other amputations of lower extremities	26		26	5	4	1	2	
Amputation of one upper and one lower extremity	15	—	8	5	—	—	—	28
Other multiple amputations	18	—	17	5	—	—	—	40
Diseases:								
Dysentery	858	571	381	152	74	114	90	2,240
Enteric	44	—	21	2	2	1	4	74
Malaria	11,842	7,125	3,073	915	321	342	181	23,799
Trench fever	269	—	97	22	7	11	—	406
Rheumatism	2,930	2,952	1,112	281	115	189	175	7,754
Pulmonary tuberculosis	2,641	}1,494	{2,654	1,685	1,215	1,167	742	}12,574
Tuberculosis not pulmonary	306		{ 302	155	88	78	47	
Affections of the respiratory system	2,780	2,951	1,351	544	364	510	432	8,932
Organic diseases of the heart	1,270	78	790	344	153	157	122	2,914
Functional diseases of the heart	2,479	4,706	1,033	286	118	116	84	8,822
Nephritis	390	—	273	122	70	56	52	963
Gastric ulcer	165	—	91	48	59	75	67	505
Appendicitis	103	—	61	25	10	14	10	223
Other diseases of the alimentary system	1,055	—	369	151	106	120	126	1,927
Hernia	447	748	214	64	41	36	43	1,593
Neurasthenia	3,654	177	1,594	539	250	259	222	6,695
Epilepsy	182	221	130	63	32	31	31	690
Tabes dorsalis	31	—	19	14	4	8	16	92
Other organic nervous diseases	126	2,604	103	53	68	50	36	3,040
Psychoses	439	593	403	179	126	160	199	2,099
Diseases of the eye resulting in complete blindness	16	}1,122	{ 7	4	4	2	—	}2,916
Other diseases of the eye	803		{ 483	160	102	85	128	
Diseases of the ear	1,518	1,639	792	338	156	194	156	4,793
Debility	3,096	—	751	124	39	20	12	4,042
Diabetes	50	—	41	22	11	19	7	150
Flat foot	147	—	93	15	8	13	12	288
Frost bite	92	89	62	17	11	7	7	285
Gas poisoning	1,321	762	372	129	24	—	—	2,608
Miscellaneous	1,339		1,046	374	134	203	164	
Diseases of the veins	532	}6,082	293	95	51	63	74	}5,015
Diseases of the joints	175		106	42	41	55	53	
Arteriosclerosis	84		35	20	12	15	9	
Bilharziasis	—	—	—	—	—	—	2	2
Loss of eye	—	—	—	—	1	3	3	7
Not recorded	29	144	17	9	—	—	1	203
	49,219	46,766	21,998	8,450	4,538	5,118	4,134	140,223
Total	95,985							

Table 8 gives the numbers of the first awards granted for different disabilities in each financial year of the period 1st April, 1920, to 31st March, 1926. The essential features in this table are made prominent in Table 9, where those disabilities which appear numerically therein to a conspicuous extent are separated out and the percentage proportion shown which each of these conditions occupies in the total of first awards in each year.

TABLE 9.—Showing Year by Year the Percentage Proportion of certain Conspicuous Disabilities in the total First Awards

Disability	Total First Awards in period	Percentage proportion in each financial year						Percentage for whole period
		1920–21	1921–22	1922–23	1923–24	1924–25	1925–26	
Wounds and amputations	28,490	21·6	17·4	17·3	15·8	18·5	20·0	20·3
Tuberculosis	12,574	4·6	13·4	21·9	28·7	24·5	19·2	8·8
Respiratory diseases	8,932	5·9	6·1	6·5	8·0	10·0	10·3	6·4
Organic diseases of the heart	2,914	1·4	3·6	4·1	3·4	3·1	2·9	2·1
Functional diseases of the heart	8,822	7·5	4·7	3·4	2·4	2·3	2·0	6·3
Neurasthenia	6,695	4·0	7·2	6·4	5·5	5·1	5·4	4·8
Malaria	23,799	19·8	14·0	10·8	7·1	6·7	4·4	17·0
Rheumatism	7,754	6·1	5·0	3·3	2·5	3·7	4·3	5·6
Diseases of the ear	4,793	3·3	3·6	4·0	3·4	3·8	3·8	3·4
Psychoses	2,099	1·1	1·8	2·0	2·8	3·1	4·8	1·5
Dysentery	2,240	1·5	1·7	1·8	1·6	2·2	2·0	1·6
Miscellaneous of small percentage	31,111	23·2	21·5	18·5	18·8	17·0	19·9	22·2
Total percentage	—	100·0	100·0	100·0	100·0	100·0	100·0	100·0
Total First Awards	140,223	95,985	21,998	8,450	4,538	5,118	4,134	—

It is manifest that wounds, malaria and functional diseases of the heart were the most prominent conditions in the total first awards made in 1920–21, in which year the majority of all first awards were made.

As time went on, however, whilst wounds maintained a constant proportion, malaria and functional diseases of the heart soon decreased to relative insignificance, whilst tuberculosis, respiratory diseases, organic diseases of the heart and psychoses increased in relative proportions. Ear diseases, rheumatism and dysentery remained remarkably even in proportion.

The general indications of "latency" are more strikingly demonstrated by Table 10, with its graphic form Fig. 1, where the total incidence of each conspicuous disability is shown by annual percentage. Thus it appears that of the total first awards for malaria, 79·5 per cent. were made in the first year of the period and 13·3 per cent. in the second year, whilst of the total for tuberculosis only 35·2 per cent. and 23·4 per cent. fell in those years. Malaria was thus a condition of relatively

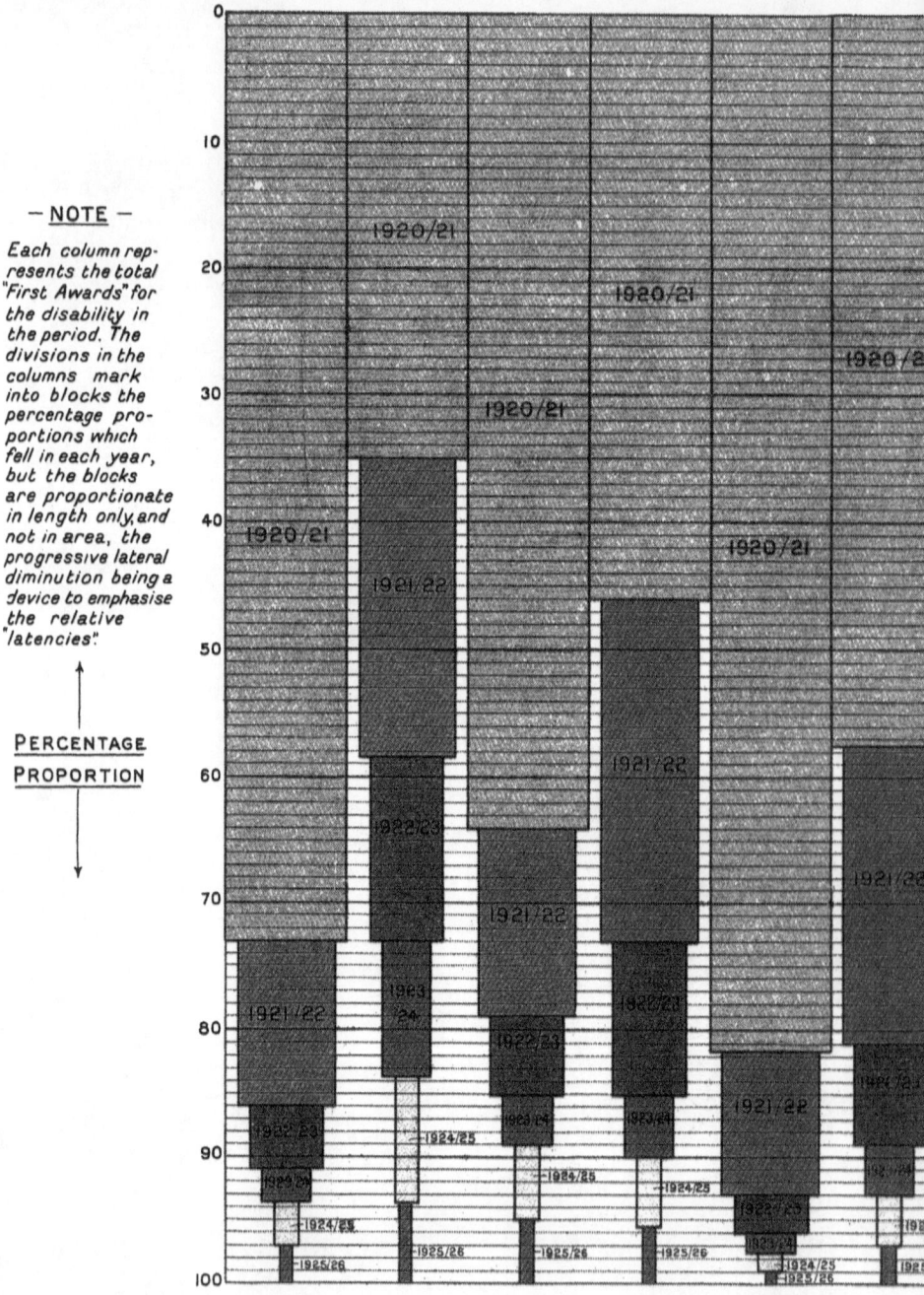

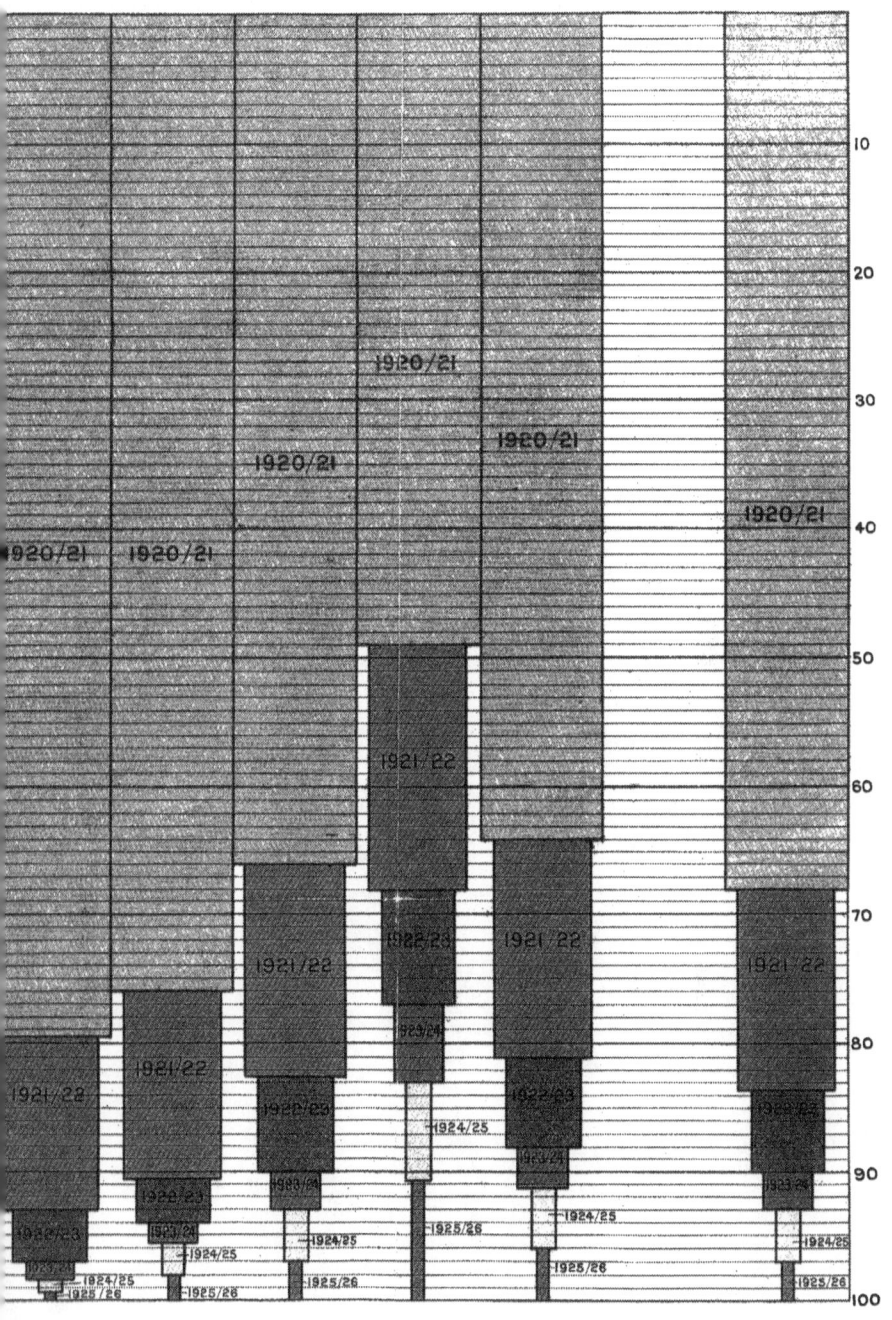

ERTAIN DISABILITIES THE PERCENTAGE PROPORTION
Y YEAR IN THE PERIOD 1920-1926.
ABLE 10.)

slight latency, whilst tuberculosis had a considerable latent period. This latency is conspicuous also in psychoses, organic diseases of the heart, and to a lesser degree in respiratory diseases, neurasthenia and dysentery. Functional diseases of the heart and rheumatism closely follow malaria in showing relatively little latency.

TABLE 10.—Analysis of the "First Awards" for certain Conspicuous Disabilities to show, for each Disability, the Percentage Proportion of its Total which occurred year by year in the period 1920–1926
(*See also* Fig. 1.)

Disability	Percentage of total in each financial year						Total percentage	Total first awards in period
	1920–21	1921–22	1922–23	1923–24	1924–25	1925–26		
Wounds and amputations	72·7	13·5	5·1	2·5	3·3	2·9	100·0	28,490
Tuberculosis	35·2	23·4	14·6	10·5	9·9	6·1	100·0	12,574
Respiratory diseases	64·2	15·2	6·1	4·1	5·6	4·8	100·0	8,932
Organic diseases of the heart	46·2	27·1	11·8	5·3	5·4	4·2	100·0	2,914
Functional diseases of the heart	81·5	11·7	3·2	1·3	1·3	1·0	100·0	8,822
Neurasthenia	57·4	23·5	8·2	3·7	3·9	3·3	100·0	6,895
Malaria	79·5	13·3	3·7	1·3	1·5	·7	100·0	23,799
Rheumatism	75·8	14·4	3·5	1·5	2·5	2·3	100·0	7,754
Diseases of the ear	65·8	16·5	7·1	3·3	4·0	3·3	100·0	4,793
Psychoses	49·2	19·2	8·5	6·0	7·6	9·5	100·0	2,099
Dysentery	64·0	17·0	6·7	3·3	5·0	4·0	100·0	2,240
All Disabilities	68·2	15·7	6·2	3·2	3·7	3·0	100·0	140,223
Total first awards in each year	95,985	21,998	8,450	4,538	5,118	4,134		

The rate of stabilisation of war disablement.—The way in which war disablement became stabilised and decreased is best revealed by a study of the statistics of the final awards included in Class II of Table 4.

Final awards in the technical sense came into operation in 1921, and have been made when the disablement, so far as it is the direct result of war service, is found to have reached a condition of virtual stability, or to have disappeared. Thus, an analysis of the rate at which these awards have been granted, and their relative proportions amongst the various disabilities, indicates the stages by which war disablement has become stabilised.

Table 11 shows the total final awards comprised in Class II of Table 4, and thus expresses the conditions which became stabilised in the second phase of the Ministry's work. It records these awards by disabilities and by the years in which the award was made. It thus, broadly speaking, shows the rate and nature of stabilisation during the period 1922–1929. It is necessary to add that the figures refer to the final awards as notified year by year, and thus the totals are totals of awards and not, as in Tables 6 and 7, of individuals. Thus, for

TABLE 11.—Final Awards made up to 31st May, 1923, and subsequently during each financial year up to 31st March, 1929. (*See Table 4, Class II*)

Disability	Up to 31.5.23	1.6.23 to 31.3.24	1.4.24 to 31.3.25	1.4.25 to 31.3.26	1.4.26 to 31.3.27	1.4.27 to 31.3.28	1.4.28 to 31.3.29	Total
Wounds:								
Complete blindness	12	68	—	1	—	—	—	81
Head	7,631	4,423	2,533	978	840	348	495	17,248
Face	6,525	3,692	1,769	689	508	199	236	13,618
Neck	1,409	612	303	153	117	47	51	2,692
Chest	5,418	2,599	1,252	556	489	269	366	10,949
Abdomen	2,276	1,024	417	168	165	64	135	4,249
Perineum	512	273	120	50	59	15	22	1,051
Back	4,717	1,745	994	495	356	159	185	8,651
Upper extremities (not amputation)	48,553	19,045	8,493	3,247	2,046	653	659	82,696
Lower extremities (not amputation)	44,970	16,801	7,508	3,218	2,388	899	1,117	76,901
Fracture of femur	2,067	1,477	793	313	221	94	208	5,173
Multiple	5,556	1,177	450	114	88	13	31	7,429
Amputations:								
Amputation of one upper extremity	100	2	191	87	53	37	25	495
Amputation of both upper extremities	1	—	—	—	2	1	—	4
Other amputations of upper extremities	1,411	772	394	138	113	33	43	2,904
Amputation of one lower extremity	350	—	966	384	318	172	163	2,353
Amputation of both lower extremities	3	1	11	7	2	3	2	29
Other amputations of lower extremities	433	233	122	42	31	17	16	894
Amputation of one upper and one lower extremity	23	6	1	5	—	—	1	36
Other multiple amputations	39	19	11	5	1	1	2	78
Total								237,433
Diseases:								
Dysentery	3,242	718	214	201	583	434	598	5,990
Enteric	104	47	26	15	21	6	11	230
Malaria	32,758	4,408	1,258	1,629	1,495	1,041	974	43,563
Trench fever	1,362	319	181	89	78	29	30	2,088
Rheumatism	14,984	5,591	3,030	1,216	857	554	1,520	27,752
Pulmonary tuberculosis	1,276	679	1,392	945	1,156	1,955	3,629	11,032
Tuberculosis not pulmonary	460	266	230	164	237	211	445	2,013
Affections of the respiratory system	12,557	6,474	3,544	1,797	1,803	1,602	2,796	30,573
Organic diseases of the heart	4,260	1,124	1,099	451	593	591	4,681	12,799
Functional diseases of the heart	16,827	6,742	5,605	3,061	3,363	1,082	2,346	39,026
Nephritis	3,851	1,435	650	337	477	267	793	7,810
Gastric ulcer	865	301	167	151	247	190	446	2,367
Appendicitis	566	169	130	64	58	33	47	1,067
Other diseases of the alimentary system	2,604	1,135	980	604	710	425	708	7,166
Hernia	2,390	682	479	250	189	92	174	4,256
Neurasthenia	18,850	9,680	7,383	3,800	4,712	2,284	2,650	49,359
Epilepsy	871	429	248	163	319	218	467	2,715
Tabes dorsalis	208	105	97	33	38	25	127	633
Other organic nervous diseases	712	647	562	238	188	171	324	2,842
Psychoses	747	578	626	314	392	307	1,051	4,015
Diseases of the eye resulting in complete blindness	4	5	10	2	6	3	2	32
Other diseases of the eye	2,274	1,661	1,049	393	413	315	673	6,778
Diseases of the ear	7,387	4,565	2,694	1,146	1,460	705	1,514	19,471
Debility	8,773	2,038	924	473	503	117	236	13,064
Diabetes	52	19	16	11	20	27	39	184
Flat foot	1,015	419	238	81	66	45	51	1,915
Frost bite	1,563	522	250	113	77	21	37	2,583
Gas poisoning	4,854	1,194	718	252	212	145	157	7,532
Miscellaneous	4,399	1,344	1,103	662	785	428	846	9,567
Diseases of the veins	3,486	1,283	636	328	350	224	542	6,849
Diseases of the joints	2,287	1,344	689	280	340	273	711	5,924
Arteriosclerosis	135	125	107	30	42	20	62	521
Bilharziasis	—	—	—	2	6	—	1	9
Loss of eye	—	94	58	3	36	9	4	204
Not recorded	104	415	979	894	272	—	1	2,665
Total								334,692
Grand Total	287,833	110,526	63,700	30,842	29,901	16,873	32,450	572,125

example, when for any reason the notification of a final award was temporarily revoked but again notified at a later date, it will appear twice in the total figures. This factor, and certain other technicalities in the final awards statistics, explain why, for individual disabilities, the totals of final awards in Table 11 are in many cases greater than those of the stabilised awards in Table 6. The actual differences in number are, however, relatively slight, and as Table 6 includes several thousand cases from Class I of Table 4 which are not included in Table 11, the grand total of the stabilised awards is considerably greater than that of the final awards. The statistical complexity of Table 11 is relieved by Table 12, which extracts the conspicuous disabilities from the mass of final awards, and shows their individual percentage incidence in the total of final awards, year by year. The disabilities thus considered make up 88 per cent. of the total final awards.

TABLE 12.—Annual Percentage Incidence of Certain Disabilities in the total Final Awards up to 31.5.23, and for each Year thereafter up to 31.3.29

Disability	Percentage incidence in period							Whole Period
	Up to 31.5.23	1.6.23 to 31.3.24	1.4.24 to 31.3.25	1.4.25 to 31.3.26	1.4.26 to 31.3.27	1.4.27 to 31.3.28	1.4.28 to 31.3.29	
Wounds and amputations	45·5	48·6	39·7	32·8	21·7	16·0	10·9	41·6
Tuberculosis	·6	·9	2·5	3·6	4·6	12·9	12·6	2·3
Respiratory diseases	4·4	5·9	5·6	5·3	6·0	9·5	8·6	5·3
Organic diseases of the heart	1·5	1·0	1·7	1·5	1·9	3·5	14·4	2·2
Functional diseases of the heart	5·8	6·1	8·8	10·0	11·3	6·4	7·2	6·8
Neurasthenia	6·5	8·7	11·6	12·3	15·7	13·6	8·2	8·6
Malaria	11·3	4·0	2·0	5·3	5·0	6·2	3·0	7·6
Rheumatism	5·2	5·1	4·8	4·0	2·9	3·3	4·2	4·9
Diseases of the ear	2·6	4·1	4·2	3·4	4·9	4·2	4·7	3·4
Psychoses	·3	·5	1·0	1·0	1·3	1·8	3·2	·7
Dysentery	1·1	·7	·3	·7	1·9	2·6	1·8	1·1
Nephritis	1·3	1·3	1·1	1·1	1·6	1·6	2·4	1·4
Other disabilities	13·9	13·1	16·7	19·0	21·2	18·4	18·8	14·6
Total percentage	100·0	100·0	100·0	100·0	100·0	100·0	100·0	100·0
Total final awards	287,833	110,526	63,700	30,842	29,901	16,873	32,450	572,125

Table 12 shows clearly that wounds and amputations, malaria, neurasthenia and functional diseases of the heart were the conditions in which stabilisation was possible at an early date. These conditions also form the main bulk of final awards as a whole. It must be remembered that, as already stated, some 70,000 cases of wounds, amputations and injuries of serious degree had been stabilised before 1922 and are not included in this table, which applies, essentially, to the period 1922–29.

On the other hand, tuberculosis, organic diseases of the heart and psychoses do not appear in more than slight percentage until the last two years of the period, some 7 to 8 years after the close of hostilities. This increase in stabilisation of these three conditions has, it may be added, continued in the period since March, 1929, and the financial year 1929–30 has added appreciably to their total of stabilised awards.

Ear diseases and rheumatism have maintained a noticeably even proportion throughout.

TABLE 13.—Proportion of Total Final Awards for certain Disabilities granted up to 31.5.23, and subsequently in each Financial Year *(See also Fig. 2)*

Disability	Total Nos.	Up to 31.5.23	Percentage proportion in period						Total percentage
			1.6.23 to 31.3.24	1.4.24 to 31.3.25	1.4.25 to 31.3.26	1.4.26 to 31.3.27	1.4.27 to 31.3.28	1.4.28 to 31.3.29	
Wounds and amputations	237,433	54·6	23·8	11·1	4·4	3·3	1·2	1·6	100·0
Tuberculosis	13,045	13·2	7·2	12·3	8·4	10·6	16·3	32·0	100·0
Respiratory diseases	30,573	41·2	21·2	11·6	5·8	5·8	5·2	9·2	100·0
Organic diseases of the heart	12,799	33·3	8·8	8·6	3·5	4·6	4·6	36·6	100·0
Functional diseases of the heart	39,026	43·1	17·5	14·4	7·7	8·6	2·7	6·0	100·0
Neurasthenia	49,359	38·3	19·7	14·9	7·7	9·6	4·6	5·2	100·0
Malaria	43,563	75·1	10·1	3·1	3·7	3·4	2·4	2·2	100·0
Rheumatism	27,752	54·0	20·2	10·8	4·4	3·1	2·0	5·5	100·0
Diseases of the ear	19,471	38·0	23·5	13·8	5·9	7·5	3·6	7·7	100·0
Psychoses	4,015	18·6	16·1	14·0	7·7	9·7	7·7	26·2	100·0
Dysentery	5,990	54·2	12·0	3·6	3·3	9·7	7·2	10·0	100·0
Nephritis	7,810	49·3	18·4	8·3	4·3	6·1	3·4	10·2	100·0
All disabilities	572,125	50·3	19·3	11·2	5·4	5·2	2·9	5·7	100·0

In Table 13 a further attempt is made to extricate the salient facts from the statistical mass of Table 11, by showing the percentage proportion of the total final awards for each conspicuous disability which fell in the successive years of the period under consideration. Fig. 2 presents these proportions graphically and shows the rate of stabilisation of the disabilities.

Thus it is apparent that the stabilised awards for malaria were given at an early date, namely, 75·1 per cent. by 31st May, 1923 ; whereas in tuberculosis, psychoses and organic diseases of the heart, such stabilisation as has occurred has been a more recent development.

It is of interest to compare Table 13 with Table 10 which shows the incidence of first awards in comparable fashion. There is seen to be a close correspondence between those conditions which show a definite latent period and those in which stabilisation was relatively late in development. In

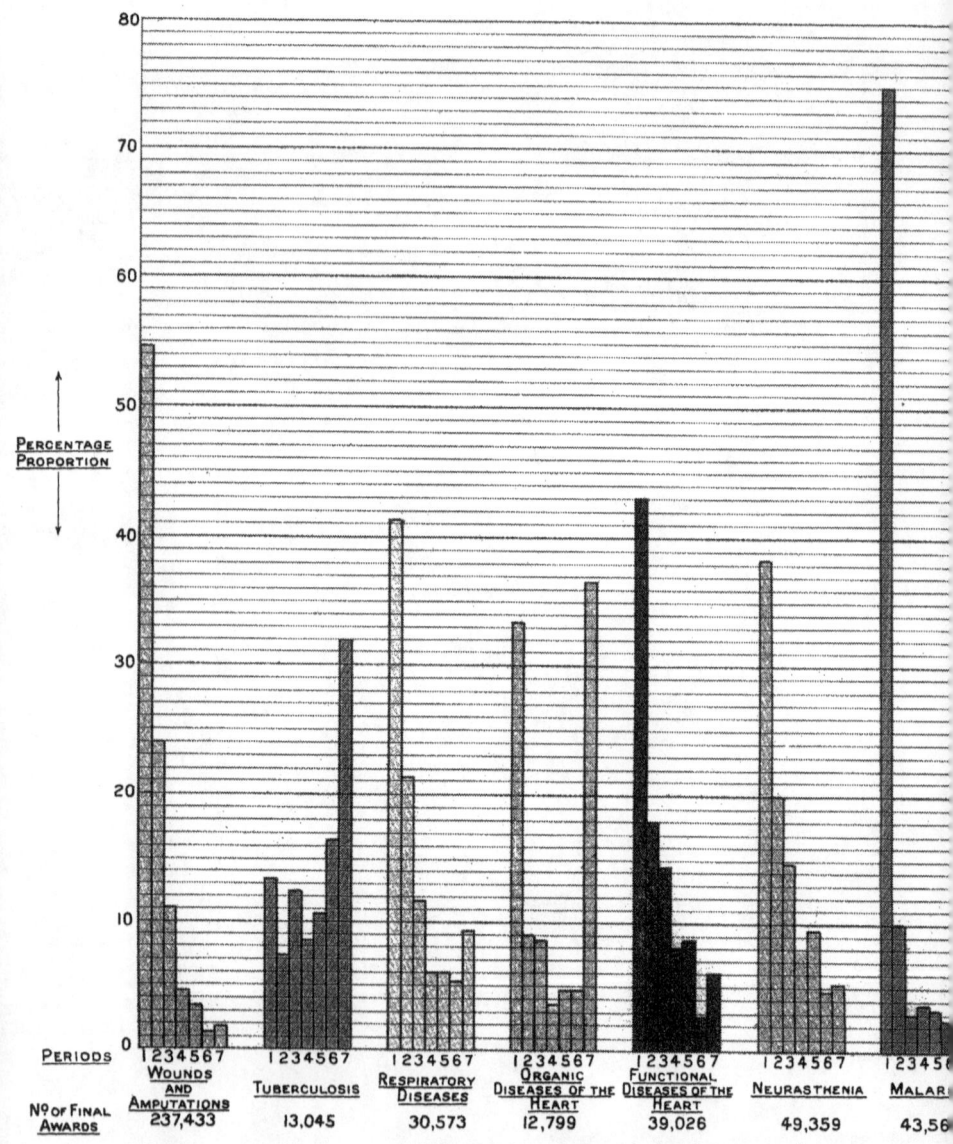

FIG. 2.—SHOWING, FOR "FINAL AWARDS" IN CERTA[IN]
GRANTED UP TO 31:5:1923 AND SUBSE[QUENT]
(COMPAR[ISON])

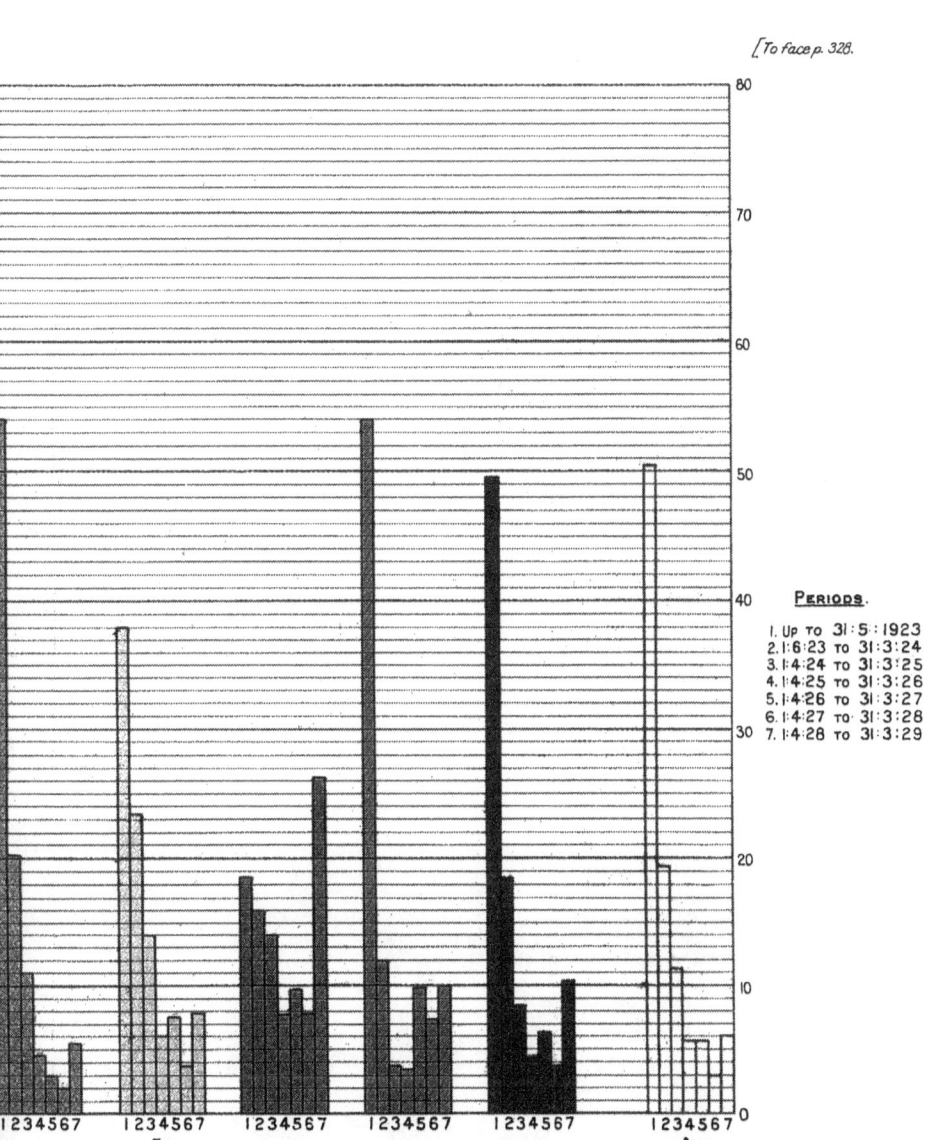

[To face p. 328.

SABILITIES, THE PERCENTAGE PROPORTION
ENTLY FOR EACH YEAR UP TO 31:3:1929.
ABLE 13.)

MINISTRY OF PENSIONS MEDICAL REVIEW 329

TABLE 14.—Analysis of the Stabilised Awards given in Table 6, showing the Distribution in Assessment Groups at 31st March, 1929

Disability	Assessments			Total
	70–100 per cent.	40–60 per cent.	30 per cent. and under	
Wounds:				
Complete blindness	794	—	—	794
Head	3,771	4,643	9,695	18,109
Face	1,840	5,541	6,749	14,130
Neck	266	475	2,149	2,890
Chest	498	1,795	9,198	11,491
Abdomen	181	680	3,626	4,487
Perineum	134	277	1,152	1,563
Back	621	893	7,549	9,063
Upper extremities (not amputation)	2,715	23,285	68,716	94,716
Lower extremities (not amputation)	1,660	10,334	67,474	79,468
Fracture of femur	756	2,163	3,171	6,090
Multiple	412	872	4,166	5,450
Amputations:				
Amputation of one upper extremity	5,397	3,656	21	9,074
Amputation of both upper extremities	45	1	—	46
Other amputations of upper extremities	244	1,745	4,512	6,501
Amputation of one lower extremity	9,229	13,643	15	22,887
Amputation of both lower extremities	925	13	2	940
Other amputations of lower extremities	108	416	1,001	1,525
Amputation of one upper and one lower extremity	139	9	12	160
Other multiple amputations	27	13	35	75
Total	29,762	70,454	189,243	289,459
Diseases:				
Dysentery	37	130	5,852	6,019
Enteric	5	6	211	222
Malaria	43	155	42,999	43,197
Trench fever	4	12	2,038	2,054
Rheumatism	364	1,022	25,030	26,416
Pulmonary tuberculosis	4,686	1,321	3,432	9,439
Tuberculosis not pulmonary	464	400	1,066	1,930
Affections of the respiratory system	2,058	3,499	23,275	28,832
Organic diseases of the heart	2,361	3,094	6,250	11,705
Functional diseases of the heart	102	818	37,447	38,367
Nephritis	200	443	6,821	7,464
Gastric ulcer	62	322	1,886	2,270
Appendicitis	10	45	989	1,044
Other diseases of the alimentary system	96	389	6,396	6,881
Hernia	37	123	4,045	4,205
Neurasthenia	1,535	3,346	42,788	47,669
Epilepsy	563	402	1,625	2,590
Tabes dorsalis	270	96	179	545
Other organic nervous diseases	1,191	432	1,127	2,750
Psychoses	1,992	656	1,515	4,163
Diseases of the eye resulting in complete blindness	123	—	1	124
Other diseases of the eye	1,167	3,492	2,547	7,206
Diseases of the ear	619	3,154	15,573	19,346
Debility	48	208	12,200	12,456
Diabetes	73	13	71	157
Flat foot	6	55	1,846	1,907
Frost bite	45	294	2,352	2,691
Gas poisoning	67	115	6,535	6,717
Miscellaneous	425	866	8,200	9,491
Diseases of the veins	47	283	6,236	6,566
Diseases of the joints	713	969	4,176	5,858
Arteriosclerosis	137	70	202	409
Bilharziasis	1	1	9	11
Loss of eye	1,782	7,360	4	9,146
Not recorded	1	16	2,650	2,666
Total	21,324	33,635	277,554	332,513
Grand Total	51,086	104,089	466,797	621,972

general, it may be said that the conditions slow in manifestation are also slow in stabilisation, whilst those conspicuous at the outset are, for the most part, quickly stabilised.

The comparative severity of disablement amongst stabilised conditions.—Having surveyed stabilised conditions as a whole, and according to their rate of stabilisation, it is of interest to consider the degrees of disablement they include. For this purpose the group of stabilised awards, given in detail in Table 6, has been divided according to certain assessment groups. The assessment of pension is based, as previously stated, on the extent to which war service has reduced the individual below the standard of a normal healthy man of the same age. This degree of disablement is expressed in percentages and graded by steps, each of 10 per cent. For the purpose of this analysis the assessments have been grouped into (a) 70–100 per cent.; (b) 40–60 per cent.; and (c) 30 per cent. and under, thus indicating three main grades of severity in the total range.

Table 14 shows the stabilised awards of Table 6 divided according to these assessment groups, whilst, for the readier comprehension of its details, Table 15 extracts the conspicuous disabilities therein and shows their percentage distribution in each assessment group.

TABLE 15.—Analysis of the Stabilised Awards, given in Table 6, to show the Percentage Distribution of the Conspicuous Disabilities in each Assessment Group at 31st March, 1929

Disability	Percentage distribution in assessment group			Percentage of all assessments
	70–100 per cent.	40–60 per cent.	30 per cent. and under	
Wounds and amputations	58·2	67·5	40·5	46·5
Tuberculosis	10·1	1·7	1·0	1·8
Respiratory diseases	4·3	3·4	5·0	4·6
Organic diseases of the heart	4·6	3·0	1·3	1·9
Functional diseases of the heart	—	—	8·0	6·2
Neurasthenia	3·0	3·2	9·2	7·2
Malaria	—	—	9·2	6·9
Rheumatism	—	1·0	5·4	4·3
Ear diseases	1·2	3·0	3·3	3·1
Psychoses	3·9	—	—	—
Dysentery	—	—	1·3	1·0
Nephritis	—	—	1·5	1·2
Percentage * of total disabilities comprised in the above conditions	85·3	81·8	80·3	84·7
Total of all disabilities	51,086	104,089	466,797	621,972

* Percentages less than 1 per cent. are not recorded.

[To face p. 331.]

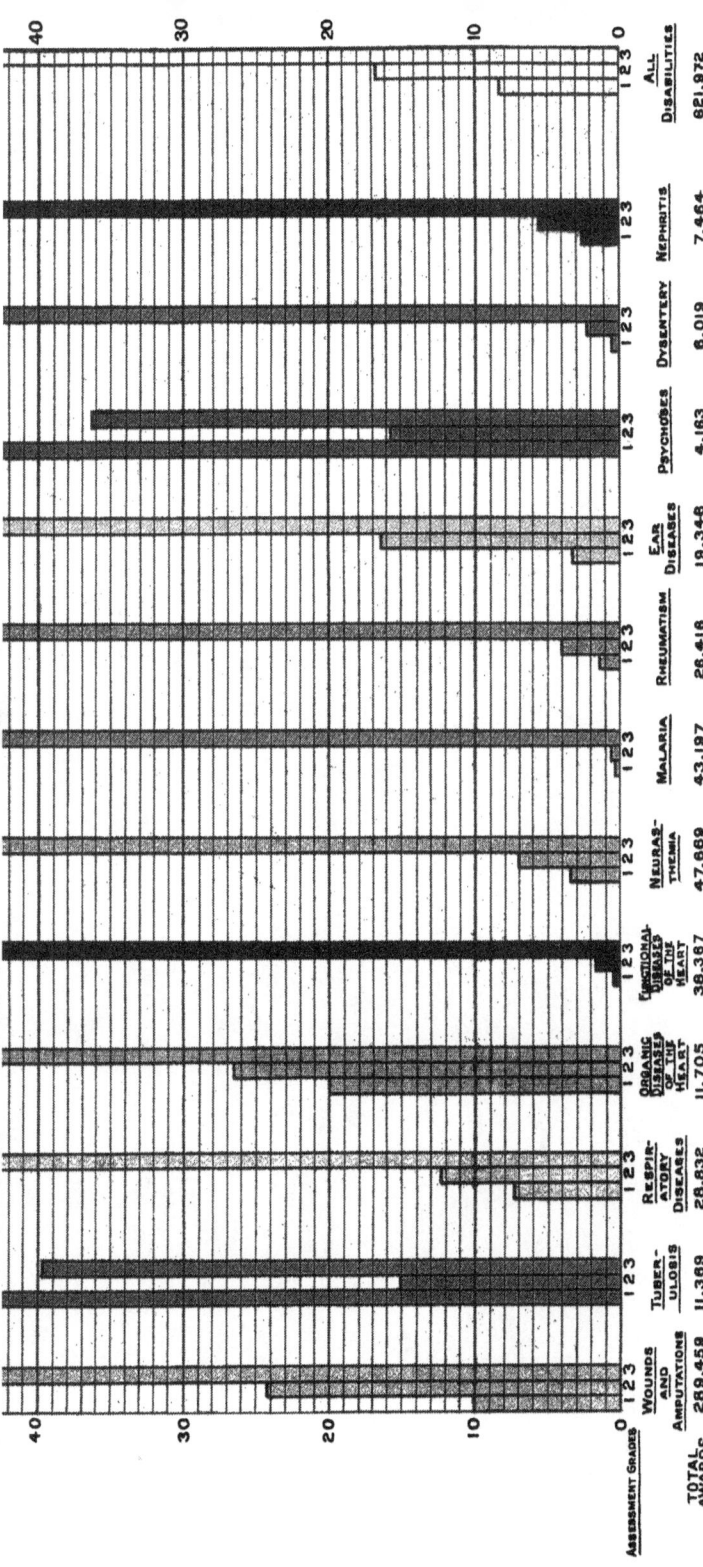

FIG. 3.—SHOWING FOR STABILISED AWARDS, THE PERCENTAGE PROPORTIONS IN WHICH AT 31:3:29 CERTAIN DISABILITIES FELL INTO THE ASSESSMENT GRADES. (COMPARE TABLE 16.)

ASSESSMENT GRADES.— 1 = 70 – 100 %
2 = 40 – 60 %
3 = 30 % and under.

It is apparent that wounds and amputations make up a fairly constant proportion of each assessment group, whereas tuberculosis and psychoses fall noticeably into the "70-100 per cent." group. Malaria, functional diseases of the heart, neurasthenia and rheumatism appear most prominently in the total of the "30 per cent. and under" category.

To represent the essential facts from another angle, Table 16 analyses each disability into the proportions in which its total numbers fall into the three assessment groups. Fig. 3 expresses this table graphically.

TABLE 16.—Analysis of the Stabilised Awards, given in Table 6, to show the Distribution of the Grades of Assessment in the Conspicuous Disabilities at 31st March, 1929

(*See also* Fig. 3)

Disability	Total numbers	Percentage distribution in assessment group			Percentage
		70–100 per cent.	40–60 per cent.	30 per cent. and under	
Wounds and amputations	289,459	10·2	24·3	65·5	100·0
Tuberculosis	11,369	45·3	15·1	39·6	100·0
Respiratory diseases	28,832	7·2	12·2	81·6	100·0
Organic diseases of the heart	11,705	20·1	26·4	53·5	100·0
Functional diseases of the heart	38,367	·3	1·7	98·0	100·0
Neurasthenia	47,669	3·2	7·1	89·7	100·0
Malaria	43,197	·1	·4	99·5	100·0
Rheumatism	26,416	1·3	3·9	94·8	100·0
Ear diseases	19,346	3·2	16·3	80·5	100·0
Psychoses	4,163	48·0	15·6	36·4	100·0
Dysentery	6,019	·6	2·2	97·2	100·0
Nephritis	7,464	2·7	5·6	91·7	100·0
All disabilities	621,972	8·2	16·8	75·0	100·0
Total of all disabilities	621,972	51,086	104,089	466,797	

The table and diagram show that the stabilisation of functional diseases of the heart, neurasthenia, malaria, rheumatism, dysentery and nephritis have been to the extent of 90 per cent. or over, in the assessment grade "30 per cent. and under," and it will be remembered that functional diseases of the heart, neurasthenia and malaria bulk largely in the total of stabilised awards. Tuberculosis, organic diseases of the heart and psychoses are conspicuous by their large proportion in the "70-100 per cent." group.

It may be said, generally, that amongst the diseases the quickly manifest and more speedily stabilised are also those with the least degree of disablement.

TABLE 17.—Unstabilised Pensions in payment at 31st March, 1929, classified by Disability and Assessment

Disability	Assessment		
	70-100 per cent.	40-60 per cent.	20-30 per cent.
Wounds:			
Complete blindness	2	—	—
Head	1,677	1,907	600
Face	275	472	213
Neck	65	97	86
Chest	386	1,494	916
Abdomen	95	396	304
Perineum	37	78	62
Back	243	450	288
Upper extremities (not amputation)	344	1,219	932
Lower extremities (not amputation)	402	2,062	2,311
Fracture of femur	218	537	128
Multiple	23	40	19
Total	*3,767*	*8,652*	*5,859*
Amputations:			
Amputation of one upper extremity	75	21	—
Amputation of both upper extremities	1	—	—
Other amputations of upper extremities	21	63	50
Amputation of one lower extremity	301	122	—
Amputation of both lower extremities	7	—	—
Other amputations of lower extremities	10	36	23
Amputation of one upper and one lower extremity	9	—	—
Other multiple amputations	—	—	—
Total	*424*	*242*	*73*
Diseases:			
Dysentery	49	310	647
Enteric	1	7	10
Malaria	43	165	344
Trench fever	1	30	79
Rheumatism	219	850	1,482
Pulmonary tuberculosis	7,782	8,701	5,799
Tuberculosis not pulmonary	464	434	316
Affections of the respiratory system	2,042	7,176	6,062
Organic diseases of the heart	2,360	5,442	2,192
Functional diseases of the heart	88	1,210	3,258
Nephritis	368	1,901	2,988
Gastric ulcer	80	361	300
Appendicitis	6	28	89
Other diseases of the alimentary system	96	416	736
Hernia	18	106	215
Neurasthenia	1,343	3,497	2,934
Epilepsy	393	572	317
Tabes dorsalis	102	110	34
Other organic nervous diseases	441	295	140
Psychoses	5,951	1,391	863
Diseases of the eye resulting in complete blindness	3	—	—
Other diseases of the eye	566	524	236
Diseases of the ear	142	1,282	1,549
Debility	29	149	345
Diabetes	59	52	12
Flat foot	—	24	38
Frost bite	5	42	68
Gas poisoning	61	323	315
Miscellaneous	294	625	723
Diseases of the veins	48	264	594
Diseases of the joints	371	742	617
Arteriosclerosis	77	34	14
Bilharziasis	—	—	2
Loss of eye	157	50	—
Not recorded	—	—	—
Total	*23,659*	*37,113*	*33,318*
Grand Total	**27,850**	**46,007**	**39,250**

NOTE.—408 unstabilised pensions at less than 20 per cent. have not been included and hence the grand total of this table is by so much less than that of Table 7.

The war disablement which remains unstabilised.—A general view has now been given of the extent to which war disablement has become stabilised. There remains the group of pensioners, numbering approximately 113,000, in which, up to 31st March, 1929, the condition of the disability was still so uncertain in prognosis, whether of improvement or otherwise, as to make it impracticable to finalise the current compensation.

The numbers of the disabilities in this group have been given in detail in Table 7.

Table 17 classifies the totals into assessment groups in the same way as the stabilised awards were analysed, except that, as current pensions for unstabilised conditions are, subject to a negligible exception, assessed at 20 per cent. or more, the third assessment group contains assessments only of 20 per cent. or 30 per cent. and is not, as in the third assessment group of Tables 14, 15 and 16, inclusive of assessments of less than 20 per cent.

Here again, for simplicity of exposition, the conspicuous disabilities have been extracted, and Table 18 shows their percentage incidence in each assessment group as well as their incidence in the unstabilised awards as a whole.

TABLE 18.—Percentage Distribution of the Conspicuous Disabilities in the Total of Unstabilised Pensions and in each Assessment Group at 31st March, 1929

Disability	Percentage distribution in assessment group			Percentage of all assessments
	70–100 per cent.	40–60 per cent.	30 and 20 per cent.	
Wounds and amputations	15·1	19·5	15·2	16·3
Tuberculosis	29·6	19·8	15·6	20·7
Respiratory diseases	7·3	15·6	15·4	13·5
Organic diseases of the heart	8·5	11·8	5·6	8·8
Functional diseases of the heart	—	2·6	8·3	4·0
Neurasthenia	4·4	7·6	7·5	6·9
Malaria	—	—	—	—
Rheumatism	—	1·8	3·8	2·3
Ear diseases	—	2·8	3·9	2·6
Psychoses	21·4	3·0	2·2	7·3
Dysentery	—	—	1·6	·8
Nephritis	1·3	4·1	7·6	4·7
Percentage * of total disabilities comprised in the above conditions	87·6	88·6	86·7	87·9
Total of all disabilities	27,850	46,107	39,250	113,207

* Percentages of less than 1 per cent. are not recorded.

In this way it is seen that, in contrast to stabilised awards, wounds and amputations are now relatively small in their proportion of the total. Tuberculosis, respiratory diseases, organic diseases of the heart and psychoses, however, bulk largely and constitute the major proportion of continuing unstabilised conditions. These conditions also constitute more than half of the " 70-100 per cent." group.

This table should be compared with Table 15, the equivalent one for stabilised awards.

Following the method of simplified analysis adopted for stabilised awards, Table 19 and Fig. 4 show the distribution of the assessment groups in each of the conspicuous disabilities, and may be compared with Table 16 and Fig. 3, the corresponding ones for stabilised awards. It is seen that about half of the remaining unstabilised wounds, respiratory diseases and organic diseases of the heart fall in the middle grades of assessment, whereas tuberculosis is more evenly distributed. Functional diseases of the heart and malaria, which comprise only 4 per cent. and 5 per cent. of the total unstabilised awards, have a negligible percentage in the 70–100 per cent. group and are mainly in the " 20–30 per cent. " grade.

TABLE 19.—Distribution of the Grades of Assessment in the Conspicuous Disabilities amongst Unstabilised Pensions at 31st March, 1929
(*See also* Fig. 4)

Disability	Total number	Percentage distribution in assessment group			Total percentage
		70–100 per cent.	40–60 per cent.	30 and 20 per cent.	
Wounds and amputations	19,163	21·9	47·0	31·1	100·0
Tuberculosis	23,515	35·2	38·8	26·0	100·0
Respiratory diseases	15,311	13·4	47·0	39·6	100·0
Organic diseases of the heart	10,001	23·6	54·4	22·0	100·0
Functional diseases of the heart	4,581	1·6	27·4	71·0	100·0
Neurasthenia	7,800	17·3	44·8	37·9	100·0
Malaria	572	1·0	28·9	70·1	100·0
Rheumatism	2,567	8·5	33·0	58·5	100·0
Ear diseases	2,987	4·8	43·0	52·2	100·0
Psychoses	8,208	71·3	16·9	11·8	100·0
Dysentery	1,021	4·9	30·4	64·7	100·0
Nephritis	5,265	7·0	36·0	57·0	100·0
All disabilities	113,207	24·6	40·9	34·5	100·0

Thus, in so far as the diseases prominent in the stabilised awards appear amongst unstabilised awards, they fall chiefly in the lower degrees of assessment, and, conversely, those conditions which are relatively few in the stabilised awards appear amongst unstabilised awards mainly in the higher grades of assessment.

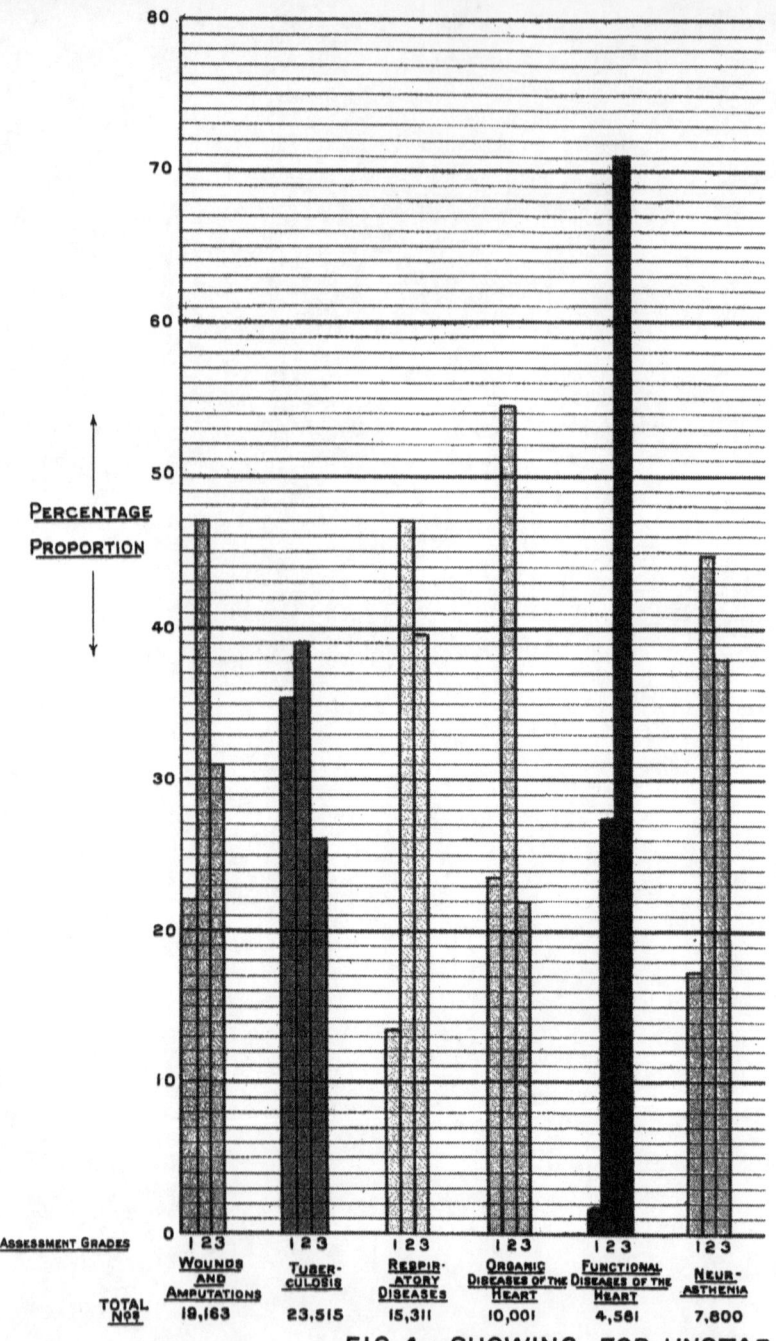

FIG. 4.— SHOWING, FOR UNSTAB
OF THE GRADES OF ASSE
(COMPARE

ASSESSMENT

	1 2 3	1 2 3	1 2 3	1 2 3	1 2 3	1 2 3	1 2 3
	MALARIA	RHEUM-ATISM	EAR DISEASES	PSYCHOSES	DYSENTERY	NEPHRITIS	ALL DISABILITIES
	572	2,567	2,987	8,208	1,021	5,265	113,207

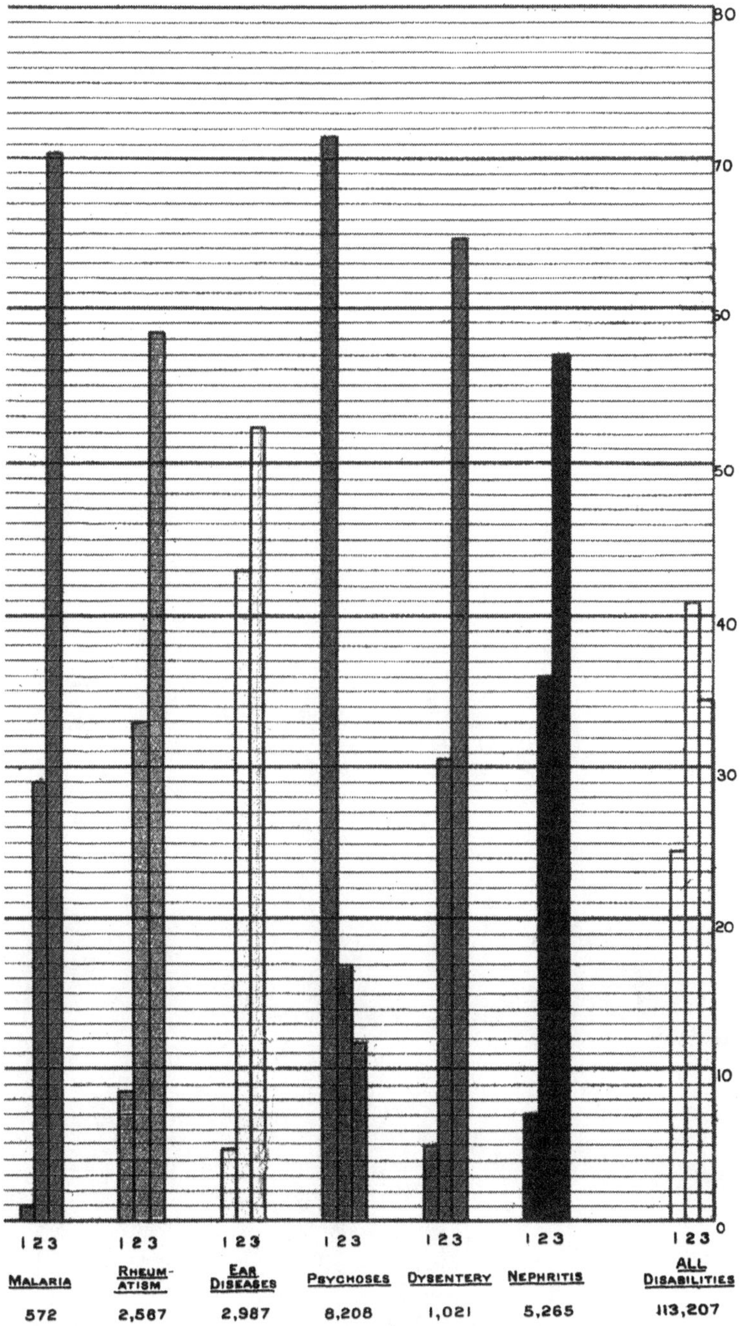

ILISED AWARDS, THE DISTRIBUTION AT 31:3:29
SSMENT IN CERTAIN DISABILITIES.
TABLE 19.)

GRADES — 1 = 70–100 %
2 = 40–60 %
3 = 20% & 30%.

MINISTRY OF PENSIONS MEDICAL REVIEW 335

TABLE 20.—Annual Discharges from Institutional Treatment (In-patient and Out-patient) for the period 1st April, 1919, to 31st March, 1929

Disabilities	Financial Year, 1st April to 31st March										Whole Period
	1919–20	1920–21	1921–22	1922–23	1923–24	1924–25	1925–26	1926–27	1927–28	1928–29	
General surgical	66,800	98,640	86,785	78,883	51,665	36,538	28,213	22,254	15,849	11,493	497,120
Aural	6,676	9,865	8,678	8,619	5,708	4,839	4,668	3,041	1,601	938	54,633
Ophthalmic	2,700	3,978	3,400	3,675	1,965	1,735	1,544	1,153	782	571	21,503
General medical	57,500	84,800	74,600	59,045	32,468	26,130	21,251	14,150	10,360	6,286	386,590
Neurasthenia	8,459	17,128	22,679	21,533	13,964	11,452	8,584	4,857	3,284	2,032	113,972
Tuberculosis	17,116	24,446	22,222	22,223	15,001	10,292	7,467	4,520	3,401	2,972	129,660
Dysentery	770	3,305	4,315	4,055	2,578	2,144	1,644	989	577	445	20,822
Malaria and other tropical	5,336	22,796	31,154	19,572	6,499	3,146	1,545	562	315	182	91,107
Paraplegic	552	727	632	570	296	173	223	169	101	88	3,531
Epileptic	1,064	2,102	2,173	2,381	1,613	1,165	821	576	374	279	12,548
Totals	166,973	267,787	256,638	220,556	131,757	97,614	75,960	52,271	36,644	25,286	1,331,486

NOTES

1. The total discharges from treatment prior to 1.4.19 were 80,920.
2. Up to 1923 the general medical, general surgical, aural and ophthalmic cases were statistically amalgamated. The totals given in this table for those conditions for the years 1919–20, 1920–21, 1921–22 are estimated proportions of the grand total of general medical and surgical.
3. Convalescent treatment, treatment and training and limb-fitting are not included. They amount to approximately 31,000, 15,500 and 28,000 respectively.

Some Outstanding Features in the Treatment of War Disablement

The main necessities of treatment, and the general provision made for in-patient, out-patient and home treatment, have already been described, while Tables 2 and 3 give general statistics of this provision.

Table 20 shows in detail, year by year, the discharges from institutional treatment, both in-patient and out-patient, during the period 1919 to 1929. A good general idea is thus obtained of the nature and extent of the institutional provision, supplementing the summary statements of Tables 2 and 3.

From Table 20 it is apparent that the totals of men treated varied considerably year by year and according to the disabilities. These variations are more readily appreciated in Table 21 where the percentage proportions are given of each disability in the total discharges for each year.

It will be noted that " general surgical " tends to increase in proportion towards the end of the period, whilst " general medical " on the whole declines. These variations stress the importance of surgical conditions as a continuing cause of institutional provision. Tuberculosis remains very level in proportion. Dysentery and epilepsy increase somewhat; malaria soon diminishes to a small fraction, whilst neurasthenia shows a definite " peak " in the middle years.

Table 22 shows the proportion of the total discharges for each disability which fell in each year. It shows, from another angle, the rise and fall in neurasthenia, the elimination of malaria and the persistence of " general surgical " as compared with " general medical." The years 1920–21, 1921–22 and 1922–23 appear as the " peak " years for all disabilities.

These tables emphasise the magnitude of the provision made by the Ministry of Pensions for institutional treatment. It is to be remembered that when an award of pension becomes stabilised the pensioner does not, *ipso facto*, cease to be eligible for treatment, and thus the progressive stabilisation of awards did not produce an equivalent diminution in the need for treatment provision.

From this general statement of treatment provision, it is of interest to pass to some of the outstanding points in the specific treatment of particular disabilities.

Wounds and injuries.—As was to be expected, an enormous number of these cases required hospital provision, especially in the early days of the Ministry's work, and special surgical

TABLE 21.—Showing, for Table 20, the Percentage Proportion of each Disability in the total Discharges of each Financial Year

Disabilities	Financial Year										Whole Period
	1919–20	1920–21	1921–22	1922–23	1923–24	1924–25	1925–26	1926–27	1927–28	1928–29	
General surgical	40·0	36·8	33·9	35·7	39·2	37·3	36·8	42·7	43·2	45·5	37·5
Aural	4·0	3·7	3·3	3·9	4·3	4·8	6·1	5·8	4·4	3·7	4·1
Ophthalmic	1·6	1·5	1·3	1·7	1·5	1·8	2·2	2·2	2·1	2·2	1·6
General medical	34·4	31·6	29·1	26·8	24·7	26·7	28·0	27·1	28·2	24·7	29·0
Neurasthenia	5·1	6·4	8·8	9·7	10·6	11·6	11·3	9·3	9·0	8·2	8·6
Tuberculosis	10·3	9·1	8·7	10·1	11·4	10·4	9·8	8·6	9·3	11·7	9·6
Dysentery	·5	1·2	1·7	1·8	2·0	2·2	2·2	1·8	1·6	1·8	1·6
Malaria and other tropical	3·2	8·5	12·2	8·9	4·9	3·2	2·2	1·1	·9	·7	6·8
Paraplegic	·3	·4	·2	·3	·2	·8	·3	·3	·3	·3	·3
Epileptic	·6	·8	·8	1·1	1·2	1·2	1·1	1·1	1·0	1·2	·9
Total of percentages	100·0	100·0	100·0	100·0	100·0	100·0	100·0	100·0	100·0	100·0	100·0
Total discharges in each year	166,973	267,787	256,638	220,556	131,757	97,614	75,960	52,271	36,644	25,286	1,331,486

TABLE 22.—Showing, for Table 20, the Percentage Proportion of the Total Discharges for each Disability which fell in each Financial Year

Disabilities	Financial year											Total percentages	Total discharges in period
	1919–20	1920–21	1921–22	1922–23	1923–24	1924–25	1925–26	1926–27	1927–28	1928–29		
General surgical	13·4	19·8	17·5	15·8	10·4	7·3	5·7	4·5	3·2	2·3	100·0	497,120
Aural	12·2	18·1	15·9	15·8	10·5	8·8	8·5	5·6	2·9	1·7	100·0	54,633
Ophthalmic	12·6	18·5	15·8	17·1	9·1	8·1	7·1	5·4	3·6	2·7	100·0	21,503
General medical	14·9	21·9	19·4	15·3	8·4	6·7	5·5	3·7	2·7	1·5	100·0	386,590
Neurasthenia	7·4	15·0	19·9	18·9	12·3	10·0	7·6	4·3	2·9	1·7	100·0	113,972
Tuberculosis	13·2	18·8	17·1	17·1	11·6	7·9	5·9	3·5	2·6	2·3	100·0	129,660
Dysentery	3·7	15·9	20·6	19·4	12·4	10·5	7·9	4·8	2·7	2·1	100·0	20,822
Malaria and other tropical	5·9	25·0	34·2	21·5	7·1	3·5	1·7	·6	·3	·2	100·0	91,107
Paraplegic	15·6	20·6	17·9	15·9	8·4	4·9	6·3	4·8	2·9	2·5	100·0	3,531
Epileptic	8·5	16·8	17·3	19·0	12·8	9·3	6·5	4·6	3·0	2·2	100·0	12,548
All disabilities	12·5	20·2	19·3	16·5	9·9	7·3	5·7	4·0	2·7	1·9	100·0	1,331,486

hospitals were needed on an extensive scale. A Ministry Massage Service was established in January, 1920, and specialised gymnastics were also arranged.

The treatment of penetrating wounds of the skull and brain was greatly advanced, and, following specialised operations, many cases gained a surprising degree of physical and mental fitness. Gun-shot wounds of the chest, often with retained foreign bodies, were also treated with success. In general, for those wounds in which there was a retained foreign body, the accepted opinion at the outset was against surgical interference if the wound appeared to be soundly healed. It became specially noticeable, however, with the progress of time, that in a large number of these cases, after varying intervals, the wound flared up suddenly into serious activity necessitating operation, often of an extensive character. For this reason the need for the provision of surgical treatment did not diminish at the rate which had been expected.

Some idea of the extent of the work of the Ministry's special surgical hospitals will be gleaned from the fact that in one hospital alone, from 1st August, 1919, to its closure in March, 1925, 771 officers and 22,641 other ranks were dealt with as surgical in-patients.

Limbs and appliances.—Table 23 shows the extent of the supply of artificial limbs and appliances made by the Ministry. The limbs provided have been of an increasingly efficient type and the Ministry has been a pioneer in their improvement. A duplicate limb has been provided for all cases. It will be seen that, in addition to artificial limbs, surgical boots and other surgical appliances, artificial eyes, spectacles, hand-propelled tricycles and invalid chairs have been issued in large numbers.

TABLE 23.—Issue of Artificial Limbs and Surgical Appliances by the Ministry of Pensions, 1920 to 1929

Financial year ending 31st March	Artificial limbs		Surgical boots	Other appliances	Tricycles	Invalid chairs	Artificial eyes	Spectacles	Totals in year
	Legs	Arms							
1920	15,621	3,546	10,000*	10,000*	1,195		6,000*	18,000*	64,362
1921	15,391	4,746	12,000*	11,000*	751		8,396	9,569	61,853
1922	9,469	3,937	14,078	12,949	568		4,000	3,000	48,001
1923	7,589	1,230	17,758	13,520	303	129	6,217	1,197	47,943
1924	9,255	1,201	18,521	13,184	285	137	3,370	798	46,751
1925	11,102	1,289	18,470	16,053	347	192	4,707	733	52,893
1926	10,058	1,169	18,388	15,476	294	189	4,881	564	51,019
1927	7,674	1,080	17,100	12,469	290	168	4,687	509	43,977
1928	5,205	1,106	17,249	12,323	223	138	4,574	354	41,172
1929	3,837	775	16,469	11,386	171	86	4,510	340	37,574
Totals	95,201	20,079	160,033	128,360	5,466		51,342	35,064	495,545

* Estimated figures, as precise records are not available

Tuberculosis.—Treatment for tuberculosis is a normal provision in the schemes of local Health Authorities as approved by the Ministry of Health, and this provision was utilised for the treatment of those pensioned for tuberculosis. The Ministry has, however, as and when required, supplemented these existing schemes, as, for example, by (*a*) arrangements with sanatoria for the treatment of officers and nurses; (*b*) arrangements for the treatment of surgical tuberculosis, including the installation in its own hospitals of full facilities for artificial light therapy ; (*c*) facilities for the observation and diagnosis of conditions alleged to be tuberculous. For some years the Ministry kept some 200 beds in its own hospitals continuously occupied with such cases, and the observation work therein undertaken was unique, both in scale and comprehensiveness ; * (*d*) special arrangements for treatment abroad ; (*e*) vocational training, for which, in conjunction with the Ministry of Health, extensive provision was made.

Mental diseases.—Responsibility for the care of the certified insane is governed by the Lunacy Acts, and the cases of ex-service men were dealt with accordingly.† The Ministry, however, made arrangements early in its history under which ex-service men suffering from certifiable mental disease due to or hastened by their war service were received into County and County Borough Mental Hospitals under the classification of " service patients " by which they enjoyed certain special privileges, including the legal status of private patients. A close liaison was established with the Board of Control, and arrangements made for the regular examination by Ministry specialists of all pensioners in mental hospitals. Although no mental hospitals were established for pensioners alone, special arrangements were made with two public mental hospitals for the allocation of separate wings for the exclusive use of service patients, carefully selected from those with hopeful prognosis and whose mental state permitted of their appreciating the advantages of the greater freedom and the enjoyment of the special amenities which it was the object of these wings to supply. Arrangements were also made whereby service patients fit for discharge from mental institutions, or to be allowed out " on trial," were received into Ministry of Pensions hospitals for a short stay, in order to re-accustom them to full liberty and thereby to minimise the difficulties inherent in a sudden return to ordinary civil life.

---

* An account was published in *The Lancet*, 1924, (i), 1195.
† The number has amounted to approximately 6,000.

Neurasthenia and like conditions.—The diagnosis and treatment of cases of neurosis and psychosis needed much time, skill and patience. In their more acute forms these conditions presented many novel features, and amidst the various theories and therapeutic suggestions it was difficult at the outset to decide on the most effective form of treatment. Indeed, treatment had often to be largely empirical. A relatively small group soon emerged in which the existing neurosis was shown to be but a reflection from a generalised or local organic condition, such as heart disease or gunshot wound, and for these the treatment was directed to the underlying organic cause.

For most of the cases comprised in the general group " neurasthenia " it was clear that the prognosis and the nature of the treatment required would mainly depend on the inherent predisposition to neurosis, apart from the factor of war stress.

In cases of true " war " neuroses (*i.e.*, those manifested in men with a minimal predisposition), the symptoms rapidly disappeared on the cessation of exposure to war conditions. In cases of neurosis occurring in men with a fairly well-marked predisposition, the subsequent progress depended largely on the environment and conditions to which the men were afterwards subjected. If the circumstances were favourable, and the men were able to obtain suitable employment, they lost all their symptoms, but if the circumstances were not favourable the condition was perpetuated and the men remained amongst those for whom the Ministry had to provide facilities for special treatment. In the more severe cases of neurosis, occurring in men with a pronounced predisposition, improvement only occurred when the environment was made exceptionally favourable. For the most part these men could not in any case have made a successful adaptation to the conditions of post-war life, and there can be little doubt that, even if there had been no war, these men would sooner or later, and from one cause or another, have been likely to break down under the stress of everyday life.

The Ministry's general scheme of treatment from the early days included the establishment of a number of neurological clinics, where men attended as out-patients, and a number of neurological institutions into which they were received as in-patients. One of the main functions of the clinic was to examine the men in order to determine what form of treatment, if any, was indicated. In addition, it was often found practicable for the necessary treatment to be undertaken at the clinic itself, by way of psychotherapy, gymnasia, and so on. This was specially advantageous, by comparison with admission to an institution, if the man was in employment, because it did not necessitate his relinquishing his work. Moreover, the fact of the man having work to go to helped the clinic specialists in their efforts to inspire the man with resolution, and sustain him in his doubts and hesitations, until self-reliance was restored.

In the more severe cases, where it was clear that the man was completely failing to adapt himself to civil life conditions, and was either unable to obtain employment or to continue in it when obtained, it was usually found necessary to remove him, at any rate for a time, from home environment and to provide the necessary treatment in the sheltered conditions of institutional life.

As time went on, the character of treatment had to undergo a change. Cases which psychotherapy was capable of restoring had ceased to need treatment, and other means than psychotherapy had to be adopted for cases in which that method had been thoroughly tried without success, and for those for which it had never been appropriate. It was soon found by experience that men who had not been restored by active treatment did nevertheless derive great benefit from unobtrusive but continuous medical supervision and discipline under the sheltered conditions of hospital life, and more especially from occupational treatment. Gradually, therefore, the need for neurological clinics began to disappear, and at the same time the character of the Ministry neurological hospitals underwent a change. The facilities for occupational treatment were extended, and reliance was placed more and more upon keeping the man steadily employed at some interesting form of occupation, thus helping to " take him out of himself," and encourage the regrowth of concentration, application and self-reliance.

The ordinary neurological institution was for men deemed to be capable of a large measure of self-control. It was, however, only possible to conduct institutions of this type in safety for so long as the means existed for the removal of relapsed cases, often urgently, to a hospital specially maintained for the treatment, observation and supervision of cases of the more extreme character, such as cases incapable of self-management but not so severe as to require certification; cases violent or erratic in behaviour, but capable of some self-control while under fairly constant supervision; or men with a-social habits. A special institution at Cosham, near Portsmouth, has been continuously maintained by the Ministry for this type of case.

While, in all the Ministry's neurological institutions, occupational treatment was the main standby, medical and psychological training and knowledge were in constant demand in dealing with the patients. This was especially so in the more severe cases, in which aches and pains that are merely imaginary, and ailments and physical disturbances that are real but of the most trivial nature, all assume in the mind of the patient an alarming significance, or an interesting importance, and cause him to ask for medical attention. The man's fears had to be allayed, and this could be done only by giving him a patient hearing and then a careful and reasoned explanation of the facts and of the needlessness of his alarms. The patient with suicidal or homicidal tendencies, and the chronic alcoholic were much less open to persuasion and more difficult to influence. Periodic segregation and close supervision were essential during their more uncontrollable outbursts, but every endeavour was made to avoid the need for certification under the Lunacy Acts, and this was only resorted to where experience had shown that the patient was so unmanageable that frequent or constant restraint was the only method of dealing with him.

Epilepsy.—The primary difficulty here was accurate diagnosis. A hospital of 300 beds was for a long period devoted to the investigation of cases of reputed epilepsy, with the result that many cases that had been labelled " epileptic " on discharge from the service proved to be suffering from other conditions, or some functional disorder. The treatment of the true cases was also undertaken at this hospital, as well as at various existing epileptic colonies.

Facial wounds.—The work done under the ægis of the Ministry at the Queen's Hospital, Sidcup, in the plastic treatment of facial wounds, is well known and justly famous. As an indication of the extent of the work of this nature, done after the immediate emergencies had been met, it may be noted that from March, 1920, to April, 1925, 2,944 facial operations were performed, of which 1,156 were cases of specialised jaw and dental work.

Diabetes.—Relatively few ex-service men were pensioned for diabetes, but, for those who were, a special hospital ward was maintained by the Ministry in connection with the provision of treatment by insulin. In this special ward the appropriate dietary and insulin dosage of each patient were determined, and the man was not discharged until he had been fully instructed in this respect and trained to administer insulin himself in case of need.

Tropical diseases.—Malaria was treated by intensive methods and soon became effectively extinguished in any active form. Great success followed the treatment of bilharziasis by antimony tartrate, and many patients who had suffered from this disease as a legacy of the South African War also had this condition cleared up by this means.

Eye and ear diseases.—In the case of the blind a close liaison was maintained with St. Dunstan's in London and its sister organisation, Newington House, in Scotland. For cases of deafness special classes were established for the purpose of providing instruction in lip-reading, in which many men obtained remarkable proficiency.

Dental defects.—Those conditions attributable to war service, or closely connected with the pensioned disabilities, were remedied on an extensive scale. For this purpose the services of dental surgeons engaged in private practice were used, a number of whole-time dental surgeons being appointed by the Ministry for supervisory duties.

Hospitals and clinics.—The " peak " period of the Ministry's treatment activities was the twelve months ended 31st March, 1921. At that time the number of institutions, including hospitals under the direct control of the Ministry, reserved for in-patient treatment of war disabilities that could not be adequately provided for otherwise was 113, with a total bed accommodation of 18,603. In addition to these facilities, use was made of such accommodation as could be secured in military and civil hospitals throughout the country.

During the same period there were in existence 319 clinics for surgical cases, 48 for neurasthenics, 61 for cases of tropical diseases, 36 for aural cases, 24 for ophthalmic patients and 19 for cardiac cases. In the following year a beginning was made in substituting for these clinics a number of general medical and surgical clinics, each constituting a comprehensive institution for the general co-ordination and control of the functions of the Ministry in the matter of treatment and its certification. These clinics, which at one time numbered 250, worked under the Ministry's direct control, the medical personnel consisting of specialists and local medical men in part-time attendance. Use was also made of the out-patient departments of most of the civil institutions in the country.

Summary

The general work of the Ministry of Pensions, briefly outlined in this chapter, has been shown in three main phases: (1) an initial influx of claims and awards; (2) a gradual stabilisation of both the disability and the award; and (3) the position at 31st March, 1929, when the conditions remaining unstabilised formed but a small proportion of the total awards. During these phases treatment had been provided on a vast scale, diminishing as time went on, but not in any precise ratio to the stabilisation of award.

From the medical point of view it has been possible to trace numerically the various disabilities throughout the decade following the war and, for the more conspicuous conditions, to discover their relative proportions in different classes of award and at successive periods. The classification of disabilities has, however, been of necessity broad, and thus, to a considerable extent, lacking in the precision necessary for detailed clinical deduction. Moreover, the magnitude of the numbers dealt with and the need for the statistical records being primarily directed towards the requirements of efficient general administration, have inevitably blurred the medical outlines of the disability classification. Thus, for example, when two or more disabilities co-exist, only the major one is statistically recorded. The statistics, moreover, can only reflect indirectly the various changes and amplification of diagnosis which necessarily occurred with fuller knowledge of the individual case. The group labelled debility, for instance, is large in numbers in early years and clearly represents a provisional diagnosis of only temporary interest. The subsequent allocation of debility cases to more accurately defined medical groups cannot, in these general statistics, be followed in detail. Nor, again, can the overlapping of such analogous conditions as functional diseases of the heart and neurasthenia be expressed in precise figures. Nevertheless, the numerical totals of the various disabilities are sufficiently large to counterbalance to a considerable extent these statistical limitations, and although the boundaries of certain classes are ill-defined they yet indicate groups of conditions which, taken in large numbers, do, by their variations in total and in proportion, indicate general tendencies and characteristics which are broadly true and worthy of consideration.

Again, it is to be remembered that the statistics are not records of the general or total occurrence of various disabilities in all ex-service men, but of the occurrence of disabilities in a way which could be attributed, either solely or in part, to the effects of war service. They are records of the acceptance of responsibility by the State for such effects and as such have been primarily influenced by the principles on which the State determined to award compensation. The statistics presented may raise questions as to how far disabilities which, unlike wounds, are not obviously due to war service, were in fact its outcome. Peace has its diseases, no less renowned than war, and as the war period recedes it becomes a problem of increasing intricacy to effect a clinical balance between the persisting effects of war service and the ordinary casualties and influences of civil life. Such questions, however, essentially relate to individual cases and as such are beyond the scope of this investigation. The broad facts remain. Acting on the best medical advice and utilising the most modern methods of investigation, the State has accepted certain cases of disability, in the numbers given, as related to war service. Had the medical criteria and evidence on which the awards were based been different, the totals would not have been the same, but the broad proportions and the general statistical picture would, in all probability, have remained constant. Thus, for example, when it is found that malaria stabilises rapidly and at a low degree of severity, that tuberculosis and psychoses remain largely unstable and severe, and that functional diseases of the heart and neurasthenia show a similarity in their rate and extent of stabilisation, it appears reasonable to regard these discoveries as expressing general characteristics of post-war disablement which would have been equally true had the total numbers been either substantially greater or less. Whilst, therefore, the total numbers of the various disabilities possess great interest as indicative of the extent to which, after a great war, a connection between the disability and service in that war has been medically demonstrated and accepted by the State for compensation, the deductions of general medical interest, and for reference in any future similar emergency, are perhaps best drawn from the study of the relative proportions of the different conditions and their modifications in the decade following the war. For this purpose the main characteristics of the more conspicuous disabilities are set out in Tables 24 and 25 which summarise the extent of war disablement remaining at 31st March, 1929.

In Table 24 the relative proportions of the disabilities are shown in Column A as to awards and in Column B as to assessment grades.

TABLE 24.—Percentage Proportions of the Disabilities in the Totals of Certain Categories of Awards and of Assessment Grades at 31st March, 1929

Disability	A Percentage of awards			B Percentage of assessment grades		
	1. Stabilised awards	2. Unstabilised awards	3. Total awards (1+2)	4. "70–100 per cent." grade	5. "40–60 per cent." grade	6. "30 per cent. and under" grade
Wounds and amputations	46·5	16·3	42·0	43·0	52·7	38·6
Tuberculosis	1·8	20·7	7·1	17·1	7·2	2·1
Respiratory diseases	4·6	13·5	6·0	5·2	7·1	5·4
Organic diseases of the heart	1·9	8·8	3·0	6·1	5·7	1·7
Functional diseases of the heart	6·2	4·0	5·8	·2	1·4	8·7
Neurasthenia	7·2	6·9	7·5	3·5	4·6	9·1
Malaria	6·9	·5	5·9	·1	·2	8·5
Rheumatism	4·3	2·3	3·9	·7	1·3	5·2
Ear diseases	3·1	2·6	3·0	1·0	3·0	3·4
Psychoses	·7	7·3	1·7	10·1	1·4	·5
Dysentery	1·0	·8	1·0	·1	·3	1·3
Nephritis	1·2	4·7	·9	·7	1·6	1·9
Other disabilities	14·6	11·6	12·2	12·2	13·5	13·6
Total percentage	100·0	100·0	100·0	100·0	100·0	100·0
Number of cases	621,972	113,515	735,487	78,936	150,096	506,455
			735,487			735,487

It is apparent that, of stabilised awards, wounds form by far the largest proportion, followed by neurasthenia, malaria and functional diseases of the heart. Of unstabilised awards, tuberculosis forms the greatest proportion, followed by wounds, respiratory diseases, organic diseases of the heart and psychoses. Neurasthenia is in almost identical proportion in both stabilised and unstabilised awards. Taking stabilised and unstabilised awards together, wounds constitute much the greatest proportion, and it is noticeable that tuberculosis, neurasthenia, respiratory diseases, functional diseases of the heart and malaria all closely approximate in their proportions. These five conditions, together with wounds, make up 75 per cent. of the total awards.

When the proportions in the assessment grades are considered, it is seen that wounds are very evenly distributed throughout the three grades, whilst tuberculosis and psychoses are markedly prominent in the most severe (70–100 per cent.) grade. On the other hand, whilst functional diseases of the heart, malaria, rheumatism, dysentery and nephritis each form less than 1 per cent. of the " 70–100 per cent." grade, they form a considerable proportion of the " 30 per cent. and under " grade.

In summary it is seen that, ten years after the war, the total cases of serious disablement still remaining are, to the extent of 81·5 per cent., composed of only five main disabilities, namely, wounds, tuberculosis, respiratory diseases, organic diseases of the heart and psychoses, of which wounds are rather more than half.

In Table 25 an attempt is made to summarise, in as comprehensive a manner as possible, the general aspect in 1929 of the disabling effects of service in the Great War. A disablement still existing on 31st March, 1929, and then assessed at 40 per cent. or more, has been taken as an indication of war disablement of serious degree, both by reason of its assessment and of its long continuance, and the columns under " A " of the table record and classify the cases complying with this standard, showing the nature of the disability, the assessment grade and the stabilisation or otherwise of award. Under " B " of the table are placed all other cases which have had an appreciable disablement, but which on 31st March, 1929, had either (1) ceased to be assessed at more than 30 per cent., or (2) were known to be deceased. It therefore comprises the Classes II and III of Table 4 together with (a) the cases in Class I of that table for which adequate medical records are available, and (b) the 120,000 who have died whilst in receipt of pension. The total of " A " and " B " may be taken as the total number of cases in which the effects of war service produced a disablement of appreciable severity and continuance, and this total is given in Column " C." Column " D " gives the percentage proportion of each disability in the grand total of Column " C "; its variations from the total of stabilised and unstabilised awards shown in Table 24 are due to the inclusion of the cases known to be deceased.

Table 25 thus gives a picture of the war disablement of 1914–18 from the standpoint of 1929. The figures for " all disabilities " show that, ten years after the war, only 26·8 per cent. of living cases of originally appreciable war disablement are still disabled to the extent of more than 30 per cent. The remaining 73·2 per cent. have ceased to be assessed at more than 30 per cent. or have died whilst in receipt of pension. As explained in connection with Table 4, it is not practicable to analyse these deaths in detail, but it may be repeated here that they number about 120,000, and that only 60–70 per cent. were associated with the effects of war service.

In the following conditions these known deaths whilst in receipt of pension are responsible for more than 10 per cent. of the totals in Column B :—Tuberculosis (73 per cent.), organic diseases of the heart (54 per cent.), respiratory diseases

MINISTRY OF PENSIONS MEDICAL REVIEW 349

TABLE 25.—Showing the Position at 31st March, 1929, of the Cases in which War Service produced Appreciable Disablement of Definite Duration

Disability		A. Cases in which war service effects were recognised as still producing disablement to an extent greater than 30 per cent.								B. Other Cases, i.e. (1) Disablement 30 per cent. or less (2), Known to be deceased	C. Grand total (A+B)	D. Percentage of total disabilities
		I. Disablement assessed at "70–100 per cent."			II. Disablement assessed at "40–60 per cent."			Total of A				
		Stabilised	Unstabilised	Total of I.	Stabilised	Unstabilised	Total of II.					
Wounds and amputations	Total No. of cases	29,762	4,191	33,953	70,454	8,894	79,348	113,301	211,421	324,722	38·2
	Percentage of grand total. Col. C.	9·1	1·4	10·5	21·6	2·7	24·3	34·8	65·2		
Tuberculosis	Total No. of cases	5,150	8,246	13,396	1,721	9,135	10,856	24,252	41,118	65,370	7·6
	Percentage of grand total. Col. C	7·9	12·6	20·5	2·6	14·0	16·6	37·1	62·9		
Respiratory diseases	Total No. of cases	2,058	2,042	4,100	3,499	7,176	10,675	14,775	40,608	55,383	6·5
	Percentage of grand total. Col. C	3·7	3·7	7·4	6·3	12·9	19·2	26·6	73·4		
Organic diseases of the heart	Total No. of Cases	2,361	2,360	4,721	3,094	5,442	8,536	13,257	18,245	31,502	3·7
	Percentage of grand total. Col. C	7·5	7·5	15·0	9·9	17·3	27·2	42·2	57·8		
Functional diseases of the heart	Total No. of cases	102	88	190	818	1,210	2,028	2,218	42,637	44,855	5·2
	Percentage of grand total. Col. C	0·2	0·2	0·4	1·8	2·8	4·6	5·0	95·0		
Neurasthenia	Total No. of cases	1,535	1,343	2,878	3,346	3,497	6,843	9,721	48,681	58,402	6·8
	Percentage of grand total. Col. C	2·6	2·3	4·9	5·7	6·0	11·7	16·6	83·4		
Malaria	Total No. of cases	43	43	86	155	165	320	406	44,343	44,749	5·2
	Percentage of grand total. Col. C	0·1	0·1	0·2	0·4	0·4	0·8	1·0	99·0		
Rheumatism	Total No. of cases	364	219	583	1,022	850	1,872	2,455	31,453	33,908	4·0
	Percentage of grand total. Col. C	1·1	0·6	1·7	3·0	2·5	5·5	7·2	92·8		
Ear diseases	Total No. of cases	619	142	761	3,154	1,282	4,436	5,197	18,575	23,772	2·7
	Percentage of grand total. Col. C	2·6	0·6	3·2	13·3	5·4	18·7	21·9	78·1		
Psychoses	Total No. of cases	1,992	5,951	7,943	656	1,391	2,047	9,990	3,040	13,030	1·5
	Percentage of grand total. Col. C	15·3	45·6	60·9	5·0	10·7	15·7	76·6	23·4		
Dysentery	Total No. of cases	37	49	86	130	310	440	526	7,499	8,025	0·9
	Percentage of grand total. Col. C	0·5	0·6	1·1	1·6	3·9	5·5	6·6	93·4		
Nephritis	Total No. of cases	200	368	568	443	1,901	2,344	2,912	12,925	15,837	1·8
	Percentage of grand total. Col. C	1·3	2·3	3·6	2·8	12·0	14·8	18·4	81·6		
Other disabilities	Total No. of cases	6,863	2,810	9,673	15,597	4,754	20,351	30,024	105,909	135,933	15·9
	Percentage of grand total. Col. C	5·1	2·2	7·3	11·5	3·5	15·0	22·3	77·7		
All disabilities	Total No. of Cases	51,086	27,852	78,938	104,089	46,007	150,096	229,034	626,454	855,488	100·0
	Percentage of grand total. Col. C	5·9	3·3	9·2	12·2	5·4	17·6	26·8	73·2		

(27 per cent.), nephritis (24 per cent.), psychoses (22 per cent.), rheumatism (16 per cent.), and dysentery (13 per cent.).

The percentage proportions given in the table show, from left to right, the extent to which the different disabilities continue, or cease, to be an active source of disablement. Malaria and psychoses show the extremes. In malaria only ·2 per cent. remain assessed at " 70–100 per cent.," and only ·8 per cent. at " 40–60 per cent." ; 99 per cent. are now less than 40 per cent. disabled or are known to be deceased, and these known deaths form in fact only about 2 per cent. On the other hand, 60·9 per cent. of the psychoses are still assessed at " 70–100 per cent.," 15·7 per cent. at " 40–60 per cent.," and there are only 23·4 per cent. who are less than 40 per cent. disabled or are known to have died. In general, tuberculosis, organic diseases of the heart and psychoses stand out as the conditions with the most continuous and severe degree of disablement, with wounds and respiratory diseases next in order. Ear diseases, nephritis and neurasthenia still show considerable severity ; functional diseases of the heart, rheumatism and dysentery show slight severity ; malaria is negligible.

So, in the aftermath of war as judged by the award of pension, it is the diseases of lungs and heart and brain which remain the most conspicuous items in the sum of the State's aggregate liability, whilst the wounds, despite their greater numbers, have relatively healed.

As was inevitable, this chapter has dealt with the mass statistics. The interesting details of the individual cases and the pros and cons of medical argument regarding the precise part played by war service in their clinical history would have been out of place, but it may be said that the files of the Ministry contain a wealth of clinical records, unique in character and pregnant with possibilities for research. It is not irrelevant to add that the necessity for accuracy of clinical record has never been more in evidence than in the work of the Ministry. Its experience has also emphasised how much depends on the medical records kept on recruitment and during service. Gaps, inaccuracies and ambiguities in recruiting and service records lead to perplexity and make difficult the balance of equity between the man and the State in the post-war decisions on pension claims. Defects in the medical organisation and records for recruitment and in service are thus a potent source of difficulty in post-service medical investigation and decision, whilst, when recruiting records are precise and the service medical history clear, the decisions on pension are greatly simplified. During hostilities it is inevitable that refinements of clinical record should be secondary to the pressing requirements of active service, but, though the dust of conflict may obscure the vision of post-war problems, their certain emergence needs to be remembered and, in so far as is possible, provided for in administrative routine during service. Such foresight is amply repaid both to the individual and to the State.

INDEX

ABSCESSES : among British troops in Italy, Forward Area, 184.

ADMISSIONS TO HOSPITAL : (*See* Disease and Injury, and Wounded).

ADVANCED OPERATING CENTRES : trial of, in France, not wholly successful, 29.

AFRICAN NATIVE MEDICAL CORPS : 10.

ALBUMINURIA : among British troops in Italy, Forward Area, 184.

AMBULANCE BARGES : numbers of sick and wounded carried by, in France 1915–18, 117 ; proportion of wounded to sick carried by, 118.

AMBULANCE TRAINS : use of, in evacuating casualties, 31–3 ; numbers of sick and wounded carried by, in France, 31, 117 ; proportion of wounded to sick carried by, 118.
    Improvised or Temporary : need for, in war, 31–2 ; use of, and accommodation in, 32.
    Regular : number of, insufficient in war, 31 ; supplementary assistance required, *ib.* ; accommodation in, and use of, 33.

AMERICAN MEDICAL DEPARTMENT : 35.

AMPUTATIONS : as common cause of pensionable disability, 318 ; percentage proportion of, 319 ; analysis of stabilised awards for, 320, by assessment groups, 329, and percentage distribution, 330–1 ; analysis of unstabilised pensions in payment for, 321–2, by assessment group, 332, and percentage distribution, 333–4 ; first award of pension for, 1920–26, 323–4–5 ; final awards for, 326–7–8 ; percentage proportions of, as to awards and assessments at 31.3.29, 347–8 ; general aspect of disabling effects from, 349–50.

ANKYLOSTOMIASIS : in Native Labour Corps in France, 1917, 165.

ANTHRAX :
    In Egypt and Palestine, at certain periods, 216 ; in XXIst Corps, 1918, *ib.*
    ,, France .. .. .. *1916*, 155 ; *1917*, 164 ; *1918*, 174
    ,, Italy 184
    ,, Macedonia, *1916*, 195 ; *1917*, 196 ; *1918*, *ib.* ; *1915–18*, 197.
    ,, United Kingdom, *1914* 99

APPENDICITIS :
    In France, *1914* 131
    ,, Italy, among troops in Forward Area 184
    ,, South-West Africa 267
    ,, United Kingdom, *1914* 100

AEROLAR TISSUE, Diseases of the : proportion of, in France 1914–15, to total sick and injured admitted to hospital, 116 ; comparison between ratios of, among British troops in France 1915 and at home and abroad in 1927, 143.
    In Dardanelles Campaign 61, 206–7
    ,, France .. .. .. *1914*, 61, 129, 132 ; *1915*, 61, 143–4–5
    ,, Italy 183–4
    ,, South African War 61, 273
    ,, United Kingdom .. .. *1914*, 61, 101 ; *1915*, 61, 103
    Sample Cases Analysed : 61, 286, 289, 293, 297, 299, 303, 306.

354 MEDICAL HISTORY OF THE WAR

ARMY COUNCIL : x, xii, 274.

ARMY DENTAL SERVICE : work of, at base in France, 1917, table showing, 118, and in army areas in 1918, 119 ; records of dental treatment by, in Italy during 1918, 185.

BALKAN WARS : strength of troops engaged in, 6.

BERI-BERI :
    In France, *1914*, 132 ; *1915*, 144–5 ; *1917*, 164–5 ; *1918*, 175.
  ,, Mesopotamia, *1914–15*, 237 ; *1916*, 238 ; *1917*, 239 ; *1918*, 240 ; *1914–18*, 241.
  ,, United Kingdom, *1914*, 101 ; *1915*, 104.
  Sample Cases Analysed : 286, 289, 293, 297, 299, 302, 305.

BILHARZIASIS (*Bilharzia hæmatobia*) :
    In Egypt and Palestine, at certain periods, 216 ; in XXIst Corps, 1918, *ib.*
  ,, France .. .. *1915*, 144–5 ; *1917*, 165
  ,, South African War 273
  ,, South-West Africa 267
  ,, United Kingdom, *1915* 104
  Sample Cases Analysed : 286, 289, 293, 297, 300, 303, 306.

  As **Pensionable Disability** : stabilised awards for, 320, showing assessment groups, 329 ; unstabilised pensions in payment for, 321, showing assessment groups, 332 ; first awards of pension for, 1920–26, 323 ; final awards for, 326 ; treatment of, by Ministry of Pensions, 344.

BLACKWATER FEVER :
    In Macedonia, *1915–16*, 195 ; *1917*, 196 ; *1918*, *ib.* ; *1915–18*, 197.
  ,, United Kingdom, *1914* 99

BLOOD, Diseases of the :
    In Dardanelles Campaign 206–7
  ,, France .. .. *1914*, 131 ; *1915*, 144–5
  ,, United Kingdom .. .. .. *1914*, 100 ; *1915*, 103
  Sample Cases Analysed : 285, 288, 292, 296, 299, 302, 305.

BOILS : among British troops in Italy, Forward Area, 184.

BREAST, Diseases of the :
    In Dardanelles Campaign 206–7
  ,, France .. .. *1914*, 131 ; *1915*, 144–5
  ,, United Kingdom .. .. .. *1914*, 100 ; *1915*, 103
  Sample Cases Analysed : 285, 288, 292, 296, 299, 302, 305.

BRONCHITIS : (*See* Respiratory system, diseases of).
    In France, *1914*, associated with gunshot wounds, 133.
  ,, Italy 184
  ,, South African War 273

BROWNLEE, Dr. J. : xii.

CASUALTIES : survey of, from standpoint of conservation of manpower in war, 11 *et seq.* ; in British Expeditionary Forces during Great War, table showing, 12.
  Battle : definition of, xvii ; subdivision of, into permanent and temporary losses, *ib.*, and percentage of, 13 ; treated by medical services, and percentages, 14 ; estimate of, by Staff, necessary to medical services

INDEX 355

CASUALTIES : (*Contd.*)
in calculating requirements, 36 ; revised methods of estimating, and tables illustrating reasons for, 37–8 ; percentages of, to average strengths in various campaigns, table showing, 38 ; percentages of, by arms of the Service, 42, and table illustrating, 43 ; approximate percentage of walking, sitting or lying-down cases among, 44 ; proportion of, to non-battle, 45–6 ; in British Expeditionary Forces during Great War, 56 ; in the battle of the Somme, 1916, as percentage of total for the year, 147.

In Dardanelles Campaign	200–2
,, East Africa	253–6
,, Egypt and Palestine	209–11
,, France, *1914–18*, 107–9 ; *1914*, 121–5 ; *1915*, 136–9 ; *1916*, 148–50 ; *1917*, 158–60 ; *1918*, 167–9.	
,, Italy	177–9
,, Macedonia	187–9
,, Mesopotamia	222–6
,, North Russia	246–8
,, South African War	269–70
,, South-West Africa	262–4

Classification of : xvi–xvii ; explanation of terms used in, xvii, 13–4.

Disposal of : table showing, 15 ; deaths, percentages of, 16–7 ; returned to duty, percentages of 16, 18 ; evacuated overseas, 16 ; wastage through invaliding, 17–8.

Estimate of : importance of, to medical services, 36–7, 39 ; in collection, evacuation and accommodation of sick and wounded, 43–54.

Evacuation of : during Great War, table showing, 15 ; supplementary assistance required in, 24–33 ; utility transport employed in, 25–7, 31 ; to Shaikh Saad, 26 ; during battle of Cambrai, 26–7 ; methods of, determined by circumstances, 30–3 ; to United Kingdom from all theatres of war, table showing, 51 ; improvements in, in France 1916, 147, continued in 1917, 156–7 ; to base, during German offensive in France 1918, 166 ; difficulties of, in Gallipoli, 198–9 ; from Force in Palestine 1918, 217 ; by River Sick Convoy Unit in Mesopotamia, 221 ; to coastal bases and overseas, from East Africa, 257. (*See* also Disease and Injury, and Wounded, evacuated overseas).

Non-battle : definition of, xvii ; subdivision of, into permanent and temporary losses, *ib.*, and percentages, 13–4 ; treated by medical services, and percentages, 14 ; estimate of, by administrative medical officer, 38 ; percentages of, to average strengths in various campaigns, table showing, *ib.* ; proportion of, to battle, 45–6 ; in British Expeditionary Forces during Great War, table showing, 56 ; preponderance of, over battle casualties in previous wars, led to investigations into the prevention of disease, 55 ; percentage of, temporarily ineffective, 57.

In Dardanelles Campaign	200–2, 205–7
,, East Africa	253–6, 258–60
,, Egypt and Palestine	209–11, 215–7
,, France *1914–18*, 107–9, 114–7 ; *1914*, 121–5, 129–32 ; *1915*, 136–9, 143–6 ; *1916*, 148–50, 154–5 ; *1917*, 158–60, 163–5 ; *1918*, 167–9, 173–5.	
,, Italy	177–9, 182–4
,, Macedonia	187–9, 194–7
,, Mesopotamia	222–6, 236–44
,, North Russia	246–8, 251
,, South African War	269–70, 272–3
,, South-West Africa	262–4, 266–7
,, United Kingdom, *1914–18*	94–5, 98–105

356 MEDICAL HISTORY OF THE WAR

CASUALTIES: *(Contd.)*
  Principal Causes of:
    In Dardanelles Campaign 205
    ,, East Africa 258–60
    ,, France, *1914–18*, 114; *1914*, 129; *1915*, 143; *1916*, 154; *1917*, 163–4; *1918*, 173–4.
    ,, Italy, Forward Area 183
    ,, Macedonia 194–7
    ,, Mesopotamia 237–41
    ,, North Russia 251
    ,, South African War 272
    ,, South-West Africa 266
    ,, United Kingdom, *1914–18* 98
  Proportions: among total casualties, 13; of sick and wounded in quiet and active periods, 45–6; of battle to non-battle casualties in Great War, table showing, 56; of gas casualties to wounded over certain periods, 112.
    In Dardanelles Campaign 202–3
    ,, East Africa 254, 256
    ,, Egypt and Palestine 209, 211–2
    ,, France, *1914–18*, 107, 109, 110; *1914*, 122, 125, 126; *1915*, 136, 139, 140; *1916*, 148, 150–1; *1917*, 158, 160; *1918*, 168, 169, 170
    ,, Italy 178, 179, 180
    ,, Macedonia 187, 189, 190
    ,, Mesopotamia 222–3, 226, 227–8
    ,, North Russia 246, 248, 249
    ,, South African War 269, 270, 271
    ,, South-West Africa 262, 264, 265
  Returned to duty: numbers of, in Great War, 15, and percentages, 18; importance of analysing casualties to show, 18–9; classification of, for administrative purposes, 19–20; improvement in, points to consider, 20; high percentage of, in total admissions in Mesopotamia, 220; estimated percentage of, among admissions in East Africa, 257. (*See* also Disease and Injury, and Wounded, returned to duty.)

CASUALTY CLEARING STATIONS: dependence of, on supplementary organisation, 27; functions of, *ib.*; table illustrating additional medical personnel required for, in France, 28; sections of, detailed as advanced operating centres in France, not entirely successful, 29; provision of, important as pivotal centre for early treatment of casualties, *ib.*, 30; allotment of, with additional personnel, depends on estimate of casualties, 44; estimate of transport in evacuating casualties from, 45; development of, in France, *1916*, 147, in *1917*, 156–7; grouping of, 147; importance of, in *1918*, 167.

CEREBRO-SPINAL FEVER: incidence of, in British Expeditionary Forces during Great War, 63; comparison with peace-time ratio of, in British Army, 64; prevalence of, among civilian population in East Africa, 258.
    In Dardanelles Campaign 206–7
    ,, East Africa *1917*, 259; *1918*, 260
    ,, Egypt and Palestine, during certain periods, 216; in XXth and XXIst Corps, 1918, *ib.*
    ,, France, *1914–18*, 114; *1914*, 130; *1915*, 144–5; *1916*, 155; *1917*, 164–5; *1918*, 174–5.
    ,, Italy 184
    ,, Macedonia, *1915–16*, 195; *1917*, 196; *1918*, *ib.*; *1915–18*, 197
    ,, Mesopotamia *1916*, 238; *1917*, 239; *1918*, 240

INDEX   357

CEREBRO-SPINAL FEVER: (*Contd.*)
   In North Russia 251
   ,, United Kingdom, *1914*, 99; *1915*, 102; *1916–17–18*, 105; *1914–18*, *ib.*
   Sample Cases Analysed : 285, 287, 291, 295, 298, 301, 304.

CHICKEN-POX : incidence of, in British Expeditionary Forces during Great War, 63.
   In Dardanelles Campaign 206–7
   ,, Egypt and Palestine, during certain periods, 216; in XXIst Corps, 1918, *ib.*
   ,, France, *1914–18*, 114; *1914*, 130; *1915*, 144–5; *1916*, 155; *1917*, 164–5; *1918*, 174–5.
   ,, Italy 184
   ,, Macedonia, *1915*, 195; *1916*, *ib.*; *1917*, 196; *1918*, *ib.*; *1915–18*, 197.
   ,, United Kingdom *1914*, 99; *1915*, 102
   Sample Cases Analysed : 285, 287, 291, 295, 298, 301, 304.

CHOLERA : 65; incidence of, in British Expeditionary Forces during Great War, 67; cause of outbreak of, in Mesopotamia, 68.
   In Dardanelles Campaign 206–7
   ,, Egypt and Palestine, in XXIst Corps, 1918, 216.
   ,, Mesopotamia, 221, 236; *1914–15*, 237; *1916*, 238; *1917*, 239; *1918*, 240; *1914–18*, 241.
   ,, United Kingdom, *1915* 102
   Sample Cases Analysed : 285, 287, 291, 295, 298, 301, 304.

CIRCULATORY SYSTEM, Diseases of the :
   In Dardanelles Campaign 206–7
   ,, France, *1914*, 131, 133; *1915*, 144–5.
   ,, Italy 184
   ,, South African War 273
   ,, South-West Africa 266–7
   ,, United Kingdom *1914*, 100; *1915*, 103
   As Pensionable Disability : stabilised awards for, 320, showing assessment groups, 329; unstabilised pensions in payment for, 321, showing assessment groups, 332–3–4; first award of pension for, 1920–26, 323; final awards for, 326.
   Sample Cases Analysed : 285, 288, 292, 296, 299, 302, 305.

COLLIE, SIR JOHN : 308.

CONJUNCTIVITIS : among British troops in Italy, Forward Area, 184; in South African War, 273.

CONNECTIVE TISSUE, Inflammation of : among British troops in Italy, 183–4.

CONTUSIONS : among British troops in Italy, Forward Area, 184.

CONVALESCENT DEPOTS : 49; development of, as a means to conserve manpower, 51–3; in France and Macedonia, table illustrating, 53; need for advanced, 52–3; benefit of, with advance troops, 54.
   Accommodation :
   In Egypt and Palestine 214
   ,, France, *1914*, 129; *1915*, 142–3; *1916*, 153–4; *1917*, 162–3; *1918*, 173.
   ,, Italy 182
   ,, Macedonia 193
   ,, Mesopotamia 236

CONVALESCENT DEPOTS: (*Contd.*)
   For Indian troops and followers :
     In France .. .. ..   *1916*, 154 ; *1917*, 163 ; *1918*, 173
     ,, Mesopotamia 236

CRIMEAN WAR : strength of troops engaged in, 6.

DARDANELLES CAMPAIGN : introductory note to chapter on, 198–9.

DEBILITY :
   In Dardanelles Campaign 205–6–7
   ,, France .. .. *1914*, 132 ; *1915*, 144–5
   ,, Italy 184
   ,, South African War 272–3
   ,, United Kingdom, *1914*, 101 ; *1915*, 104.
   Sample Cases Analysed : 285, 287, 292, 295, 298, 301, 305.

   As Pensionable Disability : stabilised awards for, 320, showing assessment groups, 329 ; unstabilised pensions in payment for, 321, showing assessment groups, 332 ; first awards of pension for, 1920–26, 323 ; final awards for, 326.

DENGUE : in South African War, 273.

DIABETES :
   As Pensionable Disability : stabilised awards for, 320, showing assessment groups, 329 ; unstabilised pensions in payment for, 321, showing assessment groups, 332 ; first awards of pension for, 1920–26, 323 ; final awards for, 326 ; treatment of, by Ministry of Pensions, 343–4.

DIARRHŒA: 81.
   In Dardanelles Campaign 205–6–7
   ,, Egypt and Palestine, 209, 215 ; in XXth Corps, 1918, 216.
   ,, France .. .. *1914*, 131 ; *1915*, 144–5
   ,, Italy 183–4
   ,, Macedonia, *1915–18*, 194, 197 ; *1915*, 195 ; *1916*, *ib.* ; *1917*, 196 ; *1918*, *ib.*
   ,, North Russia 251
   ,, South African War 273
   ,, South-West Africa 267
   ,, United Kingdom .. .. .. *1914*, 100 ; *1915*, 103
   Sample Cases Analysed : 285, 289, 293, 296, 299, 302, 305.

DIGESTIVE SYSTEM, Diseases of the : 59 ; ratio of, among British troops in France 1915, compared with that of British Army in 1927, 143.
   In Dardanelles Campaign 61, 199, 205–6–7
   ,, France .. *1914*, 61, 129, 131 ; *1915*, 61, 143–4–5 ; *1917*, 157
   ,, Italy 184
   ,, Macedonia, *1915*, 195 ; *1916*, *ib.* ; *1917*, 196 ; *1918*, *ib.* ; *1915–18*, 197.
   ,, Mesopotamia 242
   ,, North Russia 251
   ,, South African War 61, 272–3
   ,, South-West Africa 266–7
   ,, United Kingdom, *1914*, 61, 98, 100 ; *1915*, 61, 98, 103 ; *1914–18*, 98, 105 ; *1916–17–18*, 105.
   Sample Cases Analysed : 61, 285–6, 288–9, 293, 296, 299, 302, 305.

   As Pensionable Disability : stabilised awards for, 320, showing assessment groups, 329 ; unstabilised pensions in payment for, 321, showing assessment groups, 332 ; first awards of pension for, 1920–26, 323 ; final awards for, 326.

INDEX 359

DIPHTHERIA : incidence of, in British Expeditionary Forces during Great War, 63 ; comparison with peace-time ratio of, in British Army, 64.
In Dardanelles Campaign 206–7
,, Egypt and Palestine, during certain periods, 216 ; in XXth and XXIst Corps, 1918, *ib.*
,, France, *1914–18*, 114 ; *1914*, 130 ; *1915*, 144–5 ; *1916*, 155 ; *1917*, 164–5 ; *1918*, 174–5.
,, Italy 184
,, Macedonia, *1915*, 195 ; *1916*, *ib.* ; *1917*, 196 ; *1918*, *ib.* ; *1915–18*, 197.
,, North Russia 251
,, South African War 273
,, United Kingdom .. .. .. *1914*, 99 ; *1915*, 102
Sample Cases Analysed : 285, 287, 291, 295, 298, 301, 304.

DISABLEMENT, WAR : xix ; outstanding medical characteristics of post-, and compensation for, 307 *et seq.* ; summary of, 315 ; classification of principal causes of, and their variation, 318–9 ; comparative analysis of, 319–35 ; additions to, after demobilisation, 322–5 ; rate of stabilisation of, 325–8, 330 ; comparative severity of, among stabilised conditions. 329–31 ; grades of assessment in awarding pensions for, 330 ; conditions of, unstabilised, 332–4 ; extent of, remaining at 31.3.29, 346–8 ; general review of, 1914–18, 348–50.

Awards : distribution of disabilities among stabilised and unstabilised, 320–2 ; analysis of stabilised, 320, by assessment grades with diagram illustrating, 331 ; analysis of unstabilised, 321, by grades of assessment, with diagram illustrating, 334 ; first awards of pension after demobilisation, 1920–26, 322–5, with percentage proportions and diagram illustrating, 324–5 ; analysis of final, 325–8, by annual percentage incidence, 327, by percentage proportions, with diagram illustrating, 328.

Compensation for : primary duty of Ministry of Pensions to award, 307–8 ; problem of assessing degree of, 311 ; standard of assessment of, adopted, *ib.* ; extent and nature of State, 316–8.

Nature of : in relation to compensation, 315–9 ; general types of war disability and their phases, 315–6 ; main types, and corresponding form of compensation, 316–8.

Treatment : provision of medical and surgical, by Ministry of Pensions, 309 ; arrangements necessary for, 312–4 ; pensioners receiving institutional, table showing, 314 ; outstanding features in, 335–44 ; annual discharges from institutional, 1919–29, 335, with percentage proportions, 337–8 ; of wounds and injuries, 336, 339 ; of tuberculosis, 340 ; of mental diseases, *ib.* ; of nervous disorders, 341–3 ; of epilepsy, 343 ; of facial wounds, *ib.* ; of diabetes, *ib.*, 344 ; of tropical diseases, 344 ; of eye and ear diseases, *ib.* ; of dental defects, *ib.* ; hospitals and clinics employed in, 344.

DISEASE AND INJURY :
Admissions : in British Expeditionary Forces during Great War, table showing, 12 ; disposal of, 15, 20 ; mortality percentage, 16–7 ; percentage of, invalided in 1914–15, 18 ; percentage of, returned to duty, *ib.*, 19, 20 ; percentage of, sent to convalescent depots in France, 1917–18, 52 ; survey of chief causes of, 59–92 ; table showing principal causes of, in complete war records analysed, 61 ; associated with gunshot wounds in France, 1914, 133 ; comparison between principal causes of, among British troops in France 1915 and in the British Army in 1927, 143 ; in Palestine, 1918, 217.

DISEASE AND INJURY: (*Contd.*)
    In Dardanelles Campaign 201-2-3-4, 205-7
    ,, East Africa 253, 254-5-6, 258-9, 260
    ,, Egypt and Palestine 210-1-2-3, 215-7
    ,, France, *1914-18*, 108-9, 110-1; *1914*, 122-3-4-5-6-7-8, 129-33; *1915*, 136-7-8-9, 140-1, 143-6; *1916*, 149, 150-1-2, 154-5; *1917*, 158-9, 160-1, 163-5; *1918*, 168-9, 170-1, 173-5.
    ,, Italy 177-8-9, 180-1, 182-4
    ,, Macedonia 188-9, 190-1-2, 194-7
    ,, Mesopotamia 224-5, 227, 229, 230-1-2-3-4, 236-44
    ,, North Russia 247-8-9, 250-1
    ,, South African War 269, 270-1-2-3
    ,, South-West Africa 263-4-5-6-7
    ,, United Kingdom, *1914-15*, 95-6-7, 98-104; *1916-17-18*, 105; *1914-18*, *ib*.
    Rate of: in British Army during peace, 57-8; in British Expeditionary Forces during Great War, 58-9; in United Kingdom, comparison of, in peace and war, 93; in France 1916 compared with pre- and post-war ratios, 154; in Gallipoli, 199; comparison of, in Egypt and Palestine, with post-war figures, 208; in certain forces in Egypt and Palestine, 217; in Mesopotamia, reasons for high, 220-1, and measures to reduce, 221.
    Sample Cases Analysed: 275, 285-6; by arms of the service, 276, 287-90; by geographical areas, 276, 291-4; by age groups, 277, 295-7; by year of admission to hospital, 277, 298-300; by period in hospital, 277-8, 301-3; by final disposal, 278, 304-6.

Deaths: in British Expeditionary Forces during Great War, 12, 15; percentage of, 16-7, in front line medical units, 17, in Mesopotamia, 220.
    In Dardanelles Campaign 201-2, 204, 206-7
    ,, East Africa 253-4-5, 259-60
    ,, Egypt and Palestine 210-1, 213, 215
    ,, France, *1914-18*, 108-9-10-11; *1914*, 122-3-4, 127-8, 130-2; *1915*, 136-7-8, 141, 144-5; *1916*, 149-50, 152, 155; *1917*, 158-9, 161, 164-5; *1918*, 168-9, 171, 174-5.
    ,, Italy 177-8, 180-1, 183
    ,, Macedonia 188-9, 191-2, 195-6-7
    ,, Mesopotamia, 220, 224-5, 229, 230-1-2-3-4, 236-7-8-9, 240-1, 242, 244.
    ,, North Russia 247-8-9, 250
    ,, South African War 269, 270-1-2-3
    ,, South-West Africa 263-4-5, 267
    ,, United Kingdom .. *1914-15*, 95-6-7, 99, 100-1-2-3-4
    Sample Cases Analysed: 278, 304-6.

Evacuated Overseas: in British Expeditionary Forces during Great War, 15.
    In France, *1914-18*, 110-1; *1916*, 152; *1917*, 161; *1918*, 171.
    ,, Italy 180-1
    ,, Macedonia 191-2
    ,, Mesopotamia 229, 230-1-2-3-4
    ,, North Russia 249-50
    ,, South African War 271-2-3

Invalided: 17, 18, 20.
    In Dardanelles Campaign 204, 206-7
    ,, France 1914, 127-8, 130-1-2; *1915*, 141, 144-5
    ,, South African War 271-2-3
    ,, United Kingdom *1914-15*, 96-7, 99, 100-1-2-3-4
    Sample Cases Analysed: 278, 304-5-6.

INDEX

DISEASE AND INJURY: (*Contd.*)
Returned to Duty : 18–20.
    In Dardanelles Campaign 204, 206–7
    ,, France, *1914–18*, 110–1; *1914*, 127–8, 130–1–2; *1915*, 141, 144–5; *1916*, 152; *1917*, 161; *1918*, 171.
    ,, Italy 180–1
    ,, Macedonia 191–2
    ,, Mesopotamia 229, 230–1–2–3–4
    ,, North Russia 249–50
    ,, South African War 271–2
    ,, United Kingdom *1914–15*, 96–7, 99, 100–1–2–3–4
    Sample Cases Analysed : 278, 304–5–6.

DISEASES : method of tabulating statistics of, xviii ; ordinary infectious, incidence of, during Great War, 62–4, comparison with peace time ratios in British Army, 64 ; infectious, associated with the East, incidence of, 65–70 ; due to infection, causing great inefficiency, 72–86.

DYSENTERY : incidence of, in British Expeditionary Forces during Great War, 81 ; in relation to bad sanitation, 82–3, in Mesopotamia, with table illustrating, 84 ; development of sanitary organisation in the forces to combat, 84–5 ; lessons in prevention of, 85.
    In Dardanelles Campaign 205–6–7
    ,, East Africa .. .. 258 ; *1916*, 259 ; *1917, ib*; *1918*, 260
    ,, Egypt and Palestine, 209, 215 ; during certain periods, 216 ; in XXth and XXIst Corps, 1918, *ib*.
    ,, France, *1914–18*, 114 ; *1914*, 130, 133 ; *1915*, 144–5 ; *1916*, 154–5 ; *1917*, 163–4–5 ; *1918*, 173–4–5.
    ,, Italy 183–4
    ,, Macedonia, *1915–18*, 194, 197 ; *1915*, 195 ; *1916, ib.*; *1917*, 196 ; *1918, ib*.
    ,, Mesopotamia, *1914–15*, 237 ; *1916*, 238 ; *1917*, 239 ; *1918*, 240 ; *1914–18*, 241.
    ,, North Russia 251
    ,, South African War 272–3
    ,, South-West Africa 267
    ,, United Kingdom, *1914*, 99 ; *1915*, 102 ; *1916–17–18*, 105 ; *1914–18, ib*.
    Sample Cases Analysed : 285, 287, 291, 295, 298, 301, 304.

As Pensionable Disability : common cause of, 318 ; percentage proportion of, 319 ; stabilised awards for, 320, showing assessment groups, 329, and percentage distribution, 330–1 ; unstabilised pensions in payment for, 321, classified by assessment group, 332, and percentage distribution, 333–4 ; first awards of pension for, 1920–26, 323, with percentage proportions, 324–5 ; final awards for, 326, with annual incidence percentage of, 327, and percentage proportion of, 328 ; annual discharges from institutional treatment for, 335, with percentage proportions of, 337–8 ; percentage proportions of, as to awards and assessment at 31.3.29, 347, general aspect of disability due to, 349–50.

EAR, Diseases of the :
    In Dardanelles Campaign 206–7
    ,, France .. .. *1914*, 131, 133 ; *1915*, 144–5
    ,, Italy 184
    ,, South African War 273
    ,, United Kingdom .. .. .. *1914*, 100 ; *1915*, 103
    Sample Cases Analysed : 285, 288, 292, 296, 299, 302, 305.

EAR, Diseases of the : (*Contd.*)
  As Pensionable Disability : common cause of, 318 ; percentage proportion of, 319 ; stabilised awards for, 320, showing assessment groups, 329, and percentage distribution, 330–1 ; unstabilised pensions in payment for, 321, classified by assessment group, 332, and percentage distribution, 333–4 ; first awards of pension for 1920–26, 323, with percentage proportions of, 324–5 ; final awards for, 326, with annual percentage incidence of, 327, and percentage proportion of, 328 ; training of the deaf by Ministry of Pensions, 344 ; percentage proportions of, as to awards and assessment at 31.3.29, 347 ; general aspect of disability due to, 349.

EAST AFRICA, Campaign in : introductory notes to chapter on, 252–3.

ECZEMA : in United Kingdom, 1914, 101 ; in France, 1914, 131.

EGYPT AND PALESTINE : introductory notes to chapter on, 208–9.

ENDOCRINE GLANDS, Diseases of the :
  In Dardanelles Campaign 206–7
  ,, France .. .. *1914*, 131 ; *1915*, 144–5
  ,, South African War 273
  ,, United Kingdom .. .. .. *1914*, 100 ; *1915*, 103
  Sample Cases Analysed : 285, 288, 292, 296, 299, 302, 305.

ENTERIC GROUP OF FEVERS : 55, 65 ; incidence of, in British Expeditionary Forces during Great War, 66.
  In Dardanelles Campaign 205–6–7
  ,, East Africa .. .. *1916*, 259 ; *1917, ib.* ; *1918*, 260
  ,, Egypt and Palestine 215, 216
  ,, France, *1914–18*, 114 ; *1914*, 130, 133 ; *1915*, 144–5 ; *1916*, 155 ; *1917*, 164–5 ; *1918*, 174–5.
  ,, Italy 184
  ,, Macedonia, *1915*, 195 ; *1916, ib.* ; *1917*, 196 ; *1918, ib.* ; *1915–18*, 197.
  ,, Mesopotamia, *1914–15*, 237 ; *1916*, 238 ; *1917*, 239 ; *1918*, 240 ; *1914–18*, 241.
  ,, North Russia 251
  ,, South African War 272–3
  ,, South-West Africa 267
  ,, United Kingdom .. .. .. *1914*, 99 ; *1915*, 102
  Sample Cases Analysed : 285, 287, 291, 295, 298, 301, 304.

  As Pensionable Disability : stabilised awards for, 320, showing assessment groups, 329 ; unstabilised pensions in payment for, 321, classified by assessment groups, 332 ; first awards of pension for, 1920–26, 323 ; final awards for, 326.

ENTERITIS : (*See* Digestive System, Diseases of the).
  In Italy 184
  ,, North Russia 251
  ,, South African War 273

EPILEPSY : associated with gunshot wounds, 1914, 133 ; in sample cases analysed, 285, 288, 292, 296, 298, 301, 305 ; investigations into accurate diagnosis of, by Ministry of Pensions, and treatment, 343.

ERYSIPELAS :
  In Egypt and Palestine, in XXIst Corps 1918, 216
  ,, France .. *1914*, 130 ; *1916*, 155 ; *1917*, 164–5 ; *1918*, 174–5
  ,, Italy 184
  ,, Macedonia, *1915–16*, 195 ; *1917*, 196 ; *1918, ib.* ; *1915–18*, 197
  ,, South African War 273
  ,, United Kingdom *1914*, 99

INDEX

EYE, Diseases of the:
    In Dardanelles Campaign 206–7
    ,, France *1914*, 131; *1915*, 144–5
    ,, Italy 184
    ,, South African War 273
    ,, United Kingdom *1914*, 100; *1915*, 103
    Sample Cases Analysed: 285, 288, 292, 296, 299, 302, 305.
    As Pensionable Disability: stabilised awards for, 320, showing assessment groups, 329; unstabilised pensions in payment for, 321, classified by assessment groups, 332; first awards of pension for, 1920–26, 323; final awards for, 326; 344.

FIBROSITIS: in sample cases analysed, 285, 287, 291, 295, 298, 301, 304, 318.

FLAT FOOT:
    As Pensionable Disability: stabilised awards for, 320, showing assessment groups, 329; unstabilised pensions in payment for, 321; classified by assessment groups, 332; first awards of pension for, 1920–26, 323; final awards for, 326.

FLETCHER, SIR WALTER: xiii.

FOLLOWERS: employment of, with British forces, 9; study of, by medical services, important, *ib.*; medical arrangements for, 10; causes of high death rate among, in East Africa, 259.
    Strength: 3, 5; in Mesopotamia, 10, 222; in East Africa, 10, 253.

FRANCE AND FLANDERS, Campaign in: introductory notes to chapters dealing with, 106–7; *1914*, 120–1; *1915*, 134–5; *1916*, 147–8; *1917*, 156–7; *1918*, 166–7.

FRANCO-GERMAN WAR: Strength of troops engaged in, 6.

FROST-BITE AND TRENCH FOOT: 87; incidence of, in British Expeditionary Forces during Great War, 88; weekly incidence of, in France 1916–18, 89; factors tending to increase rate of, among troops, 90.
    In Dardanelles Campaign 205–6–7
    ,, Egypt and Palestine, in XXth Corps 1918, 216
    ,, France, *1914–18*, 114; *1914*, 129, 132–3; *1915*, 143–5; *1916*, 154–5; *1917*, 163–4–5; *1918*, 174.
    ,, Italy 184
    ,, Macedonia .. *1915*, 195; *1916*, *ib.*; *1917*, 196; *1918*, *ib.*; *1915–18*, 197.
    ,, North Russia 251
    ,, United Kingdom *1914*, 101; *1915*, 104
    Sample Cases Analysed: 286, 290, 294, 297, 300, 303, 306.
    As Pensionable Disability: stabilised awards for, 320, showing assessment groups, 329; unstabilised pensions in payment for, 321, classified by assessment groups, 332; first awards of pension for, 1920–26, 323; final awards for, 326.

GALWEY, MAJOR W. R.: xii.

GANGRENE: in gunshot wounds in France, 1914, 133.

GAS CASUALTIES: in France, 1915–18, 111; disposal of, admitted to casualty clearing stations, 112; proportion of, to wounded over certain periods, *ib.*; admissions and final disposal of, 1915, 113; deaths among, *ib.* 134; series of cases, analysed according to disposal, 113; average stay in hospital, 1915, *ib.*; average number of, constantly in hospital, 1915, *ib.*; admissions of, to casualty clearing stations, 1917, 157; number of "mustard," in France, 1917, *ib.*

GAS POISONING :
 Sample Cases Analysed : 286, 290, 294, 297, 300, 303, 306.
 As Pensionable Disability : stabilised awards for, 320,'showing assessment groups, 329 ; unstabilised pensions in payment for, 321 ; classified by assessment groups, 332 ; first awards of pension for, 1920–26, 323 ; final awards for, 326.

GASTRALGIA : among British troops in Italy, Forward Area, 184.

GASTRITIS : among British troops in Italy, Forward Area, 184.

GENERATIVE SYSTEM, Diseases of the :
 In Dardanelles Campaign 206–7
 ,, France .. .. *1914*, 131 ; *1915*, 144–5
 ,, South African War 273
 ,, United Kingdom, *1914*, 100 ; *1915*, 103.
 Sample Cases Analysed : 286, 289, 293, 297, 299, 303, 305.

GLANDERS : in France, 1914, 130.

GONORRHŒA : (*See* Venereal Diseases)

GOODWIN, LIEUT.-GEN. SIR J. : 19 *n*.

HÆMORRHOIDS : among British troops in Italy, Forward Area, 184.

HAMILTON, GENERAL SIR IAN : 23, 33, 33*n*, 82.

HEALTH, MINISTRY OF : 57, 340.

HEART, Diseases of the : (*See* Circulatory System, Diseases of the)
 Sample Cases Analysed : 285, 288, 292, 296, 299, 302, 305.
 As Pensionable Disability : common cause of, 318 ; percentage proportion of, 319 ; stabilised awards for, 320, showing assessment groups, 329, and percentage distribution, 330–1 ; unstabilised pensions in payment for, 321, classified by assessment groups, 332, and percentage distribution, 333–4 ; first awards of pension for, 1920–26, 323, with percentage proportions, 324–5 ; final awards for, 326, with annual percentage incidence of, 327, and percentage proportion of, 328 ; percentage proportions of, as to awards and assessment, at 31.3.29, 347–8 ; general aspect of disability due to, 348–50.
 Disordered Action of the : (*See* Circulatory System, Diseases of)
 Valvular Disease of the : (*See* Circulatory System, Diseases of)

HEAT, EFFECTS OF :
 In Dardanelles Campaign 206–7
 ,, France, *1915* 104
 ,, Macedonia, *1915*, 195 ; *1916*, *ib.* ; *1917*, 196 ; *1918*, *ib.* ; *1915–18*, 197.
 ,, Mesopotamia, 221 ; *1914–15*, 237 ; *1916*, 238 ; *1917*, 239 ; *1918*, 240 ; *1914–18*, 241 ; 243–4 ; chart of temperatures, *facing* 244.
 ,, South African War 273
 ,, South-West Africa 267
 Sample Cases Analysed : 286, 290, 294, 297, 300, 303, 306.

HERBERT, A. P. : 82.

HERNIA : among British troops in Italy, Forward Area, 184.

HORSLEY, SIR VICTOR : 219.

INDEX

HOSPITALS :
  Accommodation : In United Kingdom during Great War, 8 ; estimate of casualties required in providing, 45 ; development of, in France, 47–8 ; difficulties in obtaining, 48 ; policies regarding provision of, 49–50, and results of, 50–1 ; percentage of vacant, 50 ; benefit of, with advance troops, 54 ; use of " crisis " beds to increase the, in France *1916*, 147, 153, in *1917*, 162, and in *1918*, 172 ; policy adopted in France 1917 to relieve the situation regarding, 157, 161 ; in front area, France *1917*, 162, *1918*, 172 ; variety of nationalities given, in France 1918, 172 ; inadequate, at commencement of Dardanelles Campaign, 205 ; development of, in Mesopotamia, 235 ; daily average, occupied by allied troops in North Russia, 250 ; special arrangements for, necessary for native labour in South-West Africa, 261–2 ; provided by Ministry of Pensions, 1919–29, 314.

    In East Africa 258
    ,, Egypt and Palestine 213–4
    ,, France, *1914*, 129 ; *1915*, 142 ; *1916*, 152–3 ; *1917*, 162 ; *1918*, 171–2.
    ,, Italy 182
    ,, Macedonia 193
    ,, Mesopotamia 234–5
    ,, North Russia 250
  For Indian troops and followers :
    In East Africa 258
    ,, Egypt and Palestine 214
    ,, France .. .. .. *1916*, 153 ; *1917*, 162 ; *1918*, 172
    ,, Mesopotamia 235

  Admissions : in British Expeditionary Forces during Great War, table showing, 15 ; percentage of deaths among, 16 ; percentage of invaliding among, 17–8 ; percentage of, returned to duty, 18.
  and Disposal of Cases :
    In Dardanelles Campaign 203–4, 205–7
    ,, East Africa 256–7
    ,, Egypt and Palestine 212–3
    ,, France, *1914–18*, 110–1 ; *1914*, 125–8, 130–2 ; *1915*, 140–1, 144–5 ; *1916*, 151–2, 155 ; *1917*, 160–1, 164–5 ; *1918*, 170–1, 173–5.
    ,, Italy 179–81, 183–4
    ,, Macedonia 190–2, 195–7
    ,, Mesopotamia 227–34, 236–44
    ,, North Russia 248–50, 251
    ,, South African War 270–3
    ,, South-West Africa 265, 267
    ,, United Kingdom *1914–15*, 95–7, 98–104

  Average Period in :
    In Dardanelles Campaign 204, 207
    ,, France *1915*, 142, 145
    ,, South-West Africa 266–7
    ,, United Kingdom *1915*, 97, 102–4

  General : need for, and benefits of, at outset of a campaign, 46–7, 54 ; results of lack of, 46 ; margin of vacant beds necessary in, 48–50.

IMPETIGO CONTAGIOSA : in United Kingdom, 101 ; in France 1914, 131 ; among British troops in Italy, Forward Area, 184.

INDIGESTION : in United Kingdom, *1914*, 100, *1915*, 103 ; in France, *1914*, 131, *1915*, 144–5.

INFLUENZA : 59, 85 ; incidence of, in British Expeditionary Forces during Great War, 86 ; comparison between ratios of, among British troops in France 1915 and the British Army at home and abroad 1927, 143 ; epidemic of, in France 1918, 167 ; chief cause of wastage among British troops in Italy 1918, 176, 183.
    In Dardanelles Campaign 61, 205–6–7
    ,, East Africa 258–9
    ,, Egypt and Palestine 215
    ,, France .. .. *1914*, 61, 130 ; *1915*, 61, 143–4–5 ; *1918*, 167
    ,, Italy 183–4
    ,, Macedonia, *1915–18*, 194, 197 ; *1915*, 195 ; *1916*, ib. ; *1917*, 196 ; *1918*, ib.
    ,, Mesopotamia 242
    ,, North Russia 251
    ,, South African War 61, 273
    ,, South-West Africa 266–7
    ,, United Kingdom, *1914*, 61, 99 ; *1915*, 61, 98, 102 ; *1914–18*, 98, 105 ; *1916–17–18*, 105.
    Sample Cases Analysed : 61, 285, 286, 287, 291, 295, 298, 301, 304.

INJURIES :
    Accidental or Undefined :
    In France, *1915*, 144–5.
    ,, United Kingdom, *1915*, 104.
    Local and General : 59 ; comparison between ratios of, among British troops in France 1915 and at home and abroad 1927, 143
    In Dardanelles Campaign 61, 205–6–7
    ,, France .. .. .. *1914*, 61, 129, 132 ; *1915*, 143–4–5
    ,, South African War 61, 272–3
    ,, United Kingdom, *1914*, 61, 98, 101 ; *1915*, 61, 98, 104 ; *1914–18*, 98, 105 ; *1916–17–18*, 105.
    Sample Cases Analysed : 61, 286, 290, 294, 297, 300, 303, 306.

INTESTINES, Diseases of the : (*See* Digestive System, Diseases of the)

INVALIDS : 17 ; percentages of, in 1914–15, and later series, 18 ; approximate total percentage of, 20. (*See* also Disease and Injury, and Wounded, Invalided.)

ITALY, British troops in : introductory notes to chapter dealing with casualties among, 176.

JAUNDICE : incidence of, in British Expeditionary Forces during Great War, 91.
    In Dardanelles Campaign 205–6–7
    ,, Egypt and Palestine, certain periods, 216 ; in XXIst Corps 1918, ib.
    ,, France, *1914–18*, 114 ; *1914*, 131 ; *1915*, 144–5 ; *1916*, 155 ; *1917*, 164–5 ; *1918*, 174–5.
    ,, Italy 184
    ,, Macedonia, *1915*, 195 ; *1916*, ib. ; *1917*, 196 ; *1918*, ib. ; *1915–18*, 197.
    ,, Mesopotamia 242
    ,, South African War 273
    ,, United Kingdom .. .. .. *1914*, 100 ; *1915*, 103
    Sample Cases Analysed : 285, 289, 293, 296, 299, 302, 305.

JOINTS, Diseases of the :
    As Pensionable Disability : stabilised awards for, 320, showing assessment groups, 329 ; unstabilised pensions in payment for, 321, classified by assessment groups, 332 ; first awards of pension for, 1920–26, 323 ; final awards for, 326.

INDEX 367

KALA-AZAR : among Native Labour Corps in France 1918, 175.

KILLED IN ACTION : in British Expeditionary Forces during Great War, 12.
    In Dardanelles Campaign 200–1–2–3
    ,, East Africa 253–4–5–6
    ,, Egypt and Palestine 210–1–2
    ,, France, *1914–18*, 108–9, 110 ; *1914*, 122–3–4–5–6–7 ; *1915*, 136–7–8–9, 140–1 ; *1916*, 149, 150–1 ; *1917*, 158–9, 160 ; *1918*, 168–9, 170.
    ,, Italy 177–8, 180
    ,, Macedonia 188–9, 190
    ,, Mesopotamia 224–5, 228
    ,, North Russia 247–8–9
    ,, South African War 269, 270–1
    ,, South-West Africa 263–4–5

LABOUR BATTALIONS : strength of non-European, in France, 3, 5, 9 ; diversity of nationality, *ib.* ; admissions to hospital and disposal of cases among, in Italy, 181.

LABOUR CORPS, NATIVE : disease among, in France, *1917*, 164–5 ; *1918*, 174–5.

LABOUR, MINISTRY OF : 313.

LEISHMAN, SIR WILLIAM : xiv, 55, 65.

LEPROSY : in Native Labour Corps in France, *1917*, 165 ; in *1918*, 175.

LIMBS, ARTIFICIAL : centres for fitting, established by Ministry of Pensions, 314 ; issue of, and surgical appliances, by Ministry of Pensions, 339.

LOCOMOTION, ORGANS OF, Diseases of the : comparison between ratios of, among British troops in France 1915, and at home and abroad 1927, 143.
    In Dardanelles Campaign 205–6–7
    ,, France .. .. .. *1914*, 129, 132–3 ; *1915*, 143–4–5
    ,, Italy 184
    ,, South African War 273
    ,, South-West Africa 267
    ,, United Kingdom .. .. *1914*, 98, 101 ; *1915*, 98, 103
    Sample Cases Analysed : 286, 289, 293, 297, 299, 303, 305–6.

LUMBAGO : 318. (*See* Locomotion, Organs of, diseases of the)
    In Italy 184
    Sample Cases Analysed : 285, 287, 291, 295, 298, 301, 304.

LUNACY ACTS : 340, 343.

LYMPHATIC SYSTEM, Diseases of the :
    In Dardanelles Campaign 206–7
    ,, France .. .. *1914*, 131 ; *1915*, 144–5
    ,, Italy 184
    ,, South African War 273
    ,, United Kingdom .. .. .. *1914*, 100 ; *1915*, 103
    Sample Cases Analysed : 285, 288, 292, 296, 299, 302, 305.

MACEDONIA, Campaign in : introductory notes to chapter on, 186.

MACPHERSON, MAJOR-GENERAL SIR WILLIAM : xii, xiii.

MALARIA : 79 ; incidence of, in British Expeditionary Forces during Great War, 80, 81 ; comparison between ratios of, among British troops in France 1915 and at home and abroad 1927, 143 ; in Macedonia, principal cause of inefficiency among troops, 186, 194 ; convalescent cases of, evacuated to United Kingdom, 191–2.
    In Dardanelles Campaign 206–7
  ,, East Africa .. 258 ; *1916*, 259 ; *1917*, *ib.* ; *1918*, 260
  ,, Egypt and Palestine, 209, 215 ; during certain periods, 216 ; in XXth and XXIst Corps 1918, *ib.*
  ,, France, *1914–18*, 114 ; *1914*, 130, 133 ; *1915*, 144–5 ; *1916*, 155 ; *1917*, 164–5 ; *1918*, 174–5.
  ,, Italy 183–4
  ,, Macedonia, *1915–18*, 194, 197 ; *1915*, 195 ; *1916*, *ib.* ; *1917*, 196 ; *1918*, *ib.*
  ,, Mesopotamia, *1914–15*, 237 ; *1916*, 238 ; *1917*, 239 ; *1918*, 240 ; *1914–18*, 241.
  ,, North Russia 251
  ,, South African War 272–3
  ,, South-West Africa 267
  ,, United Kingdom, *1914*, 99 ; *1915*, 102 ; *1916–17–18*, 105 ; *1914–18*, *ib.*
  Sample Cases Analysed : 285–6–7, 291, 295, 298, 301, 304.

As Pensionable Disability : common cause of, 318 ; percentage proportion of, 319 ; stabilised awards for, 320, showing assessment groups, 329, and percentage distribution of, 330–1 ; unstabilised pensions in payment for, 321–2, classified by assessment groups, 332, and percentage distribution, 333–4 ; first awards of pension for, 1920–26, 323 ; with percentage proportions, 324–5 ; final awards for, 326, with annual percentage incidence of, 327, and percentage proportions of, 328 ; treatment of, by Ministry of Pensions, 344 ; percentage proportions of, as to awards and assessment at 31.3.29, 347 ; general aspect of disability due to, 349–50.

MANPOWER IN WAR : xvii, xviii, xx ; conservation of, in relation to medical services, 1, 11 *et seq.*, 106 ; wastage of, caused by non-battle casualties, important to study, 55–9.

MAUDE, GENERAL SIR STANLEY : 84.

MEASLES : incidence of, in British Expeditionary Forces during Great War, 63 ; comparison with peace-time ratio of, in British Army, 64.
    In Dardanelles Campaign 206–7
  ,, Egypt and Palestine, during certain periods, 216 ; in XXth and XXIst Corps, *ib.*
  ,, France, *1914–18*, 114 ; *1914*, 130 ; *1915*, 144–5 ; *1916*, 155 ; *1917*, 164–5 ; *1918*, 174–5.
  ,, Italy 184
  ,, Macedonia, *1915*, 195 ; *1916*, *ib.* ; *1917*, 196 ; *1918*, *ib.* ; *1915–18*, 197.
  ,, North Russia 251
  ,, South African War 273
  ,, United Kingdom .. .. .. *1914*, 99 ; *1915*, 102
  Sample Cases Analysed : 285, 287, 291, 295, 298, 301, 304.

MEDICAL HISTORY OF THE WAR : ix ; medical statistics for, preparation of, ix–xv ; reorganisation in office of, xii ; scheme for, includes volume on medical statistics of the Great War, *ib.* ; statistical volume of, not to be undertaken by Editorial Committee of, xiii ; 6, 20, 21, 55, 117, 274, 307.

MEDICAL RESEARCH COMMITTEE : ix, ix *n.*

INDEX

MEDICAL RESEARCH COUNCIL: organisation for compilation of medical statistics of the war established under, ix–xii; progress made by, in preparation of medical statistics of the war, xii; statistical organisation transferred from, to Ministry of Pensions, *ib.*; 129, 133, 135, 274.

MEDICAL SERVICES: relation of, to manpower, 1; wider conception of, in war, *ib.*, 6; study of problems connected with followers and labour important by, 9–10; Continental records employed in training of, 11; limitation of responsibility of, in war, *ib.*, 22–4; approximate total casualties treated by, and percentages, table showing, 14, 20; in relation to numbers returned to duty, 18–20; difficulties of, in Mesopotamia, leading to breakdown, 219.

    Co-operation of: with other branches of the Army, 19 *n*, 22; essential to successful fulfilment of functions of, 33–4; results of lack of, *ib.*; tendency to ignore need for, 34–5; necessary in estimating requirements, 36–9; in estimation of casualties, *ib.*; value of, during Great War, some instances showing, 39–43.

    Duties of: 1; to individual and State, 14, 16; in war, 21–2.

    Experience, lack of: in handling large numbers of casualties, 7; in combined naval and military operations, 23, 198.

    Organisation of: requirements for, 20, *et seq.*; objects of, on Lines of Communication, 30; reorganisation necessary after initial failures in, 35.

        Regular: limited and inadequate in prolonged battles, 22; limits of, 34; depends on co-operation of the Staff for success, *ib.*

        Supplementary: must be authorised, 22–3; additional personnel, equipment and transport required in work of front line medical units, 24–7, of casualty clearing stations, 27–30, of medical units on lines of communication, 30–3.

MEDICAL STATISTICS OF THE WAR: preparation of, history outlined, ix *et seq.*; organisation of, under Medical Research Council, ix–xii; under Ministry of Pensions, xii–xiii; under War Office, revised scheme for production of, xiv–xx; difficulties of preparing, for campaign in Mesopotamia, 218; further modification of original scheme for, considered necessary and adopted, 274–5.

MEDICAL UNITS, Sick and Wounded constantly in:
    In Dardanelles Campaign 204
    „ East Africa 257
    „ Egypt and Palestine 213
    „ France, *1914*, 128–9; *1915*, 142; *1916*, 152; *1917*, 161–2; *1918*, 171.
    „ Italy 181
    „ Macedonia 193
    „ Mesopotamia, 232; during certain periods, 234.
    „ North Russia 250
    „ South African War 272
    „ South-West Africa 266
    „ United Kingdom *1914–15*, 97

MEDITERRANEAN FEVER: 65; incidence of, in British Expeditionary Forces during Great War, 67.
    In France, *1914* 130
    „ Italy 184
    „ Macedonia .. *1915*, 195; *1916, ib.*; *1917*, 196; *1915–18*, 197
    „ South African War 273
    „ South-West Africa 267
    „ United Kingdom, *1914* 99

MENTAL DISEASES :
  In Dardanelles Campaign 206–7
  ,, France .. .. *1914*, 131 ; *1915*, 144–5
  ,, South African War 273
  ,, United Kingdom .. .. .. *1914*, 100 ; *1915*, 103
  Sample Cases Analysed : 285, 288, 292, 296, 299, 302, 305.

  As Pensionable Disability : common cause of, 318 ; percentage proportion of, 319 ; stabilised awards for, 320, showing assessment groups, 329, and percentage distribution, 330–1 ; unstabilised pensions in payment for, 321, classified by assessment groups, 332, and percentage distribution, 333–4 ; first awards of pension for, 1920–26, 323, with percentage proportions, 324–5 ; final awards for, 326, with annual percentage incidence of, 327, and percentage proportions of, 328 ; treatment of, by Ministry of Pensions, 340 ; percentage proportions of, as to awards and assessment, 347–8 ; general aspect of disability due to, 349–50.

MESOPOTAMIA, Campaign in : introductory notes to chapter on, 218–21.

METABOLISM, Diseases of :
  In Dardanelles Campaign 206–7
  ,, France, *1914*, 132 ; *1915*, 144–5 ; *1917*, 164–5 ; *1918*, 175.
  ,, United Kingdom .. .. .. *1914*, 101 ; *1915*, 104
  Sample Cases Analysed : 286, 289, 293, 297, 299, 302, 305.

MIDDLE EAR DISEASE : among British troops in Italy, Forward Area, 184 ; in South African War, 273.

MISSING :
  In Dardanelles Campaign 201–2–3
  ,, East Africa 253–4–5–6
  ,, Egypt and Palestine 210–1–2
  ,, France, *1914–18*, 108–9–10 ; *1914*, 122–3–4, 126–7 ; *1915*, 136–7–8, 140 ; *1916*, 149–50, 151 ; *1917*, 158–9, 160 ; *1918*, 168–9, 170.
  ,, Italy 177–8, 180
  ,, Macedonia 188–9, 190
  ,, Mesopotamia 224–5, 228
  ,, North Russia 247–8–9
  ,, South African War 269, 270–1

MISSING AND PRISONERS OF WAR : in British Expeditionary Forces during Great War, 12.
  In Dardanelles Campaign 200
  ,, East Africa, among followers 253–4–5–6
  ,, France .. .. *1914*, 123–4 ; *1915*, 137–8, 141
  ,, South-West Africa 263–4–5

MITCHELL, MAJOR T. J. : xiii ; preparation of statistical volume undertaken by, xiv.

MOTOR AMBULANCE CONVOY : numbers of sick and wounded carried by, from front to base, and between bases in France *1917–18*, 117 ; proportion of wounded to sick carried by, 118.

MUMPS : incidence of, in British Expeditionary Forces during Great War, 63 ; comparison with peace-time ratio of, in British Army, 64.
  In Dardanelles Campaign 206–7
  ,, Egypt and Palestine, during certain periods, 216 ; in XXIst Corps, 1918, *ib*.

MUMPS: (*Contd.*)
 In France, *1914–18*, 114; *1914*, 130; *1915*, 144–5; *1916*, 154–5; *1917*, 163–4–5; *1918*, 174–5.
 ,, Italy 184
 ,, Macedonia, *1915*, 195; *1916*, *ib.*; *1917*, 196; *1918*, *ib.*; *1915–18*, 197.
 ,, North Russia 251
 ,, United Kingdom *1914*, 99; *1915*, 102
 Sample Cases Analysed : 285, 287, 291, 295, 298, 301, 304.

MYALGIA : 318. (*See* Locomotion, Organs of)
 Sample Cases Analysed : 285, 287, 291, 295, 298, 301, 304.

MYOSITIS : 318.
 Sample Cases Analysed : 285, 287, 291, 295, 298, 301, 304.

NATIONAL SERVICE, MINISTRY OF : 308, 310.

NAVAL AND MILITARY WAR PENSIONS, ETC., ACT, 1915 : Statutory Committee constituted by, 308; powers of, transferred to Ministry of Pensions, 1917, *ib.*

NEPHRITIS : some conclusions regarding war, 90; incidence of, in British Expeditionary Forces during Great War, 91.
 In France, *1914–18*, 114; *1914*, 132; *1915*, 135, 144–5; *1916*, 154–5; *1917*, 163–4–5; *1918*, 173–4–5.
 ,, Italy 184
 ,, South African War 273
 ,, United Kingdom *1914*, 101; *1915*, 103
 Sample Cases Analysed : 286, 289, 293, 297, 300, 303, 306.
 As Pensionable Disability : common cause of, 318; percentage proportion of, 319; stabilised awards for, 320, showing assessment groups, 329, and percentage distribution, 330–1; unstabilised pensions in payment for, 321, classified by assessment groups, 332, and percentage distribution, 333–4; first awards of pension for, 1920–26, 323; final awards for, 326, with annual percentage incidence of, 327, and percentage proportion of, 328; percentage proportions of, as to awards and assessment, at 31.3.29, 347; general aspect of disability due to, 349–50.

NERVOUS SYSTEM, Diseases of the : in France, 115–6; admissions for, 1914–15, 115; proportions of, to total sick and injured, and wounded, *ib.*; admission and disposal of cases of, in army areas, 1918, *ib.*; diagnosis of, sent to Base, 116; proportion of, to sick and wounded over certain periods, *ib.*
 In Dardanelles Campaign 206–7
 ,, France *1914*, 115, 131, 133; *1915*, 143–4–5
 ,, North Russia 246
 ,, South African War 273
 ,, South-West Africa 266–7
 ,, United Kingdom *1914*, 100; *1915*, 103
 Sample Cases Analysed : 285–6, 288, 292, 296, 298, 301, 305.
 As Pensionable Disability : common cause of, 318; percentage proportion of, 319; stabilised awards for, 320, showing assessment groups, 329, and percentage distribution, 330–1; unstabilised pensions in payment for, 321, classified by assessment groups, 332, and percentage distribution, 333–4; first awards of pension for, 1920–26, 323, with percentage proportions, 324–5; final awards for, 326, with annual percentage incidence of, 327, and percentage proportion of,

376 MEDICAL HISTORY OF THE WAR

SCARLET FEVER: *(Contd.)*
    In France, *1914–18*, 114; *1914*, 130; *1915*, 144–5; *1916*, 155; *1917*, 164; *1918*, 174–5.
    ,, Italy 184
    ,, Macedonia *1915*, 195; *1916*, ib.; *1917*, 196; *1918*, ib. *1915–18*, 197.
    ,, North Russia 251
    ,, South African War 273
    ,, United Kingdom *1914*, 99; *1915*, 102
    Sample Cases Analysed : 285, 287, 291, 295, 298, 301, 304.

SCIATICA: in sample cases analysed, 285, 287, 291, 295, 298, 301, 304; as pensionable disability, 318.

SCURVY:
    In Dardanelles Campaign 206–7
    ,, France, *1914*, 132; *1915*, 144–5; *1917*, 164–5; *1918*, 175.
    ,, Mesopotamia, *1914–15*, 237; *1916*, 238; *1917*, 239; *1918*, 240; *1914–18*, 241; 242–3.
    ,, North Russia 251
    ,, South African War 273
    ,, South-West Africa 267
    ,, United Kingdom, *1915* 104
    Sample Cases Analysed : 286, 289, 293, 297, 299, 302, 305.

SEPTIC DISEASES:
  Major :
    In Dardanelles Campaign 206–7
    ,, France *1914*, 130, 133; *1915*, 144–5
    ,, South African War 273
    ,, United Kingdom *1914*, 99; *1915*, 102
  Minor :
    In Dardanelles Campaign 206–7
    ,, Egypt and Palestine, XXth Corps 1918 216
    ,, France, *1915* 144–5

SHELL-SHOCK : cases of, admitted to medical units in army areas in France over certain periods during 1918, 115–6.
    Sample Cases Analysed : 285, 288, 292, 296, 298, 301, 305.

SICK RATE : (*See* Disease and Injury, Admissions, *Rate of*)

SKIN, Diseases of the : 59; in France 1914–15, proportion of, to total sick and injured admitted, 116; wastage due to, in First Army, France 1918, 117; comparison between ratio of, among British troops in France 1915 and at home and abroad 1927, 143.
    In Dardanelles Campaign 61, 205–6–7
    ,, France .. *1914*, 61, 131; *1915*, 61, 143–4–5; *1917*, 157
    ,, Italy 184
    ,, South African War 61, 272–3
    ,, South-West Africa 266–7
    ,, United Kingdom *1914*, 61, 98, 101; *1915*, 61, 98, 103
    Sample Cases Analysed : 61, 286, 289, 293, 297, 300, 303, 306.

SMALL-POX : incidence of, in British Expeditionary Forces during Great War, 63; comparison with peace-time ratio of, in British Army, 64; prevalence of, among civilian native population in East Africa, 258.
    In Dardanelles Campaign 206–7
    ,, East Africa 258; *1918*, 260
    ,, Egypt and Palestine, during certain periods, 216.

INDEX

SMALL-POX: *(Contd.)*
    In France, *1914–18*, 114 ; *1915*, 144–5 ; *1916*, 155 ; *1917*, 164–5 ; *1918*, 174.
    ,, Italy 184
    ,, Macedonia, *1915*, 195 ; *1916*, *ib.* ; *1917*, 196 ; *1918*, *ib.* ; *1915–18*, 197.
    ,, Mesopotamia, 221, 236 ; *1914–15*, 237 ; *1916*, 238 ; *1917*, 239 ; *1918*, 240 ; *1914–18*, 241.
    ,, South African War 273
    ,, United Kingdom .. .. .. *1914*, 99 ; *1915*, 102
    Sample Cases Analysed : 285, 287, 291, 295, 298, 301, 304.

SMITH, MISS G. M.: xiv.

SMUTS, GENERAL: 252.

SOFT CHANCRE: (*See* Venereal Diseases.)

SOUTH AFRICAN WAR: ix, x, xix ; strength of British and Dominion troops engaged in, 6, 268 ; percentage of deaths in, 16–7, 19 ; percentages of battle and non-battle casualties to average strength in, 38, 55 ; proportion of battle to non-battle casualties in, 56, 269–70 ; 60, 65 ; percentage of venereal diseases in, due to gonorrhœa, syphilis and other forms, 76 ; introductory note to chapter on, 268.

SOUTH-WEST AFRICA, Campaign in: introductory notes to chapter on, 261–2.

SPLEEN, Diseases of the:
    In Dardanelles Campaign 206–7
    ,, France .. .. *1914*, 131 ; *1915*, 144–5
    ,, South African War 273
    ,, United Kingdom .. .. .. *1914*, 100 ; *1915*, 103
    Sample Cases Analysed : 285, 288, 292, 296, 299, 302, 305.

SPRAINS: among British troops in Italy, Forward Area, 184.

SPRUE: in United Kingdom, *1914*, 99.

STATISTICS, ARMY MEDICAL: peace time methods of recording, unsuitable for war, x ; medical history card for, introduced, x–xi ; accuracy in, on recruitment and during service necessary in connection with claims to pension, 350–1.

STOMACH, Diseases of the: (*See* Digestive System.)

STRENGTHS: definition of terms used in connection with, xvi ; tables of, in British Expeditionary Forces during Great War, 2–5 ; of previous wars, comparison with, 6 ; of British Army in peace, comparison with, 7 ; in relation to medical organisation, 7–8 ; of Royal Army Medical Corps, 8 ; importance of, to medical administrative officers, 8–10 ; as showing expansion of forces, 8 ; as basis of calculation, *ib.* ; of followers and labour, knowledge of, necessary, 9–10 ; in relation to estimation of casualties, and tables illustrating, 37–8 ; of Fifth Army, Ypres, 1917, 38 ; percentages of battle and non-battle casualties to average, in various campaigns, table showing, *ib.* ; percentage of hospital beds to, in France, 1914–15, 47 ; expansion of, in France, 1915, in relation to medical problems, 135 ; of different forces in Egypt and Palestine, 217 ; average daily, of native labour employed in South-West Africa, 261.

STRENGTHS : (*Contd.*)
    Average Ration : in British Expeditionary Forces during Great War, 2–5.
        In Dardanelles Campaign 199
        ,, East Africa 253
        ,, Egypt and Palestine 209
        ,, France, *1914*, 121 ; *1915*, 135 ; *1916*, 148 ; *1917*, 157 ; *1918*, 167.
        ,, Italy 176
        ,, Macedonia 186
        ,, Mesopotamia 222
        ,, North Russia 246
        ,, South African War 268
        ,, South-West Africa 262
        ,, United Kingdom, *1914–18* 94

STRETCHER BEARERS : increase of, in France, 24 ; additional personnel required, *ib.*, 25.

SYNOVITIS : (*See* Locomotion, organs of)

SYPHILIS : (*See* Venereal Diseases.)

TEETH AND GUMS, Diseases of the : comparison between ratio of, among British troops in France 1915 and at home and abroad 1927, 143.
    In Dardanelles Campaign 206–7
    ,, France .. .. *1914*, 129, 131 ; *1915*, 143–4–5
    ,, Italy 183–4
    ,, South African War 273
    ,, United Kingdom .. .. .. *1914*, 100 ; *1915*, 103
    Sample Cases Analysed : 285, 288, 292, 296, 299, 302, 305.

TETANUS :
    In Dardanelles Campaign 206–7
    ,, France, *1914*, 130, 133 ; *1915*, 144–5–6 ; *1916*, 155 ; *1917*, 164 ; *1918*, 174–5.
    ,, Italy 184
    ,, Mesopotamia 242
    ,, South African War 273
    ,, United Kingdom .. .. .. *1914*, 99 ; *1915*, 102
    Sample Cases Analysed : 285, 287, 291, 295, 298, 301, 304.

TONSILLITIS : (*See* Digestive System.)
    In Dardanelles Campaign 206–7
    ,, Egypt and Palestine, in XXth Corps, 1918, 216.
    ,, France .. .. *1914*, 131, 133 ; *1915*, 144–5
    ,, Italy 184
    ,, South African War 273
    ,, United Kingdom, *1914*, 100 ; *1915*, 103 ; *1916–17–18*, 105 ; *1914–18*, *ib.*
    Sample Cases Analysed : 285, 288, 293, 296, 302, 305.

TRACHOMA :
    In France .. .. *1915*, 144–5 ; *1917*, 164–5 ; *1918*, 174–5
    ,, Italy 184
    ,, Macedonia, *1915*, 195 ; *1916*, *ib.* ; *1917–18*, 196 ; *1915–18*, 197.
    Sample Cases Analysed : 285, 288, 292, 296, 299, 302, 305.

INDEX

TRANSFER OF POWERS ACT, 1917: 308.

TRANSPORT: benefits of utility, for medical purposes, 26-7, in Mesopotamia, 30-1 ; use of motor, to accelerate evacuation of casualties, 30, 31, 32 ; estimate of casualties necessary in calculating requirements of, 44-5 ; casualties requiring, to United Kingdom during Great War, table showing, 51.

  Ambulance: deficiencies in field, 25-6 ; supplemented by other forms of, *ib.* ; in France, 1914-18, sick and wounded carried by, 117 ; proportion of wounded to sick evacuated by, 118 ; proportion of lying-down to sitting cases evacuated by, *ib.*

TRENCH FEVER: 86, 135.
  In Dardanelles Campaign 206-7
  „ France .. .. *1915*, 144-5 ; *1917*, 157
  „ Macedonia, *1915-16*, 195 ; *1917*, 196 ; *1918, ib.* ; *1915-18*, 197.
  „ United Kingdom, *1915* 102
  Sample Cases Analysed: 285, 287, 291, 295, 298, 301, 304.

  As Pensionable Disability: stabilised awards for, 320, showing assessment groups, 329 ; unstabilised pensions in payment for, 321, classified by assessment groups, 332 ; first awards of pension for, 1920-26, 323 ; final awards for, 326.

TRENCH FOOT: (*See* Frost bite)

TUBERCULOSIS: incidence of, in British Expeditionary Forces during Great War, 69 ; comparison with peace time ratio of, in British Army, 70 ; latent development of, 71, 324-5.
  In Dardanelles Campaign 206-7
  „ Egypt and Palestine, in XXIst Corps, *1918* 216
  „ France, *1914-18*, 114 ; *1914*, 130, 133 ; *1915*, 144-5 ; *1916*, 155 ; *1917*, 164-5 ; *1918*, 174-5.
  „ Italy 184
  „ Macedonia, *1915*, 195 ; *1916, ib.* ; *1917*, 196 ; *1918, ib.* ; *1915-18*, 197.
  „ North Russia 251
  „ South African War 273
  „ United Kingdom .. .. .. *1914*, 99 ; *1915*, 102
  Sample Cases Analysed: 285, 287, 291, 295, 298, 301, 304.

  As Pensionable Disability: common cause of, 318 ; percentage proportion of, 319 ; stabilised awards for, 320, showing assessment groups, 329, and percentage distribution, 330-1 ; unstabilised pensions in payment for, 321-2, classified by assessment groups, 332, and percentage distribution, 333-4 ; first awards of pension for, 1920-26, 323, with percentage proportions, 324-5 ; final awards for, 326, with annual percentage incidence of, 327, and percentage proportion of, 328 ; annual discharges from institutional treatment for, 335, with percentage proportions, 337-8 ; treatment of, by Ministry of Pensions, 340 ; percentage proportions of, as to awards and assessment at 31.3.29, 347-8 ; general aspect of disability due to, 348-50.

TUMOURS AND CYSTS:
  In Dardanelles Campaign 206-7
  „ France .. .. *1914*, 132 ; *1915*, 144-5
  „ United Kingdom .. .. .. *1914*, 101 ; *1915*, 104
  Sample Cases Analysed: 286, 289-90, 294, 297, 300, 303, 306.

TYPHOID FEVER: (*See* Enteric Group of Fevers)

WOUNDS: percentage of, by different weapons, table showing, 40; regional incidence of, by different weapons, with percentages, tables showing, 41–2; gunshot, diseases associated with, in France 1914, 133; plastic treatment of facial, at Queen's Hospital, Sidcup, extent of work, 343.

Sample Cases Analysed: 275; by arms of the service, 276, 280; by geographical areas, 276, 281; by age groups, 277, 282; by year of admission to hospital, 277, 282; by period in hospital, 277–8, 283; by final disposal, 278, 284; by cause, nature and site, 279–84.

As Pensionable Disability: common cause of, 318; percentage proportion of, 319; analysis of stabilised awards for, 320, showing assessment groups, 329, and percentage distribution, 330–1; unstabilised pensions in payment for, 321–2, classified by assessment groups, 332, and percentage distribution, 333–4; first awards of pension for, 1920–26, 323, with percentage proportions, 324–5; final awards for, 326, with annual percentage incidence, 327, and percentage proportion, 328; special arrangements for treatment of, by Ministry of Pensions, 337, 339; percentage proportions of, as to awards and assessment at 31.3.29, 347–8; general aspect of disabling effects from, 348–50.

WRIGHT, SIR ALMWROTH: 55, 65.

www.ingramcontent.com/pod-product-compliance
Lightning Source LLC
Chambersburg PA
CBHW021827220426
43663CB00005B/157